THE VIG  *IS*

Daily Success Principles
From
Diverse American Founders

A HISTORICAL DEVOTIONAL

Joseph Holland
Copyright © 2019 by Joseph Holland

ISBN:9781705354285

TABLE OF CONTENTS:
MONTHLY VIRTUES

	Acknowledgments	i
	Introduction	ii
1	**January: Courage**	1
2	**February: Self-Discipline**	53
3	**March: Compassion**	101
4	**April: Perseverance**	153
5	**May: Teamwork**	204
6	**June: Integrity**	256
7	**July: Industriousness**	307
8	**August: Self-Reliance**	359
9	**September: Optimism**	411
10	**October: Purposefulness**	463
11	**November: Civility**	516
12	**December: Faith**	567
	About the Author	

ACKNOWLEDGMENT

Over the years of my adult life there has rarely been a day that didn't begin in Bible study and prayer. The deepest root of this devotional book has been my own devotional studies. The virtues that I discovered through my daily disciplines evolved into these vigorous virtues as I uncovered the creative intersections of two of my greatest passions: love of history and love of God. Though I recognize the importance of the former, I esteem the latter. Whatever wisdom rises from these pages, I acknowledge — and thank — the Lord of my life.

INTRODUCTION

Do not conform to the pattern of this world,
but be transformed by the renewing of your mind.
— Romans 12:2

The Vigorous Virtues ("VV") is a re-imagining of the history of America. Some look in the nation's past and only see stories of injustice and oppression. Others emphasize the narratives of American exceptionalism. This book presents a unique rendering by capturing the wisdom gleaned from the character, bravery, talent, work and spirit of men and women who led lives of virtue in pursuit of their American dreams.

VV is a different kind of devotional book. Though it offers 365 distinct entries for each day of the year, VV raises daily inspiration through diverse historical voices. Among the well-known Founding Fathers are unfamiliar founders as well as unsung heroes including women and people of color who have too often been overlooked. All of these illustrative lives exemplify principles of success.

The book is organized as monthly themes of one vigorous virtue per month delineated by one principle-driven selection per day. You will find four elucidating elements interwoven into the daily narratives:

- Introductory quote
- Historical account
- Inspirational voice
- Success principles

This structure is designed as a spiritual road map to take you on an inner journey, which is not so much about reaching a desired destination but rather about experiencing the purposeful process — evolving day-by-day into a person of strong character with rising aspirations who works hard at attaining your American dream.

I first learned about the importance of daily success principles while running Harkhomes, a homeless shelter in Harlem. My vision was holistic housing: shelter not as an end in itself but as a means to restore the whole person. Every day I led Bible-based discussions with the residents and discovered that a regular diet of principles and disciplines fostered moral fortitude in the same way that supplying food, clothing and shelter sustained physical strength. Countless challenges over many years at Harkhomes revealed an essential truth: people lead fulfilling lives because of their foundational virtues. So I committed myself to developing a set of tools that allows anyone to build a solid system of values to thrive in the of adversity, live each day with inspiration, and rise to his or her divine destiny.

The only exception to the historical accounts of the daily selections is a handful of stories from my own experiences at Harkhomes. You will see in each of the twelve chapters at least one narrative that imparts success principles rising from my work with the homeless. The virtues and life lessons are constant throughout the book; the only difference at times is the context, which shifts from historical to autobiographical when I describe what I learned while helping the homeless.

The overarching theme of this book was captured by novelist John Dos Passos in a 1941 essay.

Every generation rewrites the past . . . we are driven to the written record by a pressing need to find answers to the riddles of today. We need to know what kind of firm ground other men, belonging to generations before us, have found to stand on.

The "firm ground" that we share with the "generations before us" is the solid rock of the virtues described in this book. These life lessons from history will inform and bolster your here and now. By understanding and practicing these daily success principles and making them a part of the fabric of your life, you will be transformed by the renewing of your mind. And you will be empowered by the truth of what you're becoming on the inside is ultimately more important than what you're achieving on the outside.

Twenty-first century American malaise stems from a loss of foundational virtues. A society of justice, industriousness and virtue must possess a people of justice, industriousness and virtue. *VV* is a clarion call to individuals and society as a whole to acknowledge the richness of America's past and esteem the set of core moral and spiritual values rising from it; to revive them and to live by them, yielding transformed lives of greater joy, peace, purpose, and productivity.

The United States is a unique nation because of its founding principles, which were premised on virtue as a foundation for personal progress as well as for the collective good. The vision was — and still is — for a society in which one's fate wouldn't be determined by where one was born or who the parents were, but by individual choice in aspiration's pursuit. As you read this book and daily apply its principles, you will experience your inner journey that will bring about the fulfillment of your American dream. Just know that this book will take you to the higher moral ground, leading to your success in life. You will also be inspired to revive your neighborhood and refound the nation.

JANUARY: COURAGE
DAILY SUCCESS PRINCIPLES

1. Show Up In Quiet Strength — Rosa Parks — 1955
2. Dare To Be Great — Robert Smalls — 1862
3. Encourage One Another — Elbridge Gerry — 1776
4. Seize Your Battlefield — Joseph De Castro — 1863
5. Don't Give Way To Hating — Elizabeth Eckford — 1957
6. Tell The Truth Boldly — Frederick Douglass — 1852
7. Stay Cool Under Fire — Chew-Een Lee — 1950
8. Be A Courageous Chronicler — Helen Hunt Jackson — 1881
9. Get Ready To Ride — Paul Revere — 1775
10. Act On The Truth — Frances Kemble — 1838
11. Be Strong In War And Peace —Douglas MacArthur — 1945
12. Live What You Know To Be Right — Phoebe Cary — 1848
13. Cry Out For Justice — Samuel Hopkins — 1776
14. Take A Courageous Stand — Margaret Douglass — 1854
15. Confront Your Bitter Truth — Joseph Holland — 1986
16. Courageously Make Your Case — John Harlan — 1896
17. Sing An Encouraging Song — Marian Anderson — 1939
18. Take Your High Road — Abraham Lincoln — 1862
19. Be Strategically Courageous — Lucretia Mott — 1833
20. Demonstrate Great Courage — Martin Luther King, Jr. — 1963
21. Fight The Good Fight — Susan B. Anthony — 1872
22. Speak The Truth In Love — John Russwurm — 1827
23. Live To Fight Another Day — Ida B. Wells — 1890
24. Tackle Tough Problems — John Gardner — 1968
25. Hold Down The Fort — Dolley Madison — 1812
26. Resist Popular Opinion — Robert Louis Stevenson — 1879
27. Encourage Yourself — Thomas Edison — 1930
28. Dare To Die — Davy Crockett — 1836
29. Take A Big Risk — Harriet Tubman — 1850
30. Be Creatively Courageous — John Greenleaf Whittier — 1844
31. Fight For Rights Of Others — Samuel May — 1846

SHOW UP IN QUIET STRENGTH   JANUARY 1ST

Without a vision the people perish, but without courage dreams die.
Rosa Parks

On December 1, 1955, Rosa Parks finished her workday as a seamstress at the Montgomery Fair department store. She boarded the Cleveland Avenue bus for her ride home. The buses in Alabama reflected the segregationist policies that prevailed throughout the American South. Front seats were reserved for whites; back seats reserved for blacks; whites had preference for the unreserved middle seats; if the bus was full when a white person boarded, blacks were required to stand and give up their seat for the new white rider.

On that day Parks was sitting in the first row of the middle section when a white man boarded the bus. The bus driver told her and the three black men seated in her row to move to the back of the bus. The men moved back but Parks refused. The bus driver left and came back with a Montgomery police officer who arrested Parks. That night the Women's Political Council printed a flyer that circulated throughout the black community of Montgomery.

Don't ride the buses to work, to town, to school, or anywhere on Monday. You can afford to stay out of school for one day if you have no other way to go except by bus. You can also afford to stay out of town for one day. If you work, take a cab, or walk. But please, children and grown-ups, don't ride the bus at all on Monday. Please stay off all buses Monday!

Parks appeared in court that Monday December 5th. She was found guilty and fined ten dollars and a court cost of four dollars, which was eventually overturned on appeal. The victory achieved on December 5th was a mass boycott of Montgomery buses by blacks. Sparked by the courageous actions of Parks, the Montgomery bus boycott launched the Civil Rights Movement, marking a historic turning point that forever changed American race relations. Parks showed up in quiet strength and it paved new pathways of progress. Heed the counsel that she offered in her words. It will bring out your own quiet strength, which will help you attain your own trailblazing outcomes.

KEEP SITTING — *People always say that I didn't give up my seat because I was tired, but that isn't true. No, the only tired I was, was tired of giving in.*

KEEP FOCUSED — *I have learned over the years that when one's mind is made up, this diminishes fear; knowing what must be done does away with fear.*

2

KEEP WORKING — *There is work to do; that is why I cannot stop or sit still. As long as a child needs help, as long as people are not free, there will be work to do. As long as an elderly person is attacked or in need of support, there is work to do. As long as we have bigotry and crime, we have work to do.*

KEEP GOING — *What really matters is not whether we have problems, but how we go through them. We must keep going on to make it through whatever we are facing.*

KEEP ACTING RIGHT — *If you want to be respected for your actions, then your behavior must be above reproach. If our lives demonstrate that we are peaceful, humble, and trusted, this is recognized by others.*

KEEP THE FAITH — *I learned to put my trust in God and to see Him as my strength . . . You cannot always control the powers-that-be. You just have to have faith and stand by the things you believe in.*

You don't have to be called or chosen for greatness to be a person of courage. You don't have to stand, shout or soar. All you have to do is sit, like Rosa Parks, in the right place for the right reason at the right time. This small woman spawned significant change by a most simple thing: saying nothing with her words; her actions stating — "I'm not moving." She exemplifies the diminutive dimension of courage: quiet strength matters. You can keep your seat to take your stand. You can spark fires of change with the courage of your conscience. Just showing up in the silence of your power may be enough to move the mountain of social resistance.

Is there a roar of community change waiting to be awakened by the whisper of your courage?

DARE TO BE GREAT   JANUARY 2ND

*My race needs no special defense, for the past history of them
in this country proves them to be the equal of any people
anywhere. All they need is an equal chance in the battle of life.*
Robert Smalls

On May 12, 1862, as dusk fell over Charleston harbor, the military transport boat "CSS Planter" was docked in its usual spot at the wharf below the Confederate Army's headquarters. Robert Smalls, a slave, had been assigned to assist General Ripley in piloting the Planter as it delivered Civil War supplies, troops and land mines in its survey of South Carolina waterways. Having been hired out as a longshoreman, sail maker and wheelman throughout his teen years, Smalls had picked up knowledge about Charleston's harbor and the mechanics of maneuvering the Planter as well.

In keeping with the custom of the times, the Planter's three white officers disembarked to spend the night ashore, leaving Smalls and the slave crewmen on board. About 3 a.m. on May 13th, Smalls, wearing the captain's uniform including a straw hat similar to Ripley's, sailed the Planter to a wharf where his wife and family and those of the other escaping crewmen were waiting to be picked up. Smalls correctly signaled as he steered the ship past five Confederate harbor checkpoints, but at Fort Sumpter, the last and most precarious barrier, the alarm was raised. Undeterred, Smalls maneuvered the ship ahead to the Union-controlled enclave, moving swiftly beyond the range of Confederate guns. He had his crew flourish the white bed sheet that his wife had brought on board. As the Planter approached the Union clipper "Onward", Smalls took off his hat, waved his arms and shouted:

Good morning, sir! I've brought you some of the old United States guns, sir!

The daring escape that Smalls engineered was more than a military coup; it was a cultural breakthrough. The courageous action was a major factor in the decision by President Abraham Lincoln to allow blacks to enlist in the Union Army. Following his distinguished service as a Union soldier, Smalls used the notoriety that he gained from the great escape to build an even more remarkable career as a businessman, publisher, and politician. He led the fight in the state legislature to establish in South Carolina the first free and compulsory public school system in the United States, before serving in the United States House of Representatives throughout Reconstruction.

Small's courage was not a moment in time in a theater of war. It was a lifestyle of intrepid initiative that you can follow if you resolve to:

TEST THE WATERS — Your waters may not be as treacherous as the actual waters through which Smalls had to maneuver, but you still have to be willing to get off the shore and venture beyond the safe harbors of your life. Greatness lies before you in the deep waters. Forge ahead into the unknown. Your destiny will rise.

TACKLE YOUR FEARS — Small's faith kept him going, overcoming his fears through the perils of night. Let your faith extinguish your fears as it sparks your courage.

TAKE DOWN BARRIERS — Courage is the quality of mind and spirit that enables you to face your barriers — whether they be internal or external — and overcome them. Like Smalls, first develop your plan. As you implement it, pay attention to the barriers of your checkpoints all along the way, but keep your eyes on the horizon. That's where you'll find your victory.

TRIGGER THE FUTURE — Your greatness now leaves a legacy for future generations, as Henry Wadsworth Longfellow reminds us:

> *Lives of great men all remind us,*
> *We can make our lives sublime,*
> *And departing, leave behind us,*
> *Footprints on the sands of time.*

# ENCOURAGE ONE ANOTHER							JANUARY 3RD

> *I am exceedingly distressed at the proceedings . . .*
> Elbridge Gerry

On July 4, 1776, members of the Continental Congress gathered in Philadelphia to sign the Declaration of Independence. Less than a week before — less than one hundred miles away — one hundred British sail appeared in New York's Lower Bay. Some of General George Washington's military advisers counseled a retreat, pulling back their thinly spread and outmanned army from what would later become the boroughs of Manhattan, Brooklyn and Queens. But the Congress wasn't quite ready to give up New York City. Washington received his orders and directed his troops to fight to hold the ground.

Not all signers of the Declaration on that fateful day voiced confidence about this strategy. As they waited for the final document to return from the printer, Benjamin Harrison of Virginia said to Elbridge Gerry of Massachusetts:

> *I shall have a great advantage over you, Mr. Gerry, when we are all hung for what we are now doing. From the size and weight of my body I shall die in a few minutes, but from the lightness of your body you will dance in the air an hour or two before you are dead.*

In retrospect, it is difficult to determine the degree of seriousness with which Harrison made this comment. But Benjamin Rush of Pennsylvania, who overheard it, noted that the remark "procured a transient smile, but it was soon succeeded by the solemnity with which the whole business was conducted".

The signers put everything at risk — even their own lives — in declaring independence; none of them possessed a crystal ball to reveal the seven years of revolutionary vicissitude about to unfold, resulting in a remarkable — some characterized it as miraculous — outcomes: not only military victory but the establishment of a new political order: representative government premised on popular sovereignty and individual enterprise that evolved over the succeeding centuries as a paradigm for so many countries of the world.

The signers succeeded in large part because they encouraged one another to make it through. Follow their example. Seek to encourage others by using your:

WIT — Sometimes the best way to help someone get through a dark moment is to make light of it. This approach worked for America's Founding Fathers. Let your sense of humor ease another's burden, your wit distract from the dire mood, your smile brighten someone's day.

WORDS — Your words have the power to depress or uplift, so watch what you say. An encouraging word can light the flame of progress. A discouraging word can snuff out the spark of success. Use your words to avoid disaster and foster success as the Apostle James suggests.

> *. . . the tongue is a little member and boasts great things.*
> *See how great a forest a little fire kindles!*
> *— James 3:5*

WILL — Life isn't easy. You may have detractors, adversaries, even archenemies or saboteurs — people who seek to thwart or destroy you because of conflicting aims or outright ill will. You may not have an enemy as formidable as the British military that the Founders faced; nevertheless the question confronts you. Do you have the strength of will to face your foes - whoever they might be - to stare them down and keep going for your goal? Exercise your will. Your determination to pull yourself through will encourage someone else.

WALK — People are paying attention to what you say, to what you don't say, and even more to what you do. Encourage others by your example. Walk out ahead of the crowd. Strive to be first in line, to be at the head of the pack. Someone will be inspired by seeing you take the lead.

SEIZE YOUR BATTLEFIELD   JANUARY 4TH

*We entered Gettysburg in the afternoon, just in time to meet the enemy entering
the town, and in good season to drive him back before his getting a foothold.*
John Buford, Union Army General

The Battle of Gettysburg was fought in July 1863; it was
considered to be the turning point of the Civil War. General George
Meade's Union Army of the Potomac defeated the Confederate forces led
by General Robert E. Lee, yielding upon the Pennsylvania battlefield the
greatest casualties of the war and halting Lee's invasion of the North.

On July 3rd, the last day of the battle, the Confederate infantry
moved against the Union positions on Cemetery Ridge in an assault known
as Pickett's Charge, named after one of Confederate generals who led the
attack.

Hispanic American soldier Joseph De Castro was part of the
Union army on that fateful day. Born and raised in Boston, De Castro had
joined the all-volunteer 19th Massachusetts Infantry at the outbreak of the
Civil War. He carried the flag of Company I of his infantry into battle at
Gettysburg. During Pickett's Charge, De Castro assaulted with the staff of
his own flag a Confederate soldier bearing the 19th Virginia Infantry flag.
He prevailed in the scuffle, seizing the 19th Virginia's colors, and brought
the emblem of victory to General Alexander S. Webb, who described the
incident.

*At the instant a man broke through my lines and thrust a rebel
battle flag into my hands. He never said a word and darted back. It was
Corporal Joseph H. De Castro, one of my color bearers. He had knocked
down a color bearer in the enemy's line with the staff of the Massachusetts
State colors, seized the falling flag and dashed it to me.*

The failure of Pickett's charge, due to the valiant efforts of De
Castro and his fellow soldiers, was the military blow knocking down the
Southern war effort at Gettysburg from which it never fully recovered. For
his courageous service in battle, De Castro became the first Hispanic-
American to be awarded the Medal of Honor, the United States's highest
military decoration for valor in combat.

De Castro made a bold move and seized his battlefield, helping to
turn the tide of victory. Your victory will come as you seize your daily
battlefields. You can do so through:

PREPARATION — You cannot seize your battlefield if you're not
ready for battle. The bigger your fight, the greater the preparation must be.
Victory won't happen for you on that pivotal day unless you make it happen

before that day. Focus in on what you need to do to prepare for whatever challenge lies before you. Make a plan. Get it done.

PRINCIPLE — Get in touch with your convictions, not just your beliefs: the latter you will sing about; the former you will die for. De Castro possessed a conviction about the flag he was carrying, so strong that it motivated him to transform his flag into a weapon to vanquish the opposing flag bearer. Meditate on your convictions until they become a source of your strength . . . until they become strong enough to inspire courageous action.

PUGNACITY — Life is a fight for territory. If you don't seize your territory, someone or something else will take it. If you don't fight for truth, falsehood will occupy your mind. If you don't fight for vigor, laziness will govern your lifestyle. If you don't fight for harmony, conflict will plague your relationships. If you don't fight for prosperity, poverty will take over your life. Figure out your battlefield, then, like Castro, move forward. Seize it!

PROVIDENCE — Don't forget your spiritual battlefield. Be a prayer warrior. There are times when prayer is your most effective — and only weapon. Put on your divine armor; it could be your shelter through the storm. When all else fails, pray for the outcomes you seek, as the Apostle James advised.

The prayer of a righteous person is powerful and effective.
— James 5:16

DON'T GIVE WAY TO HATING   JANUARY 5TH

If we have honestly acknowledged our painful
and shared past, then we can have reconciliation.
Elizabeth Eckford

In the late summer of 1957 the battle over school desegregation in the South reached its terrifying climax. The racial conflict over public education had been raging since the 1954 United States Supreme Court decision in *Brown v. Board of Education* in favor of school integration. In its aftermath forty-two segregation laws were passed in Southern states. Among other such measures, in Mississippi it became illegal to file desegregation proceedings in state courts; in Virginia, public schools in some counties closed down rather than integrate; in Georgia, school officials spending tax monies on integrated schools committed a felony.

In Arkansas, Governor Orval Faubus stationed national guard troops at Central High School in Little Rock to prevent the entry of African American youth. Consequently, a federal judge ordered the withdrawal of the state troops. On September 4, 1957, Elizabeth Eckford and eight other black students, who eventually became known as the Little Rock Nine, were blocked by a white mob from entering the school. Fifteen-year-old Eckford described the horrific experience.

> *I stood looking at the school — it looked so big! Just then the guards let some white students through. The crowd was quiet. I guess they were waiting to see what was going to happen. When I was able to steady my knees, I walked up to the guard who had let the white students in. He didn't move. When I tried to squeeze past him, he raised his bayonet and then the other guards moved in and they raised their bayonets. They glared at me with a mean look and I was very frightened and didn't know what to do. I turned around and the crowd came toward me. They moved closer and closer. Somebody started yelling, "Drag her over this tree! Let's take care of that nigger!"*

Eckford and the other youth fled the scene and studied at home for the next two weeks until President Dwight Eisenhower intervened, sending in federal troops to safeguard the Little Rock Nine. On September 24th, with soldiers and police officers at their side, Eckford and her schoolmates finally entered the school building — through a side door!

Eckford went on to attain her college degree, serve in the U.S. military and held various jobs, including writing for newspapers. Though she could have felt justified in doing so, Eckford didn't give way to hate, instead developing a friendship with Hazel Bryan Massery, one of segregationist students at Central High School who protested against her entry. The two women even made speeches together during a 1997 reconciliation rally.

Though their friendship eventually frayed, their relationship shows that the courage that it took for Eckford to walk the perilous path to integrate her high school didn't end there. It takes courage to refuse to return hatred. Eckford did it; you can, too, when you:

REFUSE TO RECIPROCATE — A passage from Rudyard Kipling's "If" captures this virtue.

> *If you can keep your head when all about you*
> *Are losing theirs and blaming it on you;*
> *If you can trust yourself when all men doubt you,*
> *But make allowance for their doubting too;*
> *If you can wait and not be tired by waiting,*

Or, being lied about, don't deal in lies,
Or being hated, don't give way to hating,
And yet don't look too good, nor talk too wise.

RISE TO THE OCCASION — If someone has been hating on you, do your best to flip the script. Show them love instead of hate. Jesus did it and advised us all to follow His example:

Do good to those who hate you . . .
— Matthew 5:44

RECONCILE WITH ENEMIES — If Eckford could stand together at a reconciliation rally with a woman who had once stood in her way; then you can also reconcile with someone who has opposed you — if only you reach deep within for the courage to do so.

TELL THE TRUTH BOLDLY   JANUARY 6TH

Fellow Citizens, pardon me, allow me to ask, why am I called upon to speak here today? What have I, or those I represent, to do with your national independence? Are the great principles of political freedom and of natural justice, embodied in that Declaration of Independence, extended to us?
Frederick Douglass

On July 4, 1852, Frederick Douglass, America's leading black abolitionist, delivered the Independence Day address in Rochester, New York. Douglass had been born a slave on a Maryland plantation thirty-five years earlier but escaped as a late teen to Massachusetts. He devoted the rest of his life to the antislavery cause, renown for his searing oratory that America be held accountable for its original sin. In his Fourth of July speech, Douglass elaborated his moral argument with a graphic question.

What, am I to argue that it is wrong to make men brutes, to rob them of their liberty, to work them without wages, to keep them ignorant of their relations to their fellow men, to beat them with sticks, to flay their flesh with the lash, to load their limbs with irons, to hunt them with dogs, to sell them at auction, to sunder their families, to knock out their teeth, to burn their flesh, to starve them into obedience and submission to their masters?

He concluded his oration with challenging words.

What, to the American slave, is your Fourth of July? I answer: a day that reveals to him, more than all other days in the year, the gross injustice and cruelty to which he is the constant victim. To him, your celebration is a sham: your boasted liberty, an unholy license; your national greatness, swelling vanity . . . There is not a nation of savages, there is not a nation on the earth guilty of practices more shocking and bloody than are the people of the United States at this very hour.

It takes courage to tell the truth when you're dealing with controversial or sensitive issues, particularly when they concern wrongdoing on the part of others. Douglass' bold truth-telling made a big difference. About a decade after his Fourth of July fulmination, his powerful protests paved the way to the White House, where he met with President Abraham Lincoln and other top officials about turning his fiery declarations into federal law, yielding the Emancipation Proclamation and eventually the Thirteenth Amendments, abolishing slavery.

Like Douglass, you can boldly — and effectively — tell the truth when you resolve to be:

STRONG — Douglass' example may be a difficult one for you to follow. You may shy away from confrontation and choose the path of diplomacy. But in those moments when boldness is called for, speak from your soul. If your advocacy flows from your heart, the passion of the points you make will uplift your audience. Accept the fact that sometimes the truth is difficult for others to accept — it may cause discomfort, even pain; declare it anyway. Your bold voice just might be what's needed to spur change.

STRATEGIC — His militant language notwithstanding, Douglass did not advocate — as some of his peers did — violence in the battle for racial justice. His indignation was strategic, as he waged war with his words, preaching messages designed to pierce the heart and soul of an anguished nation. Let your indignation be strategic. Don't fight your battle with physical weapons to inflict arms and legs. Wage war with moral weapons: deploy your words and writings to move hearts and minds. Without guns and fists and with a strong and strategic approach, you will certainly win over friends and neighbors, and, as Douglass did, you just might uplift the nation.

STAY COOL UNDER FIRE   JANUARY 7TH

His outstanding courage, brilliant leadership and unswerving devotion to duty
were contributing factors in the success achieved by his company and reflect
the highest credit upon First Lieutenant Lee and the United States Naval Service.
From the Navy Cross Citation of Chew-Een Lee

On December 7, 1941, when Pearl Harbor was attacked, Chew-Een (nicknamed "Kurt") Lee, the first-born son of Chinese immigrants, was a high school student participating in the Junior Reserve Officers' Training Corps. Before the end of World War II Lee had joined the United States Marine Corps and moved to Quantico, Virginia to attend the Marines Officer Training School. His relatively small frame (5 feet, 6 inches; 130 pounds) notwithstanding, Lee excelled and became the first Asian-American officer in the Marine Corps.

With the outbreak of the Korean War in June 1950, First Lieutenant Lee received notice that his unit would ship out for the war zone in September. Lee later described the poignant moment when he said goodbye to his parents.

I came from a family of limited means. My father . . . distributed fruit and vegetables to restaurants and hotels in Sacramento. He stayed home from work that morning, and my mother . . . made a special meal. There was an awkward moment when the clock on the wall said it was time to depart. My mother was very brave. She said nothing. My father had been reading the Chinese newspaper, or pretending to. He was a tough guy, my father, and I admired his toughness. He rose from his chair and shook my hand abruptly. He tried to talk, but couldn't, and that's when my mother broke down.

On route to the theater of war, Lee's superiors endeavored to reassign him to translation duties, but he insisted on commanding his platoon. They landed at Inchon, South Korea with the assignment of forcing the North Koreans — bolstered by troops from the People's Republic of China — to retreat northward. During one night of combat, facing enemy gunfire, Lee led his men in an advance, sowing confusion by shouting at the opposing forces in Mandarin Chinese while attacking with grenades and gunfire. Lee was wounded in the knee and elbow and had to be evacuated, but before being sent to Japan for recuperation, he left the hospital and returned to his unit, walking the last ten miles to the front line when his jeep ran out of gas. With his arm in a sling, Lee drilled platoons in combat maneuvers. Lee later received, the Navy Cross, the Silver Star and the Navy Marine Corps Commendation Ribbon for bravery in battle.

Lee stayed cool under fire, and his actions led to success. Just as

Lee did, you can stay cool under fire through your:

TOUGHNESS — Lee described his father as tough; so was he. Physical toughness is important; mental toughness, more so. Discipline your thinking, to keep out distractions. Strengthen your attitude, so you can deal with whatever difficult situations arise.

TEMERITY — "The desire for safety stands against every great and noble enterprise," wrote the Roman historian Tacitus. Lee boldly lead his men in battle without concern for his personal safety. If you're going to do something worthwhile with your life, there will be times when audacity is called for. Don't shy away from those moments.

TEMPERAMENT — Don't let the heat of your circumstances determine the intensity of your emotions. When proverbial — or actual — bullets are flying at you, keep one eye on the projectiles so you can dodge them; keep your other eye on your goal so you can transcend them.

TONE — It's not easy to stay cool when the enemy attacks or calamity strikes. At such moments, be intentional about measuring your words. Say just those things — express them calmly, only shout if you have to — that you need to get through.

BE A COURAGEOUS CHRONICLER   JANUARY 8TH

*I shall be found with 'Indians' engraved on my brain when I am
dead. A fire has been kindled within me, which will never go out.*
Helen Hunt Jackson

In 1881 poet and activist Helen Hunt Jackson published "A Century of Dishonor", which chronicled the U.S. government's dealings with various Native American tribes. Jackson documented state and federal policies that resulted in broken treaties, property rights violations and other wrongs. She described the injustices suffered by these tribes, forcefully making her case in the book's concluding chapter.

*President after President has appointed commission after commission
to inquire into and report upon Indian affairs and to make suggestions as to
the best methods of managing them. The reports are filled with eloquent
statements of wrongs done to the Indians, of perfidies on the part of the
government. They counsel, as earnestly as words can, a trial of the simple and
unperplexing expedients of telling truth, keeping promises, making fair*

bargains, dealing justly in all ways and all things. . . .

Jackson not only courageously chronicled Native American history but also sent the book to every member of Congress. Her initiative helped to build momentum for a shift towards a more enlightened governmental policy towards Native Americans that took root over time. Heed Jackson's example. When you have an important story that needs to be told, keep these two points from her book in mind.

CALL OUT THE PROBLEMS

Cheating, robbing, breaking promises — these three are clearly things which must cease to be done. One more thing, also, and that is the refusal of the protection of the law to the Indian's rights of property, "of life, liberty , and the pursuit of happiness." . . . When this four things have ceased to be done, time, statesmanship, philanthropy and Christianity can slowly and surely do the rest. . . .

Jackson underscored specific harmful actions to be rectified, then identified the positive steps to be taken. Follow her approach. Specify problems and solutions. Courage means that you can face your critics and keep going, as Jackson did and Ralph Waldo Emerson advised:

Whatever you do, you need courage. Whatever course you decide upon, there is always someone to tell you that you are wrong. There are always difficulties arising that tempt you to believe your critics are right.

CLEAR THE SWAMP

There is a disposition in a certain class of mind to be impatient with any protestation against wrong which is unaccompanied or unprepared with a quick and exact scheme of remedy. This is illogical. When pioneers in a new country find a tract of poisonous and swampy wilderness to be reclaimed, they do not withhold their hands from fire and axe till they see clearly which way roads should run, where good water will spring and what crops will best grow on the redeemed land. They first clear the swamp. So with this poisonous and baffling part of the domain of our national affairs — let us first "clear the swamp."

Jackson used a compelling metaphor that made clear the incremental approach to problem-solving. Like her, don't be captive to conventional wisdom or big-picture myopia. Be willing to clarify that you don't have to fix things all at once. Let your listeners know that first "clearing the swamp" may be the best way to sow the seeds of change in individual lives and even turn the tides of history.

GET READY TO RIDE   JANUARY 9TH

There's a time for casting silver; a time for casting cannon . . .
Paul Revere

During the night of April 18, 1775, seven hundred British troops, who were quartered in Boston — the early hotbed of the American Revolution — began a fateful foray. The troops left the occupied city for a raid on Lexington to capture colonial leaders Samuel Adams and John Hancock, then on to Concord to destroy one of the larger caches of Patriot gunpowder and other military supplies. Their secret mission was soon uncovered, and Paul Revere galloped ahead of the Redcoats to warn his compatriots. His courageous journey that night is memorably rendered through several stanzas of Longfellow's poem *Paul Revere's Ride.*

A hurry hoofs in a village street,
A shape in the moonlight, a bulk in the dark,
And beneath, from the pebbles, in passing, a spark
Struck out by a steed flying fearless and fleet;
That was all! And yet, through the gold and the light
The fate of a nation was riding that night;
And the spark struck out by that steed in his flight,
Kindled the land into flame with its heat.

He has left the village and mounted the steep,
And beneath him, tranquil and broad and deep,
Is the Mystic, meeting the ocean tides;
And under the alders, that skirt its edge,
Now soft on the sand, now loud on the ledge,
Is heard the tramp of his steed as he rides.

It was one by the village clock,
When he galloped into Lexington.
He saw the gilded weathercock
Swim in the moonlight as he passed,
And the meeting house windows, blank and bare,
Gaze at him with a spectral glare,
As if they already stood aghast
At the bloody work they would look upon.

Revere accomplished his mission: the leaders escaped and the militia was forewarned. On through this consequential night until dawn, gunfire was exchanged; casualties resulted; homes were burned; a long, bloody war for a nation's independence had begun.

Lexington and Concord was not Revere's first ride for the colonial cause: as an army lieutenant, he took to horseback to carry messages; and as a courier for the Boston Committee of Public Safety, spreading the news throughout the colonies of Britain's rising aggressions against Boston. Revere was ready for the challenge the night of his historic ride. For you to be ready to ride into your challenge, you must be willing to:

FORGET about other things. Don't be distracted with other stuff. Concentrate on the task at hand.

FACE the challenge. Don't shy away from difficulty. Prioritize it. Put the hardest thing at the top of your agenda for the day. Get it out of the way. If you wait to do it, it might not get done.

FIX the problem. Be realistic in how you approach it. Think through possible solutions and keep trying them until you apply the right one. Each "ride" will yield less fear, more confidence and greater courage, preparing you for your unexpected midnight ride.

FLY to the moment. Revere had prepared himself for his pivotal moment through countless rides. Years of patriotic service equipped him to rise to the historic occasion. Check your own preparation then take off. The time for deliberation is over. Throw caution to the wind. Go for it! Beat the enemy to your appointment with destiny.

ACT ON THE TRUTH   JANUARY 10TH

. . . the sick women . . . were cowering, some on wooden settles, most of them on the ground, excluding those who were too ill to rise; and these last poor wretches lay prostrate on the floor, without bed, mattress, or pillow, in tattered and filthy blankets.
Frances Anne Kemble

In 1834 notable British actress Frances Anne Kemble married wealthy Philadelphian Pierce Mease Butler, whom she met on her American acting tour two years earlier. A couple years into the marriage, Butler inherited his grandfather's cotton, tobacco and rice plantations in Georgia and the seven hundred slaves who worked them.

Butler made several trips to the plantations without Kemble, but, at her insistence, during the winter of 1838-1839, she spent two months on the plantations with her husband. Gravely concerned about the conditions of plantation life for the slaves — and her husband's failure to share her scruples — she kept a diary of her experiences.

One episode, which she recorded, was her visit to the plantation "hospital".

> *. . . And here, in their hour of sickness and suffering, lay those whose health and strength are spent in the unrequited labor for us; those who, perhaps even yesterday, were being urged on to their unpaid task; those whose husbands, fathers, brothers, and sons were even at that hour sweating over the earth; whose produce was to buy for us all the luxuries which health can revel in, all the comforts which can alleviate sickness.*

She was anguished by what she observed.

> *I stood in the midst of them, perfectly unable to speak, the tears pouring from my eyes at this sad spectacle of their misery, myself and my emotion alike strange and incomprehensible to them. Here lay women expecting every hour the terrors and agonies of childbirth; others who had just brought their doomed offspring into the world; others who were groaning over the anguish and bitter disappointment of miscarriages. Here lay some burning with fever . . . dirt, noise, and stench, and every aggravation of which sickness is capable, combined in their condition. Here they lay like brute beasts . . . unvisited by any of those Divine influences which may ennoble the dispensations of pain and illness, forsaken, as it seemed to me, of all good; and yet, O God, Thou surely hadst not forsaken them! Now pray take notice that this is the hospital of an estate where the owners are supposed to be humane, the overseer efficient and kind, and the Negroes remarkably well-cared for and comfortable.*

Kemble was so troubled by her plantation visit — and her husband's intransigence — that the marriage didn't survive. Butler threatened that he would prevent her from seeing their two daughters if she published her diary observations. Kemble courageously took her daughters to England, endured the divorce, and published her anti-slavery *Journal of a Residence on a Georgian Plantation in 1838-1839*. As Kemble did, you can act on the truth as you:

DISCOVER — Important truth won't come looking for you; you have to go out and find it. That's what Kemble did, insisting on a trip to her husband's plantations. Go to those difficult places where you can discover the truth.

DECOUPLE — Once you discover an ugly truth, separate yourself from it. You may not have to take an extreme action like the divorce that Kemble suffered through. Don't stay connected to the problem. Step away from it, so you can gain the perspective to change it.

DESTINE — Your destiny will remain beyond your grasp if you fail to act on the truth. Fear is such a powerful emotion that it can paralyze you. Courage is also a strong emotional force, dynamic enough to break fear's hold because it comes from a deeper place. Fear resides in your mind. Courage rises from your heart. Get in touch with your spirit, release courage, and you will act on the truth in ways that liberates yourself as well as others. Remember the counsel of George Sheehan:

> *Success means having the courage, the determination, and the*
> *will to become the person you believe you were meant to be.*

BE STRONG IN WAR AND PEACE   JANUARY 11TH

> *. . . I thank a merciful God that He has given us the faith, the courage,*
> *and the power from which to mold victory. We have known the bitterness of*
> *defeat and the exultation of triumph, and from both we have learned there can*
> *be no turning back. We must go forward to preserve in peace what we won in war.*
> Douglas MacArthur

On September 2, 1945, the formal surrender documents ending the hostilities of World War II with Japan were signed in Tokyo Bay on board the warship U.S.S. Missouri. General Douglas MacArthur, commander of United States Army Forces in the Far East and soon to be appointed supreme commander of the Allied powers during the military occupation of Japan, broadcasted remarks to the American people after the execution of the documents. MacArthur began with these words.

> *Today the guns are silent. A great tragedy has ended. A great victory*
> *has been won. The skies no longer rain death — the seas bear only commerce*
> *— men everywhere walk upright in the sunlight. The entire world lies quietly*
> *at peace. The holy mission has been completed. And in reporting this to you,*
> *the people, I speak for the thousands of silent lips, forever stilled among the*
> *jungles and the beaches and in the deep waters of the Pacific which marked the*
> *way. I speak for the unnamed brave millions homeward bound to take up the*
> *challenge of that future which they did so much to salvage from the brink of*
> *disaster.*

MacArthur subsequently reiterated his determination to be just as strong in peace as he had been in war.

> *If the historian of the future should deem my service worthy of some slight reference, it would be my hope that he mention me not as a commander engaged in . . . battles, even though victorious to American arms, but rather as that one whose sacred duty it became, once the guns were silenced, to carry to the land of our vanquished foe the solace and hope and faith of Christian morals.*

MacArthur's example to be ready to do battle for peace as well as in war is worthy of your emulation; to do so, be:

PRINCIPLED — Know what you're fighting for, and make sure the goals of your battle align with life-affirming, joyful principles. Be careful that you don't end up on the wrong team fighting for the wrong things. Take a retreat from your daily battlefields to reflect on what you're fighting for. If you're unclear about the purpose of your mission or doubtful about its integrity, back off to get some advice from a new source.

POWERFUL — You have to pick your battles because you can't win them all. Once you choose, fight hard for what you believe. True power comes when you fight more for the ideas that foster peace than when you battle for the issues that foment war.

PEACE-MAKING — Remember Jesus' words:

> *Blessed are the peacemakers, for they will be called children of God.*
> — Matthew 5:9

Even after bitter battles, be resolved to peacemaking, which rises from a commitment to better understand those with whom you differ. To gain a deeper understanding of someone, get to know what she really needs and wants — then do something positive about it. People won't care how much you know until they know how much you care.

PRAYERFUL — Meditate on the words of Phillip Brooks:

> *Do not pray for easy lives. Pray to be stronger men. Do not pray for tasks equal to your power, pray for power equal to your tasks.*

LIVE WHAT YOU KNOW TO BE RIGHT   JANUARY 12TH

You may wear your virtues as a crown,
As you walk through life serenely,
And grace your simple rustic gown
With a beauty more than queenly.
Though only one for you shall care,
One only speak your praises;
And you never wear in your shining hair,
A richer flower than daisies.
Phoebe Cary

Phoebe Cary was born in 1824 and raised on an Ohio farm; her life became a profile in courage. She and her sister Alice were required to work on the farm, so they attended school only periodically, which turned more sporadic after their mother died and their stepfather was unsupportive of their educational aspirations. Phoebe and Alice continued with their obligations at home but determined to self-educate, studying late into the night after a full day's work. They were creative in sustaining their nocturnal academic pursuits. After the rest of the family had gone to bed, they used — instead of candles — a saucer of lard with a bit of rag for a wick, their only light.

In male-dominated antebellum America, Cary became a champion of women's rights. In 1848, at the time of the the Seneca Falls Convention — the first women's rights convention — she edited *Revolution*, a newspaper published by social reformer Susan B. Anthony. Cary subsequently published two volumes of e poetry: *Poems and Parodies* and *Poems of Faith, Hope, and Love* and gained renown for writing church music, her lyrics appearing in many church hymnals and on Sunday School cards as well as being sung at funerals. The following poem exemplified her very own life of courage, for she lived what she knew to be right. This verse also signifies the three success principles for your own commitment to live what you know to be right; you must be:

STERN:

Here's a hand to the boy who has courage
To do what he knows to be right;
When he falls in the way of temptation,
He has a hard battle to fight.
Who strives against self and his comrades
Will find a most powerful foe.
All honor to him if he conquers.
A cheer for the boy who says "NO!"

STRONG:

> *There's many a battle fought daily*
> *The world knows nothing about;*
> *There's many a brave little soldier*
> *Whose strength puts a legion to rout.*
> *And he who fights sin singlehanded*
> *Is more of a hero, I say,*
> *Than he who leads soldiers to battle*
> *And conquers by arms in the fray.*

STEADFAST:

> *Be steadfast, my boy, when you're tempted,*
> *To do what you know to be right.*
> *Stand firm by the colors of manhood,*
> *And you will o'ercome in the fight.*
> *"The right," be your battle cry ever*
> *In waging the warfare of life,*
> *And God, who knows who are the heroes,*
> *Will give you the strength for the strife.*

CRY OUT FOR JUSTICE   JANUARY 13TH

> *The slavery that now takes place is in a Christian land, and without*
> *the express sanction of civil government . . . is most notoriously unjust.*
> Samuel Hopkins

At the time of the American Revolution, slavery was a well-established institution in the colonies. But the Declaration of Independence proclaimed: *We hold these truths to be self-evident, that all men are created equal . . .* Consequently, a chorus of voices arose insisting on the inconsistency of slavery with America's new values. Perhaps the loudest outcry came from Congregational minister Samuel Hopkins, who authored the antislavery protest *A Dialogue Concerning the Slavery of the Africans.* Hopkins published and directed it at the Continental Congress in 1776, not long after the Congress affirmed egalitarian principles in declaring America's independence from Britain. Hopkins wrote about the contradiction and even intimated divine judgement.

> *. . . These things . . . make it duty to oppose and bear testimony, both*
> *in public and more privately, against this evil practice, which is evidently*
> *injurious to individuals, and threatens our ruin as a people. . . But if we*
> *obstinately refuse to reform what we have implicitly declared to be wrong .*

. . have we not the greatest reason to fear, yea, may we not with great certainty conclude, God will yet withdraw His kind protection from us and punish us yet seven times more?

Hopkins became one of the earliest antislavery advocates because his worldview was rooted in the moral certainties of God's word. In Hopkins' worldview slavery was wrong because it violated God's purpose for human dignity and fulfillment — *the unrighteousness of it is most apparent . . . a general and crying sin for which we are under the awful frowns of heaven.* From his perspective, to fail to denounce slavery would have been an act of disobedience to God. Hopkins knew he was going up against the prevailing ethos of colonial culture in support of slavery, but he possessed the courage to cry out for justice. Strive to do the same as you:

QUESTION YOURSELF — Do you have the courage to look deep within, to search your soul and heart for what is true and right? This is the first step: to be get in touch with your worldview, get clear how you view God, and on how you see the world. Embrace your worldview by asking yourself the following questions, taking some time to think through your responses, writing down the answers: What is my worldview or belief system? What are my deepest convictions? Where do they come from? Why do I believe them?

QUESTION OTHERS — Your second step is to get in touch with the world views of those closest to you, those with most influence over you. Whether you realize it or not, you are influenced by the perspectives of friends, family, the media you read and watch, and the places you spend your time. Are you being influenced by hedonism (whatever feels good is good), materialism (what matters most is money), fatalism (what will be will be), or narcissism (what I want comes first)? I am a Christian with a firm belief in the supremacy of God, the deity of Christ, and the inerrancy of the Bible; this book is written from that worldview. Know your worldview: take courage, dig deep inside for it; once you discover it, embrace it and proclaim it!

QUEST FOR TRUTH — Hopkins' strong stand against slavery took courage. His church was in Newport, Rhode Island, one of the hubs of the colonial slave trade. He spoke out even though his congregation was full of not only slaveholders but also those benefiting financially from the commerce in African slaves. The truth of his voice confronted their unrighteousness and spurred a moral movement. Let your cry for justice ring with truth.

TAKE A COURAGEOUS STAND   JANUARY 14TH

> *. . . those who call the Southern Negroes ungrateful are only*
> *those who never do anything to call forth that emotion....May I ask*
> *what gratitude they owe to those who would degrade them? What gratitude*
> *does that child owe to his own father, who would coldly sell him as a slave?*
> Margaret Douglass

In January 1854, Margaret Douglass, a white resident of Norfolk, Virginia, was arrested and brought to trial for the crime of teaching free Negro children to read. Eighteen months earlier, Douglass and her daughter had opened a school in her home, charging twenty-five black boys and girls who attended three dollars per quarter. Having recently moved to Norfolk, Douglass was unaware that it was against Virginia law to assemble any African Americans, free or enslaved, for the purpose of instructing them to read or write.

Douglass did not intend to practice civil disobedience. But she was intentional in her own way, speaking for herself at the trial about the righteousness of her conduct. Douglass took a courageous stand. Strive to be courageous in similar ways as you show:

SACRIFICE — For eleven months prior to her arrest Douglass and her teenage daughter brought free black children into their home, teaching them to read and write. Such sacrifice is exemplary. Take steps to put your self-interested agenda to the side to benefit those in need.

SINEW — Declining to be represented by an attorney, Douglass exhibited strength, courageously defending herself, asserting that she was not an abolitionist and that she only taught free blacks with the objective of improving their lives. She asserted in her defense:

> *When they are sick, or in want, on whom does the duty devolve to*
> *seek them out and administer to their necessities? Does it fall upon you,*
> *gentlemen? Oh no, it is not expected that gentlemen will take the trouble to seek*
> *out a negro hut for the purpose of alleviating the wretchedness he may find*
> *within it. Why then persecute your benevolent ladies for doing that which you*
> *yourselves have so long neglected? Shall we treat our slaves with less compassion*
> *than we do the cattle in the field?*

Her impassioned plea notwithstanding, the court ruled against her, in the judge's words:

> *For these reasons, as an example to all others in like cases disposed to*
> *offend, and in vindication of the policy and justness of our laws, which every*

individual should be taught to respect, the judgment of the court is, in addition to the proper fine and costs, that you be imprisoned for the period of one month in the jail of this city.

SERENDIPITY — About ten years later, free blacks of Douglass' community took formal action to abolish Norfolk's restrictive literacy and assembly laws. Their successful initiative stemmed from the notoriety of Douglass' case. It takes a special courage to help others when the cultural tide and legal establishment are firmly against you. Steps of civil disobedience should not be taken lightly but deliberately, circumspectly, prayerfully — as a last resort after all other remedies have been exhausted. Even then, because of the severity of the consequences. Only then is suffering — even persecution — for righteousness' sake justified. Remember Douglass: her courageous actions not only led to unjust laws being overturned during her lifetime; she also became a role model for Rosa Parks and others of the Civil Rights era a century later, conscientious citizens just like her, facing unjust laws and nonetheless taking action on behalf of others. Make sure that the cause that you're suffering for is morally right, ethically pure, and perfectly just; your burden will soon be lifted; your example will eventually be exalted; and your actions — even if it wasn't your original intent — will forge a better society. Douglass fulfilled the meaning of the following words of Jesus. You should do the same.

*Blessed are those who are persecuted for righteousness'
sake, for theirs is the kingdom of heaven.*
— Matthew 5:10

CONFRONT YOUR BITTER TRUTH   JANUARY 15TH

If you go through life half-stepping, you will never hit full stride.
Joseph Holland

After a few months at Harkhomes, Slim had tired of the regimen, so he initiated a "make nice" campaign with his wife to return home. He not only started calling her everyday, but he saved some of each paycheck from his part-time job toward sending her flowers, contributing to the rent, and helping out with other household expenses and the kids' school supplies. Slim soon moved back in with the family.

Just a week after having left the shelter, Slim was back, late at night, knocking on the Harkhomes door. I let him in and we talked until dawn. I'd sensed that he'd been living a lie, so I challenged him to come clean. He said that, after a lifetime of wearing a mask of chuckles and grins, this was the hardest thing he'd ever done.

"I'm afraid, Rev," he admitted.

I encouraged him to own up by sharing a verse that I'd committed to memory long ago.

> *Two natures beat within my breast,*
> *The one is foul, the other blessed.*
> *The one I love, the other I hate;*
> *The one I feed will dominate.*

"Stop thinking about your fears," I counseled him, "and they will go away."

"I'm a gambler," he finally confessed. "And I'm an alcoholic, too."

For years Slim had been slipping away from his job at lunch and scurrying around after work, stealing time for a card game, slot machine, or dice throw wherever he could, concealing his habit from his family. His wife had finally busted him — short on the rent money one too many times — and put him out of the house, landing him at Harkhomes the first time around. Still skeptical upon his return home, she enlisted her brother to follow Slim after work one day; an incriminating photo was taken and presented to the suspicious spouse, and Slim was back out on the streets within a week of his homecoming.

Slim's confession was the key to his personal breakthrough. He confronted his bitter truth, and his life turned around. You can experience similar positive outcomes by confronting your own bitter truth as you:

STATE YOUR TRUTH — Slim was a very long time in denial. Be honest: first with yourself about your challenges; then with those whom you trust. It is trite but true: confession is good for the soul. Find a confidant to confide in. To free yourself from the bondage of your problems, you have to put them on the table and enlist a trustworthy adviser to sort through them, putting the pieces of your life back together. Mark Twain's point is relevant.

Courage is resistance to fear, mastery of fear, not absence of fear.

STARVE YOUR FEARS— Emotions can be unruly, hard to control and manage. Take a deep breath and step back from the emotional turmoil to separate the negative inner forces from the positive. Be self-aware enough to feel the fears rising within you. Be intentional about isolating them: withdraw your time and energy from your stressors. If you refuse to feed them by not talking about them, thinking about them, focusing on them; they will soon shift to a diminished place in your consciousness and have less negative influence on you, and you will have more positive influence on others, as Nelson Mandela advised:

As we are liberated from our fear, our presence automatically liberates others.

SEED YOUR COURAGE — It is just as important to feed your courage. Slim was able to overcome because I gave him Bible verses, inspirational sayings and encouraging words to feast on, which built his inner strength. A diet of spiritually nutritious readings will fill you with the courage not only to confront your bitter truth but also to overcome the related challenges. Meditate on Robert Louis Stevenson's formula:

Keep your fears to yourself but share your courage with others.

COURAGEOUSLY MAKE YOUR CASE   JANUARY 16TH

The white race deems itself to be the dominant race in this country, so it is, in education, in wealth, and in power. . . . But in view of the Constitution, in the eye of the law, there is in this country no superior, dominant, ruling class of citizens. There is no caste there. Our Constitution is color-blind and neither knows nor tolerates classes among citizens.
John Harlan

In 1890, similar to all Southern states, Louisiana enacted the Separate Car Act, which required separate railway cars for black and white riders. To test the constitutionality of the law, African American Homer Plessy sat in a white car and refused to move, resulting in his arrest and conviction, which he appealed.

The case eventually made its way to the United States Supreme Court, which issued its decision in "Plessy versus Ferguson" in 1896. The court ruled against Plessy, holding that "separate but equal accommodations" in railway cars were constitutional. The ruling established the separate but equal precedent that sanctioned segregation of all kinds in the South and throughout the country for almost sixty years.

The lone dissent came from Associate Supreme Court Justice John Harlan, who opposed the majority opinion, arguing for racial unity: laws should be made with the consequence of bringing people together instead of driving them apart.

Sixty millions of whites are in no danger from the presence here of 8 million blacks. The destinies of the two races in this country are indissolubly linked together, and the interests of both require that the common government of all shall not permit the seeds of race hate to be planted under the sanction of law. What can more certainly arouse race hate, what more certainly create and perpetuate a feeling of distrust between these races than state enactments, which, in fact, proceed on the ground that colored citizens are so inferior and degraded that they cannot be allowed to sit in public coaches occupied by white citizens? . . .

The history of U.S. race relations since the "Plessy" decision has vindicated Harlan's position. Divisiveness won out over unity, and the spirit of this fractious legacy lingers to this day. Like Harlan, you may be the only one in your circle to make a case for unity. Be bold enough to do it anyway. You — and society — will be better for it. To courageously make your case, strive to be:

HUMBLE — Don't be the smartest person in the room. If you're feeling superior to another because of your race, background, class, gender, or for any other reason, be intentional about growing out of such arrogance. Remember Jesus' words:

The greatest among you is the one who serves
— Matthew 23:11

A HEARER — Work at becoming a good listener. Harlan heard the historic voice crying out for a more enlightened approach to race relations and he incorporated those perspectives into his legal opinion. Do your best to discern inspired voices. Once you gain knowledge of them you will be in a better position to show others respect, which will help lower cultural barricades.

HARD — Like Harlan, take the contrary view, even if you are the only one. People may consider you difficult. It's okay. Be difficult, if it means furthering a righteous cause.

HEARTFELT — Be approachable, even vulnerable. Share something that humanizes the conversation, that harmonizes differences. Your perspective should be: I can learn something from every person I meet. Seek interaction that's mutually open.

A HELPER — Everyone needs help of some kind, including you. Think about your own needs: for support, direction, to be understood. Figure out how to help others in areas where you've received help. Share the wisdom of your own experience. Whatever barriers that existed will start to come down.

SING AN ENCOURAGING SONG   JANUARY 17TH

As long as you keep a person down, some part of you has to be down there
to hold him down, so it means you cannot soar as you otherwise might.
Marian Anderson

On April 9 1939, Easter Sunday, celebrated singer
Marian Anderson gave a free open-air concert at the Lincoln Memorial in
Washington, D.C. More than 75,000 people turned out to hear Anderson,
and millions of Americans listened on radio. The concert was such a
sensation in large part due to the controversy that precipitated it.

Earlier that year, the Daughters of the American Revolution (DAR)
denied Anderson the right to sing at Constitution Hall. Anderson and
others protested, and a furor ensued, causing First Lady Eleanor Roosevelt,
among thousands of others members, to resign from the DAR. The First
Lady prevailed upon President Roosevelt, who worked with Walter White,
then-executive secretary of the NAACP, to arrange Anderson's
unprecedented concert on the steps of the Lincoln Memorial.

Anderson courageously continued to break racial barriers. On
January 7, 1955, she became the first African American to perform at
the Metropolitan Opera in New York City; it was her only operatic
performance. She also sang at the March on Washington for Jobs and
Freedom on August 28, 1963, preceding Martin Luther King, Jr.'s "I Have
A Dream" speech.

Anderson's courage manifested through her inspired singing as well
as her shared views. Over the years she used her songs and words to
proclaim important truths about principled living. Take note of Anderson's
advice imparted in the following statements. You, too, can sing encouraging
songs through your:

EXAMPLE — *The minute a person whose word means a great*
deal to others dares to take the open-hearted and courageous way, many others
follow.

Like Anderson, be willing to let your voice resound to make a
difference in the quest for greater justice in the world.

ECSTASY — *A singer starts by having his instrument as a gift*
from God . . . when you have been given something in a moment of grace, it is
sacrilegious to be greedy.

Whatever your divine gift, express it; cherish it; share it. Be joyful
with it. Use it to bless the lives of others.

EQUALITY — *When I sing, I don't want them to see that my face is black. I don't want them to see that my face is white. I want them to see my soul. And that is colorless.*

Like Anderson, refuse to wear racial blinders. Let people see you beyond your skin color, and see beyond theirs. Let your voice be a clarion that calls people to come together.

EXPERIENCE — *I suppose I might insist on making issues of things. But that is not my nature, and I always bear in mind that my mission is to leave behind me the kind of impression that will make it easier for those who follow.*

Don't wait for others to take the righteous step. Take a great initiative. Let your passion drive you to break barriers and ceilings. Strive to go where no one has gone before you. Create a legacy that sings songs, broadens pathways, lifts horizons and makes the sun shine brighter wherever you go.

TAKE YOUR HIGH ROAD   JANUARY 18TH

The dogmas of the quiet past are inadequate to the stormy present. The occasion is piled high with difficulty, and we must rise with the occasion. As our case is new, so we must think anew, and act anew. We must disenthrall ourselves, then we shall save our country.
Abraham Lincoln

In December 1862, when the lame duck Thirty-seventh U.S. Congress gathered to hear President Abraham Lincoln's annual message, he was already in the political cauldron: many Northerners were condemning Lincoln's recently announced Emancipation Proclamation as reckless; Democratic victories in the midterm elections indicating a turn in public opinion against him; some in Congress condemning his administration for violating civil liberties; mounting opposition to the war effort among members of his own party; and temperamental military commanders leading to combat defeats.

The torrent of criticism and opposition notwithstanding, Lincoln did not succumb to the temptation of recrimination in his remarks but took the high road, elaborating that the survival of the country was tethered to the freeing of the slaves.

Fellow citizens, we cannot escape history. We of this Congress and this administration, will be remembered in spite of ourselves. No personal significance, or insignificance, can spare one or another of us. The fiery trial through which we pass, will light us down, in honor or dishonor, to the latest generation. We say we are for the Union. The world will not forget that we say this. We know how to save the Union. . . . We — even we here — hold the power, and bear the responsibility. In giving freedom to the slave, we assure freedom to the free — honorable alike in what we give, and what we preserve. We shall nobly save, or meanly lose, the last best hope of earth. Other means may succeed; this could not fail. The way is plain, peaceful, generous, just — a way which, if followed, the world will forever applaud, and God must forever bless.

Taking the high road takes courage because most people travel other pathways, moving in directions that in end in tension, conflict, accusation and hostility. Lincoln took the high road; you can also take it when you:

TRAVEL TOUGH — The high road is likely a rocky road for you to travel. Don't be thin-skinned, looking for ways to bring others down as they endeavor to drag you down into the pit of backbiting and bitterness. Though criticism will come, your commitment to excellence and ethics will bolster you through any public relations storms. Don't get bogged down riding the low road of acrimony. Instead, seek to exalt people up to common ground of mutual affirmation.

TRAVEL LIGHT — Cast off the intense conflictual mores of today's cultural movements. Refuse to practice the finger-pointing, partisanship and social media warfare that have become societal norms. Live according to your highest standards. It's likely not the natural or acceptable thing to do — do the right thing anyway! And taking your high road will place you in a very special group — those representing "the last best hope of earth."

TRAVEL TRUE — Lincoln possessed the courage to say things that were unpopular but true. He called his fellow countrymen to take the high road of heartfelt confession, acknowledging their shared history of prejudice, leaving it behind. He also summoned them to transcend that tainted track record and instead to embrace the greater calling of righteousness and destiny, to live in accordance with their highest ideals. To travel true, you have to be committed to your highest ideals. You have to walk with them, no matter how bumpy the road, no matter how inclement the weather. Shakespeare drove this point home:

To thine own self be true.

BE STRATEGICALLY COURAGEOUS   JANUARY 19TH

*Let our lives be in accordance with our convictions
of right, each striving to carry out our principles.*
Lucretia Mott

During the 1850's, 338 Arch Street in Philadelphia was a "station" on the Underground Railroad — the network of secret routes, passageways and safe houses established in pre-Civil War America for slaves to escape from southern to northern states and Canada. The "station masters" of this "depot" were European American Quakers Lucretia and James Mott, who, along with their six children, used their home to harbor the runaways fleeing from Maryland and Delaware. The risks were great: if their station was uncovered, the Motts faced not only ostracism but fines in the thousands of dollars. The objective was to succor the fugitives until "conductors" like Harriet Tubman could safeguard them to areas in states much further north.

Lucretia Mott was also an outspoken abolitionist, having been a founding member of both the Philadelphia Female Anti-Slavery Society in 1833 and the National Anti-Slavery Coalition of American Women in 1835. During the 1838 National Women's Convention in Philadelphia, a rioting mob attacked Pennsylvania Hall, which had been recently built by abolitionists to host their meetings. Mott linked arms with her fellow women delegates and led them through the violent crowd to safety. Afterward, when the mob targeted her home, Mott relocated her family and waited there to face her ominous opponents, who decided to assault black residences instead. Mott reflected on the reasons for her courageous stand:

> *I have no idea of submitting tamely to injustice either on me or on the slave. I will oppose it with all the moral powers with which I'm endowed. I am no advocate of passivity. . . . If our principles are right, why should we be cowards?*

Mott took her anti-slavery crusade throughout antebellum America, lecturing in major Northern cities like New York and Boston as well as giving speeches in Baltimore, Richmond and other slave-owning states. Mott secretly continued to operate her station on the Underground Railroad. To follow her example of being strategically courageous, strive to be:

SILENT — Showing courage doesn't mean you have to be the loudest person in the room. There are times when acting courageously means biting your tongue. Mott acted in both public and private ways; you should, too. Pick your moments to be public, proclaiming your views. Pick your moments to be private, harboring them, until revelation is most opportune.

SURREPTITIOUS — It's okay to keep a secret, especially if it's for a righteous cause. But don't conceal the truth of your actions when you're pursuing selfish ends. And, like Mott, if you're involved in a project that's fostering justice for others, maintain both the power of your tactics and the purity of your motives.

SAGE — Be wise. Know your limitations and concentrate in the areas where you have leverage, where you know you can make a difference. Remember: you have to choose your battles because you can't win them all. Memorize Reinhold Niebuhr's prayer and deploy it.

God grant me the serenity
To accept the things I cannot change;
Courage to change the things I can;
And wisdom to know the difference.

DEMONSTRATE GREAT COURAGE   JANUARY 20TH

You speak of our activity in Birmingham as extreme. . . . But though I was initially disappointed at being categorized as an extremist, as I continued to think about the matter I gradually gained a measure of satisfaction from the label.
Martin Luther King, Jr.

In the spring of 1963 Martin Luther King Jr. was placed in solitary confinement for leading nonviolent protests in Birmingham, Alabama. Responding to a published statement from fellow clergymen who argued that the battle against racial segregation should be fought in the courts — not in the streets — King wrote "Letter from Birmingham City Jail", scribbling it out on the margins of a newspaper because it was the only paper available to him. He asserted that civil disobedience was justified in the face of unjust laws and enumerated Biblical and historical leaders who had taken similar stands for justice.

Was not Jesus an extremist for love: "Love your enemies, bless them that curse you, do good to them that hate you, and pray for them which despitefully use you, and persecute you." Was not Amos an extremist for justice: "Let justice roll down like waters and righteousness like an ever-flowing stream." Was not Paul an extremist for the Christian gospel: "I bear in my body the marks of the Lord Jesus." Was not Martin Luther an extremist: "Here I stand; I cannot do otherwise, so help me God." ... And Abraham Lincoln: "This nation cannot survive half slave and half free." And Thomas Jefferson: "We hold these truths to be self-evident, that all men are created equal ..." So the question is not whether we will be extremists, but what kind of extremists we will be. Will we be extremists for hate or for love? Will we be extremists for the preservation of injustice or for the extension of justice? ...

King showed great courage by taking a stand against unjust laws that had preserved systems of white supremacy. You, too, can be greatly courageous as you:

RESIST YOUR ANGER — King could have written from his jail cell a letter of righteous indignation. He put his emotion to the side and instead expressed compelling moral points. Strive to control your temper so you can speak the truth in love. Embrace this Biblical counsel:

> *Be angry and do not sin; do not let the sun go down on your anger.*
> — Ephesians 4:26

RECKON THE FACTS — King articulated the historical facts — quoting the luminaries — to make his points. Do your research. Substantiate your positions with data that is difficult to refute. If you've done your homework and know your stuff, your courage will manifest.

RESIST YOUR DETRACTORS — King was assailed by his enemies. You also should expect to be assailed, even if you're not involved in protesting against injustice. You may have the most wonderful personality in the world, but not everyone with whom you cross paths will like you. It's one of those unfortunate facts of life that someone will come along to mess up your plans, not necessarily because you did something to warrant adversaries, but because envy, jealousy, pride, mean-spiritedness, ill will and preservation of self-interest are human forces that we all have to deal with at one point or another. Don't falter or faint in the face of opposition. Stare them down. Write them a letter from a solitary place. Take a stand by turning the other cheek.

RIGHT SOCIETAL WRONGS — Suffering for a righteous cause is not a fun thing to do. Do it with the knowledge that the greatest value you can add to your life is by serving others — even if that serving hurts. You may not end up in jail like King but be prepared to sacrifice in some way. In whatever ways you might suffer for righteousness, it will be worth it. Your courageous act will be requited by the satisfaction of your being a blessing to others. At the end of the day, selflessness beats self-centeredness every time.

FIGHT THE GOOD FIGHT   JANUARY 21ST

Organize, agitate, educate, must be our war cry.
Susan B. Anthony

In November 1872 in Rochester, New York, Susan B. Anthony cast a ballot in the presidential election. Since women did not have the right to vote in New York or any other state at that time, she was soon arrested and charged with illegally entering the voting booth.

Anthony had been raised in antebellum America as a Massachusetts Quaker, greatly influenced by her faith. Quaker daughters were affirmed at home as no less important than sons. Growing up, Anthony experienced women speaking at religious meetings and voting on church matters. As a young adult, she became active in the Daughters of Temperance and as an abolitionist, working for the immediate end of slavery.

Anthony became an early leader of the women's suffrage movement with the conviction that women could not achieve equality without the right to vote. In 1869 she and Elizabeth Cady Stanton founded the National Woman Suffrage Association, aimed at passing a constitutional amendment guaranteeing women's voting rights. She worked indefatigably, in one year alone giving 171 lectures and traveling 13,000 miles, some nights sleeping in railroad stations.

During her 1873 criminal trial in federal court, Judge Ward Hunt — after directing a guilty verdict — asked if Anthony had anything to say. She responded with passionate protest.

> *Yes, your Honor, this is high-handed outrage upon my citizen's rights . . . you have trampled under foot every vital principle of our government. My natural rights, my civil rights, my political rights, my judicial rights, are all alike ignored.*

Furious at her outburst, Judge Hunt ordered her to sit down and be silent; at the risk of immediate arrest, Anthony did neither. The judge further directed her to "pay a fine of $100 and the costs of prosecution." Anthony fought on.

> *May it please your honor, I shall never pay a dollar of your unjust penalty. And I shall earnestly and persistently continue to urge all women... that resistance to tyranny is obedience to God.*

Anthony never paid her $100 fine and did not serve any time. The courage that she demonstrated at her trial proved a turning point in the struggle for women's suffrage. Her spirited defense elevated her cause, gradually swinging public opinion in her favor. Almost a half-century later — fourteen years after Anthony's death — the Nineteenth Amendment passed in 1920 — granting women nationwide the right to vote.

Anthony's intrepid court appearance rose from her vigorous virtue: her courage about the righteousness of her cause — the fight for women's rights — vanquished her fear of going to jail.

In light of Anthony's example, take a moment to evaluate your convictions relative to your fears. Which ones are stronger? You may have courage, but that doesn't mean that you will never be afraid. Both courage and fear are present within you. The emotion to which you give your time and energy will be the one to shape your personality and dictate your actions. So implement this strategy:

FIGHT YOUR FEARS — Decrease the time and energy you give to it; don't talk about them; if you have to express them, confess them to a trusted confidant or in prayers to God. If you give into your fears by harping on them, you will never overcome them.

FUEL YOUR COURAGE — But to overcome your fears, reverse the process: increase the time and energy with positive thoughts and feelings that bolster you to face the circumstances you find yourself in; you will foster encouragement as you focus on your strengths and achievements; such concentration will help you to steer clear of inner negativity.

The emotional calculus of courage versus fear varies with each situation that you face. If your present fears are paralyzing you from needed action, fight the good fight: strengthen your convictions to overcome your fears. If you, like Anthony, are courageous enough to take action in the face of your fears, your initiative might also spur a movement of historic consequence.

SPEAK THE TRUTH IN LOVE   JANUARY 22ND

In the spirit of candor and humility we intend . . . to lay our case before the public, with a view to arrest the progress of prejudice . . . We wish to conciliate all and to irritate none, yet we must be firm and unwavering in our principles and persevering in our efforts.
Editors of Freedom Journal

On March 16, 1827, John Russwurm, the first black graduate of Bowdoin College, joined with Samuel Cornish, to publish the first weekly edition of *Freedom's Journal*, the first newspaper owned and operated by African Americans in the United States. Russwurm, Cornish and other leading free blacks launched the periodical in New York City, committed to blaze trails in the marketplace of ideas in support of their double-edged message — directed not only against the institution of slavery in the South but also to foster equal opportunities and respect for their peers in the North.

In the first edition, which was targeted to the 500,000 free African Americans throughout the states, the founders demonstrated their courage by publishing an editorial that proclaimed their high purpose.

We wish to plead our own cause. Too long have others spoken for us. Too long has the public been deceived by misrepresentations in things which concern us dearly, though, in the estimation of some, mere trifles; for though there are many in society who exercise toward us benevolent feelings, still (with sorrow we confess it) there are others who make it their business to enlarge upon the least trifle which tends to the discredit of any person of color, and pronounce anathemas and denounce our whole body for the misconduct of this guilty one. We are aware that there are many instances of vice among us, but we avow that it is because no one has taught its subjects to be virtuous; many instances of poverty, because no sufficient efforts accommodated to minds contracted by slavery and deprived of early education have been made, to teach them how to husband their hard earnings and to secure to themselves comforts.

The publishers made sure to pledge their support for their brothers in bondage.

We would not be unmindful of our brethren who are still in the iron fetters of bondage. They are our kindred by all the ties of nature; and though but little can be effected by us, still let our sympathies be poured forth, and our prayers in their behalf ascend to Him who is able to succor them.

Though the paper lasted only a couple of years, the courageous initiative of the publishers helped to set the tone and build the momentum for the Abolitionist movement, leading to the legal prohibition of slavery in the next generation. The editorialists endeavored to strike that delicate balance between confrontation and conciliation. You can do the same as you:

CUSHION — Protect those who cannot protect themselves. Russworm and Cornish used their status as free blacks to advocate for slaves. As you experience success and rise towards your destiny, make sure to look out for those still stuck in the circumstance from which you've ascended.

CONFRONT — Like the Freedom Journal editors, confront wrongdoing. Don't be silent in the face of injustice. Position yourself head-on at the challenging circumstance and declare victory over it. Let your voice resound for truth and justice. You'll have greater peace and end up on the right side of history.

CONCILIATE — Don't get carried away with confrontation; don't do it for its own sake. Conciliation is often the better approach. Look for ways to bring people together, emphasizing those things that cause the least conflict with others. Use the strategy of the Freedom Journal editors: blend confrontation with conciliation, as the Apostle Paul directed.

Speak the truth in love.
— Ephesians 4:15

LIVE TO FIGHT ANOTHER DAY   JANUARY 23RD

Virtue knows no color line.
— Ida B. Wells

From 1884 to 1900 lynchings in America soared to 2,500 victims, most of whom were African Americans. One collective response rose from a group of Massachusetts blacks in a 1899 open letter to President William McKinley. A passage from their letter reflected the outrage of Northern blacks at the unwritten law — no intervention by Northern politicians in Southern affairs.

The struggle of the Negro to rise out of his ignorance, his poverty, and his social degradation   . . . to the full stature of his American citizenship, has been met everywhere in the South by the active ill-will and determined race hatred and opposition of the white people of the section. Turn where he will, he encounters this cruel and implacable spirit. He dare not speak openly the thoughts which rise in his breast. He has wrongs such as have never in modern times been inflicted on a people, and yet he must be dumb in the midst of a nation which prates loudly of democracy and humanity, boasts itself the champion of oppressed peoples abroad, while it looks on indifferent, apathetic at appalling enormities and iniquities at home, where the victims are black and the criminals white.

The most consequential individual response came from journalist Ida B. Wells, who led an antilynching crusade, lecturing throughout America and Europe and publicizing the racist terror through well-research articles. In one of her writings — excerpted below — Wells debunked the Southern white male storyline that lynching was necessary to protect their women.

This almost universal tendency to accept as true the slander which the lynchers offer to civilization as an excuse for their crime might be explained if the true facts were difficult to obtain; but not the slightest difficulty intervenes. The Associated Press dispatches, the press clipping bureau, frequent book publications and the annual summary of a number of influential journals give the lynching record every year. This record, easily within the reach of everyone who wants it, makes inexcusable the statement and cruelly unwarranted the assumption that Negroes are lynched only because of their assaults upon womanhood.

Throughout the 1890s Wells pressed forward with her mission to expose lynching as a barbaric practice by whites to oppress blacks. Her advocacy was so effective that her Memphis printing presses and office were destroyed by a white mob, and she had to flee to Chicago because of incessant threats against her life.

Taking a courageous stand sometimes means facing perils. Wells confronted and overcame them, and her courage fueled her moral crusade. Principles from her life should inform any challenging initiative you're involved with or considering. Do your best to be:

SMART — Choose wisely the battles you decide to fight because you can't take on all the worthy causes of this world. And don't get too complicated with your tactics. Follow Wells' straightforward advice.

The way to right wrongs is to turn the light of truth upon them.

STRONG — You can't overcome social injustice working alone. Like the letter-writing Massachusetts blacks, plan a joint effort. Your strength rises from the number of those committed to your cause. Build a strong team.

SINCERE — Check your motives. Make sure you're doing the right thing for the right reason. If you're not, it's better to get off the train before it gets too deep into enemy territory.

SAFE — Don't be afraid or ashamed to retreat from the battlefield. Wells retreated from Memphis to Chicago, living to fight another day. If your circumstances get too ominous, step back. Use the break from the battle to renew your energy and strategize afresh! Remember the words of Mary Anne Radmacher.

> *Courage doesn't always roar. Sometimes courage is the quiet*
> *voice at the end of the day saying, "I will try again tomorrow."*

TACKLE THE TOUGH PROBLEMS   JANUARY 24TH

> *The American dream is based on the conviction that every*
> *individual is of value. . . . . A free society should produce free and*
> *responsible individuals as a tree bears fruit. That is its purpose.*
> John Gardner

In the 1960s the problem of poverty — symbolized by urban blight — was vexing. Mass media images of comfortable, fun-loving middle class Americans bombarded the poor, exacerbated by the fact that the images were of whites, and the impoverished were disproportionately black. Voices of protest cried out in anger about both the material need and the psychological debility.

Other voices, such as Health, Education and Welfare Secretary John Gardner, focused on new approaches to intractable problems. Gardner left his Cabinet post to take on poverty on a national scale as chairman of a new organization — the Urban Coalition. In March 1968 Gardner contributed an article to a special report in "Life Magazine" titled "The Cycle of Despair: the Negro and the City". He began by contrasting the ideals with the challenges.

> *Poverty is not easy to eliminate, whether the poor are black or white.*
> *In the case of the Negro it is made harder by the evil of racism. . . . But we*
> *cannot afford to be discouraged by the difficulty of the problems. If they were*
> *easy, we would have solved them long ago. When we formed this free society we*
> *did not commit ourselves to solve only the easy ones. The tough problems are the*
> *ones that test our resolve.*

Gardner then pointed to the solution.

We must begin with a massive resolve on the part of the great, politically moderate majority of whites and blacks — to transform destructive emotion into constructive action. The time has come when the full weight of the community opinion, white and Negro, should be felt against those within their own ranks who hate and destroy . . . We can solve our problems. But it will take moral courage, intelligence, and stamina. We have summoned these qualities before at critical times in our history. At no time has the need been greater than it is now.

Gardner was willing to tackle one of the toughest problems of his era. His Urban Coalition brought together leaders from labor, industry, and government to address poverty, racism and other underlying problems that fueled the 1960's riots. Implement his problem-tackling strategy by getting involved in:

RISK-TAKING — If you're willing to tackle the tough problems, you can't play it safe. Gardner left a top government position and created an entrepreneurial position to gather new resources and champion new approaches. Be bold; be willing to take some chances; you won't be able to coast your way to answering the big challenges; have the courage to climb to reach the solutions that lie uphill from where you are.

RECRIMINATION-AVOIDING — Don't be a hater, throwing bombs of negativity back and forth across the table, the aisles and the tracks. Stay away from verbal bomb-throwers and refuse to use their tactics. Gardner brought people, who wouldn't ordinarily be together, onto the team with a shared mission. What new person or group can you start or join to make a difference?

RIGHT-THINKING — Your victory lies in your strategy. Any intractable problem has been been around for awhile, confounding many, waiting on someone with some new thinking to fix it. Let that someone be you. Be creative, innovative. New ideas may strike some as crazy at first, but don't let that stop you from casting fresh vision and sharing it with others. Be the one whose thinking shines the bright light of solution.

You cannot discover new oceans unless you have the courage to lose sight of the shore.

HOLD DOWN THE FORT   JANUARY 25TH

Two messengers covered with dust come to bid me fly, but here I mean to wait for him.
Dolley Madison

The War of 1812 was America's second war of independence, waged on two fronts — land and sea. Wanting to keep their forts around the Great Lakes, the British allied with Native Americans and fought along the western frontiers, attacking the settlers flooding Ohio, Kentucky and the Illinois Territory. Because of troubles with Napoleon, England assaulted American merchant ships, impressing sailors into naval service against France.

The U.S. plight took a turn for the worst when the British entered the Chesapeake Bay on August 14, 1814, landed and began their march towards Washington, D.C., to torch the nation's capital. With this threat looming, First Lady Dolley Madison penned a letter to her sister.

> *Dear Sister: My husband left me yesterday morning to join General Winder. . . . I have since received two dispatches from him . . . The last is alarming, because he desires I should be ready at a moment's warning to enter my carriage, and leave the city . . . I am determined not to go myself until I see Mr. Madison safe . . . as I hear of much hostility toward him. Disaffection stalks around us. My friends and acquaintances are all gone . . . Since sunrise I have been turning my spy-glass in every direction, and watching with unwearied anxiety, hoping to discover the approach of my dear husband . . . and here I am still, with sound of the cannon! Mr. Madison comes not. May God protect us! . . . I insist on waiting until the large picture of General Washington is secured, and it requires to be unscrewed from the wall. This process was found too tedious for these perilous moments; I have ordered the frame to be broken and the canvas taken out. It is done! and the precious portrait placed in the hands of two gentlemen of New York, for safekeeping. And now, dear sister, I must leave this house, or the retreating army will make me a prisoner of it by filling up the road I am directed to take. When I shall again write to you, or where I shall be tomorrow, I cannot tell!   Dolley*

Learn from Dolley Madison's experience. Hold down your own fort as you:

EXERCISE DISCRETION — Be clear-eyed about any approaching peril. Expect them at inopportune times and from unknown places. If the coming menace threatens to burn down your house, first be prepared to defend your fort. But have a Plan B. If there's no way to hold off the enemy, be realistic. If you must, abandon the fort. Be wise; stay alive!

ESCAPE WITH SPEED — Dolley Madison took flight from the White House, just before the arrival of British troops, who found the evening meal yet warm on the dining room table. They decided to first eat before burning down the house. If you have to get away through the back door, do it quickly. When you make the decision to move, go quickly.

EXPRESS YOUR STRENGTH — Dolley Madison risked her life for a righteous cause. You may not be faced with a challenge as dire as an invading army; whatever the challenge, determine to be courageous. Like Madison, don't get bent out of shape when your enemies approach or your saboteurs appear. Stare them down. Rise to the occasion. Overcome evil with good.

EMBRACE YOUR HOPE — Do whatever you have to do to get through the present battle. See the brighter day on the other side of your crisis. Look to the future more than the present and the past. That hope will get you through.

RESIST POPULAR OPINION   JANUARY 26TH

. . . no emigrant direct from Europe, save one German family and a knot of Cornish miners . . . All the states of the North had sent out a fugitive to cross the Plains with me. From Virginia, from Pennsylvania, from New York, from far-western Iowa and . . .
Robert Louis Stevenson

In 1879 Scottish novelist Robert Louis Stevenson traveled from New York to San Francisco on an emigrant train. He documented his journey in "Across the Plains", in which he described his fellow passengers as well as the Chinese emigrants on board.

Of all stupid ill-feelings, the sentiment of my fellow Caucasians toward our companions in the Chinese car was the most stupid and the worst. . . . The Chinese are considered stupid because they are imperfectly acquainted with English. They are held to be base because their dexterity and frugality enable them to underbid the lazy, luxurious Caucasian. They are said to be thieves; I am sure they have no monopoly of that. They are called cruel; the Anglo-Saxon and the cheerful Irishman may each reflect before he bears the accusation. I am told, again, that they are of the race of river pirates and belong to the most despised and dangerous class in the Celestial Empire. But if this be so, what remarkable pirates have we here! And what must be the virtues, the industry, the education, and the intelligence of their superiors at home!

Stevenson resisted the opinions of the other passengers about the Chinese, asserting his own view.

> *For my own part, I could not look but with wonder and respect on the Chinese. Their forefathers watched the stars before mine had begun to keep pigs. Gunpowder and printing, which the other day we imitated, and a school of manners which we never had the delicacy so much as to desire to imitate, were theirs in a long-past antiquity. They walk the earth with us, but it seems they must be of different clay. They travel by steam conveyance, yet with such a baggage of old Asiatic thoughts and superstitions as might check the locomotive in its course. Whatever is thought within the circuit of the Great Wall; what the wry-eyed, spectacled schoolmaster teaches in the hamlets round Pekin; religions so old that our language looks a halfling boy alongside; philosophy so wise that our best philosophers find things therein to wonder at; all this traveled alongside of me for thousands of miles over plain and mountain.*

It takes courage to resist popular opinion, to declare your position against the prevailing view. Stevenson did it; follow his example as you:

KNOT YOUR CONVICTIONS — Be strong in what you believe, then state your convictions with purpose and passion. Don't be wedded to the views of your upbringing that are now outdated. Dig deep inside for your core values and tie them to your daily living.

KICK YOUR CONCERNS — It is natural to be concerned when you're swimming against the tide of opinion, especially if it's a rising tide. Stephenson didn't let it intimidate him. You shouldn't either. Acknowledge your fears, then rise above them.

KNIT YOUR CONSCIOUSNESS — Take time to think through your views, to bring them together into a compelling position. Do your research. Break down your argument into bullet points. You'll be convincing if you logically connect the dots of your ideas and coherently express them.

KINDLE YOUR COURAGE — Make sure your statement is more than idle chatter. Fashion your ideas into thoughts that challenge the status quo, that uplift popular opinion from gutter to glory. When your words are making a difference, you'll be inspired to proclaim them. As Moses instructed Joshua when he passed the mantle of leadership:

> *Be strong and very courageous.*
> — Joshua 1:8

ENCOURAGE YOURSELF   JANUARY 27TH

I am not discouraged, because every wrong attempt discarded is another step forward.
Thomas Edison

Thomas Edison, America's greatest inventor, never retired, his creative genius in full throttle up to his final days. Edison had long championed an overhead catenary system using direct electric current for commuter rail service. When the the Lackawanna Railroad launched suburban electric train service in September 1930 — about a year before his death — Edison was the conductor of the inaugural Multiple-Unit train, departing Hoboken for South Orange. This fleet of cars would serve northern New Jersey commuters for the next half-century.

During Edison's twilight years the Great Depression dawned, which concerned him greatly. Sensing that the hard times at hand would be a great challenge to America, he often spoke about how he had encouraged himself through the trials early in his legendary career. In the following account he reminisced about finding strength in adversity.

I was paying a sheriff five dollars a day to postpone a judgment on my small factory. Then came the gas man, and because I couldn't pay his bill he promptly cut off my gas. I was in the midst of certain very important experiments, and to have the gas people plunge me into darkness made me so mad I at once began to read up on gas technique and economics, and resolved I would try to see if electricity couldn't be made to replace gas and give those gas people a run for their money.

Several decades earlier, the prodigious nineteenth century poet Ralph Waldo Emerson had proclaimed the same theme of inner virtue manifesting as uplifting fortitude, affirming the truth that individual courage is the foundation of national greatness.

Not gold, but only man can make
A people great and strong;
Men who, for truth and honor's sake,
Stand fast and suffer long.

Brave men who work while others sleep,
Who dare while others fly —
They build a nations' pillars deep
And lift them to the sky.

As Edison exemplifies and Emerson extols, it's important to

encourage yourself as you:

KNOW YOUR THOUGHTS — What are you spending most of your time thinking about? Your problems or your opportunities? Your assets or your liabilities? Your friends or your enemies? The only way you can encourage yourself is to focus on your inner positives instead of negatives. Doing so will bolster you through the hard times.

KNOW YOUR PAST — You are still here today because you made it to today. Consider the mountains you've already climbed. Sometimes the best way to overcome the obstacle before you is to remember how many past hurdles you've bounded over. You did it before. You can do it again.

KNOW YOUR STRENGTHS — Edison worked on his potential with electricity instead of worrying about his problem with gas, and he forever changed the energy industry. Cultivate your areas of strength and encouragement will rise.

KNOW YOUR DESTINY — Believe in your future, and you will ride the wave of encouragement over every shipwrecked plan. Make hope your constant companion, and you will never get lost in the valley of despair.

DARE TO DIE   JANUARY 28TH

I know not whether a brilliant death is not preferred to an obscure life of rectitude. Most men are remembered as they died not as they lived. We gaze with admiration on the glories of the setting sun, yet scarcely bestow a passing glance upon its noonday splendor.
Davy Crockett

In the last months of 1835 the Texas Revolution commenced: U.S. colonists rebelled against the centralist government of General Antonio López de Santa Anna of Mexico. By the end of the year, the armed resistance of Texian soldiers had driven all of Santa Anna's troops out of Mexican Texas. In early 1836 the military contingent comprised mostly of U.S. colonists in the area established a garrison at the Alamo Mission, a former Spanish religious outpost now converted to a makeshift fort.

Alamo reinforcements, including co-commanders James Bowie and Wiliam Travis, trickled in to support the one hundred Texians garrisoned there. General Santa Anna moved swiftly, marching fifteen hundred of his troops on San Antonio de Béxar on February 23rd; the siege of the Alamo had begun. Aware of his dire straits, Travis sent out couriers with urgent pleas for assistance, including this one.

COMMANDANCY OF THE ALAMO, TEXAS February 24, 1936
To the People of Texas and All Americans in the World.
FELLOW CITIZENS AND COMPATRIOTS:
I am besieged by a thousand or more of the Mexicans under Santa Anna. I have sustained a continual bombardment and cannonade for twenty-four hours and have not lost a man. **I shall never surrender nor retreat.** *Then, I call on you in the name of Liberty, or patriotism, and of everything dear to the American character, to come to our aid with all dispatch . . . I am determined to sustain myself as long as possible and die like a soldier who never forgets what is due to his honor and that of his country.* *VICTORY OR DEATH.*
WILLIAM BARRET TRAVIS, Lieutenant Colonel, Commandant

In the ensuing days the Alamo defenders were joined only by just over a couple dozen men, of little consequence against the daily bombardments and the March 6th assault, which overwhelmed the Alamo, killing the entire garrison of one hundred eighty men including former U.S. Congressman Davy Crockett. Six weeks later the newly formed Republic of Texas army under the command of Sam Houston defeated the Mexican Army at the Battle of San Jacinto and captured Santa Anna. Committed to their cause, Travis and his troops dared to die. As you reflect on the legacy of their courage, consider these points.

DELIBERATION — Be careful not to rush into precarious circumstances. Be willing to give all for a worthy cause, but make sure the cause is worthy. When your life is at risk, count the cost upfront; make sure your mission is worth the ultimate sacrifice.

DOUGHTY — Henry van Dyke's poem *Doors of Daring* best captures this principle.

> *The mountains that inclose the vale*
> *With walls of granite, steep and high,*
> *Invite the fearless foot to scale*
> *Their stairway toward the sky.*
> *The restless, deep, dividing sea*
> *That flows and foams from shore to shore,*
> *Call to its sunburned chivalry,*
> *"Push out, set sail, explore!"*
> *The bars of life at which we fret,*
> *That seem to prison and control,*
> *Are but the doors of daring, set*

Ajar before the soul.
Say not "Too poor," but freely give;
Sigh not, "Too weak," but boldly try;
You never can begin to live
Until you dare to die.

Have you ever been greatly committed to a worthy cause for which you would dare to die?

TAKE A BIG RISK   JANUARY 29TH

Every great dream begins with a dreamer. Always remember, you have within you
the strength, the patience, and the passion to reach for the stars to change the world.
Harriet Tubman

Nicknamed "Moses" in reverential reference to the Old Testament leader who freed his people from Egyptian captivity, Harriet Tubman first escaped alone from a Maryland plantation to Philadelphia in 1849.
The next year the U.S. Congress passed the Fugitive Slave Law, which increased the risks for escaped slaves because it compelled law enforcement officials — even in states that had outlawed slavery — to help capture the fugitives. Undeterred, Tubman took on great risks as a conductor on the Underground Railroad, the secret passageway through which she brought her family members and many others from bondage to freedom.

Tubman made 19 trips on the Underground Railroad throughout the 1850's. Of her legendary work it has been reported — she never lost a passenger. With the outbreak of the Civil War her bravery went public. She worked for the Union Army as an armed scout and spy. When Tubman engineered the raid at Combahee Ferry, which liberated more than 700 slaves, she became the first woman to lead an armed expedition in the war.

Tubman courageously took on big risks; she not only survived but succeeded. If you want to do something great with your life, you will also have to take on big risks. You can follow Tubman's example as you:

MYSTIFY — Tubman was a dreamer:

In my dreams and visions, I seemed to see a line, and on the other
side of that line were green fields, and lovely flowers, and beautiful white ladies,
who stretched out their arms to me over the line, but I couldn't reach them no-
how. I always fell before I got to the line.

Many were mystified by Tubman, whose intrepid acts defied

47

common sense. She wasn't constrained by logic but followed her inner vision. Cultivate your own visionary powers. If people misunderstand you and your dreams, keep dreaming. Follow them; you just may lead yourself and others to greater freedom.

MANAGE — If you're going to do worthwhile things with your life, you are going to have to take some risks. Playing it safe all the time won't lead to accomplishment and fulfillment. You may not be inclined to live every day as a daring adventure, putting your life on the line as Harriet Tubman did. The key is — not to avoid risk — but how you manage risk. Whenever you try something new and different — even bold and daring — you increase your risk of failure. Courage means possessing the mental strength to take your great risk in order to achieve your great thing. First assess the risks; put together a plan of action, then move forward. It's always a risk worth running, if it leads to the freedom of others as well as your own.

MENTOR — Tubman carried along countless others:

> *I was a stranger in a strange land. My father, my mother, my brothers, and sisters, and friends were in Maryland. But I was free, and they should be free.*

Whatever advantage you gain, take the greater risk of sharing it with others.

MASTER — As you confront risks, they don't go away. You will just have to master them. Overcome them by casting aside their attendant fears. Heed the words of the Apostle Paul:

> *We are hard pressed on every side, but not crushed;*
> *perplexed, but not in despair;*
> *persecuted, but not abandoned;*
> *struck down, but not destroyed.*
> — 2 Corinthians 4:8-9

BE CREATIVELY COURAGEOUS   JANUARY 30TH

> *For of all sad words of tongue or pen,*
> *The saddest are these,*
> *"It might have been".*
> John Greenleaf Whittier

On October 4, 1842, George Latimer and his wife, Rebecca, escaped from slavery in Virginia, making their way to Massachusetts. Latimer's slave owner offered a $50 reward, which led to him being seized without warrant in Boston. Latimer's arrest sparked a tremendous uproar throughout the state: "Latimer Meetings" were held; "Latimer Committees" were formed; issues of the "Latimer Journal" were published every other day; fundraising events collected the four hundred dollars, which eventually purchased Latimer's freedom.

This movement resulted in the "Great Massachusetts Petition" — presented to the state legislature with 64,526 signatures — which created momentum for the passage of the 1843 Personal Liberty Act (aka "Latimer Law"). This law prevented Massachusetts officials from involvement in the detention of suspected fugitive slaves; it also banned state facilities from being used to detain such suspects. The "Great Petition to Congress" contained a similar number of signatures and called for new federal laws and Constitutional amendments relieving Massachusetts of any participation in slavery.

Perhaps the most lasting impact of these Latimer activities came from creative writing by poet and abolitionist John Greenleaf Whittier. Because of his anti-slavery stand, Whittier had on several occasions been assaulted, mobbed and stoned. But he kept on writing, and in the aftermath of Latimer's arrest, Whittier penned "Massachusetts to Virginia". Whittier was creatively courageous in writing this poem; his words and the principles they project signify strategies for you to follow. Be creatively courageous as you:

TESTIFY TO THE TRUTH —
All that a sister State should do, all that a free State may,
Heart, hand and purse we proffer, as in our early day;
But that one dark loathsome burden ye must stagger with alone,
And reap the bitter harvest which ye yourselves have sown.

Lower than plummet soundeth, sink the Virginia name;
Plant, if ye will, your fathers' graves with rankest weeds of shame;
Be, if ye will, the scandal of God's fair universe;
We wash our hands forever of your sin and shame and curse.

Look to it well, Virginians! In calmness we have borne,
In answer to our faith and trust, your insult and your scorn;
You've spurned our kindest counsels; you've hunted for our lives;
And shaken round our hearths and homes your manacles and gyves.
But for us and for our children, the vow which we have given
For freedom and humanity, is registered in heaven;
No slave-hunt in our borders — no pirate on our strand!
No fetters in the Bay State —- no slave upon our land!

Like Whittier, communicate truth in compelling ways through your creativity.

THINK OUTSIDE YOUR BOX — Whatever your gifting happens to be, let your commitments and your creativity come together to make a bigger difference in the world. Combine your artistry with your activism. Imagine involvement beyond your present environment. Think big: bring greater attention to your righteous cause and fulfill your singular calling.

TRY A NEW APPROACH — If you are writer, be poetic in your advocacy; if a singer, raise anthems of justice; if a speaker, give voice to issues of freedom; if an actor, dramatize your convictions; if a painter, add colors to your cause; if a dancer, gracefully move your body in favor of fairness . . . whatever your talent, be creatively courageous . . . to make a difference.

FIGHT FOR THE RIGHTS OF OTHERS   JANUARY 31ST

This entire disfranchisement of females is as unjust as the disfranchisement of the males
would be; for there is nothing in their moral, mental or physical nature that disqualifies
them to understand correctly the true interest of the community or to act wisely . . .
Samuel May

Even before the suffrage movement was formally launched in 1848, male voices courageously cried out, fighting for women's rights. On November 8, 1846, Reverend Samuel May delivered a sermon to his congregation at the Unitarian Church of the Messiah in Syracuse, New York entitled "The Rights and Condition of Women." May had first distinguished himself as an abolitionist: serving as general agent for the New England Anti-Slavery Society; attending the 1840 World Anti-Slavery Convention in London; and raising money for escaped slaves traveling the Underground Railroad.

In his 1846 sermon on behalf of women, May articulated physical gender differences as his context for his moral argument.

> *To prove, however, that woman was not intended to be the equal of man, the argument most frequently alleged is that she is the weaker vessel, inferior in stature, and has much less physical strength. . . . But allowing women generally to have less bodily power, why should this consign them to mental, moral or social dependence? Physical force is of special value only in a savage or barbarous community. It is the avowed intention and tendency of Christianity to give the ascendancy to man's moral nature; and the promises of God, with whom is all strength and wisdom are to the upright, the pure, the good, not to the strong, the valiant, or the crafty.*

May's advocacy places him in the pantheon of courageous male souls who stepped out early onto the battlefields for women's rights. You should also fight for the rights of other. To possess the courage to do so, keep these points in mind.

TEMERITY — It's challenging enough to find the courage to press for your own rights. But to go to the mat for others calls for boldness. There are times when it's best for you to throw caution to the wind, as Teddy Roosevelt advised:

> *. . . far better it is to dare mighty things, to win glorious triumphs, even though checkered by failure, then to take rank with those poor spirits who neither enjoy much nor suffer much, because they live in the gray twilight that knows neither victory nor defeat.*

TRAILBLAZING — Say and do the things that haven't been said or done before. You will make a way for those who need a breakthrough. Edgar Guest's poem strikes the right chord for you to harmonize with. Get in rhythm with his words.

> *A few strike out, without map or chart,*
> *Where never a man has been,*
> *From beaten paths they draw apart*
> *To see what no man has seen.*
> *There are deeds they hunger alone to do;*
> *Though battered and bruised and sore,*
> *They blaze the path for the many, who*
> *Do nothing not done before.*
>
> *The things that haven't been done before*
> *Are the tasks worthwhile today;*

Are you one in the flock that follows, or
Are you one that shall lead the way?
Are you one of the timid souls that quail
At the jeers of a doubting crew,
Or dare you, whether you win or fail,
Strike out for a goal that's new?

FEBRUARY: SELF-DISCIPLINE
DAILY SUCCESS PRINCIPLES

1. Discipline Your Way To Success — Lewis Latimer — 1876
2. Build Your Own Runway — Amelia Earhart — 1932
3. Discipline Your Finances — Benjamin Franklin — 1748
4. Make A Way Out Of No Way — Jerome Holland — 1938
5. Discipline Your Words — Abraham Lincoln — 1863
6. Establish Strong Boundaries — John Woolman — 1740
7. Make Every Day Count — Jesse Applegate — 1843
8. Beware The Shiny Object Syndrome — Helen Lynd — 1925
9. Develop Transformative Habits — François Michaux — 1804
10. Pay Attention To Details — William McGuffey — 1879
11. Adjust Your Expectations — Joseph Holland — 1987
12. Aspire, Perspire, Inspire — Irish Immigrant Handbook — 1816
13. Don't Lose Your Self-Control — Daniel Freedman — 1968
14. Discipline Your Emotions — Alexander Hamilton — 1804
15. Innovate With Your Discipline — Calvin Woodward — 1880
16. Prepare Through Discipline — Martin Luther King, Jr. — 1968
17. Take Daily Steps To Your Goals — Andrew Downing — 1848
18. Discipline Away From Trouble — Benjamin Rush — 1798
19. Discipline From Where You Are — Booker T. Washington — 1895
20. Master Your Anger — Cotton Mather — 1692
21. Discipline Your Environment — Catholic Plenary Council — 1866
22. Endure Pain For Gain — Samuel Harrison Smith — 1797
23. Discipline Your Work — Orville and Wilbur Wright — 1903
24. Give Up To Get Ahead — Philip Lindsley — 1825
25. Appreciate The Grind — Edward Purinton — 1920
26. Set High Standards — Theodorus Frelinghuysen — 1720
27. H E E D Your Body — Joseph Holland — 1989
28. Be Disciplined To Benefit Others — Abraham Lincoln — 1837

DISCIPLINE YOUR WAY TO SUCCESS   FEBRUARY 1ST

We create our future, by well improving present
opportunities: however few and small they are.
Lewis Latimer

In July 1865, after serving in the U.S. Navy during the Civil War, sixteen-year-old African American Lewis Latimer got a job earning a salary of $3.00 per week as an office boy in a Boston law firm specializing in helping inventors protect their patents. Fascinated by the creativity and diligence of the draftsmen, Latimer started reading books on drafting. Whenever he had a spare moment, Latimer would study the draftsmen at work, read about what he observed, then practice drawing himself. He repeated this process — using compasses, rulers, T squares, triangles — every day, for many months. In this way he taught himself mechanical drawing.

When his boss discovered that Latimer had learned the tools of the trade so well that he'd become more talented at sketching patent drawings than other staff, he promoted him to the position of head draftsman earning $20.00 a week.

Years later Latimer reflected on the personal attributes that paved the way for his precocious breakthrough.

Habit is a powerful means of advancement, and the habit of eternal vigilance and diligence, rarely fails to bring a substantial reward.

While continuing with draftsmanship for this Boston law firm Latimer met Alexander Graham Bell, who recruited him to draft the necessary drawings for his new invention — the telephone. With the advantage of Latimer's expertise and discipline — sometimes working together late into the night — Bell was able to file his telephone patent on February 14, 1876, before the rival inventors registered a similar device.

Soon after this breakthrough, Latimer transitioned his expertise in mechanical draftsmanship into the field of electric incandescent lighting, where there was fierce competition for patents. He developed his own patent for a light bulb with a carbon filament — an improved version of Thomas Edison's paper filament. Latimer sold the patent to the United States Electric Company in 1881.

Edison took notice and hired Latimer — by this time an expert electrical engineer — to protect his company from patent infringement through proper submissions to the U.S. Patent Office. With Edison's encouragement Latimer wrote "Incandescent Electric Lighting: A Practical Description of the Edison System", published in 1890.

Just as Latimer did, you can discipline your way to success through your:

TRAINING — Your biggest battle will be disciplining your thoughts and impulses. Beware a wandering mind. Like Latimer, stay focused on the task at hand and keep doing it until you master it. Success will follow, as author/speaker Albert Gray expounded:

The common denominator of success lies in forming the habit of doing things that failures don't like to do.

TENACITY — Latimer had to join the military as a teenager because his father — an escaped slave — feared recapture and left home. The youthful Latimer worked through that ordeal, which helped to develop his fortitude. Latimer's future boss, Thomas Edison, was regarded unteachable as a teenager. Don't let failure define you. Hold onto your dream and refuse to let it go. Your self-discipline will flow from your tenacity.

TURNING POINTS — The challenges of your life can lead to breakdowns or breakthroughs. It's your choice. Latimer could have complained about his low-paying menial job at the law firm; instead he used it as an opportunity to learn new skills; it proved to be his turning point. Will you turn your awful obstacles into awesome opportunities?

TRIUMPH — Check your circumstances. If you fish in a sea that's too shallow, you won't catch anything, no matter how hard you try. Explore the territory, find the fertile ground and go there. Latimer went from a prominent law firm to the legendary inventor Bell to the most prolific inventor ever Edison. Keep moving up towards the summit. Your greatness awaits at the top of the hill.

BUILD YOUR OWN RUNWAY   FEBRUARY 2ND

The most effective way to do it is to just do it.
Amelia Earhart

In December 1920, spending a leisurely afternoon with her father, Amelia Earhart took a 10-minute airplane ride and remarked after the flight, "I knew I had to fly." In her early twenties, Earhart worked several jobs — truck driver, stenographer, photographer — to save the $1,000 that she needed for flying lessons. To reach the airfield for those lessons, she had to walk four miles after taking the bus to the end of the line.

Her airborne training regimen continued over the next decade, leading to a historic moment. On May 20, 1932, Earhart took off from Harbour Grace, Newfoundland, in her single engine Lockheed Vega 5B, intending to land in Paris. Icy conditions, strong winds and mechanical problems confronted her throughout the almost 15-hour flight. When Earhart touched down in a pasture at Culmore, north of Derry, Northern Ireland, she became the first woman to fly solo nonstop across the Atlantic. Earhart's self-discipline paid off with an epochal breakthrough. Lessons from her experience — articulated in her own words — will help you take off with great success.

HARDSHIP CONFRONTS YOU — *Some of us have great runways already built for us. If you have one, take off. But if you don't have one, realize it is your responsibility to grab a shovel and build one for yourself and for those who will follow after you.*

Making decisions that are adverse to your economic self-interest may be one of the hardest things you'll ever face. Earhart sacrificed more lucrative opportunities to pursue her passion of flying. Like her, give up to go up!

HORIZONS BEFORE YOU — *Experiment! Meet new people. That's better than any college education . . . By adventuring about, you become accustomed to the unexpected. The unexpected then becomes what it really is . . . the inevitable.*

Go somewhere you haven't been before. When you venture out to new territory, you stretch yourself in new ways. First imagine the new you, then life your life accordingly.

HEART WITHIN YOU — *Everyone has ocean's to fly, if they have the heart to do it. Is it reckless? Maybe. But what do dreams know of boundaries?*

Keep your eyes on the summit; your heart fixed on your dream; it's the best way to make it up the rough side of the mountain. Look to the silver lining in the clouds to get across your oceans of discipline.

HOPE AWAITS YOU — *The most difficult thing is the decision to act. The rest is merely tenacity. The fears are paper tigers. You can do anything you decide to do. You can act to change and control your life and the procedure. The process is its own reward.*

One of the ironies about personal sacrifice is that somehow the struggle actually makes the achievement that much more satisfying in the end. The inner journey to discipline is not suffering for suffering's sake; it's the hopeful process of daily progress towards a fulfilling goal. Find joy in the trek past the pain to the gain. Learn to celebrate each step you take along the pathway to success.

DISCIPLINE YOUR FINANCES   FEBRUARY 3RD

Early to bed, early to rise makes a man healthy, wealthy and wise.
Benjamin Franklin

Benjamin Franklin ran away from home — from Boston to Philadelphia — when he was   seventeen. He launched an entrepreneurial career and acquired a fortune by the time he was forty-two, when he retired from business. He epitomized the self-made man, one of the first of this American archetype. He was self-made through self-discipline — in his lifestyle generally, and particularly concerning his finances.

In 1748 he published Advice to a Young Tradesman, which, among his many writings, best summarized his personal accomplishments as a life lesson for those seeking their own success. Franklin's Advice is timeless. It is about maximizing and managing your money, not by placing it with a Wall Street investment advisor or Main Street banker, but by your financial discipline; to make it happen in your own life, keep these points from Franklin — expressed in his own words — in mind.

BALANCE — *The most trifling actions that affect a man's credit are to be regarded. The sound of your hammer at five in the morning or nine at night, heard by a creditor, makes him easy six months longer; but if he sees you at a billiard table, or hears your voice at a tavern when you should be at work, he sends for his money the next day; demands it, before he can receive it, in a lump.*

Balance your work and play. To be successful, you'll need more the former than the latter. But if you have no play, you'll become a workaholic, and that's unhealthy. Quality over quantity is the rule of thumb you should apply to your play time.

BUDGET — . . . *keep an exact account for some time, both of your expenses and your income. If you take the pains at first to mention particulars, it will have this good effect: you will discover how wonderfully small, trifling expenses mount up to large sums, and will discern what might have been, and may for the future be saved, without occasioning any great inconvenience.*

Be financially disciplined. Develop a detailed budget that you adhere to so that you know exactly where your money is going and that you are spending responsibly. If you spend wisely and save aggressively, you will be making decisive steps toward your financial security and destiny.

> BOUNTY — *In short, the way to wealth, if you desire it, is as plain as the way to market. It depends chiefly on two words, industry and frugality; that is, waste neither time nor money, but make the best use of both. Without industry and frugality nothing will do, and with them everything. He that gets all he can honestly and saves all he gets (necessary expenses excepted) will certainly become rich, if that Being who governs the world, to whom all should look for a blessing on their honest endeavors, does not, in His wise providence, otherwise determine.*

Franklin's pecuniary point was plain: make it, then save it. Start with the pennies in your pocket. Instead of buying that lottery ticket, open up a bank account. Forget about the get-rich-quick scheme or the casino slot machine and use the money you just saved toward an investment in your own business, the down payment on a home, or your retirement fund. If you're having trouble saving, let a trustworthy friend or relative hold your earnings until you've developed the habit for yourself.

Applying these principles, Franklin attained financial independence in twenty-five years, freeing him up to help attain America's independence. Discipline your finances to attain your financial freedom. It could lead to promising possibilities more important than personal wealth.

MAKE A WAY OUT OF NO WAY   FEBRUARY 4TH

My dream was to play pro ball. I worked hard for the opportunity, was ready for it. I was told change was on the way, it didn't come. I shook off disappointment, I didn't let it stop me. I had learned the discipline of making a way out of no way.
Jerome Holland

In 1938 Jerome "Brud" Holland, the first African American to play football at Cornell University, gained All-American status, widely acknowledged as one of the best college players in the country. His athletic prowess notwithstanding, Holland had no opportunity to play professional football because of the color line: blacks were not permitted to play professional sports until Jackie Robinson's breakthrough in baseball a decade later.

Holland first learned to work through adversity in high school, as a student-athlete in Auburn, New York. His guidance counselor advised him to stop wasting his time with football and get a job because there was no way he was going to college. Holland rejected this counsel and instead worked harder at sports and school, even taking a year of post-high school remedial courses — while working full-time — to prepare for college. During that gap year he saved enough for tuition to one of Cornell's statutory colleges, but, once at Cornell, he had to live in the basement of a fraternity house and shovel coal in the furnace to earn his room and board.

> *I got up early to shovel coal and stayed up late to study. In between it was all going to classes and football practice — no time for anything else. It was really hard at first but it got easier as I stuck with it, and the self-discipline I developed stayed with me for the rest of my life.*

Holland's self-discipline led to remarkable career of trailblazing success. After receiving his PhD from the University of Pennsylvania in 1950, he became president of Delaware State College (now Delaware State University) then of Hampton Institute (now Hampton University) before his appointment as U.S. Ambassador to Sweden in 1970. Holland also served as the first African American chair of the American Red Cross Board of Governors, was the first African-American to sit on the board of the New York Stock Exchange, and received posthumously the Presidential Medal of Freedom. Holland made an excellent way out of no way, and you can follow his disciplined example if you:

REFUSE TO CUT CORNERS — Shortcuts seldom lead to long-run success. Don't underestimate the time and effort it takes to reach your goals. If you're looking for the easy way, forget about making a way out of no way. You'll stay stuck at square one.

REPLACE MOODS WITH STANDARDS — Living according to shifting moods will not help you attain your breakthrough. Set high standards and hold yourself accountable. Be your hardest critic and your own best drill sergeant. Push yourself to reach higher.

REIFY YOUR GOALS AS DISCIPLINES — Possessing abstract ideas won't get you to your destination in life. You have to get real: take your lofty goals and figure out how to do the daily things that bring about their fulfillment. Brud Holland had to shovel coal to make his way. Are you willing to work in your basement to get to your penthouse? Holland and legendary coach Vince Lombardi played college football during the same era, and they shared the same values, as Lombardi affirmed:

> *Leaders aren't born they are made. And they are made just like*

anything else, through hard work. And that's the price we'll have to pay to achieve that goal, or any goal.

RISE TO YOUR DESTINY — A great vision for your life will fuel you through the pain of self-discipline. Like Brud, take it one career opportunity at a time, make it a success, use it to springboard higher and higher and higher . . . If you strategically take one rung up at a time, there's no telling how high on the ladder of achievement you will climb.

DISCIPLINE YOUR WORDS   FEBRUARY 5TH

. . . in a larger sense, we can not dedicate, we can not consecrate,
we can not hallow this ground. The brave men, living and dead, who
struggled here, have consecrated it, far above our poor power to add or detract.
Abraham Lincoln

On November 19, 1863, at the dedication of the Soldiers' National Cemetery in Gettysburg, Pennsylvania, President Abraham Lincoln delivered an address honoring the dead soldiers. Because of the words he chose — 271 words in 3 minutes — Lincoln transformed the talk into an oration about national purpose. His speech was more powerful than that of the main speaker Edward Everett, whose address was over two hours. Lincoln disciplined his words and presented an oratorical masterpiece. Follow his example Take note of the words of his speech and the precepts they signify as you; discipline your own words in your everyday communication by using:

BREVITY — *Four score and seven years ago our fathers brought f worth on this continent a new nation, conceived in liberty and dedicated to the proposition that all men are created equal.*

Like Lincoln, make every word count. What's important is not how much you say, but it's how you say it. Lincoln's terseness versus Everett's long-windedness demonstrates that there are times when less is more. If you can make the same point in a sentence rather than a paragraph . . . in a phrase rather than a sentence . . . be succinct.

BOLDNESS — *Now we are engaged in a great civil war, testing whether that nation or any nation so conceived and so dedicated can long endure.*

Lincoln characterized the military conflict as a test of national principles. Your words can also carry great meaning, so phrase them for influence. Say things that others won't in ways that they wouldn't. Know the difference between being bold and being obnoxious. Communicate with challenging language, but also in respectful, sensitive and supportive ways.

> BLESSING — *The world will little note nor long remember what we say here, but it can never forget what they did here. It is for us, the living, rather, to be dedicated here to the unfinished work which they who fought here have thus far so nobly advanced.*

In this passage Lincoln connected the sacrifice of the soldiers to the destiny of the nation. Use language that blesses people in similar ways. Your words can tear people down or build them up; discourage or encourage; curse or consecrate. Don't be negative when speaking to others. If you have nothing good to say, practice holding your tongue. If you have criticism, be constructive with it. And if you're angry, it's best to wait until the storm passes before sharing your thoughts. You can be a blessing to people by simply complimenting them about something they did good, perhaps shining a smile in their direction; or you can curse them by flinging profanity their way. Regarding these options, heed the Apostle James' warning:

> *Out of the same mouth proceed blessing and cursing.*
> *My brethren, these things ought not to be so.*
> — James 3:10

> BEAUTY — *Now, it is rather for us to be here dedicated to the great task remaining before us — that from these honored dead we take increased devotion to that cause for which they gave their full measure of devotion; that we here highly resolve that these dead shall not have died in vain; that this nation, under God, shall have a new birth of freedom; and that government of the people, by the people, for the people shall not perish from the earth.*

In a single sentence, Lincoln concluded with eloquence, calling all Americans to the mission of fulfilling the founding promises. Use words that inspire others. Lincoln didn't use big words or many words; he used motivational words and they uplifted a nation. Paint a picture: make your listeners see something from what you're saying that will engage them in new and exciting ways. A poetic phrase can be more compelling than a lengthy lecture. Discipline your own words today, to uplift a life, or perhaps to inspire a nation.

ESTABLISH STRONG BOUNDARIES   FEBRUARY 6TH

Conduct is more convincing than language.
John Woolman

In the 1740's Quaker John Woolman gave up his thriving New Jersey retail dry goods store for a more modest living as a tailor. His purpose was to devote his life to social betterment. Woolman kept a journal about his mission; most of the entries concerned his crusade against slavery. But he also wrote about the importance of the inner life — self-discipline as the key to successful living. In one entry, Woolman pointed to the problem of excessive drinking in the colonies, explaining the collateral damage of this wanton lifestyle.

When men take pleasure in feeling their minds elevated with strong drink, and so indulge their appetite as to disorder their understandings, neglect their duty as members of a family or civil society, and cast off all regard to religion, their case is much to be pitied. And those whose lives are for the most part regular . . . adhere to some customs which powerfully draw to the use of more strong liquor than pure wisdom allows, it hinders the spreading of the spirit of meekness and strengthens the hands of the more excessive drinkers.

He concluded this particular journal writing with a spiritual point.

As I have sometimes been much spent in the heat and have taken spirits to revive me, I have found by experience that in such circumstances the mind is not so calm, nor so fitly disposed for divine meditation, as when all such extremes are avoided. I have felt an increasing care to attend to that Holy Spirit which sets right bounds to our desires and leads those who faithfully follow it to apply all the gifts of Divine Providence to the purposes for which they were intended.

Woolman emphasized a life of personal sacrifice, understanding the tradeoff of the disciplined lifestyle: establishing strong boundaries in the short term would lead to greater freedom in the long run. Establish the discipline of boundaries for yourself by taking these four steps.

DAILY — You need self-discipline to break bad habits. Take regular action; ideally, do the new thing every day. Whether going to the gym, attending a support meeting, viewing self-help instruction, seeing an advisor, whatever the task — making it happen everyday breaks the bondage of the old and births the bounty of the new.

DETAILS — Set your boundaries in specific places. Draw a bright line between acceptable and unacceptable behavior. Give yourself visual cues — markers to remind you of areas that are off limits. If drinking is a problem, stay away from the bar. And if you wind up out of bounds, hold yourself accountable. To prepare for the next time, make the boundary harder to penetrate.

DISCOMFORT — Yes, it will be uncomfortable, even painful, but only at first. The new discipline will get easier as you go along; the more you do it, the less difficult it becomes. As the regimen becomes a habit, the discomfort dissipates. Remember — as you endure the short-term pain, you can expect the long-term gain.

DESTINY — Today's sacrifice is about tomorrow's soaring: self-discipline is the launching pad to the better you. Always keep your goal in mind — you may even want to write it down or visualize it some way — so it can motivate you to stay on track.

DIVINE — This was Woolman's last point. If you're having trouble maintaining your self-discipline, ask God for help. Pray for strength. When you confess an inability to make it on your own, the amazing grace of divine intervention makes all the difference.

MAKE EVERY DAY COUNT   FEBRUARY 7TH

It is 4 A.M.; the sentinels on duty have discharged their rifles — the signal that the hours of sleep are over; and every wagon and tent is pouring forth its night tenants, and slow-kindling smokes begin largely to rise and float away on the morning air. . . .
Jesse Applegate

In the spring of 1843 Jesse Applegate was one of the leaders of more than 1,000 people — and 5,000 cattle — who left Independence, Missouri to make the overland journey to Oregon. The boundaries of the Oregon Territory were still in dispute, but that didn't deter the "Great Migration of 1943" from traveling to the Northwest frontier. Applegate kept an account of this expedition, "A Day with the Cow Column". In the following excerpt he recounted that when breakfast was finished, the day's journey began.

It is on the stroke of 7; the rushing to and fro, the cracking of the whips, the loud command to oxen, and what seems to be the inextricable confusion of the last ten minutes has ceased. Fortunately everyone has been found, and every teamster is at his post. The clear notes of the trumpet sound in the front; the pilot and his guards mount their horses, the leading division of wagons moves out of the encampment, and takes up the line of march, the rest fall into their places with the precision of clockwork, until the spot so lately full of life sinks back into that solitude that seems to reign over the broad plain and rushing river as the caravan draws it lazy length toward the distant El Dorado.

After a challenging day, the travelers settled at that night's encampment.

It is not yet 8 o'clock when the first watch is to be set; the evening meal is just over, and the corral now free from the intrusion of the cattle or horses, groups of children are scattered over it . . . It has been a prosperous day; more than twenty miles have been accomplished on the great journey. . . . the council of old men has broken up and each has returned to his own quarter. The flute has whispered its last lament to the deepening night, the violin is silent, and the dancers have dispersed. . . . . All is hushed and repose from the fatigue of the day, save the vigilant guard and the wakeful leader who still has cares upon his mind that forbid sleep.

These pioneers made every day count, as they moved along the Oregon Trail to Willamette Valley, reaching their destination in November 1843. You, too, can make every day count by practicing these four principles.

AHEAD OF TIME — The Oregon pioneers disciplined themselves to plan ahead of time; their itinerary and agenda were ready to be executed before the break of dawn. They implemented step by step their plan for any given day. Follow their example.

ADJUST TO CIRCUMSTANCES — Every day presents a unique set of challenges. Be disciplined: don't get derailed as new circumstances arise through the course of your day. Your biggest problem may be getting caught up in unexpected adversity. Adjust and stay focused. Have your day planned out before the sun comes up.

ACCEPT RISKS — Don't be reckless in your endeavors but accept the fact anything worthwhile will carry risks. Moving lots of people and animals across mostly untraveled terrain was

risky. Applegate and his fellow pioneers had to be extra organized
and prepared to manage those risks. Remember — the greater the
risks, the greater the need for discipline.

ADVANCE PER PRIORITIES — There's never enough
time to do everything that you want, need, or should do in a given
day. Be disciplined with your priorities; get them done first. Other
matters can wait and just might fall into place once you complete
the important things. As you set your priorities, reflect on this
formula, offered by Benjamin Franklin as Poor Richard:

One day is worth two tomorrows.

BEWARE THE SHINY OBJECT SYNDROME   FEBRUARY 8TH

*One of the sources of pride in being a human being is the ability
to bear present frustrations in the interests of longer purposes.*
Helen Lynd

In 1908 the Ford Motor Company created the Ford Model T,
which, five years later, hit the assembly line, becoming the first mass-
produced automobile and a national sensation. By 1927 over 15,000,000
Model T's had been produced.
In 1925 sociologist Helen Lynd and her husband Robert researched
consumer use of automobiles as part of a study of the effects of modern
inventions on American life. The Lynds spent a year in Muncie, Indiana, to
compile data through resident interviews. In their 1929 book "Middletown"
(the fictional name for Muncie) they published their findings on the impact
of the automobile on family life. The Lynds reported repercussions on the
spending habits of Muncie families.

*That the automobile does represent a real choice in the minds of some
at least is suggested by the acid retort of one citizen to the question about car
ownership: "No, sir, we've not got a car. That why we've got a home." . . . The
automobile has apparently unsettled the habit of careful saving for some
families. "Part of the money we spend on the car would go to the bank, I
suppose," said more than one working-class wife.*

The Lynds also observed impact on religious practices.

*Sharp, also, is the resentment aroused by this elbowing new device
when it interferes with old-established religious habits. The minister trying to*

65

change people's behavior in desired directions through the spoken word must compete against the strong pull of the open road strengthened by endless printed "copy" inciting to travel. Preaching to 200 people on a hot, sunny Sunday in midsummer on "The Supreme Need of Today," a leading Middletown minister denounced "automobilitis — the thing those people have who go off motoring on Sunday instead of going to church. If you want to use your car on Sunday, take it out Sunday morning and bring some shut-ins to church and Sunday school; then in the afternoon, if you choose, go out and worship God in the beauty of nature — but don't neglect to worship Him indoors too.

"Automobilitis" soon passed and cars became commonplace. Automobiles of the early twentieth century are like the smartphones of the early twenty-first century: different machine in hand; same principles are work. The new shiny object can be distracting, enervating, and counterproductive. You can be so enraptured with the new thing that you tend to pay excessive attention to it and lose sight of your priorities. To overcome the shiny object syndrome, you must:

POSTPOSE YOUR ACTIONS — Take a moment. Avoid immediate gratification. Not every new thing should be acted on, so sit on an idea, think it through, assess all your options; then take action. Meditate on this insight from Sidney Howard; it will help mitigate the pain and waste of hasty decision-making.

One half of knowing what you want is knowing what you must give up before you get it.

PRIORITIZE YOUR TASKS — The Middletown minister made it clear that the Sunday priority was worshipping, not motoring. Be committed to your priorities and refuse to be distracted by shiny objects. And it always a good idea to prioritize spiritual activity over materialistic moves.

POLICE YOUR ACTIVITIES — Moderation in all things is a good rule of thumb. If you find yourself excessively engaged with some new thing, apply self-discipline. Make the correction before the enticing attraction turns into a bad habit.

PROJECT YOUR GOALS — Set short- and long-term goals for every project. As you focus on new things, make sure that they are aligned with your objectives. If acquiring a new shiny object doesn't further your agenda or fit into your budget, let it go.

DEVELOP TRANSFORMATIVE HABITS   FEBRUARY 9TH

*The inhabitants of Kentucky eagerly recommend to strangers
the country they inhabit as the best part of the United States,
where the soil is most fertile, the climate most salubrious, where all
the inhabitants were brought through the love of liberty and independence!*
François André Michaux

In the late 1760's explorer Daniel Boone blazed his Wilderness Road through the Cumberland Mountains, opening the route from North Carolina and Tennessee into Kentucky, leading to the establishment of the American settlement of Boonesborough. Several permanent communities resulted from Boone's legendary exploits, and the Kentucky territory became the fifteenth state admitted to the Union in 1792.

As the first state west of the Appalachians, Kentucky attracted the interest of French botanist François André Michaux, who had been traveling America with his father André, also a botanist and the royal collector for France. During the summer of 1802 the younger Michaux explored Kentucky, collecting data on its peoples, lands, and customs. He wrote about his experiences in the book, "Travels to the West of the Alleghanies," published in Paris in 1804; Michaux described a regional regimen.

For some time past the inhabitants of Kentucky have taken to the rearing and training horses; and by this lucrative branch of trade they derive considerable profit . . . Almost all the inhabitants employ themselves in training and meliorating the breed of these animals.

Though much of his writing dealt with the area's foliage and commerce, Michaux also touched on quality of life, as in the following passage.

Throughout the Western country the children are kept punctually at school, where they learn reading, writing, and the elements of arithmetic. These schools are supported at the expense of the inhabitants, who send for masters as soon as the population and their circumstances permit; in consequence of which it is very rare to find an American who does not know how to read and write.

Michaux's account evinces an important success skill — habits of discipline. His example was drawn from education but disciplined habits are key in all areas of life. Develop your own disciplines — the earlier, the better — but it's never too late. Following this six-step daily approach will help you become more disciplined.

FOCUS — Identify the one area of your life where you really lack discipline, the one thing you most need a disciplined habit for — call it the issue. Make sure you focus on the most important issue you need to work on.

FIX — Come up with something you can do today, every day — a habit — to resolve the issue. It may be going to a support group, reading the Bible or another inspirational book, attending a class or workshop, watching a self-help video, praying — whatever it is, do it every day! Aristotle memorably imparted this principle:

We are what we repeatedly do. Excellence, then, is not an act, but a habit.

FORTY DAYS — Do it every day for forty days. That's how long it takes to unlearn a bad habit and establish a new one in its place. This process will renew your mind and transform your life.

FIFTEEN MINUTES — Spend at least 15 minutes in the morning, before you get busy with your day, doing your new habit. Get up earlier if you have to.

FIVE MINUTES — Take five during the course of the day to refocus on your new habit. Whatever you have to do, make the time to become more disciplined.

FOUR MINUTES — When you get back home, before you watch your favorite TV shows, chat on the phone or go to bed, spend a little more time with your habit. Reflect on how you did today so you can do better tomorrow.

PAY ATTENTION TO DETAILS   FEBRUARY 10TH

Begin, therefore, the work of forming the orator with the child; not merely by teaching him to declaim, but what is of more consequence, by observing and correcting his daily manners, motions, and attitudes.
William McGuffey

In 1836 William McGuffey and his brother Alexander published the first "McGuffey Reader", which were widely used as textbooks in school systems across America from the mid-19th century to the mid-20th century. More than 122 million McGuffey Readers were sold, placing the graded primers in a sales category with the Bible and Webster's Dictionary.

The overarching purpose of the Readers was balancing intellectual with moral instruction. The underlying premise was self-discipline as the means towards these ends. In the Sixth McGuffey Reader, published in 1879, the emphasis on disciplined conduct as the key to successful outcomes was detailed.

> *You can say, when he comes into your apartment, or presents you with something, a book or letter, in an awkward and blundering manner, "Return, and enter this room again," or, "Present me that book in a different manner," or, "Put yourself in a different attitude." You can explain to them the difference between thrusting or posing out his hand and arm, in straight lines and at acute angles, and moving them in flowing circular lines, and easy graceful action. He will readily understand you. Nothing is more true than that the motions of children are originally graceful; it is by suffering them to be perverted, that we lay the foundation of invincible awkwardness in later life.*

The Readers instructed that paying attention to details was the key in developing self-discipline. Take note of the following directive about proper posture; if such disciplines aren't already a part of your lifestyle, seek to incorporate them. The little things will make a big difference.

> GRANULARITY — *The first general direction that should be given to the speaker is, that he should stand erect and firm, and in that posture which gives an expanded chest and full play to the organ of reparation and utterance.*

Bodily movements, as articulated by the Readers, possessed both physical and moral qualities. Stand tall: you will project presence of body and soul.

> GESTURE — *Gesture is that part of the speaker's manner which pertains to his attitude, to the use and carriage of his person, and the movement of his limbs in delivery. . . . There is an expression in the extended arm, the clinched hand, the open palm, and the smiting of the breast. But let no gesture be made that is not in harmony with the thought or sentiment uttered; for it this harmony which constitutes propriety. As far as possible, let there be a correspondence between the style of action and the train of thought.*

The Readers encouraged "habitual practice" — or self-discipline — as the tool to cultivate a graceful lifestyle, which led to the effective communication skills of a successful person.

GRACE — *What is called a graceful manner, can only be attained by those who have some natural advantages of person. So far as it is in the reach of study or practice, it seems to depend chiefly upon the general cultivation of manners, implying freedom from all embarrassments and entire self-possession. The secret of acquiring a graceful style . . . lies in the habitual practice, not only when speaking but at all times, of free and graceful movements of the limbs.*

Pay attention to the details of self-discipline. Launch a new regimen of discipline with the daily practice of the 3-G principles stated above. You will crossover to great success, as Jim Rohn explained:

Discipline is the bridge between goals and accomplishment.

ADJUST YOUR EXPECTATIONS   FEBRUARY 11TH

Breaking free of mental bondage is a challenge that only daily-renewed self-discipline can surmount. And the best way to deliver the mind from imprisonment by one thing is to consume it with something else.
Joseph Holland

In 1985, when I first started Harkhomes, the homeless shelter in Harlem, I was baffled by the many men who had become homeless by spending their rent money on satisfying their drug habits. It was inconceivable to me that anyone could sacrifice the place where they live day after day for a moment's pleasure. After a while, however, I began to understand that their urge for immediate gratification was running wild, without regard to consequences.

Harry exemplified the problem of self-indulgence as a means of escape from unpleasant realities. His homelessness was the result of a complex set of problems, but at the root he was plagued by a frustrating lack of personal drive and discipline. He was lazy, too easily distracted from work, burying his head in a comic book instead of focusing on the present challenge.

Harry's story exemplified the tribulations of the homeless men at Harkhomes: he was born to a single mom on welfare; dropped out of high school; never knew his father; never had a 9-to-5 job; never had a place of his own.

I told Harry: "You have to give up to go up. You have to let go of old habits if you want to get ahead."

It took a while, but Harry eventually embraced a regimen of self-discipline. It was the key to the great strides of progress that he made.

Harry learned to practice the following principles; they worked for him. They will work for you, too, so do your best to be:

PAINFUL — Expect personal progress to hurt. Be willing to practice self-denial. Be ready to make personal sacrifices. If you want to get ahead, you're going to have to give some things up. Human nature shrinks back from this process. Get used to it. The sooner you accept the fact that pain is a good thing on the pathway to success, the quicker you'll get over it and the closer you'll be to your destination. I encouraged Harry to memorize the following scripture. He did, and it helped him.

No discipline seems pleasant at the time, but painful. Later on, however, it produces a harvest of righteousness and peace for those who have been trained by it.
— Hebrews 12:11

PREPARED — Expect things to go wrong. Life has an annoying way of upending your best-laid plans. Everyday trials can cause events to spiral out of your control: tragedies, emergencies, calamities, problems, and chaos reign. Just because life veers off track, don't give up on your goals. Be prepared for the detour. If plan A fails, be ready to move to plan B, C, or D. Get ready for the obstacles; nip disappointment in the bud; move on to the next best thing.

PATIENT — Expect outcomes to take longer than you would like. Beware of immediate gratification. People want what they want (or what they think they want) when they want it, which is invariably right now. Yet progress and inspiration usually take longer to happen than you think. So take your time; you will worry less and make fewer mistakes. Also, take the long view when estimating the time you need to achieve your goals. You will have more chances to take advantage of opportunities that you would have missed speeding by.

PLUCKY — Expect to be assailed. You may have the most wonderful personality in the world, but not everyone with whom you cross paths will like you. Don't get bent out of shape when unexpected — and undeserved — adversaries appear. Don't let them disrupt your plans. You will have friends. You will have enemies. So see the opposition coming. Be ready for the haters. Expect them at inopportune times and from unknown places. If they don't come, so much the better. If they do, be courageous. Stare them down. Turn the other cheek. Overcome evil with good.

ASPIRE, PERSPIRE, INSPIRE   FEBRUARY 12TH

*We bid you welcome to a land of freedom; we applaud your resolution;
we commend your judgment in asserting the right of expatriation — a right
acknowledged by people of all nations from the earliest ages to the present time, a
right indispensable to liberty and happiness, and which ought never to be surrendered.*
Irish Immigrant Booklet, 1816

The history of the United States is, in significant part, the story of
immigration: how almost 50 million people, who came voluntarily to
America, contributed to the making of one new nation out of many
different cultural groups. This epic is filled with countless chapters of
newcomers from all over the world. One epochal influx was in the
aftermath of the Napoleonic Wars, which coincided with a burgeoning
awareness of opportunities in America. The wave of immigration in the
1810's glutted the job market in New York City. In July 1816, the Shamrock
Society of New York, which had formed among already established Irish
immigrants to help the newcomers, published Hints to Emigrants from
Europe. The purpose of this booklet was to inform the incoming Irish
about transitional issues, preparing them for the challenges of America. It
advised the immigrants to be disciplined.

*First of all, he should regulate his diet, and be temperate in the
quantity of his food. The American laborer or working mechanic who has a
better and more plentiful table than any other man in the world of his class is,
for the most, a small eater; and we recommend to you his example . . . He
should, therefore, be quite as abstemious in the quantity of food as of strong
drink . . . after some residence here, he may preserve his health by regimen and
exercise alone.*

It concluded with some inspiration.

*You then who left the abject condition of European subjects, who will
never encounter the persecution of kings . . . who are now beyond the fantastic
tyranny of those governments that exterminate Catholics in one country, and
connive at the massacre of Protestants in another, what more is requisite to
engage your love and veneration of the free Constitution of America than to
remember who you were, what you have witnessed, what you have suffered, and
to reflect on what you are about to become, and the blessings you have it in your
power to enjoy?*

The three-pronged strategy of the booklet worked for many of the
new Americans; it remains relevant today. Success still happens through

aspiration, perspiration and inspiration. Utilize these principles to pave your own pathway of success.

ASPIRE — There's always something better up ahead. Set your sights on it. Go for the stars. Even if you land on the moon, you've ended up in a better place. The higher your expectations, the better chance you'll have of gaining the motivation to reach your goals.

PERSPIRE — The new immigrants were advised to be disciplined about their diet. It's still good advice to manage your food intake in ways that maximize your energy. This is the hard part. A disciplined approach may make you sweat. It's good sign. Work as hard as you can, until you feel the sweat. Perspiration means progress. Thomas Edison said it best:

Genius is one percent inspiration and ninety-nine percent perspiration.

INSPIRE — You will be inspired to achieve great things if, in the words of a historic booklet with a great track record, you remember:

who you were:
never forget your starting point; it will keep you grounded.
what you have witnessed:
keep a journal to chart your progress; a future book?
what you have suffered:
short-term pain leads to . . .
what you are about to become:
. . . long-term gain.

DON'T LOSE YOUR SELF-CONTROL   FEBRUARY 13TH

During the drug state, awareness becomes intensely vivid while self-control over input is remarkably diminished; thus there is the lurking threat of loss of inner control, so often reported in bad trips or in phases of mystical experiences with the drug. Customary boundaries become fluid and the familiar becomes novel and portentous.
Daniel Freedman

Students activists were at the center of the social and political ferment that characterized the 1960's. They confronted the "Establishment" — the web of industry, government and university that seemed unresponsive to their concerns. Some of the students mixed protest and pleasure-seeking. Controversy arose from the burgeoning psychedelic culture, characterized by the widespread use of LSD and other drugs. Daniel Freedman, chairman of the department of psychiatry at the University of Chicago, wrote a 1968 article assessing the countercultural challenge. Early in the essay, Freedman described one of the most unfortunate consequences of the drug culture.

> EVENTS — *internal or external, memories or perceptions — take on a trajectory of their own; qualities become intense and gain a life of their own. Redness is more interesting than the object which is red; meaningfulness more important than what is specifically meant; connotations balloon into cosmic allusiveness; the limits of sobriety are lost. . . . replaced by the old medicine show with an updated campus version complete with readings and tempting arguments, if not pills, to sell: "Tune in, turn on, drop out." A drug mystique has been welded to the serious shifts and strains inherent in the experience of the potentially most unstable group of any society — the adolescent and young adult.*

He concluded by pointing to a more general concern.

> *We should not forget to assess the cost of sustained euphoria or pleasure states; we have to wonder whether the mind of man is built to accommodate an excess of either pleasure or rationality. We do not know whether or not there are individuals with sufficient strength to take these drugs for growth or pleasure within the social order without increased and credulous alienation from it. . . .*

Freedman articulated the perilous consequences of the loss of self-control. To help you avoid these outcomes when confronted by temptations and challenges, here's your self-control management plan, in three steps; you have to manage your:

ENVIRONMENT — This is your moral environment: the values of life determine the success of life. Be clear on right from wrong, on where to draw the line. If you know temptation is up ahead, steer clear. Take the less risky road. Avoid people, places and things that bring moral hazards into your life. There are times when it's best to say "NO!"

EMOTIONS — Work on knowing the difference between the time to display your emotions and to delay them. Emotional extremes like rage or depression can cause you to escape the negativity by resorting to alcohol or drugs, which is short-term fix

74

creating long-term problems. Though psychedelic culture or getting high may feel good, such distractions are anathema to personal fulfillment and divine destiny.

EVERY MOMENT — A New Testament verse is on point: "making the best use of the time, because the days are evil" (Ephesians 5:16). Carpe Diem! (Seize the day!) If you adopt the attitude that every moment is a precious opportunity to take a step of progress, you'll stay on the pathway of self-control and earned success. If you want to fulfill your dreams, you have to avoid the psychedelic detours that will eventually derail them. Meditate on these words from Mahatma Gandhi; they will strengthen your resolve to exercise self-control.

There's always a limit to self-indulgence, but none to self-restraint.

DISCIPLINE YOUR EMOTIONS   **FEBRUARY 14TH**

*Men often oppose a thing merely because they have had no agency in
planning it, or because it may have been planned by those whom they dislike.*
Alexander Hamilton

Founding Father Alexander Hamilton was one of the most accomplished men of his era: the first Secretary of the Treasury; an influential interpreter and promoter of the U.S. Constitution; and the main author of the economic policies of George Washington's administration. But in 1804 he met a tragic end, killed at forty-nine in his infamous duel with Aaron Burr.

The circumstances surrounding his death are complicated. Hamilton had served with Burr in the Revolutionary Army but afterwards their personal and political feud raged more and more out of control. Hamilton felt betrayed by Burr and expressed his anger in published statements, like the following.

*As to Burr there is nothing in his favour. His private character is
not defended by his most partial friends. He is bankrupt beyond redemption
except by the plunder of his country, His public principles have no inter spring
or aim than his own aggrandizement. . . . If he can he will certainly disturb
our institutions to secure himself permanent power and with it wealth. He is
truly the Catiline of America.*

The reference to Catiline, the abject and treacherous figures whose machinations almost brought down the Roman Republic, was the ultimate insult. Burr soon issued the invitation for the fatal duel.

The historical record shows that Hamilton had ample opportunity and justification to reject the invitation and move on with his life. But his emotions wouldn't let him. Whether his indignation towards Burr had justification is beside the point. Blaming Burr is also beside the point. Hamilton could have — should have! — declined the invitation to the shooting match. But he chose not to, instead indulging the hostile feelings, rejecting counsel to mediate, escalating matters with his dismissiveness and counter-threats.

Hamilton represents a negative role model. Don't make his mistake. Be emotionally disciplined as you:

GIVE UP — Discipline is hard because it entails the determination to give things up in order to get ahead. Practice self-denial. Decide what you need to sacrifice and keep fighting with yourself until you let it go for good. Overcoming something that you've grown accustomed to because it's been there seemingly forever is a mountain to climb. Be intentionally sacrificial when it comes to your emotions. One of the most important things to discipline is your anger, as the Apostle James advised:

My dear brothers and sisters, take note of this: Everyone should be quick to listen, slow to speak and slow to become anger.
—James 1:19

GO DEEP — Emotional discipline is harder because it means getting in touch with those deeply buried feelings and bringing them to the surface. If you've been badly hurt, don't be like Hamilton, allowing the ill feelings to fester, becoming ever more ingrained and intractable. Instead acknowledge the inner wounds and forgive those who caused them. Letting go of long-held negative feelings about someone may be the most difficult thing you to do, but you've got to do it. Do everything you can to keep your emotions from getting the best of you.

GET ON — You won't be able to get on with your life as long as you fail to discipline your emotions. Don't get stuck in a rut of bitterness. Govern your life by principles, not sentiments. Refuse to let unbridled feelings dictate your actions. Otherwise you might end up like Hamilton — successful life, undisciplined emotions, tragic ending.

INNOVATE WITH YOUR DISCIPLINE   FEBRUARY 15TH

When manual training has been generally adopted for boys in their teens, the world will see a multiplication of useful inventions such as not even the past twenty-five years can parallel. The era of invention is now in its infancy.
Calvin M. Woodward

In 1880, Calvin M. Woodward, dean of the school of engineering at Washington University in St. Louis, founded the St. Louis Manual Training School for young men. An educational innovation, the school soon became the the the largest and best attended public high school in St. Louis. Woodward described the purpose of the school, which operated under the auspices of Washington University, as the "systematic study of tools, processes, and materials" to help boys discover their "inborn capacities and aptitudes whether in the direction of literature, science, engineering or the practical arts."

The key to Woodward's success at his Manual Training School was his pioneering approach to instilling self-discipline. He was intentional and strategic about transforming typically rigorous and challenging academic regimens into novel, engaging processes for his students. You should take note of his approach and apply its principles. Be innovative about how you bring discipline into your own life. Four precepts stood out in Woodward's efforts to impart self-discipline, which are stated in his own words below. Use his perspectives to help you think outside of the box about disciplining yourself and others.

DEVOTION — *It awakens a lively interest in school and invests dull subjects with a new life. . . . "My son never was so interested in his school, never studied so hard, and never had so much to tell about schoolwork as now." That is the way scores of parents have reported. . . The habit of applying what one reads or hears to what one does makes things interesting.*

With his signature wit, Mark Twain drives home the point about discipline:

Training is everything. The peach was once a bitter almond; cauliflower is nothing but cabbage with a college education.

DISTANCE — *It keeps boys out of mischief, both in and out of school. This result is most marked . . . The pupils are so earnest, so impressed with the value of what they are receiving that mischief and foolishness seem rather out of place. Fellow principals in other cities bear the same testimony. One says that the moral influence of manual training is worth all the manual training costs.*

Distance yourself from "mischief and foolishness". You will stay out of trouble and on the road to success.

> DIRECTION — *It aids one who must choose his occupation. Most children step from the schoolroom into the working world with no just conception of what the world is nor what it is doing. In a great majority of cases one's occupation is the result of chance or environment. There is no intelligent choice because there is not intelligence in such matters. Boys who live near the wharves become sailors; the son of the schoolmaster teaches school, etc. If they break away from the influences that would thus hedge them in, they are apt to take their chances with the odds against them. It is more than likely that the square plug gets into the round hole. To change the figure, the boy fresh from school sees a variety of roads before him. How is he to know which to choose unless he knows not only the roads but himself? Clearly, intelligent choice can be exercised only when the chief characteristics of both roads and traveler are fairly comprehended . . . .*

> DIGNITY — *It raises the standards of attainment in mechanical occupations and invests them with new dignity. Man became man when he made his first tool, and he becomes more manly as he continues to invent and use more tools. Man subdues nature and develops art through the instrumentality of tools. . . . Through the instrumentality of tools, the intellect is gradually doing away with the lower forms of labor. Every occupation becomes ennobled by the transforming influence of thought and skill.*

Apply these four D's to your own life; then impart them to young people you know; they will bring innovative thinking and dynamic progress to your life and theirs.

PREPARE THROUGH DISCIPLINE   FEBRUARY 16TH

> *There is an old Testament prophecy of the "sins of the fathers being visited upon the third and fourth generations." . . . Now, almost a century removed from slavery, we find the heritage of oppression and racism erupting in our cities, with volcanic lava of bitterness and frustration pouring down our avenues.*
> Martin Luther King, Jr.

In the early spring of 1968, Martin Luther King, Jr. arrived in Memphis to lead a nonviolent protest on behalf of striking garbage collectors in that city. On April 4th, standing on a motel balcony, King was shot down by an assassin's bullet. The tragic irony of his death was that

King had been the foremost American apostle of nonviolence throughout the Civil Rights Movement. And building on the success of his earlier initiatives in Birmingham, Selma and elsewhere, King had been planning a nationwide nonviolent movement — the Poor People's Campaign. In an article that appeared shortly before his assassination, King articulated his anti-poverty protest strategy.

> *We've selected fifteen areas — ten cities and five rural districts — from which we have recruited our initial cadre. We will have 200 poor people from each area. That would be about 3,000 to get the protests going and set the pattern. They are important, particularly in terms of maintaining nonviolence. They are being trained in this discipline now.*

At the conclusion of the essay King juxtaposed the negative phenomenon of peril against the positive force of hope, as he summoned America to overcome injustice and fulfill its ideals.

> *The American people are infected with racism — that is the peril. Paradoxically, they are also infected with democratic ideals — this is the hope. . . . But they do not have a millennium to make changes. Nor have they a choice of continuing in the old way. . . . To end poverty, to extirpate prejudice, to free a tormented conscience, to make a tomorrow of justice, fair play, and creativity — all these are worthy of the American ideal.*

King's practice of preparing his nonviolent protesters through discipline was an effective approach, yielding victorious outcomes throughout his singular career as a civil rights leader. Preparing through discipline is also important for you to practice, in the following ways.

SEARCH FOR OPPORTUNITIES TO PREPARE — Strive to do your best whatever situation you're in, even if your circumstances are far from perfect. Greatness is earned in the trenches, in those hard places where you never thought you'd be and you can't wait to move beyond. Be disciplined about working through the small things and with the little opportunities; you're simply preparing yourself to excel with the big things.

> *The future belongs to those who prepare for it today.*
> — Malcolm X

SECURE SUCCESS HABITS — Success doesn't just happen. You have to make it happen. One of the most important things you can do towards that end is to develop success habits. Self-discipline is key. If you want to achieve something great in life, you have to be disciplined about developing the right habits. If becoming a great athlete is your quest, the habit of smoking cigarettes is self-defeating; but the daily habit of working out at the gym, the weight room, the practice field, wherever — provides both strength and edification. Discipline is the means to the end of breaking bad old habits and forming new good ones.

SEEK HIGH IDEALS — Holing on to your ideals will sustain your discipline. Just because long-sought-after ideals are still in the making, refuse to surrender; keep believing and pursuing them. Almost 200 hundred years after their proclamation, King hadn't given up on America's ideals. Don't give up on them either. Work to complete the unfinished business of liberty and justice for all.

TAKE DAILY STEPS TO YOUR GOALS   FEBRUARY 17TH

Plant spacious parks in your cities, and loose their
gates as wide as the morning, to the whole people.
Andrew Jackson Downing

With the rise of nineteenth century industrialization and urbanization throughout America, agricultural life seemed to be waning. Architect and horticulturist Andrew Jackson Downing publicized the contrary view. Considered to be the founder of American landscape architecture, Downing was commissioned by President Millard Fillmore to create a plan for beautify the National Mall. Downing's most important writings — "Rural Essays" — appeared in the periodical "The Horticulturist", which he edited from 1846 to 1852. In a June 1848 essay Downing underscored the excellence of the farm worker, highlighting timeless features of their self-discipline. Study Downing's words and seek to incorporate the principles they represent as you take daily steps to your goals.

WORK HARDER THAN OTHERS — *The cultivators of the soil constitute the great industrial class in this country. They may well be called its "bone and sinew"; for, at this moment, they do not only feed all other classes but also no insignificant portion of needy Europe, furnish the raw material for manufactures, and raise the great staples which figure so largely in the accounts of the merchant, the shipowner and manufacturer, in every village, town, and seaport in the Union.*

If you're expecting to take it easy, you will never excel. Excellence doesn't abide in places of leisure. If you want to be extraordinary, your work ethic cannot be ordinary. Resolve to work harder than everyone else around you . . . harder than you ever have before . . . and do it everyday: you will be laying bricks in your house of greatness.

WASTE NOT TIME — *He who will do this most successfully must not waste his time, labor, and capital by working in the dark . . . He must plant and prune so as to aid and direct nature, that neither time nor space are idly squandered.*

How you spend your time — putting the non-priorities to the side — will shape your excellence. Put aside those things that tether you to mediocrity. Free yourself to excel.

WELCOME DAILY CHALLENGES — *He must learn gardening and orcharding . . . He must collect the lost elements of the soil from the animal and mineral kingdoms, and bring them back again to their starting point. He must seek out the food of plants in towns and villages where it is wasted and thrown away.*

Excellence rises over time, from what you do every day towards self-improvement. The only path to greatness is as you overcome daily challenges, so welcome them. Take on a challenging task today, even if it puts you in deep water. Keep swimming with the right attitude and you will come through it stronger, ready to achieve. Harry Truman's word resonate here.

. . . In reading the lives of great men, I found that the first victory they won was over themselves . . . self-discipline with all of them came first.

WAIT NOT ON HELP — *The farming class is the great nursery of all the professions and the industrial arts of the country. From its bosom go out the shrewdest lawyers and the most successful merchants of the towns: and back to the country return these classes again, however successful, to be regenerated in the primitive life and occupation of the race.*

Your helper isn't right around the corner about to show up. Get started by yourself on what needs to get done. The needed assistance may just show up at the appropriate time, but don't depend on it to get going. If you take the initiative, your pathway to excellence will be easier and shorter that if you're waiting on someone to flash the green light. Be a self-starter.

DISCIPLINE AWAY FROM TROUBLE   FEBRUARY 18TH

Without virtue there can be no liberty.
— Benjamin Rush

Physician, patriot and scholar Benjamin Rush was a strong advocate of establishing a national school system for the American Experiment. In a 1798 essay, Rush emphasized values-driven public education as the key to a successful life. Though he didn't shy away from writing about religious determinants of ethical behavior, Rush explained that his purpose was not to proselytize but only to provide youth with the moral foundation for individual progress.

It is foreign to my purpose to hint at the arguments which establish the truth of the Christian revelation. My only business is to declare that all its doctrines and precepts are calculated to promote the happiness of society and the safe and well-being of civil government . . . every precept of the Gospel inculcates those degrees of humility, self-denial, and brotherly kindness which are directly opposed to the pride of monarchy and the pageantry of court . . . a Christian cannot fail of being wholly inoffensive, for his religion teaches him in all things to do to others what he would wish, in like circumstances, they should do to him.

Rush's approach of asserting the centrality of religion in the formation of ethics was controversial in post-Revolutionary War America; it has become even more so since then. Whatever your religious background or views, it's vital to note that a commitment to virtuous living helps to steer you clear of trouble. You can discipline yourself away from trouble by keeping these points in mind.

MAKE A MISTAKE — Temptation happens to us all; at some point it will stare you in the face. When you're confronted with temptation, the question is: will you resist it or succumb to it. A Biblical reference is illustrative.

One evening David got up from his bed and walked around on the roof of the palace. From the roof he saw a woman bathing. The woman was very beautiful . . .
— 2 Samuel 11:2

David, the greatest king of Israel, was attracted to the bathing Bathsheba and, instead of resisting the temptation, committed adultery with her. Once the mistake is made, the question becomes: will you admit it, or will you cover it up?

MAKE AN EXCUSE — Making an excuse means jumping from the frying pan into the fire. David tried to cover up his mistake by orchestrating the death of Bathsheba's military husband on the battlefield. So David went from bad to worse, adulterer to murderer, which led to disastrous consequences for himself, his family and his kingdom. To help you stop making excuses, memorize this precept from Ralph Waldo Emerson.

Excuses always replace progress.

MAKE A COVENANT — Avoiding David's fate starts with a promise: declare to yourself that you will live according to virtue, not vice. The Ten Commandments of Old Testaments and Jesus' Sermon on the Mount overflow with positive values; they are good places to begin. If not there, choose a good source of personal ethics. Become a student of morality and covenant to yourself to live a virtuous lifestyle.

MAKE A MOVE — There's a high cost to pay for having no self-discipline. Rush's point was that, given what's at stake, society should prioritize instilling it and other vigorous virtues at a young age. If you didn't get it at home, school or elsewhere, make sure you prioritize self-discipline for your own life. Disciplining yourself, especially when confronted by temptation is a must; it will help you stay out of trouble. Your failure to possess self-discipline — and practice it daily — will not end well.

DISCIPLINE FROM WHERE YOU ARE   FEBRUARY 19TH

To those of my race . . . who underestimate the importance of cultivating friendly relations with the Southern white man, I say: Cast down your bucket where you are: cast it down in making friends of the people of all races by whom we are surrounded.
Booker T. Washington

On September 18, 1895, educator Booker T. Washington delivered a speech at the Cotton States and International Exposition in Atlanta that received national attention. Representative of the last generation of African American leaders born into slavery, Washington elaborated in his Atlanta address his philosophy that industrial education and racial accommodation were the best strategies for black progress in the post-Reconstruction, Jim Crow-era South. The speech was called by some the Atlanta Compromise because it advocated conciliation over confrontation. In the following passage Washington proclaimed cultivating virtues like self-discipline.

> *Our greatest danger is that, in the great leap from slavery to freedom, we may overlook the fact that the masses of us are to live by the productions of our hands and fail to keep in mind that we shall prosper in proportion as we learn to dignify and glorify common labor, and put brains and skill into the common occupations of life; shall prosper in proportion as we learn to draw the line between the superficial and the substantial, the ornamental gewgaws of life and the useful. No race can prosper till it learns that there is as much dignity in tilling a field as in writing a poem. It is at the bottom of life we must begin, and not at the top. Nor should we permit our grievances to overshadow our opportunities.*

Washington's Atlanta speech catapulted him into the role of national Negro leader, rising from his Alabama base as president of Tuskegee Institute to found the National Negro Business League and advise U.S. Presidents. His rallying cry for self-discipline encouraged his listeners to "Cast down your bucket where you are": be disciplined about working with what's presently in your hands, making your way from there. Casting down your buckets means focus, being intentional about doing whatever you need to do to forge your pathway of personal progress. Washington's principles of self-discipline transformed countless lives. Apply them to your life; start practicing discipline from wherever you are as you:

PAY YOUR PRICE — Life — if it's to be worthwhile — demands an investment from you, a payment that represents personal sacrifice. Don't worry that what you have to pay — your time, your effort, the pain — may be greater than what your sibling, friend or neighbor may be sacrificing. Just focus on paying your price. You may have to cast down your bucket where you are; in other words, make the best of your present circumstances. If that's the case for you, figure out a way to get through it.

PUNT YOUR PLEASURES — Be clear: you will have to make personal sacrifices to achieve your goals. It may not feel like it in the moment but it's always worth it to put off present pleasures for future goals. Make the hard decisions to delay gratification. Choose to punt your pleasures. A New Testament Scripture establishes the trade-off — punt now, score later. Jesus' teaching to his followers is relevant here.

> *Whoever wants to be my disciple must deny themselves and take up their cross and follow me.*

— Matthew 16:24

POSITION YOUR PRIORITIES — Discipline is difficult, but it gets easier the more you do it. In the initial stage, you must be intentional about it. Prioritize it — the most important thing you do every day — until it becomes a habit.

PICTURE YOUR PURPOSE — Discipline for discipline's sake doesn't work. Make sure your discipline is short-term pain for long-term gain. If your effort isn't purpose-driven, you'll never get through it. See the goal; use it to motivate you through the trial.

MASTER YOUR ANGER   FEBRUARY 20TH

The afflicted state of our poor neighbours, that are now suffering by molestations from the invisible world, we apprehend so deplorable, that we think their condition calls for the utmost help of all persons in their several capacities.
Cotton Mather, letter to Chief Magistrate William Stoughton, 1692

From February 1692 to May 1693 during the Salem witch trials in colonial Massachusetts, of the more than two hundred people accused of sorcery, fourteen women, five men, and two dogs were executed by hanging. Historians have long debated the ethical lessons of this infamous episode. One conclusion seems unassailable: anger at the witchcraft turned into rage, then to hatred and hysteria, jeopardizing the fair administration of justice.

The Salem witch ignominy is a cautionary tale about out-of-control anger, which was metaphorically captured by British poets Charles and Mary Lamb in Anger.

Anger in its time and place
May assume a kind of grace.
It must have some reason in it,
And not last beyond a minute.
If to further lengths it go,
It does into malice grow.
'Tis the difference that we see
'Twixt the serpent and the bee.
If the latter you provoke,
It inflicts a hasty stroke,
Puts you to some little pain,
But it never stings again.

Close in tufted bush or brake
Lurks the poison-swelled snake
Nursing up his cherished wrath;
In the purlieus of his path,
Wheresoever fate may bring you,
The vile snake will always sting you.

You can master your anger or be mastered by it. Don't let the intensity of your feelings provoke you to do things you shouldn't do. Don't just manage your anger. Take these five steps and master it!

COOL OFF — Thomas Jefferson gave good advice: *When angry, count ten before you speak; if very angry, an hundred.* In other words, let the fire of your anger burn out and give your raging emotions a chance to settle down before they affect what you say and do. Be disciplined about Jefferson's advise: count to ten or more, depending on how angry you are, before you speak or act.

CARETAKE YOUR FEELINGS — Own your emotions, however negative they might be. Taking responsibility for your anger means refusing to blame someone or something else for it. When you make a mistake and get really upset about it, hold yourself accountable; then you can move on.

CONNECT TO THE SOURCE — Find the original trigger for your anger. A parent who has a bad day at work gets angry at his children when he/she gets home, but the real reason — not the misbehavior of the kids — occurred earlier in the day. Don't miss the root cause.

CUT IT OFF — Distinguish between anger and rage. The former can be positive — a feeling of personal power that can be harnessed into controlled expressions of righteous indignation; whereas the latter is negative — a breakdown of that power into scattered, blind outbursts.

CREATE AN OUTLET — Share your emotions. Do it honestly with those you can trust. Such transparency will help you to better understand how you're feeling. It can also help build the constraint of mutual accountability and a sense of shared community.

DISCIPLINE YOUR ENVIRONMENT   FEBRUARY 21ST

Whether from poverty or neglect . . . a large number of parents have no idea of the responsibility imposed on them of providing for the moral training of their offspring.
American Catholic Pastoral Letter of 1866

On October 7, 1866, the Second Plenary Council, a national council of Roman Catholic American clergy convened in Baltimore. The purpose of this provincial gathering was to set policy in the aftermath of "the national crisis" of the Civil War. Of the many issues that were addressed the problem of wayward youth received significant attention. The Pastoral Letter of 1866 summarizing the conclusions of the Plenary Council recommended establishing new schools for wayward youth because . . .

. . . day after day these unhappy children are caught in the commission of petty crimes, which render them amenable to the public authorities; and day after day are they transferred by hundreds from the sectarian reformatories in which they have been placed by the courts to distant localities . . .

The 1866 Letter emphasized the importance of creating disciplined environments in which the lives of these young people could be given a new trajectory — from a downward spiral to steady progress.

. . . we cannot too earnestly exhort our venerable brethren of the clergy to bring this matter before their respective flocks, to endeavor to impress on Christian parents the duty of guarding their children from the evils above referred to, and to invite them to make persevering and effectual efforts for the establishment of institutions wherein, under the influence of religious teachers, the waywardness of youth may be corrected . . .

Discipline is a key virtue in the success of any individual; it is especially important for those who have — for whatever reason — ended up with self-destructive habits on a gloomy pathway towards dismal ends. The religious leaders of the mid-nineteenth century understood that dynamic intervention was needed to turn such lives around. This strategy holds true not only for you to rise to success but also for your family members, friends, co-workers — all who fall under your influence. Create a disciplined environment for yourself and others to move ahead by implementing these principles.

HEAVY REGULATIONS — When the goal is to attain

greatness, especially if you're rising up from hard times, you need to impose hard rules on yourself. Don't shy away from the list of do's and don't's. Hold yourself accountable to daily milestones. The more pressure you put on yourself now, the less stress you'll have in the future.

HIGH EXPECTATIONS — Go for the gold medal. Whether you're a teenager, in the throes of middle age or a senior citizen, use your imaginative powers to conceive the best possible outcomes. If you get stuck on the rough side of the mountain today, keep striving for the summit. Tomorrow will bring a new opportunity to climb. Keep your eyes on the mountaintop!

HUGE HOPE — The wayward youth of which the religious leaders spoke have not gone away as a pressing social problem two centuries later. Complex, intractable issues raise challenges for young people, especially from hard-hit communities, as they pursue their American Dream: family instability/ disintegration; mass incarceration, mental illness; unemployment; poor education/drop-out status; addiction; etc. But there seems to be a deeper root, shared by those falling through sociological cracks, a more personal determinant stemming from the gloomy circumstances out of which so many of the socially dislocated come. It is hopelessness; no vision for the future; limited opportunities; few if any options; no dream to motivate you to play by the rules because of a conviction that the game is stacked against you. Do everything you can to change the hopeless mindset by making hopefulness the center of your life and of whatever environment you're in; this Old Testament verse outlines the consequences:

Hope deferred makes the heart sick, but a longing fulfilled is a tree of life.
— Proverbs 13:12

Resolve to find the silver lining in every cloud. Search hard for it. Keep hope alive!

ENDURE PAIN FOR GAIN   FEBRUARY 22ND

. . . it is the duty of a nation to superintend and even to coerce the education of children.
Samuel Harrison Smith

In 1797 the American Philosophical Society sponsored a contest for the best essay on education and public schools. One of the Society's members, Philadelphia banker and newspaper publisher Samuel Harrison Smith, won the first prize for a submission entitled Remarks on Education: Illustrating the Close Connection between Virtue and Wisdom, To Which is Annexed, a System of Liberal Education. In the essay, Smith elaborated his vision for American public education as a collaboration between home and school. The goal was to create academic and moral environments: for the child to gain knowledge as well as to develop good habits.

Smith's essay drew the attention of Thomas Jefferson; consequently Smith moved to Washington, D.C. and started the triweekly periodical "National Intelligencer", influencing national policy on education and other issues.

In his prize-winning essay, Smith explained the value of self-discipline: one endures short-term pain while expecting long-term gain. As Smith elucidated in his own words, manage your process of self-discipline — enduring pain for gain — by focusing on the following.

HARD THINGS — *To be deprived of that which we love is in some degree painful to us all; to children it is painful in the highest degree. Yet a habit of voluntary or compulsory abstinence from pleasure is absolutely necessary to human happiness.*

Do your hard things — the undesirable, even difficult tasks — first, at the beginning of your day. Get the painful stuff out of the way early. Finish it before you start some less challenging activity. Completing the unpleasant, mundane agenda — wash the dishes, make your bed, do your drudgery — will develop your discipline. Drill sergeant yourself until you get it done, like the Apostle Paul:

I strike a blow to my body and make it my slave . . .
— 1 Corinthians 9:27

HEURISTIC APPROACH — *. . . the daily attendance at a school will withdraw the mind of the child from an entire dependence on its parents, will place it in situations demanding the exercise of its faculties, and will strengthen instead of weakening, its attachment to domestic scenes.*

Handle your discipline in ways that enable you learn things on your own. Parents, teachers and friends should be helpful, but your greatest life lessons will be those you embrace independent of any outside influence.

HABITS DEVELOPED — *Let this plan, partly domestic and partly public, be pursued till the mind begins boldly to expand itself and to indicate an ability and an inclination to think for itself.*

The key is developing a constructive daily routine. Keep repeating the good actions until they become second nature. It may take longer than expected to break the bad habits and hone the new. Don't give up. Your good habits will determine your future success.

HEED THE MOMENT — *We have now reached the period which claims the closest attention. The mind now feels its vigor and delights in displaying it. Ambition is kindled, emulation burns, a desire of superiority and distinction are roused . . . The indulgence of parental tenderness should now be exchanged for the patient and unobstructed exercise of the mental powers . . .*

One of the most important habits for you to develop is punctuality. Commit to be on time. Even strive to be early. Paying attention to being punctual means you're getting disciplined about handling your most precise asset — your time. Don't miss your transformative moment because you were late to the gate.

DISCIPLINE YOUR WORK   FEBRUARY 23RD

It is possible to fly without motors, but not without knowledge and skill.
— Wilbur Wright

On December 17, 1903, at Kitty Hawk, North Carolina, Orville and Wilbur Wright flew for the first time the heavier-than-air machine that they had built. Orville's account of the final of the four flights that they took that day (Orville, the first and third; Wilbur, the second and fourth) follows.

Wilbur started the fourth and last flight at just about 12 o'clock. The first few hundred feet were up and down, as before, but by the time three hundred ft had been covered, the machine was under much better control. The course for the next four or five hundred feet had but little undulation. However, when out about eight hundred feet the machine began pitching again, and, in one of its darts downward, struck the ground. The distance over the ground was measured to be 852 feet; the time of the flight was 59 seconds. The frame supporting the front rudder was badly broken, but the main part of the machine was not injured at all. We estimated that the machine could be put in condition for flight again in about a day or two.

The Wright Brothers' invention of the first motor-driven flying machine entailed years of disciplined endeavor. Starting in their workshop in Dayton, Ohio, Orville and Wilbur developed the mechanical skills critical to their aeronautical achievement working on machines of all kinds including printing presses and bicycles. Their labors on the latter convinced them that unstable modes of transportation — even flying vehicles — could be controlled through practice. Countless tests yielded accurate data, which led to more efficient designs of wings, propellers and pilot control mechanisms. This regimen allowed them to solve piece by piece the puzzle of the flying machine, which up to this point in history had hardly been more than an object of curiosity.

After the successful first flight the Wright Brothers continued their disciplined approach, as recounted by aeronautical engineer Octave Chanute.

. . . spending the season of 1904 in learning how to fly in circular courses, they succeeded in 1905 in perfecting modes of control with which they made at last continuous flight of eleven, twelve, fifteen, twenty, twenty-one, and twenty-four miles at speeds of about thirty-eight miles per hour, alighting in every case safely, ready to start again upon the replenishing of the fuel supply.

The discipline of the Wright Brothers' work yielded their invention of the world's first successful airplane, which revolutionized the transportation industry. You can develop new and great things through disciplined work as you:

HUMBLE YOUR EFFORT — Don't be discouraged or distracted by humble beginnings. The Wright Brothers started in a print shop. Just get started. Let the little idea grow into the grand project, as the Old Testament prophet Zechariah declared:

Who dares despise the day of small things . . .
— Zechariah 4:10

HIKE OVER MOUNTAINS — Be prepared for the long haul. It took the Wright Brothers decades of discipline to create a flying machine. Make sure you set realistic expectations. Bringing a breakthrough to life will not happen overnight.

HONE YOUR SKILLS — Be committed to the process of living your dream, which happens day by day. For Orville and Wilbur, the short-term pain of incessant glider test failures turned into the long-term gain of becoming trailblazing aviators. Through the disappointment and defeat, keep working on your project. Your daily discipline will develop your skill set, which will lead to singular success.

HOLD ONTO YOUR VISION — Your turning point is coming. Your day of breakthrough is on its way, as long as you hold onto your vision. Achieving great things means having great faith in yourself and the future. Let your sense of destiny drive you through the suffering of your discipline. It worked for the Wright Brothers. You, too, can change the world.

GIVE UP TO GET AHEAD   FEBRUARY 24TH

A free government like ours cannot be maintained
except by an enlightened and virtuous people.
— Philip Lindsley

Presbyterian minister Philip Lindsley was educated at the College of New Jersey (now Princeton University) and later served as its President — but not for long. Believing education to be "a great equalizer, a special right for the poor", Lindsley left the security and privilege of the educational establishment of the North and went South, moving to Tennessee. Sensing a divine calling, he took on the presidency of Cumberland College (soon to become under his leadership the University of Nashville); it was his mission to address the relative deficiencies of educational programming in the Southern inland states.

On January 12, 1825, he delivered his inaugural address at Cumberland. He began by setting the educational quest in a national context.

To the people, our rulers are immediately responsible for the faithful discharge of their official duties. But if the people be incapable of judging correctly of their conduct and measures, what security can they have for their liberties a single hour?

Lindsey also stressed the great hope of those committed to disciplined endeavors.

*Such is the peculiar genius and excellence of our republican
institutions that moral and mental worth is the surest passport to distinction.
The humblest individual, by the diligent cultivation of his faculties, may,
without the aid of family or fortune, attain the most exalted stations within the
reach or gift of freemen. What an encouragement to studious effort and
enterprise! What an incentive to the generous aspiring and honorable ambition
of our youth! Why should not the door be opened wide for their entrance upon
the fast theater of useful action and noble daring?*

Lindsley's point about paying the price of success not only applies
to education but to all other other pursuits as well. Whatever you're trying
to accomplish, you have to give something up in order to get ahead. These
four strategies provide guidance.

COST — Success comes at a price. What do you have to
give up to get ahead? Maybe it's turning off the TV or your
smartphone; perhaps it's cutting off a bad habit or transforming a
negative attitude? Whatever the cost, the sooner you start paying it,
the better chance you'll have of attaining your goal.

CONSISTENCY — It's not a one-time cost. You have to
keep paying it until the sense of sacrifice goes away, until the long-
term gain overcomes the short-term pain. Discipline means doing
the right thing over and over and over . . . until it becomes second
nature.

CLIMATE — Change your social environment. Assess
your relationships. Are they working for you or against you? People
in your life can be an asset or a liability. Set your climate controls
for the former, not the latter. Surround yourself with accountability
partners — it may take a while getting used to them, but they will
help you do the right thing!

CHOICE — It's always up to you. You can choose to give
up to get ahead — or not. But let's be clear. If you choose not to
pay the price of discipline upfront, you will pay in some other
more costly ways in the future. Choices have consequences — and
they're not always good. Choose wisely: sacrifice now; succeed
later! Profess this Jewish proverb to inspire your choices today.

I ask not for a lighter burden but for broader shoulders.

APPRECIATE THE GRIND   FEBRUARY 25TH

Happiness for a human being lies in his work, or nowhere. And the way to make people good is to make them know they are good for something.
— Edward Purinton

World War I helped to foster the greatest economic boom in American history, paving the way for the postwar prosperity that defined the 1920's. During this period American business experienced unprecedented success: profits soared; investments abounded; salesmanship spread; consumer credit expanded; and wealth reached down to grow the middle class. The Roaring Twenties resulted, when leisure and luxury, sports legends and movie icons, heroes and hokum, became commonplace in American life.

Reverence for free enterprise was widespread; nowhere was it more memorably captured than in "Big Ideas from Big Business", published by lecturer and efficiency expert Edward Purinton in 1921. In the book Purinton stated several lessons "to be gleaned from a tour of the world's greatest business plants and a study of the lives of their founders", the first of which was discipline.

The biggest thing about a big success is the price. It takes a big man to pay the price. You can measure in advance the size of your success by how much you are willing to pay for it. I do not refer to money. I refer to the time, thought, energy, economy, purpose, devotion, study, sacrifice, patience, care that a man must give to his lifework before he can make it amount to anything.

Whether you're striving to make it in the corporate environment, the sports arena, on your first job, or just trying to do your best in school, discipline is essential. Start with it. Make sure it's part of your lifestyle. You'll make a lot more progress with a lot less aggravation than without it. Discipline yourself and:

GRIND IT — Success in life demands climbing uphill to your goal, and it's likely not a pleasant journey a good part of the way. No matter — grind through it. You'll have time for a vacation break after you've reached your objectives. You'll appreciate your attainment all the more having survived those most difficult of days. Legendary football coach Vince Lombardi imparted this principle to his players and they won championships:

I've never known a man worth his salt who in the long run, deep down in his heart, didn't appreciate the grind, the discipline. I firmly believe that any man's finest hour—this greatest fulfillment to all he holds dear—is that moment when he has worked his heart out in a good cause and lies exhausted on the field of battle—victorious.

GAS IT — Develop the discipline of daily filling your tank. You'll need a nutritious diet: healthful food for physical energy and meditating on Bible verse and inspirational sayings for spiritual energy. Get properly fueled up — every day! If you're not energized, you won't make it through the grind. Ask yourself the hard question: "Do I the energy and strength to get through this?"

GUFFAW IT — But don't take yourself — and your crucible — too seriously. Realize you're not alone in your struggle to get ahead. Sometimes the best thing to do is to step back from your ordeal, take a deep breathe, and laugh at the impossibility of your situation. Just keep believing, stay the course, get some rest. Try again tomorrow.

GAIN IT — Submit to your disciplines. You will gain mastery over those bad habits that have long plagued your progress. Easier said than done? Don't throw in the towel. You just might need some assistance. Keep your eyes open for a helping hand. Explore new directions. Walk into a house of worship. Attend a neighborhood meeting. Check out a support group. Call an old friend. Pray. Do something positive. Just don't give up and you will gain the mastery you've been seeking. Heed the words of John Locke.

He that has not a mastery over his inclinations; he that knows not how to resist the importunity of present pleasure or pain, for the sake of what reason tells him is fit to be done, wants the true principle of virtue and industry, and is in danger of never being good for anything.

SET HIGH STANDARDS   FEBRUARY 26TH

I seek not praise, of blame I am not afraid.
Theodorus Frelinghuysen

In 1664 the British completed their conquest of New Netherland — present-day New York City and its environs — to end the Anglo-Dutch wars. In the decades following Dutch settlers found their way to other areas of the New World, such as Raritan in the New Jersey colony. One of the immigrants was Theodorus Frelinghuysen, a Dutch Reformed minister who settled there in 1720.

Frelinghuysen distinguished his ministry by his emphasis on church discipline. He preached on the high scriptural standards of salvation, endeavoring to stir the New Jersey congregations that he pastored to more vigorous expressions of faith. He insisted on various forms of religious discipline to incentivize his congregants to examine their lives, encouraging consistency with Biblical guidelines for holy living.

To alert worshippers to the imperative of righteous living, Frelinghuysen established the stringent practice of "fencing the table": people were prevented from fully participating in the the sacrament of the Lord's Supper unless they had first confessed the sins of their heart and demonstrated acts of righteousness evidencing their salvation. He often passionately preached on these precepts, stressing that an individual's faith be supported by exemplary outward behaviors. An excerpt from one of his revivalist sermons follows.

> *Reflect, therefore, upon and bear in mind this truth; and remember that, though moral and outwardly religious, if still you be unregenerate and destitute of spiritual life, you have not warrant for an approach to the table of grace. Ye ignorant, worldly minded and ungodly persons who live in your sin, know that we dare not grant you access but are under obligation to debar you; not to your destruction but for your good, that you may thus amend your lives and turn to the Lord; and if you give evidence of real amendment, with good conscience and the utmost cheerfulness, will we admit you.*

"Fencing the table" provoked criticism from some colonists, but Frelinghuysen's commitment to high ecclesiastical standards galvanized his flock, leading to a religious awakening within the Middle Colonies, setting the stage for the First Great Awakening that would soon sweep through the colonies. And his efforts sparked social enlightenment, resulting in 1766 to the establishment of Queen's College in New Brunswick, now Rutgers University.

Setting high standards for your life means being disciplined about doing the right thing at the right time for the right reason. Start practicing this principle by asking yourself the questions that follow.

RIGHT THING — What is the one thing you need to move forward towards your dreams? Avoid the tendency to take on too much at once. Slow down. Focus. Living to high standards means working on the most important thing, and to keep working on it, until you learn to excel at it. Don't settle for average. Strive to be the best.

RIGHT TIME — What are the things holding you back

from reaching for your goals today? This is not a stop-and-start exercise. Fling away the distractions, fix on the standards for your life; once you get committed to fighting the battle of self-discipline, there's no looking back. You may have heard this before; it's worth repeating to drum the point: Today is the first day of the rest of your life. Apostle Paul articulated the principle in this way:

> *Behold, now is the favorable time . . .*
> — 2 Corinthians 6:2

RIGHT REASON — What are your highest ideals, your deepest convictions, your core values? Don't be concerned about what others are thinking or saying. Get in touch with your motives. Turn off all the crowd noise and turn up the volume on your inner voice. If your highest standards rise from your deepest spiritual place, it will be easier for you to stick with them.

H E E D YOUR BODY   FEBRUARY 27TH

> *I will concentrate on my long-term gain to get me through my short-term pain, determined to give something up in order to get ahead, willing to pay the price of personal progress, no matter the cost!*
> Joseph Holland

"How come you're the only one who visits me?" Big Mike queried, during one of my visits to Harlem Hospital. I was a frequent visitor at the outset of Harkhomes in the mid 1980's. Big Mike had collapsed at the homeless shelter, on the floor motionless until the ambulance came. In addition to his chronic diabetes and obesity, Big Mike's recent bout with the flu had turned into pneumonia.

Big Mike wasn't a Harkhomes favorite — he didn't pull his weight; always complaining; thought he was funnier than he was — no one wanted to visit him. To avoid telling him this difficult truth, I decided to change the subject.

"When was the last time you worked out?" I asked him.

"What do you think, Rev? Just look at my buffed body." He laughed, and I shook my head as he flopped his flabbiness.

"When you get out of here, you got to get some exercise."

"Don't you see me running the New York Marathon in a few months?" he snickered.

"Walking around the block a couple times a day would be a good start. One of the most important things for you to do is to H E E D."

"H E E D?!"

I explained the H E E D principle to Big Mike and encouraged him to start practicing it right away. He grudgingly turned over his stash of junk food and cigarettes. Putting H E E D into practice made a difference for Big Mike. It can make a difference for you, too. You can put H E E D to work in your life by paying attention to your:

H = HEALTH — Don't take your physical health for granted. There's a ton of truth in Ben Franklin's adage: an ounce of prevention is worth a pound of curse. Big Mike missed this point. The first time he had any medical attention in ten years is when we rushed him to the emergency room. A visit to the doctor is imperative, especially if you've recently been through a stormy crisis.

E = ENERGY — The most important thing for you to manage throughout the course of your days is your energy. The best way to do it is through disciplines. Really get to know your body. How many hours of sleep do you need to function at your highest level? When is it best for you to eat to keep a good energy flow all day long? I've discovered that the spiritual energy produced by prayer and fasting magnifies my physical energy. Figure out what maintains and maximizes your energy and develop a discipline for it.

E = EXERCISE — To keep the body performing at its highest level, it's not enough to get checked out; you also need to work out. It's the only way to fill the body with vigor. You don't have to go jogging or light weights at the gym; but you do have to get some kind of physical exercise. Break a sweat in your own way. Getting in good physical condition means that the energy, the vigor, and the strength will be there in abundance to help you fight the good fight of personal progress.

D = DIET — Regard your body as a temple of God, a sacred and holy place created in God's image. This perspective creates a more careful approach to what goes into the body. You should avoid being a junk food junkie but also avoid abusing the body with drugs, alcohol and cigarettes. And to generate the extra energy, proper nutrition is crucial. Put the right fuel in your body's tank and you will have higher levels of daily productivity.

BE DISCIPLINED TO BENEFIT OTHERS   FEBRUARY 28TH

Whenever this effect shall be produced among us; whenever the vicious portion of population shall be permitted to gather in bands of hundreds and thousands and burn churches, throw printing presses into rivers, shoot editors, and hang and burn obnoxious persons at pleasure, and with impunity — depend on it, this government cannot last.
Abraham Lincoln

On November 7, 1837, rioters in Alton, Illinois, murdered journalist Reverend Elijah Lovejoy, who was defending his abolitionist newspaper press from mob attack. Lovejoy had moved across the river from the slave state of Missouri to the free state of Illinois after his printing press in St. Louis had been destroyed three times by mobs there. The Alton violence took place about a week after the charter convention of the Illinois antislavery society.

Twenty-four year old Abraham Lincoln had entered politics in 1832 running for the Illinois legislature from nearby Sangamon County. He lost that race but won two years later and was a state legislator at the time of Lovejoy's death. On January 27, 1838, Lincoln addressed the mob-killing in a speech to the Young Men's Lyceum of Springfield, Illinois. At his talk's climax, he challenged his audience to rise up as a disciplined citizenship, taking preemptive action as responsible people against future atrocities.

Let every American, every lover of liberty, every well-wisher to his posterity, swear by the blood of the Revolution never to violate in the least particular the laws of the country; and never to tolerate their violation by others. As the patriots of '76 did to the support of the Declaration of Independence, so to the support of the Constitution and laws, let every American pledge his life, his property, and his sacred honor; let every man remember that to violate the law is to trample on the blood of his father and to tear the character of his own and of his children's liberty. Let reverence for the laws be breathed by every American mother to the lisping babe that prattles on her lap; let it be taught in schools, in seminaries, and in colleges . . . let it be preached from the pulpit . . . let it become the political religion of the nation; and let the old and the young, the rich and the poor . . . of all sexes and tongues, and colors and conditions, sacrifice unceasingly upon its altars.

Lincoln's words still ring true — and loudly so. They are a clarion call for you and me — for all of us — to be disciplined for the benefit of others. Four ways — personal management techniques, so to speak — stand out for you to practice this principle and become a positive influence in the lives of others.

MANAGE YOUR THOUGHTS — Mental discipline is the hard part because your thoughts are so easily influenced by external forces. Memorizing Bible verses and other inspirational materials will help defend against assaults on your soul. Daily reading of uplifting writings will help discipline your thinking.

MANAGE YOUR WORDS — Herein lies great benefit or great danger, because your words possess the power to speak life or death over your life as well as other lives. The mob that murdered Lovejoy spoke words of death and acted in accordance with them. Eschew their example. Align your words and actions with the shining lights of kindness and self-control. You words are very powerful instruments, which can be used to produce good or bad consequences. Use your words to spawn the former and spurn the latter.

MANAGE YOUR ACTIONS — Lincoln exhorted his crowd to live out founding principles of liberty and justice. Look for ways to make those values come alive in your life as a lighthouse to lives in your community.

MANAGE YOUR RELATIONSHIPS — Stay away from mobs of ill-will and violence — whether in person or online. Use whatever influence you have to steer others clear of destructive associations. Fill your relationships with love, not hate.

MARCH: COMPASSSION
DAILY SUCCESS PRINCIPLES

1. Return To Your Roots To Revitalize — Wilma Pearl Mankiller — 1955
2. Make Your Generosity Count — Tadeusz Kościuszko — 1798
3. Focus On Meeting The Need — Clara Barton — 1861
4. Be Creative With Your Compassion — Alain Locke — 1925
5. Be The One To Help — Edwin Booth — 1865
6. Reach Out, Touch Somebody's Hand — Margaret Sangster/Diana Ross — 1970
7. Become Great By Serving Others — Alexis de Tocqueville — 1831
8. Uplift The Disadvantaged — Ella Baker — 1943
9. Take A Compassionate Stand — Germantown Mennonites — 1688
10. Be A Game-Changer — Helen Keller — 1887
11. Give With No Strings Attached — John Mahoney — 1920
12. Cultivate Your Compassion — Emma Lazarus — 1886
13. Get Under The Burdens Of Others — Henry Ford — 1932
14. Count That Day Lost — Dorothea Dix — 1843
15. Collaborate With Your Compassion — Joseph Holland — 1985
16. Be An Inspiration — Ralph Waldo Emerson — 1844
17. Gain Power To Serve Others — Dolores Huerta — 1960
18. Be A Gift — Abraham Lincoln — 1864
19. Advocate For The Needy — Florence Kelley — 1906
20. Be Holistic With Your Compassion — Mathew Carey — 1833
21. Get A Move On — Florence Converse — 1932
22. Possess An Abundant Mindset — William Cobbett — 1819
23. See The Potential In Everyone — Aimee McPherson — 1923
24. Be Gutsy With Your Compassion — Lewis Coffin — 1850
25. Shed The Light Of Possibility — Michael Harrington — 1962
26. Heed Your Call To Compassion — Katharine Drexel — 1887
27. Make A Difference For Those In Need — George Boardman — 1866
28. Widen Your Circle Of Compassion — Roberto Clemente — 1972
29. Love Your Enemies — Herman Melville — 1866
30. Choose To Be A Plus Person — Robert Morse Lovett — 1933
31. Be Effective With Your Compassion — Walt Whitman — 1846

RETURN TO YOUR ROOTS TO REVITALIZE   MARCH 1ST

The happiest people I've ever met, regardless of their profession, their social standing, or their economic status, are people that are fully engaged in the world around them.
Wilma Pearl Mankiller

In 1955 a severe drought hit the area around Tahlequah, Oklahoma, where ten-year-old Wilma Pearl Mankiller lived with her parents and five siblings. Because the family hunted, fished, and maintained a vegetable garden for food, the extreme conditions decimated their livelihood. So they moved to San Francisco as part of a federal program to urbanize Native Americans. Mankiller lived there for many years; she went to school, started her own family, worked as a social worker and became active in Native American issues.

In 1976 Mankiller returned to Oklahoma, first volunteering for the Cherokee Nation before gaining employment teaching young Cherokees about environmental science. She wrote a grant for a community development project, attaining funding for self-help initiatives that built housing and laid piping for a new water system. Mankiller expounded the philosophy behind her commitment.

The most fulfilled people are the ones who get up every morning and stand for something larger than themselves. They are the people who care about others, who will extend a helping hand to someone in need or will speak up about an injustice when they see it.

Mankiller's efforts proved paradigmatic; she was appointed to lead the Community Development Department of the Cherokee Nation and raised millions of dollars to implement her community development model on many reservations. She was so successful that trailblazing leadership ensued, becoming the first woman elected to be Principal Chief of the Cherokee Nation. She described the distinctive qualities of her leadership.

Recognizing the good, not just in one's own personal circumstances, but in the world, makes anything possible. When I am asked about the important characteristics of leadership, being of good, positive mind is at the top of my list. If a leader can focus on the meritorious characteristics of other people and try to play to their strengths as well as find value in even the most difficult situation, she can inspire hope and faith in others and motivate them to move forward.

Mankiller expanded her influence through her bestselling

autobiography, "Mankiller: A Chief and Her People". She was later recognized with the Presidential Medal of Freedom, the nation's highest civilian honor. Mankiller returned to her roots to revitalize the community. Heeding her example, these principles will guide your compassion in similar ways.

RELOCATION — Like Mankiller, return to your roots, especially if it's one of those places where the needs are the greatest. Make sure you're strong enough to pull others up, and not get pulled back down. First get in touch with who you are; you will be better able to touch others souls.

REDEVELOPMENT — Are you making things better or worse for those in your life? Be a catalyst for positive change by helping people help themselves. True development does not foster dependency but self-determination. Individuals with a stake in their own redevelopment will find their way to progress that lasts.

RISING UP — Be a leader from wherever you are in your organization or community. Mankiller didn't start at or near the top of the Cherokee Nation. She wasn't even looking to be top dog. She started as a volunteer. Your greatness as a leader will not be on account of your power; it's all about your ability to empower others.

It is one of the most beautiful compensations of life, that no man can sincerely try to help another without helping himself.

Mankiller lived out these words from Ralph Waldo Emerson. You should do the same.

MAKE YOUR GENEROSITY COUNT   MARCH 2ND

I beg Mr. Jefferson that in case I should die with will or testament he should buy out of my money so many Negroes and free them, that the remaining sum should be sufficient to give them education and provide for their maintenance.
Tadeusz Kościuszko

In June 1776, when he learned about the American Revolution, Polish-Lithuanian military engineer Tadeusz Kościuszko sailed for America to join the Continental Army. Kościuszko received his assignment on

August 31, 1776 and started building fortifications at Fort Billingsport in New Jersey to protect against the British troops advancing up the Delaware River to Philadelphia. Because of his brilliant work constructing defense structures — his fortifications at West Point were praised as innovative for that era — Kościuszko was first promoted to chief engineer by Major General Nathanael Greene, commander of the Southern Department, and by war's end, by Congress, to brigadier general.

During the war Kościuszko befriended Thomas Jefferson, who wrote this about him.

> *. . . the purest son of liberty . . . that I have ever known, the kind of liberty which extends to all, not only to the rich.*

After the war, when he received his back pay, he also exercised his right to buy 500 acres of land in the Ohio territory. Fifteen years later, as Kościuszko was about to return to Europe, he executed his American will and testament, which reflected his generosity as an expression of the new nation's ideals. On May 5, 1798, Kościuszko executed the will and entrusted it to Jefferson; the document provided not only that proceeds from the sale of his real estate be used to buy the freedom of slaves, but also stipulated conditions for the freed citizens to live by.

> *That is to say, each should know before the duty of a citizen in the free government . . . to have good and human heart sensible for the sufferings of others; each must be married and have 100 acres of land, with instruments, cattle for tillage, and know how to manage and govern it as well; to know how to behave to neighbors, always with kindness and ready to help them; to themselves they must be frugal; to their children give good education; and in gratitude to me, to make themselves happy as possible.*

Kościuszko made his generosity count, bequeathing his estate to better the lot of African American slaves. Follow his example; make your own generosity count as you:

GLEAN YOUR RESOURCES — You may not have real estate or other monetary assets to dedicate in support of a worthy cause but dig deep into your non-monetary resources to assist those in need. Be resourceful: you may be able to make something of value by volunteering and/or impart your knowledge in ways that eventually becomes a financial blessing to someone else.

GOOGLE YOUR EFFORTS — Do your research. Kościuszko knew first-hand what needed to happen to improve the condition of slaves because he'd witness the calamity of American slavery. Look around. Explore new territory. Get to know those in need: their background, skills, challenges, aspirations. Such knowledge may put you in a position of facilitating that person's freedom. Find ways to truly make a difference.

GUIDE YOUR BENEFICIARIES — Kościuszko stipulated in his will that his beneficiaries were to their children give good education. He was concerned about the present and the future of those he was trying to help. Make your generosity really count by inspiring others to take constructive action. Sow seed that will bear the fruit of transformed lives.

GIVE OF YOURSELF — Kościuszko returned to Europe so he wasn't available to personally help. It's okay to enlist capable hands to carry out your compassionate purposes. But it's even better to be present to give of yourself. If at all possible, share in ways where you can be dynamically engaged in securing the optimal outcomes of your generosity, which could very well prosper you in ways so you'll have more to give in the future.

FOCUS ON MEETING THE NEED   MARCH 3RD

You must never so much think as whether you like it or not, whether it is bearable or not; you must never think of anything except the need, and how to meet it.
Clara Barton

One of the many Union soldiers wounded on a Civil War battlefield, Jack Gibbs was holding to life and hope, but both were slipping slowly away. He could not lift his body off the cold, rocky ground, so he languished there, looking around for help that never came, until he fell unconscious.

When Jack regained consciousness, he wasn't sure if he was still on the battleground or somewhere in the afterlife. His eyes beheld a woman . . . a woman?! On the battlefield?! He became even more incredulous as this woman worked with two soldiers to get him onto a cot and move him to a horse-drawn van, where she bandaged his wounded leg, saving his life.

This woman was Clara Barton, who served as a hospital nurse during the Civil War until she discovered that too many wounded soldiers were dying before arriving at the hospitals. Barton took the initiative, convincing Union generals to break the gender barrier and allow a woman on the battlefield.

Barton became a light amidst the military gloom, a pioneering nurse, loading medical supplies onto vans and going to numerous battlefields to care for countless soldiers. And she was on the front lines. One harrowing incident was when a bullet tore through the sleeve of her dress; it didn't strike her but killed the man to whom she was tending. Her heroism earned her the title "Angel of the Battlefield", which gave her the post-war stature to found the American Red Cross, expanding her service beyond those wounded in military combat to those suffering as a result of calamities of all kinds. Barton described her compassion in these words:

> *I have an almost complete disregard of precedent, and a faith in the possibility of something better. It irritates me to be told how things have always been done. I defy the tyranny of precedent. I go for anything new that might improve the past.*

Barton's legacy of kindness has endured across the generations. She focused on meeting needs, and to do so, she went someplace that no woman had gone before. Emulate her focus on meeting needs as you give in:

NEW WAYS — Barton's compassion broke the gender barrier on the Civil War battlefield. Think outside of the box with your giving. Meet a need in an unprecedented way.

ENDURING WAYS — Barton's acts of kindness in times of war paved the way to a charitable organization — the Red Cross — whose work, whether war or peace, continues to this day. Meeting the little needs around you can lead to lasting compassionate outcomes around the world.

IMMEDIATE WAYS — One night at Harkhomes, feeling discouraged after a long, hard day of disappointing outcomes among the homeless, unsure what to say to another dejected resident, I shrugged my shoulders. He responded: "Don' worry, Rev. You just being here for me is enough." Sometimes to make a difference among those in need you have to take Barton-like action, moving with a hero's grace onto the battlefields of life. But at other times just being there for the hurting person is sufficient for the moment. Let this poem be your prayer today:

> *My life shall touch a dozen lives before this day is done,*
> *Leave countless marks for good or ill ere sets the evening sun,*
> *This is the wish I always wish, the prayer I always pray;*
> *Lord, may my life help other lives it touches by the way.*

BE CREATIVE WITH YOUR COMPASSION   MARCH 4TH

Art must discover and reveal the beauty which prejudice and caricature have overlaid.
Alain Locke

In 1925 The New Negro, a collection of African-American writings, was published, edited by Alain Locke. Locke — a Harvard PhD and the first African American Rhodes Scholar — wrote that "The New Negro" would no longer accept white subjugation; instead he described "the new spirit" that had arisen among the black masses. Locke's theme was to establish a new black self-identify, transforming African Americans from a stereotype of obsequiousness to one where proud, enterprising, self-confident actors took their place on national and global stages — men and women strong enough to throw off the shackles of two centuries of slavery and another of Jim Crow. His strategy was to bring together African-American artists, writers, and musicians to create works that affirmed their own heritage. One of those writers, Langston Hughes, captured the spirit of this cultural movement in his poem "I, Too, Sing America."

> *I, too, sing America.*
> *I am the darker brother.*
> *They send me to eat in the kitchen*
> *When company comes,*
> *But I laugh,*
> *And eat well,*
> *And grow strong.*
> *Tomorrow,*
> *I'll be at the table*
> *When company comes.*
> *Nobody'll dare*
> *Say to me,*
> *"Eat in the kitchen,"*
> *Then.*
> *Besides,*
> *They'll see how beautiful I am*
> *And be ashamed--*
> *I, too, am America.*

Though part of an ethnic group known more for brute force than artistic agility or the pursuits of the mind, Locke, Hughes and their artistic peers used their imaginative powers to create cultural strength through intellectual endeavor for political purposes, which spawned the Harlem Renaissance. You can bring their historic example to life as you exercise your:

MUSE — William Shakespeare exemplified the use of art to evoke compassion through the heiress Portia in The Merchant of Venice, as she pleaded with the moneylender Shylock to extend mercy.

The quality of mercy is not strain'd.
It dropped as the gentle rain from heaven
Upon the place beneath. It is twice blest:
It blest him that gives, and him that takes.

Though three centuries apart, Shakespeare and the Harlem Renaissance writers shared a mission: to use their literary gifts to touch the needy. Join their mission. Use your muse to make a difference.

MIGHT — Alan McGinnis underscored the power of compassion.

There is no more noble occupation in the world than to assist another human being.

Be creative in your compassion. If you're a poet, conceive some verse that inspires light amidst gloom. If you're a novelist, write a story that chronicles the journey of a Mother Teresa-like community servant. If you're a painter, use colors that speak compassion. If you sing, proclaim lyrics that send hope to the hopeless. The question for you today: how can you use your artistic power to uplift others?

BE THE ONE TO HELP   MARCH 5TH

Upon turning to thank my rescuer I saw it was Edwin Booth, whose face was of course well known to me. I expressed my gratitude to him, and in doing so, called him by name.
Robert Todd Lincoln

On April 14, 1865, President Abraham Lincoln was assassinated at the Ford's Theater in Washington, D.C. by John Wilkes Booth. The shocking murder devastated countless Americans; one man was so distraught that his singular career was derailed. Edwin Booth — the brother of the assassin — had toured U.S. cities and European capitals, performing Shakespearean plays; he had been acclaimed the greatest American actor of his generation. But Edwin left the stage and went into seclusion for quite some time, overcome by shame and the infamy associated with the family name.

A few months after his brother killed Lincoln, Booth received a letter from Colonel Adam Badeau, who worked for General Ulysses S. Grant. The correspondence thanked Booth for a past good deed, when he saved the life of a young man at the Jersey City train station. Booth never knew the identity of the man whom he'd helped until the revelation of letter. It was the late President's son — Robert Todd Lincoln — who described Booth's heroism in these words.

> *The incident occurred while a group of passengers were late at night purchasing their sleeping car places from the conductor who stood on the station platform at the entrance of the car. The platform was about the height of the car floor, and there was of course a narrow space between the platform and the car body. There was some crowding, and I happened to be pressed by it against the car body while waiting my turn. In this situation the train began to move, and by the motion I was twisted off my feet, and had dropped somewhat, with feet downward, into the open space, and was personally helpless, when my coat collar was vigorously seized and I was quickly pulled up and out to a secure footing on the platform.*

Knowing that he had saved the life of the son of Abraham Lincoln — the man his own brother had shot to death — brought unexpected consolation to Booth. The emotional uplift from this twist of fate helped him break free from his isolation and return to the stage with such renown that his illustrious career is commemorated by a statue in Manhattan's Gramercy Park and by Booth Theatre, the first and oldest Broadway theatre named in honor of an actor. You can make Booth's compassionate legacy come to life as you determine to be:

SUPPORTIVE — Though there were many others on the Jersey City train platform that night, Edwin Booth was the one on the scene to help. Maintain an attitude of compassion wherever you are. Look to extend support to those you don't know.

SPONTANEOUS — Be the first to help someone in trouble. You may not always have time to think it through. Be bold to extend a hand to someone in need. Yes, you may have to act quickly, break your routine, experience discomfort, take some risks. Seek to live out the words of Emily Dickinson's poem:

> *If I can stop on heart from breaking,*
> *I shall not live in vain;*
> *If I can ease one life the aching,*
> *Or cool one pain,*
> *Or help the fasting robin*
> *Unto his nest again,*

I shall not live in vain.

SAVED — Your service to others will come back to bless you in unknown ways. Booth's career was saved because of consequences from his compassionate act. Keep this in mind: the hand you extend to pull someone out of harm's way could be helping a person of inestimable value to yourself and the world.

REACH OUT, TOUCH SOMEBODY'S HAND   MARCH 6TH

It isn't the thing you do, dear,
It's the thing you leave undone
That gives you a bit of a heartache
At the setting of the sun.
Margaret Sangster

In the 1870's, during the height of her literary career, author and editor Margaret Sangster published her most famous poem, "The Sin of Omission"; in it she laments "our slow compassion" that leaves too many good things undone and that misses too many opportunities to extend "the loving touch of the hand."

The tender word forgotten,
The letter you did not write,
The flowers you did not send, dear,
Are your haunting ghosts at night.
The loving touch of the hand, dear,
The gentle, winning tone
Which you had no time nor thought for
With troubles enough of your own.
For life is all too short, dear,
And sorrow is all too great,
To suffer our slow compassion
That tarries until too late

Just about a century later another creative American woman — celebrity songstress Diana Ross — embraced this same compassionate theme, with the same metaphor. In April 1970 Ross released her debut solo single "Reach Out and Touch Somebody's Hand". The song soared on all the charts, selling 500,000 copies during its first year. What distinguished "Reach Out and Touch" was that it was one of the few songs Ross made with lyrics expressing her social conscience. The song was also notable for the special way Ross performed it at concerts, encouraging the audience members to turn to their neighbors to "reach out and touch" their hands as they sang along.

Reach out and touch somebody's hand
Make this world a better place if you can
Take a little time out of your busy day
To give encouragement to someone who's lost the way
Or would I be talking to a stone
If I asked you to share a problem that's not your own
We can change things if we start giving
If you see an old friend on the street and he's down
Remember his shoes could fit your feet
Try a little kindness you'll see
It's something that comes very naturally

KEEP IT SIMPLE — Both their creations — Diana's song and Margaret's poem — evoke the touch of your hand as a meaningful gesture to show that you care. Or it could be a "tender word", "the letter", "the flowers", that you offer to uplift another. Keep it simple with your compassion. It's noble to travel to other continents to extend a helping hand to the needy, but what about your next-door neighbor or somebody just across the tracks? Touch a hand that's close by.

KEEP IT REAL — Trying to touch a hand over instagram or facebook is just not the same as the real thing. Staying connected via internet is important but face-to-face contact is sometimes required to meet the need. Be prepared to initiate sincere, immediate communication; it may be the only thing that will work.

KEEP IT GOING — From the nineteenth century muse Sangster to the twentieth century legend Ross, their advice is timeless: don't miss the little opportunities to serve another. Let your hand be their twenty-first century extension.

BECOME GREAT BY SERVING OTHERS   MARCH 7TH

Although the Americans have in a manner reduced egotism to a social and philosophical theory, they are nevertheless extremely open to compassion.
Alexis de Tocqueville

In 1831 French diplomat and historian Alexis de Tocqueville came to United States, sent by his government to study the American penal system. Tocqueville did visit prisons and penitentiaries during his nine-month tour, but his travels took him to many different destinations throughout the states, which enlarged his project. The result was Democracy In America: a voluminous analysis of the individual living standards and social conditions under U.S.-style democracy.

Tocqueville assessed the diverse aspects of the American way of life. One of his most telling observations concerned how democracy had created a compassionate environment.

When men feel a natural compassion for their mutual sufferings — when they are brought together by easy and frequent intercourse, and no sensitive feelings keep them asunder, it may readily be supported that they will lend assistance to one another whenever it is needed. When an American asks for the cooperation of his fellow citizens it is seldom refused, and I have often seen it afforded spontaneously and with great good will. If an accident happens on the highway, everybody hastens to help the suffering; if some great sudden calamity befalls a family, the purses of a thousand strangers are at once willingly opened, and small but numerous donations pour in to relieve their distress.

He concluded with an insight about the dynamic between selfishness and service: less of the former leads to more of the latter.

In democracies no great benefits are conferred, but good offices are constantly rendered: a man seldom displays self-devotion, but all men are ready to be of service to one another.

From Tocqueville's work rises a challenging question: when you compare yourself to his positive depictions of American compassion, how do you measure up? If you're not quite there, practice these principles.

HUMBLE TRAVELS — If you've been on an ego-trip, get off that bus. Start going places and doing things where it is not all about gratifying you. Start expressing your selflessness through your travels: cross the tracks to a different neighborhood; cross the ocean to a different continent; or cross the street to the house of a

hurting neighbor. to discover your calling. Be willing to go to places
— near and far — to meet a need.

HEAVENLY HIDEAWAYS — Spend more time in
spiritual spots, whether at a house of worship, a home fellowship
gathering — maybe hosted by you? — or in your own prayer
closet. Meditating on divine things like Bible verses or inspirational
sermons will take your mind off yourself and put it where it
belongs — on others!

HEART OF A SERVANT — Strive to be a leader, which,
in the words of Jesus, means serving others.

. . . whoever wants to become great among you must be your servant . . .
— Matthew 20:26

By living out a heart of service, you will eventually ascend to that
higher ground of loving one another.

HOPEFUL PERSPECTIVE — Give people the benefit
of the doubt until they prove themselves unworthy of it. Don't be
cynical; it will limit your ability to serve. Keep looking for the best
in needy persons. You will eventually find a gem of encouragement
to offer them.

UPLIFT THE DISADVANTAGED   MARCH 8TH

*Remember, we are not fighting for the freedom of the Negro alone, but for the
freedom of the human spirit, a larger freedom that encompasses all mankind.*
Ella Baker

In 1943 civil rights activist Ella Baker was named Director of
Branches of the National Association for the Advancement of Colored
People ("NAACP"). Traveling throughout the South to organize new
chapters, Baker laid the foundation not only for the expansion of the
NAACP in this region but also for the launch of the Civil Rights
Movement a decade later.

Baker believed that organizational strength stemmed from
individuals working together at the grassroots. She emphasized treating
everyone with dignity and respect, especially those at the bottom rung of
society, seeking to rise from underprivileged circumstances. Baker's quest
was not to be in the public limelight but to work in the neighborhood

trenches where she could make a difference.

> *You didn't see me on television; you didn't see news stories about me. The kind of role that I tried to play was to pick up pieces or put together pieces out of which I hoped organization might come. My theory is: Strong people don't need strong leaders.*

Baker's commitment to uplift disadvantaged people moved her from the NAACP to the Southern Christian Leadership Conference, to the Student Nonviolent Coordinating Committee, to the Southern Conference Education Fund. Her mission transcended the struggle for racial justice; her vision was the inner liberty that propelled every individual.

Heed Baker's example. Disadvantaged people should not be ignored, rejected, mistreated or stereotyped. The best thing to do is to uplift them, affirming their dignity by extending opportunity, helping them to see themselves in a different light. If you have encountered the disadvantaged in your personal universe, engage them instead of dismissing them. Help guide them on an inward journey that will change the trajectory of their lives. Challenge them with these questions.

WHERE ARE YOU? — This was the first question God asked Adam in the Garden of Eden after he and Eve had sinned. The query was more about their emotional and spiritual condition than a physical location. Ask this question to help individuals get beyond surface symptoms to root causes, so they can understand more objectively where they are on life's journey in relation to their goals. Help them delve deeply into this question, to understand better their inner strengths and weakness; this is the first step in helping them make a positive move to rise out of whatever situation they're in.

WHAT DO YOU WANT? — Some people never get to respond to this question because they're too troubled by what they don't have. Keep it simple. Your mission in asking it is not to psychoanalyze but only to shift the perspective from past problems to future goals. Baker stayed in people's homes to create the comfort level for them to open up. You must get close enough to gain understanding, to help them connect the dots: once they're on solid emotional and spiritual ground it's easier for them to reach for their true desires. Share your own story — highlighting your challenges — to help them be transparent about theirs.

HOW CAN I HELP? — This question is the most important one for you to ask the person in need. Listen carefully to the response, discern between and beneath the words. The homeless need more than a place to stay, a hungry person more than a meal, an angry person more than someone to strike. Uplifting people starts with your understanding where they are stuck — what the true need is. From there your mission is to help them get into a position to solve the problem themselves. That's the only way to bring about a permanent solution. That's what compassion is really all about.

TAKE A COMPASSIONATE STAND   MARCH 9TH

These are the reasons why we are against the traffic of mens-body
as follows: Is there any that would be done or handled at this
manner, to be sold or made a slave for all the time of his life?
17th Century Germantown Mennonites

In 1619 Dutch traders brought the first Africans to colonial America. These twenty men arrived in Jamestown, Virginia as indentured servants, holding the same status of numerous white immigrants. It was not until 1670 that the Virginia assembly legislated chattel slavery for Africans.

Eleven years later English king Charles II granted Quaker William Penn the charter for vast region called "Sylvania". "Liberty of conscience" and freedom of religion were established in this colony soon known as Pennsylvania, which attracted the Mennonites, a persecuted Quaker sect who settled at Germantown near Philadelphia in 1683. With the institution of slavery spreading throughout the colonies, the Mennonites took a compassionate stand in their monthly meeting of February 1688, passing the following resolution.

For we hear that the most part of such Negroes are brought hither against their will and consent, and that many of them are stolen. Now, though they are black, we cannot conceive there is more liberty to have them slaves as it is to have other white ones. There is a saying that we shall do to all men like as we will be done ourselves, making no difference of what generation, descent, or color they are . . . But to bring men hither, or to rob and sell them against their will, we stand against . . .

They concluded their statement by asserting the moral strength of their position.

Now consider well this thing, if it is good or bad. And in case you find it to be good to handle these blacks at that manner, we desire and require you hereby lovingly that you may inform us herein, which at this time never was done, viz., that Christians have liberty to do so, to the end we shall be satisfied in this point, and satisfy likewise our good friends and acquaintances in our native country, to whom it is a terror or fearful thing that men should be handled so in Pennsylvania.

The late 17th century Mennonites advocated for African slaves. It was the first protest of its kind in the American colonies, and their peerless precedent resonated for generations. Let them be your timeless role model as you:

CONFRONT THE WRONG — If you find unfairness or injustice in your circumstances, confront it. Like the Mennonites of centuries ago, take a compassionate stand. And if the injustice reaches beyond just you and touches others outside of your immediate environment, find them; resolve to stand together; speak out as one voice.

CREATE YOUR HAPPINESS — When you're compassionate towards others, your psychology shifts: you take your mind off yourself and your own problems, so you end up being more content. This truth is wonderfully expressed by the following Chinese proverb.

If you want happiness for an hour—take a nap.

If you want happiness for a day—go fishing.

If you want happiness for a month—get married.

If you want happiness for a year—inherit a fortune.

If you want happiness for a lifetime—help others.

If you want happiness now, take a compassionate stand today.

If you want justice, take a compassionate stand with others.

BE A GAME-CHANGER   MARCH 10TH

*The most important day I remember in all my life is the one on
which my teacher, Anne Mansfield Sullivan, came to me. . . . It was
the third of March, 1887, three months before I was seven years old.*
Helen Keller

When Helen Keller was not yet two years old, illness robbed her of
sight and hearing. Several years later a woman arrived at her Alabama home,
beginning a relationship that forever changed her life.

*On the afternoon of that eventful day, I stood on the porch, dumb,
expectant. . . . The afternoon sun penetrated themes of honey suckle that
covered the porch, and fell on my upturned face. My fingers lingered almost
unconsciously on the familiar leaves and blossoms which had just come forth to
greet the sweet Southern spring. I did not know what the future held of marvel
or surprise for me. Anger and bitterness had preyed upon me continually for
weeks and a deep languor had succeeded this passionate struggle. . . . Have you
ever been at sea in a dense fog, when it seemed as if a tangible white darkness
shut you in, and the great ship, tense and anxious, groped her way toward the
shore with plummet and sounding-line, and you waited with beating heart for
something to happen?*

That day launched a lifelong friendship between Keller and
Sullivan. Largely because of it, Keller went on to become the first deaf-
blind person to earn a bachelor of arts degree, leading to a singular career
as an author, political activist, and lecturer. Her distinctions included
induction into the Alabama Women's Hall of Fame, one of twelve
inaugural inductees to the Alabama Writers Hall of Fame, and a presidential
proclamation by President Jimmy Carter on the one hundredth anniversary
of her birth.

As Anne Sullivan was to Helen Keller, be a game-changer in
someone's life today as you:

SHOW UP — *I felt approaching footsteps. I stretched out my hand
as I supposed to my mother. Someone took it, and I was caught up and held
close in the arms of her who had come to reveal all things to me, and, more
than all things else, to love me.*

Show up in a special way for a person in need. If a big act of
kindness is not on your agenda today, a little act will do. Be a light to
someone's gloom. Intervene to meet a need. Give a hug. Refrain from
indiscretion. Forgive an old hurt. Sacrifice your seat on a crowded bus or

train. Point the way to the lost. Throw a lonely starfish back into the sea. Share a moment of silent grief. Brighten someone's day with a smile. A small gesture can be what's needed to make a big difference.

SOW MUCH — *I learned a great many new words that day. I do not remember what they all were; but I do know that "mother, father, sister teacher" were among them — words that were to make the world blossom for me, "like Aaron's rod, with flowers".*

Listen attentively. Be discerning. Share from your heart. Turn the tables. Change the conversation. Shift the mood. Create an edge. Be the X factor. In these ways you will foster personal transformation.

STAY LONG — *It would have been difficult to find a happier child than I was as I lay in my crib at the close of that eventful day and lived over the joys it had brought me, and for the first time longed for a new day to come.*

Do be there for the crisis, to put out the fire. But make sure you're there for the long haul, as the house is being restored, as the pieces of the individual life are being put back together. It may take a while as well as blood, sweat, and tears. But don't just be a firefighter. Stay around. Be a builder, bolstering others through their struggles. Share an inspirational saying, a Bible, this book, or some other uplifting text. Pray — sometimes it's your best and only option. And it just might change the game.

GIVE WITH NO STRINGS ATTACHED   MARCH 11TH

Blanket statements about the immigrant are unsafe and misleading. There are immigrants and immigrants, of every nationality and of every degree of repute, just as in the case of native-born . . . Is the immigrant a menace? There are undesirables among our newcomers, as among our native-born. There are also the chosen from many lands.
John Mahoney

During the early 1900's the challenge of assimilating millions of recent immigrants spawned the Americanization movement. Over thirty states passed laws establishing after-school and Saturday classes as school boards worked together with chambers of commerce and charities. In 1920 John Mahoney, state supervisor of Americanization for Massachusetts, published a training manual; in one section, Mahoney emphasized the importance of individuality.

Individuals differ, and races differ also. The person who would deal with immigrants must know racial backgrounds and characteristics. These differ. There is no magic process the can be applied to all national groups with any assurance of the same result. The approach to any group must be based upon the psychology of the folk, their customs, beliefs and apperceptive bases. One cannot gain the confidence of and help those whom he does not know and those in whom he does not believe.

Compassion, Mahoney asserted, was the key.

In the final analysis the major part of the burden of Americanizing the immigrant rests on the shoulders of the teacher. Her task is a meaningful one, and she should approach it as one who engages not for hire. She must be an American 100 percent pure. She must be sane and sympathetic and able to see things whole. She must be ready to give and give, and reckon not the return.

Compassion isn't easy, especially when you're dealing with those much different than you. But whether you're dealing with someone from across the ocean or a member of your own household, treat that individual with a loving attitude. The more different they are, the more you should endeavor to connect. Follow Mahoney's advice by practicing these principles.

SEE — Don't focus on the shortcomings and weaknesses in people. Look for the best in others. It's easy to harp on the negative; pointing out what's wrong in another might make you feel better about yourself. Prejudice rises when you fix on what you don't like about that person. Resist that temptation and search for the good things.

SHARE — Once you discover the positive attributes in someone else, share them with that person. By doing so you will be sowing seeds of success into that life. If you don't tell them the good news, they may stay stuck on the bad news. Speak encouraging words as a way to break the ice, foster good relations, and seed motivation.

STRENGTHEN — Fertilize the seed you have sown. Opportunities for growth abound. You strengthen others when you help them find places of employment, education, personal development, spiritual advancement, etc., where their gifts can get rooted and watered. Find ways to bring people into environments where they can start flourishing.

STRINGS UNATTACHED — Mahoney concluded with the most important point: "She must be ready to give and give, and reckon not the return." Give to others with no strings attached. Serve, expecting nothing in return. Adopt an attitude of generosity. Give sacrificially; you will not only be a blessing to others; a blessing of abundance will also flow into your life at unexpected times from unknown places. An Old Testament scripture asserts this truth.

One person gives freely, yet gains even more; another withholds unduly, but comes to poverty. A generous person will prosper; whoever refreshes others will be refreshed.
— Proverbs 11:24-25

CULTIVATE YOUR COMPASSION   MARCH 12TH

To the world you may be one person, but to one person you may be the world.

On October 28, 1886, the Statue of Liberty was dedicated in New York Harbor, with part of "The New Colossus" — a poem by Emma Lazarus — as the inscription on its pedestal. Lazarus had written the poem a few years earlier to help raise funds to build the Statue's pedestal. The title of the poem evokes the Colossus of antiquity, one of the seven wonders from that world that overlooked the harbor of the Greek City Rhodes. The poem, which, along with the statue, has come to symbolize America's compassionate spirit to provide a refuge for immigrants, follows.

> *Not like the brazen giant of Greek fame,*
> *With conquering limbs astride from land to land;*
> *Here at our sea-washed, sunset gates shall stand*
> *A mighty woman with a torch, whose flame*
> *Is the imprisoned lightning, and her name*
> *Mother of Exiles. From her beacon-hand*
> *Glows world-wide welcome; her mild eyes command*
> *The air-bridged harbor that twin cities frame.*
> *"Keep, ancient lands, your storied pomp!" cries she*
> *With silent lips. "Give me your tired, your poor,*
> *Your huddled masses yearning to breathe free,*
> *The wretched refuse of your teeming shore.*
> *Send these, the homeless, tempest-tossed to me:*
> *I lift my lamp beside the golden door!"*

Compassion is the virtue that compels you to come to the aid of others in their distress. In her poem Lazarus eloquently makes the case for a national policy of compassion, but that's Phase Two. The first step is for you to cultivate your own compassion, and that will happen as you:

READ — I read the Bible to take my mind off my own problems, nurture my spiritual life and understand better how to serve others. Whether it's the Bible, some other religious book, or inspirational writing, you should spend more time learning about the King of Kings and Mother Teresa than listening to the King of Pop and the Queen of Soul. Research those who have made a difference in the world; it will help you live your life in similar ways.

RESPOND — Compassion means that you go forth, meeting in some concrete way the reality of another person's need: it could be an emotional challenge rising from the inner life or a deprivation plaguing one's external circumstances. Just know you can't be compassionate lying on the couch, sitting on the bar stool, or playing games on your smartphone. Decide where you can best serve; put aside your self-centered preoccupations; get up and go . .

RISK — . . . and go beyond your comfort zone. Step across the cultural tracks. Travel to the place of greatest need. It may feel risky, especially if it's somewhere far removed from your current reality. Be wise: take a supportive posse and a seasoned guide if the new territory is both uncharted and treacherous. Don't hold back. The chance to uplift the downtrodden is a risk worth taking.

REACH INSIDE — If you really want to change the world, first work on changing yourself. If you make it a priority to change the world inside of you — start with your attitude! — you will have more spiritual resources — a special kind of love! — to share with the world outside of you. If you want your home, your neighborhood, even your nation to be more compassionate, let that larger compassion begin with you. And let your attitude reflect the words of William Penn.

I expect to pass this world but once. Any good therefore that I can do, or any kindness that I can show to my fellow-creature, let me do it now. Let me not defer or neglect it, for I shall not pass this way again.

GET UNDER THE BURDENS OF OTHERS   MARCH 13TH

The only true charity . . . was to get under their burdens with them and lend them the value of our experience to show them what can be done by people in their circumstances.
Henry Ford

As the Great Depression intensified in 1932, the number of the U.S. unemployed soared towards thirteen million people. Business magnate Henry Ford, the founder of the Ford Motor Company and a captain of American industry, believed that industrial corporations had a responsibility to address the unemployment problem. Ford used an article in the June 1932 issue of "Literary Digest" to share an experience that laid out his strategy.

> *One of our responsibilities, voluntarily assumed — not because it was ours but because there seemed to be no one else to assume it — was the care of a village of several hundred families whose condition was pretty low. Ordinarily, a large welfare fund would have been needed to accomplish anything for these people. In this instance, we set the people at work cleaning up their homes and backyards, and then cleaning up the roads of their town, and then plowing up about 500 acres of vacant land around their houses. We abolished everything that savored of "handout" charity, opening instead a modern commissary where personal I O U's were accepted, and a garment-making school, and setting the cobblers and tailors of the community to work for their neighbors. We found the people heavily burdened with debt, and we acted informally as their agents in apportioning their income to straighten their affairs. Many families are now out of debt for the first time in years. There has appeared in this village, not only a new spirit of confidence in life but also a new sense of economic values and an appreciation of economic independence which we feel will not soon be lost.*

Getting under the burdens of others means easing the load they are carrying, which is important way of demonstrating compassion for them. You will excel at your own burden-bearing as you:

LISTEN — The true purpose of getting under someone else's burden is to help that person get out from under it. Listen closely so you can find out the best positioning to bear the load. Each individual will have a particular area of need. Pay attention, heed the urgent voice, so you can go right to the spot where the suffering is most severe.

LIFT — One of the best ways to lift others up is to encourage them, especially if they're confronted by challenging circumstances. You can encourage with your words: thank them for their effort, praise them for their ideas, or cast a vision for their future.

LIGHT — Like Henry Ford, you can light a fire under folks by forging opportunities to work. Energize them to reach their potential by creating a collaborative environment where everyone believes in pulling their own weight. Motivate people by setting an industrious, entrepreneurial example.

LEAD — An account from the life of Abraham Lincoln is illustrative. On a visit to the South, Lincoln, then a young lawyer, observed a plantation owner bidding for a slave girl. Lincoln quickly concluded that the owner would buy and abuse her, so he intervened, put in his own bid and won; then he set the girl free. "Does this mean I can go anywhere I want?" "Yes, you're free!" Lincoln affirmed. Tears streaming down her face, she asserted, "Then, sir, I will go with you." Like Lincoln, once you listen, lift, and light, be prepared to lead.

LIVE TO GIVE—

We make a living by what we get, we make a life by what we give.
— Winston Churchill

Your livelihood is important, but you will lead a more fulfilling life as you make time and room to ease the burden of others.

COUNT THAT DAY LOST   MARCH 14TH

I cannot suppose it needful to employ earnest persuasion, or stubborn argument, in order to arrest and fix attention upon a subject only the more strongly pressing in its claims because it is revolting and disgusting in its details.
Dorothea Dix

In March 1841 writer and teacher Dorothea Dix visited a jail near Boston and found insane persons living in deplorable conditions. Alarmed by such neglect and abuse, Dix proceeded to investigate care for the mentally ill poor throughout Massachusetts. Excerpts from her 1843 report to the state legislature follow.

I found, near Boston, in the jails and asylums for the poor, a numerous class brought into unsuitable connection with criminals and the general mass of paupers. I refer to idiots and insane persons, dwelling in circumstances not only adverse to their own physical and moral improvement, but productive of extreme disadvantages to all other persons brought into association with them.

Dix testified about the extremely bad conditions of this unregulated and underfunded system.

I come to present the strong claims of suffering humanity. I come to place before the legislature of Massachusetts the condition for the miserable, the desolate, the outcast. I come as the advocate of helpless, forgotten, insane and idiotic men and women; of beings sunk to a condition from which the most unconcerned would start with real horror; of beings wretched in our prisons, and more wretched in our almshouses.

The political leaders responded, passing legislation to reform the state's mental health system. Dix's successful lobbying there led her to reach out to those in similar need throughout the United States and Europe, resulting in the first generation of mental health asylums, which eventually led to the establishment of modern psychiatric hospitals. To following Dix's trailblazing example, you must:

COMMIT TO GO FORTH — If Dorothea Dix had never visited the prison to experience the atrocities there, she would not have lobbied on behalf of the mentally ill, and no reform movement would have risen. Leave your comfort zone. Travel to uncharted territory to reach out to the needy. Stepping into the crucible of another's hardship will yield a special reward.

COUNT THAT DAY LOST — Dix's nineteenth century contemporary, British writer, Mary Ann Evans — better known by her pen name George Eliot — poetically captured a compassionate theme. If you've done nothing today beyond your own self-interest — not a word written; not a sentiment spoken; not a hand extended; not a smile offered; nothing of compassion; then do yourself a favor and meditate on the truths of Eliot's poem.

If you sit down at set of sun
And count the acts that you have done,
And, counting, find
One self-denying deed, one word

That eased the heart of him who heard,
One glance most kind
That fell like sunshine where it went —
Then you may count that day well spent.
But if, through all the livelong day
You've cheered no heart, by yea or nay —
If, thought it all
You've nothing done that you can trace
That brought the sunshine to one face —
No act most small
That helped some soul and nothing cost —
Then count that day as worse than lost.

COLLABORATE WITH YOUR COMPASSION   MARCH 15TH

Can two walk together, except they be agreed ?
Amos 3:3

In 1982 I founded a nonprofit, Harlem's Ark of Freedom (a/k/a Hark), through which we offered food and clothing in front of the countless Harlem vacant buildings and empty lots. Homeless, hungry, hurting, Henry was a regular at these Saturday street outreaches. After a few months I realized that Henry needed more than the hearty sandwiches, passionate preaching, winter coats, encouraging counseling, gospel singing and heartfelt prayers that my charity provided.

But by then he'd stopped showing up, so I went looking for him at his "residence" — the Harlem armory shelter. I didn't find him, but discovered hundreds of Henrys in a sea of cots adrift across the drill hall floor. I watched the staff drag men out of bed, giving up my search when guns were brandished in a fight over a broken crack-pipe stem. I fled the scene. I never saw Henry again.

Though I had the best of intentions, I kept leading my outreach group into burned-out blocks with Henry-like outcomes. There had to be a better way, I thought, so I went to see one of my Harlem mentors, Pastor Ezra Williams of Bethel Gospel Assembly (a/k/a Bethel).

"Three hots and a cot won't turn a life around," explained Reverend Williams, making it clear that it was Henry's poverty of spirit that gave rise to his material destitution. "The Henrys of Harlem will be transformed by the renewing of their minds," he elaborated, paraphrasing a New Testament scripture.

As we continued to talk and pray about these challenges, we decided to work together. Reverend Williams' church had recently taken over an abandoned Harlem school building. The collaboration was straightforward: Bethel provided unused classrooms as program space; Hark brought its street ministry experience, counseling insights and youthful energy to the partnership. The Beth-Hark Christian Counseling Center (www.bethharkccc.org) launched in 1985 and continues to serve the community's neediest to this day.

Just like Bethel and Hark, you can collaborate in your compassion by:

CONNECTING — If I had stayed in the closet with my problem, I would have never discovered the collective solution. If you have a great mentor like I did in Reverend Williams, be sure to avail yourself of that person's wisdom and resources. Even if you don't have someone close with whom can connect, go out of your way to find someone who shares your vision and values. Whatever good you're doing as an individual, you can extend your compassion by connecting with others.

COMMUNICATING — Share your need. I was failing to effectively serve the Henrys of Harlem. When I opened up and disclosed my shortcoming, I stepped onto the pathway of communication leading inevitably to solution and partnership. Tell the truth of your trials to those you trust. Answers — and allies — will rise through your transparency.

CONQUERING — Fear, doubt, anger, envy . . . these and other sins separate you from others. Working together with others starts with humility, so begin with the admission: "I can't do this alone." Conquer your pride: it lays the foundation for constructive relationships.

CREATING — Create a win-win-win: you win by joining forces to attain your goal; your allies wins through the mutual benefit of shared endeavor that furthers their objectives; and the community wins with an enterprise of unity.

BE AN INSPIRATION   MARCH 16TH

In every age of the world there has been a leading nation, whose eminent citizens were
willing to stand for the interests of general justice and humanity . . . Which should be
that nation but these states? . . . Who should lead the leaders but the Young American?
Ralph Waldo Emerson

The two decades leading up to the Civil War years have been
regarded as the golden age of American literature. An amazing array of
enduring writings flowed through this epoch: Melville's "Moby Dick";
Hawthorne's "The Scarlet Letter"; Thoreau's "Walden"; Dana's "Two Years
Before The Mast"; Poe's poems and stories; Whitman's "Leaves of Grass";
and Emerson's essays and poems.

The relationship of last two named, Walt Whitman and Ralph
Waldo Emerson, illustrates how small gestures of compassion make a big
difference. At a time when Whitman was feeling discouraged with the lack
of interest in his writing, Emerson sent him a note:

Dear sir, I am not blind to the worth of the wonderful gift of Leaves
of Grass. I find it the most extraordinary piece of wit and wisdom that
America has yet contributed. I greet you at the beginning of a great career.

Inspired, Whitman kept writing and his poetry attained historic
stature. Emerson took the same inspirational approach in a lecture entitled
"The Young American", delivered in Boston on February 7, 1844. He
began with a general point about America's destiny.

It seems so easy for America to inspire and express the most
expansive and humane spirit: newborn, free, healthful, strong, the land of the
laborer, of the democrat, of the philanthropist, of the believer, of the saint, she
should speak for the human race. It is the country of the future. From
Washington, proverbially "the city of magnificent distances," through all its
cities, states and territories, it is a country of beginnings, of projects, of designs,
of expectations. . .

As Emerson concluded, he made one final point about America's
high calling as an inspiration to the world.

Gentlemen, . . . One thing is plain for all men of common sense and
common conscience, that here, here in America, is the home of man. After all
the deductions which are to be made for our pitiful politics, which stake every
gravest national question on the silly die whether James or whether Robert shall
sit in the chair and hold the purse; after all the deduction is made for our
frivolities and insanities, there still remains an organic simplicity and liberty,

which, when it loses its balance, redresses itself presently, which offers opportunity to the human mind not known in any other region.

Emerson was an inspiration to his poet peer as well as to the youth of his day. Make it your intention to inspire others by keeping Emerson's strategies in mind.

LITTLE GESTURE — Emerson did it in a small way. You, too, should write a note of encouragement to someone who's feeling down. Sometimes just showing up with a thumbs-up or a smile is enough to lift an individual's spirit. Do whatever you can do one-on-one — even the apparently insignificant thing — to touch a life.

LARGE VENUE — Emerson also did it in a big way. If an opportunity to give a speech to an audience of young people — or of senior citizens — comes your way, seize it. And strive to shape your social media platform to reach lots of people with uplifting posts.

LOVE ABOVE ALL — Let compassion fuel your inspiration. If love is your motivation, your soaring words and deeds could likely be breeze of encouragement into another's life, or perhaps even the wind into the full-blown sails of the life of a nation.

GAIN POWER TO SERVE OTHERS   MARCH 17TH

We must use our lives to make the world a better place to live, not just to acquire things. That is what we are put on the earth for.
Dolores Huerta

In 1960 farm worker and women's rights advocate Dolores Huerta co-founded the Agricultural Workers Association. As a result of her earlier work fighting for economic progress for Latinos, Huerta had reached the conclusion that farm laborers were the most poverty stricken workers. She had witnessed them living without clean water, sleeping on floors in shacks, working in the fields from sun up to sun down, making little to nothing in wages.

Huerta committed her career to gaining the power to improve the farmers' conditions. To achieve this end, she used several strategies, which follow, in her own words. Seek to emulate her tactics.

PEDAGOGY — *Giving kids clothes and food is one thing, but it's much more important to teach them that other people besides themselves are important and that the best thing they can do with their lives is to use them in the service of other people.*

It is important to combine meeting material needs with providing a sense of mission — a cause larger that one's own challenges. Teach people that they are not alone in their struggles, that their quest for a better life is shared by many. Help them to learn from their fellow travelers.

POWER — *We just have to convince other people that they have power. This is what they can do by participating to make change, not only in their community, but many times changing in their own lives. Once they participate, they get their sense of power.*

Huerta organized farm workers to march in protest, to go on strike, to take matters into their own hands. In doing so, they were empowered to press for and attain improvements on the job. Organize people to give them a sense of their own power.

POLITICS — *I couldn't tolerate seeing kids come to class hungry and needing shoes. I thought I could do more by organizing farm workers than by trying to teach their hungry children.*

Huerta lobbied for laws to be passed to further the rights of workers in agricultural fields, championing better compensation and working conditions. In 1975 California Agricultural Labor Relations Act was enacted, the first time farm workers' right to collective bargaining was established in U.S. history. Following Huerta's example, lobby for new laws that yield greater opportunities for people in need.

PASSION — *Walk the street with us into history. Get off the sidewalk.*

Huerta's passion took her to the front line in the battle for farm worker rights. She was arrested 22 times for participating in strikes and nonviolent acts of civil disobedience. In September 1988 in San Francisco, during a peaceful protest, Huerta was severely beaten by a police officer, incurring broken ribs and other internal injuries. She recovered and kept fighting. Be willing to suffer for the opportunity to serve others.

PANOPLY — *We can't let people drive wedges between us . . . because there's only one human race.*

Bring people together around a righteous cause, emphasizing that the human values we all share are greater than the cultural realities that tend to separate us. Rally for unity.

PARVENU — *When you choose to give up your time and resources to participate in community work, that's what makes a leader.*

It doesn't matter where you start in life. Commit yourself to sacrifice and hard work, and you can rise to the top.

BE A GIFT   MARCH 18TH

The letter wove its awful implication that human freedom so often was paid for with agony as though he might be a ship captain at midnight by lantern light, dropping black roses into the immemorial sea for mystic remembrance and consecration.
Carl Sandburg

The Civil War was a costly conflict, not only in the hundreds of thousand of lives lost on the battlefields but also in the hearts of the grieving families. Perhaps no one of these mourning loved ones suffered more than the Boston widow whose five sons served in the Union army. The historical record shows that one was taken prisoner, two deserted while two were killed in action. But President Abraham Lincoln was told by an aide that all five sons had died in combat. This misinformation notwithstanding, the letter that Lincoln wrote to comfort the lamenting mother transformed this official rite into a heartfelt testament.

Executive Mansion, Washington, Nov. 21, 1864
To Mrs. Bixby, Boston, Mass.

Dear Madam,

I have been shown in the files of the War Department, Statement of the Adjutant General of Massachusetts that you are the mother of five sons who have died gloriously on the field of battle. I feel how weak and fruitless must be any word of mine which should attempt to beguile you from the grief of a loss so overwhelming. But I cannot refrain from tendering you the consolation that may be found in the thanks of the republic they died to save. I pray that our Heavenly Father may assuage the anguish of your bereavement, and leave you only the cherished memory of the loved and lost, and the solemn pride that must be yours to have laid so costly a sacrifice upon the altar of freedom.

Yours very sincerely and respectfully,
A. Lincoln

Lincoln's letter was a special offering of support to Mrs. Bixby in her moment of profound need. His actions were like a gift to her; you can be a gift to others as you:

GIVE FROM YOUR HEART — Don't give someone something as the gift. Give yourself as the gift. Your words as well as your actions can be that gift. Lincoln didn't have to write a heartfelt letter; he could've sent a template to check the bureaucratic box. Transform a the simple things — a smile, a handshake, a pat on the back — into an uplifting gesture. Poet Spencer Michael Free poetically captured this theme.

> *'Tis the human touch in this world that counts,*
> *The touch off your hand and mine,*
> *Which means far more to the fainting heart*
> *Than shelter and bread and wine;*
> *For shelter is gone when the night is o'er,*
> *And bread last only a day,*
> *But the touch of the hand and the sound of the voice*
> *Sing on in the soul alway.*

GIVE OUT OF THE ORDINARY — You don't have to wait for the tragedy of lost lives to motivate you to lift someone who is struggling. Like Lincoln, do something out of the ordinary; step out of the customary; go the extra mile. Don't just pay for someone's lunch; pay for their training workshop so next year the individual can get a job and pay for your lunch. Remember: grassroots engagement is just as valuable as monetary support. Go beyond the year-end charitable contribution handout and go to the place of need, where you can touch another with your time and energy. Volunteer at the soup kitchen; pray at a sick person's hospital bed; fulfill a school or work requirement of community service by mentoring a young person in need of support. Give sacrificially. What if Jesus had thought about the challenge before him and decided, "I don't do crosses." Don't be someone's worst nightmare. Be the answer to someone's prayer.

ADVOCATE FOR THE NEEDY   MARCH 19TH

The trouble is with ourselves. We get exactly the sort of care for the children that the community determines they shall have; and we register our indifference, obscuring the actual conditions of the working children in nearly all the states. . . . this is a national evil, and we must have a national law abolishing it.
Florence Kelley

In December 1906, at the third annual meeting of the National Child Labor Committee, social reformer Florence Kelley updated the committee members on the progress of various states' child labor laws in addressing the distressing conditions and long hours children were forced to work. Part of her report featured the strides that were being made in Chicago.

There is a chart showing the attendance of the children of Chicago at school in the year 1902. A small block symbolizes the attendance in that year. For the following year the same block repeated symbolizes the attendance; but the next year, 1904, when the present drastic child labor law of Illinois had taken effect, the enrollment in the Chicago schools of the children of compulsory school age trebled. . . . That statute carried 1,000 children out of the stockyards in a single week; and later it carried 2,200 children out of the mines of Illinois in another week . . .

Because of ongoing pressure from the the National Child Labor Committee and the National Consumers League, of which Kelley was the general secretary, the first federal child labor law was enacted ten years later. Kelley's success in advocating for the disadvantaged suggest four strategies. Put your own compassionate advocacy into action as you:

LIMN — Bring power to your advocacy by telling it in compelling ways. Kelley used charts to depict Chicago's progress. Create visuals and other dramatic media to illustrate the engaging truths that will generate support for your cause. Tell your own story and find others to tell their stories; it's the best way to give abstractions reality and bring the truth to light.

LAMBAST — This is sometimes referred to as tough love. There are times when you have to speak the truth — and it comes across critically. When Kelley called child labor practices in America a "national evil", she was practicing very tough love, and it brought attention to the problem. Use dramatic language to highlight your cause. It will help to rally support.

LEGISLATE — Some people in need will only get help when laws are passed in their favor. Be strategic about taking political steps. Like Kelley, begin local and build on your success with your municipality; then move on to take legislative initiatives at the state and federal levels. But don't start in the corridors of powers; begin to make changes closer to home, in your community, maybe inside your own home. Then when you enter into the political chambers, you will have a good handle on how best to advocate for the needy, having done it in your own surroundings.

LOVE — Kelley's life mission was helping others. Make your compassionate advocacy a personal mission. Let helping others become a priority. Embrace Jesus' words as a daily mantra: "Love your neighbor as yourself"; or in the words of George Washington Carver:

How far you go in life depends on you being tender with the young, compassionate with the aged, sympathetic with the striving and tolerant of the weak and strong. Because someday in your life you will have been all of these.

BE HOLISTIC WITH YOUR COMPASSION   MARCH 20TH

I propose to consider and attempt to refute certain pernicious errors which too generally prevail respecting the situation, the conduct, the characters, and the prospects of those whose sole dependence is on the labor of their hands.
— Mathew Carey

The American economic expansion of the 1820s created in the Northeastern cities of Boston, New York and Philadelphia an urban working class. The massive immigrant influx increased the labor pool, keeping wages low and leaving some unemployed. The plight of the urban poor emerged for the first time in America; it hasn't gone away.

Irishman Mathew Carey had fled to Paris from persecution at home where he met Benjamin Franklin in 1781. Franklin's influence led to Carey's eventual immigration to Philadelphia where he established a book shop and publishing business. Carey witnessed the growing poverty in the city, and, out of his concern, he published in 1833 Appeal to the Wealthy of the Land. He noted some "erroneous opinions" about the poor.

. . . That the poor, by industry, prudence, and economy, may at all times support themselves comfortably, without depending on eleemosynary aid. . . . That their sufferings and distresses chiefly, if not wholly, arise from

their idleness, their dissipation, and their extravagance.

Carey also pointed out that wrong thinking about how to help the poor had worsened the problem.

> *These opinions, so far as they have operated — and, through the mischievous zeal and industry of the school of political economists by which they have been promulgated, they have spread widely — have been pernicious to the rich and the poor. They tend to harden the hearts of the former against the sufferings and distresses of the latter, and of course prolong those sufferings and distresses.*

Carey believed it was important to be holistic in your compassion — to reach out in ways to meet the totality of an individual's needs. Make this your approach as you help people to:

LOVE THEIR BODY — About 150 years after Carey's writing, when I finished Harvard Law School and moved to Harlem, I observed a similar myopia in dealing with the New York City poor of the 1980's. So I started Harkhomes, an emergency shelter for fifteen homeless men in a Harlem church basement. Though Harkhomes was about holistic housing — shelter not as an end in itself but as a means to restore the whole person — the assistance prioritized meeting the physical needs: food, clothing and shelter. Start your compassion with the imperatives of the body.

LOVE THEIR SOUL — Then strive to go beyond the material basics of "three hots and a cot" to provide discipline, skills, family-like support, opportunity — the stuff out of which lives are transformed. The Chinese proverb rings ever true.

> *Give a man a fish and he'll eat for a day.*
> *Teach him how to fish and he'll eat for a lifetime.*

LOVE THEIR FUTURE — Instead of allowing individuals to harp on the mistakes of the past, help them to embrace hope for the future as the best medicine for present problems. Cast vision for brighter days ahead; this visionary perspective will bring motivation to those seeking to overcome immediate challenges.

LOVE THEIR NEIGHBOR — You will be better able to help others if you first help yourself. Though this is a fundamental truth to impart to those in need, let your compassion be contagious. Role-model selfless service. Help them to understand that what you're doing to assist them, they should also do for others still stuck in the dismal places that they're trying to step beyond. Helping others can be the best way to help yourself. Teach them to embrace Jesus' second great commandment:

Love your neighbor as yourself.
— Mark 12:31

GET A MOVE ON   MARCH 21ST

What's the meaning of the queue,
Tailing down the avenue,
Full of eyes that will not meet
The other eyes that throng the street . . .
Florence Converse

The Great Depression, the longest and severest economic depression of the twentieth century, reached its nadir in1932; more than twelve million Americans were unemployed, an increase of fifty percent from the previous year. Businesses and families defaulted on record numbers of loans; thousands of banks failed; hundreds of thousands found themselves homeless; and breadline, soup kitchens, tar-paper cities, shanty towns (also known as Hoovervilles) and Bonus Army camps defined both urban and rural landscapes all across America.

Author Florence Converse memorably captured the dire mood of Depression-era America in her poem "Bread Line", published in January 1932 in the "Atlantic Monthly".

. . .
The questing eyes, the curious eyes,
Scornful, popping with surprise
To see a living line of men
As long as round the block, and then
As long again? The statisticians
Estimate that these conditions
Have not reached their apogee.
All lines end eventually;
Except of course in theory.
This one has an end somewhere.
End in what? — Pause, there.

What's the meaning in these faces
Modern industry displaces,
. . .

What if our breadline should be
The long slow-match of destiny?
. . .

It took America a decade to recover from this crisis. If you know individuals in a "Bread Line" crisis, your response should be: assist them to meet their physical need but also to empower them so they no longer have to be on the Bread Line. Practicing these principles will help you more effectively help others.

GET OUT — Get out of your self-consciousness. Shift your focus from conspicuous consumption to compassionate service. Once your basic needs are meet, create the time and space in your life to meet the needs of others. Take off the blinders of your self-centeredness so you can see how best to serve.

GET THROUGH— Get through the geographic and institutional barriers that limit your ability to uplift the needy. You may have to relocate to a new place beyond your comfort zone; or spend some time after work or on weekends in a neighborhood far removed from where you live; or even travel abroad on a summer missions trip to an impoverished destination. Wherever you have to go, break through a sociological wall; make a move in a new direction to serve.

GET TO — Get to the person in need. Don't just donate to the Bread Line. Go to the Bread Line and get to know the individual on line. Advise and support that person in ways to make a return to the Bread Line unnecessary.

GET A MOVE ON — Show up to be a light amidst the gloom. Get moving beyond your usual places. Sometimes just being present in the place of need — without saying or doing anything — is enough to make a difference. So many are without food and shelter but even worse — without hope. It is better to light one candle than to curse the darkness.

POSSESS AN ABUNDANT MINDSET   MARCH 22ND

When one sees this sort of living, with the houses full of good beds,
ready for the guest as well as the facility to sleep in, we cannot help perceiving
that this is that "English hospitality" of which we have read so much; but,
which boroughmongers' taxes and pawns have long since driven out of England.
William Cobbett

The English politician and journalist William Cobbett came to America in 1817 as a political refugee, fearful that he might be arrested again in Britain for his arguably seditious writings. Living on a farm on Long Island, Cobbett spent much of time writing about his observations of American society and customs. He returned to London in 1819 and published the following year A Year's Residence in the United States, which contrasted the American way of life with that of his home country. Cobbett elaborated the uniqueness of American compassion; it offered physical as well as spiritual provision.

It is not with a little bit of dry toast so neatly put in a rack; a bit of
butter so round and small; a little milkpot so pretty and so empty; an egg for
you, the host and hostess not liking eggs. It is not with looks that seem to say,
"don't eat too much , for the tax gatherer is coming." It is not thus that you are
received in America. You are not much asked, not much pressed, to eat and
drink; but, such an abundance is spread before you, and so hearty and so
cordial is your reception, that you instantly lose all restraint, and are tempted to
feast whether you be hungry or not. And, though the manner and style are
widely different in different houses, the abundance everywhere prevails. This is
the strength of the government — a happy people — and no government ought
to have any other strength.

Cobbett's perspective evokes three mindsets. Assess the following to see which best characterizes you.

SCARCITY — This mentality asserts that there's not enough to go around so I have to protect my stuff and watch my back; if I share anything with others, I will lose out.

SURPLUS — If I share what I have — money, food, ideas, love — with others, I'll be inspired with resourcefulness; I'll be motivated to replace what I've offered to others and to get even more. This mindset is best captured by the words of Henri Nowen.

When we refrain from giving, with a scarcity mentality, the little we have will become less.
When we give generously, with an abundance mentality, what we give away will multiply.

It's up to you whether you're bringing to life a never-enough or always-enough attitude. That's why your optimal mindset is:

SACRED — Life is not just about material things. Your best offerings are those that come from your soul and spirit; they come anointed with humility, which makes it a greater blessing for those on the receiving end of your gift. Be assured of this truth: when you make up your mind to give what you have, and you give it faithfully, whatever it is, Providence intervenes to create reciprocity: you will receive a blessing even as you give one. Add faith-inspired sharing to your compassionate giving and you will be rewarded with abundance. Keep in mind the divine principle, which Jesus so memorably proclaimed.

Give and it will be given to you. A good measure, pressed down,
shaken together and running over, will be poured into our lap.
For with the measure you use, it will be measured to you.
— Luke 6:38

SEE THE POTENTIAL IN EVERYONE   MARCH 23RD

I ponder and pray in the stillness, I dream as a dreamer of dreams. A steepled church
stands before me — a church with open doors. Within it I see the preacher stand . . .
But 'tis the throng that flows through the street outside that holds my anxious gaze.
Aimee McPherson

In 1918 traveling evangelist Aimee McPherson moved to Los Angeles, settling her ministry in the fast-growing city. McPherson began holding services in the 3,500-seat Philharmonic Auditorium but soon outgrew it. She decided to build a new church, raising $250,000 from her supporters to do so.

In 1923 McPherson consecrated Angelus Temple, which became the first Pentecostal megachurch with membership exceeding 10,000 and over 40 million visitors during its first seven years. But McPherson's vision was to serve people beyond the four walls of the church, meeting physical as well as spiritual needs.

McPherson's strategy was to engage her large congregation in community outreach, requiring every member to get involved in charity work. Her preaching emphasized both spiritual healing and social service.

Let us ever strive to lighten our brother's load and dry the tears of a sister; race, creed or status make no difference. We are all one in the eyes of the Lord. . . True Christianity is not only to be good but to do good.

McPherson organized her ministry to address everyone in need. Donations for humanitarian relief of all kinds were collected: local earthquakes and floods as well as international disasters in Europe and Asia. McPherson's "Brotherhood" found jobs for men released from prison; her "Sisterhood" came along side impoverished mothers with newborn babies. The commissary at Angelus Temple was open seven days a week, 24 hours a day, providing free clinics, food, clothing, and blankets to everyone — even newly arrived immigrants — no questions asked. As the demand for such services intensified through the Great Depression, with some government programs shutting down, Angelus Temple — according to a 1936 survey — served more families than any other public or private institution in Los Angeles.

McPherson saw the potential in everyone and endeavored to uplift them. Endeavor to emulate her compassionate work by practicing these principles.

SENSITIVITY — Do no harm: when someone is damaged, be sensitive; the first thing is not to do any more damage. If you don't have anything encouraging to say, keep quiet. Your words are like fire. They can simmer the stew or burn down the house. Use them wisely to create a recipe of success for those less fortunate than you.

SELFLESSNESS — Spend some time figuring out how to slice some time away from activities centered around you, to create opportunities to serve others. Is there something you can give up to put you in a better position to give to others? . . . Putting others before your own agendas isn't easy. It may steal some time away from your hobbies and other leisure activities. Make the sacrifice anyway. The rewards are priceless.

STRATEGY — Look for the good in everyone. It's there — it may be buried pretty deep under years of disappointment, disadvantage and despair. Everyone's different. Understand the real issues and customize your response. Find out what works best for each individual and reach out accordingly. Heed Mother Teresa's counsel:

Spread love everywhere you go. Let no one ever come to you without leaving happier.

STANDARD-BEARER — Model the behavior you want others to follow. You shouldn't demand of others what you're not demanding of yourself. When you serve others, set high standards. Just make sure you're living by them so those in need can aspire to your level. Be an inspirational example!

BE GUTSY WITH YOUR COMPASSION   MARCH 24TH

Our willingness to aid the slaves was soon known, and hardly a fugitive came to the city without applying to us for assistance. There seemed to be a continual increase of runaways, and such was the vigilance of the pursuers that I was obliged to devote a large share of time from my business to making arrangements for their concealment . . .
Lewis Coffin

Known as the "President of the Underground Railroad", Quaker businessman Levi Coffin facilitated throughout the 1850's the branch of the vast interstate network that aided slaves to freedom northward through the midwestern states on to Canada. In his autobiography, "Reminiscences of Levi Coffin", published many years after his anti-slavery exploits, Coffin reflected on efforts to help slaves escape through such places as southern Indiana and Ohio, key locations because of their proximity to slave states.

His compassion entailed not only a big commitment of time but also of money and of his own residence, which some called the "Grand Central Station" of the Underground Railroad.

They sometimes came to our door frightened and panting and in a destitute condition, having fled in such haste and fear that they had no time to bring any clothing except what they had on, and that was often very scant. The expense of providing suitable clothing for them when it was necessary for them to go on immediately, or of feeding them when they were obliged to be concealed for days or weeks, was very heavy. . . . Our house was large and well adapted for secreting fugitives. Very often slaves would lie concealed in upper chambers for weeks without the boarders or frequent visitors at the house knowing anything about it.

His life incessantly threatened by slave hunters, Coffin courageously continued his crusade, holding fast to his religious convictions.

If by doing my duty and endeavoring to fulfill the injunctions of the Bible, I injured my business, then let my business go. As to my safety, my life was in the hands of my Divine Master, and I felt that I had his approval. I had no fear of the danger that seemed to threaten my life or my business. If I was faithful to duty, and honest and industrious, I felt that I would be preserved, and that I could make enough to support my family.

If you're faced with a big mission like Coffin's and you need to be gutsy in your compassion, be sure to:

GO OUT OF YOUR WAY — Take some risks. Be careful to manage them as Coffin did, but understand that to reach some needy people you have to take the road less traveled. If you go out of your way to serve, you will find, like Coffin, divine grace and guidance all along that journey.

GRIND FROM YOUR GUT — Selfless compassion can be hard work. Be willing to labor before work, after hours, on weekends and holidays, to uplift the needy. You may feel you don't have the strength to do it all. Reach down deep inside your soul; you will find the mettle there. Remember — when you make great personal sacrifices to serve others, you open the door to unexpected, overflowing blessings.

GET OTHERS EMPOWERED — This kind of compassion is about much more than giving a needy person a few dollars. It takes guts to bring liberty into the life of another. Make this your goal: to take the person in need to a whole new place of life, to set the captive free.

GRIP YOUR FAITH — Because of the risks, don't endeavor to work on contemporary "Underground Railroads" without divine help. Coffin is the role model here. Without a strong faith to support your compassion, you may find yourself without access to supernatural protection and miraculous provision when you need them most.

SHED THE LIGHT OF POSSIBILITY   MARCH 25TH

In the other America each group suffers from a psychological depression as well as from simple material want . . .
Michael Harrington

During the 1960's affluence embraced America: the nation experienced greater wealth than any country in the history of the world.

But the abundance was not shared by all Americans, as the plight of the poor became more pronounced in the midst of prosperity. In his 1962 book "The Other America", Michael Harrington articulated various manifestations of U.S. poverty. The following passage depicted a particularly devastating aspect of the problem.

> *Some commentators have argued that Negroes have a lower level of aspiration, of ambition, than whites. In this theory, the Jim Crow economy produces a mood of resignation and acceptance. . . an even more serious situation: one in which Negro children had more aspiration than whites from the same income level, but less opportunity to fulfill their ambition.*

To elaborate this point, Harrington made a historical comparison between the immigrant and the African American experiences.

> *The Negro child, coming from a family in which the father has a miserable job, is forced to reject the life of his parents, and to put forth new goals for himself. In the case of the immigrant young some generations ago, this experience of breaking with the Old Country tradition and identifying with the great society of America was a decisive moment in moving upward. But the Negro does not find society as open as the immigrant did. He has the hope and the desire, but not the possibility. The consequence is heartbreaking frustration.*

Harrington's emphasis on possibility was key for the poor of the past; it's also vital for the needy of the present. If you want to truly show compassion to someone, you must shed the light of possibility for that person, even as you meet the material needs. You can do so by fostering:

ENGAGEMENT — Start helping by listening. It's the only way to figure out what's really needed to make a difference, because everyone is different. Customize your intervention to the individual in need. You may give gentle advice to one person and show tough love to another. Someone will require some handholding; someone else will need you to extend some breathing room. You'll have to draw up a daily plan of action for one individual, whereas a self-starter simply needs a template. Engage to learn, then act to serve.

ENCOURAGEMENT — Encourage others by asking questions. Choose queries that will help an individual launch the inner journey, the process by which one gets more deeply in touch with soul and spirit. "What are you most passionate about?" (Where's your joy?) . . . "What makes you cry?" (Where's your pain?) . . . "What are your values?" (What's most important to you?) . . . "What are your dreams?" (Where is your destiny?) Don't make it feel like an interview. Guiding people softly through this inquiry will encourage their hearts.

ENTERPRISE — Possibilities arise through opportunities extended. If you really want to help a poor person — or anybody — help that individual see hope in the future. For the disadvantaged, that means both getting them ready for work and helping them find it. Yes, easier said than done. But be enterprising about employment opportunities, even if you have to create direly needed jobs yourself. When I was running the Harkhomes homeless shelter I took over a failing travel agency and revived it as Harlem's first American Express Office; then I trained and hired homeless men to work part-time at the agency as a stepping stone to other full-time jobs. Employ your creativity to employ those in need.

HEED YOUR CALL TO COMPASSION   **MARCH 26TH**

If we wish to serve God and love our neighbor well, we must manifest our joy in the service we render to Him and them. Let us open wide our hearts. It is joy which invites us. Press forward and fear nothing.
Saint Katharine Drexel

In January 1887 Katharine Drexel and her two younger sisters Elizabeth and Louisa received a private audience with Pope Leo XIII. Heiresses to a sizable fortune, the sisters were committed to direct some funding to address the societal disadvantages of Native Americans and African Americans. They discussed this mission with the Pope and requested missionaries to staff the work that they were looking to establish in the southwestern United States. The Pope encouraged Katharine to become a missionary herself, and she eventually accepted that calling; she described the process of her submitting to the divine direction for her life.

It is a lesson we all need - to let alone the things that do not concern us. He has other ways for others to follow Him; all do not go by the same path. It is for each of us to learn the path by which He requires us to follow Him, and to follow Him in that path.

Drexel established with a dozen other nuns the Sisters of the Blessed Sacrament and built the motherhouse in Bensalem, Pennsylvania. In 1894 they launched their first school, St. Catherine's Indian School, in Santa

Fe, New Mexico. In addition to starting missions and schools through her own Blessed Sacrament congregation, Drexel encouraged then financed the work of friars among the Navajo and Pueblo tribes of Arizona and New Mexico. Over the decades of her ministry, Drexel launched 145 missions, 12 schools for Native Americans, 50 schools for African Americans, and Xavier University, which, located in Louisiana, is the only historically black Catholic college in the United States. Largely because of her prodigious works of compassion, Drexel was canonized by the Roman Catholic Church in 2000, becoming only the second American to be canonized a saint, the first who was actually born a U.S. citizen.

Drexel heeded her call to compassion and bore great fruit as a result. You can have similarly positive impact if you heed your own call; to do so, be sure to be:

CALLED — To be called, you have to be listening. If you're so full of your own thinking, there won't be any space in your consciousness for a divine voice to be heard. Do your best to quiet the noise of your ideas. Incline your ear heavenward. Discern the truth in the spiritual whispers. Drexel made her move after she heard the Pope's voice. Wait on your godly sign.

Be still, and know that I am God.
Psalm 46:10

CENTERED — Embrace your core values. Try to avoid running to every conference with a nice slogan or a big promise. Drexel was committed to social justice and directed her ministry accordingly. Set your moral compass to keep clear the difference between acceptable and unacceptable behavior. Maintain your calling at the center of all you do.

CRUSADING — There are so many young people who live in environments that lead them into early confrontations with the criminal justice system, landing them in jail or a juvenile delinquency program. Drexel set up academic and spiritual interventions to guide youth in positive directions. She believed that a compassionate society should create nurturing environments to bring young people to moral maturity without suffering through the severity of penal sanctions. Do as much as you can to steer individuals, especially young ones, away from detours of trouble and onto pathways of achievement.

MAKE A DIFFERENCE FOR THOSE IN NEED   MARCH 27TH

He who preaches the gospel to the poor will have no doubt . . . that
governments and all social institutions are to based on positive virtue, on
morality, not on selfishness, not on each man's ability to take care of himself.
George Boardman

Post-Civil War America experienced the greatest period of expansion and innovation the nation had yet seen. The industrial development of oil, steel, railroads, telephones, among others, was accompanied by huge personal fortunes. On the opposite end of the income ladder was the proliferation of poverty, especially among urban immigrants and other low wage-earners.

In 1866 Rev. George Boardman published an article "Political Economy and Christian Ministry" in which he argued for governmental action on behalf of the poor. A Presbyterian minister from Binghamton, New York, Boardman asserted the disadvantage and suffering of working men, women and children in light of the tremendous growth of industry and the consequent concentration of economic power. He was particularly concerned about the plight of the American family, which the following passage indicates.

> *Nor will the clergyman be satisfied when those to whom he preaches*
> *are barely sustained in life; there are some moral qualities indispensable to the*
> *family which extreme poverty destroys . . . there are families to be found in*
> *every land in which fathers and mothers are obliged to labor till their muscles*
> *are knotted . . . till weariness is ingrained in the very tissues, till complaint,*
> *sighing, faultfinding have settled down upon the family circle like a blight . . .*

Boardman advocated that government and civil society should work together to alleviate the conditions of the poor. His insistence that we all make a difference for those in need is as important today as it was 150 years ago. Don't wait on government to legislate another poverty initiative or to make existing programming more effective. Show government the way; make a difference for those in need as you:

GO TO THE PLACE OF NEED — Don't just send in a check to support your local soup kitchen. Go volunteer at the soup kitchen. When I finished Harvard Law School, I relocated to Harlem — a place where I had never lived — to position myself to help the community. Boots on the ground at the front lines is the best way to make a difference. Reflect on Old Testament Prophet Isaiah's message about the actions that comprise true spirituality.

Is it not to share your food with the hungry and to provide the
poor wanderer with shelter, when you see the naked, to clothe
them, and not to turn away from your own flesh and blood?
— Isaiah 58:7

GATHER RESOURCES TO SHARE — Think beyond a
financial contribution to people within your network. Bring
someone else — perhaps even a team — with you the next time
you help the needy. Strive to be a compassionate role model to
inspire others to do the same.

GAIN A FOOTHOLD — Get to know someone who
needs a hand up the socio-economic ladder and lead the way.
Become a mentor — you may help guide an individual away from
the hopeless gloom towards a brighter future. Sometimes all it takes
is speaking the right words to the right person at the right time to
transform a life.

GROW OTHERS INTO SELF-SUFFICIENCY — You
don't have to have a lot of money or possess a special set of skills
to help lift someone out of poverty. It's all about imparting
encouragement and strategy: assisting the needy individual to
formulate a plan towards self-sufficiency and to gain the
confidence to pursue it. The bonds of generational dependency
can only be broken by the efforts of the one in bondage, but you
can help that person grow into freedom.

WIDEN YOUR CIRCLE OF COMPASSION   MARCH 28TH

Any time you have an opportunity to make a difference in this
world and you don't, then you are wasting your time on Earth.
Roberto Clemente

In the 1971 World Series Roberto Clemente of the Pittsburgh
Pirates was the hero, leading his team to the championship in seven games
over the Baltimore Orioles. Voted the Most Valuable Player of the series,
Clemente not only excelled consistently at the plate with a .414 batting
average (12 hits in 29 at-bats); he also proved to be the clutch performer,
hitting a home run in the 2–1 victory in the decisive Game Seven.

Clemente's performance represented the capstone of his 18-year
Hall of Fame career. His professional baseball start was in Puerto Rico,
where he was born and raised. In 1955, he broke through with the Pirates,

just a year after the team became the ninth to break the color line in Major League Baseball when Curt Roberts joined the team — seven years after Jackie Robinson had been the first black player in the league with the Brooklyn Dodgers.

Clemente soon became a star, both at the plate — winning the batting title several times during the 1960's; and in the field — garnering 12 consecutive Gold Glove awards. In the off season Clemente would return to his native Puerto Rico, where he was known for his commitment to charitable work.

After the 1972 season Clemente's compassion took him to Managua, Nicaragua. Three weeks after his visit the region was struck by a massive earthquake. Clemente was moved to arrange emergency relief to be flown to the quake victims, but the first three flights of aid packages never got to them, diverted by corrupt government officials. Consequently, Clemente joined the fourth relief flight to ensure the delivery of aid to the survivors. Tragically, the chartered New Year's Eve flight crashed due to engine failure. Clemente and the other passengers perished into the Atlantic Ocean.

Clemente sacrificed his life in a heroic initiative to widen his circle of compassion. You don't have to go to that extreme to touch someone outside of your typical range of activities. To widen your own circle of compassion, keep these points in mind.

> NO LIMITS — *A human being is a part of the whole called by us universe, a part limited in time and space. He experiences himself, his thoughts and feeling as something separated from the rest, a kind of optical delusion of his consciousness. This delusion is a kind of prison for us, restricting us to our personal desires and to affection for a few persons nearest to us. Our task must be to free ourselves from this prison by widening our circle of compassion to embrace all living creatures and the whole of nature in its beauty.*

These words from scientist Albert Einstein articulate the meaning of Clemente's charitable commitment — compassion knows no bounds. Free yourself from the limitations of cultural background as you reach out to serve others.

> NO SELFISHNESS — *Do nothing out of selfish ambition or vain conceit. Rather, in humility value others above yourselves, not looking to your own interests but each of you to the interests of the others.* (Philippians 2:3-4)

This directive from the Apostle Paul to the church at Philippi depicts the compassionate ideal — an attitude that puts others before yourself. Start thinking in this way and you will make a difference for many more lives.

NO FEAR — Clemente was a baseball superstar, but that status didn't get in the way of his fearless charity. Put aside any trepidation you might have and reflect on this question: what is the one thing you can do today to widen your own circle of compassion, touching the lives of those you don't know?

LOVE YOUR ENEMIES   MARCH 29TH

We cannot live only for ourselves. A thousand fibers connect us with our fellow men.
Herman Melville

In 1866 novelist Herman Melville (He had already published his most famous book "Moby-Dick".) wrote an essay that was published with his collection of poems entitled "Battle-Pieces and Aspects of the War". In it Melville advocated North-South reconciliation in the aftermath of the Civil War. In one passage Melville paraphrased the Golden Rule to accentuate the Christian precept of loving one's enemies.

In imagination let us place ourselves in the unprecedented position of the Southerners — their position as regards the millions of ignorant manumitted slaves in their midst, for whom some of us now claim the suffrage. Let us be Christians toward our fellow whites, as well as philanthropists toward the blacks, our fellowmen. In all things and toward all, we are enjoined to do as we would be done by. Nor should we forget that benevolent desires, after passing a certain point, cannot undertake their own fulfillment without incurring the risk of evils beyond those sought to be remedied. Something may well be left to the graduated care of future legislation, and to heaven.

Melville's counsel was to love your enemies; it is a most difficult thing to do, but it is one of the most compassionate things you can do. It takes both commitment and strategy, both of which you can live out through these precepts.

RUBICON — Refuse to go to your point of no return. You may be angry about someone's behavior, and your anger may be well justified. But don't let it turn into a bitterness that takes deep root in your soul. Confess those feelings in prayer, and to others, which will help to nip raging hatred in the bud and start the process of transforming negative feelings into positive sentiments.

RELEASE — Let go of the past. Hundreds of thousands Northerners lost their lives in the Civil War, yet Melville counseled against holding grudges against Southerners. He insisted on the Golden Rule. Do your best to practice it in your daily living: treat others as you would like to be treated. Love your enemies by eschewing the breakdowns and conflicts of past while emphasizing the breakthroughs of the present and the possibilities of the future.

REACH OUT — Follow Melville's advice: use your imagination and put yourself in your enemies' shoes. Envisage what they're going through and discover reasons to connect with them. Be the bigger person and reach out across whatever physical and emotional barriers exist. Surprise your enemy with attention, even affection — it just might demolish some long-standing barriers. Jesus' counsel is timeless:

Love your enemies, do good to those who hate you, bless those who curse you, pray for those who mistreat you.
— Luke 6:27-28

RECONCILIATION — Live graciously and generously toward others, even those who have been hostile and abusive to you and your loved ones. The higher ground of compassion is reconciliation — that exalted space that many are unable to attain. Strive to step up to it. To be there, be humble, magnanimous, and forgiving; you will ascend to divine spheres of life where only the compassionate dwell, and where your blessings will overflow.

CHOOSE TO BE A PLUS PERSON   MARCH 30TH

The achievements of science were there in abundance, and their applications; but where, one was moved to ask, was the evidence of the larger life for mankind, or even the promise of it?
Robert Morse Lovett

In 1933 Chicago celebrated its centennial of the city's incorporation with "A Century of Progress", an international exposition commemorating "the achievements of science and their application through industry to the creation of a larger life for mankind." University of Chicago English professor Robert Morse Lovett wrote an article about the world's fair: "Progress — Chicago Style." In the essay Lovett observed the myopia of the exposition that featured exhibitions with attractions for the prosperous but neglected the things that would have demonstrated concern for the poor and needy.

> *A conspicuous omission was in the matter of popular housing. There were examples of houses of steel, of glass, of concrete, but none of model tenements. There were hundreds of appliances for household comfort, all of them beyond the means of the poor. . . . In this rendering of the century of progress, the problem of poverty did not exist.*

Near the essay's conclusion Lovett highlighted the paradox of the glitter and glamor of the world's fair against the backdrop of a city known for organized crime, gang wars, intractable indigence and official corruption.

> *The enormous irony of the Century of Progress was to be appreciated in the unescapable contrast between the combination of natural beauty of lake, island, lagoons, with lavish architectural decoration and brilliant illumination, against the imposing skyline of the city's facade and the sordid background of civic life in which official corruption was never more arrogant nor human misery more appalling.*

True compassion means looking beyond your own needs and those of your loved ones, even beyond those in your immediate circumstances and social group — to embrace the needs of those who are less fortunate than you. No matter how dire your present situation may be, there is always someone in this world who's in some way needier than you are. To meaningful serve such people, keep these two points in mind.

PERSPECTIVE — How you treat others is determined by your perspective of them. Lovett's critique of the Chicago world's fair was its narrow perspective, exhibiting progress — during the Great Depression when many millions of Americans were unemployed — as if "the problem of poverty did not exist." Whatever success you've had in life, take some time to think how you can use your assets of advantage to address the needs of the disadvantaged. Be clear that your life does not simply consist of the abundance of your possessions. For true abundance, embrace what you have while giving generously from what you have.

PLUS — The decisions you make in life will affect others positively or negatively. Choose to be a Plus Person — adding value by serving others. The value can be an emotional asset that you offer, making someone feel special, affirmed or worthwhile. The

plus that you bring can also be tangible things — buying a hungry
person lunch, giving the homeless person a coat or offering the
unemployed the opportunity to work. Or it may be as simple as
encouraging words to brighten another's day. Surprise someone
with service, as Jesus did when he washed his disciples' feet. Jesus
added value to the lives of his disciples by that selfless act; you, too,
can add value by serving others. What can you do today — right
now — to add value to someone's life through an act of service?

BE EFFECTIVE WITH YOUR COMPASSION   MARCH 31ST

> *Indeed, sensible men have long seen that "the best government is
> that which governs least." And we are surprised that the spirit of
> this maxim is not oftener and closer to the ears of our domestic leaders.*
> Walt Whitman

One of the most influential of American poets, Walt Whitman was
also a journalist, working as editor of the newspaper Brooklyn Eagle. In an
editorial published on April 4, 1846, Whitman began with a quotation from
another periodical, the New York Globe.

> *The end of all government is the happiness of the whole
> community; and whenever it does not secure that, it is a bad
> government, and it is time it was altered.*

Whitman criticized this statement as an ineffective approach.

> *We snip out this little paragraph from our New York contemporary
> because it affords us a chance of nailing a very wide though very foolish error.
> It is only the novice in political economy who thinks it the duty of government
> to make its citizens happy. Government has no such office. To protect the weak
> and the minority from the impositions of the strong and the majority, to prevent
> anyone from positively working to render the people unhappy (if we may so
> express it), to do the labor not of an officious intermeddler in the affairs of
> men but of a prudent watchmen who prevents outrage — these are rather the
> proper duties of a government.*

Whitman concluded this article with a more effective strategy for
governmental intervention.

> *Under the specious pretext of effecting "the happiness of the whole
> community," nearly all the wrongs and intrusions of government have been*

carried through. The legislature may, and should, when such things fall in its way, lend its potential weight to the cause of virtue and happiness, but to legislate in direct behalf of those objects is never available and rarely effects any even temporary benefit.

Whitman's emphasis on limited, strategic governmental intervention underscores the difference between compassion and effective compassion; the former can embrace platitudinous gestures and political grandstanding, while the latter emphasizes fruitful efforts on behalf of those in need. Be effective in your compassion; to do so, practice these principles.

ASK PROBING QUESTIONS — Effective compassion is tough love. If you really want to help someone, ask questions that challenge individuals to push beyond symptoms to causes. You're not being unfair or harsh when your assistance is piercing, guiding an individual to a greater understanding of personal breakdowns, which is the first step in moving beyond them.

ABUNDANCE PERSPECTIVE — Effective compassion is not a zero-sum game: moving someone forward doesn't mean trampling over others or pushing them out the way. Come to help with an abundant mind-set: there are always enough opportunities to go around for those who are prepared to seize them. Commit yourself to help others discover what pieces of the progress puzzle they are missing; create opportunities for them put their lives together.

ACTION PLAN — Dependency means others are doing things for persons in need that they should be doing for themselves. A daily plan of action corrects this: it guides the disadvantaged to do constructive things for themselves. Whether it's working on getting more education or training, finding or upgrading work, gaining or enhancing sobriety — whatever — your work is to assist the striver in developing a customized action plan that can be followed daily.

ACCOUNTABILITY PROCESS — "How are you doing with your action plan?" . . . "Did you reach your goal this week?" . . . "Did you make progress today?" . . . "Did you make it to your support group on time?" . . . These are the questions you need to ask to hold people you're trying to help accountable. To be effective in your compassion, you have to make sure that they stick to their plans for moving forward.

APRIL: PERSEVERANCE
DAILY SUCCESS PRINCIPLES

1. Persevere With Your Virtues — George Washington Carver — 1896
2. Persevere With Grace — Eleanor Roosevelt — 1932
3. Declare It's Not Over — Benjamin Rush — 1787
4. Keep On Being Yourself — Zora Neale Hurston — 1937
5. Get Through It Somehow —Equiano — 1745
6. Be A Voice Of Endurance And Triumph — William Faulkner — 1949
7. Persevere Through Inner Turmoil: The Black Experience — Charlotte Forten Grimke — 1837
8. Persevere Through Inner Turmoil: The White Experience — Mary Boykin Chesnut — 1864
9. Avoid The Words: I Can't — Elbert Hubbard —1899
10. Affirm The Words: I Can — Redoshi — 1860
11. Keep Going For It — Bessie Coleman — 1922
12. Learn To Labor And To Wait — African American Bostonians — 1844
13. Make It Through Your Turning Point — Emma Willard — 1819
14. Keep Marching Towards Your Goal — A. Phillip Randolph — 1941
15. Stick To The Fight When You're Hardest Hit — Joseph Holland — 1988
16. Persevere Through Suffering — Charles Sumner — 1856
17. Transform Failure Into Success — Frances Wright — 1825
18. Ride Your Momentum — W.E.B. DuBois — 1903
19. Surmount Difficulties Through Perseverance —Abigail Adams — 1775
20. Keep Playing Your Music — William Handy — 1905
21. Persevere In Your Calling — Antoinette Blackwell — 1853
22. Persevere For Your Rights — African American South Carolinians — 1791
23. Overturn Your Obstacles — Elizabeth Cady Stanton — 1860
24. Possess The Spirit To Go On —John Steinbeck — 1939
25. Persevere Through Dreary Days — African American Virginians — 1865
26. Push Yourself Through Hard Times — Irvin Wilson — 1932
27. Blaze Your Trails — Lorenzo Dow — 1804
28. Persevere As A Leader — Oliver Ellsworth — 1787
29. Persevere To Be Who You Truly Are — Anna May Wong — 1922
30. Draw Lessons As You Go — Andrew Jackson — 1837

PERSEVERE WITH YOUR VIRTUES   APRIL 1ST

Start where you are, with what you have. Make something of it and never be satisfied.
George Washington Carver

Born into slavery in Diamond Grove, Missouri in the early 1860's, George Washington Carver was kidnapped by night raiders from Arkansas when he was only a week old. His white master Moses Carver was able to recover baby George but not his mother and sister. The boy's educational journey was rocky. Because African American children weren't allowed at Diamond Grove public schools, he had to travel ten miles to a school for black kids.

Carver persevered in his educational pursuits. After being accepted at Highland University, he was rejected when he arrived on campus because of his race. He didn't give up, earning money at odd jobs as well as maintaining a small farm. His agricultural work opened the door to his becoming the first black student at Iowa State Agricultural College.

In 1896 Carver was recruited by trailblazing educator Booker T. Washington to head the Agriculture Department at Tuskegee Institute (now Tuskegee University). Drawing from his own experiences, Carver focused on the intellectual advancement and character development of his students, imparting the virtues to his students that he himself had lived out. And because of the renown that he gained from his innovative agricultural applications for peanuts, sweet potatoes and other plants, he developed a national platform, meeting with three U.S. Presidents and touring white Southern colleges for the Commission on Interracial Cooperation. Carver persevered with his moral messaging, from his college students to a national audience.

TO THE STUDENTS —

Be clean both inside and out.

Neither look up to the rich nor down on the poor.

Lose, if need be, without squealing.

Win without bragging.

Always be considerate of women, children, and older people.

Be too brave to lie.

Be too generous to cheat.

Take your share of the world and let others take theirs.

TO THE NATION —

Education is the key to unlock the golden door of freedom.

Happiness and moral duty are inseparably connected.

It is impossible to reason without arriving at a Supreme Being.

Worry is the interest paid by those who borrow trouble.

It is better to be alone than in bad company.

It is better to offer no excuse than a bad one.

Heed the lessons of Carver's singular life. Build your own perseverance by taking his virtues with you. Pick the three from each of the above lists that mean the most to you. Memorize them. Put them into practice. This strategy will lead you breakthroughs, for yourself and perhaps even for those in your community who will benefit from your example.

PERSEVERE WITH GRACE   **APRIL 2ND**

People grow through experience if they meet life
honestly and courageously. This is how character is built.
Eleanor Roosevelt

In 1918, after thirteen years of marriage, future First Lady Eleanor Roosevelt discovered a bundle of love letters to her husband from her social secretary Lucy Mercer. The revelation that Franklin was considering divorcing her to marry Mercer devastated Eleanor. Yet she persevered through the traumatic marriage by emphasizing their political partnership and becoming more active in social work and public life.

Three years later, Franklin was diagnosed with a paralytic illness that permanently limited the mobility of his legs. Eleanor's steadfast care of her disabled husband stabilized his health and sustained his hope in a political career. Throughout Franklin's electoral ascent, first as New York State governor followed by his election as U.S. President, Eleanor served as a surrogate for her incapacitated husband, traveling widely to make speeches and public appearances on his behalf, becoming a key adviser on political matters.

As First Lady for Franklin's four terms, Eleanor pressed on as a trailblazer: outspoken on civil rights for African Americans as well as being the first presidential spouse to write daily newspaper and monthly magazine columns, hold regular press conferences, speak at a national party convention and host a weekly radio show. Even after Franklin's death in 1945, Roosevelt kept up her exemplary service as the first chair of the United Nations Commission on Human Rights and the Presidential Commission on the Status of Women.

Enduring the hard times, Roosevelt persevered with grace and rose to positions of legendary influence. Her example is yours to emulate, and her wise counsel — expressed in her own words — yours to follow. Persevere with grace through your:

POWER — *A woman is like a tea bag - you can't tell how strong she is until you put her in hot water.*

PERSISTENCE — *Courage is more exhilarating than fear and in the long run it is easier. We do not have to become heroes over night. Just a step at a time, meeting each thing that comes up, seeing it is not as dreadful as it appeared, discovering we have the strength to stare it down. . . . Nothing has ever been achieved by the person who says, 'It can't be done.'*

PLUCK — *Do one thing every day that scares you.*

PARTNERS — *Many people will walk in and out of your life, but only true friends will leave footprints in your heart.*

PERSPECTIVE — *To handle yourself, use your head; to handle others, use your heart.*

PLEASE-NOT — *I can't tell you how to succeed, but I can tell you how to fail: Try to please everybody.*

PRUDENCE — *Someone once asked me what I regarded as the three most important requirements for happiness. My answer was: A feeling that you have been honest with yourself and those around you; a feeling that you have done the best you could both in your personal life and in your work; and the ability to love others.*

PATRIOTISM — *True patriotism springs from a belief in the dignity of the individual, freedom and equality not only for Americans but for all people on earth, universal brotherhood and*

156

*good will, and a constant and earnest striving toward the principles
and ideals on which this country was founded.*

PRESENT — *Tomorrow is a mystery. Today is a gift. That is
why it is called the present.*

DECLARE: IT'S NOT OVER!   APRIL 3RD

*The American war is over, but this is far from being the case with American
Revolution. On the contrary, nothing but the first act of the great drama is closed.
It remains yet . . . to prepare the principles, morals, and manners of our citizens.*
                              Benjamin Rush

In May 1787, delegates from the thirteen states were arriving in
Philadelphia for the Federal Convention to determine the new form of
American government. Renowned medical doctor (He had served
as Surgeon General of the Continental Army.) Benjamin Rush was a
member of the Pennsylvania host delegation. He was one of the strongest
voices for discarding the existing Articles of Confederation and creating a
brand new governing system — a strategy receiving a lukewarm reception.
To foster support for the work of the gathering Constitutional Convention
delegates, Rush delivered an address to inspire his fellow citizens to
persevere as American revolutionaries, in which he contrasted the American
Experiment with the governmental experience of Great Britain and other
European countries.

> *Look at the steps by which governments have been changed or
rendered stable in Europe. Read the history of Great Britain. Her boasted
government has risen out of wars and rebellions that lasted above 600 years.
The United States are traveling peaceably into order and good government.
They know no strife but what arises from the collision of opinions; and in three
years they have advanced further in the road to stability and happiness than
most of the nations in Europe have done in as many centuries.*

He concluded his remarks, challenging his countrymen.

> *. . . the patriots and heroes of the war. They resemble skillful
mariners who, after exerting themselves to preserve a ship from sinking in a
storm in the middle of the ocean, drop asleep as soon as the waves subside, and
leave the care of their lives during the remainder of the voyage to sailors
without knowledge or experience. Every man in a republic is pubic property.
His time and talents, his youth, his manhood, his old age — nay, more, his*

life, his all —belong to his country. . . . Patriots of 1774, 1775, 1776 — heroes of 1778, 1779, 1780! Come forward! . . . Your country forgives your timidity and demands your influence and advice! Hear her proclaiming, in sighs and groans, in her governments, in her finances, in her manufactures, in her morals, "The Revolution is not over!"

Regarding his life's overarching mission, Rush declared: "It's not over!" To reinforce your persevering spirit, you should do the same; you will declare your own mission as not over as you:

ADORE IT — Love what you do. Your passion will spawn a persevering a state of mind, a heroic attitude, making it easier for you to say:

I'll get through it, no matter what it takes!

AFFIRM IT — Memorize baseball legend Yogi Berra's simple statement:

It ain't over til it's over.

ALLURE IT — Declare it to others; they will be attracted to your cause. Rush exhorted his contemporaries to get over the disappointment and frustration that prevailed in the minds of so many. It's also time for you to grab any lingering negative feelings — emotional barriers to your personal progress — and leave them behind you so you can decree to others:

I'm greater than my circumstances. They won't hold me back!

ASCEND IT — Rise up through your declarations. Let refreshing thoughts and feelings rise from your soul. Speak empowering words. Activate your persevering state of mind. You'll get through anything when you declare:

You're not in you control of me. I'm in control of you!

## KEEP ON BEING YOURSELF							APRIL 4TH

Such as I am, I am a precious gift.
Zora Neale Hurston

In 1937 African American writer Zora Neale Hurston published the novel "Their Eyes Were Watching God", widely regarded as her master work. The attainment was a long time coming. Hurston was born in Alabama in 1891 and had a literary awakening a decade later when some northern schoolteachers visited her town with a trove of books. But she was suffered an educational setback as a teenager, dismissed from boarding school because her parents couldn't keep up with tuition. Hurston didn't graduate from high school until she was 27. She so distinguished herself as a Howard University student that she earned a scholarship to Barnard College of Columbia University, where she became the only black student. Hurston graduated with a bachelor's degree in anthropology at 37.

Through all her academic journeying, she managed to find time to write creatively, which eventually connected her to Langston Hughes and other Harlem Renaissance writers. This association fueled her passion. Her creative perseverance yielded several short stories, a play, musical revues, the critically acclaimed "Mules and Men", all of which paved the way for "Their Eyes Were Watching God", which firmly established her literary reputation.

A significant part of her writing explored her struggles as African American woman, and the wisdom she gain enduring through the challenges. Hurston kept on being herself, boldly and creatively expressing her identity in ways that elevated the black experience in America. Her insights are priceless and timeless; the following passages project principles for you to follow as you persevere in living out the person you're destined to be.

COURAGE — *I have the nerve to walk my own way, however hard, in my search for reality, rather than climb upon the rattling wagon of wishful illusions.*

CONTENTMENT — *Sometimes, I feel discriminated against, but it does not make me angry. It merely astonishes me. How can any deny themselves the pleasure of my company? It's beyond me.*

CONFRONTATION — *If you are silent about your pain, they'll kill you and say you enjoyed it.*

CONFIDENCE — *I am not tragically colored. There is no great sorrow dammed up in my soul, nor lurking behind my eyes. I do not mind at all. I do not belong to the sobbing school of Negrohood who hold that nature somehow has given them a lowdown dirty deal and whose feelings are all hurt about it. Even in the helter-skelter skirmish that is my life, I have seen that the world is to the strong regardless of a little pigmentation more or less. No, I do not weep at the world — I am too busy sharpening my oyster knife.*

CONSCIOUSNESS — *Everybody has some special road of thought along which they travel when they are alone to themselves. And his road of thought is what makes every man what he is.*

CURIOSITY — *Research is formalized curiosity. It is poking and prying with a purpose.*

CLAIRVOYANCE — *Learning without wisdom is a load of books on a donkey's back.*

CLARITY — *If you haven't got it, you can't show it. If you have got it, you can't hide it.*

COWARDICE — *Bitterness is the coward's revenge on the world for having been hurt.*

CONQUEST — *I have been in Sorrow's kitchen and licked out all the pots. Then I have stood on the peaky mountain wrapped in rainbows, with a harp and sword in my hands.*

As you meditate upon and apply these "Zora Principles" to your life, you will discover new strength to keep on being yourself.

GET THROUGH IT SOMEHOW   APRIL 5TH

I now saw myself deprived of all chance of returning to my native country.
Olaudah Equiano

Olaudah Equiano was born in 1745 in the Igbo region of what is today southeastern Nigeria. When he was eleven, Equiano was captured and sold to European slave traders who transported him to Barbados. Through several transactions he ended up working on Virginia plantations, traveling extensively on the seas (A Royal Navy lieutenant who owned him renamed him Gustavus Vassa.), eventually moving in Philadelphia where he worked for an American merchant from whom he bought his freedom.

Through his journeying away from the grind of American plantation life, Equiano learned to read and write, one of the few slaves to gain an education. Once free, he moved to London, became active in the abolitionist movement and was encouraged to write his story. In 1789 Equiano's autobiography, The Interesting Narrative of the Life of Gustavus Vassa, The African, was published and became a best seller, not only widely read in England but it went on to be published in Germany, Holland, Russia and and the United States.

The first influential slave narrative, the book gave a detailed account of Equiano's experience on the slave trip from Africa to the West Indies. An excerpt follows.

> *. . . I was soon put down under the decks, and there I received such a salutation in my nostrils as I had never experienced in my life; so that, with the loathsomeness of the stench and crying together, I became so sick and low that I was not able to eat, nor had I the least desire to taste anything. I now wished for the last friend, death, to relieve me; but soon, to my grief, two of the white men offered me eatables; and, on my refusing to eat, one of them held me fast . . . the other flogged me severely.*

Equiano also described how the slave traders' inhumanity was not limited to his race.

> *I feared I should be put to death, the white people looked and acted, as I thought, in so savage a manner; for I had never seen among any people such instances of brutal cruelty; and this not only shown toward us blacks but also to some of the whites themselves. One white man in particular I saw, when we were permitted to be on deck, was flogged so unmercifully with a large rope near the foremast that he died in consequence of it; and they tossed him over the side as they would have done a brute. . . .*

Equiano's book helped to build momentum for the abolitionist movement leading to the milestone legislation — the British Slave Trade Act of 1807 — which abolished the transatlantic slave trade for Great Britain and its colonies. To achieve great things, he somehow got through the worst things. Let his example live for you. Whatever hard time you're going through, get through it somehow. To do so, keep these four factors of your inner life in mind.

FATIGUE — The stormy circumstances of life can wear you out. Don't let it happen. Remember, whatever you're going through, it's not worse than a slave ship. If Equiano got through that, you can get through yours. There's no formula for survival. Just make up your mind to do so. Hold onto Winston Churchill's advice:

If you're going through hell, keep going.

FRUSTRATION — "Why is this happening to me?" Stop asking questions; instead focus on finding the silver lining in your clouds.

FEAR — This is your biggest enemy; it will make you feel like giving up. That's why you need the next point.

FAITH — This is the X-factor. If your faith is strong enough, it's the one positive force that will countervail and overcome the three negative ones listed above. At times your best option — your only option — is to simply believe.

BE A VOICE OF ENDURANCE AND TRIUMPH   APRIL 6TH

Never be afraid to raise your voice for honesty, truth and compassion against injustice, lying and greed. If people all over the world...would do this, it would change the earth.
William Faulkner

The 1949 Nobel Prize for Literature was awarded to William Faulkner, one of the most celebrated writers of twentieth century America. On December 10, 1950, William Faulkner delivered his Nobel Prize acceptance speech in Stockholm. Faulkner's creative work — mostly set in the fictional Yoknapatawpha County, based on his Mississippi home — had been better known for exploring the complexities and evils of human nature rather than affirming its straightforwardness and virtue. His remarks came in the midst of the new uncertainties of the nuclear age; his words confronted this challenge.

I decline to accept the end of man. It is easy enough to say that man is immortal simply because he will endure; that when the last ding-dong of doom has clanged and faded from the last worthless rock hanging tideless in the last red and dying evening, that even then there will still be one more sound: that of his puny, inexhaustible voice, still talking.

At other points throughout his literary career, Faulkner exalted hope over despair, asserting that in persistence there is triumph. His was a voice of endurance and triumph. As you read his words and reflect on the corresponding principles, consider how your own voice can ring with endurance and triumph.

VOICE — *I believe that man will not merely endure: he will prevail. He is immortal, not because he alone among creatures has an inexhaustible voice, but because he has a soul, a spirit capable of compassion and sacrifice and endurance. The poet's, the writer's duty is to write about these things. It is his privilege to help man endure by lifting his heart, by reminding him of the courage and honor and hope and pride and compassion and pity and sacrifice which have been the glory of his past. The poet's voice need not merely be the record of man; it can be one of the props, the pillars to help him endure and prevail.*

Watch what you say. If you are constantly stating you won't make it, then you will end up giving up. It's just a matter of time.

VISION — *Always dream and shoot higher than you know you can do. Don't bother just to be better than your contemporaries or predecessors. Try to be better than yourself.*

It's more important for you to set standards for yourself — and set them high — than for you to pay attention to what others are doing. And once you set those personal standards, hold yourself accountable to them; it will add fuel to your endurance.

VIGILANCE — *At one time I thought the most important thing was talent. I think now that the young man must possess or teach himself, training himself, in infinite patience, which is to try and to try until it comes right.*

Faulkner's right on point: keep trying and trying and you will eventually get it right, which will lead to . . .

VICTORY — *If we Americans are to survive it will have to be because we choose and elect and defend to be first of all Americans; to present to the world one homogeneous and unbroken front, whether of white Americans or black ones or purple or blue or green . . .*

Once you succeed in achieving your personal goals, don't stop there. The greater success happens when you shine your victorious example to bring people together.

PERSEVERE THROUGH INNER TURMOIL — THE BLACK
EXPERIENCE   APRIL 7TH

Would that those with whom I shall recite tomorrow could sympathize with me
in this; would that they could look upon all God's creatures without respect to
color, feeling that it is character alone which makes the true man or woman!
Charlotte Forten Grimké

Charlotte Forten Grimké was born in 1837 into a distinguished
African American family in Philadelphia. Her abolitionist parents decided to
send the teenage Charlotte north to Salem, Massachusetts for education.
Just sixteen, she heard about the capture and return of fugitive slave
Anthony Burns and wrote about it in her journal.

Our worst fears are realized. The decision was against poor Burns
and he has been sent back to a bondage worse, a thousand times worse, than
death. . . . I can write no more. A cloud seems hanging over me, over all our
persecuted race, which nothing can dispel.

Subsequent journal entries reveal how very difficult it was for this
young woman to live through the racial challenges of her day. Study her
writings and the principles they project. Her words can help open a window
to your own soul as you persevere through inner turmoil.

SEARCH FOR ESCAPE — *Oh, England, my heart yearns*
toward thee . . . far from the land, my native land, where I am hated and
oppressed because God has given me a dark skin. How did this cruel, this
absurd prejudice ever exist? How can it exit?

SINCERE REFLECTION — *. . . . hatred of oppression seems*
to me so blended with hatred of the oppressor I cannot separate them. I feel
that no other injury could be so hard to bear, so very hard to forgive, as that
inflicted by cruel prejudice. How can I be a Christian when so many in common
with myself, for no crime, suffer so cruelly, so unjustly?

SUFFER THROUGH REJECTION — *. . . . I have met*
girls in the schoolroom — they have been thoroughly kind and cordial to me;
perhaps the next day met them in the street — they feared to recognize me;
these I can but regard now with scorn and contempt. Once I like them, believing
them incapable of such meanness. . . . O! It is hard to go through life . . .
fearing, with too good reason, to love and trust hardly anyone whose skin is
white, however lovable, attractive, and congenial in seeming.

SEEK ANSWERS — *In the bitter, passionate feeling of my soul, again and again there rises the questions — "When, oh! When shall this cease?" "Is there no help?" "How long, oh! How long must we continue to suffer, to endure?"*

Forten Grimké persevered through her inner turmoil and rose from these trials to become a prominent anti-slavery activist, poet, and educator. During the Civil War she was the first black teacher to go to the South Carolina Sea Islands and participate in the Port Royal Experiment, a federal initiative to instruct 10,000 former slaves in their transition to freedom. While there, Forten Grimké befriended Robert Gould Shaw, the Commander of the all-black 54th Massachusetts Regiment. Shaw led his men into the Sea Islands Campaign, when they stormed Fort Wagner on the night of July 18, 1863. Forten Grimké was present that night, when Shaw and most of his regiment were killed; she volunteered as a nurse to help the surviving members.

Whatever mental anguish or emotional distress you're going through, your experience is likely not as anguishing as Forten Grimké's experience growing up a free black woman in antebellum America. She persevered and contributed greatly to the cause of her people. If she got through her inner turmoil, you can get through yours.

PERSEVERE THROUGH INNER TURMOIL — THE WHITE EXPERIENCE   APRIL 8TH

These stories of our defeats in the valley fall like blows upon a dead body. Since Atlanta fell, I have felt as if all were dead within me forever. . . .
Mary Boykin Chesnut

In 1823 Mary Boykin Chesnut was born into the upper-class circles of Southern planter society and married a lawyer, living comfortably on a South Carolina estate. With a husband who eventually became a Confederate officer and U.S. Senator, Chesnut kept her anti-slavery views private. With the advent of the Civil War, she transformed her journal into a diary describing the war, detailing her emotional turmoil and downfall of her way of life.

Her journal entries described the challenges of her era, on the battlefield and in her soul. They also point to principles for you to follow.

DESPONDENCY — *February 19, 1861, Montgomery, Alabama. I am despondent once more. . . . We have to meet tremendous odds by pluck, activity, zeal, dash, entrance of the toughest, military instinct. . . .*

Everywhere political intrigue is as rife as in Washington. . . .

DESPARATION — *April 13, 1861, Charleston, South Carolina. Fort Sumter has been on fire. . . . But the sound of those guns makes regular meals impossible. None of us go to table. Tea trays pervade the corridors going everywhere. Some of the anxious hearts lie on their beds and moan in solitary misery.*

DIET — *May 24, 1862, Columbia, South Carolina. The enemy are landing at Georgetown. . . . If it be true, I hope some cool-headed white men will make the Negroes save the rice for us. It is so much needed. They say it might have been done at Port Royal with a little more energy. . . .*

DREAD — *March 24, 1864. Columbia, South Carolina. Yesterday, we went to the capitol grounds to see our returned prisoners. We walked slowly up and down until Jeff Davis was called upon to speak. There I stood, almost touching the bayonets when he left me. I looked straight into the prisoners' faces. . . . These men were so forlorn, so dried up and shrunken, with such a strange look in some of their eyes . . . A poor woman was too much for me. She was searching for her son. . . . he was taken prisoner at Gettysburg. She kept going in and out among them with a basket of provisions she had brought for him to eat. It was too pitiful. She was utterly unconscious of the crowd. The anxious dread, expectation, hurry, and hope which led her on showed in her face.*

Chesnut persevered with her writing throughout the military conflict; by the war's end her diary contained over 400,000 words. Facing the post-war financial hardships of a debt-ridden plantation, Chesnut plodded on, preparing herself to revise her diary as a book by translating French poetry and writing essays, a family history and three unpublished novels. In the 1880s she edited the diary into a book for publication, featuring slavery's complexities, especially the sexual abuses of black women at the hands of white men. She died, however, before the book was ever published. It was eventually published three times, the last a Pulitzer Prize-winning edition in 1982. And extensive readings from the book were included in Ken Burns' documentary television series, "The Civil War".

If Mary Boykin Chesnut made it through the collapse of her world and the concomitant emotional distress to create an important record of crucial moments in America history, you can make it through your present turmoil, no matter how trying it is. And her legacy has endured over century; yours could, too!

AVOID THE WORDS — "I CAN'T"   APRIL 9TH

A little more persistence, a little more effort, and what
seemed hopeless failure may turn to glorious success.
Elbert Hubbard

In April 1898, just prior to the outbreak of the Spanish–American War, President William McKinley decided to reach out surreptitiously to General Calixto García, commander of the Cuban insurgent forces in their fight against Spain. All McKinley and his top advisers knew was that Garcia was stationed somewhere in the Sierra Maestra Mountains of Cuba. They chose U.S. Army Lieutenant Andrew Rowan for the mission of finding Garcia and delivering McKinley's letter to him.

Posing as a civilian, Rowan traveled alone on this secret foray. In Kingston, Jamaica, he connected with some members of the Cuban Revolutionary Junta, who helped him on his journey to see Garcia. They first traveled by boat to Cuba, then over a week on horseback through hostile territory, sometimes trekking through the jungle. Rowan eventually discovered Garcia's hideout in the mountains and delivered the President's letter to him, which was instrumental in shaping a collaborative military effort leading to a U.S. invasion of Cuba and victory in the war against Spain.

In March 1899 writer Elbert Hubbard published "A Message to Garcia", a piece of creative nonfiction based on the true story of Rowan's successful mission the year before. The essay highlights Rowan's determination as he overcame myriad obstacles and delivered the message to Garcia. Hubbard exalts Rowan as a role model of hard work and perseverance in delivering "A Message to Garcia".

My heart goes out to the man who does his work when the "boss" is away as well as when he is at home. And the man who, when given a letter for Garcia, quietly takes the missive, without asking any idiotic questions, and with no lurking intention of chucking it into the nearest sewer, or of doing aught else but deliver it, never gets "laid off," . . . Civilization is one long, anxious search for just such individuals. Anything such a man asks shall be granted; his kind is so rare that no employer can afford to let him go. He is wanted in every city, town, and village — in every office, shop, store, and factory. The world cries out for such; he is needed, and needed badly — the man who can carry a message to Garcia.

If you want to achieve anything important in life, perseverance is an essential quality. Just as Hubbard lionized the persistence of Rowan in pursuit of Garcia, poet Edgar Guest memorably affirmed similar themes in

"Can't." Meditate on this poem and its principles to strengthen your commitment to avoid using the words — "I Can't".

DO NO HARM:
Can't is the worst word that's written or spoken;
Doing more harm here than slander and lies;
On it is many a strong spirit broken,
And with it many a good purpose dies.
It springs from the lips of the thoughtless each morning
And robs us of courage we need through the day;
It rings in our ears like a timely sent warning
And laughs when we falter and fall by the way.

DARE TO SUCCEED:
Can't is the father of feeble endeavor,
The parent of terror and halfhearted work;
It weakens the efforts of artisans clever,
And makes of the toiler an indolent shirk.
It poisons the soul of the man with a vision,
It stifles in infancy many a plan;
It greets honest toiling with open derision
And mocks at the hopes and the dreams of a man.

Here's your challenge. Strive to possess the persistence of Rowan by making a promise to your yourself never to proclaim the words: "I can't". Do this and your goals will track you down.

AFFIRM THE WORDS — "I CAN!"   **APRIL 10TH**

Mama exhorted her children at every opportunity to 'jump at the sun.'
We might not land on the sun, but at least we would get off the ground.
Zora Neale Hurston

In 1860, twelve-year-old Redoshi was taken from her village in West Africa; the men who kidnapped her killed her father. She sailed across the Atlantic, surviving the treacherous Middle Passage on board the Clotilda, the last recorded slave ship to come to the United States after 240 years of slavery. She landed along the Mobile-Tensaw River Delta in Alabama, where Redoshi began her journey as a slave girl in America.

Redoshi was soon sold to a man named Washington Smith and made a child bride to an enslaved man. Given the name Sally Smith, she later described the experience.

I was 12 years old and he was a man from another tribe who had a family in Africa. I couldn't understand his talk and he couldn't understand me. They put us on block together and sold us for man and wife.

Redoshi was moved to a plantation in Bogue Chitto, Alabama, where she lived through the Civil War. Though she became a free woman when the ratification of the 13th Amendment abolished slavery in 1865, she remained on the Smith plantation for the remainder of her life. Until her death in 1937, Redoshi's perseverance made her the last living survivor of the trans-Atlantic slave trade in the United States.

A few years earlier, while doing research in the South for her literary works, the Harlem Renaissance author Zora Neale Hurston discovered Redoshi, who emerged in some of Hurston's unpublished writings. Redoshi also appeared in "The Negro Farmer: Extension Work for Better Farming and Better Living," a U.S. Department of Agriculture instructional video released in 1938. This film is the only known footage of a woman who survived the Middle Passage.

Redoshi persevered through the physical and psychological trauma of her West African capture, transport to America, young life as a slave, and through many years of plantation servitude. The fact that she lived to eighty-four demonstrates her exceptional fortitude, a life that refutes the words "I can't" and affirms "I can". The concluding lines of the Edgar Guest poem best capture Redoshi's "I can" spirit; and they project precepts for you to embrace.

DREAM EXALTED:
Can't is a word none should speak without blushing;
To utter it should be a symbol of shame;
Ambition and courage it daily is crushing;
It blights a man's purpose and shortens his aim.
Despise it with all of your hatred of error;
Refuse it the lodgment it seeks in your brain;
Arm against it as a creature of terror,
And all that you dream of you someday shall gain.

DEMON DEFEATED:
Can't is the word that is foe to ambition,
An enemy ambushed to shatter your will;
Its prey is forever the man with a mission
And bows but to courage and patience and skill.
Hate it, with hatred that's deep and undying,
For once it is welcomed 'twill break any man;
Whatever the goal you are seeking, keep trying

And answer this demon by saying: "I can."

The next time you're feeling like there's something you can't do —
remember Redoshi. Whatever you're facing pales in comparison to the
challenges of her life. Declare the words: "Redoshi can, and I can, too!" . . .
And keep saying — "I can!" . . . Let the spirit of this great woman energize
you to defeat every "I Can't" Demon on your way to success.

KEEP GOING FOR IT!   APRIL 11TH

The air is the only place free from prejudices. I knew we had no aviators,
neither men nor women, and I knew the Race needed to be represented along
this most important line, so I thought it my duty to risk my life to learn aviation.
Bessie Coleman

On January 26, 1892, Bessie Coleman was born to
Texas sharecroppers George (of Native American and African American
descent) and Susan (African American). To make it through grade school
Coleman had to endure the cotton harvests disrupting her education as well
as the daily 4-mile walk to her segregated, one-room school. She worked
throughout her teenage years to save enough to enroll in the Oklahoma
Colored Agricultural and Normal University but left after one semester
without the money to continue.

Hearing accounts of World War I pilots returning home from war,
Coleman was inspired to become a pilot, but American flight schools of her
era didn't admit women or blacks. She worked two jobs and found
sponsorship to gather the funds to study abroad. She learned French in
Chicago then left for Paris, where she became the first woman of African-
American and Native American descent to earn an aviation pilot's license.

Coleman's commitment to keep going for it paid off. First
appearing in a 1922 event honoring veterans of the all-black 369th Infantry
Regiment of World War I, she became an airborne celebrity, known as
"Queen Bess" for her daring aviation in flight shows all across the U.S. Like
Coleman, you can fulfill your dreams if you keep going for it. Do your best
to follow her example by living out these principles.

LISTEN FOR DIRECTION — Growing up, Coleman
didn't have any exposure to flying. She didn't know anyone
involved in aviation; it just wasn't a part of her world. But as a
young woman, she overheard some conversations of military pilots
sharing their experiences. That moment so intrigued her that it
changed the direction of her life. Pay attention to what's happening

in your immediate environment — what people around you are saying and doing. Clues to your destiny may be discoverable, if you open a little more your ears and eyes. Be vigilant. Learn something from every encounter, even the unexpected ones. Embrace every moment as a potential key to the door of your brighter future. Say to yourself — "Today, and everyday, I will keep going for it!" — and you will discover new opportunities in surprising places.

LEVERAGE YOUR OPPORTUNITIES — You may be asking yourself: how do I fulfill my dreams without the money to do so? Take note of Coleman's pursuit. She leveraged her work ethic — holding down two jobs — and her relationships — working her contacts. In these ways she succeeded in putting together the resources to travel to Europe and access knowledge unavailable to her in her own country. Don't focus on what you don't have. Concentrate on what you can create. Be proactive about using your work ethic and relationships to generate the resources you need to pursue your dream.

LEARN FROM YOUR EXPERIENCES — Reflect on your past mistakes. Figure out what went wrong and draw lessons from it. You won't be able to persevere if you keep getting stuck in the revolving door of doing the same thing in the same way, which will leave you in emotional stagnation, causing you to feel like throwing in the towel. Resolve to use your past as experiential building blocks to develop the fortitude leading to your success.

LIFT YOUR LEGACY — Coleman lost her life in a plane crash when she was 36. Her friends and family had discouraged her from flying a plane with mechanical issues that she had recently purchased. Though she died young, she lifted a legacy that long endured. Mae Jemison, the first African American woman astronaut, who soared decades after Coleman, shared about her example.

It's tempting to draw parallels between me and Ms. Coleman . . .[but] I point to Bessie Coleman and say here is a woman, a being, who exemplifies and serves as a model for all humanity, the very definition of strength, dignity, courage, integrity, and beauty.

What you do today — if you keep going for it — can live on to touch future generations. Fly high with your life; create a star in the sky for those who come after you to reach for.

LEARN TO LABOR AND TO WAIT   APRIL 12TH

Resolved, that we consider the late action of the School Committee,
in regard to our petition asking for the entire abolition of separate
schools for colored children, as erroneous and unsatisfactory.
Black citizens of Boston

Not all efforts to attain racial justice in antebellum America were focused on slavery in the Southern states. In the early 1840's African Americans in Boston petitioned the School Committee there to abolish segregated schools and had their several petitions rejected. On June 24, 1844, a mass meeting of black Bostonians objected to these denials and demanded the School Committee reconsider.

Whereas, we, the colored citizens of the city of Boston, have recently
sent a petition to the School Committee respectfully praying for the abolition of
the separate schools for colored children, and asking for the rights and privileges
extended to other citizens in respect to the common-school system, the right to
send our children to the schools established in the respective districts in which we
reside . . .

The Boston School Committee did not reconsider; segregation continued; the black Bostonians persevered. In addition to incessant petitions, a court case — Roberts v. Boston — was brought in 1850. The plaintiff was five-year-old African American Sarah Roberts, attending an underfunded all-black common school far from her home in Boston, denied admittance to the white-only school much closer to where she lived. When the Massachusetts Supreme Judicial Court ruled against Sarah, her father Benjamin Roberts, with the assistance of his attorneys, U.S. Senator Charles Sumner and Robert Morris (one of the first African-American lawyers in the U.S.), lobbied the state legislature. Finally, in 1855, the Commonwealth of Massachusetts passed a law prohibiting segregated schools in the state, the first such law in the United States.

Their fellow New Englander, Henry Wadsworth Longfellow, might have had the perseverance of the black Bostonians in overturning school segregation in mind when he penned the following poem. Note the principles that rise it; apply them to your own life.

PROGRESS:
Not enjoyment, and not sorrow,
Is our destined end or way;
But act, that each tomorrow
Find us further than today.

PROVIDENCE:
Trust no Future, howe'er pleasant!
Let the dead Past bury its dead!
Act — act in the living Present!
Heart within, and God o'erhead!

PARADIGM:
Lives of great men all remind us
We can make our lives sublime
And, departing, leave behind us
Footprints on the sands of time;

PULL UP:
Footprints, that perhaps another,
Sailing o'er life's solemn main,
A forlorn and shipwrecked brother,
Seeing, shall take heart again.

PATIENCE:
Let us, then, be up and doing,
With a heart for any fate;
Still achieving, still pursuing,
Learn to labor and to wait.

MAKE IT THROUGH YOUR TURNING POINT   APRIL 13TH

In those great republics which have fallen, the loss of republican manner and virtues has been the invariable precursor of their loss of the republican form of government. But is it not the power of our sex to give society its tone, both as to manners and morals?
Emma Willard

In 1819 women's rights activist and educator Emma Willard addressed the New York Legislature about greater support for women's education. It had been a long and windy road for Willard to reach this turning point. Born in Berlin, Connecticut, she was largely self-taught, not attending her first school until she was fifteen. As Willard worked hard on her education, she became increasingly aware that public funds were being used to raise academic standards in men's schools, but schools for women lacked sufficient resources, sound facilities, and substantial curricula. She made it her mission to establish the first women's school for higher education.

After holding several teaching jobs, she gained in 1807 the position of principal at the Middlebury Female Seminary in Vermont. Frustrated by the inadequate curriculum and her inability to change things, she left there to start in 1814 a women's boarding school in her own home. Willard was committed to improving upon the subjects taught at finishing schools by adding topics like philosophy and mathematics to her educational agenda. Believing that her cause would receive more serious attention on the road, she traveled from Vermont to New York in 1819 to present her pamphlet A Plan for Improving Female Education. In her speech to Albany leaders, she emphasized the larger implications of her strategy, placing her mission in the context of American destiny.

> *In calling on my patriotic countrymen to effect so noble an object, the consideration of national glory should not be overlooked. Ages have rolled away; barbarians have trodden the weaker sex beneath their feet . . . Nations calling themselves polite have made us the fancied idols of a ridiculous worship, and we have repaid them with ruin for their folly. But where is that wise and heroic country which has considered that our rights are sacred, though we cannot defend them?*

The all-male legislature rejected her proposal, but Willard persevered, following up with New York Governor DeWitt Clinton, who eventually promised financial support for her to open a school in Waterford, New York. That assistance did not materialize, but she did not give up, moving her school to a solid base of funding in Troy, New York. Willard's Troy Female Seminary opened in September 1821, the first school to offer higher education for women in the United States, and it operates as a top-rated, all-girls boarding school to this day.

Like Willard, things may not be going as planned for you, but you have to persevere, to make it through your turning point. To do so, you have to make these principles happen in your life.

THINK — The challenges of your life represent a fork in your road — this is your turning point. You have to think through the options. Which way will you turn? Forward or backward? . . . When you lose your job? . . . Go through a divorce? . . . Get a bad doctor's report? . . . Have your proposal rejected? . . . What will you do? . . .

TURN — Make a positive move. If not, don't do anything; it's better to wait. Don't jump from the frying pan into the fire. Willard made it through her turning point in Albany because she kept at it and found a new approach that generated the resources to attain her goal. Do your best to follow her lead. Keep turning towards the light. Remember:

A bend in the road is not the end of road unless you fail to make the turn.

TODAY — Be alert. Pay attention to potential breakthroughs. Resolve to take a new step towards your destiny , to make today the first day of the rest of your life. Plant a seed:

Great oaks from little acorns grow.

KEEP MARCHING TOWARDS YOUR GOAL   APRIL 14TH

Salvation for a race, nation or class must come from within. Freedom is never granted; it is won. Justice is never given; it is exacted.
A. Philip Randolph

In 1925 A. Philip Randolph organized the Brotherhood of Sleeping Car Porters, the first predominantly African-American labor union. His tireless efforts against unfair labor practices in relation to people of color and to gain greater employment opportunities for them led him to plan a March on Washington in 1941. The march didn't take place, so Randolph published the article "Why Should We March?", in which he explained the strategic victory that he and the other organizers had nevertheless won.

When the defense program began and billions of the taxpayers' money were appropriated for guns, ships, tanks, and bombs, Negroes presented themselves for work only to be given the cold shoulder. . . . Not until their wrath and indignation took the form of a proposed protest march on Washington, scheduled for July 1, 1941, did things begin to move in the form of defense jobs for Negroes. The march was postponed by the timely issuance of the famous Executive Order No. 8802 by President Roosevelt.

Roosevelt's Executive Order banned discrimination in war industries but not in the armed forces, so Randolph persevered.

For the plan of a protest march has not been abandoned. Its purpose would be to demonstrate that American Negroes are in deadly earnest and all out for their full rights.

After World War II Randolph continued to press for an end to discrimination in the armed services. As President Truman prepared for a tough election fight in 1948, Randolph understood that a key to Truman's electoral strategy was to gain the support of the burgeoning black population in northern states. He made it clear to the powers-that-be what black voters wanted. On July 26, 1948, President Truman issued Executive Order 9981, abolishing racial segregation in the armed forces.

Randolph kept up his strong advocacy for civil rights, finally fulfilling his goal for a March on Washington on August 28, 1963. The March attracted 250,000 people and is best remembered for Martin Luther King Jr.'s "I Have A Dream" speech. Randolph and the other leaders built on the momentum from the rally and attained breakthrough legislative triumphs: the Civil Rights Act of 1964 and the Voting Rights Act of 1965.

Randolph's perseverance helped paved the way to monumental attainments. The key was that he never stopped marching towards his goal. For you to do the same, keep these points in mind.

HEART — Determination starts on the inside; it's a matter of the heart. Randolph could have given up on his vision for a Washington March after he made his deal for black jobs in war industries. But he believed in it strongly enough that twenty-two years later he realized a dream far greater than he could have imagined.

HEAD — Learn the lessons of perseverance as you persist down the long and windy road. Randolph organized strategically, using his base of support as leverage to negotiate for advantage. Keep your head in the journey so you don't miss opportunities to pick up wins along the way.

HAND — The story of a little boy who lost his right hand in an accident is illustrative here. The boy told the doctor inquiring about his disability: "I don't have a disability; I just don't have a right hand." The boy went on to star as leading scorer on his high school basketball team. You, too, may have lost something really important, but don't give up because of what you've lost. Focus on what you have left and make the most of it.

STICK TO THE FIGHT WHEN YOU'RE HARDEST HIT
APRIL 15TH

You have to get through the short-term pain to attain the long-term gain.
Joseph Holland

Harkhomes resident Sandi had been homeless for quite some time; his biggest problem was a habit of giving up too easily. He shrank back from challenges, habitually waving the white flag of surrender at the first sign of crisis.

The first objective was for Sandi to obtain a G.E.D. He was afraid of failing the prep course and found every excuse not to try. Despite his reluctance, however, he responded to my direction and started the course. He got discouraged the first week, dropped out, refusing to go back.

To encourage Sandi, I shared with him the Biblical example of Namaan. This Old Testament figure was a great military leader, but he had a problem — he had leprosy. One day he went to the prophet Elisha for healing. His expectation was that Elisha would pray and he would be healed. Instead Elisha sent a message: go dip yourself in the river seven times to attain your healing. Namaan was outraged and stormed off. He didn't like the prophet's arduous process. But Namaan's assistant persuaded him to follow Elisha's directions, and Namaan experienced a miraculous healing.

I told Sandi: "You're just like Namaan. You want immediate, easy results. But that's not how success works; it takes times and requires doing things over and over again."

What happened next to Sandi reveals three important principles of perseverance for you to apply in your own life.

CONFESSION — Sandi heeded my counsel and started the course again, finished it, took the exam, failed miserably. Sandi was devastated — "I've had enough!" — he declared.

CLARITY — I pulled out a dog-eared sheet of paper out of my wallet, a poem kept handy for my own inspiration. I forced him to take the poem by Rudyard Kipling as he stormed out.

When things go wrong, as they sometimes will,
When the road you're trudging seems all uphill,
When the funds are low and the debts are high,
And you want to smile, but you have to sigh,
When care is pressing you down a bit,
Rest! if you must—but never quit.
. . .
Success is failure turned inside out—

The silver tint of the clouds of doubt—
And you never can tell how close you are,
It may be near when it seems afar;
So stick to the fight when you're hardest hit—
It's when things seem worst that YOU MUSTN'T QUIT.

Sandi returned to Harkhomes well before curfew. He had started reading the poem right away and read it over and over, so many times that he began to memorize it. He went back to the GED course and passed the exam on his third try. Soon thereafter a friend of a friend called with news of a job opening as a dishwasher at a nearby restaurant. Sandi went in for the interview and got the job.

CHOICE — You should heed Sandi's example. The journey of life is not a sprint but a marathon with detours and obstacles all along the way. At some point the adverse conditions will make you feel like giving up. Don't do it. Don't give up. To persevere is a spiritual endeavor, a matter of your will, strength found in your inner life. When your body is overwhelmed with fatigue, when your soul is overcome with fear and doubt, it is your spirit that empowers you to stay the course. Determine in your heart that you will never, ever give up. Perseverance is a choice: you choose—to give up or go on. Which will it be for you? Vince Lombardi said it best:

Winners never quit and quitters never win!

PERSEVERE THROUGH SUFFERING   APRIL 16TH

Moral excellence is the bright consummate flower of all progress.
Charles Sumner

On May 20, 1856, U.S. Senator Charles Sumner spoke on the Senate floor denouncing the Kansas–Nebraska Act, arguing against the spread of slavery and for the immediate admission of Kansas as a free state. He used graphic language in his "Crime Against Kansas" speech, ascribing to slavery's supporters the motivation to rape a virgin territory.

Not in any common lust for power did this uncommon tragedy have its origin. It is the rape of a virgin Territory, compelling it to the hateful embrace of slavery; and it may be clearly traced to a depraved desire for a new Slave State, hideous offspring of such a crime, in the hope of adding to the

178

power of slavery in the National Government.

Two days later, South Carolina Representative Preston Brooks assaulted Sumner in the Senate chamber, beating him with a thick cane into unconsciousness; Sumner collapsed near death in a pool of blood.

It took three years for Sumner to recover from this attack and return to the Senate. Yet he persevered through this suffering, his first speech back in the Senate chamber, delivered on June 4, 1860 — entitled "The Barbarism of Slavery". He continued to campaign far and wide for slavery's abolition. His efforts bore fruit in 1863 with the Emancipation Proclamation freeing slaves and in 1865 with the Thirteenth Amendment outlawing slavery.

When suffering comes your way — even unwarranted assault — heed Sumner's example. Don't give up. Persevere through your suffering as you:

TAKE A STAND — Winston Churchill lets you know what to expect when you take a moral stand:

You have enemies? Good. That means you've stood up for something, sometime in your life.

TOUGH IT OUT — Sumner's suffering was light compared with what the Apostle Paul endured:

Three times I was beaten with rods; once I was stoned; three times I was shipwrecked; a night and a day I have been in the deep . . .
— 2 Corinthians 11:25

If your opposing forces are fierce, get ready to tough it out.

TAKE A BREAK — Though the pain of suffering makes you feel like surrendering, keep fighting. If you have to, take a break to heal from your wounds, giving yourself time to recover. Come back stronger than ever. If you persevere, you will not have suffered in vain. Your season of brokenness will lead to showers of blessing.

TIME TO RISE — Be strong in character. Even through vicious assaults, you will rise again. The Old Testament declares your victorious outcome.

. . . for though the righteous fall seven times, they rise again . . .
— Proverbs 24:16

TENACIOUS TO THE END — *The highest greatness, surviving time and stone, is that which proceeds from the soul of man. Monarchs and cabinets, generals and admirals, with the pomp of court and the circumstance of war, in the lapse of time disappear from sight; but the pioneers of truth, though poor and lowly, especially those whose example elevates human nature, and teaches the rights of man, so that "a government of the people, by the people, for the people, may not perish from the earth;" such a harbinger can never be forgotten, and their renown spreads co-extensive with the cause they served so well.*

This statement from Sumner demonstrates that he was tenacious to the end. Whatever pain and suffering you must go through, hold on. The rewards you attain will be commensurate with the rigors you endure.

TRANSFORM FAILURE INTO SUCCESS   APRIL 17TH

What were the glories of the sun, if we knew not the gloom of darkness?
Frances Wright

Originally from Scotland, social reformer Frances Wright first traveled to America in 1818 when she was twenty-three. Wright toured the United States for two years, advocating for the immediate abolition of slavery, free public education and women's rights. In 1825 she founded the Nashoba Commune near Memphis, Tennessee, a model farm community for the purpose of educating emancipated slaves: they could work to earn their own freedom while being provided with education and being prepared to live in society. The following account of Nashoba was written in 1828 by John Humphrey Noyes, founder of the Oneida community in New York State.

This experiment was made in Shelby County, Tennessee, by the celebrated Frances Wright. The objects were to form a community in which the Negro slave should be educated and upraised to a level with the whites and thus prepared for freedom; and to set an example which, if carried out, would eventually abolish slavery in the Southern states; also to make a home for good and great men and women of all countries who might there sympathize with each other in their love and labor for humanity. She invited congenial minds from every quarter of the globe to unite with her in the search for truth and the pursuit of national happiness. Herself a native of Scotland, she became imbued with these philanthropic views through a knowledge of the sufferings of a great portion of mankind in many countries, and of the condition of the

Negro in the United States in particular.

Wright's Nashoba experiment was short-lived, plagued by a plethora of problems including an outbreak of malaria from the mosquito-infested land. After her work there failed, Wright became a leader of the New York Workingmen's Party, another ill-fated initiative. But she persevered through these failures, incorporating lessons from her experiences into speeches and books. Her Course of Popular Lectures, a special speaking tour during the 1830's that visited cities throughout the United States, drew large, enthusiastic audiences and inspired ongoing associations that were called "Fanny Wright" societies. Wright motivated her following with challenging statements:

> *All that I say is, examine, inquire. Look into the nature of things. Search out the grounds of your opinions, the for and against. Know why you believe, understand what you believe, and possess a reason for the faith that is in you.*

Just as Wright transformed failure into success, you should follow her example; to do so:

LIGHTEN UP ON YOURSELF — Don't personalize it. The fact that you experienced failure doesn't make you a failure; take the "u" out of failure. Release any shame you feel about what happened; shift your emotions; it will make room for you to grow beyond the disappointment.

LEARN FROM THE PAST — Be willing to admit — "I was wrong." Confess the breakdown to someone you trust, talk it over. Discussing the situation will help you own the failure.

LOOP IN LESSONS — Like Wright, transform your failure into success by looping your learning into new understanding, not just for your own edification. Create a platform of wisdom to share with others.

LOOK TO THE FUTURE — Take your eyes off the past and fix them on the future, where your success awaits. Recover. Be patient. Your timing is coming, if you do not give up. The Apostle Paul highlighted this truth.

> *Let us not become weary in doing good, for at the proper time we will reap a harvest if we do not give up.*
> — Galatians 6:9

RIDE YOUR MOMENTUM   APRIL 18TH

There is in this world no such force as the force of a person
determined to rise. The human soul cannot be permanently chained.
W.E.B. Du Bois

In 1903 African American leader W.E.B. Du Bois published his seminal book "The Souls of Black Folks". The first black to earn a doctorate degree from Harvard, Du Bois used a collection of fourteen essays to advocate equal economic, social and political status. He memorably captured the book's theme in its first sentence: "The problem of the Twentieth Century is the problem of the color line." Du Bois elaborated this motif in eloquent prose.

After the Egyptian and Indian, the Greek and Roman, the Teuton and Mongolian, the Negro is a sort of seventh son, born with a veil, and fitted with a second-sight in this American world — a world which yields him no true self-consciousness, but only lets him see himself through the revelation of the other world. It is a peculiar sensation, this double-consciousness, this sense of always looking at oneself through the eyes of others . . . One ever feels his twoness — an American, a Negro; two souls, two thoughts, two unreconciled strivings; two warring ideals in one dark body, whose dogged strength alone keeps it from being torn asunder.

Du Bois described black persistence along the pathway towards educational attainment.

Up the new path the advance guard toiled, slowly, heavily, doggedly; only those who have watched and guided the faltering feet, the misty minds, the dull understandings of the dark pupils of these schools know how faithfully, how piteously this people strove to learn. It was weary work . . . the inches of progress here and there . . . a foot had slipped or someone had fallen. To the tired climbers, the horizon was ever dark, the mists were often cold, the Canaan was always dim and far away. . . . it changed the child of Emancipation to the youth with dawning self-consciousness, self-realization, self-respect.

Du Bois himself persevered to become the leading voice of his generation for black civil and political rights, helping to found the National Association for the Advancement of Colored People. His persistence along with others in his generation created the momentum for the breakthroughs of the Civil Rights Movement a half-century later. Such perseverance can also forge your progress. These points will help guide your journey.

REDEFINE SUCCESS — Most historians have made Du Bois and his contemporary Booker T. Washington epochal adversaries. The following statement by Washington is one that Du Bois would have surely affirmed. Let it help you think about your own success journey in new ways.

Success is to be measured not so much by the position that one has reached in life as by the obstacles that he has overcome while trying to succeed.

RESCUE THOSE IN NEED — Once you get yourself on the success track, pull some others on board with you. Du Bois wrote a book to reach out to the historically downtrodden. Figure out how you can best build a pathway for those less fortunate. The trail you blaze for a few just might become a highway for many.

RIDE YOUR MOMENTUM — Du Bois fought the battle for racial equality throughout his ninety-five years of life. Each achievement — such as founding the monthly journal "The Crisis" as a periodical to combat racism — was fuel that carried him towards his goal of a more just society. Momentum can also be your best friend as you journey to reach your objectives. Let each victory — no matter how small — propel you to higher ground.

SURMOUNT DIFFICULTIES THROUGH PERSEVERANCE
APRIL 19TH

. . . whatever occurs, may justice and righteousness be the stability of our times, and order arise out of confusion. Great difficulties may be surmounted by patience and perseverance.
— Abigail Adams

The twelve hundred letters that were written between John and Abigail Adams constitute a colorful canon of candor more consequential than any other correspondence between eminent spouses in American history. A self-educated woman through her voracious reading of English and French literature, Abigail's incisive erudition helped her become her husband's political confidant, a treasured adviser as he rose in prominence to the Presidency. She offered her sagacity through steadfast letter writing. Her inquisitive style is evident in one of her earliest letters, dated November 27, 1775, in which she shared her doubts about the emerging American Experiment.

The building up a great empire, which was only hinted at by my correspondent, may now, I suppose, be realized even by the unbelievers. Yet, will not ten thousand difficulties arise in the formation of it? The reins of government have been so long slackened that I fear the people will not quietly submit to those restraints which are necessary for the peace and security of the community. If we separate from Britain, what code of laws will be established? How shall we be governed so as to retain our liberties? . . . Who shall frame these laws? Who will give them force and energy? It is true your resolutions, as a body, have hitherto had the force of laws: but will they continue to have?

It was twenty-two long years from the the time she wrote this letter to her ascendence as the Second First Lady of the United States — and perhaps the most influential in American history. In her literary persistence through the trials of establishing and forming a viable new government, she was not only a role-model for vigorous virtues but also one of the first American voices for women's rights. Her March 1776 letter to her husband and fellow delegates to the Continental Congress possessed a prophetic ring.

. . . remember the ladies, and be more generous and favorable to them than your ancestors. Do not put such unlimited power into the hands of the Husbands. Remember all Men would be tyrants if they could. If particular care and attention is not paid to the Ladies we are determined to foment a Rebellion, and will not hold ourselves bound by any Laws in which we have no voice, or Representation.

Though mostly in the background, Abigail inspired John to surmount his difficulties through perseverance, which had positive influence on his Founding peers and the young nation. Her success is worthy of your emulation. Surmount your own difficulties through perseverance as you strive to be:

PROLIFIC — Abigail never stopped counseling John through correspondence: letter after letter after letter gave her and the women of her era an indefatigable voice. She possessed a singular role as wife and confidant of a Founding Father; through her persevering commitment she elevated her status to that of Founding Mother. Whatever your commitment happens to be, keep expressing it, and you will make splendid impact. Whatever happens, just keep writing!

PROFOUND — You have to be deep-rooted in your perseverance before you can rise above your difficulties. You must confront the challenge and refuse to waver, vacillate or falter. Whether it's writing political advice, staying on a demanding job, enduring a bad relationship, or going through a business failure — just hang in there. Have a deep enough resolve to work through it to the best possible outcome. It may take longer than you like, it may be harder than you expect, but you will surmount the difficulty through your perseverance.

PANOPTIC — Take the long view. You can hope for a quick resolution but be prepared for a protracted process. Manage your expectations to mitigate disappointment and frustration. See yourself in a marathon, not a sprint. It may still be a rocky road to travel, but you will have a less traumatic time reaching your destination if you anticipate — and prepare for — a long and winding pathway. If it turns out to be shorter success journey than expected (Don't bet on it!), so much the better.

KEEP PLAYING YOUR MUSIC   APRIL 20TH

Life is like a trumpet - if you don't put anything into it, you don't get anything out of it.
William Christopher Handy

Born in Alabama in 1873, William Christopher Handy exhibited his love of music as a young boy. Handy had to secretly learn to play the guitar, organ and cornet because of his father's belief that musical instruments were tools of the devil. He started his career as a schoolteacher but soon shifted to musical endeavors: first tenor in a minstrel show, choral director, cornetist, trumpeter and bandmaster. Handy kept playing his music, eventually conducting his own orchestra that toured the South and Midwest.

In 1905, on one of those tours, Handy experienced a revelation that forever changed his style of music.

My own enlightenment came in Cleveland, Mississippi. I was leading the orchestra in a dance program when someone sent up an odd request. . . . Would we object if a local colored band played a few dances. . . . We eased out gracefully as the newcomers entered. . . . their band consisted of just three pieces, a battered guitar, a mandolin, and a worn-out bass. . . . They struck up one of those over-and-over strains that seem to have no very clear beginning . . . no ending at all. The strumming attained a disturbing monotony, but on and on it went . . . Thump-thump-thump went their feet on the floor. . . . A rain of silver dollars began to fall around the outlandish, stomping feet. The dancers went wild. Dollars, quarters, halves — the shower grew heavier and continued so long I strained my neck to get a better look. There before the boys lay more money than my nine musicians were being paid for the entire engagement. Then I saw the beauty of primitive music. They had the stuff the people wanted. It touched the spot.

From this moment of discovery a new art form arose. Handy created and orchestrated the "Memphis Blues", followed by the "St. Louis Blues". These and other compositions and performances made him the first famous jazz musician in America, earning him the title "Father of the Blues". His perseverance with this new musical genre established the "blue" lowered seventh as the defining feature of the Blues, which became not only widely popular music but also an important cultural designation, as Handy explained.

Most white people think that the Negro is always cheerful and lively, but he isn't, though he may seem that way when he is most troubled. The Negro knows the Blues as a state of mind, and that's why his music has that name.

Handy kept playing the Blues, and he even wrote a book, "Blues: An Anthology —Complete Words and Music of 53 Great Songs". When it was published in 1926, Small's Paradise in Harlem hosted "Handy Night" to celebrate the achievement. Handy's perseverance paved the way for artistic breakthroughs. Heed his example. Whatever your calling, keep playing your music as you:

RHYTHM WELL — Whatever your groove is, find it . . . flow with it. You'll be able to make it all the way through your trials if you keep it moving.

REDEFINE FAILURE — The turning point for Handy came when he was asked to step aside for a less accomplished band. He used that failure to learn a new way of musical expression. Learn from your failures; use them as a bridge to new success.

REGULATE ATTITUDE — Handy could've stormed out of the club when the other band proved to be the crowd-pleaser. Don't get upset when things don't go your way. And don't be concerned with the things you can't control and focus on the things you can. Control your thoughts and feelings on the inside and you will overcome the circumstances on the outside.

RISK IT ALL — Handy embraced his revelatory moment

and rode it to trailblazing success. He went all in for the new musical thing. When the time comes, make sure you go for it. Let your new discovery generate the momentum for its fulfillment. Whatever life brings your way, compose your own melody to stay upbeat and keep playing your music!

PERSEVERE IN YOUR CALLING   APRIL 21ST

One thing is certain. I am not afraid to act as my
conscience dictates, no matter what the world may think.
Antoinette Brown Blackwell

In 1833, when she was eight years old, Antoinette Brown Blackwell surprised her family by offering a simple prayer as they gathered to give thanks to God. A year later, at the Congregational Church in Henrietta, New York, Young "Nettie", as she was called, answered the pastor's altar call. Her quest to serve in ministry has begun.

Blackwell excelled as a student and graduated from the only secondary school in her county at fifteen. She immediately got a job as a teacher, saving her money towards her goal of pursuing theological studies. In 1844 Blackwell was accepted to Oberlin College in Ohio, the only college in the nation at that time that regularly admitted women. When the administration opposed her studying theology, Blackwell persisted and gained a compromise: she was allowed to enroll in the courses but would only receive formal recognition or a license to preach upon graduation.

Despite counsel from teachers, friends and family advising her to forgo a career in ministry, Blackwell refused to give up on her divine calling. She used her splendid oratorical skills in eloquent support of the temperance movement, abolition of slavery and women's rights, making a living as a public speaker. Brown continued to apply for her ministerial credentials and was finally granted a license to preach by the Congregational Church in 1851.

During one of her temperance speaking tours, Brown spoke at a Congregational church in upstate New York. The church membership was so impressed that they asked Brown to fill their vacant pastorate. On September 15, 1853, Brown became the first woman to be ordained into church ministry in a mainstream denomination in the United States.

Brown's ordination provoked a storm of protests from pulpits, the public and the press. Her response at a temperance conference in the aftermath of her ordination captured the inner strength of her divine calling.

There were angry men confronting me and I caught the flashing of defiant eyes, but above me and within me, there was a spirit stronger than them all.

Brown's perseverance paid off, yielding a prodigious clerical career and rich legacy. In 1975 the United Church of Christ (which includes the former Congregational denomination), began presenting Antoinette Brown Awards to outstanding women ordained within their denomination. To persevere in your own calling:

REFUSE TO COMPLAIN — When tough circumstances tempt you to complain, remember these words from the Apostle Paul.

Do everything without complaining or arguing, so that you may become blameless and pure, children of God without fault in a crooked and depraved generation, in which you shine like stars in the universe . . .
— Philippians 2:14-15

REFOCUS ON STRONG WORDS — Memorizing the following passage from Mahatma Gandhi and others like it will engender strength.

Strength does not come from winning. Your struggles develop your strengths. When you go through hardships and decide not to surrender, that is strength.

RELEASE YOUR SPIRITUAL ENERGY — Starting when she was a little girl, Antoinette Brown spoke about her faith. Follow her example: testify; share; pray. You will find the strength to keep going through your testimony. Speaking encouraging words to others will bolster your persistence.

RISE TO THE OCCASION — Brown was talking about temperance when her divine calling beckoned. Since you don't know when the day of your destiny will dawn, be ready for it. Rise to the occasion when your moment comes.

PERSEVERE FOR YOUR RIGHTS   APRIL 22ND

That as your memorialists have been and are considered as free citizens of this state, they hope to be treated as such . . . and are willing to take upon them any duty for the preservation of the peace in the city or any other occasion if called on.
Thomas Cole, P. B. Mathews and Mathew Webb

In the early 1790's as the infant government of the United States worked through controversial issues like the establishment of a national bank, the individual states faced political challenges of their own. South Carolina's laws placed some of the most severe restrictions on Negroes — slave or free — who were prohibited from testifying under oath in court or bringing suit against another party. In January 1791 three black men from Charleston petitioned the South Carolina legislature for equality under the law. Some sections of their January 1791 submission appear below.

The memorial of Thomas Cole, bricklayer, P. B. Mathews and Mathew Webb, butchers, on behalf of themselves and others, free men of color humbly shows: Your memorialists show that they have at all times since the independence of the United States contributed and do now contribute to the support of the government by cheerfully paying their taxes proportionable to their property with others who have been during such period, and now are, in full enjoyment of the rights and immunities of citizens, inhabitants of a free independent state. . . . Your memorialists do not presume to hope that they shall be put on equal footing with the free white citizens of the state in general. They only humbly solicit such indulgence as the wisdom and humanity of this honorable House shall dictate in their favor by repealing the clauses in the act before mentioned, and substituting such a clause as will effectually redress the grievance which your memorialists humbly submit . . .

It had been fifteen years since the passage of Declaration of Independence to which they referred in their petition, but Cole, Mathews and Webb persevered to make their claim for equality. Whatever adversity or injustice you're facing — whether big or small — the change that you're seeking won't happen overnight. You must persevere to further your rights; to do so, you have to:

UNDERSTAND YOUR RIGHTS — You cannot persevere for your rights unless you know what they are. Demonstrate cultural literacy by studying not only history but also current events. Know the facts, data, and statistics concerning the sociology and legalities pertaining to your rights. Move intelligently forward; it will inform your journey in pivotal ways.

UPROOT YOUR DOUBTS — It's important to distinguish between internal obstacles, such as insecurities, and external obstacles, like the institutionalized racism that the free Negroes of South Carolina faced over two hundred years ago. Identify your doubts and fears and seek to overcome them. Emotionally equip yourself to take on the foes on the outside by being strong on the inside.

UNDERGIRD YOUR QUEST — Like Cole, Mathews and Webb, the institutional barriers will have to be addressed by working together with others for change. You will strengthen your quest — and make it harder to give up — through united action. Though the wheels of justice grind slowly, you can keep them moving by making your collective voice heard . . . and heard . . . and heard . . .

UPLIFT OTHERS — As you persevere for your rights, you will cause others to pay attention to — and even support — your mission. Note the impact reflected by George Washington's letter to J.F. Mercer, dated September 9, 1786:

I never mean, unless some particular circumstance should compel me to it, to possess another slave by purchase, it being among my first wishes to see some plan adopted by which slavery in this country may be abolished by law.

OVERTURN YOUR OBSTACLES   APRIL 23RD

You, by your unwise legislation, have crippled womanhood by closing to her all honorable means of employment, have driven her into the garrets of our cities where she now revenges herself on your innocent sons, sapping the very foundations of national virtue.
Elizabeth Cady Stanton

A dozen years after she led the first women's rights convention in Seneca Falls, New York in 1848, Elizabeth Cady Stanton addressed the New York State legislature on a pending bill for woman suffrage. Stanton's commitment to social activism preceded her work on women's issues. She had been an active abolitionist with her husband Henry Brewster Stanton, a co-founder of the Republican Party. While on their honeymoon in the spring of 1840, they attended the the World Anti-Slavery Convention in London, England. At the convention Stanton met Quaker minister Lucretia Mott; they became allies when the male delegates voted to deny women participation in the proceedings, requiring them to sit in a roped-off section hidden from the view of the men in attendance. This experience was a turning point for Stanton, shifting her devotion into the fight for women's rights.

Her 1860 speech to New York political leaders demonstrated her strategy. Stanton understood that her biggest obstacle was the attitude of men toward women, so she used language to challenge the deep-seated male perspective. She elaborated her moral points with dramatic imagery designed to overturn the attitudinal obstacles. She depicted women as the "crowning glory" of American democracy.

> *We are building a model republic; our edifice will one day need a crowning glory. Let the artists be wisely chosen. Let them begin their work. Here is a temple to liberty, to human rights, on whose portals behold the glorious declaration, "All men are created equal." The sun has never yet shone upon any of man's creations that can compare with this. The artist who can mold a statue worthy to crown magnificence like this must be godlike in his conceptions, grand in his comprehensions, sublimely beautiful in his power of execution. The woman — the crowning glory of the model republic among the nations of the earth — what must she not be?*

Her arguments did not prevail that day; but Stanton kept proclaiming her wisdom and she eventually won over hearts and minds when New York granted women the right to vote in 1917; three years later the Nineteenth Amendment established women's suffrage as a constitutional right for all Americans. Stanton persevered to overturn her obstacles; follow her example by practicing these principles.

TACTICS — Obstacles in your life are unavoidable. No matter how hard you might try to travel a pathway without them, they will keep popping up to frustrate — even derail — your goals. Don't focus on the obstacle; it will force too much of your attention into the rearview mirror. Be aware of the challenges but focus on developing the strategy that you need to overcome them. Your victory is in your strategy.

TALK — Think about how you might use your words — Stanton is your role model here — to shift the negative thinking of others. Overturning obstacles, especially attitudinal ones, is not easy, so get some strong talking points. Deploy them as your arsenal in the battle for truth.

TIMING — Though the triumphant milestones didn't occur until years after Stanton's death in 1902, her perseverance led to victories all along the journey of her life. Her first breakthrough came in 1869 when Wyoming became the first — it was still a territory at that time — to legislate a woman's right to vote. Every obstacle you overturn — even if it's not the giant you dream to defeat — is an important one.

TRIUMPH — Your victory first happens on the inside then manifests in your circumstances; Helen Keller put it this way:

Character cannot be developed in ease and quiet. Only through experience of trial and suffering can the soul be strengthened, ambition inspired and success achieved.

POSSESS THE SPIRIT TO GO ON   APRIL 24TH

The free exploring mind of the individual human is the most valuable thing in the world.
John Steinbeck

In 1939 John Steinbeck won the Pulitzer Prize for "The Grapes of Wrath", his novel about a family driven by the dust storms of the 1930's from the Great Plains to the West Coast. Steinbeck depicted the plight of these migrant workers as they struggled from rural stability to uncertain mobility. In the following passage he described the challenging transition from settled life on the farm to endless days behind the wheel.

Thus they changed their social life — changed as in the whole universe only man can change. They were not farm men any more, but migrant men. And the thought, the planning, the long staring silence that had gone out to the fields, went now to the roads, to the distance, to the West. That man whose mind had been bound with acres lived with narrow concrete miles. And his thought and his worry were not any more with rainfall, with wind and dust, with the thrust of the crops. Eyes watched the tires, ears listened to the clattering motors, and minds struggled with oil, with gasoline, with the thinning rubber between air and road. Then a broken gear was tragedy. Then water in the evening was the yearning, and food over the fire. Then health to go on was the need and strength to go on, and spirit to go on. The wills thrust westward ahead of them, and fears that had once apprehended drought or flood now lingered with anything that might stop the westward crawling. . . .

Steinbeck vividly portrayed the perseverance of these westward travelers. Through the hard times, they possessed the spirit to go on. When you face hard times, you need to possess that same spirit. Steinbeck's words point to principles to help you attain it.

SHOOT HIGHER — *Always dream and shoot higher than you know you can do . . . Try to be better than yourself.*

Let your imagination take you to places you haven't been before. Settle your mind there. Seeing beyond the clouds will get you through their gloom.

STUDY HARD — *Books are the best friends you can have; they inform you, and entertain you, and they don't talk back.*

Feed your soul some spiritual nutrition. Read a religious or inspirational book. You will be encouraged to keep moving forward towards your goal.

SUCCEED WELL — *It has always seemed strange to me . . . the things we admire in men, kindness and generosity, openness, honesty, understanding and feeling, are the concomitants of failure in our system. And those traits we detest, sharpness, greed, acquisitiveness, meanness, egotism and self-interest, are the traits of success. And while men admire the quality of the first they love the produce of the second.*

Steinbeck highlights a troubling irony of success: the vices seems to yield more than the virtues. Stick with the virtues. Their greater value will be vindicated over time.

STAYING POWER — *Don't worry about losing. If it is right, it happens. The main thing is not to hurry. Nothing good gets away.*

Resolve to stay the course. Whether you're making a long, arduous drive through new, perilous territory or striving to overcome a challenging circumstance right in your own background, your commitment to work through it — and to keep working through it — will get you through it and on to success. When a dustbowl brings adversity into your life, remember — it's a matter of your will, as Vince Lombardi affirms:

The difference between a successful person and others is not a lack of strength, not a lack of knowledge but rather in a lack of will.

PERSEVERE THROUGH DREARY DAYS   APRIL 25TH

We are "sheep in the midst of wolves." And nothing but the military arm of the government prevents us and all the truly loyal white men from being driven from the land of our birth. . . . Trusting that, we remain yours for our flag, our country, and humanity.
Colored Convention Delegates of Virginia

During the first week of August 1865, African Americans gathered in Alexandria where they held the "Convention of the Colored People of Virginia". Among them were some of the four million blacks who gained their freedom as a result of the Civil War. They felt compelled to organize with the rise of the Black Codes and other systemic maneuvers by former slaveholders to block their social advancement.

Before the Civil War the Colored Conventions Movement was centered in the Northeastern cities of Philadelphia, New York City, Albany, and Boston; conventions also took place in Kansas, Louisiana, and California. After the war colored conventions were hosted in major cities across the South. The Virginia Colored Convention delegates declared their sentiments that they lived in perilous times.

Well, the war is over, the rebellion is "put down," and we are declared free! Four-fifths of our enemies are paroled or amnestied, and the other fifth are being pardoned, and the President has, in his efforts at the reconstruction for the civil government of the states late in rebellion, left us entirely at the mercy of these subjugated but unconverted Rebels, in everything save the privilege of bringing us, our wives, and little ones to the auction block. . . .

Fully aware of their challenging circumstances, these blacks resolved to persevere through their rainy days, which evokes the "Rainy Day" penned by their contemporary Henry Wadsworth Longfellow. As you read the words of this poem, consider how best to apply its principles to your life.

DARKNESS:
The day is cold, and dark, and dreary;
It rains, and the wind is never weary;
The vine still clings to the moldering wall,
But at every gust the dead leaves fall,
And the day is dark and dreary.

DESPAIR:
My life is cold, and dark, and dreary;
It rains, and the wind is never weary;

My thoughts still cling to the moldering Past,
But the hopes of youth fall thick in the blast,
And the days are dark and dreary.

DAWN:
Be still, sad heart! And cease repining;
Behind the clouds is the sun still shining;
Thy fate is the common fate of all,
Into each life some rain must fall,
Some days must be dark and dreary.

19th century African Americans did in fact persevere through the dreary days of Reconstruction, which turned into decades of darkness as Compromise and Jim Crow extended the gloom; clouds of prejudice linger to this day. Though their persistence took place well over a century ago, let their example be an inspiration to you. These disadvantaged citizens made it through the dark days filled with pervasive racism, oppression and violence. Face the facts. Challenges surely confront you, but they are less ominous than the social climate plaguing your predecessors. You are therefore in a better position to rise up beyond whatever storms of inequity are still encircling you. Seize those dark and dreary days; persevere through them; your sunshine will soon break through.

PUSH YOURSELF THROUGH HARD TIMES   APRIL 26TH

. . . we believe that that situation if permitted to continue will finally result in but one thing, the complete collapse of the Chicago pubic school system, which would be a blot upon the good name, not only of that city but upon the records of this nation.
Irvin Wilson

On May 9, 1932, Irvin Wilson, president of the Chicago Principals Club, testified before the U.S. Senate Subcommittee on Federal Cooperation in Unemployment Relief. Wilson described the devastating impact of the Great Depression on Chicago's school teachers. He reported on the results of a survey that was distributed to the 14,000 teachers of his city.

The teachers of Chicago, 3,177 of those teachers out of 6,315 reported a total loss of $2,367,00 in bank failures. Two thousand eight hundred and sixty-nine of those teachers reported a loss of time of $621,293 because of personal illness, that at a time when salaries were not forthcoming. . . . Seven hundred and fifty-nine lost their homes, lost an equity in the homes which they were buying. There were large amounts due on rent

195

and food, doctors' and dentist' bills, and all those things.

The financial hardships notwithstanding, the teachers organized and pushed for change. Concerned about plans to close schools, five thousand teachers marched on Chicago's Loop, protesting at the five largest banks and City Hall as well. Some of the teachers even managed to feed and clothe needy students in their districts. Through it all, they continued to teach, not receiving back pay until years later.

The Great Depression struggles of the Chicago teachers present lessons of perseverance for today, to push <u>and</u> pace yourself through hard times.

PUSH YOURSELF THROUGH HARD TIMES —
Every major difficulty you face in life represents an opportunity for you to grow, or not. The challenge can stretch you into a stronger person, or cause you to break down and give up. In the hardest of times, perseverance becomes a matter of focus. When your circumstances exalt the bad aspects of life over the good, your attitude must fight back, concentrating on the good aspects. Even though you can't see them, or even feel them, the good stuff is still there. You just have to push yourself to discern the bright horizon through the encircling gloom. Keep pushing, keep believing, until the rays of sunshine glimmer through. Take seriously Martin Luther King, Jr.'s advice.

> *If you can't fly, then run. If you can't run, then walk. If you can't walk, then crawl, but by all means, keep moving.*

PACE YOURSELF THROUGH HARD TIMES — The account of the annual dogsled derby in a small Wisconsin town illustrates this point. All of the racers were older boys with big sleds pulled by several dogs, except for one little boy with only one dog tied to a small sled. When the race began the boy with the small sled and dog quickly fell far behind. Way ahead of him, halfway through the race, the second-place sledder tried to take the lead. But he got too close to the first-place sled, the dogs got entangled, got into a fight, and the other dogs as they arrived at the battleground joined the ruckus. Only the forgotten little guy with his little sled and dog was able to maneuver around the chaos and finish the course, winning the race. So when the chaos of hardship confronts you, take it easy, pace yourself, let the others prance ahead and around. Slow and steady will help you figure out how to make it through. Albert Einstein elucidates this point.

It's not that I'm so smart, I just stay with problems longer.

BLAZE YOUR TRAILS   APRIL 27TH

*Solitary shrieks were heard in these woods, which he
told me were said to be the cries of murdered persons.*
Lorenzo Dow

Since church buildings were rare on the early nineteenth century American frontier, people came from miles away and camped together for several days to listen to traveling preachers. Evangelist Lorenzo Dow appeared at countless of these camp meetings. He was a trailblazer who gave the first sermons within the bounds of what later became Mississippi and Alabama and gained renown for having preached to more people than any other preacher of his era. Dow was also a popular writer, his autobiography at one time selling better in the United States than any other book except the Bible.

His eloquence and eccentricity drew big crowds wherever he went. In over thirty years of ministry he spoke in town halls, open fields and farmers' barns to Methodists, Baptists, Quakers, Catholics, and atheists — whoever would gather to listen — mostly along the frontier.

Dow's determination sustained him through the challenging circumstances of his missionary travels. In February 1804 he journeyed to Knoxville, Tennessee, for a camp meeting. It was tough getting there, as he recorded in his journal.

*In the night I grew uneasy, being twenty-five miles from my
appointment for next morning at 11 o'clock. I prevailed on a young man to
attempt carrying me with horses until day, which he thought was impracticable,
considering the darkness of the night and the thickness of the trees. At
day we parted, being still seventeen miles from the spot, and the ground covered
with a white frost.*

The next part of his journey revealed the strength of his perseverance.

*I had not proceeded far before I came to a stream of water, from the
springs of the mountain, which made it dreadful cold. In my heated state I had
to wade this stream five times in the course of an hour, which I perceived so
affected my body that my strength began to fail. Fears began to arise
that I must disappoint the people, till I observed some fresh tracks of horses,
which caused me to exert every nerve to overtake them in hopes of aid or*

assistance on my journey; and soon I saw them on an eminence. I shouted for them to stop till I came up. They inquired what I wanted. I replied, I had heard there was a meeting at Seversville by a stranger and was going to it. . . . perceiving that I was weary, they invited me to ride. And soon our company was increased to forty or fifty, who fell in with us on the road from different plantations.

Dow was determined to blaze his trails, and it paved the way for him to touch many lives. Blaze your own trails as you:

REACH IN FOR STRENGTH — "Great Men", a poem by Ralph Waldo Emerson, resounds Dow's perseverance and articulates this principle:

Not gold, but only man can make
A people great and strong;
Men who, for truth and honor's sake,
Stand fast and suffer long.
Brave men who work while others sleep,
Who dare while others fly —
They build a nation's pillars deep
And lift them to the sky.

REACH OUT TO SERVE — As you draw the power from the inside, you'll discover the pathway on the outside. And as you devote yourself to serve others, you will — like Dow — experience Providential assistance: the help to stay the course when you need it the most. Educator Marian Wright Edelman affirmed this point.

Service is the rent we pay for being. It is the very purpose of life . . .

PERSEVERE AS A LEADER   APRIL 29TH

That is the best form of government which returns the greatest number of advantages in proportion to the disadvantages with which it is attended.
Oliver Ellsworth

In the first few months of 1788, major obstacles loomed before the leaders of the American Experiment. Though the Constitutional Convention had adopted the new constitution in October 1787, only six states had ratified it, and nine were required to do so.

Oliver Ellsworth had been one of the many attorneys (Of the fifty-five delegates, more than half were lawyers.) to serve as a delegate to the 1787 Convention. An early and active champion of the constitution, Ellsworth proposed using the name the United States to identify the government under constitutional authority. When the Convention deadlocked over congressional representation, he led the negotiation of the Connecticut Compromise: a bicameral federal government with two members of the Senate elected by each state legislature, with House of Representatives members elected proportionately among the states based on share of the entire population of the states.

Ellsworth persevered in his efforts for constitutional passage, playing a significant role in ratification. He first rallied support in his home state of Connecticut to ratify the document, then wrote and disseminated the Letters of a Landholder to promote ratification in other states. When New Hampshire proved a holdout, Ellsworth wrote an open letter to its cautious citizenry, which is excerpted below.

> *Measured by this rule, the state of New Hampshire cannot expect a Constitution preferable to that now proposed for the Union. In point of defense it gives you the whole force of the empire, so arranged as to act speedily and in concert, which is an article of greatest importance to the frontier states. With the present generation of men, national interest is the measure by which war or peace are determined; and when see the British nation by a late treaty paying an enormous annual subsidy to the little principality of Hesse Cassel for the purpose of retaining her in military alliance, it should teach us the necessity of those parts in the Constitution which enable the efficient force of the whole to be opposed to an invasion of any part.*

On June 21, 1788, New Hampshire became the ninth state to ratify, putting the U. S. Constitution into effect. Ellsworth went on to serve as United States Senator from Connecticut, and the third Chief Justice of the United States. And in the 1796 presidential election, he received 11 electoral votes.

Ellsworth fulfilled his goal of shaping the new American government because he persevered as a leader. You will persevere as a leader as you:

SHARPEN YOUR ABILITIES — To be successful as a leader — whatever your goals — you will have to keep getting better over time. If your perspective is static or your work stagnant, your leadership will not last. Use your persevering seasons as opportunities to self-improve. At the end of a particular challenge, make sure you're coming out ahead of where you were when it first confronted you.

SACRIFICE FOR OTHERS — Many people underestimate the sacrifice that leadership entails. There's a price to pay for being in charge — shifting time away from your own agendas to look out for others. The best leaders are those who are devoted to serve.

STRENGTHEN YOUR COMMITMENT — As you stick with your mission over time, your commitment to lead others will grow stronger. It may not get any easier, but you will become wiser, especially as you keep this precept in mind:

The road to success is always under construction.

SOAR WITH YOUR SUCCESS — Ellsworth soared from a delegate, a U.S. Senator, Chief Justice of the U.S. Supreme Court and a Presidential candidate winning electoral votes. Persevere as a leader, and your own success will soar.

PERSEVERE TO BE WHO YOU TRULY ARE   APRIL 29TH

There seems little for me in Hollywood, because, rather than real Chinese, producers prefer Hungarians, Mexicans, American Indians for Chinese roles.
Anna May Wong

In 1922 Hollywood released its first technicolor feature, "The Toll of the Sea." 17-year-old Chinese American actress Anna May Wong starred in her first leading role, playing Lotus Flower, a young Chinese girl who falls in love with an American man, but she drowns herself after he breaks her heart. This denouement was consistent with the culture of that era that forbade interracial marriages. The New York Times described her performance:

Miss Wong stirs in the spectator all the sympathy her part calls for and she never repels one by an excess of theatrical 'feeling'. She has a difficult role, a role that is botched nine times out of ten, but hers is the tenth performance. Completely unconscious of the camera, with a fine sense of proportion and remarkable pantomimic accuracy . . . She should be seen again and often on the screen.

Her captivating screen presence and exceptional acting ability notwithstanding, Wong was incessantly cast as either the naïve "Butterfly" innocent or, more often, as the deceitful "Dragon Lady" villain. She reflected on the discrimination that plagued her career.

> *Why is it that the screen Chinese is always the villain? And so crude a villain — murderous, treacherous, a snake in the grass! We are not like that. How could we be, with a civilization that is so many times older than the West.*

Confronted by the prevailing prejudice against mixed race onscreen couples, Wong humbled herself to play supporting roles in numerous films and eventually gained international recognition as the first Chinese American movie star. She endeavored to escape this stereotypical type casting by going abroad. In 1928 she left for Europe and was a sensation in Germany, Austria and England, starring in opera, film, and on stage.

Wong's success abroad eventually led her back to Hollywood with greater stature if not better roles, so she branched out. Wong performed on radio and developed a cabaret act, touring globally throughout the 1930's and 1940's. She sang songs in Cantonese, English, German, French, Swedish, Danish and other languages. During World War II she played the lead in "The Lady from Chungking", a Hollywood war film that flipped the script: the Chinese heroes were portrayed by Chinese Americans while the Japanese villains by European Americans. And in 1951 Wong starred on television in "The Gallery of Madame Liu-Tsong", a primetime series that was written specifically for her; she played a Chinese art dealer in the title role that used her birth name.

Wong endured a career of vicissitude and held on until she garnered roles that allowed her to be who she truly was. You, too, should persevere to be who you truly are by putting the 7 R-Principles into practice:

RECOGNIZE the things outside of your control and don't worry about them.

RECALL all of your successes and meditate on them.

REDUCE the volume of your critics and increase the volume of your supporters.

REFLECT on your talents and abilities, embracing and cultivating the gifts that make you special.

REFUSE to think too much about the failures of the past or the possibilities for future; focus on being your best self in the present.

RESEARCH solutions instead of complaining about problems.

REHEARSE your inspirational sayings and uplifting prayers; memorize them; declare them often.

DRAW LESSONS AS YOU GO   APRIL 30TH

We have passed triumphantly through all these difficulties. Our Constitution is no longer a doubtful experiment; and we find that . . . our country has improved and is flourishing beyond any former example in the history of nations.
Andrew Jackson

On March 4, 1837, at the end of his two terms as the seventh U.S. President, Andrew Jackson delivered his farewell address. The first president from outside the Virginia/Massachusetts "aristocracy", Jackson was elected on and proclaimed a platform representing the "common man". In his final speech, he summarized the major accomplishments of his administration: "humble efforts" leading to "this great people prosperous and happy, in the full enjoyment of liberty and peace, and honored and respected by every nation of the world." Jackson began by setting the historical context.

We have now lived almost fifty years under the Constitution framed by the sages and patriots of the Revolution. The conflicts in which the nations of Europe were engaged during a great part of this period . . . and our intimate commercial connections with every part of the civilized world rendered it a time of much difficulty for the government of the United States. We have had our seasons of peace and war, with all the evils which precede or follow a state of hostility with powerful nations. We encountered these trials with our Constitution yet in its infancy, and under the disadvantages which a new and untried government must always feel when it is called upon to put forth its whole strength, without the light of experience to guide it or the weight of precedents to justify its measures.

As Jackson emphasized, it is crucial to draw upon and apply the lessons from the past to succeed in the present and future. Heed his words and the principles they represent. You will draw lessons as you go when you:

REFLECT — *Any man worth his salt will stick up for what he believes right, but it takes a slightly better man to acknowledge instantly and without reservation that he is in error.*

Take a real break from your busy routine — more than a dog walk or coffee break. Give yourself some meaningful time to think through your experiences, connecting the dots from pit to summit. Draw some conclusions. Figure out what went wrong. Don't sit on it. Acknowledge it. Resolve to move forward.

> RECKON — *We behold systematic efforts publicly made to sow the seeds of discord between different parts of the United States and to place party divisions directly upon geographical distinctions . . .*

As Jackson did, define the key problem. Reckon with the truth, even if it's a difficult pill to swallow.

> RECTIFY — *But you must remember, my fellow-citizens, that eternal vigilance by the people is the price of liberty, and that you must pay the price if you wish to secure the blessing.*

Come up with a plan of action based on you've learned from your past. Don't be bound by your history but let it inform so you can take well-reasoned steps to improve your life as well as the world around you.

> REVERENCE — *Finally, it is my most fervent prayer to that Almighty Being before whom I now stand, and who has kept us in His hands from the infancy of our Republic to the present day, that He will so overrule all my intentions and actions and inspire the hearts of my fellow-citizens that we may be preserved from dangers of all kinds and continue forever a united and happy people.*

Sometimes the best way to end things — the only way — is in prayer. Just say: Amen!

MAY: TEAMWORK
DAILY SUCCESS PRINCIPLES

1. Go The Extra Mile — Jesse Owens — 1936
2. Bring On Board A Leader — Sacagawea — 1804
3. Collaborate For Change — Harry Truman — 1948
4. Take Off Your Mask — Paul Laurence Dunbar — 1872
5. Bring Down Your Walls — Frances Perkins/Robert Frost — 1933
6. Prioritize Your People Skills — Benjamin Franklin — 1787
7. Endeavor As A Family — John Audubon — 1839
8. Work Together Strategically — Sacheen Littlefeather/Marlon Brando — 1973
9. Be Loyal To Your Teammates — James Gooding — 1863
10. Harmonize As A Team — Benny Goodman — 1936
11. Organize For Justice — African Americans From Kentucky — 1871
12. Strive To Connect With All Your Teammates — Thomas Jefferson — 1789
13. Advocate For Your Teammates — Doris Stevens — 1917
14. Flee The Menace — Joseph Holland — 1987
15. Fence The Mystery — Joseph Holland — 1988
16. Find The Mentor — Joseph Holland — 1989
17. Bridge Difficult Relationships — Red Jacket — 1805
18. Refuse To Label Yourself And Others — Lyndon Johnson — 1958
19. Affirm The Individuals On Your Team — Ole Raeder — 1847
20. Become A Team Player — Alexander Hamilton — 1787
21. Pick The Right Teammates — Jane Addams — 1889
22. Enrich Your Relationships — Henry Wallace — 1934
23. Unify Your Team — Philip Schaff — 1854
24. Fight For Your Team — African American Soldiers in Viet Nam — 1968
25. Be A Value-Add Teammate — William Elery Channing — 1830
26. Strengthen Your Team — Fredrika Bremer — 1853
27. Work As A Team — Thomas Jefferson — 1826
28. Dream As A Team — James Madison — 1826
29. Build Your Best Team — Herbert Croly — 1909
30. Communicate Effectively With Others — John Neal — 1843
31. Align With Your Teammates —John Adams — 1818

GO THE EXTRA MILE   MAY 1ST

*I am here, Jesse, where it seems there is only the dry sand and the wet
blood. I do not fear so much for myself, my friend, I fear for my woman
who is home, and my young son Karl, who has never really known his father.*
Luz Long, in a letter to Jesse Owens

During the 1936 Olympic Games in Berlin, American Jesse Owens
competed in twelve events and won four gold medals. What made Owens'
feat even more remarkable was that he did it as a black person at an athletic
event in the heart of Nazi Germany hosted by Adolf Hitler who was
trumpeting Aryan superiority.

Owens' gold medal in the long jump held meaning that
transcended the athletic attainment. He was competing against German and
European record holder Luz Long. They battled throughout the long jump
competition, exceeding the old Olympic record five times. Owens set a new
world record on his final winning jump, besting Long who earned the silver
medal. He warmly congratulated Owens in full view of Hitler, taking
photographs together and strolling arm-in-arm to the locker room.

Having bonded in Berlin, Long and Owens corresponded
afterwards. While stationed with the German Army in North
Africa during World War II, Long wrote his last letter to Owens.

*My heart tells me, if I be honest with you, that this is the last letter I
shall ever write. If it is so, I ask you something. It is something so very
important to me. It is you go to Germany when this war is done, someday find
my Karl, and tell him about his father. Tell him, Jesse, what times were like
when we not separated by war. I am saying — tell him how things can be
between men on this earth.*

*If you do this something for me, this thing I need the most to know
will be done . . . I tell you something I know you want to hear . . . it is true.
That hour in Berlin when I first spoke to you, when you had your knee upon
the ground, I knew that you were in prayer. . . . And you, I believe, will read
this letter . . . I believe this shall come about because I think now that God will
make it come about. This what I have to tell you, Jesse. I think I might believe
in God. And I pray to him that, even while it should not be possible for this to
reach you ever, these words I write will still be read by you.*

Your brother, Luz

During the Allied invasion of Sicily in 1943, Long was killed in
action, but his heart's desire lived on. Owens received Long's letter and,
after the war, travelled to Germany to meet Long's son Karl. Going the
extra mile, Owens befriended Karl and even served as best man at his
wedding. You should also go the extra mile to develop relationships with

others; to do so:

BREAK YOUR ROUTINE — Yes, go out of your way to get to know someone better. You may not have to go to Europe like Owens, but what about crosstown? Share your life story and get to know theirs. Spend time together outside of the usual habitat. If you work in the same place, visit each other's house of worship, or favorite workout spot, outdoor space, or sporting event. One of Jesus' directives from the Sermon on the Mount pronounced this precept:

> *If anyone forces you to go one mile, go with them two miles.*
> — Matthew 5:41

BARE YOUR SOUL — Be transparent: share some things about yourself to establish a comfort level, so the other person will open up. Be careful not to ventilate and suck all the emotional air out the room. Remember — it's not just about you. It's about us: you and others experiencing the mutual benefit of heartfelt sharing.

BUST THROUGH BARRIERS — Be the one to do that something special to deepen the relationship; that special stride to cross the cultural border; that insightful initiative to strengthen the bond. Reach out to affirm that the individual connection is more powerful than the cultural barrier.

BRING YOUR BEST — Owens served as best man in the wedding of his friend's son. Like him, seek to do something extraordinary for someone else. When you go the extra mile, you touch others in transformational ways.

BRING ON BOARD A LEADER   MAY 2ND

> *Amazing the things you find when you bother to search for them.*
> Sacagawea

On January 18, 1803, President Thomas Jefferson submitted a confidential message to Congress requesting that the members appropriate funds for an expedition led by Meriweather Lewis and William Clark to explore the region being acquired by the United States from France in the Louisiana Purchase. This acquisition doubled the size of the country, encompassing land from fifteen present U.S. states and two Canadian provinces: $15 million for over 529 million acres — 3 cents an acre; it turned out to be by far the largest territorial gain in U.S. history.

On May 30, 1804, Lewis, Clark and their team of explorers calling themselves the Corps of Discovery launched the expedition. Knowing the myriad of challenges before them, they decided to hire as an interpreter Canadian trapper Toussaint Charbonneau because he was married to Sacagawea, a Native American who spoke Shoshone.

Sacagawea proved to be much more than an interpreter during the 30-month, eight-thousand mile journey. She was a guide as well as a peacemaker. During an arduous stretch of the journey through what is now Franklin County, Washington, Clark noted in his journal.

> *The Indian woman confirmed those people of our friendly intentions, as no woman ever accompanies a war party of Indians in this quarter . . . the wife of Shabono our interpeter we find reconsiles all the Indians, as to our friendly intentions a woman with a party of men is a token of peace.*

As they approached the Pacific Ocean, the corps faced a shortage of food and had run out of funds to purchase provisions from neighboring tribes. Lewis decided to take a vote about whether to move their camp to a location promising less inclement weather; Sacagawea participated in the vote — a historic milestone for a Native American woman in democratic decision-making. The group moved its camp and survived its second winter.

In July 1806, approaching the Rocky Mountains on their return trip, the corps faced another crossroads. Clark recorded the moment.

> *The Indian woman informed me that she had been in this plain frequently and knew it well . . . She said we would discover a gap in the mountains in our direction.*

Sacagawea soon led the group along the route through the Yellowstone River basin, which not only paved the way to their final destination in St. Louis; her directive evolved into the future route for the Northern Pacific Railway.

If you want success, do what Lewis and Clark did. Bring on board your team a leader like Sacagawea; do do so, be strong in:

CALCULATION — You need a thinker on your team who can help you figure things out. Since your victory lies in your strategy, work together to work out your plan step by step. The Devil is in the details, so make sure to dot every "I" and cross every "T".

COMMUNICATION — Lewis and Clark had received written instructions from Jefferson, but they needed Sacagawea, an intermediary who listened to their dictates then imparted these directives to others. Be that someone who communicates in ways to make crooked paths straight; be the one described by John Maxwell:

A leader is one who knows the way, goes the way, and shows the way.

CONNECTIVITY — Look for those who can connect to people beyond your network. Make sure you cultivate the relationship before making the ask. Touch a person's heart, then request help.

CHARACTER — If the folks you're trying to reach can't trust your teammates, they won't trust you. Sacagawea successfully led her team because she was trustworthy. Can the same be said of you and your team?

COLLABORATE FOR CHANGE   MAY 3RD

Today the American people enjoy more freedom and opportunity that ever before. Never in our history has there been better reason to hope for the complete realization of the ideals of liberty and equality.
Harry Truman

On July 26, 1948, President Harry Truman issued an executive order that paved the way for the desegregation of the United States Armed Forces. Several months earlier Truman built momentum for this initiative when he presented his first major civil rights program to Congress. His message of February 2, 1948 articulated the social challenges facing the nation.

We shall not, however, finally achieve the ideals for which this nation was founded so long as any American suffers discrimination as a result of his race, or religion or color, or the land of origin of his forefathers. . . . We cannot be satisfied until all our people have equal opportunities for jobs, for homes, for education, for health, and for political expression, and until all our people have equal protection under the law.

He concluded with a call for collaboration to bring about the changes that the society so direly needed.

This will take the strong efforts of each of us individually, and all of us acting together through voluntary organizations and our governments. . . .

The protection of civil rights begins with the mutual respect for the rights of others, which all of us should practice in our daily lives. Through organizations in every community — in all parts of the country — we must continue to develop practical, workable arrangements for achieving greater tolerance and brotherhood.

Truman's point was that social change won't happen unless people work together to make it happen. Collaboration was the key in fostering greater civil rights in American society. Collaboration will also be a critical factor in bringing about change in your personal circumstances and community, which you can achieve through initiatives in these four areas.

CORRECTION — Be open to a course correction. If you find yourself too often at odds with others, adjust your approach to them: perhaps try listening more and talking less; maybe you should spend less time alone on social media and playing games on your smartphone, and more time hanging out with family, colleagues, classmates and friends. Check your emotional security. Are you easily threatened by those around you? Stop thinking about meeting your own needs through your teammates; instead make it a priority to serve them.

CONTRIBUTE — You can't add value to others if you don't first value them. Check your attitude. If you think negatively about your neighbors — "He's worthless. . . . She's a nobody." — you will devalue them and create tension. Instead contribute positivity. Give them the benefit of the doubt. Look first for the positive in others. Let them prove you wrong.

CONSTRUCT — Build a strong team by strategically supporting one another. Work together with others who are strong in the areas where you are weak and who are weak in the areas where you are strong. Make each other better. The example of basketball legend Bill Russell is one to emulate:

The most important measure of how good a game I played was how much better I'd made my teammates play.

CELEBRATE — If you want to attain the big victories, build confidence and excitement in your team by celebrating the little wins. Don't wait for a birthday or an anniversary. Throw a party for someone who earned a G.E.D., finished reading a self-help book like this one, started a new training program, or reached a sobriety milestone. Start at home, with family and close friends.

Applaud those in your inner circle for a good thing they've accomplished. You will be lighting the fire of individual progress that will lead to collective betterment.

TAKE OFF YOUR MASK   MAY 4TH

I hope there is something worthy in my writings and not merely the novelty of a black face associated with the power to rhyme that has attracted attention.
Paul Laurence Dunbar

In 1872 Paul Laurence Dunbar was born in Dayton, Ohio, to parents who had been antebellum slaves in Kentucky. Dunbar was precocious with his literary gifts, writing his first poem when he was six, giving his first public recital at nine. The support of his mother Matilda fueled the child prodigy. She read to him daily, often from the Bible, hoping he might become an African Methodist Episcopal Church minister. Dunbar so benefited from his mother's tutelage that at only sixteen years of age his poetry was published in a Dayton newspaper; and as the only black student during his time at Dayton's Central High School, he became literary society president, a debate club member, and the school newspaper editor.

Though he died at thirty-three of tuberculosis, Dunbar was so prolific — numerous books of poetry and short stories, a play and four novels — that he gained a national reputation as the first African American writer of distinction. He even wrote the lyrics for the 1903 Broadway show "In Dahomey", the first musical entirely written and performed by African Americans. Dunbar was referred to by the New York Times as "a true singer of the people – white or black." His most famous poem was "We Wear The Mask".

We wear the mask that grins and lies,
It hides our cheeks and shades our eyes,—
This debt we pay to human guile;
With torn and bleeding hearts we smile,
And mouth with myriad subtleties.

Why should the world be over-wise,
In counting all our tears and sighs?
Nay, let them only see us, while
We wear the mask.

We smile, but, O great Christ, our cries
To thee from tortured souls arise.

We sing, but oh the clay is vile
Beneath our feet, and long the mile;
But let the world dream otherwise,
We wear the mask!

Dunbar's eloquent words are ironic as well as timeless, providing important counsel for how you should manage your relationships. His advice is simply — take off your mask as you relate to others. To take off your mask, you must be:

TRANSPARENT — Work hard to be honest as you communicate with others. Be an authentic rather than a counterfeit person. People will eventually see through any phoniness you bring to the table so better to leave bogus tendencies behind.

TETHERED — Know your core values and stick to them. Connect to your principles and let them govern your life. People with whom you deal will not only appreciate you more, they will respect you more.

TENACIOUS — You have to be committed to taking off your mask. It's easy to dissemble, to live in the shadows. Discipline yourself to walk in the light so that others can experience who you really are.

TIMELY — Taking off your mask will help others take theirs off. When they do, follow Maya Angelo's advice:

When someone shows you who they are; believe them — the first time.

TRUE — Shakespeare's words resonate here: "To thine own self be true." Take off your mask so you can be true to yourself. There is nothing more important in deepening your relationship with others.

BRING DOWN YOUR WALLS   MAY 5TH

A government should aim to give all the people under its jurisdiction the best possible life.
Frances Perkins

In 1933 Frances Perkins became the first woman appointed to the U.S. Cabinet when President Franklin Roosevelt named her Secretary of

Labor. One of only two Cabinet members to serve the entire twelve years of Roosevelt's presidency, Perkins was a key architect of the New Deal, overseeing the establishment of government entities like the National Labor Relations Board. In a March 1936 article she described the benefits of government helping to facilitate better labor/management relations.

> *That the government should encourage mutuality between labor and employers in the improvement of production and in the development in both groups of a philosophy of self-government in the public interest. This means not merely that strikes and lockouts may be fewer but that the fundamental causes of such disorders may be diagnosed and remedies provided for the purpose of keeping industrial peace for the benefit of employers and workers and in the public interest. . . .*

Frances Perkins used her government position to bring down walls between employers and employees. A couple of decades earlier, poet Robert Frost explored this same theme of opposing sides working together in "Mending Walls." In the poem Frost depicted two farmers who converse as they consider repairing the stone wall that divides their properties.

> *There where it is we do not need the wall:*
> *He is all pine and I am apple orchard.*
> *My apple trees will never get across*
> *And eat the cones under his pines, I tell him.*
> *He only says, "Good fences make good neighbors."*
> *Spring is the mischief in me, and I wonder*
> *If I could put a notion in his head:*
> *"Why do they make good neighbors? Isn't it*
> *Where there are cows? But here there are no cows.*
> *Before I build a wall I'd ask to know*
> *What I was walling in or walling out,*
> *And to whom I was like to give offense.*

Robert Frost used poetry to argue for bringing down the wall between two neighboring farmers who had come together to mend the wall, suggesting three key questions for you to consider concerning bringing down the walls — those things that separate you from others — in your life:

QUESTION 1 — What am I walling in?
Consider your inner life, those submerged thoughts and buried feelings, the hidden things that you don't want anyone to discover about you. To be free from those secrets, to release yourself from those burdens, the walls that you've built around them need to come down, so that you can

grow in transparency . . . so you can share your soul with others.

QUESTION 2 — What am I walling out?

Consider your relationships, especially those who have hurt you, those whom you haven't forgiven. You've put up a wall to keep them at a distance, so they can't do anymore damage. But the walls you've put up are isolating you from family members, close friends, even those potential teammates who could add value to your life. Because of these unintended consequences of unfortunate isolation, these walls that you've built need to come down, so that you can extend forgiveness and experience social enrichment.

QUESTION 3 — Whom does my wall offend?

You may have no idea who's offended by your walls. Specific identities of the alienated ones are not the real issues. Just know that walls by their nature are offensive. You, like all of humanity, are a relational being, created for fellowship, for community. Walls get in the way of our divinely ordained social harmony. What walls can you bring down, which, when gone, will remove the shadows and cause new light to shine on the relationships of your life?

PRIORITIZE YOUR PEOPLE SKILLS   MAY 6TH

. . . for when you assemble a number of men to have the advantage of their joint wisdom, you inevitably assemble with those men all their prejudices, their passions, their errors of opinion, their local interests, and their selfish views. From such an assembly can a perfect production be expected?
Benjamin Franklin

On September 17, 1787, after almost four months of endeavoring to form the new American government, the delegates gathered for the closing day of the Federal Convention. Benjamin Franklin prefaced his motion that the recently drafted Constitution be signed by the delegates present with a speech.

Mr. President, I confess that there are several parts of this Constitution which I do not at present approve, but I am not sure I shall never approve them. For having lived long, I have experienced many instances of being obliged, by better information or fuller consideration, to change opinions, even on important subjects, which I once thought right but found to be otherwise. It is therefore that the older I grow the more apt I am to doubt my own judgment and to pay more respect to the judgment of others. . . .

213

Franklin continued by emphasizing their success in working together despite their differences.

> *In these sentiments, sir, I agree to this Constitution with all its faults, if they are such; because I . . . believe farther that this is likely to be well administered for a course of years, and can end in despotism, as other forms have done before it, when the people shall become so corrupted as   to   need despotic government, being incapable of any other. I doubt, too, whether any other convention we can obtain may be able to make a better Constitution . . .*

Thirty-nine of the fifty-five delegates signed the constitution that day, then left Philadelphia to gain approval from their respective states. They were able to work through the magnitude of their differences by prioritizing their people skills. You can prioritize your people skills as you:

PACE YOURSELF — Slow down to really connect with people. Take time to study them, understand them, meaningfully interact with them. Staying behind the closed door of your office, incessantly preoccupied by your smart phone or hidden in the dark corner of the library is not the best way to cultivate relationships. And don't forget to slow down your tongue: listen more than you talk. It's important to share your thoughts and feelings but don't let them crowd out the communication flowing from others.

POSITION FOR STRENGTH — Put your teammates in position where they can add most value to the team. A baseball player skilled at catcher should not be playing centerfield. Your football teammate with a strong throwing arm should be at quarterback, not linebacker. Size up the strengths of your teammates and purpose them accordingly. In this way you are affirming them, and you and they are now in the best position to win.

PRIORITIZE THE INTERESTS OF OTHERS — Like the history-makers of 1787, your success in life will depend in large part on your determination to put people first. So prioritize them. Book knowledge is important. Trend knowledge is vital. Financial knowledge is need for survival. But people knowledge is most crucial. If people don't like you, they'll be disinclined to assist, mentor, promote or do business with you. Knowing how to get along with others is a skill. Do your best to learn it well, as Theodore Roosevelt emphasized:

The most important single ingredient in the formula
of success is knowing how to get along with people.

When you put people ahead of projects, you are building an effective team, which is better for the projects in the long run, and, in the process, you just might make some history of your own.

ENDEAVOR AS A FAMILY   MAY 7TH

. . . they are persons who, having a family of strong and hardy children,
are anxious to enable them to provide for themselves. They have heard from
good authorities that the country extending along the great streams of the West
is the richest in its soil, the growth of its timber, and the abundance of its game.
John James Audubon

Between 1826 and 1839 naturalist and painter John James Audubon published The Birds of America, which resulted from his many years traveling the American Frontier. The monumental work is regarded as one of the finest ornithological works ever compiled, identifying twenty-five new bird species among the 435 hand-colored, life-size prints of 497 total specimens. Audubon included in the book explanatory text — Delineations of American Scenery and Character — to give social context to his natural renderings. In one Episode he described the life of a frontier family — he referred to them as Squatters — as they endeavored together towards success. Whether you're a part of a natural, extended, professional or spiritual family, pay attention to Audubon's account of this frontier family and the principles that their success imparts.

MISSION — *Days and weeks . . . of unremitting toils pass before they gain the end of their journey. The have crossed Carolina, Georgia, and Alabama. They have been traveling from the beginning of May to that of September, and with heavy hearts they traverse the state of Mississippi. But now, arrived on the banks of the broad stream, they gaze in amazement on the dark, deep woods around them.*

To make it on the frontier, the family took on their mission together. On the success journey that you take every day, figure out a way — as much as possible — to take your family along. Do more than just playing cards, watching TV or going to the movies together. Plan a trip, or, like the nineteenth century settlers, blaze new trails; adventure will enrich and strengthen your relationships.

MEASURE — *The sons by this time have discovered a swamp covered with excellent timber, and as they have seen many great rafts of saw logs bound for the mills of New Orleans floating past their dwelling, they resolve to try the success of a little enterprise. . . . A few cross-saws are purchased . . . their first raft is made on the shore and loaded with cordwood. . . . the husband and sons embark on it and float down the mighty stream . . . they arrive in safety at New Orleans, where they dispose of their stock, the money obtained for which may be said to be all profit . . .*

Don't let work, play, charity or anything else detract you from spending time with your family. Like these settlers, find a project that can become the object of family devotion. Such an initiative will lead to what really counts in life — being respected and loved by those who are closest to you. The true measure of your personal success is family success.

MOUNTAINTOP — *And now the vessel approaches their home. See the joyous mother and daughters as they stand on the bank! A store of vegetables lies around them, a large tub of fresh milk is at their feet, and in their hands are plates filled with rolls of butter. As the steamer stops, three broad straw hats are waved from its upper deck; and soon, husband and wife, brother and sisters are in each other's embrace . . . The husband gives his bag of dollars to the wife, while the sons present some token of affection to their sisters. Surely, at such a moment, the Squatters are richly repaid for all their labors.*

Endeavor to take family members along on your success journey. Incorporating them into the different arenas of your life will not only yield deeper meaning but will also bring you — like the reunited frontier family — to the mountaintop of joy. In the long run, investing in family teamwork will yield financial, social and personal profit.

WORK TOGETHER STRATEGICALLY   MAY 8TH

Hello. My name is Sacheen Littlefeather. I'm Apache and I am president of the National Native American Affirmative Image Committee. I'm representing Marlon Brando this evening . . .

On February 27, 1973, protesters representing the American Indian Movement occupied the Pine Ridge Indian Reservation in Wounded Knee, South Dakota, criticizing a range of issues including the failure of the United States government to fulfill its obligations under its treaties with Native Americans.

One month later, during the 45th Academy Awards Ceremony in

Los Angeles, Liv Ullmann and Roger Moore took the stage to present the Best Actor Award. When they announced that Marlon Brandon had won for his performance in The Godfather, actress Sacheen Littlefeather (also known as Marie Louise Cruz) came out as Brando's representative to decline the Oscar. Littlefeather's speech was Met by a plethora of jeers as well as some cheers.

> *. . . and he has asked me to tell you in a very long speech which I cannot share with you presently, because of time, but I will be glad to share with the press afterwards, that he very regretfully cannot accept this very generous award. And the reasons for this being are the treatment o f American Indians today by the film industry – excuse me – and on television in movie re-runs, and also with recent happenings at Wounded Knee. I beg at this time that I have not intruded upon this evening . . . in the future, our hearts and our understandings will meet with love and generosity. Thank you on behalf of Marlon Brando.*

Brando's strategy to boycott the ceremony and deploy Littlefeather as his surrogate had two aims: to draw attention to the Wounded Knee incident and, more generally, to critique Hollywood's portrayal of Native Americans. The tactic had been years in the making. Brando's activism with the American Indian Movement had started in the 1960s. Engaged with Native American issues since her college days, Littlefeather reached out to Brando and the shared commitment that they discovered evolved into a collaboration that blossomed at the Oscars event.

The publicity that Littlefeather garnered from that occasion fueled her ongoing activism and eventually led to her co-founding the National American Indian Performing Arts Registry, sharing an Emmy for PBS's "Dance in America: Song for Dead Warriors" and producing films about Native Americans. Working strategically together with Brando yielded success for Littlefeather. Whether or not you agree with a social protest at the Academy Awards, strategic collaboration can work for you, too, as you:

ASSERT YOUR INTERESTS — Brando and Littlefeather were able to work strategically together because they were both interested in supporting Native Americans. Littlefeather knew to check out Brando as a potential collaborator because of his track record on the issue. Assert your interests then pay attention to who has been tracking in the same direction. Ask yourself the key question: do we share the same core values? Determine whether you're on common ground and that it's solid enough to move forward together.

ASSESS YOUR OPTIONS — Find someone to brainstorm with, especially when you're trying to come up with a strategy to address a big problem. Put all your options on the table so you can figure out which one is the missing piece to your puzzle. Think outside of the box. No one was expecting Brando to send an Apache woman to decline his Best Actor Oscar.

ACCELERATE YOUR JOURNEY — Balance your solo endeavors with team effort. Littlefeather invested in a relationship of social activism with Brando, and it paid dividends, yielding her an opportunity to take her issue to one of the biggest stages imaginable. If you tend to do everything yourself, develop the collective approach. To start thinking about building strategic collaborations, meditate on Mother Teresa's words:

We don't have to be extraordinary in any way. I can do what you can't do, you can do what I can't do, and together we can do great things.

BE LOYAL TO YOUR TEAMMATES   MAY 9TH

And now he is in the war, and how has he conducted himself? Let their dusky forms rise up out the mires of James Island and give the answer. . . Obedient and patient and solid as a wall are they. All we lack is a paler hue and a better acquaintance with the alphabet.

James Gooding

The 54th Regiment Massachusetts Volunteer Infantry was was the first African American regiment of the Civil War, organized in early 1863 in the aftermath of the Emancipation Proclamation. The regiment served extensively during the war, notably on July 18, 1863, at the Second Battle of Fort Wagner, when the black infantry, in concert with other Union regiments, executed a frontal assault against Fort Wagner and suffered major casualties.

This exemplary service notwithstanding, Negro soldiers received less pay than their white counterparts. War Department regulations set pay for the latter at $13 per month but for the former at only $10 per month.

On September 28, 1863, 54th Regiment Corporal James Gooding wrote to President Lincoln requesting equal pay. Gooding asserted his appeal by affirming the loyalty of the black troops and asking for the same loyalty in return.

Now, Your Excellency, we have done a soldier's duty. Why can't we have a soldier's pay? . . . We appeal to you, sir . . . to have us justly dealt with. The regiment do pray that they be assured their service will be fairly appreciated by paying them as American soldiers, not as menial hirelings. . . . If you, as chief magistrate of the nation, will assure us of our whole pay, we are content. Our patriotism, our enthusiasm will have a new impetus to exert our energy more and more to aid our country. Not that our hearts ever flagged in devotion, spite the evident apathy displayed in our behalf, but we feel as though our country spurned us, now we are sworn to serve her.

In July 1864, Congress established equal pay for black and white soldiers, and, a couple months later, Gooding and his fellow 54th Regiment troops received their full back pay.

One of the most important qualities for you to possess for whatever team you're on — family, work, sports, community organization — is loyalty. Gooding was loyal to his military team; follow his example. To be loyal to your teammates, be:

FIRM — Be solid as a rock in support of your teammates, even when they've done something wrong. If that's the case, share with them out of the public eye. Do nothing to expose or embarrass until you've had a chance to confront them with the truth behind close doors. Helping them understanding the importance of repentance should be your goal.

FORTHRIGHT — Speak out for your teammates. Take a stand on their behalf, especially if they're not strong enough to speak for themselves. Baseball legend Yogi Berra hit a grand slam on this point:

You stand up for your teammates. Your loyalty is to them. You protect them through good and bad, because they'd do the same for you.

FASTIDIOUS — Pay close attention to what others are saying, doing, and feeling. Loyalty means that you care about the interpersonal details. Don't dismiss the little things that happen to offend a teammate. If team members know you got their back in the small matters, they'll know you'll be there for them when it really counts; and they'll be there for you!

FAIR — If your teammates are treating you unfairly, do what Gooding did: let the leader know. Teams will fall apart without fair and equal treatment among its members. Good leaders understand this truth. Make sure you treat others fairly and if you see unfairness in your organization, make sure the leaders know so they can rectify the wrong.

HARMONIZE YOUR TEAM   MAY 10TH

This is really composition on the spot, with the spirit of jazz strongly over all of them but the iron laws of harmony and rhythm never lost sight of; and it is a collective thing, the most beautiful example of men working together seen in public today.
Otis Ferguson, writing about the Benny Goodman Quartet

America of the 1920's was the birthplace of jazz, and the style of music garnered such widespread popularity by the 1930's that the era gained the reputation as the Jazz Age. Four of the most famous jazzmen — Benny Goodman, Gene Krupa, Teddy Wilson and Lionel Hampton — played together to sold-out audiences in the fall of 1936 in New York City. Their performances at the Cafe Rouge in the Pennsylvania Hotel were reviewed by music critic Otis Ferguson in the New Republic.

They play every night — clarinet, piano, vibraphone, drums, and they make music you would not believe. No arrangements, not a false note, one finishing his solo and dropping into background support, then the other, all adding inspiration until with some number like "Stomping at the Savoy" they get going too strong to quit — four choruses, someone starts up another, six, eight, and still someone starts — no two notes the same and no one note off the chord, the more they relax in the excitement of it the more a natural genius in preselection becomes evident and the more indeed the melodic line becomes rigorously pure.

Ferguson concluded his essay by explaining the enduring effect of the experience.

And if you leave at the end, before the "Good-Bye" signature, you will seem to hear this great rattling march of the hobos through the taxis, lights, and people, ringing under the low sky over Manhattan as if it were a strange high thing after all (which it is) and as if it came from the American ground under these buildings, roads and motor cars (which it did). And if you leave the band and quartet and piano of the Goodman show and still are no more than lightly amused, you may be sure that in the smug absence of your attention a native true spirit of music has been and gone, leaving a message for your grandchildren to study through their patient glasses.

The Benny Goodman Quartet exemplified a harmonized team, individuals working together to create beautiful outcomes. To harmonize your team, practice these principles.

COMPLEMENTARY FELLOWSHIP — Work with people whose skills and talents complement your own. Be humble enough to recognize your deficiencies and bring others on board who are strong where you are weak, who are the percussion to your piano; your voice to their violin.

CRUCIAL FLOW — Like the jazzmen, find your rhythm. You will unearth it by discovering what feels special — in you and in others. Let your emotions flow in positive directions as you offer compliments, affirmation, encouragement. Bringing your best work will bring out the best in someone else, raising not only the individual but the collective level of performance. Another accomplished jazzman, Max Roach, elaborates this point.

Jazz is a very democratic musical form. It comes out of a communal experience. We take our respective instruments and collectively create a thing of beauty.

CERTAIN FOLLOWSHIP — Outsiders know when the insiders are working together, and they will flock to embrace the excellence of the experience. Crowds assembled before dawn to hear the Goodman ensemble's afternoon concerts. The harmony of your teamwork will be a magnet to others.

CRUSADING FREEDOM — Everyone wants a better tomorrow, so help those in your social environment see that brighter day. Show them hope. Make their destiny ring loud like music in their ears. Start working together towards a victorious future and you and your teammates will harmonize towards greater freedom; and the beauty of your composition will be heard far and wide.

ORGANIZE FOR JUSTICE   MAY 11TH

We the colored citizens of Frankfort and vicinity . . . would respectfully state that life, liberty, and property are unprotected among the colored race of this state.
Negro Coalition of Kentucky

On March 25, 1871, African Americans from Kentucky made an appeal to the U.S. Congress for protection of their life and property. Many such appeals were made by Southern blacks during the Reconstruction era following the Civil War because of the violence and persecution of white extremists attempting to restore their social and political supremacy. The Kentucky petition made its case from the opening paragraph.

> *Organized bands of desperate and lawless men, mainly composed of soldiers of the late Rebel armies, armed, disciplined, and disguised, and bound by oath and secret obligations, have by force, terror, and violence subverted all civil society among colored people, thus utterly rendering insecure the safety of persons and property, overthrowing all those rights which are the primary basis and objects of the government which are expressly guaranteed to us by the Constitution of the United States . . . We believe you are not familiar with the description of the Ku Klux Klan's riding nightly over the country, going from county to county, and in the county towns spreading terror wherever they go by robbing, whipping, ravishing, and killing our people without provocation, compelling colored people to break the ice and bathe in the chilly waters of the Kentucky River.*

On April 20, 1871, largely in response to these pleas for federal intervention, Congress passed the Enforcement Act — one of three such legislative initiatives from 1870 to 1871 — empowering President Ulysses Grant to suspend the writ of habeas corpus and take other action to combat the terrorist campaigns of Ku Klux Klan. Also known as the Klan Act, the bill empowered President Grant to send federal troops to Southern states to enforce the law. Consequently, hundreds of Klansmen were fined or imprisoned, causing the decline of the white supremacist group until its return in 1915. Unfortunately, with the Compromise of 1876, the Klan Act under President Rutherford Hayes was mostly shelved.

African Americans of Kentucky and other Southern states experienced some success in confronting the existential threats of post-Civil War America because they came together for change. When you're facing big, seemingly insurmountable challenges, don't go at it alone. Close ranks with those of common interest and overturn barriers to change by working together. Keeping the following points in mind will help you organize for justice.

STATUS QUO — Recognize right up front that there are long-standing systems in place that are resistant to social change. That's why big changes don't happen without a team. You may start with the vision; it's necessary but not sufficient. If your goal is to reform the status quo, you'll need help. Surround yourself with like-minded people. Like the Kentucky blacks of 150 years ago, come together with a committed cohort and you'll be in a better position to be heard; societal improvement will follow.

STRATEGY — And come together around a shared mission. A focused strategy is key to implementing change. If you're not on the same page with your teammates, step back; slow down; brainstorm; plan. It's better to wait on clear and coordinated tactics then to venture onto the battlefield moving in different directions. Remember — your victory rises from your strategy.

STRENGTH — The petition of the Kentucky coalition demanded that President Grant send in federal troops to quell the Klan; the blacks knew that state militias weren't up to the task. Grant heeded their call for intervention because the masses had lined up in support behind the initiative. Strength comes in numbers. Keep building your team, adding more and more members, to create such enormous strength that change becomes irresistible . . . inevitable . . . impending . . . irreversible. The words of Andrew Carnegie captured this precept.

Teamwork is the ability to work together toward a common vision . . .
It is the fuel that allows common people to attain uncommon results.

STRIVE TO CONNECT WITH ALL YOUR TEAMMATES
MAY 12TH

Hamilton was, indeed, a singular character.
Thomas Jefferson

In December 1789, Thomas Jefferson returned to Virginia from his diplomatic tour of duty as Minister to France. Four months later, he moved to New York City, joining President George Washington's cabinet as Secretary of State. He immediately found himself in political and ideological conflict with another cabinet member, Treasury Secretary Alexander Hamilton. In notes of his early days in the President's inner circle, Jefferson wrote about his consternation with Hamilton.

For he avowed the opinion that man could be governed by one of two motives only, force or interest; force, he observed, in this country was out of the question, and the interests, therefore, of the members must be laid hold of to keep the legislative in unison with the executive. And with grief and shame it must be acknowledged that his machine was not without effect; that even in this, the birth of our government, some members were found sordid enough to bend their duty to their interest, and to look after personal rather than public good.

He elaborated on his adversary's chief flaw.

> *Of acute understanding, disinterested, honest, and honorable in all private transactions, amiable in society, and duly valuing virtue in private life, yet so bewitched and perverted by the British example as to be under thorough conviction that corruption was essential to the government of a nation.*

Jefferson failed to connect with Hamilton during his four-year cabinet tenure (Jefferson left after Washington's first term.). In fact he stopped trying to connect, instead exacerbating the tension through surreptitious newspaper attacks and rising political warfare. Don't follow his example. If you're having trouble connecting with some on your team — no matter how intense the disagreement or difficult the relationship might be — strive to connect with them. To do so, you should:

RESET YOUR OPINIONS — Try to take a different view of your adversaries. Endeavor to cultivate a higher opinion of them. Everyone possesses valuable qualities, even some redeeming features. The antagonism notwithstanding, Jefferson had to acknowledge that Hamilton was "honest, and honorable in all private transactions, amiable in society, and duly valuing virtue in private life." If you look hard enough, you'll find good qualities in people with whom you're at odds. Focusing on the attributes will help you transition the challenging relationship to a more positive place.

RELEASE YOUR ANGER — You're upset, offended about something that was said or done concerning you. Get over it. Don't ignore it or bury it. Talk to a friend about it. Pray about it. If need be, go see a counselor or lawyer. Just don't let it fester. Releasing your hostility will help you cultivate a forgiving spirit.

REFLECT ON YOUR BAGGAGE — Make sure the biggest problem in the conflictual relationship is not you. Look in the mirror. If you're harboring negative feelings and having trouble overcoming them, acknowledge that it's a normal reaction, as Maya Angelou surmised:

> *People will forget what you said, people will forget what you did, people will never forget how you made them feel.*

If it's your baggage that's the major factor in the relational breakdown, empty it. The lighter load will make it easier to reconcile.

REACH FOR THE GREATER GOOD — Jefferson led the opposition to Hamilton, organizing the anti-Federalist forces into a new political party, splitting the young nation into competing groups. Make it about the goals of the team, not your personal agendas. Subordinate your role for the greater good. Put the team's interests ahead of your own. If you fail to connect with all of your teammates, let it be someone else's fault.

ADVOCATE FOR YOUR TEAMMATES   MAY 13TH

We decided, in the face of extended imprisonment, to demand to be treated as political prisoners. We felt that, as a matter of principle, this was the dignified and self-respecting thing to do, since we had offended politically, not criminally.
Doris Stevens

Beginning in 1917 suffragist Doris Stevens participated in the Silent Sentinels vigil in front of the White House, urging the passage of a constitutional amendment for a woman's right to vote. Stevens targeted President Woodrow Wilson, arguing that it was "arrogant of Wilson to fight for democracy abroad when women were not included in democracy at home." Along with other protesters, she was arrested and jailed. In her book "Jailed for Freedom", published in 1920, Stevens wrote about the woman who led the fight to get them released.

. . . Lucy Burns . . . the leader of the new protest . . . possessed the 'voice' of the modern suffrage movement. . . . She had no sooner begun to organize her comrades for protest than the   officials sensed a 'plot' and removed her at once to solitary confinement. But they were too late. Taking the leader only hastened the rebellion. A forlorn piece of paper was discovered on which was written their initial demand. It was then passed from prisoner to prisoner through holes in the wall surrounding leaden pipes, until a finished document had been perfected and signed by all the prisoners.

In a letter of protest to the Commissioners of the District of Columbia, Stevens and other women leaders advocated for their imprisoned sister-in-arms.

Conscious, therefore, of having acted in accordance with the highest standards of citizenship, we ask the commissioners of the District to grant us the rights due political prisoners. We ask that we no longer be segregated and confined under locks and bars in small groups, but permitted to see each other, and that Miss Lucy Burns, who is in full sympathy with this letter, be released from solitary confinement in another building and given back to us.

Largely as a result of the efforts of Stevens, Burns and their suffrage teammates, the 19th Amendment to the U.S. Constitution was enacted in 1919, securing women's voting rights. Teamwork fueled their success, especially when they advocated for one another. To raise an effective voice on behalf of your teammates, make it a priority to:

PROCLAIM FOR YOUR TEAMMATES — Speak up your teammates. Stevens led her team in writing a letter of protest for Burns. See yourself in a common plight, as Martin Luther King, Jr. asserted:

We may have all come on different ships, but we're in the same boat now.

When someone on your team is in need, especially if it's a crisis, make sure your voice is heard!

PUNCH FOR YOUR TEAMMATES — Sometimes you have to fight. Stevens verbally assaulted the U.S. President to further the cause of her team. But before you throw the first punch (figuratively speaking), make sure you've exhausted all the more peaceful approaches. You should go to battle as the last resort.

PUT YOUR TEAMMATES FIRST — Do you value your own agenda more than the goals of the team? If so, it's time to reassess your motives and objectives. Are you willing to make personal sacrifices for the sake of the team? Think of ways you can do it. Focus on the most important project you can take on that puts the welfare of your team ahead of your own. Stevens and her cohort risked greater punishment for their teammate. Be willing to take a sacrificial step for a teammate in need. Take a step in that direction today.

FLEE THE MENACE   MAY 14TH

Ahab son of Omri did more evil in the eyes of the Lord than any of those before him.
1 Kings 16:30

Tuck had been homeless for a while and was doing well as a resident at Harkhomes. It was after ten weeks of progress when trouble hit. Drug addiction had precipitated his broken life, but the drill-sergeant regimen had helped him achieve thirty days "clean", i.e., without any drug use. Randy, his main "get-high" buddy from his street days, was coming regularly to visit Tuck but was not allowed to see him.

"Whatever you do, stay away from Randy," I advised Tuck. "Randy is your Ahab," I used a Biblical analogy, referring to the most evil king of the Old Testament. I gave him an urgent warning:

Don't spend any time with him or you'll end up in trouble.

He agreed with this prohibition, understanding that Randy presented too great a temptation for him to violate his new lifestyle and return to his old ways. But Randy's persistence paid off. On his birthday, he dropped by to see Tuck and passed him a note inviting him to attend his birthday party. Tuck couldn't resist the offer. So, after his N.A. meeting one afternoon, instead of sticking with his routine and returning to Harkhomes, he detoured to hang out at Randy's party.

As soon as he arrived that evening, Tuck knew he had made a bad decision. He was tremendously tempted to indulge again in drugs offered by the many crack smokers there. But even as he struggled to resist that temptation, what he did not expect was the police raid that swept him up that night along with the drug abusers. Tuck had an outstanding warrant, so he was detained, while most of the others, including Randy, were released.

The consequent jail term derailed his progress. We maintained some contact with him for a while but eventually lost track of him in the prison system. He stopped answering our letters, and we never heard from him again.

Tuck had been heading in the right direction before he became the classic innocent victim. His downfall stemmed not so much from his behavior as from his association. Who he was with had more to do with bringing about his crisis than who he was or what he had done.

To avoid Tuck's tragic outcome, your key is to:

BEWARE — A menace is someone who is a major distraction, preventing you from making progress toward your goals. If you want to get better at work, at school, at whatever, and there's a person in life who distracts you from getting it done, then keep it simple — FLEE THE MENACE: create as much distance between you and that person as possible; or, put another way, spend as little time with that person as possible. If you're an athlete and your goal is to get into the best physical shape possible, then the last thing you want to do is to hang around people who are smoking cigarettes, drinking alcohol, and doing drugs, because they might influence you to do the same things. Steer clear of negative influencers, lest they trip you up, breaking your strides of progress, or drag you down into the rut of failure with them. It's trite but true: misery loves company. Lose the losers in your life so that you'll be free to win. Once you've won your battle, you can always go back and show them the way to victory.

FENCE THE MYSTERY   MAY 15TH

The old prophet answered, "I too am a prophet, as you are. And an angel said to me by the word of the Lord: 'Bring him back with you to your house so that he may eat bread and drink water.'" (But he was lying to him.)
1 Kings 13:18

Jimmie had done well at Harkhomes. After about seven months with us, he had kicked his heroin habit and had saved enough money from his part-time job to get his own room. Not long after he moved out, he came back for a visit. He told me that his girlfriend, Val, had become homeless. He wanted her to move in with him. I counseled him against it. I sensed he wasn't yet strong enough to maintain his own progress while also shouldering her burdens.

More important than the strength of his character was the effect of this association. I sensed that Val's unrepentant drug habit would be too great a temptation for Jimmie. I advised him to limit his association with her. I gave him some information on programs for homeless women to share with Val. Using an Old Testament example, I compared Val to the old prophet, who lied to the younger prophet, which led to the latter's downfall. Jimmie seemed resistant to my counsel so I admonished him:

Help her in any way you can, advise her to seek the assistance she needs, but don't let her move in with you under any circumstances.

He rejected my advice, and his recalcitrance led to the worst possible outcome. Val moved in with him, and through this close association with her drug habit, he started using drugs again. They consumed all their rent money supporting their addictive lifestyle, and eventually both ended up homeless again.

To avoid Jimmie's unfortunate outcome, your key is to:

BE WARY — Jimmie didn't need to flee Val; he needed to fence her. It wasn't clear at first that his relationship with her would be destructive; it was a bit of mystery. Jimmie didn't have to completely cut Val off, but should have played it safe, strategically regulating the relationship, keeping her at arm's length, creating and maintaining some degree of separation from his shaky friend. If Jimmie had maintained a safe distance from Val, he would have run less risk of falling back into the broken life himself. This strategy is important as you handle relations with family, coworkers, friends, classmates, colleagues, and significant others who you must deal with out of obligation, tradition, or necessity. Your objective is simple — FENCE THE MYSTERY: find a way to manage the uncertain relationships of your life in a cautious, circumspect, and self-protective way, so that their necessary presence doesn't become a negative influence. Such people may be a mystery—not obviously destructive but possessing negative traits or character defects that can adversely affect you. Or perhaps the person could be operating in a way that is intentionally deceptive, claiming to help you out when he's really using you to further his own agenda. If so, put up that fence; keep him at a safe distance until you find out if he's friend or foe. I'm not suggesting that you go through life governed by cynicism, suspicious of others' motives, but encouraging you to take it slow when faced with decisions about relationships: be careful, discerning, and wise. Fence the proverbial wolf in sheep's clothing!

FIND THE MENTOR   MAY 16TH

> *Elijah said to Elisha, "Stay here; the Lord has sent me*
> *to Bethel." But Elisha said, "As surely as the Lord lives*
> *and as you live, I will not leave you." So they went down to Bethel.*
> 2 Kings 2:2

Having recently lost his job, Chester was a willing and tireless worker who eventually took over the cooking duties at Harkhomes. He had never finished high school, so he studied and took the G.E.D. test — several times — but couldn't pass it. Chester kept working hard in the kitchen and liked it so much that he began to volunteer with the cooking chores at his church; he spent as much time as he could helping out in the church kitchen. His diligence there distinguished him, and one day one of the church leaders opened the door of opportunity. He got Chester a job working as a part-time cook in the home of an elderly couple.

I encouraged Chester by sharing a Biblical illustration. I explained to him how Elisha had Elijah as his mentor, and the relationship with the older prophet benefited the younger prophet greatly. I counseled him:

> *Keep working hard! There may be some greater opportunity as*
> *you get to know that couple; and don't give up on your education.*

Chester spent all his time helping out his elderly employers, not worrying about punching the clock. He worked hard at his cooking duties, but he also constantly went beyond the call of duty, cleaning, gardening, driving, shopping. He became so useful that his employers decided to expand his responsibilities. He eventually moved into the couple's home as live-in cook, housekeeper, gardener, and chauffeur.

Through his relationship with them, Chester not only overcame his joblessness and his homelessness; he also found mentors. His employers were both retired teachers. When they found out about Chester's aspirations, they volunteered to help prepare him for the G.E.D. test. With such abundant assistance, it wasn't long before Chester passed his exam with flying colors. Chester attained his educational goal through the bounty of a mentoring relationship.

To follow Chester's example, your key is to:

BE WATCHFUL — Let's also keep your goal here simple: FIND YOUR MENTOR. The best way to do it is to keep your eyes open for one. Accept the fact that you can't achieve success and fulfillment on your own. So be on the lookout for a person who builds your confidence, brings encouragement, and sows inspiration into your life. Be creative in finding your mentors. If no one in your "real life" appears, go virtual. Search online for mentors and role models. Explore history for inspirational figures or the contemporary scene for exemplary celebrities or public figures. Books, magazines, movies, plays, TV, the Internet — let the full range of your experience of people, direct and indirect, bring you the positive influences you need to succeed. Once you find a mentor, if he or she is someone who is a part of your life, make time to see that person on a regular basis as time allows and always be honest, courteous, punctual, and respectful. Your mentor is probably taking time away from other priorities to spend time with you, so be careful to honor that commitment. Go out of your way to show how much you appreciate your mentor: be early for appointments; come prepared with written questions or updates; have meetings at the place of greatest convenience; don't make contact at awkward or inopportune times; and from time to time, send a thank-you note or a letter updating your progress.

BRIDGE DIFFICULT RELATIONSHIPS   MAY 17TH

Brother, the Great Spirit has made us all, but He has made a great difference between His white and red children. He has given us different complexions and different customs. To you He has given the arts. To these He has not opened our eyes. We know these things to be true . . .
Red Jacket

In the summer of 1805, Seneca Chief Red Jacket participated with other Native American chiefs and warriors in a meeting in upstate New York with Jacob Cram, a New England missionary. Red Jacket, whose Native American name was Sagoyewatha (Keeper Awake), had been a key figure in the history of Indian-white relations since the Revolutionary War. His Seneca nation had been allies of Great Britain during the war, so they were forced to cede land following the British defeat. Red Jacket became a chief negotiator on behalf of his nation with the new United States, eventually leading a delegation of fifty Native American leaders to meet with President George Washington in 1792; for his peacemaking efforts, Washington presented Red Jacket with a special peace medal.

The 1805 meeting had been called by Reverend Cram in an attempt to evangelize among the Seneca Tribe. Red Jacket responded for the group, first acknowledging the divine favor upon their meeting.

> *Friend and Brother, it was the will of the Great Spirit that we should meet together this day. He orders all things and has given us a fine day for our council. He has taken His garment from before the sun and caused it to shine with brightness upon us . . .*

He then explained how important it was to place any religious discussion in historical context.

> *There was a time when our forefathers owned this great island. Their seats extended from the rising to the setting sun. The Great Spirit had made it for the use of Indians . . . But an evil day came upon us. Your forefathers crossed the great water and landed on this island. Their numbers were small. They found friends and not enemies . . . They asked for a small seat. We took pity on them, granted their request; and they sat down amongst us . . . At length their numbers had greatly increased. They wanted more land; they wanted our country. Our eyes were opened and our minds became uneasy. Wars took place. Indians were hired to fight against Indians, and many of our people were destroyed . . . our seats were once large and yours were small. You have now become a great people, and we have scarcely a place left to spread our blankets. . . .*

Red Jacket elucidated that he and his nation were unwilling to give up their traditions, but he communicated this truth in a way that affirmed both a common belief in a divine being and a shared hope in peaceful relations. He had justification to be negative but resolved to stay positive. Embrace his example; bridge your own difficult relationships as you:

LEARN TO RESPECT — Red Jacket established a common ground of understanding at the outset of the meeting, which is a good protocol for you to emulate. It's hard to respect those who have disrespected you. It takes humility and grace, which Red Jacket extended. You should do the same.

LISTEN TO UNDERSTAND — You can be in a conversation and not really hear what others are saying. Avoid the misunderstandings that lead to arguments. Demonstrate your listening skills by deliberately repeating what you've heard before responding. By doing so, you are building a bridge across difficult relationships.

LEAN IN TO FORGIVE — Red Jacket was willing to forgive. Think of forgiveness as a gift you can extend, even if the recipient doesn't deserve it. Meditate on the words of Martin Luther King Jr. to help you develop the habit of forgiveness:

Forgiveness is not an occasional act; it is a permanent attitude.

LIVE TO SERVE — In all true belief systems, greatness comes by serving others. Whatever tensions exist, acts of service will mitigate them.

REFUSE TO LABEL YOURSELF AND OTHERS   MAY 18TH

There are no problems we cannot solve together,
and very few that we can solve by ourselves.
Lyndon Johnson

In February 1950 Joseph McCarthy, the U.S. Senator from Wisconsin, first made the charge that Communists had infiltrated the highest levels of the federal government, particularly the State Department. The political and social turmoil of the McCarthy era ensued, provoking labels of communist and anti-communist to fly across the political aisles and elsewhere.

In 1958 then-U.S. Senate Majority Leader Lyndon B. Johnson (He was soon to become Vice-President, then President.) wrote an article to address the hostility-fraught, guilt-by-association cultural environment. Published in the "Texas Quarterly", Johnson's essay commenced.

I am a free man, an American, a United States Senator, and a Democrat, in that order. I am also a liberal, a conservative, a Texan, a taxpayer, a rancher, a businessman, a consumer, a parent, a voter, and not as young as I used to be or as old as I expect to be — and I am all these things in no fixed order.

Johnson went on to explain his disdain for the oversimplifying distortions of labeling.

> . . . *I am not able — nor even the least interested in trying — to define my political philosophy by the choice of a one-word or two-word label. This may be against the tide, but, if so, the choice is deliberate. . . . At the heart of my own beliefs is a rebellion against this very process of classifying, labeling, and filing Americans under headings: regional, economic, occupational, religious, racial, or otherwise. . . . we seem bent today on reducing every man's philosophy to a mere vital statistic, to the next question asked — of professors, students, public officials, job applicants, business executives, labor leaders, and many more — after age, weight, height, and color of eyes and hair.*

Labeling yourself and others — whether in Johnson's era or our own — creates misunderstanding and leads to tension and divisiveness. Your quest should be to use language that strengthens relationships rather than simplistic, insensitive words that break them down. You can avoid labeling and be a team-builder by making these concepts a reality in your daily life.

CUT SMALL-MINDEDNESS — Like Johnson, don't put yourself in narrow or small-minded categories. And don't let others define you in negative ways. If you believe the labels that others put on you, you allow them to make your world too small. Lose all the labels. Think expansively about who you are and what you're about.

COOL DOWN — Labeling represents extremes, so refusing to use them will moderate your conversations, especially with those on the other side of the political or cultural fence from you. Be intentional about deescalating your interactions, starting with your own temperament; if it's been boiling too much, turn it down. Manage yourself better so you can manage your relationships better. And if someone flings a label at you that you don't like, don't fly off the handle. Use it as an opportunity to change the conversation: talk de-labeling. Johnson did it. Why not you?

CAST VISION — Shift your focus from the past — where labels persist — to the present and future — where new identities emerge. Be open to new ideas and open to the opinions of others. Stay outside-the-box in the way you view your present and future. Johnson's insight on this point is timeless:

Yesterday is not ours to recover, but tomorrow is ours to win or lose.

CREATE VALUE — Labels devalue people. Refusing to use them creates value by diminishing the superficialities and highlighting what really matters — an individual's character. Bring people together by taking the spotlight off labels and shining it on attributes.

AFFIRM THE INDIVIDUALS ON YOUR TEAM   MAY 19TH

Let them become Americans . . . elevated and improved, rather than changed;
they lose their sharp edges and adopt some the good qualities of others.
Ole Raeder

Among the waves of European immigrants throughout the nineteenth century, Scandinavians — due to crop failures, job shortages and religious persecution at home — came to America in increasing numbers. Because of this rising emigration, the Norwegian government sent prominent jurist Ole Raeder to the United States to study its legal system and culture. Raeder arrived in 1847 and transmitted many letters reporting his findings, which were published in Norwegian newspapers. In one of his letters, he described the the distinctiveness of the American cultural environment: a demographic mix in which the "sharp edges" of the past could be lost but those "peculiar qualities" preserved and incorporated into a new social blend with distinct individual and demographic flavors.

Even if America, shall in the end absorb and mold together into a compact whole all the various nationalities which now are making their contributions in such rich measure, and shall not only blot out the many prejudices which now separate people in their home countries but also a b s o r b some of the individual characteristics which now constitute the peculiar qualities of each nation; even if such be the case, then surely it will be for us, as well as for every other European nation, not merely a source of satisfaction as an historical fact, but perhaps also, in the course of events, a factor of real benefit that our Scandinavian North has become one of the parent nations for this nation to whose lot will undoubtedly some day fall the place of leadership in the affairs of the world.

Raeder discerned the distinctive cultural attributes that made America stand out among nations: affirm individuality even as those individuals transformed to become a participating member of the larger body. In much the same way, you should affirm individuals on your team: allow them to be themselves while becoming a part of the collective. To do so, strive to:

BE AN EXAMPLE — You are divinely created—made a composite of spirit, soul, and body. Make sure you're in touch with all three parts of you, and exemplify your holistic lifestyle as an inspiration to your teammates as well as others to live life to the fullest. Affirm and express your uniqueness. People will notice and be motivated to do the same; and they may even be touched to seek higher purposes, as Jesus directed:

> *Let your light so shine before men that they may see your*
> *good works and glorify your Father who is in heaven.*
> Matthew 5:16

BE A GATHERER — Look for ways to include on your team those with differences: of nationality, of race, of gender, of ethnicity, of political persuasion, even of opinion. You will never be on a high-performing team if everyone on that team looks and acts and thinks just the same as you. Gathering such team members will affirm individuals by giving them new strength, as the Old Testament establishes:

> *Though one may be overpowered, two can defend themselves.*
> *A cord of three strands is not quickly broken.*
> Ecclesiastes 4:12

BE AN ENCOURAGER — Try to see the best in your team member, then help them to discover what you've found. That's the best way to affirm them. And if you can direct them into the areas where they are the strongest, both they and the team will prosper. This scriptural directive raises the standard for you to follow:

> *And let us consider how to stir up one another to love and good works, not*
> *neglecting to meet together, as is the habit of some, but encouraging one another . . .*
> Hebrews 10:24-25

BECOME A TEAM PLAYER   MAY 20TH

We are attempting, by this Constitution, to abolish
factions, and to unite all parties for the general welfare.
Alexander Hamilton

Between October 1787 and August 1788, the three writers of the Federalist Papers — Alexander Hamilton, James Madison and John Jay — published eighty-five essays in New York newspapers. Their goal was to make the case for New York and the other states to ratify the United States Constitution. Of the three scribes, Hamilton was the most prolific, producing fifty-one of the articles. In Federalist No. 1, he asserted the broader terms of the debate that was raging with the anti-Federalists.

It has been frequently remarked, that it seems to have been reserved to the people of this country, by their conduct and example, to decide the important question, whether societies of men are really capable or not, of establishing good government from reflection and choice, or whether they are forever destined to depend, for their political constitutions, on accident and force.

In Federalist No. 84, Hamilton covered several major issues such as the Bill of Rights and the expense of the federal government. At one point, he focused on the the the value of a collaborative citizenry, emphasizing the importance of teamwork to make the American Experiment work.

It ought also to be remembered that the citizens who inhabit the country at and near the seat of government will, in all questions that affect the general liberty and prosperity, have the same interest with those who are at a distance, and that they will stand ready to sound the alarm when necessary and to point out the actors in any pernicious project. The public papers will be expeditious messengers of intelligence to the most remote inhabitants of the Union.

Hamilton's assertion of the value of teamwork affirmed a truth that has become a sports maxim: individuals play the game, but teams win championships. Hamilton, his co-founders and early fellow citizens were successful in launching the United States of America because they managed — through all the conflicts and challenges — to work together as a team.

If you want to be successful, you cannot do it alone. One is too small a number to attain anything of real value. Strive to become a team player by practicing these four principles.

TREAT people differently, as individuals, not the all the same as one another, not as a statistic in a demographic sampling, not as just somebody else in a cultural grouping. Work to develop better relational skills, so you can get beyond the superficialities ("Nice weather today") to the what's really going on in the moment with the person you're dealing with ("I notice you're not smiling like you usually do . . . upset about something?").

TAKE a break from your agenda, so you can better understand what others are thinking and feeling. If you're always on an ego trip, you'll find it difficult to journey together with others; they will look to get off your bus.

TEST your teammates. Challenge them to get better. Becoming a team player doesn't mean you always have to play nice in the sandbox. To further the collective interest, tough love will sometimes be called for. Be willing to confront others with the truth, even if it's a difficult pill to swallow. But as you get to grips with them, be careful not to judge them. Remember Jesus' words.

> *Do not judge, or you too will be judged. For in the same way you judge others,*
> *you will be judged, and with the measure you use, it will be measured to you.*
> Matthew 7:1-2

TRY sacrifice. Do something you wouldn't ordinarily do for someone else, even give something up to benefit that person. Go out of your way — out of your comfort zone — to help the person. To build a house, you have to invest the brick and mortar in the structure. To build a team, you have to invest yourself in others. Take your precious resource of time, shift it away from your usual stuff, spend it on getting to know a team member better. Relational investment will eventually pay dividends for you and your team.

PICK THE RIGHT TEAMMATES   MAY 21ST

> *The lessons of great men and women are lost unless they reinforce upon*
> *our minds the highest demands which we make upon ourselves; they are lost*
> *unless they drive our sluggish wills forward in the direction of their highest ideas.*
> Jane Addams

In 1889 social worker Jane Addams co-founded Hull House, a run-down Chicago mansion, which she transformed into a trailblazing settlement house. Addams established this residence for twenty-five women, including herself and her college roommate, as much more than a provider of social services; it became a destination for innovation in education, research, training, art, neighborhood outreach and cultural understanding. Hull House eventually grew into a 13-building settlement complex and a national paradigm of immigrant uplift and social reform.

The first American woman to be awarded the Nobel Peace Prize, Addams learned from her grassroots work how important it was for individuals to work together to achieve personal progress. In her 1902 book "Democracy and Social Ethics" she discussed cooperation as an essential ingredient in positive individual and social change.

> *The man who disassociates his ambition, however disinterested, from the cooperation of his fellows, always takes the risk of ultimate failure. He does not take advantage of the great conserver and guarantee of his own permanent success which associated efforts afford. Genuine experiments toward higher social conditions must have a more democratic faith and practice than those which underlie private venture . . . and associated effort toward social progress, although much more awkward and stumbling than that same effort managed by a capable individual, does yet enlist deeper forces and evoke higher social capacities.*

Addams drew an example from the business world to illustrate the power of effective teamwork.

> *By the very exigencies of business demands, the employer is too often cut off from the social ethics developing in regard to our larger social relationships and from the great moral life springing from our common experiences. This is sure to happen when he is good "to" people rather than "with" them. When he allows himself to decide what is best for them instead of consulting them. . . .*

One truth from Addams' narrative about the challenging realities of self-improvement might be summarized — pick the right teammates. It is crucial for you to do so because your relationships will impact you both positively or negatively. Think about this principle in these ways; your teammates will either:

DETAIN YOU — When you're in a relationship with someone who doesn't share your convictions, values and priorities, you run the risk of being held back from your goals. If people in your life are dragging you down, or blocking your pathway, it's time to make changes. You can only be detained if you're not strong enough — mentally as well as physically — to break free. If need be, recruit a friendly cohort to unshackle you.

DEFINE YOU — I'm reminded of the story of the little boy playing outside when a neighbor asked him where his brother was. "He's inside the house," he responded. "We were playing a duet on the piano — but I finished first!" If you've started something as a team, work hard to stay in place, so you can finish as a team. Let collective commitment define you and your team.

DEVELOP YOU — If you're naturally introverted or not particularly outgoing, be intentional about picking the right teammate. It's about quality, not quantity. To reach for your dreams, you don't need a lot of people in your life, just the right people. And once you pick the right person, get out the way, as Theodore Roosevelt counseled:

The best executive is the one how has sense enough to pick good men to do what he wants done, and self-restraint to keep from meddling with them while they do it.

ENRICH YOUR RELATIONSHIPS   MAY 22ND

Power and wealth were worshipped in the old days. Beauty and justice and joy of spirit must be worshiped in the new.
Henry A. Wallace

In 1933 Henry A. Wallace was appointed Secretary of Agriculture, a cabinet post his father had held a decade earlier. Having grown up on an Iowa farm, Wallace brought firsthand knowledge of agricultural issues to his policy-making. In his 1934 book, "New Frontiers", he contrasted the old American frontier with the new, explaining that the quest of the twentieth century frontiersman went beyond profiting himself to enriching others.

. . . the new frontiersman will be continually seeking for his fellows those satisfactions which are mutually enriching. The nature of these satisfactions can only be faintly shadowed now. . . . In this land of ageless desire we are all striving newcomers. It is not a mushy, sentimental frontier, but one of hard realities, requiring individual and social discipline beyond that of the old frontiers. It lies within us and all about us. A great seer of the human heart who lived nineteen hundred years ago called it the Kingdom of Heaven. He knew that the tiny spark of divine spirit found in each individual could be fanned into an all-consuming flame, an intense passion for fair play, man to man, and man to woman, in the little time that we are here.

Wallace concluded with a vision of the glorious results of teamwork.

> *The land beyond the new frontier will be conquered by the continuous social inventions of men whose hearts are free from bitterness, prejudice, hatred, greed and fear; by men whose hearts are aflame with the extraordinary beauty of the scientific, artistic and spiritual wealth now before us, if only we reach out confidently, together.*

Wallace emphasized that enriching your relationships can have extraordinary outcomes, principles that you can exercise by being:

EXALTING — Lift people up by expressing appreciation for them. Let them know how much they mean to you and others. Go out of your way to give a compliment, or perhaps take them out for a bite to celebrate their success. It's easy for people to feel taken for granted if you fail to put into words just how wonderful they are; tell them; boost their self-esteem; make their day.

EXACTING — Learn someone's name — and use it the next time around. It takes effort to ask for the name and commit it to memory, but it personalizes interaction, making people feel valued. Titles alone don't affirm in the same way as a name. "Sir" and "M'am" are better than "Hey" and "Howdy", but saying the name is best; it's a little thing that can have big impact on others. And it'll help you remember the name of the person you just met if you repeat it during the conversation, stating the name one last time before you leave.

ENJOYABLE — Nothing enriches fellowship more than finding something you can enjoy doing together. Yes, this should be your goal for romance but also cultivate enjoyment beyond your personal relationships. Plan special activities that you can share outside of the normal course of business. New and different experiences will be a source of team joy, as you share "the extraordinary beauty of the scientific, artistic and spiritual wealth" of which Wallace wrote. Add richness to both your professional relationships by leading them along the roads less traveled.

EXPANSIVE — Your greatest fulfillment will come by fostering mutual inspiration. Follow Mark Twain's advice:

> *Keep away from people who try to belittle your ambitions. Small people try to do that, but the really great make you feel that you, too, can become great.*

UNIFY YOUR TEAM   MAY 23RD

The United States of North America are a wonder in the annals of the human race. Their development, in its gigantic proportions, far outstrips all former experience, and their significance for the future mocks the boldest calculation. Though not a hundred years old, they have become already one of the mightiest empires of the civilized world . . .
Philip Schaff

Swiss-born, German-educated Protestant theologian Philip Schaff immigrated to America in 1843. He had been called to become Professor of Church History and Biblical Literature at the German Reformed Theological Seminary of Mercersburg, Pennsylvania. Schaff spent much of the rest of his life teaching and living in the United States.

In 1854, on a sabbatical trip to Europe, Schaff gave a series of lectures on American life at the ecclesiastical diet at Frankfurt am Main and at the Swiss pastoral conference at Basel. These talks evolved into his book, "America", in which he wrote about the emergence of a national character. Schaff perceived divine handiwork orchestrating the diversity of the young nation into a unified country.

Providence, who creates nothing in vain, has there made physical preparations on the grandest scale, and formed an immeasurable territory . . . as a tempting asylum for all European nations, churches, and sects, who, there freed from the fetters of antiquated institutions . . . swarm and jostle each other, and yet, are molded by the process into one powerful nationality.

His was not a rose-colored-glasses view; he saw major problems to be overcome.

We can and must . . find fault with many things in them and their institutions: slavery, the lust of conquest, the worship of Mammon, the rage for speculation, political and religious fanaticism and party spirit, boundless temerity, boasting, quackery . . .

Yet he embraced the distinctive traits of the American character as a resource to attain exalted ends.

But we must not overlook the health, vital energies that continually react against these diseases: the noble love of liberty in connection with deep-rooted reverence for the law of God and authority; its clear, practical understating; its talent for organization; its inclination for improvement in every sphere; its fresh enthusiasm for great plans and schemes of moral reform; and its willingness to make sacrifices for the promotion of God's kingdom and every good work.

241

Schaff saw the destiny of America as diverse groups coming together through a shared vision. You, too, can bring people together by casting vision. To unify your team, keep these points in mind.

REVVED UP WITH VISION — Your team will succeed only when you have imparted a vision to which all can commit to work together. Vision conquers division. Cast a big picture for your project, the bigger the better; get them excited about it. No matter how different the individuals might be, your vision-casting can be the unifying force. A bright picture of a promising future will illuminate the pathway of unity.

READY FOR THE CRUCIBLE — Schaff possessed a true perspective: the valleys always follow the visions. Apostle Peter underscored this point.

Dear friends, do not be surprised at the fiery ordeal that has come on you to test you, as though something strange were happening to you.
1 Peter 4:12

Balance optimism with realism. Realize that adversity is inevitable. Be clear-eyed about the obstacles that challenge your objectives and communicate them to the team, so that all can work together to effectively address them. If you get them ready for the crucible, they'll more likely get through it.

RIDING STRONG WITH MOMENTUM — You will build momentum by taking daily steps towards fulfilling your goals. Lead your teammates to take those steps together and they will get stronger as they go.

FIGHT FOR YOUR TEAM   MAY 24TH

The Negro is 9.8 percent of all United States military forces here, close to 20 percent of the combat forces, about 25 parent of the front-line c ombat leaders, and currently 14.1 percent of those killed in action.
Thomas Johnson

During the first several months of 1968, New York Times reporter Thomas Johnson traveled to Saigon to investigate the morale of African American soldiers serving in Viet Nam. Johnson interviewed dozens of black servicemen during his three-and-a-half-month visit. Two of the military men in the article acknowledged an awareness of the civil rights struggles back home; but they were more focused on waging a different kind of battle, fighting together for the good of the team.

> *"We were working our show the same as Negroes back home," said Sgt. George Terry of the Army. "We brought democracy to the service by sticking it out." . . . "Many people called us Uncle Toms, but we were actually holding the line," said Lieut. Col. Felt L. Goodwin, a twenty-seven-year veteran who is information officer for the First Logistical Command.*

Another soldier emphasized the teamwork that made all the difference and caused the relationships to endure.

> *Melvin Murrel Smith, a Negro from Syracuse who served as a Marine sergeant, maintains that "the friendships formed between whites and Negroes in Vietnam will never die because of what we went through together." Mr. Smith, whose organization of self-defense units in the Vietnamese village of Tuylaon caused the Viet Cong to place a $1,700 price on his head, said that he and several white buddies form Vietnam now often telephoned and visited on another. "Civilians can't see this because they've never been through what we went through together," Mr. Smith said.*

Johnson reported a fighting spirit among the U.S. soldiers, regardless of race; it wasn't an attitude that put them at odds but a mettle that brought them together. Such shared moral strength bolstered these servicemen through the hardship, opposition, and danger that they daily faced. Their exemplary teamwork is worthy of your emulation. Fight for your team by following this playbook.

SACRIFICE FOR PROGRESS — Adopt the attitude that the progress of the mission is more important than the welfare of any individual, including you. Ask yourself — what can I do to make the team better? When you make a sacrifice for the team, everyone gets stronger, including you!

SHARE A COMMON PERSPECTIVE — Bear Bryant, the legendary Alabama football coach, taught his players to think team first. He was famous for saying:

> *I'm just a plow-hand from Arkansas, but I've learned to hold a team together. How to lift some men up, how to calm others down, until finally they've got one heartbeat together. There are   just three things I'd ever say: If something goes bad, I did it. If it goes semi-good, we did it. If anything goes*

really good, then you did it.

Whatever team you're on, think first of your teammates.

STRIVE FOR WINS — When you fight for your team, you produce wins. Some might be triumphs in the military or professional arenas; others could be breakthroughs in your social environment, which are the ones to really cherish. Sergeant Smith said it best when he stated that the interracial relationships "will never die because of what we went through together." Be a team warrior — fight for unity — and you'll bring down cultural walls.

STRONG IN BATTLE — As you enter your daily battlefields, look to bring those who share your vision and values on the team for the fight. You will end up — not fighting against each other — but fighting for each other, which will generate the strength that only unity can bring.

BE A VALUE-ADD TEAMMATE   MAY 25TH

*One of the most remarkable circumstances or features of our age is
the energy with which the principle of combination, or of action
by joint forces, by associated numbers, is manifesting itself.*
William Ellery Channing

Private association, as opposed to governmental intervention which emerged a century later, was the heartbeat of nineteenth century societal initiative. During the early 1800's clubs and groups for private and public benefit grew widely and rapidly, and they were being formed for every conceivable purpose. Clergyman William Ellery Channing described this cultural phenomenon in an essay published in 1830.

*It may be said without much exaggeration that everything is done
now by societies. . . . You can scarcely name an object for which some institution
has not been formed. Would men spread one set of opinions, or crush another?
They make a society. Would they improve the penal code or relieve poor debtors?
They make societies. Would they encourage agriculture, or manufactures, or
science? They make societies. . . .*

The leading Unitarian preacher of his day, Channing asserted that not all the societies were good and that the best ones were those who added value to their members.

Associations aiming to purify and ennoble the character of a people, to promote true virtue, a rational piety, a disinterested charity, a wise temperance, and especially aiming to accomplish these ends by the only effectual means, that is, by calling forth men's own exertions for a higher knowledge of God and duty, and for a new and growing control of themselves — such institutions are among the noblest . . .

The American tradition of community-based organizations that Channing observed has continued and expanded over the centuries. You may be part of such a group, or perhaps more than one. Channing emphasized that these grassroots associations should add value to their participants. Whatever team you're on, your goal should also be to add value to your teammates. You can do so by living out these four principles.

MANIPULATE NOT— The first rule is to do no harm. Don't diminish or disadvantage people by manipulating them to meet your selfish needs. Exploiting others will eventually come back to haunt you. Double-check your motives. If your sole purpose for being involved is your agenda, quit the team and go back home — before you end up hurting yourself and others.

MOTIVATE WELL — Your goal should be to inspire others. Sometimes it doesn't take much: a bright smile, a pep talk, an unexpected gift, a surprise invitation. Strive to understand the needs of your teammates and do something to meet them. The more special your intervention on behalf of others, the more you will motivate them.

MUTUAL BENEFIT — Look for the win-win. This is the best outcome because a mutually beneficial idea or initiative takes you and your teammates to common ground where you can together experience added value. Take care of your own interests while attending to the interests of others. The benefits of this approach are great, as Dale Carnegie explained:

You can make more friends in two months by becoming interested in other people than you can in two years by trying to get other people interested in you.

MAKE SALAD — Move your metaphor from melting pot to tossed salad. You're in the bowl of destiny together with your teammates but your distinct identity is not blended away. Affirm the value of others even as you affirm your own. In this way, you will add value by fostering both individuality and unity, which is the victorious mix.

STRENGTHEN YOUR TEAM   MAY 26TH

*Wherever the sons and daughters of the Pilgrims find their way there are
established homes, schools, and churches, shops, and legislative assemblies, the
free press, hotels for strangers, and asylums for the unfortunate or the orphaned. . . .
Wherever the Anglo-American advances, the the same vitality arises.*
Fredrika Bremer

In 1849 Swedish writer and social reformer Fredrika Bremer came
to the United States and traveled extensively over the next two years.
Bremer was struck by how people tended to work together as a team
through associations. She wrote about her observations on American life,
which were published in 1853.

> *There is principle of movement in the United States which seems to
> me creative, or, at all events, a power of organization. This is the movement of
> association. The association, founded already in the federal government — an
> association of states, governed by a general law, or Constitution — exists as a
> fundamental feature of popular life. These people associate as easily as
> they breathe.*

Bremer also shared her view on the power of American teamwork
through conventions.

> *Whenever any subject or question of interest arises in society which
> demands public sympathy or cooperation, a "convention" is immediately called
> to take it into consideration; and immediately, from all ends of the city or the
> state, or from every state in the Union, all who feel an interest in the subject fly
> upon wings of steam to the appointed place of meeting. The hotels and
> boardinghouses of the city are rapidly filled; people come together in the great
> hall of assembly, they shake hands, they become acquainted with one another,
> they make speeches, they vote, they carry their resolutions. . . . .*

Being a part of a strong team — whether at home, work, or in the
community — is vital to your success. Whatever team you're on, your goal
should be to strengthen it. You will do so as you:

SHARE YOUR STORY — Don't talk about the weather.
Talk about things that really matter. Start by sharing your story. Tell

about those tough times when you didn't give up, when you overcame obstacles to achieve success. Then encourage your teammates to share their stories of triumph with you. Pushing past the superficialities and getting know each other at a deeper level is the foundation to building a stronger team.

SPEND TIME TOGETHER — Step away from the water cooler, get out of the conference room. Spend time with the team members in new and creative ways. Gather outside of the workplace; go together to the community center, seminar, sporting event, museum, or park. This exercise is more than a water cooler visit; it's a group adventure to stretch folks to grow as a team, building collective strength. If you have children, this principle works with them. Do activities outside of the home to bolster family relationships.

SOW SEEDS — Look for ways to seed in your teammates new skills and abilities. Help them to make invest in themselves to develop their talents and capabilities. Advise them to go back for additional education and trailing. Fertilizing the soil of individual growth will foster team advancement.

SOAR YOUR TEAMMATES — The best way to inspire your team is by example. If you want them to perform at a higher level, you first need to get to that higher level in your own performance. If you want a co-worker to show up for meetings on time or your kid to get to an after-school activity on time, role model the behavior by punctuality in your own life. Your team will ascend as they see you soar. And let your self-confidence exemplify strength, as Eleanor Roosevelt advised:

No one can make you feel inferior without your consent.

WORK AS A TEAM   MAY 27TH

To myself you have been a pillar of support through life. Take care of me
when dead, and be assured that I shall leave you with my last affections.
Thomas Jefferson, in a letter to James Madison

In 1826 — not long before he died — Thomas Jefferson wrote to James Madison, reflecting on their friendship. Jefferson and Madison, the third and fourth Presidents of the United States, had met for the first time in 1776. Over the next fifty years they worked together on conceiving and implementing the American Revolution as well as formulating and leading the new government. Jefferson's correspondence demonstrated not only the depth and strength of their association but also the truth that great things are accomplished through great teamwork.

> *The friendship which has subsisted between us now half a century and the harmony of our political principles and pursuits have been sources of constant happiness to me throughout that long period. It has also been a great solace to me to believe that you are engaged in vindicating to posterity the course we have pursued for preserving to them in all their purity the blessings of self-government which we had assisted in acquiring for them. If ever the earth has beheld a system of administration conducted with a single and steadfast eye to the general interest and happiness of those committed to it, one which protected by truth can never know reproach, it is that to which our lives have been devoted.*

The key to the history-making success of Madison and Jefferson is that they worked together as a team. They exemplify teamwork as a success strategy for you to follow. To be successful, you must be able to work as a team with others. Applying these principles to your life will help you achieve effective teamwork.

COMMONALITY — Throughout their epochal collaboration Madison and Jefferson were committed to the same goal — creating the American Experiment. In the face of countless challenges that could have derailed the project, their working relationship, which became a strong friendship, focused on this objective. Make sure your values and goals are aligned with those of your teammates. Sharing a common vision will be the foundation of your successful enterprise.

CAMARADERIE— You can be a part of a team of two or a team of two hundred; your achievements will rise from the quality of relationship that allows you to develop and collaborate on common goals and values. Imagine Madison, Jefferson and their peers not possessing the rapport to work through their differences. Without the trustfulness of their teamwork, the American Experiment would have eventually broken down amidst the conflicts inherent in the founding of a new nation. Work on developing friendships with those on the job, in the classroom, at your house of worship or community group, wherever. Prioritize your relationships over your projects. Building strong relationships will lead to long-term success.

COST — In deciding which teammates to work with, ask yourself: do they add value to me and my teammates or subtract value from us? Open the door to team members who come with fresh skills and cooperative personalities. Close the door on those who carry conflictual baggage and offer nothing new. To enhance the work of your team, especially if you're a leader, be intentional and strategic with those you bring on board.

COMMITMENT — As you get to know your classmates, coworkers and associates better, don't let petty differences or conflicting opinions derail the relationships. Step back if you need to. Take a break if necessary. Your ability to work through the potential breakdown and stay on track with others will be the main factor in whether you reach your goals. As with the Founders, your commitment to teamwork will pave the way to individual and organizational success. With the right teammates, you have a better chance of changing yourself, changing your community, perhaps even the nation — for the better.

DREAM AS A TEAM   MAY 28TH

We cannot be deprived of the happy consciousness of the pure devotion to the pubic good with which we discharged the trust committed to us.
James Madison, in a letter to Thomas Jefferson

James Madison responded to Thomas Jefferson's letter within a week. His heartfelt reply affirmed their extraordinary teamwork.

You cannot look back to the long period of our private friendship and political harmony with more affecting recollections than I do. If they are a source of pleasure to you, what ought they not be to me? . . . And I indulge a confidence that sufficient evidence will find its way to another generation to insure, after we are gone, whatever of justice may be withheld whilst we are here.

Jefferson died about five months after receiving Madison's letter. In his final days he was no doubt comforted by this communication confirming the continuing of their American crusade. The letter highlighted the enduring value of their collective vision casting. They dreamed together about America's greatness and shared it with others, believing in imparting their soaring dream to others, casting vision in ways to help their fellow citizens achieve success. They became legendary leaders with generational influence by dreaming as a team.

You would be wise to embrace the example of these Founders and dream as a team; to do so, you must:

TALK THE TALK — Share your vision and encourage others to share theirs with you. Don't hold back your dream, and don't trivialize anybody else's dream. Be a moral gardener: cultivate the fertile social environment around the dreamers so that their inspirations will flourish.

WALK THE WALK — Live your dream. Conduct your lifestyle to be consistent with your vision-casting. If you dream of becoming a professional athlete, but you spend your time getting high instead of working out, you will frustrate any efforts to build a team of support for your vision. If you want to be an elected official, but you hang out in strip clubs, you will have a hard time recruiting supporters. Don't be a pretender. Set a strong example that's consistent with your dream, so that your potential team members know that you're both sincere and serious about your future. And as you seek to walk every day with your dream, take heed of Ralph Waldo Emerson's directions:

> *Do not follow where the path may lead.*
> *Go instead where there is no path and leave a trail.*

BE THE BOARD — Be a sounding board, so that others can dream with you first, getting your reactions to their ideas, before going public with them. And as you listen to opinions, suggestions and concerns, don't be dismissive of them and don't prejudge them. If you want to have your own thoughts listened to and affirmed, first do your best to listen to and affirm the thoughts of others. If you want your dreams fulfilled, seek to help fulfill the dreams of others, learning as much as you can along the way. This Biblical advice from the Apostle James speaks volumes:

> *Be quick to listen, slow to speak and slow to become angry.*
> James 1:19

PROCLAIM THE PRAISE — Let your fellow dreamers know how much you appreciate them and their vision. Without being disingenuous, err on the side of expressing too much rather than too little commendation. Let your voice of praise be heard, so that people know that their dream is important and that they are an important part of the team. Dreaming as a team means making time to ride the waves of shared enthusiasm.

BUILD YOUR BEST TEAM   MAY 29TH

The national school is not a lecture hall or a library. Its schooling consists chiefly in experimental collective action aimed at the realization of a collective purpose.
Herbert Croly

In 1909 editor Herbert Croly published "The Promise of American Life", regarded as one of the most influential books in American political history. One of the many leaders the book touched was Theodore Roosevelt, whose signature "New Nationalism" was drawn from Croly's ideas. In the following passage Croly described the importance of teamwork, encouraging people to work together in pursuit of worthy ends.

While all men are imperfect, they are not all imperfect to the same extent. Some have more courage, more ability, more insight, and more training than others; and an efficient organization can accomplish more than can a mere collection of individuals precisely because it may represent a standard of performance far above that of the average individual. Its merit is simply that of putting the collective power of the group at the service of its ablest members; and the ablest members of the group will never attain to an individual responsibility commensurate with their powers until they are enabled to work efficiently toward the redemption of the collective responsibility.

For Croly, the highest expression of teamwork was the "religion of human brotherhood."

It is very easy and in a sense perfectly true to declare that democracy needs for its fulfillment a peculiarly high standard of moral behavior; and it is even more true to declare that a democratic scheme of moral values reaches its consummate expression in the religion of human brotherhood. Such a religion can be realized only through the loving kindness which individuals feel toward their fellowmen and particularly toward their fellow countrymen; and it through such feelings that the network of mutual loyalties and responsibilities woven in a democratic nation become radiant and expansive.

Croly clearly understood that one of the keys to success in life was to build the best team possible. You, too, need to build your best team. Teamwork means a commitment to go somewhere together. Your goal should be to convince others with strong commitment to work with you to get there. To build your best team, endeavor to bring the following kind of people on board.

POSITIVE PEOPLE — Keep in mind the story of the man who was about to jump off a bridge. A policeman confronted him: "Surely nothing could be that bad. Tell me about it." When the man finished talking, they both jumped! Don't hesitate to dump the dangerous folks or the deadweight. If someone is holding you back — whether intentionally or not — let that person go. Make sure you steer clear of destructive relationships and stay close to constructive ones.

PARALLEL PEOPLE — You want people who share your goals as well as your values. Make sure you set high ethical standards for your teammates to follow. Meditate on this precept from leadership expert John Maxwell:

Who you are is what you attract.

POWERFUL PEOPLE — The bigger the goal, the better the team needs to be. Start with your inner circle: those closet to you will have the most impact on your success. If they already have their own track record of success, they add value to you and what you're trying to do. Bring people of influence around you who can motivate you and others. Remember this process; it will generate power for your team:

Coming together is a beginning; keeping together is progress; working together is success.

PROVIDENTIAL PEOPLE — Seek people who take their spiritual lives seriously; they will bring faith, hope, love and other virtues to the team. The outcome will be, as Croly stated, broad impact that will become "radiant and expansive."

COMMUNICATE EFFECTIVELY WITH OTHERS   MAY 30TH

The mightiest engine of our day is a newspaper. What are armies and treasuries, navies and forts, and magazines and foundries, or senate chambers and laws in comparison with newspapers . . .
John Neal

Newspapers and periodicals proliferated during 1830's and 1840's.

Several factors of pre-Civil War America contributed to their extraordinary expansion: new technologies like the lightning printing press and telegraph; improved transportation to disseminate the information; and the profusion of business/social organizations (corporations, churches, reform societies, labor unions, etc.) with their own publications.

Literary critic John Neal departed from the formal traditions of literature, establishing a reputation as the first American author to employ colloquialism in his many and varied writings. In his fiction and the several New England magazines that he edited, Neal popularized the new and expanding power of 19th century media. In one of his articles published in 1843, he made historical references to substantiate that the new media created opportunities for people to communicate and connect in more constructive ways.

> *Time was when . . . we had but few newspapers; and they were written for by the ablest men of the country, without pay. At the outbreak of the Revolutionary War, and after the Treaty of 1783, our whole literature was a newspaper literature, and the strongest minds and best hearts alive were engaged in wholesome newspaper controversies that shook the world. The Adamses, the Otises, the Franklins, the Hamiltons, the Jeffersons, the Madisons, the Jays were always at work upon the public mind through the newspapers . . . after this, papers went on multiplying over the land, as a mere experiment in business, a new branch in the book trade or job printing, till every village in the country had its one, two, or three, and sometimes its half a score of newspapers . . .*

The internet-based media revolution of the early 21st century is analogous to the major media movement of Neal's era. The social media of today allows people to interact in more direct and immediate ways that Neal — as innovative as he was — couldn't have imagined. You should use the devices of modern technology to communicate with others. You can do by implementing these principles.

RELATIONAL — Your people skills are key to your success. Use social media as a strategic tool to build and maintain successful relationships at home, at work, in the community. Your goals will rise or fall based on the quality of your relationships. Seek to communicate in ways to strengthen them.

RESPONSIBLE — Be very careful how you use social media to communicate. Don't use easy media access in immature, unethical or abusive ways. Take advantage of the promising opportunities instead of taking advantage of others. It's just as unacceptable to be a social media bully as a neighborhood brute. If you're spending most of your time on your online, your responsibility starts there.

REAL — You will attract people based on who you project yourself to be. Don't be an online phony. If you're not willing to share the real you in positive, constructive and uplifting ways, don't post. And don't try to use social media as a substitute for in-person encounters. Get face-to-face — be authentic — for important interactions; then use media to enhance the real thing.

REACH OUT — Be a connector. Make introductions to people who wouldn't otherwise be in touch. Start by building fellowship close to home, then reach out remotely across communities and oceans. As you enhance your team, whether in-person or online, meditate on this truth:

He who thinks he leads, but has no followers, is only taking a walk.

RIGHTEOUS — Use social media as a tool to build uplifting messaging. Avoid demeaning and hostile communication. If you don't have anything positive to post, don't post! Resolve to bring the sunshine of truth and love to cyberspace; you will make the universe of the internet a better place.

ALIGN WITH YOUR TEAMMATES   MAY 31ST

. . . a people possessed of intelligence, fortitude, and integrity sufficient to carry them with steadiness, patience, and perseverance through all the vicissitudes of fortune, the fiery trials, and melancholy disasters they may have to encounter.
John Adams

As American continued to grow in 1818 — Illinois became the twenty-first state that year — enduring patriot and former President John Adams labored with his pen through the twilight of his life. One of his most significant essays was a piece on the meaning of the American Revolution, published in March 1818 by Hezekiah Niles, editor of the Weekly Register. Adams put the revolutionary movement in context to depict what an amazing achievement it was.

The colonies had grown up under constitutions of government so different; there was so great a variety of religions; they were composed of so many different nations; their customs, manners, and habits had so little resemblance; and their intercourse had been so rare and their knowledge of each other so imperfect that to unite them in the same principles in theory and the same system of action was certainly a very difficult enterprise. The complete accomplishment of it in so short a time and by such simple means was perhaps a singular example in the history of mankind. Thirteen clocks were made to strike together: a perfection of mechanism which no artist had ever before effected.

Adams' point was clear. The Thirteen Colonies shared the common goal of gaining independence from Britain, but it was not until they came together around common values that the American Revolution proceeded towards success. The challenge was getting all the disparate individuals from divergent groups in different regions all on the same page. When the colonial leaders declared their common values on July 4, 1776, they were able to avoid internal conflict and dissension and forge the teamwork necessary for the launch of the American Experiment.

Before you join a team — whether a job, nonprofit, social club, political or religious organization — make sure you share its values; and they, yours. The following checklist will help you determine whether you're aligned with your teammates.

AWARENESS — Know the values and goals of your team. Ask questions right up front to find out about them. Check to see if there's organizational commitment to virtues similar to those of this book. If not, you may be inviting conflict and chaos into your life. Sometimes it's better to stay on the sidelines than to jump on the field without the full roster and a clear and compelling playbook.

ALIGNMENT — Communicate your values and goals to your team. The best way to ensure that your values align with theirs is by discussing them before you sign up. If there's no alignment, be willing to make reasonable adjustments but don't compromise on your core values. Your teammates may be the ones who need to change.

ACTION — After you publish and perfect your statement of values, act on it. Since you're already on the same page intellectually and morally, you'll have a better chance of taking steps together practically. Executing a successful collective project will vindicate the strength of your alignment. The Founders took action with their values in the Declaration of Independence, and fought a war to realize them. If you and your team members want to make a difference and perhaps some history, follow their example and craft your values and goals into a written statement.

Publish it and take note of the feedback. Take the initiative to make necessary revisions. Once it's ready, declare it far and wide; take concrete step to fulfill it.

ALMIGHTY — Keep in mind the spiritual dimension: divine alignment is key. Martin Luther King Jr. said it best:

Human progress never rolls in on the wheels of inevitability; it comes through the tireless efforts of people willing to be co-workers with God.

JUNE: INTEGRITY
DAILY SUCCESS PRINCIPLES

1. Refuse To Take The Stage — Lena Horne — 1945
2. Hold Onto Your Virtues — George Washington — 1789
3. Let Others Know Who You Truly Are — Zitkála-Šá — 1884
4. Win With Integrity — Bobby Jones — 1925
5. Work On Your Character — Charles Remond — 1842
6. Break Free To Be Whole — Maya Angelou — 1969
7. Declare Words Of Justice — James Smith — 1797
8. Act On What You Know — James Baldwin — 1962
9. Start Early With Integrity — Abraham Lincoln — 1816
10. Fight For Righteousness — Ho Feng-Shan — 1938
11. Show Your Sincerity — Davy Crockett — 1821
12. Live Life To The Full — Martha Graham — 1926
13. Refuse To Believe The Hype — John Williams — 1895
14. Live By The Golden Rule — Cotton Mather — 1701
15. Don't Play The Blame Game — Joseph Holland — 1988
16. Affirm Fundamental Truths — Dred Scott — 1846
17. Hold Yourself Accountable — Ida Tarbell — 1904
18. Battle For Integrity — Theodore Weld — 1839
19. Maintain Moral Standards — Commission On Law Enforcement — 1967
20. Insist On Integrity — T. Thomas Fortune — 1884
21. Start Small To Build Big — Frank Lloyd Wright — 1945
22. Treat People Fairly — William Seward — 1841
23. Get To Know You — Margaret Mead — 1975
24. Be True To Your Calling — Daniel Webster — 1830
25. Make Integrity Your Referee —William Cushing — 1783
26. Resolve Difficult Questions — Benjamin Butler — 1861
27. Raise A Strong Voice — Ida Harper — 1901
28. Walk Your Talk — Abraham Lincoln — 1854
29. Follow Through On Your Commitments — Lewis Blair — 1889
30. Build Strong Morals For Leadership — Theodore Roosevelt — 1885

REFUSE TO TAKE THE STAGE   JUNE 1ST

You have to be taught to be second class; you're not born that way.
Lena Horne

1963 was an eventful year for celebrity entertainer Lena Horne. As she continued to headline at top night clubs and appear on TV variety shows and specials, Horne intensified her activities with the Civil Rights Movement. She was with Medgar Evers at a NAACP rally in Mississippi the weekend before he was assassinated there. She attended the March on Washington and heard Martin Luther King Jr. give his historic "I Have A Dream" speech. She met with writer James Baldwin and with President John Kennedy at the White House on November 20, 1963, two days prior to his assassination.

Horne's involvement in civil rights had begun two decades earlier, even before her live album — "Lena Horne At The Waldorf-Astoria" — became a trailblazing hit in 1957, the biggest-selling record to date by a female artist on the RCA label. Throughout World War II she entertained troops for the USO but refused to take the stage when the audience was segregated. During one of her USO performances for an integrated audience in which the German POWs were seated in front of African American soldiers, Horne walked off the stage to where the black servicemen were seated, giving the front row view with the German troops behind her. Horne eventually stopped giving USO performances because of its segregationist policies but instead took the stage on her own terms; she financed her performances at military camps herself. She described her commitment in these words:

Nobody black or white who really believes in democracy can stand aside now; everybody's got to stand up and be counted.

Horne refused to take the stage when the values of the sponsoring organization were different from her own. Compromise was not an option concerning fair treatment of racial groups. No matter how much you're getting paid, how far you've traveled or how strongly you feel about a cause, refuse to take the stage when you're faced with:

IMBROGLIO — When Horne was faced with an audience of foreign prisoners seated in front of her uniformed countrymen, she refused to take the regular stage, creating an impromptu stage that was consistent with values of fairness and integrity. When you're confronted with an extremely confused, complicated, conflicted or embarrassing situation, take a step back. Refuse to move forward in any way until the predicament is rectified; unless you, like Horne, can take the initiative and come up with an immediate, creative and fair solution.

IMMISERATION — Never support policies or programs undergirding economic injustice. If making people more miserable and impoverished is the outcome, be sure to move away. Do your homework. Research the opportunity that you're considering to find out what it's really about. Don't rely simply on word of mouth. Get the facts!

IMPERIOUSNESS — If the leadership lacks integrity, it will trickle down through the organization. Everyone makes mistakes but the arrogant refuse to admit them and make necessary changes. Things are not always as they appear. Remember Jesus' words.

Beware of false prophets, who come to you in sheep's clothing, but inwardly they are ravenous wolves. You will know them by their fruits. Do men gather grapes from thorn bushes or figs from thistles?
Matthew 7:15-16

INJUSTICE — The litmus test is: is everyone better off through this activity, or are some ending up worse off because others have an unfair advantage? Safeguard your integrity. Answer this question before you get involved. Just because others are in the mud doesn't mean you have to get down and dirty with them.

HOLD ONTO YOUR VIRTUES   JUNE 2ND

Few men have virtue enough to withstand the highest bidder.
George Washington

On April 30, 1789, George Washington was sworn in as the first President of the United States. The very next day, in its first matter of business, the United States Senate dealt with the title of president. Vice President John Adams focused the senators' attention on this procedural issue, recommending — reminiscent of European monarchical appellations — "His Highness, the President of the United States, and Protector of their Liberties."

Though some senators favored "His Elective Majesty" or "His Excellency", William Maclay, one of the two Pennsylvania senators, would have none of it. Maclay kept a journal of these early legislative proceedings, which represents their only record since there was no official record keeping at this incipient stage. His notes revealed a protracted, contentious senate debate over this issue, though the House of Representatives had quickly disposed of it, with one of its leaders James Madison clarifying pretentious European titles as ill-suited for the "genius of the people" and "the nature of our Government." The below entry from Maclay's journal displayed both his passion and frustration with this issue.

> *I collected myself for a last effort. I read the clause in the Constitution against the titles of nobility; showed that the spirit of it was against not only granting titles by Congress but against the permission of foreign potentates granting any titles whatever; that as to kingly government, it was equally out of the question, as a republican government was guaranteed to every state in the Union; that they were both equally forbidden fruit of the Constitution. I called the attention of the House to the consequences that were like to follow; that gentlemen seemed to court a rupture with the other House. The Representatives had adopted the report, and were this day acting on it, or according to the spirit of the report. We were proposing a title. Our conduct would mark us to the world as actuated by the spirit of dissension, and the characters of the Houses would be as aristocratic . . .*

Embarrassed by this controversial debate — and with characteristic humility — Washington insisted that the senators drop the matter, opting for a more modest title. He decided that he would simply be called the President of the United States or Mr. President, making sure to differentiate emerging American mores with European customs. With a clear opportunity to self-aggrandize, Washington held to his virtues; he's a good role model on this one; hold onto yours as you:

DETERMINE TO BE TRUE — Washington's circumspect approach was consistent with his careful distancing from European symbolism, like ordering his tailor to make his inauguration suit out of simple broadcloth rather than the more traditional black velvet. The wisdom of Washington's decision was in its integrity. He chose to be true to who he was, refusing to succumb to the pressure of fitting someone else's — even his second-in-command's — image for him. Take the same self-effacing approach, especially if you're in or aspiring to leadership. Pressures will come upon you to sacrifice humility on the altar of titles and positions. Refuse to put on fancy robes that just don't fit. Be true to you!

DESICCATE YOUR VICES — Be honest with yourself about your shortcomings. Set a high standard and strive to meet it.

If you fall short, admit it. Figure out why. Shine a bright light on your vices. Whatever they are, starve them of your time and energy so that they'll shrivel up and fall out of your lifestyle. Remember Jesus' example, when he was offered all the kingdoms of the world if he would only bow down to the Devil (Matthew 4:8 - 11). He resisted the temptation of fame and fortune, held on to virtue, and the Tempter went away for a while. Battle against your temptations, resist them with your vigorous virtues, and they will eventually leave you alone.

DEEPEN YOUR CHARACTER — Your vices and your virtues are at war. Devote yourself to this book and other inspirational materials; you will strengthen your virtues to win the daily skirmishes. Prioritize your inner journey. Go to a deeper place within. You will find the power to invigorate your virtues and make them victorious over the sins that threaten your stability and progress.

LET OTHERS KNOW WHO YOU TRULY ARE   JUNE 3RD

The voice of the Great Spirit is heard in the twittering of birds,
the rippling of mighty waters, and the sweet breathing of flowers.
Zitkála-Šá

In 1884 eight-year-old Zitkála-Šá left the Yankton Indian Reservation in South Dakota where she had been born, traveling to Wabash, Indiana to attend the Indiana Manual Labor Institute. Though Zitkala learned to read and write English and play the violin, she was concerned about the assimilationist zeal of the Quaker missionary school: she was forced to cut her traditionally long hair and to distance herself from the mores of her tribe. She articulated her distress:

Perhaps my Indian nature is the moaning wind which stirs my
schoolteachers now . . . But, however tempestuous this is within me, it comes out
as the low voice of a curiously colored seashell, which is only for those ears that
are bent with compassion to hear it.

Zitkala left the missionary school then returned a few years later, passionate about her musical studies, eventually doing advanced work in the violin at the New England Conservatory of Music in Boston. She taught music at Carlisle Indian Industrial School in Pennsylvania and performed with the school's band at the Paris Exposition in 1900. She later collaborated with American composer William F. Hanson, playing Sioux melodies on the violin, for which she wrote libretto and songs. Her creative work led to "The Sun Dance Opera"; based on Sioux and Ute cultural themes, it was the first opera adapted from the Native American oral musical tradition.

Zitkala's other passion was writing, which featured her struggles with cultural identity: the tension between her Native American traditions and majority white society. She wrote both autobiographical narratives and legendary stories from Native American history. Zitkala also served as editor the "American Indian Magazine", to which she contributed numerous articles. Rising from her literary activism, she co-founded and was president of the National Council of American Indians, whose influence fostered the Indian Reorganization Act of 1934, which became known as the "Indian New Deal".

Zitkala used her music, writings and activism to let others know who she truly was. Let others know who you truly are by practicing these principles.

REFLECTION — The first step is for you to realize who you truly are on the inside, to get in touch with your character. One of the best ways to do it is reflection: take some time each day in prayerful meditation; let your mind focus on your actions and motivations for doing them. As you get disciplined about this quiet time, you will realize more and more whether there's consistency or conflict between what you say and what you do. Start your quiet discipline by reflecting on Molière's words.

Men are alike in their promises. It is only in their deeds that they differ. The difference in their deeds is simple: People of character do what is right regardless of the situation.

REVELATION — Zitkala sang and wrote about her struggles as well as her triumphs. Be transparent about your flaws and weakness, about your quirks and idiosyncrasies. Reveal your inner truth, open a window to your soul. Share with someone you trust what you're truly feeling; you will be making a step towards emotional maturity. Sing your own song. Write your own story.

RAMIFICATION — Make a move to get out of your own little world. Don't be a prisoner of your own mind — nor of your narrow circumstances. Stretch your mind by reading a new book. Branch out by visiting a different neighborhood or a distant shore. Zitkala ended up performing music in Paris. A change of perspective and a change of place will broaden your understanding as you communicate it to others.

REWARD — Zitkala worked hard to help others win; her advocacy led to passage of federal legislation that furthered the rights of all Native Americans. Your greatest reward in life is helping other people win. Zitkala did it. Why not you?

WIN WITH INTEGRITY   JUNE 4TH

You might as well praise me for not breaking into banks. There is only one way to play this game.
Bobby Jones

In June 1925 the U.S. Open Golf Championship was held in Worcester, Massachusetts; one sportswriter called it "easily the greatest Open Championship of them all." American Bobby Jones and Scotsman Willie McFarlane battled in a second 18-hole playoff for the championship. A lawyer by profession, Jones was at an early moment in his amateur golf career; he eventually won thirteen major tournaments in his fifteen years on the tour and became the only golfer in history to win the Grand Slam — all four major championships — in the same calendar year.

During the first round of the 1925 Open Jones' 11th hole tee shot sailed a little right, finding the rough. Jones selected his club for the next shot and, as he addressed the ball, he inadvertently moved it a little — according to Jones! No one else saw the ball move — not his competitor, not the officials, not a gallery member, not even his caddy. Jones reported the infraction but the inquiry of the tournament officials couldn't verify the fact that his ball had moved. Jones insisted that it had shifted a smidge and assessed himself a one shot penalty. He ended up losing the tournament to McFarlane by one stroke.

The only way Jones knew to play the game was with integrity. Though he lost that tournament he won something much greater — an inspirational legacy. As one journalist put it:

In the opinion of many people, of all the great athletes, Bobby Jones came the closest to being what we call a great man.

Because he exemplified principles of integrity and fair play, the United States Golf Associations's Sportsmanship Award is named the Bob Jones Award in his honor. The United States Postal Service also commemorated Jones by issuing an 18 cent stamp in 1981. You, too, can win with integrity as you strive to be:

HUMBLE — Bring real meaning back to the word integrity. Turn those blank stares into big smiles through your humility, as people experience your determination to rise to the high ground of a principle-driven lifestyle. The big win for you will be this: in a nation of far too many pretenders, panderers, partisans, and flashes in the pan, your life of integrity will shine as something to emulate, and, like Bobby Jones, you may just end up enduring as a moral hero.

HUNGRY — Since we live in a culture that celebrates talent over integrity, models of virtue are hard to come by. Examples of strength of character — like Bobby Jones — are rare commodities in contemporary society. So it's really important for you to understand that your true victory lies with your integrity. You may pick up some points for your good looks, quick wit, impressive intellect or engaging personality — all good attributes in the game of life. But it's good character that will score big for you in today's world — the resolve to be relentlessly honest in all situations in your life. Experience the meaning of Jesus' words.

Blessed are those who hunger and thirst after righteousness, for they will be filled.
Matthew 5:6

HELPFUL — Your goal should be to win, but helping others win is also important. Be a champion at supporting others to attain their very best. Your greatest reward may be watching someone else hold today's trophy.

HOPEFUL — Possess a perspective that emphasizes long-term benefits. As hard as it may be in the moment to prioritize honest over expediency, do it anyway. Your future reward — earned by your integrity — will far outweigh your present gratification.

WORK ON YOUR CHARACTER   JUNE 5TH

The grievances of which we complain are not imaginary but real; not local but universal; not occasional but every-day, matter-of-fact things, and have become, to the disgrace of our common country, matter of history.
Charles Remond

Though not as well known as his fellow black abolitionist Frederick

Douglass, Charles Remond was also a force to be reckoned with. From Salem, Massachusetts, Remond was the eldest son of eight children raised by two successful entrepreneurs: his mother was a caterer; his father, a hairdresser. In his twenties Remond began lecturing at public gatherings throughout the Northeastern states, gaining the reputation as the first black public speaker on abolition. In February 1842 Remond testified before a Massachusetts House of Representatives committee that had been convened to address the segregated state railroad system.

> *With reference to the wrongs inflicted and injuries received on railroads by persons of color, I need not say they do not end with the termination of the route, but in effect, tend to discourage, disparage, and depress this class of citizens. All hope of reward for upright conduct is cut off. . . . In the present state of things, they find God's provisions interfered with in such a way, by these and kindred regulations, that virtue may not claim her divinely appointed rewards. Color is made to obscure the brightest endowments, to degrade the fairest character, and to check the highest and most praiseworthy aspirations . . . Nay, the higher our aspirations, the loftier our purpose and pursuits, does this iniquitous principle of prejudice fasten upon us.*

The Massachusetts railroads were desegregated in 1848. Remond's words helped to pave the way for this historic reform, but his message wasn't just about changing laws; it was also about changing character. As you work on changing your character, reflect on Alice Cary's poem "Nobility" and the principles it represents.

WORK KINGLY —
True worth is in being, not seeming —
In doing, each day that goes by,
Some little good — not in dreaming
Of great things to do by and by.
For whatever men say in their blindness,
And spite of the fancies of youth,
There's nothing so kingly as kindness,
And nothing so royal as truth.

WORK JUSTLY —
We get back our mete as we measure —
We cannot do wrong and feel right,
Nor can we give pain and gain pleasure,
For justice avenges each slight.
The air for the wing of the sparrow,
The bush for the robin and wren,
But always the path that is narrow

And straight, for the children of men.

WORK PATIENTLY —
Through envy, through malice, through hating,
Against the world, early and late,
No jot of our courage abating —
Our part is to work and to wait.
And slight is the sting of his trouble
Whose winnings are less than his worth;
For he who is honest is noble,
Whatever his fortunes or birth.

Whatever your background, race, gender, or ethnicity happens to be, the content of your character is the most important thing. Are you working to improve it?

BREAK FREE TO BE WHOLE   MAY 6TH

My mission in life is not merely to survive, but to thrive; and to do
so with some passion, some compassion, some humor and some style.
Maya Angelo

In 1969 poet and civil rights activist Maya Angelou published her first autobiographical work, "I Know Why the Caged Bird Sings". The book was a coming-of-age story that described the struggles of a young Maya with trauma and racism. "Sympathy", a poem by Paul Laurence Dunbar inspired her title:

I know why the caged bird sings, ah me,
When his wing is bruised and his bosom sore,
When he beats his bars and would be free;
It is not a carol of joy or glee,
But a prayer that he sends from his heart's deep core,
But a plea, that upward to Heaven he flings –
I know why the caged bird sings

The caged bird, a symbol for the chained slave, endured as a theme through much of Angelou's writings, as in the final stanza of her poem entitled "Caged Birds":

The caged bird sings
with a fearful trill

of things unknown
but longed for still
and his tune is heard
on the distant hill
for the caged bird
sings of freedom.

In her "Caged Birds" book this motif gained expression as Angelou's character breaks free from being a victim of childhood rape and Southern racism to grow into a self-confident individual with the ability to respond to racism with dignity and to pursue her dreams. The book was a sensation, nominated for a National Book Award; a fixture on The New York Times paperback bestseller list; a standard text for countless high schools and universities; and the subject of a made-for-TV movie of the same title that aired in 1979. The international acclaim of "Caged Birds" propelled Angelou's career, which ascended in 1993 when she recited her poem "On the Pulse of Morning" at Bill Clinton's first inauguration.

"Caged Birds" captures Angelou's story of breaking free to become whole. That can be your story as well, if you build your:

CHARACTER — Break free from duplicity. Be consistent, especially in making sound decisions. And if you make a poor decision, don't cover it up. To be a person of good character, you have to admit your mistakes and work to rectify them. If you want to live a life of integrity, you have to own your shortcomings and fix them.

CONFIDENCE — Break free from perceived failure. Work to change your perception of failure. Look at it as your price of success. Angelou's youthful journey weathered many setbacks on her way to a self-aware, self-confident individual. To build your self-confidence, transform your stumbling blocks into stepping stones towards greatness.

COMMUNICATION — Break free from gossip. Keep in mind that great people talk about ideas, average people talk about themselves, and small people talk about others. Neither spread nor receive gossip. Strive to be great, which means you must leave gossip to the minions mired in mediocrity.

COHORT — Break free from aloneness. If you've been trying to overcome your problems on your own and falling short, you need some help. Don't be afraid to ask for it. Avoid the cage of pride, where you feel like you can do it all yourself, when you're too proud to seek and accept support. Be humble. Admit to yourself that you'll stay stuck in your rut unless you reach out for that helping hand to pull you out.

Declare Words Of Justice   June 7th

This ardent wish I at length see accomplished and in this infant country behold the features of true felicity and greatness. Here I see genuine liberty and national happiness growing up together, on the firm foundation and under the guardian protection of constitutional authority.
James Smith

Enacted on July 13, 1787 by the Congress of the Confederation of the United States, the Northwest Ordinance created from lands beyond the Appalachian Mountains a territory which was eventually formed into six states: Ohio (1803); Indiana (1816); Illinois (1818); Michigan (1837); Wisconsin (1848); and Minnesota (1858). Slavery was prohibited in the Northwest Territory. Reverend James Smith, a Methodist minister from Virginia, explored the Territory just northwest of the Ohio River in 1795 and 1797, assessing the possibilities of preaching the gospel in these wilderness regions. He kept a journal of his travels. Smith wrote about the land that he was visiting, declaring justice over it. Take note of his poetic language and the principles rising from it — examples for you to heed; you can declare your own words of justice as you:

PROCLAIM — *Yes, I anticipate, O land, the rising glory of thy unequaled fame. Thy forests, now wild and uncultivated, soon shall the hand of industry sow with golden grain. Thy unequaled soil, cultivated by the fostering hands of freemen, shall e'er long display its beauties and yield an increase worthy a land of liberty. . . .*

Smith's dynamic voice made him a true advocate of justice and liberty. Like Smith, speak up on behalf of someone who's hurting. Be a voice for those without a platform to project their own cause. Help people win by addressing their issues, especially when there's injustice involved. Though Smith had died before the Abolitionist movement rose in the 1840's, he was one of strongest early voices for the antislavery cause. As you declare words of justice, you are giving others a voice through yours.

PRAY — *Thy large and noble rivers, which silently flow in gentle currents, shall e'er long waft thy rich products to distant markets in foreign climes; and thou, beautiful Ohio, shalt stand an impenetrable barrier to guard this sacred land. And though the tears of the oppressed on thy southeastern border may help increase thy crystal tide, yet the galling yoke, should it attempt to cross thy current, shall sink beneath thy wave and be buried in thy bosom. The voice of the oppressor may spread terror and dismay throughout the eastern and southern states, but farther than thy delightful   banks it cannot, it dare not, it shall not be heard.*

Give your voice a divine dimension. A call for justice resonates heavenward. Seek supernatural intervention for your righteous mission, as the Old Testament leader Amos did, when he prayed:

But let justice roll on like a river, righteousness like a never-failing stream!
Amos 5:24

PROPHESY — *I must now leave this fair land of happiness with offering to Heaven this humble request: May the foot of pride never come against thee, nor human good stain thy lovely plains. May thy aged never feel the loss of liberty, nor the yoke of slavery rest on the necks of thy children. May thy gates remain open to the oppressed of all nations and may those that flock thither be the excellent   ones of the earth; and if the still continued oppressions of enlightened Virginia should at length bring down the just judgments of an incensed Deity, may it be when I or those that pertain unto me have found an asylum in thy peaceful borders. . .*

As Smith departed the territory, he offered a prophetic benediction. He looked to the future with the hope that all who came to this Territory would step onto a land of justice. Like Smith, be a visionary. Envisage more justice coming to your present circumstances and declare it to be so. Let others catch your vision through your words. Believe that your declarations of justice will indeed come to pass.

ACT ON WHAT YOU KNOW   JUNE 8TH

I can't believe what you say, because I see what you do.
James Baldwin

In December 1962 African American writer James Baldwin sent a letter to his fourteen-year-old nephew James, advising him about race relations in America. Baldwin was corresponding with his young black relative to deepen his understanding of white people and suggest strategies about how best to relate to them. In one passage he counseled acceptance and love as the pathway to greater racial understanding.

Please try to be clear, dear James, through the storm which rages about your youthful head today . . . There is no reason for you to try to become like white people . . . You must accept them and accept them with love. For these innocent people have no other hope. They are, in effect, still trapped in a history which they do not understand; and until they understand it, they cannot be released from it. They have had to believe for many years, and for innumerable reasons, that black men are inferior to white men. Many of them, indeed, know better, but, as you will discover, people find it very difficult to act on what they know.

Baldwin directed his nephew to understand whites as "your brothers" and pointed him to his family and racial roots not only as a source of strength, but also as an example of dignity and a beacon of hope.

But these men are your brothers — your lost, younger brothers. And if the word "integration" means anything, this is what it means: that we, with love, shall force our brothers to see themselves as they are, to cease fleeing from reality and begin to change it. For this is your home, my friend, do not be driven from it; great men have done great things here, and will again, and we can make America what America must become. It will be hard, James, but you come from sturdy, peasant stock, men who picked cotton and dammed rivers and built railroads, and, in the teeth of the worst terrifying odds, achieved an unassailable and monumental dignity.

Concerning race relations, Baldwin's clearcut message to his nephew was: act on what you know. In all areas of your life, you should also act on what you know; to do so, you must be:

CIRCUMSPECT — Be prudent: carefully consider your circumstances and all the possible consequences of your actions. Once you've done so, you're better prepared to act on what you know.

CONNECTED — Know you who are. Baldwin counseled his nephew to connect to his roots. You should do the same. If you dig deep enough, you will discover new understanding and new strength. This process will empower you to act on what you know, reach out and make deeper connections with those of different backgrounds.

CONSISTENT — "It will be hard", Baldwin advised. So many people find it easier to know and say one thing, and do something else. Don't fall in with the inconsistent folks. Pay attention to what you're saying and what you're doing; make sure they're matching up; it will make it easier to build trust with others.

CELEBRATORY — Baldwin concluded the letter on a historic note: the 100th anniversary of the Emancipation Proclamation was not an event to celebrated but a signpost to point to the long road ahead.

You know, and I know, that the country is celebrating one hundred years of freedom one hundred years too soon. We cannot be free until they are free.

Celebrate milestones at the appropriate time. Achieving "an unassailable and monumental dignity" should be celebrated. Freedom is also worthy of celebration. Act on what you know, thus freeing yourself to relate to others in ways that will help all get free from cultural bondage. Fostering this kind of mutual freedom just might shorten the time that Baldwin predicted would be needed to celebrate the fulfillment of American freedom.

START EARLY WITH INTEGRITY   JUNE 9TH

*I think my young readers will begin to see that the name so often given,
in later times to President Lincoln, of "Honest Old Abe," was well deserved.
A man who begins by strict honesty in his youth is not likely to change as he
grows older, and mercantile honesty is some guarantee of political honesty.*
Horatio Alger

Honest Abe — the nickname by which the 16th U.S. President Abraham Lincoln is most known — is a moniker that emerged early in his life. In 1816, when Abraham Lincoln was seven years old, his family moved from Kentucky to Indiana. Two years later, his mother Nancy died; soon Abe had to work as a store clerk, giving all he earned to his dad Thomas to help support the household.

As told by Horatio Alger in Abraham Lincoln, The Backwoods Boy, published in 1883, the proverbial honesty of teenage Abe manifested in his daily dealings with customers.

A woman entered the store and asked for a half a pound of tea. The young clerk weighed it out, and handed it to her in a parcel. This was the last sale of the day. The next morning, when commencing his duties, Abe discovered a four-ounce weight on the scales. It flashed upon him at once that he had used this in the sale of the night previous, and so, of course, given his

271

customer short weight. I am afraid that there are many country merchants who would not have been much worried by this discovery. Not so the young clerk in whom we are interested. He weighed out the balance of the half pound, shut up the store, and carried it to the defrauded customer.

Lincoln started with honesty early, and the virtue stayed with him, helping to pave the way for historic success. If you haven't already started, or if you need an ethical boost, jumpstart your integrity by focusing on your:

ASSESSMENT — Take a moment to assess your integrity. Determine whether you're an honest person — or not. And be honest with yourself about this. Take the Honest Abe test. Would you have gone back the next day to refund the customer, when the customer hadn't realized the mistake, when no one knew about it but you? If you can answer yes, you are a person of integrity; you don't worry about who knows and who doesn't know, you do the right thing regardless. But if your answer is no, then spend some time focusing on your inner life, connecting to your core values, making a commitment to live according to moral principles, no matter where you are, whom you're with, what kind of situation you're facing.

ACCOUNTABILITY — This account demonstrates that early individual morality paves the way for public trust later in life. Since trust is the most important factor in building strong personal, professional and political relationships, your integrity is essential because it helps you to be accountable, allowing others to trust you. If you haven't already developed habits of honesty and truthfulness, you need to start cultivating these virtues like yesterday. Without them, you lack the moral substance for true bonding — the glue that holds relationships together. Albert Einstein enhances our understanding of this principle:

Whoever is careless with the truth in small matters cannot be trusted with important matters.

ALACRITY — Your commitment to honesty will transform you. It will quicken your conscience and make you heartily ready for today's challenge. People will observe the change in you as you manifest a more ethical lifestyle, and and they will naturally extend trust your way. You may or may not rise to become a national leader but you will definitely gain greater respect from those who know you.

ALL-IN — Don't hold back when it comes to honesty. Put all your cards on the table — face up. Half-truths build weak relationships. Transparency builds strong ones. And it's never too late to be honest. If you didn't start as early as Lincoln did — no worries! Start today!!

FIGHT FOR RIGHTEOUSNESS   JUNE 10TH

The cause of righteousness never failed to bring out the fight in my father.
Monto Ho, son of Ho Feng-Shan

In 1938, Nazi Germany annexed Austria, making life precarious for the almost 200,000 Austrian Jews. Jews couldn't escape Nazism by fleeing Europe without receiving visas, but nations were refusing to accept Jewish immigrants with the exception of the Dominican Republic.

During the early years of World War II Chinese diplomat Ho Feng-Shan served as consul-general in Vienna. Defying the orders of his superiors, Ho issued visas for Austrian Jews to Shanghai. Throughout 1938 Ho issued almost 2,000 of these visas, and continued to do so until he was ordered to leave his post in May 1940. Nicknamed the "Chinese Schindler", Ho even issued visas to Jews who sought to flee to countries other than China. Though the exact number is unknown, it is estimated that Ho opened the door for many thousands of Jews to leave Austria and escape death.

After several decades of diplomatic service, Ho retired in 1973 and settled in San Francisco. Ho's memoir, "My Forty Years as a Diplomat" was published on 1990; his son, Monto Ho, translated it into English. In the introduction of 2010 translation, the younger Ho shared a signature story about his father.

A few days after the Kristallnacht (November 9, 1938), when Nazi hoodlums smashed Jewish windows all over Germany after the Third Secretary of the German Embassy in Paris was assassinated by a Polish Jew, Father had an appointment to see a Jewish couple, the Rosenbergs, off. They had obtained from Father a visa to Shanghai. On that day, all Jews throughout Germany were ordered restricted to their homes. Mrs. Rosenberg called and advised Father not to come. Father insisted he had to keep the appointment. On arriving at their house, she advised him that her husband had already been taken away by the police. A short while later, two rough plainclothes policemen came to search the household. Father was asked by them to identify himself. He refused to do so until they had identified themselves. His effrontery threw them off. They asked Mrs. Rosenberg who Father was. She said he was the Chinese Consul General. They left abruptly without searching the house.

Ho fought for righteousness and safeguarded countless lives. Let his example inspire you to fight for righteousness in your own circumstances; to do so, you must:

LOSE YOUR EGO — Humbling yourself doesn't mean you think less of yourself but you think of yourself less. The Apostle Paul put it best:

. . . in humility value others above yourselves, not looking to your own interests but each of you to the interests of the others
Philippians 2: 3-4

LOCK IN PRINCIPLES — Let principles — not sentiments — determine what you do. Ho decided it was the right thing to help the Jews escape, and he did it, even in the face of great danger. Whatever the right thing is for you to do, just do it!

LEAD BY EXAMPLE — It's trite but true: actions speak louder than words. Seek alignment between what you say and do. At the end of the day, the way you live outweighs the words you use. Jesus affirmed this truth:

You will know them by their fruit.
Matthew 7:20

LIVE BY RISK — If you're going to do something worthwhile with your life, you'll have to take a risk. Do it to benefit another.

LOVE TO SERVE — Check your motives. It is less important to prove a point than to make a difference. John Maxwell made it clear:

People don't care how much you know until they know how much you care.

Show Your Sincerity   June 11th

I would rather be beaten and be a man than to be elected and be a little
puppy dog. I have always supported measures and principles and not men.
I have acted fearlessly and independent and I never will regret my course.
                    Davy Crockett

Frontiersman Davy Crockett was a Tennessee backwoodsman
turned popular politician, who served two terms in the state legislature and
three terms in Congress. Known as the "King of the Wild Frontier",
Crockett transitioned from a hunter of animals to a hunter for votes in
1821, running for a Tennessee General Assembly seat. In his first campaign,
Crockett had been asked to make remarks at a local event but, as a political
novice, wasn't sure what to say.

I got up and told the people, I reckoned they know'd what I come for,
but if not, I could tell them. Had come for their votes . . . But the worst of all
was, that I couldn't them anything about government. I tried to speak about
something, and I cared very little what, until I choked up as bad as i f   m y
mouth had been lam'd and cram'd chock full of dry mush. There the people
stood, listening all the while, with their eyes, mouths, and ears all open, to catch
every word I would speak.

Crockett then pivoted, showing some sincerity and his lighter side.

At last I told them I was like a fellow I had heard of not long
before. He was beating on the head of an empty barrel near the roadside, when
a traveler, who was passing along, asked him what he was doing that for. The
fellow replied that there was some cider in that barrel a few days before, and he
was trying to see if there was any then, but if there was he couldn't get at it. I
told them that there had been a little bit of a speech in me a while ago, but I
believed I couldn't get it out. They all roared out in a mighty laugh, and I told
some other anecdotes, equally amusing to them . . . But I took care to remark
that I was as dry as a powder horn, and that I thought it was time for us all to
wet our whistles a little; so I put off to the liquor stand, and was followed by
the greater part of the crowd. I was elected, doubling my competitor, and nine
votes over.

Crockett's success speaks to the importance of being sincere. He
could have played the phony politician but instead was simply himself, and
his integrity connected with the crowd. Showing sincerity is a key strategy in
successful social relations. To show your sincerity, you should:

SHARE A JOKE — Lighten up. If you take yourself too seriously, you can turn others off. When all else fails, tell a joke. Crockett's example may not be the best one to follow in most situations; it's better to come with prepared remarks. But keep this in mind: laughter can help bring people together, in the words of Victor Borge:

Laughter is the shortest distance between two people.

Just make sure it's good, clean, relevant humor. It's a risky approach that could backfire if not well executed.

SING YOUR PERSONAL STORY — We all make mistakes. Talk about one of yours, how you survived it, how you overcame it. Make it a song of success that will inspire others to work hard to attain their goals.

SIT IN SILENCE — It's okay not to say anything sometimes, especially in a one-on-one encounter. Body language — a blink of the eye, a nod of the head, a touch of the hand — can speak volumes. In the right moment, silence can be golden. Just being present — without words — is enough.

SHINE YOUR VIRTUE — Meditate on Davy Crockett's words.

I would rather be politically buried than be hypocritically immortalized.

The deeper your commitment to integrity, the greater your freedom from hypocrisy. Be a lighthouse to someone's ethical gloom.

LIVE LIFE TO THE FULL   JUNE 12TH

I have spent all my life with dance and being a dancer. It's permitting life to use you in a very intense way. Sometimes it is not pleasant. Sometimes it is fearful. But nevertheless it is inevitable.
Martha Graham

In 1926 Martha Graham founded the Martha Graham Center of Contemporary Dance and went on to reshape American modern dance. By the time of her final performance in 1970, when she was 76 years old, Graham had become known as "the Picasso of Dance", revered as the creative spirit who had modernized American dance, ushering it into the 20th century. She had been the first dancer to perform at the White House, traveled worldwide as a cultural ambassador, composed 181 choreographies and received the Presidential Medal of Freedom, America's highest civilian award. Graham's remarkable success stemmed not only from her artistic brilliance but also from her conviction to live life to the full. Her example should inspire you to pursue this goal. To live your life to the full, learn how she did it; meditate on her words that follow; then seek to apply her success principles in your own daily experience. You don't have to be a dancer or aspire to be one. You just have to want to live your life to the full.

FEELING — *I believe that dance was the first art. A philosopher has said that dance and architecture were the first arts. I believe that dance was first because it's gesture, it's communication. That doesn't mean it's telling a story, but it means it's communicating a feeling, a sensation to people.*

FOREORDAINED — *People have asked me why I chose to be a dancer. I did not choose. I was chosen to be a dancer, and with that, you live all your life.*

FOCUS — *There is a vitality, a life force, a quickening that is translated through you into action, and because there is only one of you in all time, this expression is unique, and if you block it, it will never exist through any other medium, and be lost. The world will not have it. It is not your business to determine how good it is, not how it compares with other expression. It is your business to keep it yours clearly and directly, to keep the channel open.*

FERVOR — *Great dancers are not great because of their technique, they are great because of their passion.*

FREQUENCY — *I believe that we learn by practice. Whether it means to learn to dance by practicing dancing or to learn to live by practicing living, the principles are the same. In each, it is   the performance of a dedicated precise set of acts, physical or intellectual, from which comes shape of achievement, a sense of one's being, a satisfaction of spirit. One becomes, in some area, an athlete of God. Practice means to perform, over and over again in the face of all obstacles, some act of vision, of faith, of desire. Practice is a means of inviting the perfection desired.*

FELICITY — *No artist is pleased. There is no satisfaction whatever at any time. There is only a strange, divine dissatisfaction, a blessed unrest that keeps us marching and makes us more alive than the others.*

FLOW — *Movement never lies. It is a barometer telling the state of the soul's weather to all who can read it.*

FRISSON — *All that is important is this one moment in movement. Make the moment important, vital, and worth living. Do not let it slip away unnoticed and unused.*

FREEDOM — *Freedom to a dancer means discipline. That is what technique is for — liberation.*

FLIGHT — *I feel that the essence of dance is the expression of man — the landscape of his soul. I hope that every dance I do reveals something of myself or some wonderful thing a human can be.*

FULFILLMENT — *The main thing, of course, always, is the fact that there is only one of you in the world, just one, and if that is not fulfilled then something has been lost. Ambition is not enough; necessity is everything.*

REFUSE TO BELIEVE THE HYPE   JUNE 13TH

Before I came here I was told the niggars were a most treacherous,
devilish lot of people to deal with and the only way to manage them
was to knock them down with anything at hand, at any light offense on
their part . . . I expected to have a jabbering, semi-wild lot of people to deal with.
John Williams

In November 1895 newly arrived Welsh immigrant John Williams wrote a letter back home to his friend William Thomas. Williams had moved to work in the coal mines of West Virginia. His letter revealed a clash between what he had been told to expect and the American realities, especially concerning race relations. Corresponding with his friend, Williams wrote about his first experience of African Americans upon arriving in West Virginia.

Being easily tired of the train, I got into a large dining saloon. Presently two niggar young women came to me: They were about eighteen years old and they had delightfully melodious sweet voices and spoke in most guarded and beautiful English. "By jove," says I to myself, "if all the niggars are like these girls, I am jolly glad I came down here."

Willams' account of his ongoing interactions with blacks demonstrates how negative perceptions can be transformed by actual encounters, improving social relations.

I came in contact with several of them, men this time, while waiting at Poco and found them all extremely well-behaved and enlightened people. I am extremely fond of them and have not had the lightest trouble with them since I have been here. And I would rather manage 500 of them than half a dozen of the white people of this country. . . . I treat them very respectfully and show them that I respect their race and they appreciate that more than words can tell, for most white people treat them otherwise, which is the greatest mistake.

The uprightness that Williams experienced in the African Americans he met caused him to act respectfully towards them instead of with the violence he had expected. He refused to believe the hype and made his own assessments, which led him to truthful conclusions. Over a century later his example holds special relevance in the hype-saturated realities of our current times. To refuse to believe today's hype, make your own assessments.

ASSESS YOUR VIEWS — Williams learned through actual experience that the negative reports about African Americans were false. Always do your own research to inform your opinions based on facts and realities. Check your sources of information and be open to revise your thinking as you make new discoveries. Prioritize in-person, immediate encounters and observations over media-generated data.

ASSESS YOUR ACTIONS — Be willing to go in a different direction than the one to which you're accustomed. Like everyone else, you're a creature of habit. But if those habits were developed from misinformation, it's time to make a change. Let go of your old ways so your new actions can be consistent with your new views.

ASSESS YOUR RELATIONSHIPS — As with Williams, assessments of integrity can bring out positive rather than negative responses from others, sowing harmony instead of hostility. If you're holding untrue stereotypes due to the prejudicial limitations of the culture in which you were raised, get first-hand exposure; reassess relations; cast the dated things aside. Deal with people as they really are.

ASSESS YOUR DESTINY — Williams defied expectations and improved racial relations of his day. Refuse to believe the hype, and you, too, can be a force for good.

LIVE BY THE GOLDEN RULE   JUNE 14TH

Let a principle of honesty cause you to keep your word, in all your business.
You sometimes give your word, let that word then be as good as your bond.
Cotton Mather

Cotton Mather was the head of the Puritan church in New England and because he wrote more than four hundred fifty books and pamphlets, he was one of the most influential religious leaders in colonial America. Mather succeeded his father as pastor of Boston's original North Church; he turned many of his sermons into tracts. One of them, A Christian at His Calling, was printed and distributed in 1701. In it, Mather stated that a Christian's general calling to faith in God must be balanced by a personal calling to morality in business and professional dealings. The moral code he delineated had universal application across religions and occupations, which helped to shape the ethical environment of America as it began to rise as the world's industrial and entrepreneurial leader over the next couple of centuries.

Mather's overarching point was to be trustworthy in all your business dealings as well as in your personal relationships. It's good advice because trust is the most important factor in developing good relationships across the board. You cannot grow clients or customers for a successful business, or create fellowship or companionship for a strong relationship, if people don't trust you. Build trust one day at a time by paying attention to Mather's words and the principles they project.

TOUCHSTONE — *In your business you have dealings with other persons; but a certain vein of honesty, unspotted and resolved honesty, should run through all your dealings. You aim at the getting of silver and gold by your occupation; but you should always act by the Golden Rule. . . .*

Jesus defined the Golden Rule.

So in everything, do to others what you would have them do to you,
for this sums up the Law and the Prophets.
Matthew 7:12

Live by the Golden Rule: do to others as you would have them do to you. This lifestyle will come back to bless you in myriad ways.

TONE — *Are there also any manufactures that you are to work up for others? Cheat no man with anything that shall be unserviceable to him. Do nothing slightly, do nothing baseby, do nothing deceitfully. . . . Let a principle of honesty cause you carefully to pay the debts which in your business must fall upon you.*

Watch the way you interact with others. Be accountable at all times. Show sensitivity and respect. Use non-verbal cues to deepen connection: steady eye contact, handshake, thumbs up, pat on the back, nod of encouragement, shoulder to lean on. And don't be in a rush. Invest the time necessary to hear someone out, to be transparent, to promote understanding.

> TEMPTATION — *In every bargain that you make in your business, let a principle of honesty keep you from every fraudulent or oppressive action. . . . Wherefore, take no advantage, either from the necessity or from the unskillfulness of those with whom you are concerned. It is uncharitable, it is disingenuous, it is inhuman for one man to prey upon the weakness of another. . . .*

When you're tempted to use your intelligence, status or relationships to take advantage of someone, resist the temptation to do so. Instead turn the tables on privilege. Step away from your better position and practice self-denial. Your trustworthiness will rise through your selfless actions.

> TRUTH — *I say then: Let a principle of honesty in your occupation cause you to speak the truth, and nothing but the truth, on all occasions. . . .*

The words of Alexander Pope punctuate this principle:

> *A honest man's the noblest work of God.*

DON'T PLAY THE BLAME GAME   JUNE 15TH

Accept the role you played to create your present circumstances, which in turn prepares you mentally and emotionally to change them for the better.
Joseph Holland

Having been at Harkhomes for an exceptionally long time, Lawrence was someone I was constantly trying to motivate. This day I decided to share an adage about personal responsibility.

"If you give a man a fish, he'll eat for a day," I asserted, staring at him. "If you teach him how to fish, he'll eat for a lifetime."

He indignantly glared back at me. "I'm a black man in America. I don't do fishing. I'm the one on the hook." Lawrence then covered the spectrum of his racial difficulty. He bought his first drugs from a "white pusher," lost a fortune when he was swindled by a "white hustler," and got arrested when he was hoodwinked by a "white mole."

When I cautioned him against making Caucasians his favorite scapegoats, he exploded with a new round of complaints.

"We're always the last hired and the first fired." He'd lost his job because his foreman was a racist; of course, it had nothing to do his raging temper and the fight where he knocked out a white coworker. He'd lost his apartment because he was black and the landlord was white; of course, it had nothing to do with the fact that he had not paid rent in six months.

"Don't you know there's a conspiracy to emasculate the black man that's been going —"

I cut him off, not because I disagreed with everything he was saying but because it was important to make a point about the blame game. "The problems of too many people are always someone else's fault. People blame God, kids blame parents, wives blame husbands, husbands blame wives, and you're always blaming the white man. Won't you take any responsibility for your problems?"

Such conversations between Lawrence and me persisted, until he embraced a new Christian commitment, which shifted his thinking towards forgiveness. Just as God had forgiven his sins, he was called to forgive the sins of others, no matter how grievous. This realization and the personal responsibility that it fostered eventually — it took a while — put Lawrence on high road of individual aspiration, fair-minded perspectives and educational pursuit, eventually obtaining his college degree.

Playing the blame game is never the right thing to do. For you to avoid playing it, it's important for you to:

ASK YOUR CONSCIENCE — If you're constantly pointing the finger of blame at others for your own problems, it's time to take a hard look at yourself, asking some challenging questions. Do your words and actions match? Do you insist on a bold, bright line between right and wrong, and staying on the true and noble side of that line? Don't forget to answer Jesus' question:

Why do you look at the speck of sawdust in your brother's eye and pay no attention to the plank in your own eye?
Matthew 7:3

ASSERT YOUR CALIBER— You are someone special, born that way: you are made in the image of God and in His likeness; thus you are created great by God. Believe in your specialness, your uniqueness. Be less concerned with what role others play in your life and more aware of your distinctive gifts and talents. Stay focused on your own abilities, and you won't be inclined to look elsewhere if things don't go according to plan.

ASCEND TO YOUR CALLING—Be purpose-driven. Once Lawrence embraced his divine calling, he lost interest in the blame game; he was too busy working towards his destiny. Get busy creating your glorious future, and all the blame game-playing will quickly fade away.

AFFIRM FUNDAMENTAL TRUTHS   JUNE 16TH

A man is a man, until that man finds a plan, a plan that makes that man, a new man.
Dred Scott

In 1846 Dred Scott, an enslaved African American man, filed a lawsuit for his freedom on the ground that he and his family had lived in free states and territories for over two years. The Dred Scott case eventually made it to the United States Supreme Court, which ruled, on March 6, 1857, against Scott, asserting that he was not a U.S. citizen, thus had no right to sue; that residence in free territories does not make him free; and that the Missouri Compromise, which had resulted in new states to the North being admitted as free states, was unconstitutional.

Though the Southern states applauded the Court's opinion, the Northern states vigorously denounced it. On April 17, 1857, the Ohio legislature adopted a resolution condemning the legal decision, an excerpt of which follows.

That the General Assembly, in behalf of the people of Ohio, hereby solemnly protest against these doctrines as destructive of personal liberty, of states' rights, of constitutional obligations, and of the Union; and, so protesting, further declares its unalterable convictions that in the Declaration of Independence the fathers of the republic intended to assert the indestructible and equal rights of all men, without any exception or reservation whatever, to life, liberty, and the pursuit of happiness; and in the Constitution by the comprehensive guaranty the no person shall be deprived of life, liberty, or property, without due process of law, designed to secure these rights against all invasion but the federal government, and to make the establishment of slavery outside of slave states a constitutional impossibility.

The Ohio political leadership reaffirmed the founding principles of America, holding on to the truth that equal rights declared at the nation's outset applied just as much to Dred Scott as to any American, regardless of race. Since truth is timeless, affirming it is a good idea; note the following poem and the principles it projects.

DOGGEDNESS OF TRUTH

Though unreceived and scoffed at through the years;
Though made the butt of ridicule and jest;
Though held aloft for mockery and jeers,
Denied by those of transient power possessed,
Insulted by the insolence of lies,
Truth never dies.

DISCIPLINE OF TRUTH

It answers not. Does not take offense,
But with a mighty silence bides its time;
As some great cliff that braves the elements
And lifts through all the storms its head sublime,
It ever stands, uplifted by the wise;
And never dies.

DISCOVERY OF TRUTH

As rests the Sphinx amid Egyptian sands;
As looms on high the snowy peak and crest;
As firm and patient Gibraltar stands,
So truth, unwearied, waits the era blessed
When men shall turn to it with great surprise.
Truth never dies.

Yes, the poem makes clear that the power of truth — respecting it, affirming it — is as important for you today as it was 160 years ago. Truth should be the standard that governs all your interactions: be dogged and disciplined in affirming it; always seek to discover it; and you will rise victorious over all the relativities, vagaries and adversities of this world.

HOLD YOURSELF ACCOUNTABLE   JUNE 17TH

There is no man more dangerous, in a position of power, than he who refuses to accept
as a working truth the idea that all a man does should make for rightness and soundness.
Ida Tarbell

In 1904 journalist Ida Tarbell published "The History of the Standard Oil Company", regarded as a classic of investigative journalism. Tarbell was the leading woman among a small group of reform-minded journalists committed to expose the social evils of big business in the early years of the 20th century. Their writings — especially her book about the oil industry — had far-reaching impact, leading to the breakup of the Standard Oil monopoly, the passage of legislation regulating big corporate interests such as the Clayton Antitrust Act, Hepburn Act, and Mann-Elkins Act as well as the creation of the Federal Trade Commission.

Adapted from a series of magazine articles, the success of Tarbell's "Standard Oil" book made her the pioneer of her crusading peers — Lincoln Steffens, Ray Stannard Baker, Jacob Riis and Upton Sinclair, among them — who came to be known as muckrakers. The following passage from the book represents Tarbell's caustic critique, taking on not only a corporate giant but the questionable ethics of the entire business establishment.

> . . . *"it's business" has come to be a legitimate excuse for hard dealing, sly tricks, special privileges. It is a common enough thing to hear men arguing the the ordinary laws of morality do not apply in business. Now, if the Standard Oil Company were the only concern in the county guilty of the practices which have given it monopolistic power, this story never would have been written. Were it alone in these methods, public scorn would long ago have made short work of the Standard Oil Company. But it is simply the most conspicuous type of what can be done by these practices. The methods it employs with such acumen, persistency, and secrecy are employed by all sorts of businessmen, from corner grocers up to bankers. If exposed, they are excused on the ground that this is business. If the point is pushed, frequently the defender of the practice falls back on the Christian doctrine of charity, and points that we are erring mortals and must allow for each other's weaknesses! — an excuse which, if carried to its legitimate conclusion, would leave our businessmen weeping on one another's shoulders over human frailty, while they picked one another's pockets.*

Tarbell challenged America to hold itself accountable for the Robber Barons and business practices generally; public opinion was stirred and legislative changes ensued. Tarbell's clarion call for integrity still rings true today. Accept the challenge to hold yourself accountable. These principles will help you heighten the ethical standards for your own life.

REMOVE GREED — Check your motives. If you're so driven by making as much money as possible that greed has overtaken your principles, you're a train wreck waiting to happen. Ask Bernie Madoff!If necessary, strengthen your accountability and be really hard on yourself in regard to financial matters. Don't compromise yourself in selfish pursuit of a treasure chest. Keep your spiritual values always in full view.

RISK TAKING — It was risky for Ida Tarbell to take on John D. Rockefeller, an icon of American industry. She was able to do it because her convictions overruled her trepidations. Make sure your beliefs are stronger than your fears. Remember Old Testament leader David defeated the giant warrior Goliath because he set his bar higher than anyone else dared to do.

RESET PRIORITIES — Attaining your goals happens by choice, not by chance. Assess your agenda every day: figure out what's working and what's not. Set your priorities for today accordingly; reset them for tomorrow . . . and the next day . . . but before you set them, assess your outcomes. Make sure you're meeting your goals, then move forward.

ROBUST VISION — Holding yourself accountable today means you can set your bar high tomorrow. Be watchful — clouds of adversity will come to block your vision. Keep renewing your dream, keep pushing it up beyond the gloom towards the sun of your destiny.

BATTLE FOR INTEGRITY   JUNE 18TH

Reader, you are impaneled as a juror to try a plain case and bring in an honest verdict. The questions at issue is not one of law but of fact — What is the actual condition of the slaves in the United States? . . .
Theodore Weld

One of the architects of the antebellum anti-slavery movement, Theodore Weld was well regarded as a speaker and organizer — the most influential abolitionist of his era. Weld had greatest impact as a writer. He published numerous pamphlets marshaling his case against slavery, which were incorporated into his book, American Slavery As It Is: Testimony of a Thousand Witnesses, published in 1839. In his most popular pamphlet — he sold 100,000 copies — Weld delineated the evidence in support of his case.

We will prove that the slaves in the United States are treated with barbarous inhumanity; that they are overworked, underfed, wretchedly clad and lodged, and have insufficient sleep; that they are often made to wear round their necks iron collars armed with prongs, to drag heavy chains and weights at their feet while working in the field, and to wear yokes, and bells and iron horns . . . have some of their front teeth torn out or broken off that they may be easily detected when they run away . . . they are frequently flogged with terrible severity, have red pepper rubbed into their lacerated flesh, and hot brine, spirits of turpentine, etc., poured over the gashes to increase the torture . . . they are often stripped naked, their backs and limbs cut with knives, bruised and mangled by scores and hundreds of blows with the paddle, and terribly torn by the claws of cats, drawn over them by their tormentors; that they are often hunted with bloodhounds and shot down like beasts, or torn in pieces by dogs; that they are often suspended by the arms and whipped and beaten till they faint, and, when revived by restoratives, beaten again till they faint, and sometimes till they die. . .

Weld did in fact prove his case, enlisting many in his battle for American integrity. One of his most important converts was Harriet Beecher Stowe, whose Uncle Tom's Cabin — the most widely read anti-slavery publication — was partly based on Weld's writings. His work led to major changes in the institution of slavery in the 1860's. Just as Weld battled to make America's practices consistent with her founding principles, you should battle for your own integrity. To do so, you must:

DENY ANY COMPROMISE — If an activity is financially profitable, the morality surrounding it can easily become fungible. The slave owners whom Weld critiqued found many rationales — even those that cited Biblical passages — for their immoral practices. This is your inner battle, so draw strengths from your convictions. Don't compromise your core values for self-indulgence or profit-making.

DISCLOSE YOUR SECRETS — If you're hiding anything that falls short of your ethical standards, don't sweep it under the rug or keep it in the closet. Battling for integrity means striving to open up, resolving to come clean. Find someone trustworthy to confide in. You'll not only feel better by disclosing the thing, but it will also help you preempt a past ghost from haunting your present.

DRAW YOUR BOUNDARIES — Draw a moral line in the sand of your life. Don't cross it no matter how lucrative or gratifying it looks on the other side. Be tough on yourself. Set your standards high and hold yourself accountable to keep them. If you cross the boundaries you've set for yourself, be sure to enforce a severe penalty.

DO THE RIGHT THING — When it comes to integrity, talk is really cheap. Here's the moral battleground: say the right thing, then let your actions support your words. Do your best to be ethically consistent. Fight the good fight of integrity. You will never regret. Keep the words of John Wooden in mind:

Be more concerned with your character than your reputation, because your character is what you really are, while your reputation is merely what others think you are.

MAINTAIN MORAL STANDARDS   JUNE 19TH

No agency of government has ever in our history undertaken to probe so fully and deeply into the problems of crime in our nation . . . But the very difficulty which these problems present and the staggering cost of inaction make it imperative that this task be undertaken.
President Lyndon Johnson's Commission on Law Enforcement

In response to the rise in crime throughout America, President Lyndon Johnson established the Commission on Law Enforcement and Administration of Justice to study the criminal justice system. In February 1967 the Commission issued its final report entitled "The Challenge of Crime in a Free Society". Among the many challenges expounded in report, shrinking moral standards was prominent.

What appears to be happening throughout the country, in the cities and in the suburbs, among the poor and among the well-to-do, is that parental, and especially paternal, authority over young people is becoming weaker. The community is accustomed to rely upon this force as one guarantee that children will learn to fit themselves into society in an orderly and peaceable manner, that the natural and valuable rebelliousness of young people will not express itself in the form of warring violently on society or any of its members. The programs and activities of almost every kind of social institution with which children come in contact — schools, churches, social service agencies, youth organizations — are predicated on the assumption that children acquire their fundamental attitudes toward life, their moral standards in their homes. The social institutions provide children with many opportunities: to learn, to worship, to play, to socialize, to secure expert help in solving a variety of problems. However, offering opportunity is not the same thing as providing moral standards. . . .

The Commission's report asserted the importance of providing moral standards; but you can't provide them to others unless you possess your own. Develop and maintain your own set of moral standards by committing to:

LEARN THEM — Be teachable. Every day presents opportunities for you to grow your character, but if you're not humble enough to be open to them they will pass you by. Challenge yourself with some questions: When was the last time you took a moral inventory or you read a self-help article or religious book? How long has it been since you examined the openness of your soul? How can I move my ethical meter higher? What new steps can I take today to clarify my moral standards, to become a better person?

LIVE THEM — One day Mark Twain was conversing with a ruthless yet religious New England businessman who told him: "Before I die, I intend to visit the Holy Land, climb Mount Sinai and read aloud the Ten Commandments." Twain responded: "I have a better idea — just stay here and keep them!" Follow Twain's advice. Do your best — today and every day — to live your moral standards.

LEVERAGE THEM — Learning and living moral standards will benefit others in your life. To help maintain your standards, take some more counsel from Twain:

Always do right; this will gratify some and astonish the rest.

LIGHT THEM — By maintaining moral standards you will lighten the pathway of success for others.

The integrity of the upright guides them, but
the unfaithful are destroyed by their duplicity.
Proverbs 11:3

LET THEM GO FAR — As the Commission report indicated, imparting moral standards to your loved ones at home is imperative. But don't stop there. Your nation needs them as well.

INSIST ON INTEGRITY   JUNE 20TH

> *. . . the United States took the slave and left the thing which gave birth*
> *to chattel slavery and which is now fast giving birth to industrial slavery;*
> *a slavery more excruciating in its exactions, more irresponsible in*
> *its machinations than that other slavery, which I once endured.*
> T. Thomas Fortune

In 1884 former slave and journalist T. Thomas Fortune published "Black and White: Land, Labor and Politics in the South". In the book Fortune assessed the consequences of the collapse of Reconstruction, precipitated by the 1877 withdrawal of federal troops from the South, leaving African Americans of that region to fight their own battles. Fortune described the consequent loss of black opportunities — educational, economic and political — in an incisive analysis.

> *The chattel slaveholder must, to preserve the value of his property,*
> *feed, clothe, and house his property, and give it proper medical attention when*
> *disease or accident threatened its life. But industrial slavery requires no such*
> *care. The new slaveholder is only solicitous of obtaining the maximum labor*
> *for the minimum of cost. He does not regard the man of any consequence when*
> *he can no longer produce. Having worked him to death, or ruined his*
> *constitution and robbed him of his labor, he turns him out upon the world to*
> *live upon the charity of mankind or to die of inattention and starvation. He*
> *knows that it profits him nothing to waste time and money upon a disabled*
> *industrial slave. The multitude of laborers from which he can recruit his*
> *necessary laboring force is so enormous that solicitude on his part for one that*
> *falls by the wayside would be a gratuitous expenditure of humanity and charity*
> *which the world is too intensely selfish and materialistic to expect of him.*

Fortune's contrast between the pre-Civil War chattel slavery and the industrial slavery of the Jim Crow era underscored the chronic conflict between the nation's ideals and its practices. In his excoriating critique, Fortune insisted on integrity. You should insist on integrity as well, in the following ways.

IN YOUR OWN LIFE — Take some time today to examine the condition of your character. Fortune exposed the contradiction between America's words and actions. How are you doing with your words and actions? Do they match up? When you make a commitment to do something, do you fulfill it? When you promise to attend a family or work event, do you follow through consistently or just some of the time? When it comes to deficiencies in your integrity, be hard on yourself until you correct it. Let your life reflect the challenging words of Ralph Waldo Emerson:

What you do speaks so loudly that I cannot hear what you say.

IN THE LIVES OF PEERS — Steer clear of such people who lack integrity, lest they trip you up, breaking your strides of progress, dragging you down into the rut of moral failure with them. Keep your distance from them until you're strong enough to determine the relational dynamics: instead of them being a negative influence on you, you're a positive influence on them. If they're going to remain in your life, insist on their integrity. And let your integrity be the light that draws them to the higher ground of exemplary behavior.

IN THE LIVES OF LEADERS — Leadership is a great responsibility. Leaders not only have decision-making power but role-model influence. Insist on their integrity. If their behavior fails to meet high ethical standards, don't let them off the hook for the sake of political expediency. Call them out — and keep calling them out — until they come around to integrity.

IN THE LIFE OF THE NATION — With the unfinished business of equality and justice for all ever before the United States as a hard-to-reach goal, don't sit on the sidelines. Step onto the playing field of history as a Refounder — one committed to fulfill the founding principles of the nation, to complete the unfinished moral business of America. Every ethical step you take helps to lift the nation closer to its long-sought aspirations.

START SMALL TO BUILD BIG   JUNE 21ST

. . . all architectural values are true human values. . . . Architecture may again be the true shield for whatever aspiration, glory, or privacy humanity desires or most needs.
Frank Lloyd Wright

During an architectural career that spanned 70 years, Frank Lloyd Wright designed more than a 1,000 structures, over half of which were built. In 1945 Wright published "When Democracy Builds", in which he philosophized "Organic Architecture": an architecture that harmonized with its natural surroundings. Wright wrote about the coordination of design elements, envisioning the integrity of man-made construction into the natural environment.

> *Perhaps because it is chiefly concerned with integrity of structure, Organic Architecture first grasps the integrity of this modern demand of modern life of a new and higher Spiritual Order of all things and living persons. Perhaps only the Mind imbued with a deep sense of structure can perceive this fine Integrity as a fundamental necessity demanding and creating the more livable and gracious human simplicities.*

Wright's passion was to conceive improvements that brought people in better touch with their natural surroundings — and one another.

> *Everywhere I see the warm upsurging Love-of-Life that should be our heritage in a country truly Free. Great woods, fields, streams, mountains, ranges of hills, the windblown sweep of plains, all brought into the service of Man without doing violence to them, Man reconciled to their service, proud preserving their Beauty. Citizens now, who understand, revere, and conserve all natural resources whether of Materials or Men.*

Wright started small with a simple idea of harmonizing structure and humanity, which turned into magnificent buildings like the Johnson Wax headquarters and Guggenheim Museum. You can also start small and build big by using these principles:

SMALL THINGS — Integrity means paying attention to the little things in your life. Major lapses begin with minor shortcomings. Don't belittle the white lies; they are still lies. Strive to be holistically ethical. Make it your goal to be of sound moral character in all areas of and at all times in your life — and especially at the beginning stages of things. Jesus highlighted this truth in the Parable of the Talents.

> *'Well done, good and faithful servant; you were faithful over a few things, I will make you ruler over many things. Enter into the joy of your lord.'*
> Matthew 25:21

SECURE THINGS — Don't get distracted or disturbed by others, whether they're thriving beyond you or criticizing you. Be secure in who you are and what you're about. Know your own strengths and weaknesses; grow with the former, limit the latter. You won't even approach the bigger projects if you don't believe in your ability to handle them.

SILENT THINGS — Don't be afraid of the spotlight but don't do things to get noticed — that's the wrong motivation. Do things that bring you fulfillment and make a difference for others. Be willing to work in obscurity. Let the solitude of silence surround you — and inspire you. There will be times when your moments of greatest discovery will happen because you have achieved alone.

SCALE THINGS — Just because you start small doesn't mean you have to stay small. Commit yourself to self-improvement, becoming better and better each day of your life. Think paradigmatically: make what you're doing scalable by seeing how your creation might serve not just the immediate beneficiary but many others. Like Frank Lloyd Wright, conceive organically, believe in your small ideas and watch your big monuments manifest.

TREAT PEOPLE FAIRLY   **JUNE 22ND**

Injustice to the Indians is repugnant to the settled policy of this state, and the feelings and sentiments of its people. This state has endeavored to pursue a benign policy toward them.
William Seward

During the 1830's the Indian removal policies of President Andrew Jackson's administration displaced Native American peoples from some states west of the Mississippi River to the Kansas Territory (now the states of Kansas and Oklahoma), where lands had been statutorily reserved for them. This federal policy forced some members of the Seneca tribes of western New York State to move, but others remained on their reservations there.

Not all political leaders supported this Jacksonian initiative. On June 15, 1841, New York Governor William Seward published a letter stating his opposition in no uncertain terms.

We have suffered every tribe to remain unmolested and have ever discouraged the desire of small factions among them to effect the sale of their lands without the general consent of the tribe. We have left the Indians to debate and consider the subject without interference. When a portion of a tribe have made arrangements to purchase lands elsewhere, and obtained the consent of the whole nation to a partition, we have bought that portion of the lands equitably belonging to those who had determined to emigrate, requiring, in all cases, the consent of the whole tribe to such partial sales.

Seward concluded his letter with an appeal to change the unfair treaty.

> *. . . I cannot hesitate to declare may full conviction, derived from history now open to the world, that the treaty which has been made by the United States with the Senecas was made in open violation of the policy I have described. I am fully satisfied that the consent of the Senecas was obtained by fraud, corruption, and violence, and that it is therefore false, and ought to be held void. The removal of the Indians would, under such circumstances, be a great crime against an unoffending and injured people; and I earnestly hope that, before any further proceedings are taken to accomplish that object, the whole subject may be reconsidered by the United States.*

A year after Seward's letter, due to his lobbying and that of countless others, the U.S. government entered into a new treaty with the Senecas allowing these Native Americans who chose not to leave to remain on their reservations. Seward's initiative exemplifies the importance of treating people fairly. Keep these points in mind as you commit to do the same.

RECOGNIZE PAST INJUSTICE — Don't bury your head in the sand to avoid history's unjust realities. Even if you have no direct responsibility in the injustice, take a stand against it, and do something to rectify it. It's the right thing to do, and your influence, combined with others, can build momentum for change.

RECALIBRATE YOUR RESPONSE — Be character-driven, not emotion-driven. It's human nature for feelings to dictate choices. Resist that tendency. If you feel strongly about something, take a step back before deciding what to do . . . think about it . . . talk about it . . . pray about it . . . all of which will help you determine the right thing to do.

RECTIFY EXISTING WRONGS — Seward wrote a letter objecting to the injustice of his day. Creating correspondence may not be enough but it's a place to start. Understand the legacies of long-standing unfairness. Know your history. Connecting the dots between past misconduct and its present day consequences will inform the action you take to address societal inequities. Yes, start with treating your neighbors fairly, then take on the institutional wrongs.

RALLY YOUR TROOPS — Seward bright about an important policy change by rallying people to his cause. In addition to treating people fairly in your immediate surroundings, join with others to extend fairness far and wide. Cultivating coast-to-coast support could move the needle of fairness and justice towards greater realization.

GET TO KNOW YOU   JUNE 23RD

Be who you really are, do what you want to do, in order to have what you really want.
Margaret Mead

In 1975 Margaret Mead was appointed president of the American Association for the Advancement of Science, a pinnacle in her distinguished career as a cultural anthropologist. Almost five decades earlier Mead had received her master's and PhD degrees from Columbia University, which launched her academic career and research initiatives; one of the areas that she studied concerned the debate in the early 20th century about race and intelligence. Mead concluded that social environment has so much influence over one's intellectual development that a physical characteristic such as race is not a dispositive factor. Her research also explored family stability — or lack thereof — and its impact on individual advancement. Mead's work in this area yielded sociological theory as well as practical principles; these principles speak to self-improvement; specifically ideas for people to get to know themselves as they pursue personal progress. It starts with you getting to know yourself. Some of her views about this are set forth below as advice to you to follow. Consider all her points and focus on those that most directly relate to you. Apply the relevant principles that will help you get to know yourself better and embrace the success that will rise from such deeper personal knowledge.

INFANT — *Children must be taught how to think, not what to think.*

INDIVIDUAL — *The most intractable problem today is not pollution or technology or war; but the lack of belief that the future is very much in the hands of the individual.*

INTENSITY — *I learned the value of hard work by working hard.*

INSPIRATION — *Never depend upon institutions or government to solve any problem. All social movements are founded by, guided by, motivated and seen through by the passion of individuals.*

INTROSPECTION — *For the human species to evolve, the conversation must deepen.*

INTERCONNECTEDNESS — . . . *recognize and respect Earth's beautiful systems of balance, between the presence of animals on land, the fish in the sea, birds in the air, mankind, water, air, and land. There must always be awareness of the actions by people that can disturb this precious balance.*

IMPOSSIBLE — *Nobody has ever before asked the nuclear family to live all by itself in a box the way we do. With no relatives, no support, we've put it in an impossible situation.*

INTERDEPENDENT — *We must have . . . a place where children can have a whole group of adults they can trust.*

INTERGENERATIONAL — *Everyone needs to have access both to grandparents and grandchildren in order to be a full human being.*

INSIGHT — *The solution to adult problems tomorrow depends on large measure upon how our children grow up today.*

INTREPID — *Never doubt that a small group of thoughtful, committed citizens can change the world; indeed, it's the only thing that ever has.*

INTEGRITY — *Whatever advantages may have arisen, in the past, out of the existence of a specially favored and highly privileged aristocracy, it is clear to me that today no argument can stand that supports unequal opportunity or any intrinsic disqualification for sharing in the whole of life.*

IDEAL — *If we are to achieve a richer culture, rich in contrasting values, we must recognize the whole gamut of human potentialities, and so weave a less arbitrary social fabric, one in which each diverse human gift will find a fitting place.*

BE TRUE TO YOUR CALLING   JUNE 24TH

If all my possessions were taken from me with one exception, I would choose to keep the power of communication, for by it I would soon regain all the rest.
Daniel Webster

In January 1830 one of the great debates in American political history took place on the floor of the United States Senate. The heated exchange between Robert Hayne of South Carolina and Daniel Webster of

New York was precipitated by a resolution calling for the temporary suspension of the sale of public lands. Hayne argued for strict constructionism and state sovereignty characteristic of the political positioning of the Southern states. Webster countered with the ultimate sovereignty of the national government and Constitution over states' rights.

Webster's eloquence was memorable. He depicted the U.S. government as "made for the people, made by the people, and answerable to the people," language that Abraham Lincoln paraphrased over thirty years later as "government of the people, by the people, for the people" in his Gettysburg Address. In the conclusion of his Second Reply to Hayne, Webster challenged America to be true to her calling:

> *God grant that in my day, at least, that curtain may not rise! God grant that on my vision never may be opened what lies behind! When my eyes shall be turned to behold for the last time the sun in heaven, may I not see him shining on the broken and dishonored fragments of a once glorious Union; on states dissevered, discordant, belligerent; on a land rent with civil feuds, or drenched, it may be, in fraternal blood! Let their last feeble and lingering glance rather behold the gorgeous ensign of the republic, now known and honored throughout the earth, still full high advanced, its arms and trophies streaming in their original luster, not a stripe erased or polluted, nor a singe star obscured, bearing for its motto, no such miserable interrogatory as "What is all this worth?" nor those other words of delusion and folly, "Liberty first and Union afterwards"; but everywhere, spread all over in characters of living light, blazing on all its ample folds, as they float over the sea and over the land, and in every wind under the whole heavens, that other sentiment, dear to every true American heart — Liberty and Union, now and forever, one and inseparable!*

The integrity of which Webster spoke represents a high standard of national destiny that the American Experiment is still trying to attain. Being true to your calling is also an important standard for individual lives including your own. Answer these questions to assess how you're doing in being true to your calling.

CORE VALUES — Integrity is choosing your thoughts and actions based on values rather than personal gain. What are your core values? Are they consistent with your livelihood and lifestyle? If not, what changes do you need to make? What are some examples of your core values manifesting in your daily life?

CLARITY — Are you clear on your calling? You can't be true to your calling if you're confused about it. What is the one thing you most want to accomplish during your lifetime?

Sometimes the connection between your core values and your calling is hard to see. Have you connected the dots between your calling and your core values? Do they work in your life in mutually supportive ways?

COMMUNICATION — Are you comfortable enough and confident enough to talk about your calling? Do you have a vision statement: can you describe your calling in a few words or in a short written paragraph? Are you ready to speak publicly about it or share it with a few close friends? Meditate on your vision so you can conceive the right words. The more you talk and write about your calling, the truer it will become to you.

COMMITMENT — Being true to your calling is a daily commitment. The small steps you take in your present make a big difference in your future. What can you do today to bring you closer to fulfilling your calling?

MAKE INTEGRITY YOUR REFEREE   JUNE 25TH

I think the idea of slavery is inconsistent with our own conduct and constitution; and there can be no such thing as perpetual servitude of a rational creature . . .
William Cushing

Before becoming one of the original five associate justices of the United States Supreme Court in 1789, William Cushing served as chief justice of the Massachusetts Supreme Court. In 1783 the Quock Walker case came before him for decision. Born a slave Walker had been promised his freedom when he reached adulthood. But his new master, Nathaniel Jennison, the widower of the promisor, refused to honor it and severally beat Walker when he ran away.

Walker sued Jennison, citing the new Massachusetts constitution of 1780. Though the constitution did not explicitly prohibit slavery, its first article reflected the language of Declaration of Independence, declaring all men to be born free and equal. In his opinion finding Jennison guilty — part of which appears below — Cushing based his decision on new American values of liberty.

As to the doctrine of slavery . . . It has been a usage — a usage which took its origin from the practice of some of the European nations, and the regulations of British government respecting the then colonies, for the benefit of trade and wealth. But whatever sentiments have formerly prevailed in this particular or slid in upon us by the example of others, a different idea has taken place with the people of America, more   favorable to the natural rights of mankind, and to that natural, innate desire   of liberty, which with heaven (without regard to color, complexion, or shape of noses) . . . has inspired all the human race. And upon this ground our constitution of government . . . sets out with declaring that all men are born free and equal — and that every subject is entitled to liberty, and to have it guarded by the laws, as well as life and property — and in short is totally repugnant to the idea of being born slaves.

Cushing's legal decision had social consequences: slave owners manumitted their slaves and paid them for their labor; other masters transitioned their slaves into indentured servants; and some slaves were freed and moved on. By 1790 the federal census recorded no slaves in Massachusetts, making it the first state of the union to effectively abolish slavery. Cushing's far-reaching ruling was based on integrity, aligning his decision with the egalitarian values of America's founding. Integrity was his referee, helping him to make render a sound decision. Let integrity be your referee as you manage:

CONFLICT — Think of integrity as your inner umpire that guides, dictates and enforces the moral ground rules of your life. When you're faced with tensions about what decision to make — a conflict between what is right and what is expedient — let your referee of integrity rule, compelling you to decide based on the virtues that you hold dear. Integrity means wholeness; it's the inner force that shapes and molds what you think, say and do into the whole person you truly are.

CUPIDITY — Gratification is the enemy of integrity. Moderate your desires to keep them from steering your choices in selfish — even self-destructive — directions. Keep your passions under control. Good self-management will lead to good choices.

COMPROMISE — Your integrity is who you are — your system of values — which determines what you do. Cushing's integrity derived from his resolve to exalt natural rights as legal precedent that had far-reaching individual and societal ramifications. He didn't compromise concerning core values. Don't compromise yours; hold them sacred.

CONDUCT — Do your best to base your decisions on your values, aligning your thoughts and actions with your highest principles. Billy Graham's quote underscores the importance of this virtue.

Integrity is the glue that holds our way of life together.

Make integrity your referee and you will not only make good decisions; you will be at peace with them.

RESOLVE DIFFICULT QUESTIONS   JUNE 26TH

The first question, however, may perhaps be answered by considering the last. Are these men, women, and children slaves? Are they free? Is their condition that of men, women, and children, or of property, or is it a mixed relation? . . . What has been the effect of rebellion and a state of war upon that status?
Benjamin Butler

Massachusetts lawyer and Civil War General Benjamin Butler was commander of Fortress Monroe in Virginia and later led the Union forces in the capture of New Orleans. Butler was confronted with the challenge of thousands of slaves fleeing the Confederacy, seeking refuge behind Union lines. He refused to return them, pioneering the idea of freeing these fugitive slaves by treating them as contraband of war in service of military objectives.

Butler's approach to Negro refugees presented the military leadership with difficult legal problems. On July 30, 1861, he sent a report to Secretary of War Simon Cameron, in which he elaborated the rationale for his new policy.

When I adopted the theory of treating the able-bodied Negro fit to work in the trenches as property liable to be used in aid of rebellion, and so contraband of war, that condition of things was insofar met, as I then and still believe, on a legal and constitutional basis. . . .

He then gave his answer, posing some final questions that led to the justification of his actions, asserting a basis for the course of action.

No longer under ownership of any kind, the fearful relicts of fugitive masters, have they not, by their masters' acts and the the state of war, assumed the condition, which we hold to be the normal one, of those made in God's image? Is not every constitutional, legal, and moral requirement, as well to the runaway master as their relinquished slaves, thus answered? I confess that my own mind is compelled by this reasoning to look upon them as men and women. If not freeborn, yet free, manumitted, sent forth from the hand that held them never to be reclaimed.

The Lincoln administration upheld his judgment and Butler's rationale evolved into military policy on the issue, which led to the political consequences of general emancipation and the end of slavery as official war goals.

Butler serves as a role model for anyone confronted by difficult questions. If you are faced with your own quandaries, you'll make progress in resolving them as you determine to:

BE OPEN — Don't ask rhetorical questions. Be genuinely open to input. You don't have to follow every piece of advice that you're given but listen carefully to all viewpoints about the issue; paying attention to the divergent perspectives will help you develop a well-reasoned and straightforward course of action.

BE TEACHABLE — Make sure you're willing to change your opinion based on new information. And do your best not to be defensive when someone expresses a different approach, or even criticizes you. Hold your tongue. Listen intently. You just might gain some wisdom, which is the most important thing in resolving difficult questions. The Old Testament reinforces this point.

> *The beginning of wisdom is this: Get wisdom.*
> *Though it cost all you have, get understanding.*
> Proverbs 4:7

BE CREATIVE — Think outside the box. Experiment with new ideas. Butler's concept — fugitive slaves as contraband of war — was novel, and proved to be trailblazing. Invest some time brainstorming with others. Interact with a new cohort of thinkers. Finding the answer could very well result from working together to discover the missing pieces of the puzzle.

BE INTREPID — Much opposition confronted Butler as he considered a new approach to black war refugees. He didn't back off but pressed on. Follow his example.

RAISE A STRONG VOICE   JUNE 27TH

Men have two ways of righting their wrongs, by force and by the
ballot. Both are denied to women, one by nature, the other by man.
                        Ida Husted Harper

Around the turn of the twentieth century journalist and suffragist
Ida Husted Harper wrote weekly syndicated columns advocating for
women's rights that appeared in newspapers in major cities across America.
In article after article Harper countered the traditionalists who asserted that
the rise of the professional woman endangered the American home. In a
piece written for "The Independent" in 1901 Harper argued against the
stereotypes used to limit workplace opportunities for women.

The countless thousands who have listened to the eloquence of a
Willard or an Anthony, and have seen the great reforms they have
accomplished, would take issue with him who would characterize them as
"stump speakers, misguided and unseemly," or would name theirs as a calling
which makes women "bold, fierce, muscular, and brawny in body or mind." It
is a mistaken kindness which would doom a woman to inhale the poisonous
fumes of "artificial flower making," or to bend her back over a sewing
machine, or to depend on the poor rewards of the artist's pencil, rather than
engage in some employment which will develop "muscle."

Harper concluded the article with a moral affirmation: society
should ensure a workplace environment with a level playing field and high
ethical standards for both women and men.

. . . It is no longer practicable to shut women up within four walls to
preserve their virtue, and, instead of demanding a return to that medieval
custom, it is the duty of society to recognize the new order and, through
individual effort, public sentiment, and law, to improve the conditions which
surround wage-earning women; to invest them with every right and privilege
possessed by workingmen; and in every possible way help them develop strength
of character to resist temptation and to fix a higher standard not only for
themselves but also for the men with whom they come in contact.

As the primary author of the six-volume "History of Woman
Suffrage", Harper consistently raised a strong voice on behalf of women's
rights. She spoke to the strengths of women generally and to her own
strengths in particular. Heed her example. If you're facing disadvantage,
unfairness or wrongdoing, you're the best person to raise a strong voice on
your behalf. To do so, be sure to:

REPEL STEREOTYPES — Know who you are. Be comfortable in your own skin. Be prepared to correct any view that distorts or depreciates your true identity. Depending on who's asserting the stereotype and their reasons for doing so, you may have to repel it. Raise your voice in righteous indignation. Bring clarity to any misrepresentation. Be strong in taking a position against untruth, especially when it's about a distortion of your identity.

RECRIMINATE NOT — No matter how offensive the comments concerning you might be, don't go negative in your response. Stay positive: elaborate your position without hostility. If your opponents are throwing stuff your way from the garbage can, refuse to get into the trash with them. Root your response in humility and self-control.

RESONATE TRUTH — It's hard to stay on the side of truth when someone is hurling falsehoods at you. Yet it's the wise strategy because truth will ultimately prevail. Harper kept speaking and writing the truth about political equality for women, and she witnessed the passage of the Nineteenth Amendment in 1920, guaranteeing women the right to vote. So always speak strongly for truth. Your veracious stand will eventually pay off.

REINFORCE VIRTUES — Your integrity will help you maintain a strong voice in the face of adversity. Strength rises from your resolve to live the vigorous virtues day by day. Eleanor Roosevelt got this principle right:

With a new day comes new strength and new thoughts.

WALK YOUR TALK   JUNE 28TH

In our greedy chase to make profit of the Negro, let us beware lest we "cancel and tear in pieces" even the white man's charter of freedom.
Abraham Lincoln

After serving one term in Congress from 1847 - 1849, Lincoln stepped out of the public eye and returned to his Illinois law practice. The passage of the Kansas-Nebraska Act in 1854, which made slavery theoretically possible in all territories, compelled Lincoln to step back into the political arena.

Illinois Senator Stephen A. Douglas — Lincoln's future political opponent — had backed the bill during debates in Washington, D.C., and had returned home to tour the state in the summer of 1854, defending the new law. In response, Lincoln gave a speech in Peoria opposing the expansion of slavery that the Congressional legislation permitted. After quoting the key section of the Declaration of Independence's preamble, he asserted:

> *. . . according to our ancient faith the just powers of governments are derived from the consent of the governed. Now the relation of master and slave is pro tanto (to that extent) a total violation of this principle. The master not only governs the slave without his consent but he governs him by a set of rules altogether different from those which he prescribes for himself. Allow all the governed an equal vote in the government, and that, and that only is self-government . . .*

Lincoln elevated his argument and relegated Stephen Douglas and the law's other supporters to the denigrated status of those would assault the very integrity of the American Experiment.

> *Fellow countrymen, American — South as well as North — shall we make no effort to arrest this? Already the liberal party throughout the world express the apprehension "that the one retrograde institution in America is undermining the principles of progress and fatally violating the noblest political system the world ever saw." This is not the taunt of enemies but the warning of friends. Is it quite safe to disregard it, to despise it? Is there no danger to liberty itself in discarding the earliest practice and first precept of our ancient faith?*

Lincoln challenged his opponents to walk their talk — to have their actions match their words. His challenge rings true for you today. Strive to walk your talk as you:

CLARIFY INTENTIONS — If you give some thought to the consequences of pushing integrity to the side, you might have some second thoughts about doing it. Remember — integrity means doing the right thing when no one is looking except God, who is always looking! You may kick yourself after the fact about a lot of your choices, but you will never regret your decision to choose integrity. Remember the words of Norman Vincent Peale.

Nothing is more confusing than people who give good advice but set a bad example.

304

CALL FOR SUPPORT — Lincoln raised his voice in a clarion call to do the right thing. His noble initiative amassed a following that led him to the highest office in the land. Recruit as many as possible to join your righteous call. It's easier to walk your talk when others are walking with you.

CHOOSE INTEGRITY — Lincoln's point was clear. America can't simply declare that all men are created equal. To have integrity, America must choose to govern herself in a way that makes that declaration a reality in the lives of her citizens. The failure to do so is "danger to liberty itself". Likewise with you, integrity is a choice: You can't just say you have integrity. Your actions must match your words. It can be a hard choice because it involves surrendering what is expedient to what is right. It is unjust to enslave another human being but it is profitable to the slaveholder. It may be advantageous for you to deceive another — maybe it leads to financial gain, public stature or ego gratification — but it's not right to conceal or distort the truth. Whatever other choices you're making today, choose integrity.

FOLLOW THROUGH ON YOUR COMMITMENTS
JUNE 29TH

The first, the most important and most difficult step to take is to mollify and finally to obliterate race and color prejudice.
Lewis H. Blair

Though the Declaration of Independence affirmed the principle of human equality, the slave trade was not abolished during the the Federal Constitutional Convention of 1787. Instead a compromise was reached protecting slavery for twenty years, codified in Article 1 Section 9 of the United States Constitution:

The Migration or Importation of such Persons as any of the States now existing shall think proper to admit, shall not be prohibited by the Congress prior to the Year one thousand eight hundred   and eight . . .

On March 2, 1807, a federal law was passed following through on this commitment which stated:

. . . it shall not be lawful to import or bring into the United State or the territories thereof, from any foreign kingdom, place, or country, any Negro,

mulatto, or person of color with intent to hold, sell, or dispose of such Negro, mulatto, or person of color as a slave, or to be held to service or labor.

The Civil War and the consequent Emancipation Proclamation and 13th, 14th and 15th Amendments notwithstanding, social, political and legal equality for African Americans was still being challenged towards the end of the 19th century. In 1887 Henry W. Grady, the editor of the Atlanta Constitution, stated:

The supremacy of the white race of the South must be maintained forever . . . because the white race is the superior race.

In response to Grady and other "New South" proponents, Virginia businessman Lewis H. Blair published in 1889, "The Prosperity of the South Dependent upon the Elevation of the Negro", in which he wrote:

. . . . And the first duty resting upon us in this respect is to see that in criminal matters — that is to say, in matters of life and liberty — the scales of justice hang more level between whites and blacks; that the hand of justice bears more equally upon the two colors, and that both are punished alike for similar offenses . . .

This argument about equality between the races continues to this day. Just as it's important for America to follow through on its commitment to human equality, it's imperative that you follow through on your commitments. To help you to achieve this goal, focus on these three keys.

CONNECTION — Connect to someone who can hold you accountable. You increase your chances of following through on your commitments when you have someone in your corner who can help you stay true to them. Be circumspect in your choice of accountability partners. Make sure you have someone who's as serious as you are. And make it mutual. Share the intention of keeping each other on track.

CONTENTION — You can't avoid the reality that challenging individual or circumstances, which might be no fault of your own, lie up ahead. Countless Henry Gradys have confronted America's commitment to equality. Don't let adversity take you by surprise. Be prepared — emotionally and strategically — so you won't be derailed when opposing forces hit hard. Contend for the truth!

COMMITMENT — If you're half-hearted about your commitment, you'll never follow through. Examine your heart and soul. Make sure your commitment runs deep, grounded and rooted in your core values. Excelling at individual follow through will position you to help others follow through. Consider helping America and her commitment to racial equality. With Henry Gradys still abounding and Lewis Blairs in short supply, she still needs all the help she can get.

BUILD STRONG MORALS FOR LEADERSHIP   JUNE 30TH

I have never in my life envied a human being who led an easy life; I
have envied a great many people who led difficult lives and led them well.
Theodore Roosevelt

In 1882 future President Theodore Roosevelt was elected to the New York State Assembly at the age of 24. In his three terms, Roosevelt became a leader on anti-corruption issues, especially concerning corporate interests. In 1885 he wrote about his experiences in the legislature, highlighting the precarious conflicts between holding public office and pursuing private gain.

Many men go to the legislature with the set purpose of making money; but many others, who afterward become bad, go there intending to do good work. These latter may be well-meaning, weak young fellows of some shallow brightness, who expect to make names for themselves; perhaps they are young lawyers, or real-estate brokers, or small shopkeepers. They achieve but little success; they gradually become conscious that their business is broken up, and that they have not enough ability to warrant any expectation of their continuing in public life; some great temptation comes in their way (a corporation which expects to be relieved of perhaps $1 million taxes by the passage of a bill can afford to pay high for voters); they fall, and that is the end of them. Indeed, legislative life has temptations enough to make it inadvisable for any weak man, whether young or old, to enter it.

Roosevelt's account of the moral pitfalls of elected officials highlight the higher ethical standards to which leaders are called. Integrity demands that you live your life in adherence to the moral principles of honesty and trustworthiness. Because the temptations pulling against such probity grow stronger the higher in life you go, you must build strong morals for leadership. Like Roosevelt, you should strive to be a leader; if so, four areas merit your extra special attention to build moral strength.

AVARICE — Greed was Roosevelt's main point. If making a lot of money is your passion, stay out of public life. And don't aspire to be a leader. The best leadership model is the servant leader: you gain power to empower others, especially those who aren't in a position to help themselves. Even if you don't want to be a leader, living by such values will make you one. Meditate on Jesus' words:

The person who is greatest among you must be your servant.
Matthew 23:11

ADULTERY — Sexual indiscretions have always presented a major challenge for those in leadership. In the Me Too era, such shortcomings are a fatal character flaw. Even past missteps will haunt present initiatives. Harvey Weinstein and Jeffrey Epstein are prime examples. Really check your closet before stepping into daylight. Whether or not you go into public life, you should be very disciplined regarding your sexual conduct. You fail to do so at great peril.

APPARATCHIK — Your independence is key. If you are controlled by a someone of wealth or an organization of influence with interests likely to be affected by your leadership position, you are walking into a hornet's nest. If you're stuck doing someone else's bidding, your risk of compromising conduct goes through the roof. First be your own person; then you can be a leader who truly can make a difference.

ARROGANCE — Check your ego at the door before you enter into the arena of public leadership. If your trip to higher ground is really just a joy ride of self-aggrandizement, get off the rollercoaster before it's too late. Pride will get you into trouble in any environment, but especially those places where the spotlight in on you! Abraham Lincoln captured this truth:

Nearly all men can stand adversity, but if you
want to test a man's character, give him power.

JULY: INDUSTRIOUSNESS
DAILY SUCCESS PRINCIPLES

1. Just Keep Working — Thomas Edison — 1869
2. Work Hard To Uplift Others — Betty Mae Tiger — 1928
3. Sweat The Small Stuff — Henry Wadsworth Longfellow — 1840
4. Prosper Through Your Work — Benjamin Franklin — 1771
5. Work Towards Your Dream — Booker T. Washington — 1881
6. Bring Creativity To Your Industry — Walt Disney — 1923
7. Get Through The Hard Work — Chinese Immigrants — 1869
8. Work Your Way To The Top — Madam C.J. Walker — 1906
9. Walk Through Your Open Door — Michel de Crèvecœur — 1759
10. Work Beyond Your Barriers — William Johnson — 1835
11. Let Diligence Develop Your Dignity — Andrew Furuseth — 1927
12. Be Wise As A Serpent, Harmless As A Dove — Mary Ellen Pleasant — 1852
13. Work A Double Bottom Line — Robert Morris — 1776
14. Forge Work Habits — Abraham Lincoln — 1848
15. Don't Be Your Own Worst Enemy — Joseph Holland — 1989
16. Take Your Skills To A Higher Level — Jacob Bigelow — 1816
17. Work Your Inventiveness — Robert Fulton — 1777
18. Beat The Economic Odds — Richard Coulter — 1874
19. Work On New Things — Richard Scammon — 1965
20. Add Value To Yourself — Michel Chevalier — 1835
21. Work Your Talent — Eli Whitney — 1792
22. Seek The Strenuous Life — Theodore Roosevelt — 1899
23. Make The Most Of Your Opportunity — William Benton — 1949
24. Work To Attain Justice — Myra Bradwell — 1873
25. Work On Your Ingenuity — Job Durfee — 1843
26. Commit To Be Competent — Peter Kalm — 1748
27. Let Your Passion Drive Your Pursuits — William Gregg — 1845
28. Stick To Your Strengths — Anonymous Farmer — 1818
29. Work Through Your Adversity — John Urmstone — 1711
30. Enrich Yourself To Enrich Others — Andrew Carnegie — 1889
31. Raise Your Economic Power — Hugo Münsterberg — 1897

JUST KEEP WORKING   **JULY 1ST**

There is no substitute for hard work.
Thomas Edison

Known as America's greatest inventor for his prolific creations, Thomas Edison holds 1,093 U.S. patents, as well as countless patents in the United Kingdom, France, and Germany. Edison's prodigious work led to the establishment of new industries such as sound recording, motion pictures and electric light and power. It was indeed his work ethic that defined him, which his son Charles makes clear in these reflections about his father.

Shuffling about his laboratory at Menlo Park, New Jersey, a shock of hair over one side of his forehead, sharp blue eyes sparkling, stains and chemical burns on his wrinkled clothing, Thomas Alva Edison never looked like a man whose inventions had revolutionized the world in less than his lifetime . . . Father himself usually worked eighteen or more hours a day. "Accomplishing something provides the only real satisfaction in life", he told us. . . . His successes are well known. In the phonograph, which invented when he was thirty, he captured sound on records; his incandescent bulb lit the world. He invented the microphone, mimeograph, medical fluoroscope, the nickel-iron-alkaline storage battery, and the movies. He made the inventions of others — the telephone, telegraph, typewriter — commercially practical. He conceived our entire electrical distribution system . . .His remarkable succession of inventions made him appear to possess almost magical powers, so that he was called "The Wizard of Menlo Park." The notion alternately amused and angered him. "Wizard?" he would say. "Pshaw. It's plain hard work that does it."

Thomas Edison just kept working and it led to legendary success. You, too, can achieve great success by applying principles from Edison's life to shape your tireless work ethic.

POSSESSED — Edison was possessed with the desire to succeed; he spent entire days as a teenager reading in the public library! When was the last time you spent an hour in the library, or even read a book? In 1869 he came to New York City as a penniless twenty-something without a degree, but worked tirelessly on making it as an inventor. The rest is history, of which all humankind is a beneficiary. How badly do you want to succeed? How hard are you willing to work for it?

PREPARATION — Edison worked his way to his American Dream. Work on developing your natural talents and gifts, whatever they may be, as much as possible. Invest in yourself to gain or improve your skill set and upgrade your capabilities,

310

thereby increasing your value to potential employers or to potential investors in your entrepreneurial pursuits.

PROFUSION — You may have to start small in order to get where you want to be. An internship, menial job, or even volunteer work can lead to a flourishing career. Edison started selling sandwiches on a train but he kept working hard and long. If you just keep working, even from the humblest beginnings, there's no limit on how prosperous and influential you might become.

PERSPIRATION — Whatever your God-given talent, gift, or ability, cultivate it to its highest level. Whether you use your capability in the business office, the tradesman's shop, the official's household, the athletic arena, the concert hall, or in some form of ministry or community service, work it as though it is a divinely inspired vocation, and keep working at it . . . and keep working and working and working . . . This formula worked really well for Thomas Edison . . . When was the last time you put in an eighteen-hour day?

WORK HARD TO UPLIFT OTHERS   JULY 2ND

When you were born, you cried and the world rejoiced.
Live your life so when you die the world cries and you rejoice.
Native American Proverb

In 1928, when she was five years old, Betty Mae Tiger, also known as Potackee, was forced to move from the Seminole camp near Indiantown, Florida, because her life was in danger. Some medicine men in Tiger's Seminole tribe were so strongly against intermarriage that they threatened to kill her because her father was white. Tiger's great-uncle intervened, relocating her family to a reservation in another county where they would be safe.

Reflecting later on the lessons of her early life, Tiger stated:

I had three goals in my life. To finish school, to take nurse's training and come back and work among my people, and to write three books.

Education was a challenge. Seminole children were not accepted in white or black schools in Florida's segregated school system. Tiger had to go to North Carolina to attend a federal Indian boarding school. She worked hard at her studies, becoming the first of her Seminole tribe to read and write English. After graduating high school — also the first from her tribe to achieve this — Tiger was off to Oklahoma where she enrolled in the nursing program at the Kiowa Indian Hospital.

With her nursing degree in hand, Tiger returned to Florida and was confronted by the tribal tradition of health care only being administered by medicine men. She decided to get additional training, understanding that health care education would be as important as service delivery. She went on to do nursing for forty years, traveling to various Native American communities, inoculating countless children with vaccinations for the first time, convincing patients to go to hospitals as needed — laboring to provide better health care for the Seminole tribe.

The tribe recognized her hard work, electing Tiger its first female chief. She took over a near-bankrupt organization; before the end of her tenure the tribe was well in the black. She also co-founded and served as editor of the tribe's first newspaper, wrote three books, and was appointed by President Nixon to the National Congress on Indian Opportunity.

Tiger worked hard and she uplifted others in the process. You can do the same when you:

SET YOUR GOALS — When she was young Tiger figured out what she wanted to do with her life. The earlier you figure it out for yourself, the sooner you will plug into what really motivates you. What makes you tick? Once you put your finger on it, write down the goals to get you there. And give yourself a head start in this competitive world by working towards your dreams just as soon as they're clear to you.

STRENGTHEN YOUR WORK ETHIC — Your willingness to work hard — not your natural talent or good looks — is the most important factor in achieving success. Whether at school or on the job, Tiger just kept working hard. Check yourself — your time: are you spending more time playing games than self-improving? Your energy: is my diet/exercise/rest regimen preparing me for maximum output? Your heart: am I really willing to give things up in order to get ahead?

SECURE YOUR SKILLS — To secure the necessary skills to pursue her dream, Tiger first went from Florida to North Carolina, then to Oklahoma. By securing her skills, Tiger put herself in the best position to succeed and to serve. Her example highlights this precept.

Before you try to climb the ladder of success, make sure it's leaning against the right wall.

SEEK TO HELP — In everything you do, approach it with a servant mindset. Endeavor to add value to others. Always remember — at the end of the day, making a difference is worth more than making a dollar.

SWEAT THE SMALL STUFF   JULY 3RD

Success is not something to wait for, it is something to work for.
Henry Wadsworth Longfellow

The most popular poet of his day, Henry Wadsworth Longfellow published "The Village Blacksmith in 1840. Though Longfellow wrote the poem as a tribute to an ancestor who had been an 18th century New England blacksmith, he fashioned the poetic laborer after an actual blacksmith — one of his neighbors in Cambridge, Massachusetts. The poem's theme is industriousness — to keep working to overcome challenges and to solve problems. Great things stem from the commitment to do the small — even menial — things well. Longfellow not only poetically captured this principle but he also created a road map, delineating steps for you to take as you learn to sweat the small stuff.

STAND TALL —
Under a spreading chestnut tree
The village smithy stands;
The smith, a mighty man is he,
With large and sinewy hands;
And the muscles of his brawny arms
Are strong as iron bands.

Whatever you're presently involved in — no matter how small and insignificant it might seem — give yourself wholeheartedly to the task at hand. No matter how menial the task seems, take pride in it. Whatever small thing you have to do, the attitude you bring to it will ennoble it.

SWING SLOW —
Week in, week out, from morn till night,
You can hear his bellows blow;
You can hear him swing his heavy sledge,
With measured beat and slow,
Like a sexton ringing the village bell,
When the evening sun is low.

Take your time. Strive to be better, not bigger. If you get better at what you're doing, the bigger will naturally follow.

SOMETHING DONE —
Toiling — rejoicing—sorrowing
Onward through life he goes;
Each morning see some task begin,
Each evening sees it close;
Something attempted, something done,
Has earned a night's repose.

Work with what you've got, and give it all you've got, and great things like ingenuity, inventions and other creative outcomes can come from your commitment. Just make sure you get something done every day.

SHINE BRIGHT —
Thanks, thanks to thee, my worthy friend,
For the lesson thou has taught!
Thus at the flaming forge of life
Our fortunes must be wrought;
Thus on its sounding anvil shaped
Each burning deed and thought!

If you happen to be in the day of drudgery, perhaps in a season of seemingly endless suffering, don't despise the moment. Instead dedicate yourself to swing your sledge of daily labor and you will forge upon the anvil of sacrifice the beauty of your dreams.

PROSPER THROUGH YOUR WORK   JULY 4TH

Motivation is when your dreams put on work clothes.
Benjamin Franklin

Benjamin Franklin began his autobiography in 1771 while visiting friends in England. Though he worked on it at three subsequent periods (1784, 1786 and 1788), Franklin did not complete it during his lifetime. Published after his death, the Autobiography has become a classic of American literary history and a work of world renown in its genre. The following account from Autobiography reveals how passionate and entrepreneurial Franklin was with his writing; it also shows how seminal he was in shaping and spreading the success values at the heart of American culture.

In 1732 I first published my Almanac, under the name of Richard Saunders; it was continued by me about twenty-five years and commonly called "Poor Richard's Almanac." I endeavored to make it both entertaining and useful, and it accordingly came to be in such demand that I reaped considerable profit from it, vending annually near 10,000. And observing that it was generally read (scarce any neighborhood in the province being without it), I considered it as a proper vehicle for conveying instruction among the common people, who bought scarcely any other books. I therefore filled all the little spaces that occurred between the remarkable days in the calendar with proverbial sentences, chiefly such as inculcated industry and frugality as the means of procuring wealth, and thereby securing virtue . . .

Franklin had many talents but he worked hardest at his creative writing ability, and he was able to prosper with it — greatly so. Heed Franklin's words to prosper through your work. Pay attention to your:

PROBITY — *Only a virtuous people are capable of freedom. As nations become corrupt and vicious, they have more need of masters.*

PARTICULARS — *A little neglect may breed great mischief. ... For want of a nail, the shoe was lost; for want of a shoe, the horse was lost; for want of a horse, the battle was lost; for want of the battle, the war was lost.*

PERSPECTIVE — *Little minds think and talk about people. Average minds think and talk about things and actions. Great minds think and talk about ideas.*

PERSONALITY — *Be cheerful -- the problems that worry us most are those that never arrive.*

PROVISION — *In my youth, I traveled much, and I observed in different countries, that the more public provisions were made for the poor, the less they provided for themselves, and of course became poorer. And, on the contrary, the less was done for them, the more they did for themselves, and became richer.*

PETULANCE — *Remember not only to say the right thing in the right place, but far more difficult still, to leave unsaid the wrong thing at the tempting moment.*

PROMOTION — *All highly competent people continually search for ways to keep learning, growing, and improving. They do that by asking WHY. After all, the person who knows HOW will always have a job, but the person who knows WHY will always be the boss.*

PURSUIT — *The U. S. Constitution doesn't guarantee happiness, only the pursuit of it. You have to catch up with it yourself.*

PROVIDENCE — *When you're down to nothing, God is up to something. The faithful see the invisible, believe the incredible and then receive the impossible.*

WORK TOWARDS YOUR DREAM   JULY 5TH

I reached Hampton, with a surplus of exactly fifty cents with which to begin my education. To me it had been a long, eventful journey; the first sight of the large, three-story brick school building seemed to have rewarded me for all that I had undergone.
Booker T. Washington

In 1856 Booker T. Washington was born into slavery in Virginia; after emancipation his mother moved the family to West Virginia to become reunited with his father. In his autobiography, Up From Slavery, Washington recounts his rise from these very humble beginnings to become a college president, advisor to U.S. presidents, and a trailblazing African-American leader. The key to his remarkable achievements was the great effort he put in working towards his dreams, which started with getting an education.

One day, while at work in the coal mine, I happened to overhear two miners talking about a great school for colored people somewhere in Virginia. . . . I heard one tell the other that not only was the school established for the members of my race, but that opportunities were provided by which poor but worthy students could work out all or part of the cost of board, and at the same time be taught some trade or industry. . . . I resolved at once to go that school, although I had no idea where it was, or how many miles away, or how I was going to reach it.

His journey towards his dream was more difficult than anticipated; he recounted the challenges.

Finally the great day came, and I started for Hampton. . . . By walking, begging rides both in wagons and in the cars, . . . after a number of days, I reached the city Richmond, Virginia, about eighty-two miles from Hampton. When I reached there, tired, hungry, and dirty, it was late in the night. . . . I was completely out of money. . . . I must have walked the streets till after midnight. . . . Just about that time when I reached extreme physical exhaustion, I came upon a portion of a street where the board sidewalk was considerably elevated . . . and lay for the night upon the ground, with my satchel of clothing for a pillow. . . . As soon as it became light . . . I noticed that I was near a large ship . . . unloading a cargo of pig iron. I went at once to the vessel and asked the captain to permit me to help unload the vessel in order to get money for food. . . .

Like Washington, you're going have to work to overcome obstacles to reach your American Dream. To do so, work on your:

CAPABILITIES — In biblical times, Jesus was a carpenter; his disciple Peter, a fisherman; the great apostle Paul, a tentmaker. Just as they had the ability to provide something of value in the marketplace of over two thousand years ago, you need to focus on developing your natural talent into a skill relevant in today's economy. Invest in yourself to gain or improve your skill set and upgrade your capabilities, thereby increasing your value to potential employers. Whatever your God-given talent, gift, or ability, cultivate it to its highest level. This is where the hard work comes in. Devote yourself to be the best at what you do — and to work harder than anyone else to become the best. One of the keys is to cultivate a learning style that's continual because of the ever-shifting twenty-first century job market. In today's globally competitive economy, employers want you to be adaptable, to be ready to plug in and play to dynamic, new environments. That means self-upgrade as you go. Become a lifelong learner.

CREDENTIALS — Capabilities are important, but your pathway of personal progress will be paved, to a large extent, by your attaining credentials: high school to trade school to community college to four-year college to graduate and/or professional school to on-the-job training to professional certifications to continuing education — the list goes on and on. It doesn't matter where you start in life. Booker T. started as a slave and ended up a college president and trailblazing leader! Keep getting those degrees! The further you go on the educational/credential road will fuel your journey towards economic success and personal fulfillment. Don't get mad at the person who got the job you wanted. Get busy. Get better. Work harder. There'll be another opportunity. Get ready for it. It doesn't matter whether you are white collar, blue collar, or no collar. The decisions you make every day — both big and small — will greatly influence how socially mobile you are, how self-sufficient you will be, how high up the socioeconomic ladder you will climb, how happy you will be. Your dreams are attainable. Keep working with all you've got to reach it.

BRING CREATIVITY TO YOUR INDUSTRY   JULY 6TH

The four Cs of making dreams come true: Curiosity, Courage, Consistency, Confidence.
Walt Disney

In 1923 Walt Disney moved from Kansas City to Hollywood and, with his brother Roy, formed the Disney Brothers Studio. His initial work, such as Alice's Wonderland, combined live action with animation. But Disney's vision — rising from his background as a commercial illustrator — was to bring his drawings to life by making them move. Disney's breakthrough in animation was in 1928, using synchronized sound to create the first post-produced sound cartoon, featuring Mickey Mouse in "Steamboat Willie".

Disney brought greater creativity to his animation in the 1930's, introducing full-color three-strip Technicolor and advanced camera technology to his feature-length cartoons; his work grew in popularity, attaining international recognition. David Low, the leading British cartoonist of this era, wrote about the significance of Disney's innovations.

> *Cinema audiences can hardly be expected to perceive his true significance. They are too preoccupied with sound accompaniment and idea content. Put on one side, please, the music and noise. . . . Consider moving drawings. . . . His last three features, "Snow White", "Pinocchio", and "Fantasia" reveal a growing understanding of the meaning of observed movement and therefore greatly increased powers of creating imagined movement.*

In December 1937 "Snow White" opened to critical acclaim, becoming the top motion picture of 1938 and, by the following year with box office receipts of $6.5 million, the most successful movie to date. Soaring from this singular success, the Walt Disney Company went on to produce countless animated and live-action movie features, earning 26 Academy Awards (22 competitive, 4 honorary), 3 Golden Globe Awards, and 1 Emmy Award.

Low placed Disney's attainments in a historical context, comparing the "imagined movement" of Disney's animation to the legendary artistic achievements of Renaissance Italian painter and engineer Leonardo da Vinci.

> *. . . the constant aiming after improvement in the new expression, the tackling of its problems in an ascending scale and seemingly with aspirations*

over and above mere commercial success. It is the direction of a real artist. It makes Disney, not as a draftsman but as an artist who uses his brains, the most significant figure in graphic art since Leonardo.

Disney used his imaginative powers and innovated with artwork to build an iconic business brand. Heed his example by incorporating "the four C's of making dreams come true" into your life.

CURIOSITY — Keep searching for new ideas. Let your imagination soar to unknown destinations. Even if your idea sounds crazy at first, play with it, refine it, write it down, revise it. And don't be afraid to share it. Like Disney, surround yourself with individuals who are aligned with your mission. Brainstorming works best with a team of generous spirits. As you share ideas with each other, you will inspire mutual creativity. Reflect on Albert Einstein's insight.

Logic will get you from A to Z. Imagination will get you everywhere.

COURAGE — Boldly pursue your work. Let nothing or no one stop your pursuit. Risk putting all your heart and soul into it, and that's where your imaginative powers will be found. Have the courage to go beyond your comfort zone. Travel to new destinations to broaden your horizons but take the inner journey as well, where revelatory discoveries are made.

CONSISTENCY — Whatever you're good at, work to become the best at it. The only way to excel at your craft is to be consistent with it, to be devoted to daily practice it. Strive for perfection. Early in his career Disney kept drawing cartoons until he had honed his skill as an illustrator, which positioned him to use his craft in new and dynamic ways. Let your consistency cultivate your craft!

CONFIDENCE — The more you trust your creativity — letting it just flow — the greater confidence you'll have in it . . . and the more your confidence, the greater your creativity . . . Believe in your ability to bring something new to this world!

GET THROUGH THE HARD WORK   **JULY 7TH**

A man grows most tired while standing still.
Chinese Proverb

On May 10, 1869, at Promontory Summit, Utah, the First Transcontinental Railroad, which linked the Pacific coast with the railway network of the Eastern United States, was completed. Construction had begun six years before on the Central Pacific Railroad that stretched 1,912 miles connecting Omaha and Oakland. This railroad line eventually transformed the economy of the American West and united the country.

10,000 to 15,000 Chinese workers, comprising 90 percent of the Central Pacific Railroad workforce, built this transportation network. Large Chinese labor gangs were recruited — many on five-year contracts — because blacks were not available because of slavery and its legacy, and whites were unwilling to take on the arduous and perilous labor. Some of the Chinese workers lost their lives due to the explosives required to blast tunnels through the Sierra Nevada and Rocky Mountains.

The dangers notwithstanding, these immigrants did the hard work: clearing dense brush, filling riverbeds, carrying steel tracks, digging with picks and shovels, chiseling through solid rock. Their extreme effort literally paved the way to the consummation of the grand transportation plan.

These unsung heroes deserved a better reward. In the decades following their groundbreaking transcontinental work thousands of the Chinese laborers went eastward to work on railroad lines in Alabama, Tennessee and New York. Some of them sought and found employment in manufacturing, agriculture, garment industries, and paper mills. But they faced pervasive discrimination — and   even violence — from whites. The Chinese Exclusion Act of 1882 outlawed all Chinese immigration to America and denied   citizenship to those who had already settled in the United States. The anti-Chinese sentiment did not begin to mitigate until the Chinese Exclusion Repeal Act of 1943.

The Chinese immigrants did the hard work no one wanted to do. They got it through it triumphantly; you will also get through the hard work as you:

GET IT GOING — Do the most difficult thing first. Prioritize the hard stuff; get it done ASAP. Be urgent about it. If you put it off to the end, you may never get to it. And even if you do get to it, you may not have the vigor for it.

GRIND IT OUT — Drudgery is the work that's very far removed from your ideal activity. You'd like to avoid it; sometimes there's no way around it. Prepare your attitude for the grind. Don't think about it while you're doing it. Put on your best playlist . . .

Sing your favorite song . . . recite an inspirational poem . . . dream about your upcoming date . . . anything to take your mind off the hard work. That's the best way to get through it.

GEAR IT UP — Build enthusiasm for the tough tasks by setting a standard of excellence and striving to meet it. No matter how challenging the task, do it the best you can, and you will find the energy to work it through to completion.

GO FOR ROSES — This Edgar Guest poem says it all.

The man who wants a garden fair,
Or small or very big,
With flowers growing here and there,
Must bend his back and dig.

The things are mighty few on earth
That wishes can attain.
Whate'er we want of any worth
We've got to work to gain.

It matters not what goal you seek
Its secret here reposes:
You've got to dig from week to week
To get Results or Roses.

WORK YOUR WAY TO THE TOP   JULY 8TH

Don't sit down and wait for the opportunities to come. You have to get up and make them for yourself! I got my start by giving myself a start!
Madam C.J. Walker

In 1906 Madam C.J. Walker founded in Denver the Madam C. J. Walker Manufacturing Company, which developed and marketed hair care products and cosmetics for African American women. By the time of her death thirteen years later, Walker had expanded her business through a nationwide sales force and had become the first female self-made millionaire in America.

Walker climbed a steep mountain to attain her success. One of six children, she was the first of her family born into freedom in 1863 after the signing of the Emancipation Proclamation. She recalled the challenges of her early years: "I had little or no opportunity when I started out in life, having been left an orphan and being without mother or father since I was seven years of age."

Walker's only formal education was in church: three months of Sunday school literacy lessons. In her early twenties, due to a hygiene-related scalp disease, she started to lose her hair. The curative shampoo and ointment that she developed led to the launching of her hair care company and eventually to her wildly successful "Walker System of Hair Culture" brand, in which she trained thousands of women. Walker opened an office in Harlem in 1913; she and her daughter A'lelia became luminaries of the Harlem Renaissance.

Madam C.J. Walker worked her way to the top as she lived out certain principles of success. Heed her words and apply the strategies and virtues that benefited her to your own life. Strive to be:

PRODUCTIVE — *I am a woman who came from the cotton fields of the South. From there I was promoted to the washtub. From there I was promoted to the cook kitchen. And from there I promoted myself into the business of manufacturing hair goods and preparations....I have built my own factory on my own ground.*

It doesn't matter where you start, no matter how humble your beginnings. What matters is your determination to do the best with what you've been given and rise up from there.

PASSIONATE — *There is no royal flower strewn path to success. And if there is, I have not found it, for whatever success I have attained has been the result of much hard work and many sleepless nights.*

Success will come if you learn to love what you do and work at it, and keep working at it!

PROMOTIONAL — *Having a good article for the market is one thing. Putting it properly before the public is another.*

Be strategic in presenting yourself for whatever opportunity you're seeking.

PLUCKY — *Girls and women must not be afraid to. . .wring success out of a number of business opportunities that lie at their very doors.*

Let your courage take you through apparently closed doors.

PARADIGMATIC — *I want young people to see what can be accomplished by thrift, industry and intelligent investment of money.*

Be a role model of visionary fulfillment. Let others embrace hope through your shining example.

PHILANTHROPIC — *Now my object in life is not simply to make money for myself or to spend it on myself in dressing or running around in any automobile, but I love to use a part of what I make to help others.*

Like Walker, as you rise up, never forget the mountains you've had to climb, even the valleys from which you've come and those who are still struggling down below.

WALK THROUGH YOUR OPEN DOOR   JULY 9TH

There is room for everybody in America. Has he any particular talent or industry? He exerts it in order to procure a livelihood, and it succeeds.
Michel Guillaume Jean de Crèvecœur

In 1755 Michel Guillaume Jean de Crèvecœur migrated to North America and served as a lieutenant in the French Colonial Militia during the French and Indian War. With the British victory over the French Army, he moved to the New York colony in 1759 and settled in Orange County where he bought a farm. He began to write about his experiences and two decades later his book of narrative essays, Letters from an American Farmer, was published in London. The first literary success by an American author in Europe, the book distinguished American society as a place full of opportunity and self-determination. The following passage highlights a stark contrast between the prospects for success that he observed in his adopted country versus back home.

I do not mean that everyone who comes will grow rich in a little time; no, but he may procure an easy, decent maintenance by his industry. Instead of starving, he will be fed; instead of being idle, he will have employment; and these are riches enough for such men as come over here. The rich stay in Europe; it is only the middling and poor that emigrate. . . . Europe with all its pomp is not to be compared to this continent for men of middle stations or laborers.

Crevecoeur concluded his counsel by invoking Mother America, who offered encouraging words of her own.

Welcome to my shores, distressed European; bless the hour in which

323

thou didst see my verdant fields, my fair navigable rivers, and my green mountains! If thou wilt work, I have bread for thee; if thou wilt be honest, sober, and industrious, I have greater rewards to confer on thee - ease and independence. . . .   Go thou, and work and till; thou shalt prosper, provided thou be just, grateful, and industrious.

Crevecoeur trumpeted the message: success belongs to those who are bold enough walk through their open door; to walk through yours, you have to:

SEE IT — The story of a man applying for welfare assistance is illustrative. He went to the government office and submitted his paperwork. The official inquired, "Why are you applying for public assistance?" The man responded, "I'm having some trouble with my eyes." "You're not wearing glasses," the official observed. "You look fine. What's wrong with your eyes?" The man said, "I just can't see myself going to work everyday." Thomas Edison makes this same point in another way.

Opportunity is missed by most people because it comes dressed in overalls and looks like work.

SEIZE IT — Opportunity is before you; it's before us all. It may not be right in front of you. Like the European immigrants in Crevecoeur's account, you must be willing to move to your opportunity. You probably won't have to cross an ocean, but you still have to be ready to go in a new direction. Seize the day! If you look hard and long enough, you will find your open door.

SIZE IT — Several factors dictate whether or not you will succeed in finding new opportunities: luck — you can't count on it; timing — you can't control it; talent — necessary but not sufficient. What is more important than all these variables is your work ethic. The stronger your determination and drive to get the job done, the better are your chances for success. Work harder than you've ever worked before, and you will force the door of opportunity open. Your destiny awaits.

SURGE IT — You keep coming to the door of your future and instead of finding it open, it is closed and locked — no way to get it. Resolve to come with a new wave of vision and energy. Build a new house of personal progress offering a different set of door of opportunity. Be open to forging a totally new pathway to get to your destination.

WORK BEYOND YOUR BARRIERS   JULY 10TH

To Day I went up to the Agricultural Bank and Received in
cash Seventeen Hundred and Fifty Dollars being the amount
of a note that I Received from Flecheaux given him by Mr R. Bledsoe
for Land that I sold to Flecheaux which Said Flecheaux Sold to Mr R. Bledsoe.
William Johnson

In antebellum America black disfranchisement was pervasive, not only in Southern states; even in some Northern states — New York, New Jersey, Ohio, and Pennsylvania, among them — voting rights for Negro freemen had been abrogated. And as slavery expanded in the South due to the burgeoning cotton industry, legal restrictions on the rights and activities of free African Americans increased: observing curfews, holding licenses to sell merchandise, carrying freedom certificates.

Mississippi resident and free African American William Johnson was able to work beyond these barriers. Born a slave in 1809, an offspring — like countless others — of a black slave mother and a white father who owned him, Johnson was emancipated as a teenager to train to become a barber. Against all odds, he attained great success as an entrepreneur, owning three barbershops, a bath house, a bookstore, real estate as well as his own slaves.

Johnson kept a diary in which he recorded his numerous business transactions with white men. The following entry demonstrates that Johnson's lack of formal education didn't impede his commercial activity.

November 5, 1835. The Dayly Paper anoncees the Result of the Election Col Bingaman & Mr McMurran, Representatives, Mr Chambers, Shreriff. Miss Sara Newman gets married to a Mr Foster of Woodville, a merchant — I paid Phill $3.00 for water Out of the pond for seven Days — Mr Duolon paid me for two months shaving $2.00 I paid Mr Mellen five Dollars for One years Subscription to the Weekly Courier & Journal for Mr Jas Miller — Mr Smith paid me for One months Shaving 1.50 I paid Mr Bledsoes Boy $11 for 2 Gunea pigs.

Johnson's remarkable accomplishments exemplify that anything is possible in life, if you're willing to work hard enough to achieve it. He worked beyond his barriers; you can as well, but you will have to:

ENVISAGE — If you can't see beyond your barriers, then you won't work to get there. Set your inner vision on your destiny and keep it there, as William Jennings Bryan encouraged:

*Destiny is not a matter of chance, it is a matter of choice; it
is not a thing to be waited for, it is a thing to be achieved.*

ENDEAVOR — Stop focusing on what you don't have, all the mistakes you've made, what went wrong. Thinking about the barriers will keep you from even trying to overcome them. Instead concentrate on your strategy: this is what I'm going to do, how I'm going about it, when I'm going to execute it. Keep your mind on tactics and you'll defeat whatever's holding you back.

EARN — If you want to succeed, you have to earn it. You earn it by working hard. Some, like Johnson, have to work harder than others because their barriers are so high. You will just have to keeping working until you get over them. It's all worth it, as Theodore Roosevelt explained:

*Extend pity to no man because he has to work. If he's worth his salt, he'll
work. I envy the man who has work worth doing, and does it well . . . far and
away the best prize that life offers is the chance to work hard at work worth doing.*

ESCALATE — Believe in yourself. Increase you intensity to succeed. You are greater than your circumstances. You can work beyond your barriers, whether legal, racial, gender, class, religious, etc. — no matter how insurmountable they appear to be . . . if you believe strongly enough that you can. If former slave William Johnson could conquer the indomitable barriers facing a black man in the American South two hundred years ago, you can overcome yours today.

LET DILIGENCE DEVELOP YOUR DIGNITY   JULY 11TH

*Work is worship — to labor is to pray — because that is to exercise
the highest, the divine faculties implanted in us as the sons of God.*
Andrew Furuseth

In 1927 merchant seaman and an American labor leader Andrew Furuseth gave the Labor Day address to students at the University of California. Furuseth's renown stemmed in large part from his efforts to enact the Seamen's Act of 1915, which became known as "The Magna

Carta of the Sea". He was esteemed posthumously by the "SS Andrew Furuseth", a ship built for the United States Maritime Commission that carried troops and prisoners of war during World War II. In his Labor Day remarks to the college students, Furuseth set a divine context for his comments on the importance of work.

> *When God made man in His own image — like Himself — it must mean that He gave creative powers to man and that henceforth man was to continue creation, and in freely working — creating — he is obeying the fundamental law of his being. Whatever we may think of the narrative in the Bible, we cannot doubt that man has creative powers and that creation has continued.*

Furuseth emphasized that work was so important that it should be regarded as a sacred act and, if properly exercised, it would lead to fulfillment, dignity and charity.

> *It matters not if the labor be the writing of a thesis or the digging of a ditch, it is the use of the same divine faculty to labor — to create — and upon its proper and free use depends the life of individuals, nations and races.*

Furuseth's main point is this: life owes you — and everyone else — nothing but the opportunity to succeed. You gain that success by working — and working hard — for it; and by such diligence you develop dignity. Keep the following factors in minds as you let your diligence develop your dignity.

DIVINE OPPORTUNITY — We have all been blessed in our human nature with the ability to work. Don't simply look at your work as a job — a way to make money and pay bills. Instead take the perspective that whatever work you're doing is a God-given opportunity; it's in your life not only to address practical responsibilities but also to express divine capabilities and to bring personal fulfillment.

DILIGENCE OVERALL — A conversation between two teens illustrates this point. "I'm really worried," says the first teen. "Dad slaves away at his job so I'll never want for anything. He pays all my bills and sends me to college. Mom slaves every day washing, ironing, cleaning up after me, and even takes care of me when I'm sick." Perplexed, throwing up his hands, the other teen queried, "I wish I had it that good. What in the world do you have to be worried about?" His friend responded, "I'm worried that the slaves might escape!" Don't just observe diligence in others. Work hard to obtain it for yourself. There's nothing more important in your success journey.

DIGNITY OBTAINED — If you've been out of work, working beneath your potential or away from your dreams, be diligent in finding, maintaining, even upgrading your employment. Your quest will not only improve your finances; it will enhance your dignity. Both outcomes are super important. The words of Thorstein Veblen underscore this point:

Labor wants pride and joy in doing good work, a sense of making or doing something beautiful or useful - to be treated with dignity and respect as brother and sister.

DESTINY OFFERED — Strive to see your work as more than a job or career. Regard it as a calling. Don't be satisfied with earning a better income. Make it your goal to extend the impact of what you do for a living to make your home, school, neighborhood — the world — a better place! Work hard to rise to that higher ground where you can hear the commendation that Jesus promised to the divinely diligent:

Well done, good and faithful servant.
Matthew 25:23

BE WISE AS A SERPENT, HARMLESS AS A DOVE   JULY 12TH

She was quite a different kind of woman and yet strangely effective and influential. . . . Here was a colored woman who became one of the shrewdest business minds of the State. She was the trusted confidante of many of the California pioneers and for years was a power in San Francisco affairs.
W.E.B. DuBois

In 1852, heeding the call of the California Gold Rush, former slave Mary Ellen Pleasant arrived in San Francisco. Pleasant had been a conductor on the Underground Railroad along the East Coast before she had to flee to New Orleans for safety. On the West Coast, she shrewdly passed as white, working as a waitress in exclusive men's eating establishments, eavesdropping on the wealthy patrons. Pleasant used the financial information that she overheard at the dining tables to make money from investments. She was able to buy restaurants of her own as well as boardinghouses. Her investments included a range of businesses: laundries, dairies, even a Wells Fargo Bank.

Pleasant worked hard to attain prosperity, and she kept working to help her people. She didn't conceal her race from other African Americans, with whom she labored on the Underground Railroad along the West Coast, deploying her money to finance its activities as well as helping escaped slaves find jobs. Historians have hailed her as "The Harriet Tubman of California." Pleasant's achievements — and the methods by which she succeeded — are compellingly captured by Jesus' instructions to his disciples.

> *Behold, I send you forth as sheep in the midst of wolves:*
> *be ye therefore wise as serpents, and harmless as doves.*
> Matthew 10:16

Pleasant was shrewd as well as innocent — calculating as to tactics; genuine as to motives — in her phenomenal work. Pay attention to her words, her example, and the success principles that they represent.

SELF-CONFIDENCE — *I don't like to be called mammy by everybody. Put that down. I am not mammy to everybody in California. I received a letter from a pastor in Sacramento. It was addressed to Mammy Pleasant. I wrote back to him on his own paper that my name was Mrs. Mary E. Pleasant. I wouldn't waste any of my paper on him.*

Pleasant had to work cleaning homes and waiting tables, but she didn't let that define who she really was. If you have to take on a task that you consider beneath your abilities, do the work but maintain your self-confidence; you will soon rise above it.

SAVVY — *I often wonder what I would have been with an education . . . I have let books alone and studied men and women a good deal . . . I have always noticed that when I have something to say, people listen. They never go to sleep on me.*

Pleasant was studious; she researched in the realities of her experience instead of in libraries on campus. Both kinds of study are important, but if you don't get all the opportunities you want to get book-smart, work on becoming savvy. Focus on interpreting and applying practical realities and let your wisdom flow from there. Like Pleasant, you can make lots of money and help lots of people without lots of degrees.

SANGFROID — Pleasant stayed cool, keeping her composure, under very trying circumstances. Do your best to do the same. There will always be situations to ignite your anger or bend you our of shape. Manage your unruly emotions by starving them. Shift your thoughts away from the negative to the positive, as the Apostle Paul advised in his letter to the church at Philippi (Philippians 4:8).

Finally, brothers and sisters, whatever is true, whatever is noble,
whatever is right, whatever is pure, whatever is lovely, whatever is
admirable — if anything is excellent or praiseworthy — think about such things.

SUB ROSA — Both on the Underground Railroad and in her entrepreneurial work, Pleasant acted undercover, making things happen out of the limelight. There are times you may have to work behind the scenes to move forward with your agenda. When that time comes, work confidentially.

WORK A DOUBLE BOTTOM LINE   JULY 13TH

I am a native of England but from principle am American in this dispute.
Robert Morris

Robert Morris, who came to be known as the Financier of the American Revolution, immigrated from England to Pennsylvania as a teenager and became a successful businessman in his twenties. Morris' merchant firm had interests in shipping, real estate, and several slave trading voyages as well as handling slave auctions for other importers.

But Morris soon reached the conclusion that the slave trade was neither financially or socially profitable. He and his partner Thomas Willing authored non-importation agreements leading to the end of trade with England, including the importation of slaves. Later, as a government official, Morris endeavored to tax the domestic slave trade and battled the Southerners who resisted these measures. His efforts in his home state of Pennsylvania led to legislation for gradual abolition of slavery in 1780, setting an important precedent for elimination of the slave trade in the northern colonies during the Revolutionary period.

Morris put his money where his mouth was at two critical points during the Revolutionary War. As Continental Army awaited the crossing of the Delaware River for the pivotal Battle of Trenton, General Washington — his troops exhausted and downtrodden — wrote to Morris requesting $10,000 for much-needed provisions. Morris promptly donated the funds, helping to pave the way for the decisive Trenton victory in December 1776. He was such a well-regarded businessman and civic leader that he secured several loans on behalf of the government throughout the war with nothing but his integrity as collateral. Morris summed up his commitment in these words:

> *It is the duty of every individual to act his part in whatever station his country may call to him in times of difficulty, danger, and distress.*

Morris became a confidant of Washington, who penned more than 130 letters to him from 1776 to 1798, though he did decline Washington's invitation to be the first Secretary of the Treasury, deferring to Alexander Hamilton. But Morris was a signer of the Declaration of Independence (after some initial reluctance about the colonies' fiscal readiness), worked assiduously on the Articles of Confederation and the United States Constitution, as well as overseeing the striking of the first coins of the United States.

For most of his career Morris did well financially and during those times he also did good for society. Morris was committed to the double bottom line — doing good for the community while at the same time doing well financially. You can also make a practice of this dual strategy by a daily commitment to bring something of:

VALUE ECONOMICALLY — Like Morris, I practiced the double bottom line as a Harlem entrepreneur, starting the first inner city Ben & Jerry's scoop shop, attempting to run a profitable business while creating stepping-stone jobs for the formerly homeless as scoopers in the shop. But the shop didn't last long because the economic bottom line wasn't solid and strong. As you practice the double bottom line, first be certain of the financial stability and strength of your venture. It should be your goal to focus on both the social and economic aspects of the enterprise, but prioritize the latter until you're sure that the financial resources are in place to sustain the project.

VALUE SOCIALLY — Whatever economic value you've created through business ventures or wise investments, don't stop there. Generating good finances is only part of the wealth equation. True wealth happens when you bring something of social value to the table. Cultivate the vision for your social dimension early on, while you're making the money to support it. Endeavor to transform whatever you've been working on professionally or entrepreneurially into some tangible benefit for others. There's no formula to how this works so be creative in making your double bottom line. If you work really hard at producing this kind of holistic wealth, you will attain both financial success and personal fulfillment. And, like Morris, you may even make some history in the process.

FORGE WORK HABITS   JULY 14TH

We can complain because rose bushes have thorns,
or rejoice because thorn bushes have roses.
Abraham Lincoln

Before his rise to the Presidency, Abraham Lincoln was a lawyer and politician in Illinois. During this time his stepbrother, John D. Johnston, was in financial difficulty on the family farm in Coles County, Illinois, and reached out to Lincoln for a loan. Lincoln responded with a letter, which follows.

Dec. 24, 1848
Dear Johnston:
   Your request for eighty dollars, I do not think it best to comply with now. At the various times when I have helped you a little, you have said to me, "We can get along very well now," but in a very short time I find you in the same difficulty again. Now this can only happen by some defect in your conduct. You are not lazy, and still you are an idler. I doubt whether since I saw you, you have done a good whole day's work, in any one day. . . . This habit of uselessly wasting time, is the whole difficulty; it is vastly important to you, and still more so to your children, that you should break this habit . . . what I propose is, that you shall go to work "tooth and nail" for somebody who will give you money for it. . . . If you hire yourself at ten dollars a month, from me you will get ten more, making twenty dollars a month for your work. . . . Now if you will do this, you will soon be out of debt, and what is better, you will have a habit that will keep you from getting in debt again. . . .
   Affectionately, Your Brother,
   A. Lincoln

TOIL — Heed Lincoln's timeless wisdom. If you don't already possess the habit of work — and working hard — make it a priority to develop it. Nothing is more important to your pursuit of success than the commitment to work. If you are already industrious "at work worth doing", then follow Lincoln's example and offer a matching grant to someone plagued by "this habit of uselessly wasting time". First forge your own work habit, then be a role model and effective supporter to forge the work habit of another.

TOUGH — Be hard on yourself, to force the habit of work, with severe consequences if you fail to do so. Lincoln was tough on his stepbrother, not making the loan until he had borrowed an amount that could be matched. The Apostle Paul was even tougher to encourage work, as this scripture reveals:

For even when we were with you, we gave you this rule:
The one who is unwilling to work shall not eat.
2 Thessalonians 3:10

TODAY — The poet Nixon Waterman raises questions
for you to ask yourself; try to answer them today!

We shall reap such joys in the by and by,
But what have we sown today?
We shall build us mansion in the sky,
But what have we built today?
'Tis sweet in the idle dreams to bask;
But here and now, do we our task?
Yet, this is the thing our souls must ask,
What have we done today?

DON'T BE YOUR OWN WORST ENEMY   JULY 15TH

Work harder on yourself than on anything else,
to keep from becoming your own worst enemy.
Joseph Holland

Mack was uncomfortable about seeking employment. After five
months at Harkhomes, he was still making excuses about looking for work.
It wasn't until I gave him an ultimatum that he confessed his secret: he was
35 years old and had never worked a regular job in his life.

The inventiveness of Mack's welfare ethic was striking: stretch his
government check as far as possible; and supplement it with various
schemes ranging from selling drugs to bootlegging to running numbers to
"playing the doctors."

Mack had no notion of a standard work ethic: holding down a job,
getting to work on time, applying himself to an assigned task, submitting to
a supervisor, being accountable, cooperating with coworkers. Because he
had developed an expertise in street hustling, the thought of finding a real
job had never crossed his mind.

Mack had the intelligence to pass the GED exam, which he did on
his first try. And he had the good looks and personality — the gift-of-gab
— to impress a potential employer, which he did, garnering a job as a
security guard within a few weeks. But he was lukewarm about the position,
stating that working as a guard was beneath his level of intelligence. I

encouraged him with a quote from Martin Luther King Jr.

> *If a man is called to be a streetsweeper, he should sweep streets even as Michelangelo painted, or Beethoven composed music or Shakespeare wrote poetry. He should sweep streets so well that all the hosts of heaven and earth will pause to say, here lived a great streetsweeper who did his job well.*

Leading up to his first day, I also reminded him to keep his character in check, not to make any mistakes that would jeopardize his new job.

Mack failed to follow my advice, turning out to be his own worst enemy. Soon after starting the job, after dinner at Harkhomes, he went outside for a cigarette. An old girlfriend walked by, inviting him to get high. He fell to temptation and stayed out, missing the next two days of work without calling in.

Mack not only lost the job but his hard-earned self-confidence. It took him quite a while to recover with a new agenda to avoid womanizing, his biggest character flaw. He excelled at his new job as a waiter at a Harlem restaurant. His tips were so big that it didn't take him long to save the money to move out to his own room.

To keep from becoming your own worst enemy, you have to:

LOOK IN THE MIRROR — Strengthen your inner values as you prepare for the workplace or to upgrade your job status. If you change your circumstances without changing your character, the change will not last. Remember Mack as a negative role model; do no harm to yourself; don't be your own worst enemy. But when Mack learned that character work and career work go hand in hand, he was on his way.

LOOK BEYOND YOUR CRITICS— Refuse to let the opinions of your critics dictate the opinion you have of yourself. Learn to work with others without being controlled by their moods and views. Don't let a negative opinion that someone expresses about you hold you back. Be strong in who you are!

LOOK AT YOUR OPTIONS — Don't think too little or too much of yourself. Be humble to assess all your options, even the ones that don't fit your preferred profile. Do your best with whatever skills and talents you possess and stay focused on gaining opportunities that are a good fit. Like Mack, if Plan A doesn't work out for whatever reason, go on to Plan B and PLAN C and . . .

LOOK TO THE FUTURE — And like Mack, we all make mistakes, including you. Just don't repeat them! The most important thing to learn are the lessons from the past about how to improve yourself. Grab hold of these personal truths, and you use them to build the pathway to your brighter future.

TAKE YOUR SKILLS TO A HIGHER LEVEL   JUNE 16TH

The progress of our internal improvements and the high state of the mechanic arts among us, as well as in our sister states, has entitled us to the character of a nation of inventors.
Jacob Bigelow

Harvard Medical School professor Jacob Bigelow, who held a position endowed for the application of science to the useful arts, coined the term technology in his lectures on mechanics and non-biological sciences. In a December 1816 address, Bigelow described those who had inspired his hope for a bright future of the arts and sciences.

. . . yet we have had men of original talents who have been fortunate enough to discover some province in which they were qualified to be serviceable to their country and mankind. We have had ingenious mechanics, skillful projectors, profound mathematicians and men well-versed in the useful learning of their time.

Bigelow concluded the lecture by highlighting the special role that Americans were playing in innovation.

The individuals who have originated and promoted such improvements have often been men unambitious of fame, whose lives have passed in obscurity; yet there have sometimes been those among us whose labors have attracted the honorable notice of foreigners, and reflected luster upon the country of their birth. . . . There are some things which, if gathered from the ashes of obscurity, might serve to shed a gleam upon our literary reputation, and to make known at least the light they have kindled for others.

Bigelow's passion of bringing academic excellence to industrial pursuits laid the foundation for technological attainments in America over the centuries way beyond what he could have imagined. He advocated using knowledge to take skills to a higher level. You should embrace his philosophy to take your skills to a higher level. Work towards that goal as you:

FERRET OUT YOUR SKILLS — This is the internal work. Dig deep inside of yourself to discover what you're really good at . . . what you really want to do . . . what you're really passionate about. It's never too early or too late in life to work on what you love, but you have to make the discovery; the sooner you find it, the better.

FORGE YOUR SKILLS — This is the hard work. You can be innovative, even invent new things, but you will likely have to work harder than everyone else to do it. Be willing to pay the price to create at the cutting edge. Technology is vital but keep in mind Elbert Hubbard's assessment.

One machine can do the work of 50 ordinary men.
No machine can do the work of one extraordinary man.

FOCUS YOUR SKILLS — To take your skills to the next level you have to concentrate on them, leaving other things — even pleasurable things — to the side. You can't be good at everything. Choose that one thing and make it your labor of love, the thing you're so excited about you can't stop working at it. Specialize in it. Devote your efforts there, and you will see your skills grow.

FLOURISH WITH YOUR SKILLS — One way to take your skills to the next level is to add new skill sets. You may have to go back to school or take a special training workshop. Be adventurous. Let inspiration rise from exploring new intellectual and professional territory. Through this approach you will not only flourish with your skills; you will also affirm yourself and uplift those within your spheres.

WORK YOUR INVENTIVENESS   JULY 17TH

The American dream of rags to riches is a dream for a reason — it is hard to achieve; were everyone to do it, it wouldn't be a dream but would rather be reality.
Robert Fulton

In 1777, at the age of twelve, Robert Fulton went from his small Pennsylvania farm home to Lancaster, where he paid a visit to state delegate William Henry. The young Fulton had read about Henry's travels to England and his time there with steam engine inventor James Watt.

Fulton's interest in all things mechanical motivated him to find out more.

He kept reaching out. A few years later, while working in Philadelphia, he met with Benjamin Franklin, with whom he discussed his ideas and passion for mechanical inventions. Fulton moved to Europe, working in London and Paris on projects like dredging machines, torpedoes, canal construction and submarines. He even tried a steamboat on the River Seine in Paris but it sank.

While in Paris, Fulton met then U.S. Ambassador to France Robert R. Livingston, who had been a member of the Committee of Five that drafted the Declaration of Independence and had administered the Presidential Oath of Office to George Washington. When both men returned to the United States in 1806 they partnered to develop the North River Steamboat, the first commercially successful steamboat, which transformed transportation and trade on major American rivers.

On August 17, 1807, the steamboat with passengers aboard launched, traveling up the Hudson River, a round trip of three hundred miles in sixty-two hours from New York City to Albany. Fulton described the inaugural voyage in these words.

> *I had a light breeze against me the whole way, both going and coming, and the voyage has been performed wholly by the power of the steam engine. I overtook many sloops and schooners, beating to the windward, and parted with them as if they had been at anchor. The power of propelling boats by steam is now fully proved. The morning I left New York, there were not perhaps thirty persons in the city who believed that the boat would ever move one mile an hour . . .*

Fulton's life and work exemplifies his commitment to work his inventiveness. It's not enough to be naturally creative; you have to develop those gifts. Follow these steps to work your own inventiveness.

FIGURE OUT YOUR TALENT — You can't be all over the place if you want to be successful. Figure out that one special natural gift you possess, the thing you are called to do, and spend your time and energy on it. Let everything else go while you work to turn your talent into treasure.

FASTIDIOUS ABOUT YOUR WORK — Details are really important when you're creating and inventing stuff so pay close attention to every little thing. Fulton did research, traveling near and far to gather relevant information. Balance imagination with grittiness.

FERVENT WITH YOUR PROJECTS — There's no substitute for passion. If you don't love the work, you'll never get through the process. Find out what excites you most and commit to working at it.

FASTEN ONTO YOUR DREAMS — Fulton started pursuing his dream of the steamboat when he was twelve. It's never too early to start developing your creative gifts — and it's never too late! Fulton learned this truth from his experience:

> *The fear of meeting the opposition of envy, or the illiberality of ignorance is, no doubt, the frequent cause of preventing many ingenious men from ushering opinions into the world which deviate from common practice. Hence for want of energy, the young idea is shackled with timidity and a useful thought is buried in the impenetrable gloom of eternal oblivion.*

Whatever you do, never stop dreaming!

BEAT THE ECONOMIC ODDS   JULY 18TH

> *Nothing more dispiriting could be imagined than the atmosphere of this lowland plantation over which imminent disaster seemed breaking. From right and left came stories of trouble and affliction.*
> Edward King

During 1873 and 1874 journalist Edward King traveled throughout the South on assignment for "Scribner's Monthly" magazine. Visiting many plantations, King reported on the economic potential of the area. His findings were not promising; the biggest reason for the dismal report were his observations concerning the now free African Americans of the South.

> *The thing that struck me as most astonishing here, in the cotton lands, as on the rice plantations of South Carolina, was the absolute subjection of the Negro. Those with whom I talked would not directly express any idea. They gave a shuffling and grimacing assent to whatever was suggested; or, if they dissented, would beg to be excused from differing verbally and seemed to be much distressed at being required to express their opinions openly.*

There are exceptions to every rule. Richard C. Coulter was indeed an exceptional black man of his era, rising out of slavery, becoming a minister and starting several churches. After attending the National Theological Institute in Washington, D.C., Coulter returned to Augusta,

Georgia in 1866 with a letter that authorized him to establish a school for ex-slaves. He worked with white businessman William Jefferson White to found the Augusta Institute in 1867. They moved the college to Atlanta in 1879; the school eventually became Morehouse College.

Coulter beat the economic odds weighing so heavily against blacks of the post-Civil War South. The educational institution that he was instrumental in launching evolved into the country's only HBCU (Historically Black Colleges and Universities) for men as well as into the nation's top producer of black males receiving doctorates. The legendary civil rights leader Rev. Dr. Martin Luther King, Jr. was a Morehouse graduate.

Beating the economic odds is not easy. To get it done, you need a strategy. Focusing your energies in the following six areas will bolster you to beat any economic odds that you presently face.

EXCEPTION SURFACED — Like Coulter, be the exception to the rule. Rise up from the masses of the status quo. Don't be afraid to take the road less traveled. It's okay to be different from the crowd as long as you're moving forward and not falling back. Talk is cheap. Stand out by your work, not your words.

EXPECTATION SURPASSED — Starting at the bottom of the economic ladder means staying there only when you're not willing to work to climb the rungs. In the 1930s at his upstate New York high school my father Jerome Holland was told blacks didn't go to the college. He ended up with three Ivy League degrees, a college president (He led HBCU Hampton University; while there he mentored Hugh M. Gloster, a future Morehouse College president.), and U.S. Ambassador. Don't let what others think about you hold you back.

EXCUSES SWEPT — When you face great odds of any kind, there's always an excuse to keep you from taking them on. Keep your mental broom handy. When excuses rise up, sweep them away.

EXCELLENCE SOUGHT — Don't worry about others possessing a status, title or position that you don't. Never let your good be good enough. Let every day be an opportunity for you to learn more, get better and grow into excellence.

EDUCATION SECURED — Securing your education is the key to beating the economic odds. The sooner you get serious about working hard at your books, the greater chance you'll have of rising to the top of the socio-economic ladder. Countless blacks found the educational pathway — and success — because of Coulter's legacy. Make sure you discover your own pathway to brilliance.

ENDURANCE SUSTAINED — Just keep working and working and working . . .

WORK ON NEW THINGS   JULY 19TH

Today, the car, television, the printing press, electricity, and the wheel
all seem well entrenched — but so did the steamboat and the trolley car.
Richard Scammon and Ben Wattenberg

In 1965 U.S. Census Director Richard Scammon collaborated with journalist Ben Wattenberg to publish "This U.S.A.", a book that popularized the results of the 1960 Census. The authors wrote about what they believed were the social implications of the ninety volumes of statistics and demographic analysis. One of their salient conclusions was American industriousness.

It is true that automation eliminates may jobs, but it is also true that society, in its relentless march, sometime rolling, sometimes limping, creates jobs as it eliminates others. . . . if we continue to say we want to go to the moon, the price tag is 30 billion dollars in jobs and materials. And if the moon costs 30 billion dollars for the first ride, how many jobs is it going to cost to go to Venus, for we'll be headed for Venus and Mars within forty years, just as fifty years after the invention of the airplane we were in orbit.

The authors also looked back to look forward.

The past forty years brought spacecraft, television, dishwashers, air conditioners, penicillin, florescent lights, computers, synthetic fibers, polio vaccines, and atomic bombs. What new things the next forty years will see is anybody's guess, but this much can be postulated without much fear of going wrong: we face an America of new, newer, newest things . . .

Scammon and Wattenberg emphasized the importance of working on new things. The future belongs to those who share their perspective. You should embrace their approach and be intentional about working on new things; to do so, you have to be:

POSTULATING — To work on new things, you first have to come up with them. Imagine some things . . . Conjure up some things . . . Assume some things . . . Devise a hypothesis and test it out. Let your mental laboratory be the center of experimentation. You will find new things as you explore the creative territory within your soul.

PROBING — The story is told of a Great Depression farmer who had fallen way behind on his mortgage payments. Facing foreclosure, the farmer decided to lease a portion of the land to an oil speculator, which started drilling and eventually hit a gusher. The farmer made millions because of the decision to probe his land. You, too, can make great discoveries if you start digging beneath the surface of things. And dig deep within yourself to unbury that hidden talent. Keep probing until you hit your gusher. Search your heart for your most deeply held desires and drives. Once you get in touch with your gifts, be sure to use them — just get started. The advice of Henry Van Dyke is apropos:

Use what talent you possess: the woods would be very
silent if no birds sang except those that sang best.

PERIPATETIC — Don't just stay where you've been, especially if being stationary has brought stagnation. To work on new things you may have to move to new places. Consider making a bold move, taking a journey down the road less traveled. The point is not aimless wandering but strategic traveling, going to those destinations where resources flow, opportunities abound and unearthing flourishes.

PROPHETIC — Scammon and Wattenberg wrote about venturing to the moon and beyond just over a half-century after the first airplane took off. They envisaged a future with space travel to Venus and Mars. What represents the launching pad in your life that can send you into orbit? Endeavor to dream about how your new thing can shape your future. Let your visionary work soar, and you will be inspired to work on new things.

ADD VALUE TO YOURSELF   JULY 20TH

The man of leisure is a variety of the human species who the Yankee does not suppose to exist, and he knows that, though rich today, his father may be ruined tomorrow. . . .
Michel Chevalier

In 1833 the French government commissioned engineer and economist Michel Chevalier to observe railroad and canal construction in the United States. Once in America, Chevalier broadened his mission to study the state of her industrial and financial affairs as well the economic life of individual citizens. After returning to France in 1835, he wrote a book about his American experiences, in which he compared the past conduct of the French and the present conduct of Americans on the frontier.

On the same rivers, therefore, where our colonists floated, carelessly singing in the bark canoe of the savage, they launched fleets of superb steamers. Where we fraternized with the redskins, sleeping with them in the forests, living like them on the chase, traveling in their manner over rugged trails on foot, the persevering American has felled the aged trees, guided the plough, enclosed the fields, substituted the best breeds of English cattle for the wild deer, created farms, flourishing villages, and opulent cities, dug canals, and made roads. . .

Chevalier keenly observed that the citizens of this young republic were committed to activities that would make them more valuable in their chosen field of endeavor.

The American is brought up with the idea that he will have some particular occupation, that he is to be a farmer, artisan, manufacturer, merchant, speculator, lawyer, physician, or minister, perhaps all in succession, and that if he is active and intelligent he will make his fortune. He has no conception of living without a profession, even when his family is rich, for he sees nobody about him not engaged in business.

Chevalier wrote the industriousness of almost 200 years ago, but his insights still apply to you today. If you want to add value to yourself at whatever job you're working or in whatever mission you're on, you must take action; move forward to:

ACQUIRE KNOWLEDGE — Studying to get another degree — or your first one! — is a good thing, but go beyond the course work. Self-study is the key, so the new knowledge you acquire inside — and outside — of the classroom will add value by bringing you the power to excel.

ATTAIN SKILLS — Be willing to work for a while without pay to attain the skills you need to get a job with better pay; or keep your job and moonlight; or get a weekend or evening internship in your area of interest. Be humble — and strategic — enough to work for nothing to achieve a breakthrough goal: to pick the brains of the more advanced to enhance your skill set.

ACCESS EXPERIENCES — There's no substitute for experience, so go out of your way to access relevant ones. Don't just watch a video. Go to a conference, attend a workshop, see and hear first-hand how it's done. Travel to a new place to gather new ideas and broaden your horizons. Kicking the tires before jumping in for the ride goes a long way.

ACCEPT THE CHALLENGE — Resolve to work harder than you ever have before. That's the best way for you to add value. In our competitive world, if you work harder than whomever you're up against, your diligence will become your outstanding qualification as the best person for the job . . . as the best person period! Meditate on this truth from Vince Lombardi.

The only place success comes before work is in the dictionary.

WORK YOUR TALENT   JULY 21ST

One of my primary objects is to form the tools so the tools themselves
shall fashion the work and give to every part its just proportion.
Eli Whitney

A graduate from Yale College in 1792, Eli Whitney accepted a job as a private tutor in South Carolina, postponing his plan to attend law school. Whitney detoured to Savannah, Georgia, where he observed the slow and tedious process of removing the seeds from cotton by hand. In a letter to his father the following year, he described the sequence of events of his breakthrough invention of the cotton gin.

During this time I heard much said of the extreme difficulty of ginning cotton, that is, separating it from its seeds. . . . all agreed that if a machine could be invented which would clean the cotton with expedition, it would be a great thing both to the country and to the inventor. I involuntary happened to be thinking on the subject and struck out a plan of a machine in my mind . . .

Whitney recounted his conversation with plantation owner Catharine Greene and her agent Phineas Miller, which encouraged him to pursue the project.

> *I concluded to relinquish my school and turn my attention to perfecting the machine. I made one before I came away which required the labor of one man to turn it and with which one man will clean ten times as much cotton as he can in any other way before known, and also cleanse it much better than in the usual mode. . . . It makes the labor fifty times less, without throwing any class of people out of business.*

Whitney's cotton gin was an amazing success, a single gin generating up to fifty-five pounds daily compared with only one pound processed in the same time by hand. The invention transformed Southern agriculture and the national economy; it had such exponential impact that cotton became America's chief export, representing over half the value of the nation's exports from 1820 to 1860. The gin's unintended and unfortunate consequence was strengthening the institution of slavery; it made growing cotton with slave labor very profitable, exalting "King Cotton" and leading inexorably to the Civil War.

Whitney worked his talent, yielding significant personal and social outcomes. Like Whitney, your talent alone is not enough to make you a success; you have to work it. To do so, add these four P's to your life.

PASSION enhances your talent with enthusiasm and energy. Make sure to align what you're good at with what you love to do; it builds the momentum of success and might even result in you creating life-changing things, as John Ruskin predicted:

> *When love and skill work together, expect a masterpiece.*

PARTNERS bring the needed human resources to your talent. Whitney had to work closely with Greene and Miller to bring his ideas to fruition. You will never fulfill the purpose to which you've committed your abilities working alone.

PARTAKE of opportunities to apply your talent; use it to work on what lies before you. Whitney did it and made a difference. Why not you? Take note of Thomas Carlyle's insight.

> *Our main business is not to see what lies dimly*
> *at a distance, but to do what lies clearly at hand.*

344

PERSISTENCE sustains you through the application of your talent. Chances are — no matter how much talent you have — you will not gain success the first time around. Keep at it! Make sure you keep pressing forward to develop your talent, as Will Rogers advised:

> *Even if you're on the right track, you'll get run over if you just sit there.*

SEEK THE STRENUOUS LIFE   JULY 22ND

. . . our country calls not for the life of ease, but for the life of strenuous endeavor.
Theodore Roosevelt

In 1899 Theodore Roosevelt, governor of New York at the time (He later became U.S. Vice-President then President), spoke in Chicago about the American ideal of the strenuous life. The speech emphasized hard work as the core value for the individual success as well as for the collective progress.

> *I wish to preach not the doctrine of ignoble ease but the doctrine of the strenuous life; the life of toil and effort; of labor and strife; to preach that highest form of success which comes not to the man who desires mere easy peace but to the man who does not shrink from danger, from hardship, or from bitter toil, and who out of these wins the splendid ultimate triumph.*

Roosevelt called on individuals to work hard to benefit themselves and the nation.

> *A life of ignoble ease, a life of that peace which springs merely from lack either of desire of or of power to strive after great things, is as little worthy of a nation as of an individual. I ask only that what every self-respecting American demands from himself, and from his sons, shall be demanded of the American nation as a whole. . . .*

He even challenged the wealthy to get to work on charitable projects.

> *If you are rich, and are worth your salt, you will teach your sons that though they may have leisure it is not to be spent in idleness; for wisely used leisure merely means that those who possess it, being free from the necessity of working for their livelihood, are all the more bound to carry on some kind of nonremunerative work in science, in letters, in art, in exploration, in historical*

research — work of the type we most need in this country, the successful carrying out of which reflects most honor upon the nation.

Roosevelt's plea for "the strenuous life" seeks a balance of career work – that which you do to earn a livelihood, and character work – that which you do to foster inner strength and virtue. Seeking the strenuous life will position you for success as you must focus on both:

> CAREER WORK — Most people are inclined to work harder on their career — external goals (school, work, hobbies, etc.) — while not paying enough attention to their character — inner life of values, disciplines and principles. Working hard at school, the job, your business, wherever, is crucial to your success. There's no easy path to achievement, as Vince Lombardi made clear.

The price of success is hard work, dedication to the job at hand, and the determination that whether we win or lose, we have applied the best of ourselves to the task at hand.

Though vital, career work is only half the battle. You must also do the:

> CHARACTER WORK — Turning the focus of yours efforts inward is a difficult undertaking — it is hard work. The key is to work harder on yourself than anything else to keep from becoming your own worst enemy. Developing character begins with this understanding: we all have flaws, weaknesses, shortcomings that lead to bad choices. If you work hard at correcting your flaws, strengthening your weaknesses, rectifying your shortcomings, you can limit – and even eliminate – the bad choices and start making good decisions. The critical point is this – decisions are not made in a moment in time but they're rooted in character. If you have good character, you reflexively make productive choices. If you don't, you risk making bad choices and destroying opportunities. Examples abound of successful people who have squandered celebrity and fortune because of character flaws. Seek the strenuous life by working harder on yourself; you will make better decisions; and you might even help make a better nation.

MAKE THE MOST OF YOUR OPPORTUNITY   JULY 23RD

Most Americans would agree on the economic goals for America: a community permanently rich in opportunity and security. We can secure both if we work together. We can work together only if we understand one another.
William Benton

In 1944 University of Chicago vice-president and Encyclopedia Brittanica publisher William Benton published the pamphlet "The Economics of a Free Society." Benton's timely essay generated much interest. With America's rise as a world power in the twilight of World War II, the ideals and practices of her economic system drew global attention. The opening paragraph of the piece projected its theme of making the most of one's opportunities.

In a free society all men are common in their rights and opportunities. They are frequently uncommon in their individual capacities to contribute to the common good.

Benton clarified his point about the countless opportunities before an individual to fulfill personal calling and contribute to the world.

Opportunity is an indispensable part of true security — the opportunity to earn an adequate income through work, the opportunity to risk one's energy and savings for profit, the opportunity to live decently, to aspire to live better, to educate one's children, and to develop the highest powers inherent in every man.

Benton's emphasis on creating opportunities — and making the most of them — should be yours as well. You will make the most of your opportunities as you keep these four principles in mind.

PREP — Tony Dematteo, whose coaching propelled me to become the first All-American football player from my high school in Yonkers, New York, often encouraged his players: "You will only be as good on game day as your preparation leading up to it!" In other words, opportunities will pass you by unless you're prepped to capitalize on them. The tricky part is that it's difficult know just how and when opportunity will appear. You just have to work really hard to be ready when your door of opportunity opens. As you fight the battle of preparation, hold on to Mark Twain's insight.

It's not the size of the dog in the fight, it's the size of the fight in the dog.

347

PRACTICE — Be the best you can be by developing good habits. Personal empowerment happens through dynamic habits that you determine to deliberately practice. Researchers report that new habits are formed by doing the same thing for at least forty consecutive days. So start your new enlightened practice today and keep going until it becomes second nature.

PRIORITIZE — Today is the first day of the rest of your life, so focus on today's priority, even as you wait on tomorrow's opportunity. Don't get this order confused. If you spend too much time and energy thinking about tomorrow, the things that need to get done now to get ready for later will slip through the cracks. Today gives you — and everyone — 24 hours. If you fill that time with a tireless and strategic work ethic, better opportunities will fill your tomorrows. Memorize Henry Wadsworth Longfellow's poem as a reminder to embrace daily progress.

Not enjoyment and not sorrow is our destined end or way;
But to act that each tomorrow find us further than today.

PANTHEON — Opportunities seldom happen in a vacuum, which was one of Benton's main points. Be a relational opportunist. Don't exploit others for your own gain but identify people who can bring something of significance into your life. If you want to be great, hang out with great people. Move in their circles; network at their functions; play on their teams. Work to cultivate a good rapport with folks who can be the keys to your future's open door.

WORK TO ATTAIN JUSTICE   JULY 24TH

The natural and proper timidity and delicacy which belongs to the
female sex evidently unfits it for many of the occupations of civil life.
Justice Joseph Bradley, U.S. Supreme Court, Bradwell v. Illinois

In 1869 Myra Bradwell passed the Illinois Bar Exam with high honors in pursuit of her goal to become one of America's first female lawyers. Bradwell applied for her law license with the support of a federal judge and the state's attorney. When the Illinois State Supreme Court refused her admission because of her gender, she appealed the case to the U.S. Supreme Court, arguing that her 14th amendment rights had been violated. In 1873 the Supreme Court affirmed the lower court decision, denying her admission to the Illinois bar because of her sex, asserting:

The paramount destiny and mission of woman are to fulfill the noble and benign offices of wife and mother. This is the law of the Creator.

Despite these inequitable judgments against her, Bradwell kept working to attain justice. Several years earlier she had founded the Chicago Legal News, which published information about laws, ordinances, and court opinions. She served as both the paper's business manager and editor, orchestrating stories that targeted corruption within the local bar and judiciary. Bradwell also used its pages to speak out for women's property rights with a column entitled "Law Relating to Women". She was also instrumental in creating Chicago's first women's suffrage convention.

Her steadfast efforts paid off. The Illinois legislature enacted an anti-discriminatory statute, and in 1892 both the Illinois Supreme Court and the U.S. Supreme Court ruled in favor of her admittance to law practice, retroactive to her initial application made over two decades earlier. Bradwell worked to attain justice and her commitment is worthy of your emulation. You can do the same when by practicing these four principles.

INTUITIVE CALL — While book knowledge and practical experience are important, also pay attention to your sixth sense. Your intuition will sometimes provide that spiritual compass letting you know the best way to go. Don't ignore the inner tugging. Test it out. You won't know truth of that still, small voice within if you're too busy to listen.

INDIVIDUAL COMMITMENT— The injustice that Bradwell faced was a personal matter. She was confronted by laws that stood between her and her dream of becoming a lawyer. Yet her commitment was so strong that she worked as a legal journalist, publishing materials that helped to shift public opinion in her favor. If a door is unfairly closed in your face, don't give up; don't get mad. Get smart and stay committed. And find ways to express that commitment that moves the ball down the field towards your goal line. Bradwell's commitment bring to mind the words of Indira Gandhi.

There are two kinds of people, those who do the work and those who take the credit; try to be in the first group; there is less competition.

INSTITUTIONAL CHANGE — When you're working to attain justice, individual commitment is necessary but not sufficient. The social institutions that perpetrate injustice must be addressed. Bradwell had to take on the upper echelons of the legal establishment. Changing long-standing laws and policies are a huge challenge. Get ready for monumental battles. So don't go at it unprepared and unsupported. Build a strong team with a sound strategy.

INSPIRATIONAL CAUSE — Be careful about which cause you join. Make sure it's worthy of your devotion. There are so many groups that sound good in their promotions but fall short in their integrity. Some people get caught up in causes that end up hurting themselves and others. Investigate the movement, its core values and its leadership right up front. If it doesn't inspire you to do righteous and compassionate things, leave it alone. And work to attain justice right where you are, and rise up from there, as Helen Keller advised:

I long to accomplish a great and noble task, but it is my chief duty to accomplish small tasks as if they were great and noble.

WORK ON YOUR INGENUITY   JULY 25TH

Change indeed must come, but then let it come by force of the necessary law of progress. So shall the present still ever build and improve on a patrimony formed by the deeds of heroic virtue, and the labors of exalted intellect.
Job Durfee

American industry surged with dramatic new inventions in the 1840s: from Samuel F. B. Morse's telegraph to Elias Howe's sewing machine (He had a patent fight with Isaac Singer.) to Robert Hoe's lightning printing press to Charles Goodyear's rubber products to Cyrus McCormick's reaper . . . the list goes on. Such prodigious industriousness created a new social brand — American ingenuity — which profoundly influenced individuals and society during this era and beyond.

On September 6, 1843, Job Durfee, Chief Justice of the Rhode Island Supreme Court, addressed the Phi Bet Kappa society of Brown University on the expanding role of technology in society. In the speech Durfee argued that persons of industry — especially the inventive ones — were the true leaders of American society.

In the realm of science and art, the most exalted geniuses and the brightest intellects that it contains, are ever at the head of affairs. They are

350

there, not by the appointment of government, nor by the election of the masses, but by a decree of the Supreme Intelligence. And, if it be true . . . that their discoveries and inventions rule in the grand course of events, it will afford some consolation to reflect, that, whether government falls into the hands of demagogue or despot, (and it suffers equally from either) this high order of intellect does, after all, by setting limits to their follies, guide and govern in the main. To it we bow with deferential awe; to it we willingly owe allegiance, and are proud to confess ourselves its subjects. . . .

Durfee affirmed that the "eternal law" of science and technology determined the progress of history.

The great truth that human progress is the result of an ever active law, manifesting itself chiefly in scientific discovery and invention, and thereby controlling legislation, and giving enduring improvement to all social and political institutions, cannot be a subject of historical question or doubt. It is a law as palpable in the history of the social mind, as the law of gravitation in the movement of matter.

Durfee's conclusion: society benefits most from those who lead with ingenuity. You'd be wise to work on your own ingenuity. To do so, cultivate these attributes.

IMAGINATION — Durfee reiterated the virtue of "exalted intellect", with good reason. Your imaginative powers are your greatest human attribute. Create mental concepts of new, beneficial things. Stay in the closet until the revelation comes connecting the theoretical dots in practical ways. Use your intellectual gifts to blaze trails where no one else has gone, destinations which put you — and those in your social environment — in a better place. Your ingenuity will flow from there. Milton Berle made the point with a compelling metaphor.

If opportunity doesn't knock build a door.

INDEFATIGABILITY — Be tireless in your creative work. Your first idea will not be the final answer; indeed, it is only the beginning of your innovative process. Get ready for the long haul and keep working until your ingenuity cultivates the perfect outcome. Be assured — it will not happen overnight.

INVESTIGATION — You will not discover a better way reading the same books as your classmates or attending the same seminars as your coworkers. Think — and research — outside the box. You will find new things at the horizon, where others haven't dared to look.

INSPIRATION — Lead by your inspirational example. If you're out front on the path of discovery, forging a new trail, establishing a better way, others will follow. You won't have to shout. Your ingenuity will compel them. Financial and social profit will rise.

COMMIT TO BE COMPETENT   JULY 26TH

From hence it appears how much a well-regulated colony
contributes to the increase and welfare of its mother country.
Peter Kalm

In 1748 Peter Kalm, a Finnish naturalist and explorer, traveled to North American colonies for scientific research. He had been commissioned by the Royal Swedish Academy of Sciences to study the native flora, collecting seeds and plants for agricultural purposes. The written account of his journeying through New York, New Jersey and Pennsylvania went beyond his botanical findings. Kalm also recorded his observations of the colonial economic activity and its ramifications, highlighting the industriousness inherent in the nascent American economy.

New York probably carries on a more extensive commerce than any
town in the English North American provinces; at least it may be said to
equal them. Boston and Philadelphia, however, come very near up to it. The
trade of New York extends to many places, and it is said they send more
ships from thence to London than they do from Philadelphia.

Kalm observed the positive economic impact of colonial America back in England.

Every year they build several ships there, which are sent to London,
and there sold; and of late years they have shipped a quantity of iron to
England. In return for these, they import from London stuffs and every other
article of English growth or manufacture, together with all sorts of foreign
goods. England, and especially London, profits immensely by its trade with the
American colonies; for not only New York but likewise all the other English
towns on the continent, import so many articles from England that all their
specie, together with the goods which they get in other countries, must altogether
go to Old England, in order to pay the amount to which they are however

insufficient.

Kalm depicted the incipient American economy. Its success so profited Britain that it fought a war to keep the colonies under its control. The foundation of this vibrant commercial system was the industriousness of the working colonists, which assumed individual competence, being fit to fulfill the task at hand. These competent workers helped to spawn — as it emerged over the succeeding centuries — the greatest economy the world has ever known. You, like them, should commit to be competent; these principles will help you in your quest.

ADEQUATE IS NOT GOOD ENOUGH — Just showing up and getting the job done won't cut it. You have to work harder to get better, to be more than adequate. Don't settle for less than your best effort.

ATTENTIVE TO DETAIL — Yes, sweat the small stuff. Taking care of the little things will pay off big time. Jesus told his faithful servant:

You have been faithful with a few things; I will put you in charge of many things.
Matthew 25:21

ACE EVERY DAY — Attaining competence means taking no time off, until you reach your goal. Even when you're on vacation, spend some time in self-improvement. Make every day count!

AGOG WILL THEY BE — If you're competent, people will demand your goods and services, as Ralph Waldo Emerson explained:

I trust a good deal to common fame, as we all must. If a man has good corn, or woods, or boards, or pigs to sell, or can make better chairs or knives, crucibles or church organs, or even better mouse traps, than anybody else, you will find a broad, hard-beaten road to his house, though it be in the woods.

LET YOUR PASSION DRIVE YOUR PURSUITS   JULY 27TH

. . . at every village and crossroad in the state, we should have a tannery, a shoemaker, a clothier, a matter, a blacksmith, a wagon maker and and a carriage maker, with their shops stored with seasoned lumber, the best of which may be obtained in our forests.
William Gregg

In the quarter century before the outbreak of the Civil War, there were voices in the South crying out for a homegrown solution to the slave-driven agrarian economy. One of the most passionate was William Gregg, a South Carolina businessman who believed that the only way the Southern states could move away from its inequitable system and towards economic independence was through the development of manufacturing. Gregg's passion for the industrialization of the South manifested in his 1845 "Essays on Domestic Industry" that appeared in the Charleston Courier. He wrote about his vision for the industrial approach.

. . . to see her worn-out and desolate old fields turned into green pastures, her villages brightened up with the hand of industry, her dilapidated farmhouses taken down to be replaced by opulent mansions, her muddy and almost impassable roads graded . . . let him use his endeavors to make the people of South Carolina think less of their grievances and more of the peaceable means of redress; let our politicians, instead of teaching us to hate our Northern brethren, endeavor to get up a good feeling for domestic industry; let them teach our people that the true mode of resistance will be found in making more and purchasing less; let them endeavor to satisfy our capitalists that we are not on the verge of revolution but that there is safety in investments in South Carolina . . .

Through his passionate commitment Gregg developed the Graniteville Mill, the largest cotton mill in the South; it was not only a driving force for economic development in the region but a source of social benefits such as a new school for poor white children. Gregg's mill became a model for the economy of the post-Civil War South.

What are you most passionate about? Is your passion driving your pursuits? To align your loves with your livelihood, be sure to:

DELVE — Look deep inside. Search your memory, go back to your favorite subjects in school, what you liked to do as a kid, your favorite hobbies, the cherished books in your personal library, your unfulfilled career goals. Take this inner journey to reconnect to those things that matter to you the most. The more you embrace your passions, the easier it will be to live them out. Norman Vincent Peale highlighted the importance of your inner mission.

Empty pockets never held anyone back. Only empty heads and empty hearts can do that.

DISENGAGE — Separate yourself from anything and anyone that doesn't support the pursuit of your passions. This is the hard part. It may be a long-standing habit; it might be a very good friend. If they're getting in the way, let them go . . . and let them know you'll see them again when you're standing atop the summit of success.

DECLARE — Write your discoveries down. Start journaling, so you can track how your aspirations change over time. Share them with a trusted friend. Passion is contagious, so seek out some folks who share your passion and spend time talking about them. Interacting with others over shared passions will deepen and strengthen them. Declaring your passions is like lighting a match, brightening the pathway you can go to live them out.

DEDICATE — Aligning your passion with your pursuits will motivate you to devote all of you to the fulfillment of your dreams. Your inner battery will be recharged, your hope for the future renewed. And you will become even more passionate as you realize that you are now building a better you and a better world!

STICK TO YOUR STRENGTHS   JULY 28TH

Of all men living, the American farmers had the least occasion to borrow money.
1818 periodical advocating for farmers

Since its founding America's most important demographic change was from a rural-agricultural society to one predominated by urban-industrial forces. This transformation didn't happen overnight. In 1790 five percent of Americans lived in cities and towns. In the period 1800 - 1860, the population of New York City increased from 60,000 to 1,080,000; Philadelphia's from 70,000 to 565,000; urban dwellers generally from six to twenty percent of the U.S. population.

One of the precipitating events for the new demography was the Panic of 1819, the first significant financial crisis in American history. The post-War of 1812 land speculation drove the new state banks and the Second Bank of the United States to generously lend money, leading inevitably to the financial crash and, consequently, to severe depression, widespread unemployment and countless farm bankruptcies. Lots of finger-pointing in the press at banks ensued. In May 1818 one such article was anonymously published in Niles' Weekly Register, blaming the fiscal machinations of "the paper system" for seducing the farmers towards financial ruin.

> *If he was born to the inheritance of a farm, that farm would support him as it did his father before him — if, like him, he was frugal and industrious. If he had no land of his own, he could get it in his neighborhood; he could buy it without money; and pay for it by his industry. The payments were always so proportioned as to give him a fair chance of meeting them from the profits of his land; He gave no security but a mortgage on his farm . . . seldom, if ever, did it happen that he was forced, as nowadays, to sacrifice his farm to some hungry bank director, to pay a loan, unexpectedly demanded, upon some frivolous pretense.*

The life lesson from this historic episode is telling: no matter how enticing the new venture or proposed arrangement seems, stick to your strengths; if it's not within your wheelhouse, let it go. Whatever opportunity lies before you, make sure it's the right fit for you before moving forward. Working hard on the wrong project is counterproductive. To make sure you're sticking to your strengths, be:

PROBING — Dig deep into whatever is being presented to you. If you don't know the right questions to ask, take a deep breath, a step back, until you figure out how best to check things out. Google makes research a lot easier than it used to be so use it. Knowledge is power, so gather as much information as you can. If it sounds too good to be true, it probably is.

PARTNERED — Before signing on the dotted line, run it by a mentor or someone whose counsel you value. Talk to people who know more about the matter than you do. They can help you determine whether it's coming from a trustworthy source — or not. Scam artists abound, so another set of eyes or a second opinion is a wise choice. If it's a big rush, see it as a STOP SIGN.

PREPARED — The key is to make sure that whatever you're considering aligns with your values and goals. That's where you're strong, in areas that excite and energize you. Don't try something beyond your expertise, and stay away from initiatives for which you're not prepared. The higher your learning curve, the greater your circumspection should be.

PLUCKY — Have the courage to say NO! If you have to disappoint a relative, friend, classmate, or business associate, so be it! Your firmness could save you a lot of headaches — and money — in the long run. Sometimes the best decisions are the ones when you decide against doing something.

WORK THROUGH YOUR ADVERSITY   JULY 29TH

I am forced to work hard with axe, hoe, and spade. I have not a stick to burn for any use but what I cut down with my own hands. I am forced to dig a garden, raise beans, peas, etc.
John Urmstone

Because of the 17th century colonization initiatives of England, Spain, France and the Netherlands in eastern North America, European settlers came from a variety of places and religious and social groups. The large Carolina proprietorship granted to Anthony Ashley Cooper by Charles II in 1663 witnessed different demographics: to southern Carolina came the wealthy French Huguenots — refugees from persecution in France; and, into the north arrived poor white settlers forced south from Virginia's slave-grown tobacco economy.

One of the Carolina settlers who faced hard times was Reverend John Urmstone, an English missionary for the Society for the Propagating the Gospel. On July 7, 1711, Urmstone wrote the following letter to the Society's Secretary; it reveals the great industriousness that frontier life demanded.

Workmen are dear and scarce. I have about a dozen acres of clear ground, and the rest woods; in all, 300 acres. Had I servants and money, I might live very comfortably upon it . . . but for want thereof shall not make any advantage of my land. At this rate I might have had anything that either this government or any of the neighboring colonies afford; but had I stock, I need not fear wanting either butter, cheese, beef or mutton, of my own raising, or good grain of all sorts. . . . He or she that cannot do all these things, or has not slaves that can, over and above all the common occupations of both sexes, will have but a bad time of it; for help is not to be had at any rate, everyone having business enough of his own. This makes tradesmen turn planters, and these become tradesmen.

Urmstone worked through his adversity; embracing these principles will help you work through yours.

DETERMINATION — When faced with adversity, you have two choices: you can let it work you over, and bring you down; or you can work through it, and overcome it. You likely will not face the extreme adversity of frontier settlers like Urmstone, who worked day and night, every day, to produce the bare necessities of life. But you have your own set of challenges between you and your goals — or between you and survival. You can overcome them if you practice this Biblical precept.

Whatever your hand finds to do, do it with all your might.
Ecclesiastes 9:10

DILIGENCE — You must make your best effort everyday to conquer the challenging circumstances of your life. If you're homeless, work on getting sober and/or skilled to get a job to pay rent. If you're unemployed, go back to school to retrain yourself for a different — even better career. If you're depressed, talk to a close friend or family member, find a counselor or go to church. Work on something positive to resolve your problem. Let your adversity motivate you to work harder than you ever have before. Start achieving small goals while dreaming big dreams. Take baby steps to transform the train wreck of your life into a new locomotive! Friedrich Nietzsche made a telling point.

What doesn't kill me, makes me stronger.

DESTINY — Trek over your rocky roads with eye on the paved pathways up ahead. Be discerning during your difficult days; you don't want to miss or undervalue experiences and relationships that are essential to your future. Always remember:

If days do not daunt dreams,
then life would be a fairy tale.

ENRICH YOURSELF TO ENRICH OTHERS   JULY 30TH

No man becomes rich unless he enriches others.
Andrew Carnegie

In 1889 industrialist Andrew Carnegie — in the midst accumulating a huge fortune — published the article "Wealth", which articulated his views on philanthropy. After selling in 1901 the Carnegie Steel Company to J. P. Morgan for over $300 million, he spent the remaining eighteen years of his life donating ninety percent of his fortune — $350 million — to establish Carnegie Mellon University, Carnegie Hall, Carnegie Endowment for International Peace and other worthy causes. Carnegie's philanthropic commitments influenced his peers, sparking a new movement of charitable giving in America. But his example is not only for rich people of a century ago. Whether you're wealthy or not — whatever resources you possess that you're able to share with others — keep Carnegie's words, and the precepts they underscore, in mind.

> DUTY — *This, then, is held to be the duty of the man of wealth: first, to set an example of modest, unostentatious living, shining display or extravagance; to provide moderately for the legitimate wants of those dependent upon him; and after doing so to consider all surplus revenues which come to him simply as trust funds which he is called upon to administer . . . in the manner which, in his judgment, is best calculated to produce the most beneficial results for the community . . .*

The truism that money doesn't buy happiness points to a deeper truth. Your greatest fulfillment in life will come from things that are not temporal but eternal, like faith, hope and love. If you've been fortunate to experience some prosperity in your life, see it as your duty to make the world a more loving place.

> DILIGENCE — *Do not think a man has done his full duty when he has performed the work assigned him. A man will never rise if he does only this. Promotion comes from exceptional work.*

Carnegie rose from a job as a telegraph boy paying $2.50 at week to become the wealthiest American of his era. He discovered his strength as a business entrepreneur and he worked hard at using his talent to exploit every opportunity. Acknowledge your weaknesses but work on developing your strengths.

> DIRECTION — *In bestowing charity, the main consideration should be to help those who will help themselves; to provide part of the means by which those who desire to improve may do so; to give those who desire to rise the aids by which they may rise . . .*

Carnegie was committed to a particular kind of philanthropy, not charity for charity's sake but rather as a tool to help build the lives of those striving to get ahead. As you give to others, make sure you're adding more than money to a person's life. Donate holistically: while meeting financial needs, contribute to the lives of others in ways that will bolster them beyond the need for financial assistance, empowering them towards independence, productivity and self-sufficiency.

DESIRE — *Show me a man of average ability but extraordinary desire and I'll show you a winner every time.*

If you want success badly enough, you'll achieve it.

DYNAMIC — *There is a power under your control that is greater than poverty, greater than the lack of education, greater than all your fears and superstitions combined. It is the power to take possession of your own mind and direct it to whatever ends you may desire.*

Realize how powerful you are; exercise it everyday.

DESTINY — *You are what you think. So just think big, believe big, act big, work big, give big, forgive big, laugh big, love big and live big.*

Develop a "bigness" mindset and your destiny will rise.

RAISE YOUR ECONOMIC POWER   JULY 31ST

> *It always strikes the European as remarkable how very industrious American society is and how relatively little bent on pleasure. . . .*
> Hugo Münsterberg

In 1897 German psychologist Hugo Münsterberg, at the direction of "Father of American Psychology" William James, came to America as a Harvard professor. Münsterberg quickly gained scholarly recognition and was chosen as vice-president of the International Psychological Congress in Paris in 1900 and to organize the International Congress of Arts and Sciences at the St. Louis World's Fair of 1904. That same year Münsterberg published "The Americans", in which he wrote about his observations about American economic life. He made it clear that any nation's destiny was tied to living out its shared values about work.

> *A nation can never do its best in any direction unless it believes thoroughly in the intrinsic value of its work; whatever is done merely through necessity is never of great national significance, and second-rate men never achieve the highest things. If the first minds of a nation look down with contempt on economic life, if there is no real belief in the ideal value of industry, and if creative minds hold aloof from it, that nation will necessarily be outdone by others in the economic field. . . .*

He illustrated the power of the virtue of American industriousness by a compelling analogy.

> *The American merchant works for money in exactly the sense that a great painter works for money; the high price which is paid for his picture is a very welcome indication of the general appreciation of his art; but he would never get this appreciation if he were working for the money instead of his artistic ideals. Economically, to open up this gigantic country, to bring the fields and forests, rivers and mountains into the service of economic progress, to incite the millions of inhabitants to have new needs and to satisfy these by their own resourcefulness . . . to raise the economic power of the individual to undreamed-of importance, has been the work which has fascinated the American.*

Münsterberg emphasized one's "resourcefulness . . . to raise the economic power of the individual to undreamed-of importance." This is timeless advice; you can raise your own economic power but only by doing your best to be:

CONSCIOUS OF WORK'S VALUE — Don't buy into the position myth. If your sole goal in the workplace is to secure a better title, you may by chance get it, only to find that you're not prepared for it or fulfilled by it. Take a carpe diem attitude to work. Seize every opportunity of each day to perfectly complete the task you've been given — and to get better at. Then your promotion will come and you'll be ready for it.

CLEAR ON WORK'S SCHEDULE — Don't ever be late, but if you're going to be because of circumstances outside of your control, let your supervisor or other leaders at the job know. Punctuality shows seriousness, and others will take note you're paying attention to the detail of time.

COMMITTED TO WORK'S DEMANDS — Success isn't easy. It's even harder to excel, to be the best at what you do, to rise to the top of your school or profession. As you go for the summit, prepared to take on all the challenges as you climb the mountainsides, remember:

Excellence is the result of caring more than others think wise, risking more than others think safe, dreaming more than others think practical, and expecting more than others think possible.

CALLED TO WORK'S MISSION — If the mission of your work is not clearly understood, you can end up lost in the quicksand of confusion. Take some time to reflect on the true purpose for your life. Be industriousness about your daily responsibilities but also embrace your high calling. You'll find your divine destiny where passion meets purpose and Providence. Follow Henry David Thoreau's counsel to start with vision then work to make it happen.

If you have built castles in the air, your work need not be lost; that is where they should be. Now put foundations under them.

AUGUST: SELF-RELIANCE
DAILY SUCCESS PRINCIPLES

1. Let Your Attitude Shine Every Day — Henry David Thoreau — 1845
2. Dare To Be Yourself — Shirley Chisholm — 1972
3. Strive To Self-Govern — James Madison — 1787
4. Live Beyond The Stereotypes — Gunnar Myrdal — 1944
5. Evict Your Victim Mentality — "Matilda" — 1827
6. Rise Beyond Your Circumstances — Franklin Roosevelt — 1933
7. Declare Your Strengths — Sojourner Truth — 1851
8. Make Your Move — Theodore Roosevelt — 1910
9. Realize Your Potential — Archibald MacLeish — 1962
10. Be Committed To Self-Improvement — Benjamin Franklin — 1770
11. Petition For What Is Yours — Sylvester Gray — 1856
12. Check Your Attitude — Peter Drucker — 1952
13. Build Your Greatness Where You Are — Russell Conwell — 1861
14. Establish Your Authenticity — Agnes de Mille — 1943
15. Build Self-Confidence To Break Through — Joseph Holland — 1986
16. Go To The Root Of The Problem — George Washington Cable — 1885
17. Take Personal Responsibility — John Jay — 1788
18. Be Strategic In Your Problem-Solving — Georgia citizen — 1821
19. Keep A Positive Attitude — William Tyler Page — 1918
20. Do What You Can Do — Harriet Beecher Stowe — 1852
21. Seek Your Own Well-Being — Alexis de Tocqueville — 1831
22. Solve Problems At Home — John F. Kennedy — 1963
23. First Remove The Plank From Your Own Eye — John Griscom — 1844
24. Endeavor Beyond Expectations — Florence Kluckhohn — 1952
25. Get Ready To Handle Change — James Hall — 1820
26. Look Without And Within To Advance — Richard Wright, Jr. — 1905
27. Pursue Personal Progress — Thomas Jefferson — 1816
28. Take The Initiative — David Ramsay — 1789
29. Take The Right Initiative — American Colonization Society — 1816
30. Learn From Your Failures — William Henry Channing — 1843
31. Turn Stumbling Blocks Into Stepping Stones — Frederick Douglass — 1883

Let Your Attitude Shine Every Day   **August 1st**

That man who does not believe that each day contains an earlier,
more sacred, and auroral hour that he has yet profaned, has
despaired of life, and is pursuing a descending and darkening way.
— Henry David Thoreau

On July 4, 1845, essayist and poet Henry David Thoreau moved to the shores of Walden Pond, just outside Concord, Massachusetts. Thoreau resided in the log cabin that he had built there for the next two years, endeavoring to live deliberately and "simply". "Walden", which became a classic of American literature, records Thoreau's reflections on this experience. In the book's second chapter, Thoreau highlighted the individual's responsibility to bring to each day an attitude that will brighten it.

We must learn to reawaken and keep ourselves awake, not by mechanical aids but by an infinite expectation of the dawn, which does not forsake us in our soundest sleep . . . It is something to be able to paint a particular picture, or to carve a statue, and so to make a few objects beautiful; but it is far more glorious to carve and paint the very atmosphere and medium through which we look, which morally we can do. To affect the quality of the day, that is the highest of arts. Every man is tasked to make his life, even in its details, worthy of the contemplation of his most elevated and critical hour.

If our attitude is shining like the new dawn, we are prepared to deal with the hard realities that may come our way.

Let us spend one day as deliberately as Nature, and not be thrown off the track by every nutshell and mosquito's wing that falls on the rails. Let us rise early and fast, or break fast, gently and without perturbation . . . Let us settle ourselves, and work and wedge our feet downward through the mud and slush of opinion, and prejudice, and tradition, and delusion, and appearance . . . till we come to a hard bottom and rocks in place, which we can call reality, and say, This is, and no mistake; and then begin . . .

Living in solitude on the shores of Walden Pond, Thoreau learned to let his attitude shine every day. You should take the same approach, using the following strategies.

NOURISH — If your attitude is malnourished, it will not shine. Check your intellectual and spiritual diet. I read Bible verses and other motivational material every day. What are you consuming to keep your attitude bright?

NOW — Right now you have a choice to make. You can say — "I got up on the wrong side of the bed" — or you can dismiss any moodiness and seize alacrity. Take charge of your attitude today! Carpe Diem!! Shine your spotlight on the words of Ty Howard.

Self-reliance is knowing and trusting that you will always be there when you need you most.

NOTE — When you hear or read something that motivates you, write it down. Keep it with you and pull it out as a reminder, to keep your attitude shining. Or maybe it's an inspirational photo or saying. Hang it up so you see it first thing in the morning. Let it be your Walden Pond.

NEXT — Look forward to tomorrow. Before you go to bed at night, resolve to make the next day better than the one that's finished. Keep shining your attitude over the next 24 hours and you will find victory. Let this be your daily mantra:

Today is the first day of the rest of my life.

Dare To Be Yourself   **August 2nd**

If they don't give you a seat at the table, bring in a folding chair.
— Shirley Chisholm

In 1968 educator Shirley Chisholm won election to New York's 12th congressional district in U.S. House of Representatives, representing the Bedford-Stuyvesant area of Brooklyn, becoming the first black woman elected to Congress. Though she was displeased with her assignment to the House Agricultural Committee, considering it irrelevant to her constituents, Chisholm thought outside the box, making lemonade out of lemons. She utilized her position to enhance the Food Stamp program and to help create the Special Supplemental Nutrition Program for Women, Infants and Children (WIC) program. She expounded her strategy.

You don't make progress by standing on the sidelines, whimpering and complaining. You make progress by implementing ideas.

On January 25, 1972, Chisholm announced her U.S. presidential candidacy, making her the first woman to run for the Democratic Party's presidential nomination as well as the first black major-party presidential candidate. At the Democratic National Convention in Miami Beach later that year, Chisholm garnered 23 delegates in the roll call tally for fourth place behind the winner Senator George McGovern — quite a feat for her long shot, underfunded candidacy. She reflected on the achievement:

> *I want history to remember me not just as the first black woman to be elected to Congress, not as the first black woman to have made a bid for the presidency of the United States, but as a black woman who lived in the 20th century and dared to be herself.*

Chisholm dared to be herself and gained great success. You can dare to be yourself as you:

MAKE AN IDEA — You have power in your thoughts. Learn to exploit that power. The way you think determines your attitudes; your attitudes determine your actions. Slow down. Take some time today to think through who you truly are. Formulate a new idea that expresses your identity. No one thought of a black woman running for U.S. President until Chisholm came up with the idea and moved forward with it. A brighter day in your life will begin with the sunshine of your new idea.

MAKE AN EFFORT — Like Chisholm, if you haven't been invited to sit at the table, come with your folding chair. Once you're in the room, listen for new opportunities. Move forward with your eyes open for the best path to take. It may not be ideal, but it's better to get going to somewhere, then adjust and improve your course once your train's on track. Follow Martin Luther King, Jr.'s advice.

You don't have to see the whole staircase, just take the first step.

MAKE A SOLUTION — Your victory is in your strategy. Be intentional about exploring solutions to your problems. If you feel like you're stuck in the box of an impossible situation, resolve to think outside of that box. Go online and do some research. Brainstorm with your buddies. Continue with your education, or if you left school — for whatever reason — go back! Your solution won't just fall in your lap; the only way you will discover it is being determined enough to keep digging for it until you strike gold.

MAKE A DESTINY — Chisholm didn't win her race for the presidency but her initiative opened future political doors for other blacks and women. When you dare to become the best you can possibly be, it's not just about yourself. You are creating the best version of you, which becomes a shining example for others to follow.

Strive To Self-Govern   August 3rd

If man is not fit to govern himself, how can he be fit to govern someone else?
— James Madison

Throughout the late spring and summer of 1787 delegates from twelve states (Rhode Island boycotted) were in Philadelphia deliberating whether to replace the Articles of Confederation with a more centralized United States Constitution. By the end of September the proposed Constitution was being submitted to the various states for ratification.

Press articles and public letters critical of the new Constitution quickly pervaded the marketplace of ideas in New York and elsewhere, prompting a response from three founders: Alexander Hamilton, James Madison and John Jay. Their writings, which appeared in New York City newspapers under the pseudonym "Publius", came be known as the Federalist Papers.

Written to support the ratification of the Constitution, these essays endeavored to elaborate the justifications for republican government. Of the collection of eighty-five articles Federalist No. 55 stood out for its emphasis on personal responsibility. Madison asseverated the virtue of individual citizens as the foundation of American democracy.

> *As there is a degree of depravity in mankind which requires a certain degree of circumspection and distrust, so there are other qualities in human nature which justify a certain portion of esteem and confidence. Republican government presupposes the existence of these qualities in a higher degree than any other form. Were the pictures which have been drawn by the political jealousy of some among us faithful show likenesses of the human character, the inference would be there is not sufficient virtue among men for self-government; and that nothing less than the chains of despotism can restrain them from destroying and devouring one another.*

Madison argued that good government cannot happen without good people, that the moral responsibilities of citizenry were the cogs in the wheels of an effective political system. In sum, he asserted: in America, the government will not work if the people do not self-govern, or, if at the very least, they fail to strive to be so. You should strive to self-govern; to do so, you must:

MAKE NO EXCUSES — Self-government begins with personal responsibility. Look for ways to hold yourself accountable for what happens — or doesn't happen — in your life. Be honest about your role. If you're the star of a great success, reward yourself accordingly. But if you're the villain of a big crisis, don't excuse the behavior. Learn from your mistakes to improve your performance.

MAKE NO EMPERORS — Though you should pay attention to the character of those in political office, it is just as important that you pay attention to your own character. Don't give elected officials a moral pass. You should expect a high standard - and hold them accountable to it - because you are living life at that caliber. Let your commitment to excellence extend beyond your personal initiatives; your exemplary behavior will add value to the body politic.

MAKE GREATER ENTERPRISES — Here's the bottom line. Your priority is not the political arena but your inner life. You are responsible for making the effort to improve yourself, to delve deeper into your truth, to step up to higher ground. You will reap what you sow. If you go through life half-stepping, you will never hit full stride. Don't build your life aiming to be better than others. Build your life to be better than you used to be, to be the best you can possibly be. Commit to that better you, whatever it takes. That is your greatest responsibility, in the words of Mother Teresa.

Give the world the best you have and it may never be enough.
Give the world your best anyway.

Live Beyond The Stereotypes   August 4th

> *American history is a history of moving toward*
> *an ever greater realization of the nation's ideals.*
> — Gunnar Myrdal

In 1944 Swedish sociologist Gunnar Myrdal completed his multi-year research into the conditions of African Americans. In his landmark book, "An American Dilemma: The Negro Problem and Modern Democracy" Myrdal presented his findings and described his mission.

> *Our task in this inquiry is to ascertain social reality as it is. We*
> *shall seek to depict the actual life conditions of the American Negro people and*
> *their manifold relations to the larger American society . . . to discover and*
> *dissect the doctrines and ideologies, valuations and beliefs,*
> *embedded in the minds of white and Negro Americans.*

A quarter-century later, in light of the myriad contemporary vindications of "An American Dilemma", Myrdal was interviewed to reflect on the key insights from his past and ongoing sociological work. His statements highlighted the importance of living beyond the stereotypes and the positive impact that such behavior can have on others. To live out this virtue in your own life, make sure to:

DEVELOP YOUR TALENT — Myrdal reflected on how African American historical figures had excelled in distinctive ways.

> *. . . . of all the various groups in America, no group on the whole*
> *has had more devoted and morally solid leaders than has the Negro. A boxer*
> *like Joe Louis, a singer like Marian Anderson, as*
> *ball player like Jackie Robinson, a trade unionist like A. Philip Randolph, a*
> *statesman like Ralph Bunche — all of them, as they were rising, have felt a*
> *great responsibility toward their own race. They have felt that they should*
> *conduct themselves in such a manner as to reflect honor on their*
> *people. Of course, you have had your Negro crooks and Negro gangsters; every*
> *race has its share of those. But fundamentally the Negro leadership is probably*
> *the soundest leadership you can find in American history.*

DEVELOP YOUR STRATEGY — Another passage from Myrdal's interview demonstrates the value of developing sound strategy.

> *Twenty-five years ago many of the so-called radical Negroes thought*
> *the legal battles waged by the NAACP were too tedious, yielded too little in*

results. My conclusion then, as it is today, was that the Negro needs all sorts of organizations. He needs to fight civil rights battles all the way to the United States Supreme Court. He needs the Urban League, which is a social welfare organization. I remember an old Mississippi Negro preacher telling me on one occasion that he was chairman of something called the the Citizens Cooperation Society. He was also a member of the NAACP. I asked him about the difference between the two. "Well," he said, "we're NAACP when we're fighting, and we're Citizens Cooperation Society when we're pussyfooting. We've got to use both feet."

To borrow this analogy, use both of your feet as a strategy to stride towards your goals.

DELIVER YOUR GOODS — The story of the Midwest dairy farmer with a cow for sale is illustrative. Several buyers were interested; one of them asked detailed questions about the cow's monthly month production, butterfat output and pedigree. The farmer responded, "I have no idea about monthly or butterfat production, and I'm not sure what a pedigree is. All I know is she's a good cow, and she'll give you all the milk she has." Whatever your family background, educational credentials or skill level, no matter how insurmountable the obstacles appear — just give all that you have: bring it strong; deliver the goods; give your very best. That's the fuel in your tank, to empower you to conduct yourself with honor and keep you moving down the highway of success.

Evict Your Victim Mentality   **August 5th**

There are difficulties, and great difficulties, in the way of our advancement; but that should only stir us to greater efforts.
— "Matilda", her Letter to the Editor of Freedom's Journal

On August 10, 1827, a noteworthy letter to the editor appeared in Freedom's Journal, the first African American newspaper in the United States. The letter was from an anonymous author — "Matilda", who identified herself as a woman of color. Hers was one of the earliest initiatives taken by an African American woman in support of women's rights. Matilda's advocacy for female education was unpretentious and to the point. She began her appeal with a humble request followed by a couple of down-home illustrations, then some challenging assertions.

Will you allow a female to offer a few remarks upon a subject that you must allow to be all- important? I don't know that in any of your papers you have said sufficient upon the education of females. I hope you are not to be classed with those who think that our mathematical knowledge should be limited to "fathoming the dish-kettle," and that we have acquired enough of history if we know that our grandfather's father lived and died. It is true the time has been when to darn a stocking and cook a pudding well was considered the end and aim of a woman's being. But those were days when ignorance blinded men's eyes. The diffusion of knowledge has destroyed those degrading opinions, and men of the present age allow that we have minds that are capable and deserving of culture.

Though she acknowledged the tremendous challenges before her, Matilda did not wallow in self-pity or succumb to a victim mentality. She refused to harp on her disadvantages as a woman and as a black and instead explained the advantages that would result from supporting her position.

We possess not the advantages with those of our sex whose skins are not colored like our own, but we can improve what little we have and make our one talent produce twofold. The influence that we have over the male sex demands that our minds should be instructed and improved with the principles of education and religion, in order that this influence should be properly directed. Ignorant ourselves, how can we be expected to form the minds of our youth and conduct them in the paths of knowledge? There is a great responsibility resting somewhere; it is time for us to be up and doing.

If you feel like a victim in any way, embrace Matilda's example and cast those feelings to the side. Victimization rises from a sense of crisis. Review the two kinds of crisis that follow, see which one(s) best fits you, and apply the principles to move beyond it.

PERSONAL — Whatever disadvantages and hardships you're faced with, they don't compare with the extreme degree of the challenges confronting Matilda as an African American woman surrounded by the prejudice of two centuries ago. You will overcome whatever personal crisis you're in by cultivating a strong attitude. Embrace the advice of Maya Angelo.

If you don't like something, change it. If you can't change it, change your attitude.

So if you've been stuck in a rut, make up your mind rise up; or housed in a victim mentality, resolve to evict it; or upset over a closed door or broken heart, decide to get over it! You may say — easier said than done. I respond — get some perspective. If

Matilda could be confronted by infinitely more racism and sexism and God only knows what else, and still stay positive and proactive in her oppressive America, you have no excuse for feeling like a victim and letting that hold you back in yours.

EXISTENTIAL — If you are struggling with questions about the meaning of your life and hope for your future, you're in an existential crisis. Start by accepting the fact that you're created in the image of God; that fact alone gives you meaning, purpose, hope and destiny. Focus on the divine dimension of your humanness: you are not a victim; you are victorious because the Lord of the universe made you so, state this truth:

I am not a victim but a victor and I affirm the great
potential of my life that awaits me today and every day.

Rise Beyond Your Circumstances   **August 6th**

I am not willing that the vitality of our people be further sapped by the giving
of cash, of market baskets, of a few hours of weekly work cutting grass, raking
leaves, or picking up papers in the public parks. We must preserve not only the
bodies of the unemployed from destitution but also their self-respect, their self-reliance.
— Franklin Roosevelt

On March 12, 1933 — eight days after his inauguration — President Franklin Roosevelt gave his inaugural Fireside Chat, the first of thirty radio addresses that he delivered to a national audience during his presidency. Roosevelt used the new technology of his day to keep the public informed as well as to cultivate support for his agenda.

In his first Fireside Chat of 1934, which was broadcast to the nation on June 28, Roosevelt summarized the success of his program by highlighting core values.

In our administration of relief we follow two principles: first, that
direct giving shall, wherever possible, be supplemented by provision for useful
and remunerative work; and second, that where families in their existing
surroundings will in all human probability never find an opportunity for full
self-maintenance, happiness, and enjoyment, we shall try to give them a new
chance in new surroundings.

Six months later, in his annual message to Congress, Roosevelt put his programmatic principles in a historical context.

The lessons of history, confirmed by the evidence immediately before me, show conclusively that continued dependence upon relief induces a spiritual and moral disintegration fundamentally destructive to the national fiber. To dole out relief in this way is to administer a narcotic, subtle destroyer of the human spirit. . . . It is in violation of the traditions of America. Work must be found for able-bodied but destitute workers.

Roosevelt's message of almost a century ago is timeless. Wherever we start in life — no matter how tough our circumstances may be — each person can rise beyond them, if vigorous virtues are applied. Follow these principles to build the momentum to overcome disadvantage and destitution on your way to great success.

BE — The goal of your inner journey is to be in control of your attitude. What happens to you is less important than what happens in you. Be a soldier of your soul, fighting to control the territory of your mind and emotions, building armaments of positive thoughts and feelings. With your fortified attitude, you'll be ready to defeat whatever circumstantial foes confront you. The words of Bruce Barton highlight this theme.

Nothing splendid has ever been achieved except by those who dared to believe that something inside of them was superior to circumstances.

BECOME — To improve your life, you have to be willing to change. To become better, you must be open to moving into new areas and trying new things. Focusing your time, energy and resources on your strengths instead of your weaknesses will help you become the person you need to be to reach your goals. Meditate on Virgil's precept.

They can because they think they can.

BUSY — As Roosevelt proclaimed generations ago, work is key. Don't get dependent on help you're receiving from others. Use the assistance strategically, not as a crutch but as a launching pad, providing the stability that positions you to get really busy, working hard every day, in pursuit of your dreams.

BEST — Expect the best, not the worst, from life. It's easier said than done when you're surrounded by the worst of circumstances. Your ability to rise above them is determined by your vision to see beyond them. Exalting your expectations will enhance your attitude. Remember: if you can't see it you will never achieve it.

Declare Your Strengths   August 7th

I am a woman's rights. I have as much muscle as any man, and
can do as much work as any man. I have plowed and reaped and
husked and chopped and mowed, and can any man do more than that?
— Sojourner Truth

In 1851 abolitionist Sojourner Truth was speaking at various venues in western and central New York State, where she'd been born a slave named Isabella Baumfree. She changed her name, motivated by her divine calling to travel, "testifying the hope that was in her". In May Truth visited Akron, Ohio to attend the Women's Rights Convention. Because she was passionate about both her rights as an African American and as a woman, Truth asked for an opportunity to speak and declared:

I have heard much about the sexes being equal. I can carry as much
as any man, and can eat as much too, if I can get it. I am as strong as any
man that is now. As for intellect, all I can say is, if a woman have a pint, and
a man a quart – why can't she have her little pint full? You need not be afraid
to give us our rights for fear we will take too much – for we can't take more
than our pint'll hold. The poor men seems to be all in confusion, and don't
know what to do. . . . man is in a tight place, the poor slave is on him, woman
is coming on him, he is surely between a hawk and a buzzard.

Frances Gage, one of the convention organizers, described the response to Truth's remarks, which came be known as the "Ain't I A Woman?" speech.

Amid roars of applause, she returned to her corner, leaving more
than one of us with streaming eyes, and hearts beating with gratitude. She had
taken us up in her strong arms and carried us safely over the slough of
difficulty turning the whole tide in our favor. I have never in my life seen
anything like the magical influence that subdued the mobbish spirit of the day,
and turned the sneers and jeers of an excited crowd into notes of respect and
admiration. Hundreds rushed up to shake hands with her, and congratulate the
glorious old mother, and bid her God-speed on her mission of 'testifyin' agin
concerning the wickedness of this 'ere people.

Truth declared her strength that day and transformed the audience

— from skeptics and observers to fans and allies. You can declare your own strength when you do your best to be:

REAL — Tell it like it is. Sojourner Truth was true to her name. She didn't mince words, and her truth-telling galvanized the crowd, opening the door to a speaking tour around the state of Ohio over the next two years. Watch what you say; impart positive — not negative — messages. As the Bible makes clear, you have the power to do both:

Death and life are in the power of the tongue.
— Proverbs 18:21

Let your own words speak strongly and truthfully, and the doors of opportunity will open for you.

REALISTIC — Know your abilities as well as your limitations. Though she was a gifted speaker, Truth understood that racism and sexism confronted her. So when she traveled, she did it under the auspices of established white abolitionists like George Thompson. Be strong but also be smart. Understand the threats that you face and prepare in advance to handle them.

RESOURCEFUL — Assess your talents and resources, then connect them to relevant opportunities. Look for the best fit between your strengths and the circumstantial deficits that must be addressed. Declare your strengths to those in need of assistance.

REGNANT — Take charge. Follow Truth's example. Sometimes you have to ask for the microphone, even if you're not on the program. And when you get the mic, know what to do with it. Proclaim new things in new ways. Inspire your listeners.

Make Your Move   **August 8th**

In any moment of decision, the best thing you can do is the right thing, the next best thing is the wrong thing, and the worst thing you can do is nothing.
— Theodore Roosevelt

On August 31, 1910, former President Theodore Roosevelt gave a speech in Kansas that was the highlight of his return to active political life that summer. In calling for far-reaching reforms, Roosevelt declared a "New

Nationalism", emphasizing government's responsibility to address social problems. He also proclaimed a "Square Deal", focusing on personal responsibility.

> *I stand for the square deal. But when I say that I am for the square deal, I mean not merely that I stand for fair play under the present rules of the game but that I stand for having those rules changed so as to work for a more substantial equality of opportunity and reward for equally good service. . . .*

Roosevelt elaborated this point, highlighting a self-reliance that entailed responsibility for one's family as well.

> *The object of government is the welfare of the people. The material progress and prosperity of a nation are desirable chiefly so far as they lead to the moral and material welfare of all good citizens. Just in proportion as the average man and woman are honest, capable of sound judgment and high ideals, active in public affairs — but, first of all, sound in their homelife, and the father and mother of healthy children whom they bring up well — just so far, and no farther, we may count our civilization a success.*

Roosevelt tied national success to individual progress, which means taking steps to improve your life. If you're committed to make your life better, you have to do something to make it better. Following these principles of life will help you make some positive moves.

PROBLEM-DRIVEN — If your life is problem-driven, you're dependent on others. You want to change but you've been unable to. The internal barriers have been just as great as the external obstacles. Acknowledge your negative attitude so you can shift to a positive perspective. Avoid being so preoccupied with your problems that you can't see the forest because of the trees. Your ability to change will improve as you begin to see your problems as temporary issues instead of permanent conditions; when you see crisis as simply an opportunity to self-improve. This new outlook will prepare you to break free from the bondage of problems. As Theodore's cousin Franklin remarked:

> *It is common sense to take a method and try it. If it fails, admit it frankly and try another. But above all, try something.*

PURPOSE-DRIVEN — If your life is purpose-driven, you're independent of others. You've found the motivation and taken the initiative to change your life for the better. You're able to deal with the symptoms of problems, like the individual who sees a raft of injured bodies floating downstream and pulls the craft over to help the needy. Such a person is focused on good purpose but there's still a higher level to go.

PROMISE-DRIVEN — If your life is promise-driven, you're interdependent with others. This is the kind of life to which Roosevelt referred because this person works together with others — "active in public affairs" — that makes "civilization a success". You're able to go beyond the symptoms to deal with the systems at the root of the problems. You're like the individual who observes the raft of injured bodies on the river then heads upstream to determine the reasons for the crisis. To be promise-driven is to be future-oriented. Keep all this in mind, including these words from John F. Kennedy, and you'll be a world-changer.

Change is the law of life. And those who look only to the past or the present are certain to miss the future.

Realize Your Potential   August 9th

. . . insofar as America is something new, it is an idea . . . which had its essential expression in the Declaration of Independence. . . an idea which affirms the supreme worth of the human individual and, through an act of faith believes that, given the opportunity, he will make for himself a good life.
— Archibald MacLeish

Acclaimed poet Archibald MacLeish served as Librarian of Congress and in the State Department in the 1940's and won three Pulitzer Prizes throughout his writing career. In 1962 MacLeish appeared with his fellow poet Mark Van Doren in a television special discussing the American Dream. One of MacLeish's comments searched for meaning back in America's roots. He personalized the American Dream by centering it in the value of every individual.

. . . the essential thing— is to realize what you are as a "person." This you can learn only in yourself. You learn it in yourself in relation to others. You learn it in relation to your mother, your father, your brothers, your sisters, your friends. But you learn it in yourself, and sooner or later, if the process of your education proceeds far enough so that you become mature, you realize that you are a person, for better or for worse, with all your faults upon you . . . but you're valuable nevertheless.

Freedom — in MacLeish's view — rises from self-realization: an individual lives through constraints and opposition to realize fullness of one's potential.

> *America is a concept of what life could be like if you have an understanding of the human self in yourself, a respect for the human self in others, and a political mechanism which would make it work. And the word "freedom," I think, is a word which simply describes the viability of this kind of relationship. It describes a man not free simply of government supervision, of policemen, of bullying Southern cops, of any of the other tyrants who gag the world. It means that a man is free of the constant attrition of other people's suspicion and denigration, and this achieved is what America is. . . .*

MacLeish's perspective on America was rooted in self-reliance: the fulfillment of individual potential as the basis for community strength and national greatness. To realize your own potential, focus on:

PERSONALIZATION — Make your potential personal. Whatever you become in life depends on who you are today . . . right now . . . in this moment. Don't get stuck on your skill level; acknowledge wherever it is; commit to improve it. Just as important — even more so — is your attitude. If your attitude hasn't been the best, resolve to turn it around. You don't have to wait for the new school year or the next job opportunity. The road to your potential runs through your positive attitude; resolve to start that journey right now!

PROCESS — The factors of process always precede the fulfillment of potential. One of the biggest factors in your success process is whether you're learning from your mistakes. If you dwell on all the things you did wrong and all the things that didn't work out, you'll never move beyond disappointment. Think through the difficult experiences and draw lessons to prepare for future challenges. Reflect on this insight from Nelson Boswell.

> *The difference between greatness and mediocrity*
> *is often how an individual views mistakes.*

PROMISE — Personalization and process always precedes the promise. Realizing your potential is promised to you, as long as you use your positive attitude to make every day an opportunity to grow and keep learning from your mistakes. The benefits of fulfilled potential will bless your life, then overflow into your community and the larger society. Realize the divine dimension of fulfilling your potential.

My potential is God's gift to me.
What I do with my potential is my gift to God.

Be Committed To Self-Improvement   August 10th

Well done is better than well said.
— Benjamin Franklin

Ben Franklin was one of the most influential Founders with a remarkably multi-faceted career of accomplishments: inventor, publisher, diplomat, humorist, scientist, politician, postmaster, abolitionist, author, statesman . . . the list goes on. Perhaps most notably, Franklin's early and indefatigable efforts in Europe on behalf of the colonies — first as a spokesman in London, then as the first United States Ambassador to France during the 1770's — earned him the title of "The First American".

Raised in a family of seventeen children, Franklin left the Boston Latin School without graduating when he was just ten; his father only had enough money to send him to school for two years. His lack of formal education notwithstanding, Franklin possessed uncommon wisdom — known for it homespun quality — rising from his habit of voracious reading. This commitment to lifelong learning — and to sharing it — not only forged his extraordinary professional success but also help him shaped an inspirational approach to life that defined the American ethos. And he scorned excuses:

I never knew a man who was good at making excuses, who was good at anything else.

Franklin no doubt became famous for his political activism: a historic opponent of British authoritarianism, which put him in the room alongside Fellow Founders at crucial moments like the signing of the Declaration of Independence. But what distinguished Franklin was his personal activities, an exemplary lifestyle of practical values: hard work, inventiveness, thrift, persistence, pursuit of knowledge, community service, and fairness in society.

Franklin excelled, standing out even among his prodigious peers, because he was committed to self-improvement and to imparting wisdom learned from his experiences with others. In his devotion to personal and social betterment, he is timeless: a beacon during his time as well as an example to us now.

Like Franklin, don't be satisfied with your status quo. Be intentional about constantly improving; you will do it as you:

GET READY — Your readiness will rise from your positive attitude, so at the beginning of each day, before you leave home for school, work, wherever — ask yourself: what are the special learning opportunities before me today? What steps of correction do I need to take? With this prepared state of mind, get ready to find those hidden gems of wisdom that will brighten your pathway to success. As Jesus said:

Seek and you will find.
— Matthew 7:7

GET QUIET — Find some time alone during your day to self-assess — How am I doing? Moments of meditation are essential to your personal growth. Take a moment . . . today . . . reflect on: What did I do wrong? What did I do right? What could I have done differently? The more time you can find to reflect on the lessons of your life, the more you will self-improve.

GET CONNECTED — Just as Franklin made a habit of sharing his life lessons, impart what you're learning through your self-improving process - this is your wisdom! - and people will feel a sense of connection to you. Purpose to give freely of your expertise and experiences and you will find people responding to you in positive ways: they will love and respect you as never before. With whom can you share one of your life lessons today?

GET BETTER — Personal change can be challenging. You may be resisting it. Following the first three steps will naturally bring change to your life. You will begin to apply life lessons in ways that will be transformative, uplifting and fun. You will become a beacon in your very own historic moment, sowing inspiration for an individual in need and raising hope for many. Getting better begins with the desire to be better.

Petition For What Is Yours   **August 11th**

. . . your petitioner further begs leave to call the attention of your honorable
body to the fact that his settlement and improvements, as aforesaid, were
made prior to the date of that (Dred Scott) decision; for which reason, and that
he may not be compelled to sustain the loss which would otherwise result to him . . .
— Sylvester Gray

In August 1856 free African American and pioneer Sylvester Gray staked his land claim, settling in the New Mexico Territory and began building a house on the property. But because of the Dred Scott case the following year, the federal General Land Office confiscated Gray's land in January 1860 because he is not a citizen, being a "man of color."

On March 23, 1860, Gray petitioned Congress that his land had been wrongfully taken. Gray's matter was referred to the Senate Committee on Public Lands, which issued its report a couple months later on May 19th, in which it quoted an earlier U.S. Attorney General opinion.

Now, free people of color are not aliens; they enjoy universally the
rights of denizens. Even in the slaveholding states, they are capable of all the
rights of contract and property. In all nations, without exception, ancient and
modern, in which domestic slavery has existed, even the slave is
distinguished from the alien. He is a part of the family and as soon as he
passes into the class of freemen, is considered as at once   capable of all the
rights which mere birth under the ligenace of a country bestows. How far a
political status may be acquired is a different question, but his civil status
is that of a complete denizenship. . . .

The Senate Committee recommended a bill granting Gray's petition, which was subsequently passed, restoring his landownership.

When he received the bad news that his land and improvements had been confiscated, Gray maintained a positive attitude, forthrightly submitting his claim to Congress. He petitioned for what was his and overcame the adversity; you can do the same, by practicing these principles.

THIRST — How badly do you want to overcome your difficulty? Start by asking yourself this question, meditate on the answer. Gray wanted his property back, so badly that he pressed his petition. Check your desire. Unless you really want to get to the mountaintop, some mountains become too steep to climb. The stronger your desire to get to the goal, the better your attitude will be in conquering your problems along the way.

TETHER — Tie your attitude to your faith, your mind to your spirit. What you're thinking and feeling on the inside will determine your outward behavior. Take it deeper: tether your thoughts and emotions to your faith. Sometimes your difficulty appears to be insurmountable; all you can do is believe. Let your attitude rise from your heart and claim all that is yours.

TAKE CHARGE — Command the moment. There are times when you just can't take no for an answer. The take-charge attitude is when you possess the confidence to take on the challenge when everyone is telling you to step aside. The Old Testament account of David versus Goliath is the classic illustration. In spite of all the naysayers, doubters and fear mongers, David took charge and took on the giant and vanquished him. To take out your giant, embrace the David attitude, which George Bernard Shaw encouraged.

People are always blaming their circumstances for what they are. I don't believe in circumstances. The people who get on in the world are the people who get up and look for the circumstances they want and if they can't find them, make them.

TREASURE — You have been created with limitless potential. Relish your future possibilities and keep going after them. Embrace George Bernard Shaw's insight.

We don't stop playing because we grow old, we grow old because we stop playing.

Check Your Attitude   August 12th

*. . . the important things are attitudes, principles, and policies
rather than techniques, machines, and processes . . .*
— Peter Drucker

In 1952 management consultant Peter Drucker published in the periodical "Nation's Business" an assessment of the growing European interest in the phenomenon of America's post-World War II economy, which had transformed the United States into the wealthiest and most powerful nation on earth. Drucker described the context of his article in an opening paragraph.

Several thousand hand-picked experts — businessmen, technicians, educators, workers, and union officials, coming from every country of Western Europe and from almost every industry — have been touring the U.S. since 1949 to find out for themselves what causes American productivity.

Drucker highlighted the report of one of the visiting European groups, for it articulated the key findings of these investigative teams.

"Productivity is an attitude of mind." The report of the team from the British letterpress printing industry summed it up . . . every team has said the same. Attitude, social organization, and moral value, those, the experts from the other side report, underlie and explain America's industrial achievement.

Drucker made it clear that what exalted the American economy over the rest of the world were the attitudes held by both management and labor. Likewise, your key to individual success is not your excellent aptitude, high IQ, gifted birth or exceptional talent; it's your positive attitude. Making excuses are the enemy of winning attitude. Check your attitude by paying special attention to the following excuses; do your best to avoid them, or they might rob you of the attitude you need to succeed.

EXCUSE 1: I CAN DO IT LATER — Procrastination is the thief of positive attitude, stealing away the timely initiative required for personal progress and achievement. These words from Ben Franklin highlight this truth:

Work while it is called today, for you know not how much you may be hindered tomorrow. One today is worth two tomorrows; never leave that till tomorrow which you can do today.

EXCUSE 2: I ALREADY TRIED IT ONCE — Disappointment, frustration or failure can sink your attitude. Managing your expectations will help you manage your attitude. Don't get upset if things don't go as planned the first time around . . . or the second . . . or the third . . . Let go of your impatience. Keep reminding yourself to maintain a good attitude, even through the unexpected challenges of a tough day.

EXCUSE 3: IT'S JUST THE WAY I AM — There are things in your life that are beyond your control; your attitude is not one of them. You control your attitude. You possess the inner power to make it positive or negative. If you usually have a negative attitude, every day presents an opportunity for you to shift it.

EXCUSE 4: THEY WILL TAKE CARE OF IT —
Leaving it to someone else to handle means you don't have to
address the problem. If you let others act, you can blame them if
things don't get fixed. It's Ben Franklin again, who this time
captures the flawed attitude of those who fail to take action
themselves.

Mr. Meant-To has a comrade,
And his name is Didn't-Do;
Have you ever chanced to meet them?
Did they ever call on you?
These two fellows live together
In the house of Never-Win,
And I'm told that it is haunted
By the ghost of Might-Have-Been.

Build Your Greatness Where You Are   August 13th

That in this country of ours every man has the opportunity
to make more of himself than he does in his own environment,
with his own skill, with his own energy, and with his own friends.
— Russell Conwell

In 1861 eighteen-year-old Yale student Russell Conwell gave his
"Acres of Diamonds" talk for the first time. Over the next fifty years, in the
many different spheres of his life — as a Civil War captain, lawyer,
journalist, Baptist minister, and the first president of Temple University —
Conwell delivered versions of this speech over 6100 times. Having spent
much of his clerical career in Philadelphia, Conwell was the founder of
Temple, which resulted largely from the income he gain from the
"Diamonds" lectures as well as from the royalties of the printed version.

In one of his sermons, Conwell drove home the main point of
self-reliance in the context of one's immediate surroundings.

Any man may be great, but the best place to be great is at home. All
men can make their kind   better; they can labor to help their neighbors and
instruct and improve the minds of the men, women and children around them;
they can make holier their own locality; they can build up the schools and
churches around them; and they can make their own homes bright and sweet. . .
. and if a man is not great in his own home or in his own school district, he
will never be great anywhere.

The sustained popularity of Conwell's message stemmed from its transcendent theme: build your greatness where you are. You would be wise to apply the truths he preached to your own life. To build your greatness where you are, you must:

REJECT MOODINESS — The challenges of your life are inevitable, even constant; you can't control the situations that test you. But you can control how you feel about them. You choose your attitude, regardless of the circumstances you find yourself in. Some people — the moody ones — let their situation dictate their attitude. Reject that approach. Embrace a good attitude; expect good outcomes; make good things happen because you believe you are greater than your circumstances.

REFOCUS ON YOU — I'm reminded of the story about a man getting his windshield washed at a gas station. He complained that the attendant had done a lousy job on the windshield and demanded that he do it again, then again. Sitting next to him in the car, the man's wife was upset and pulled off his glasses. She wiped them, stating, "It's not him but you're the problem." Make sure your spiritual lens is clear and focused in the right place. Shifting the metaphor, John Maxwell emphasized the importance of inner focus.

If you don't like the crop you are reaping, check the seed you are sowing.

RECOGNIZE WHAT YOU'VE GOT — In the Old Testament account of a widow with two sons (2 Kings 4:1-7), she was so impoverished that she was about to lose her boys to her creditors. She cried out to the prophet Elisha for assistance and he asked her, "What do you have in your house?" She replied, "Nothing, except a little oil." With the prophet's advice, she turned that afterthought into a breakthrough, transforming that meagre thing into a mighty resource — a retail oil business that boosted her out of debt. Be open and discerning as you ask yourself — What do I have in my house? What underutilized resource do I possess that I can transform into a great blessing?

REACH FOR THE STARS — Don't settle for the just enough to get by, for dependency on others, for the day-to-day hustle. You're better than those things. Dream big dreams and remember this Chinese proverb.

The person who says it cannot be done should not interrupt the person who is doing it.

Make sure you're the latter and not the former.

Establish Your Authenticity   **August 14th**

Who am I? the artist asks. And he devotes his whole life to finding out.
— Agnes de Mille

In 1943 dancer Agnes de Mille choreographed her first Broadway show "Oklahoma!" Her debut was so successful that her choreography revolutionized musical theater. Her musicals — Bloomer Girl (1944), Brigadoon (1947), Paint Your Wagon (1951), Goldilocks (1957), 110 in the Shade (1963), to name a few of her dozen shows — not only featured the dancers' wonderful technique but also projected their emotions as protagonists in the plot.

De Mille was also a prolific author, writing a half a dozen books including her memoir, "Dance to the Piper", which was translated into five languages. In 1954 she published an article about the genesis of dance as an American art form. De Mille highlighted a predominant cultural influence in the following passage.

> *The enormous influx of the alien and powerful African aesthetic during the seventeenth and eighteenth centuries, the Negroes' persistent and persuasive contribution to music, and their reliance on rhythm in all work and play has grafted a characteristic rhythm-syncopation on our main dancing forms that has heightened and perverted them forever. It was the subtle African footwork applied to the Irish clog (jigs and reels) that produced buck and wing and tap dancing. It was the African body pulse and frank sexuality that turned the waltz into our current ballroom form.*

De Mille contrasted the artistic impact of African American mores with those of its European-based counterparts.

> *Every ten years or so from the slums, the wharves, the Negro ghettos and impalements comes a new original contribution to our folk vocabulary — the Rag, the Charleston, the Lindy-hop, the Black Bottom, the Jitterbug, the Shag, the Susie Q, the Big Apple. These are as original and as expressive as the gavotte, the minuet, or the waltz, but their most unusual aspect is the rapidity with which they develop. The English and French required 250 years to change the Elizabethan Volta to the waltz. This exuberant and prolific people produce each decade a new form. No other racial group boils up constantly in such spontaneous gesture.*

De Mille expounded the powerful influence of one group's unique characteristics on the larger culture. The important lesson from her reflections about collective influence is an individual application: be who you are. You can establish individual authenticity as you strive to be:

ARDENT — Step back from the hustle and bustle of everyday life; take a breath and a break; seize the solitude to discover your inner truth: what you're most passionate about; what you've been divinely called to do; who you really are. Embrace your truth; meditate on the new revelation; live the outcome. Let your light shine, in the words of Elizabeth Kubler Ross:

People are like stained glass windows, they sparkle and shine when the sun is out, but when darkness sets in their true beauty is revealed only when there's light from within.

ASSERTIVE — Don't be preoccupied with what others are saying about you. State your own ideas. Assert yourself. Proclaim your authenticity.

ADVENTUROUS — Explore the process of becoming a better version of you. Everyone is capable of more, of new possibility, of greater capability, of reaching higher ground. You first have to resolve in your heart to become great; the rest of the journey may not always be downhill, but it will be the most exciting adventure of your lifetime.

ABOUT IT — Attitude determines action. If you're clear on and committed to your calling, the pathway of success will open up before you; as long as you go for it. Make your move and keep moving towards the goal. The novelist Nathaniel Hawthorne put it best:

Preach! Write! Act! Do anything, save to lie down and die!

Build Confidence To Break Through   August 15th

Seek to value yourself and your fondest dreams will find you.
— Joseph Holland

In 1986 I started Harkhomes, a homeless shelter in Harlem. One evening, I opened the door for Tommie, a fiftysomething-year-old black man, who'd arrived seeking shelter with good timing. An empty Harkhomes bed was a rare occurrence, but we happened to have one that night. Yet he was so disheveled, so odorous, that I wondered if I should admit him. His pleading eyes persuaded me to rescue him. He also expressed gratitude, possessed a warm, engaging smile, and had a charming way of using big words, if in a slightly confused way.

I ordered the extreme-scrub protocol, an intensive cleanup procedure I initiated for long-term, subway-dwelling homeless men like Tommie. I assigned a team for the most unpleasant task. They peeled the rancid clothes off Tommie's body; bagged and took them to the curbside garbage can; hurried him off to the shower with disinfectant soap and shampoo; and fetched clean clothes from the stash of donations. Tommie emerged from the makeover routine a new man.

He ravaged all the dinner leftovers, received his linens, and made his cot. He seemed to be settling in, but within an hour he was back in the office.

"I can't stay here," he uttered.

"Why not? What happened?" My probing questions went unanswered. I asked Tommie to wait while I quickly inquired among the residents why Tommie had been alienated so quickly. Everyone was just as perplexed as I was. I urged him to change his mind; others pleaded with him to stay, but Tommie pressed his way to the door. Finally, he broke down in tears, whispering: "I'm not good enough to stay here." With those words, he walked out the door. I never saw Tommie again.

Don't be like Tommie, who missed the opportunity for a breakthrough because of his low self-esteem. You will build your self-confidence for your breakthrough as you:

CONNECT TO A SUPPORTIVE RELATIONSHIP —
If you're struggling with diffidence and insecurity, a nurturing relationship can move you beyond the place of personal powerlessness. Leaning on another will build you up in the area of perceived deficiency, developing the confidence in your own abilities until you no longer need to depend on someone else.

CONCEIVE OF YOURSELF AS IMPORTANT —
You, like everyone else, were made in the image of God and in His likeness. Beware of generational stereotypes that limit your God-given potential: "once a failure, always a failure". Don't be like Tommie. Embrace your divine origins and see yourself from God's point of view — and not from society's narrow standards — and you will gain a new perspective imparting confidence to overcome life's obstacles.

CARE FOR SOMEONE WORSE OFF THAN YOURSELF — Showing compassion for others is the antidote for self-pity. Devote yourself to someone in need, which will not only help take your mind off your problems but will make you feel useful and therefore feel better about yourself. Meditating on this phrase will help you displace self-pity.

I cried because I had no shoes until I saw a man who had no feet.

COMMIT TO DO WELL — Nothing will help you feel better about yourself than taking on a task and seeing it through to successful completion. Start doing something you love to do; keep doing it; your self-esteem will rise.

CARRY THE SCALES OF SELF-ESTEEM — Don't ego-trip. Maintain a balanced perspective. Don't be so proud that conceit takes over; don't be so self-effacing that carelessness sets in. Be self-confident, but be careful not to think you are better than you really are. Remember that pride goes before a fall.

Go To The Root Of The Problem   August 16th

The greatest social problem before the American people today is, as it has been for a hundred years, the presence among us of the Negro.
— George Washington Cable

In 1885 former Confederate army soldier and writer George Washington Cable published "The Silent South", in which he articulated his opposition to the Jim Crow culture emerging in the Southern states. In the first chapter of the book, Cable stressed the importance of going to the root of the problem.

> *We need to go back to the roots of things and study closely, analytically, the origin, the present foundation, the rationality, the rightness of those sentiments surviving in us which prompt an attitude qualifying in any way peculiarly the black man's liberty among us. Such a treatment will be less abundant in incident, less picturesque; but it will be more thorough. . . . as we could not find in our minds to blame slavery with this perpetuation, we could only assume as a further axiom that there was, by nature, a disqualifying moral taint in every drop of Negro blood.*

He pointed to a unifying perspective as the way towards solving the problem.

> *It is the first premise of American principles that whoever elevates the lower stratum of the people lifts all the rest and whoever holds it down holds all down. For twenty years, therefore, the nation has been working to elevate the freedman. It counts this one of the great necessities of the hour. It has poured out its wealth publicly and privately for this purpose. . . . colored seminaries, colleges, and normal schools dot our whole Southern country, and furnish our public colored schools with a large part of their teachers.*

Cable's writings generated so much hostility from his fellow Southerners that he decided to leave the South, moving his family to Northampton, Massachusetts. Though he suffered resentment for it, Cable's approach was the right one. To solve a problem — whatever it is, personal or social — you have to go to the root of it. Go to the root of your own problems as you:

INHERIT — Treat the issue as your own. When you handle something as an inheritance, your perspective shifts from participatory to proprietary. Owning it will make you feel obliged to solve it, because you know it's not going anywhere. And if the issue's going to persist, it's better to solve than to suffer with it.

INVESTIGATE — Do your research. As Cable stated, be "thorough". This is where the rubber of personal responsibility hits the road. It's up to you to find out what's really going on. Probe, dig, delve beneath the surface to discover the root cause. You may have to do some google searches as well as take some inner roads that you haven't traveled before. As you journey, keep in mind Albert Einstein's insight.

Problems cannot be solved at the same level of awareness that created them.

INTERACT — There are times when you'll need help to go beyond superficial assessments. Seek sound counsel, someone who can speak from relevant experience. Don't be penny wise and pound foolish. If you have to pay something for expert advice, make the investment. The emotional return you'll receive will justify the financial outlay.

INTUIT — Rational thought is important but there are times when you have to work things out by instinct. Putting your instincts into play means discernment — getting to those hidden things that others might have missed. Try to quell the external clamor so you can hear your inner voice.

INTEGRATE — Connect the dots. Put the pieces of the puzzle together. Overcoming deep challenges means reinterpreting the various factors so you can understand the whole truth. The wholistic approach could be the best — and only way — to see the entire picture and resolve things for good.

Take Personal Responsibility   August 17th

You cannot but be sensible that this plan or constitution will always be in the hands and power of the people, and that if on experiment it should be found defective or incompetent, they may either remember its defects or substitute another in its room.
— John Jay

During the founding period of the United States, John Jay served in several important capacities: negotiator and signatory of the Treaty of Paris of 1783 which formally ended the Revolutionary War; the first Chief Justice of the United States; and the second Governor of New York. Yet his most significant founding achievement might be his work ratifying the United States constitution, which needed the approval of nine of the thirteen states. Jay's home state of New York was an anti-Federalist stronghold. To stymie the opposition and generate support, Jay not only joined Alexander Hamilton and James Madison in writing the Federalist Papers, he also created and distributed a pamphlet in 1788 laying out the key arguments for ratification.

In one section of the pamphlet Jay elaborated that the people needed to take this responsibility seriously; the success of the American Experiment depended on it.

Let us also be mindful that the cause of freedom greatly depends on the use we make of the singular opportunities we enjoy of governing ourselves wisely; for if the event should prove that the people of this country either cannot or will not govern themselves, who will hereafter be advocates for systems which, however charming in theory and prospect, are not reducible to practice. If the people of our nation, instead of consenting to be governed by laws of their own making and rulers of their own choosing, should let licentiousness, disorder, and confusion reign over them, the minds of men everywhere will insensibly become alienated from republican forms, and prepared to prefer and acquiesce in governments which, though less friendly to liberty, afford more peace and security.

Jay highlighted the choice that American citizens possess over the direction and character of their government. They can take responsibility for the quality of it — or not. You and I have a similar choice concerning our personal lives. We can take responsibility for how we're living, and the problems we're facing — or not! To take personal responsibility, be sure to:

ACQUIRE — Own your shortcomings. Be honest about your weaknesses. Admit your mistakes. Take the plank out of your own eye. Shift the focus from external factors—people, places, and things that were formerly the objects of blame—to where it fundamentally belongs: on you. Be transparent about your shortcomings to yourself and others. Are you selfish? Insecure? Arrogant? Lazy? Hardhearted? "No, not me," you might say. Take a deeper look. Sometimes the pathway to your inner truth can be as simple as asking yourself, "Why am I in this situation?" Whatever attitude or behavior got you there—identify it. Confess it. Own it. That's the first step to moving beyond it.

ACT — Don't just think about what your acquisition. Act on it! The sooner you do something about it, the better chance you'll have at leaving the challenge behind. The longer the problem remains, the deeper roots it grows.

ACCOUNT — Draw lessons from the situation to avoid similar mistakes in the future. Ask yourself: "What have I learned from working my way out of this challenge?" Write down your answer. Keep reflecting on it. Move forward with more knowledge and strength, and less regret, from the perspective of George Bernard Shaw.

A life spent in making mistakes is not only more
honorable but more useful than a life spent doing nothing.

Be Strategic In Your Problem-Solving   August 18th

Every man knows that speculators would constantly introduce into the state the dregs
of the colored population of the states north of us; that the jails of North and South
Carolina, Maryland, and Virginia would be disgorged upon this deluded state.
— Letter to the Editor of the Milledgeville Georgia Journal

The Act Prohibiting Importation of Slaves, which was enacted by the United States Congress on March 2, 1807, had unintended negative consequences. Though the legislation made it unlawful for new slaves to be imported to United States, international smuggling of Africans into America, particularly into the southern states, persisted, but that wasn't the worst problem. Because the federal law failed to outlaw the business of trading slaves within the U.S. borders, the domestic slave commerce boomed. Black and white speculators flocked to interstate slave trading, seeking to buy slaves at a discount in one state and selling at an inflated price in another.

On December 4, 1821 a letter to the editor of the Milledgeville Journal was published, signed by a Georgia "citizen", lamenting the state of interstate slave trading. This "citizen" was opposed to this immoral if not unlawful commerce but for the wrong reasons. Instead of expressing humanitarian concerns, he harbored fears of backlash from villainous slaves, as asserted in the following excerpt.

> *Negro speculators would fear none of the calamities they might bring on us, would naturally introduce among us Negroes of the worst character, because, in many instances, they would purchase them for half price; and the villain who might attempt the assassination of his master, the rape of his mistress, or the conflagration of a city, might, in a few days, be transported to Georgia and sold to an unsuspecting citizen . . . To the dealer in human flesh, it would be a matter of little consequence if the next day he perpetrated any of all those crimes!*

The "citizen" was right to be against this heinous commerce but for the wrong reasons. He should've taken the righteous and intrepid stand against the institution of slavery and argued to eliminate it. Instead his proposal that Georgia and her neighbors regulate the interstate slave trade was a nonstarter, full of posturing and complaint but without any real strategy for solving the problem.

Don't make his mistake. When you're faced with a problem, be strategic about arriving at a true solution by implementing the four items on this checklist.

CHECK MOTIVES — Make sure you're doing the right thing for the right reason. If you're like the "citizen", you'll be stuck in the revolving door, never moving forward because your decisions and values are misaligned. Start with righteous decision-making, you'll make progress and — just as important — you won't make the problem worse. And heed the counsel of Samuel Johnson:

> *He who has so little knowledge of human nature as to seek happiness by changing anything but his own disposition will waste his life in*

fruitless efforts and multiply the grief which he purposes to remove.

CHECK ATTITUDE — Doubt and fear can be major obstacles to your problem-solving. You can't avoid mistakes, failures and setbacks; they are facts of life. Expect adversity, and cultivate the self-confidence to deal with it and overcome it.

CHECK ADVICE — Spend time with your mentor; or if you don't have one, share your thoughts with a friend whose advice you trust. If you don't have one of those, seek to find one. If your efforts bear no fruit, be extra careful or even postpone your decision-making. It's always more difficult to come up with the right strategy alone.

CHECK STRATEGY — Whether you're figuring things out with someone or by yourself, focus: your victory is in your strategy. Think through your problem, break it down into pieces of a puzzle, put it together one deliberate move at a time. Have multiple approaches. If Plan A doesn't work, move on to Plan B . . . Plan C . . .

Keep A Positive Attitude   August 19th

I therefore believe it is my duty to my country to love it; to support its Constitution; to obey its laws; to respect its flag, and to defend it against all enemies.
— William Tyler Page

In 1917 the United States entered the First World War. In the patriotic fervor rising from America's historic entry into an European military conflict, Henry Sterling Chapin, New York Commissioner of Education, announced a nationwide contest for "the best summary of American political faith". Baltimore mayor John Preston supported the contest with a one thousand dollar grand prize and more than three thousand entries were received.

The winner was William Tyler Page of Maryland, whose two paragraphs were judged as best representing a U.S. citizen's beliefs and principles. Page's statement was   accepted on April 3, 1918 by the U.S. House Speaker and Commissioner of Education on behalf of the American people and became known as the American's Creed.

I believe in the United State of America as a Government of the people, by the people, for the people; whose just powers are derived from the consent of the governed; a democracy in a republic; a sovereign Nation of many sovereign States; a perfect union, one and inseparable; established upon those principles of freedom, equality, justice and humanity for which American patriots sacrificed their lies and fortunes.

Page won the contest because his words exemplified his positive attitude about his country. You will win the contests of your life if you keep a positive attitude. To keep your attitude positive, it is imperative that you:

CHOOSE IT — The true meaning of responsibility is expressed in the word itself: it is the ability to respond effectively to the situations of life. Being responsible is a sign of maturity: you accept the role you played to create your present circumstances, which in turn prepares you mentally and emotionally to change those circumstances for the better. Take ownership of your problems. Accept the fact that you're the one to solve them. You decide how to respond to them - or not! Choose to respond positively!!

CHECK IT — When things in your life don't go according to plan, check on your attitude right away. Disappointments and frustrations can quickly sour your attitude. Your job is to keep pushing it toward the light when gloomy circumstances approach. Be proactive: your attitude determines approach; your approach determines success or failure. If you keep your attitude up, if it's high enough, your mood, your outlook, your energy will stay strong, preparing you for whatever obstacles come your way, no matter how formidable they might be. It's a lot easier to dust it off than to pull it out of the ditch.

CUSHION IT — Remember — the only constant in life is change. Your plans sometimes shift, strategies fail, timelines lengthen, people betray, resources run out, storms blow in, assumptions prove false. Be prepared for the changes and challenges. Protect your attitude from adversity. You can cushion your attitude with positivity by — no matter what happens — speaking positive words, reading positive materials, going to positive places, being around positive people, etc.

CELEBRATE IT — Like Page, it's important that you become a responsible citizen, but it starts with you becoming a responsible person. "The consent of the governed" that the American's Creed lifted from the Declaration of Independence is based on the responsible conduct of individuals who comprise the governed. All the assertions in this creed are wonderful expressions of patriotism, but you must realize that your responsibility is the source of these duties and rights. Maintaining your positive attitude will move you toward being a responsible person - and citizen! Then, also like Page, you might one day be in a position to celebrate a big win, for yourself and the nation!!

Do What You Can Do   August 20th

*Witness, eternal God! Oh, witness that, from this hour, I will do
what one man can to drive out this curse of slavery from my land!*
— Harriet Beecher Stowe

Harriet Beecher Stowe was a prolific writer, publishing over the course of her career 30 books including novels, poetry, travel memoirs and drama. Her most influential writing by far was "Uncle Tom's Cabin", published in 1852. The book's searing depiction of slavery revealed how its pernicious effects impacted all of society. It became a runaway bestseller, selling an unprecedented 300,000 copies in less than a year. The novel intensified the debate over slavery and its abolition, galvanizing the North and antagonizing the South, contributing to the seemingly inexorable march towards the Civil War.

Stowe was not a fiery orator, military leader or political official, but she did what she could do to make a difference concerning the social cataclysm of her day. Understand her example and the principles that signify through her words that follow. Do what you can do to make a difference as you:

RECOGNIZE YOUR GIFT — *No ornament of a house can compare with books; they are constant company in a room, even when you are not reading them.*

Stowe used her gift of writing to bring new light to a gloomy circumstance. Get in touch with your talent. Use it in far-reaching ways.

REALIZE YOUR BOND — *Having experienced losing someone so close to me, I can sympathize with all the poor, powerless slaves at the unjust auctions. You will always be in my heart Samuel Charles Stowe.*

Stowe's loss of her eighteen-month-old son allowed her to empathize with the plight of the slaves. When you're suffering loss of some kind, don't endlessly mourn or wallow in self-pity. Bond with others who are hurting; share their pain; be moved to alleviate it.

RECEIVE YOUR CALLING — *I did not write Uncle Tom's Cabin. God wrote it. I merely did his* dictation.

Let your spirit inspire you, lifting you to the higher ground of divinely ordained mission.

REJECT THE LABEL — *I feel now that the time is come when even a woman or a child who can speak a word for freedom and humanity is bound to speak . . . I hope every woman who can write will not be silent.*

Reject any labels that would keep you from fulfilling your mission. Believe in who you are and . . .

RIGHT THE WRONG — *It's a matter of taking the side of the weak against the strong, something the best people have always done.*

. . . take action. Writing a book about slavery was not fashionable but risky. Stowe did it anyway. Whatever you can do, just do it!

RELISH YOUR REWARD — *I had a real funny interview with the President.*

So Stowe wrote to her husband about her meeting with President Lincoln in November 1862. It was reported that Lincoln greeted Stowe with the statement: "So you are the little woman who wrote the book that started this great war." Stowe's daughter Hattie accompanied her to the meeting and reported, "It was a very droll time that we had at the White house I assure you... I will only say now that it was all very funny—and we were ready to explode with laughter all the while." Like Stowe and her family, enjoy your victory. When you've done all that you can do and you're experiencing the fruit of your labors, relish the moment. You've earned it!

Seek Your Own Well-Being   August 21st

*The most important care of a good government should be
to get people used little by little to managing without it.*
— Alexis de Tocqueville

On May 11, 1831, French historian and politician Alexis de Tocqueville arrived in New York to begin a nine-month tour to study the

American prison system. While Tocqueville's travels did include some prisons, his mission broadened to countless venues throughout the United States. He took extensive notes, recording his observations about everything he saw and everyone he talked to, which blossomed into the seminal book Democracy in America. Reflections from his notebook dated September 20, 1831 follow.

> *One of the happiest consequences of the absence of government (when a people is happy enough to be able to do with it, a rare event) is the ripening of individual strength which never fails to follow therefrom. Each man learns to think and to act for himself without counting on the support of any outside power which, however watchful it be, can never answer all the needs of man in society. The man thus used to seeking his well-being by his own efforts alone stands the higher in his own esteem as well as in that of others. He grows both strong and great of soul. . . .*

Tocqueville captured in these words his observations about American self-reliance.

> *If a man gets the idea of any social improvement whatsoever, a school, a hospital, a road, he does not think of turning to the authorities. He announces his plan, offers to carry it out, calls for the strength of other individuals to aid his efforts and fights hand to hand against each obstacle. I admit that in fact he often is less successful than the authorities would have been in his place, but, in the total, the general result of all these individual strivings amounts to much more than any administration could undertake; and, moreover, the influence of such a state of affairs to the moral and political character of a people would more than make up for all the inadequacies if there were any.*

In the almost two centuries since de Tocqueville's visit, one fact remains the same: the calvary is still not riding in to rescue you from your problems. The hero of your drama is you. To take greater control of your life and seek your own well-being, keep these four points in mind.

ASSUAGE DOUBTS AND FEARS — Your biggest internal obstacle is emotional bondage: tied down by your own doubts and fears. To attain your goal, you have to believe you can reach it. Starve your doubts and fears by not thinking about them; you will then give your confidence and self-assertiveness room to breathe.

ATTITUDE MANAGEMENT — There's a difference between making good decisions and managing those decisions. To be successful, you need to do both things. Reflecting on these words from Henry David Thoreau will help you maintain a positive attitude through whatever challenge you're facing.

I know of no more encouraging fact than the unquestionable ability of man to elevate himself through conscious endeavor.

ASSUME CHEERFULNESS — Heed this Chinese proverb:

Assume a cheerfulness you do not feel, and shortly you feel the cheerfulness you assumed.

Fill today early with good cheer and let that bright mood prevail throughout the day. Make pleasantness a daily practice. Make joy a lifelong habit.

AFFIRM RESPONSIBILITY — Say to yourself: "I am the change I've been waiting for" . . . Meditate on it . . . Memorize it . . . Move forward with it.

Solve Problems at Home   August 22nd

. . . legislation, I repeat, cannot solve this problem alone. It must be solved in the homes of every American in every community across our country.
— John F. Kennedy

On June 11, 1963, Alabama Governor George Wallace, confronted by federal guardsmen shielding two black students on their way to the University of Alabama, stepped back from his promise to "stand in the schoolhouse door." That evening President John Kennedy gave a televised address to the American people, during which he historically contextualized the key issue.

. . . One hundred years of delay have passed since President Lincoln freed the slaves, yet their heirs, their grandsons, are not fully free. The are not yet freed from the bonds of injustice. They are not yet freed from social and economic oppression, and this nation, for all its hopes and all its boasts, will not be fully free until all its citizens are free.

Though Kennedy proposed new laws to help rectify intractable discrimination, he focused the domestic environment as a crucial arena for permanent problem-solving. His concluding words emphasized the pivotal role that all should play in making equality of opportunity a national reality.

> *This is one country. It has become one country because all of us and all the people who came here had an equal chance to develop their talents. We cannot say to ten percent of the population that you can't have that right; that your children can't have the chance to develop whatever talents they have . . . I am asking for your help to provide the kind of equality of treatment which we would want ourselves; to give a chance to every child to be educated to the limit of his talents. . . . not every child has an equal talent or an equal ability or an equal motivation, but they should have the equal right to develop their talent and their ability and their motivation to make something of themselves.*

Kennedy's main point was not that you should ignore government assistance but to first look to yourself, your family, your community; then to look to societal forces to come along side as a partner in your self-improvement endeavors. To start with solving problems at home:

BE THERE — Fatherless facts paint a sobering picture: boys with no father in the home are 20 times more likely to end up incarcerated; girls growing up without fathers have a 92 percent higher divorce rate; children without their fathers are five times more likely to be poor, 50 percent more likely to struggle with learning disabilities, and nine times more likely to drop out of school. . . . The list goes on. If you're a parent, grandparent, sibling, relative of some kind, de-prioritize other things and be there for your family, especially if you're a father. It will make a world of difference. And don't wait to get involved with family. The time is now, as Kennedy also advised.

> *The time to repair the roof is when the sun is shining.*

BE HERE — Expecting disadvantaged households to climb the socio-economic ladder without support targeted against historic barriers is a recipe for failure. If you're currently struggling to provide for yourself and your family, do your best to put your own house in order, which will send the message that you're looking for a hand up, not a handout. Don't stress over past wrongs or future obstacles. Be present in your quest. Make everyday count — a step in the direction of your dreams. As you move forward to find uplifting opportunities, the resources of society to fuel your upward journey will find you. And seek to apply Norman Vincent Peale's problem-solving counsel.

Positive thinking is how you think about a problem.
Enthusiasm is how you feel about a problem.
The two together determine what you do about a problem.

First Remove The Plank From Your Own Eye   **August 23rd**

Men's passions are kept in check by the restrictions of the society
in which they live. Remove those checks — take from the individuals
the moral atmosphere in which they move, and their evil passions will rise.
— John Griscom

Immigration from Europe to America started to build in the years after the American Revolution, most significantly in New York City, which became the largest U.S. city in 1800 and widened its lead throughout the nineteenth and twentieth centuries. New York City's population increased fifty percent between 1830 and 1840 — approximately 300,000 that year — the influx of immigrants yielding societal challenges.

Physician John Griscom was a pioneer in the city's public health efforts. Griscom researched the slums where the immigrant poor lived, which were called "fever nest" because of the rampant diseases. On December 30, 1844, Dr. Griscom delivered an address at the Repository of the American Institute, discussing the impact that substandard slum conditions had on public health. As he concluded his remarks, he underscored the root cause.

The tide of emigration which now sets so strongly toward our shores,
cannot be turned back. We must receive the poor, the ignorant, and the
oppressed from other lands, and it would be better to consider them as coming
filled with the energy of hope for happier days . . . whose fault is it that they
live here in cellars more filthy than the cabins of whose wretchedness we hear so
much, and for whose existence half the blame is thrown upon the government
they have left.

To his credit, Griscom refused to point the finger of blame on others but placed responsibility for the public health crisis where it belonged.

Let us first cast the beam from our own eye. We are parties to their
degradation, inasmuch as   we permit the inhabitation of places, from which
it is not possible improvement in condition or habits can come. We suffer the
sub-landlord to stow them, like cattle, in pens, and to compel them to swallow
poison with every breath. They are allowed, may it not be said required, to live

in dirt, when the reverse, rather, should be enforced.

"First cast the beam from our own eye" means getting serious about taking responsibility for the problem. The phrase stems from Jesus' Sermon on the Mount when he stated:

> *. . . first remove the plank from your own eye; and then you will*
> *see clearly to remove the speck from your brother's eye.*
> — Matthew 7:5

Griscom implemented this approach regarding the social problem of poor health in slum areas; a public health movement resulted that improved conditions for his generation and beyond.

It is on you to "cast the beam" from your eye regarding personal problems. Jesus laid out a two-step strategy; strive to follow it as you:

LEARN — Your priority should be to implement Jesus' first step. Take a really hard look at whatever situation you're in, especially if it's troubled. In short, honestly assess yourself. Ask yourself some questions: What happened? How did I get in this situation? Why am I in crisis? Am I blaming someone else? Is there something that I can change today to get out of my plight? Just answering these questions will launch a new, more responsible attitude and propel you towards personal breakthrough.

LIBERATE — Living your best life is about more than just you. Jesus instructed: remove your plank then remove their speck. In sum, help yourself then help others. Put another way: you cannot effectively deal with others' problems until you deal with your own problems. But once you address your issues, don't be long celebrating; you're called to liberate others.

Endeavor Beyond Expectations   August 24th

But need Americans cling so tenaciously to these particular values which virtually
force us to judge the worth of a person by what he is doing or may accomplish
in the job world rather than by what kind of person he is or may become?
— Florence Kluckhohn

The demands of the Second World War compelled a substantial increase of U.S. women employed outside the home — in jobs that had previously been reserved for men. The impact of these employment shifts on the status of women in American society was assessed by numerous academics in the postwar era. One of them, Harvard anthropologist Florence Kluckhohn, pioneered the "values orientation theory", which posited a cross-cultural, universal set of human values. In a 1952 article Kluckhohn examined women's changing roles and the concomitant responsibilities and freedoms. She encouraged her readers to endeavor beyond expectations, directing them to consider . . .

> . . . *some of the other interests and goals which human beings always have within them as potentials be raised to a value status that is at least the equal to that accorded to economic affairs. American men are not by nature more anti-intellectual than other men and are not more aesthetically gauche. They undoubtedly have surprising gifts of both kinds which they would enjoy expressing. Women, too, have more capacities than those of mere appreciation. But of greater importance than the gains to men as men or to women as women would be the widened area of common interests for   men   and   women, for husbands and wives.*

Kluckhohn's point transcends gender categories. Whether you're a woman or man, it's important for you to understand your social role but not to simply accept and settle in it. Your quest should be to strive beyond it, endeavoring to reach that higher ground far above whatever status or position society has imposed on you. To endeavor beyond expectations, you will need:

GREATER FOCUS — What you become in life results directly from what your mind dwells on. Concentrate on spiritual books, classic literature and self-help readings instead of social media, TV sitcoms and racy periodicals, and you will will expand your mental powers, paving the inner pathway for greater capability and character to enter your life.

GREATER OPENNESS — Be open to change. Fear and doubt can be emotional barriers to personal progress. Don't let your attitude block your destiny. Be willing to change, and be strong in your will, so that your present responsibilities and circumstances don't prevent you from moving forward.

GREATER RESPONSIBILITY — The higher you go in life, the more responsibilities you will face. But don't let this prospect hold you back. As you endeavor beyond your expectations, the journey you are traveling is preparing you to take on greater responsibility. Fulfilling your potential equips for the burdens of leadership.

GREATER FREEDOM — Understand that life is a matter of choice. You are free to live to your fullest potential. Don't rush to make decisions, big and small. Take your time to first assess the situation, examining all the options before you. If you pray before choosing, you will draw closer to making the right choice.

Get Ready To Handle Change   August 25th

The American colonies were peopled from Great Britain, and the Western states derive their inhabitants chiefly from New England and Virginia. Yet, when the American looks back at his British ancestor, he discovers few traits of similarity . . . the backwoodsman is almost as far removed from his Eastern progenitor.
— James Hall

Soldier and jurist James Hall was known as the literary pioneer of the Midwestern United States. Though he was born in Philadelphia, he moved to Illinois in 1820 where he not only served as a circuit court judge but also became a prolific writer, a champion chronicler of frontier history. In Letters from the West, he wrote about a vast array of subjects including the national character of Americans, elaborating that even with all their differences, Americans possess more in common.

In the great matters of religion and law, all of us in the United States are the same, as the children of one family, when they separate in the world, still preserve the impress of those principles which they imbibed from a common source; but, in all matters of taste and fancy, customs and exterior deportment, we find a variance. Those who live under the same government, participate in the same laws, and process the same religion — whose representatives mingle in council, whose warriors rally under the same banner, who celebrate the same victories and mourn for the same disasters — must have many feelings and sentiments in common, though they may differ in their modes of evincing them.

Hall highlighted one of the shared traits — the ability to deal with change.

Thus, he who should attempt to portray the American character must draw, not a single portrait but a family-piece containing several heads. In each of these would be discovered some strong lines common to all: the same active, enterprising and independent spirit; the same daring soul and inventive genius;

and the aptitude or capacity to take advantage of every change, and subsist and flourish in every soil and situation.

Hall asserted that the distinctiveness — and greatness — of Americans is how well they handle change, which is a key to success. To get ready to handle change, you must be willing to:

ACCEPT — Remember — the only constant in life is change, so don't be resistant to change. Accept it as an everyday fact of life. You don't have to love it, but you have to be willing to work with it. Shift your expectations. Don't be surprised or frustrated when change knocks on your door. Instead, smile and say, "Welcome, I was expecting you."

ADAPT — Be improvisational with your changing circumstances. Your victory is in your strategy, so understand what is now different and plan accordingly. See the need to adapt to evolving situations as an opportunity to try new things.

ACCELERATE — Get ahead of change. Prepare for it in advance. If you move at the same pace, you risk being left at a disadvantage by the new circumstances and by competitors who have already made the adjustment. Change won't wait for you, so focus and prioritize — that's the only way you can shift into a higher gear to keep up with it.

ANOINT — The typical attitude is to be apprehensive about change — to fear it. Take the opposite approach. Embrace change. Treat it as a sacred moment that has blessed your life. You can either ride with the wave, or be drowned by it. The consequences of change in your life can be for better or worse. . . . Your choice . . . Coach John Wooden scored big with this truth.

Things turn out the best for the people who make the best of the way things turn out.

Look Without And Within To Advance   August 26th

The relation of Negroes to industrial unrest makes it clear that whatever the Negro is to have in the labor world must be won by him against odds and held by superior force. Only as the Negro develops into a strong competitor will he be recognized.
— Rev. Richard Wright, Jr.

In the early 1900's the burgeoning African American population in Chicago and other Northern cities faced employment challenges. Rev. Richard Wright, Jr., pastor of Chicago's Trinity Mission, was troubled by the economic plight — complicated by labor unrest — of this first generation of Southern blacks in his city, some of whom were his parishioners. Wright shared his concerns in October 1905 article.

The question of earning a living — how to get a job and how to hold a job — is the most serious and most difficult question now confronting the Chicago Negro. He must work where he can rather than where he will. Times of industrial unrest, of which there are many in this city, have often offered to him opportunities for work which were before closed.

As Wright described, the Chicago stockyard strike of 1904 had significant racial impact on the labor market.

Within one month, an industry which had used 95 percent white labor now threatened to use 85 percent Negro labor. It was more than unionism could bear. The more thoughtless strikers and their friends used violence and made it positively dangerous for a black face to appear in "Packingtown". . . . Today no industry in Chicago employs more Negroes than the packing industries, where in nearly every branch they may find employment.

Wright believed that it was just important for African Americans to look within to prepare themselves as it was to look outside of themselves for job opportunities. This dual approach of looking within and without to make personal advancement is a strategy that you should execute as you:

LOOK WITHIN FOR YOUR BOUNTY— The story of the young couple with California gold rush fever is relevant here. They sold all their possessions, even their farm, and went West in search for gold but failed and ended up bankrupt. To get away from it all they moved to Europe and after many years returned to America and visited their old farm. Observing security guards and a barbed-wire fence all around their old property, they found out it was now government owned because the second largest gold reserve in America had been discovered underneath. Look within for your own goldmine. The seed of great treasure has been planted inside of you; you first have to recognize your potential then cultivate it, making your heretofore hidden bounty manifest. Remember — you won't unearth your gold if you're afraid to disrupt your routines. Galileo Galilei put it this way.

You cannot teach a man anything; you can only help him find it within himself.

LOOK WITHOUT FOR YOUR BREAKTHROUGH — Wright encouraged his contemporaries to take advantage of openings that had historically been closed to blacks but for the volatility of industry/labor relations of his era. Your breakthrough opportunities are all around you. You just have to open your eyes in new ways. The Old Testament account of a weeping Hagar is illustrative. She and her son Ishmael were dying of thirst when the revelation came.

Then God opened her eyes, and she saw a well of water. And she went and filled the skin with water, and gave the lad a drink.
— Genesis 21:19

Let your eyes be opened in revelatory ways so you can fulfill this success principle: Prepare (Look Within) + Proceed (Look Without) = Progress.

Pursue Personal Progress   **August 27th**

Enlighten the people generally, and tyranny and oppressions of body and mind will vanish like evil spirits at the dawn of day.
— Thomas Jefferson

After his many years of government service, Thomas Jefferson maintained a voluminous correspondence. One of his regular correspondents was French economist Pierre S. du Pont de Nemours, the father of the founder of the DuPont Chemical Company of Wilmington, Delaware. In 1816, as he was writing new constitutions for South American republics, Du Pont asked Jefferson's views on representative government. In a letter dated April 24, 1816, Jefferson replied, highlighting the personal responsibility of the people.

Hence, with us, the people (by which is meant the mass of individuals composing the society) being competent to judge of the facts occurring in ordinary life, they have retained the functions of judges of facts under the name of jurors; but being unqualified for the management of affairs requiring intelligence above the common level, yet competent judges of human character, they chose for their management representatives, some by themselves immediately, others by electors chosen by themselves.

Jefferson concluded the letter, underscoring the importance of self-improvement and personal change.

Although I do not, with some enthusiasts, believe that the human condition will ever advance to such a state of perfection as that there shall no longer be pain or vice in the world, yet I believe it s u s c e p t i b l e   o f   m u c h improvement, and most of all in matters of government and religion; and that the diffusion of knowledge among the people is to be the instrument by which it is to be effected.

Jefferson's point to Du Pont was that if government intended to get better, the people needed to get better — to be committed to pursue personal progress. To pursue personal progress in your own life, be willing to:

SACRIFICE — Be willing to pay the price of change. If you avoid making the sacrifices now, you will pay a bigger price of lost opportunities later on because you never improved. The things you have to do or give up will hurt, but the suffering doesn't last. Remember — it's short-term pain for long-term gain.

SWITCH — Accept the fact that the only constant in life is change, so be willing to make the necessary adjustments. If you keep doing the same old things you will end up with the same old results. If you want different — and better — results, you must change. You have to do something new. It could be something as simple as going to bed earlier so you can get up earlier to get to school or work on time. Improvement will come as you embrace positive change. Take note of Albert Einstein's insight.

The definition of insanity is doing the same thing over and over and expecting different results.

SHIFT — Be willing to change your environment. To get out of your rut, don't wait for someone to pull you out. Your hero may never show up. Make the move yourself. Take the step up and out of your situation by shifting to a different place, away from the old influences that have been holding you back. . . . Walk away . . . Keep moving . . .

SOLVE — But changing circumstances is not enough to solve your problems. You have to change yourself. You may be resistant to change; a lot of people are. That's why your inner life is key. You have to bring a positive attitude to the process of personal change every day. Permanent solutions don't happen overnight. But they will happen if you make them happen through a daily commitment to pursue personal progress.

Take The Initiative   August 28th

The American Revolution, on the one hand, brought forth
great vices; but, on the other hand, it called forth many virtues
. . . which, but for that event, would have been lost to the world.
— David Ramsay

A physician and patriot from Charleston, South Carolina, David Ramsay was captured by the British during the Revolutionary War. Though he served as a South Carolina delegate to the Continental Congress, Ramsay was better known for his historical writings. His 1789 two volume work, History of the American Revolution, was based on his knowledge gained from personal involvements in activities of the Revolutionary Period. Ramsay provided insight into the impact of the war on the character of the American people.

. . . While the Americans   were guided by the leading strings of
the mother country, they had no scope nor encouragement for exertion. . . . In
the years 1775 and 1776, the country, being suddenly thrown into a situation
that needed the abilities of all its sons, these generally took their places, each
according to the bent of his inclination. As they severally pursued their objects
with ardor, a vast expansion of the human mind speedily followed.

Ramsay highlighted how the commitment of individual Americans to take the initiative put them on the pathway to accomplish great things. He elaborated on this point below.

But the great bulk of those who were the active instruments of
carrying on the Revolution were self-made, industrious men. These who by their
own exertions had established or laid a foundation   for   establishing   personal

independence were most generally trusted and most successfully employed in establishing that of their country.

The theme that Ramsay articulated — Americans rising through sacrifice and adversity to attain moral stature and personal success — was captured decades later by Henry Wadsworth Longfellow in "Success"; the poem projects various way for you to take the initiative.

CLIMB UP ADVERSITY
We have not wings, we cannot soar;
But we have feet to scale and climb
By slow degrees, by more and more,
The cloudy summits of our time.

CARVE THROUGH CHALLENGES
The mighty pyramids of stone
That wedge-like cleave the desert airs,
When nearer seen, and better known,
Are but gigantic flights of stairs.

CROSS OVER CRISIS
The distant mountains, that uprear
Their solid bastions to the skies,
Are crossed by pathways, that appear
As we to higher levels rise.

CRADLE YOUR OPPORTUNITY
The heights by great men reached and kept
Were not attained by sudden flight,
But they, while their companions slept,
Were toiling upward in the night.

You must accept that fact that you are the person you've been waiting for — no one else is coming! Your tide is not turning to bring your ship in and Prince Charming isn't waiting for you around the next corner and the odds are against you winning the lottery. Take the initiative. Don't wait until you feel like making the change. Change your behavior first; and a change in your attitude will follow.

Take the Right Initiative   August 29th

> *Resolved, that an association or society be formed for the purpose of*
> *collecting information and to assist in the formation and execution of a plan*
> *for the colonization of the free people of color, with their consent, in Africa, or*
> *elsewhere, as may be thought most advisable by the constituted authorities of the country.*
> — American Colonization Society

In December 1816 the American Colonization Society ("ACS") was formed for the purpose of migrating free African Americans to be colonized in Africa. U.S. House Speaker Henry Clay of Kentucky chaired the ACS organizational meeting; the minutes reported the following account of Clay's leadership.

> *He understood the object of the present meeting to be to consider the propriety and practicability of colonizing the free people of color in the United States, and of forming an association in relation to that object. . . . They neither enjoyed the immunities of freemen nor were the   s u b j e c t   t o   t h e incapacities of slaves, but partook in some degree of the qualities of both. From their condition, and the unconquerable prejudices resulting from their color they never could amalgamate with the free whites of this country. It was desirable, therefore, both as it respected them and the residue of the population of the country to draw them off.*

From the ACS' founding through the Civil War, more than 13,000 African Americans immigrated to Liberia, but the colonization plan eventually collapsed. The mortality rates of immigrants arriving in Liberia was staggering, one of the the highest in human history, which discouraged potential migrants. Leading abolitionists like Frederick Douglass opposed ACS' plans because the organization was led by white Southern slaveholders like Clay with their scheme to blunt criticism of slavery in the U.S. ACS declined throughout the Reconstruction era until its dissolution in 1913.

Though it's important to take action, it's imperative to take the right kind of action. The ACS leaders failed because they took the wrong initiative. Don't follow their example. You have a better chance of taking the right initiative by paying attention to the following points.

PROBLEM — Confront your problems. Slavery was indeed problem, but truly resolving it meant fixing the problem at home instead of endeavoring to export it. Clay and his ACS colleagues should have changed the laws at home instead of shipping people abroad. Because they tried what was in effect a quick fix, their strategy didn't work and the problem got bigger, eventually bringing America a war consuming hundreds of thousands of lives. Solve your problem the right way the first time around; otherwise it will cost you.

PENETRATING — Displacing free Negroes was a flawed strategy. Look inside to check your motives before moving forward to avoid ill-advised maneuvers. The ACS' misguided approach to solving the problem of slavery evokes a scriptural illustration. The Old Testament leader King David is the relevant Biblical role model, exemplifying the wrong initiative. Attracted to a beautiful woman named Bathsheba, he committed adultery with her. His troubles deepened when he discovered she had become pregnant. David then instructed his general to send Bathsheba's husband Uriah to the front lines and then pull back the other troops, ensuring his death in battle. So David moved from a bad situation to a worse one, jumping from the frying pan into the fire: he went from being an adulterer to a murderer, which eventually led to a reign of terror on himself and his family. David acted from the wrong motives and calamity resulted. Take note of the negative role models of ACS and King David. Make sure to take a different approach.

POWER — Taking the right initiative is about effective problem-solving. The ability to solve your problem comes from your resolve to tackle it. Don't take it lightly. Take a strong approach. Get your arms around it and wrestle it to the ground. Hold it there. Study it. Get to know it. When you're face-to-face with your problem, then you're in position to really figure out what to do about it. Whatever you do, don't send it across the Atlantic, across the street, or to the cemetery. It will find its way back to haunt you until you get your initiative right. Henry Clay was wrong but Abraham Lincoln was right about slavery:

You cannot escape the responsibility of tomorrow by evading it today.

Learn From Your Failures   August 30th

Difficulties are meant to rouse, not discourage.
The human spirit is to grow strong by conflict.
— William Henry Channing

Unitarian clergyman and U.S. Congress Chaplain William Henry Channing was committed to social reform, especially the woman's rights movement. Both Susan B. Anthony, who was a member of his congregation, and Elizabeth Cady Stanton, were inspired at the beginnings of their activism in the 1850s by Channing's ministry.

About a decade earlier in September 1843, Channing's passion for human progress motivated him to write in the first issue of The Present about what he believed was America's special destiny, that the nation "has a plain and urgent duty . . . to advance the Reign of Heaven on Earth." Channing was specific and graphic in outlining America's failures.

> *That we deserve the retributions, losses, disgraces which our savage robberies of the Indians, our cruel and wanton oppressions of the Africans, our unjust habits of white serfdom, our grasping national ambition, our eagerness for wealth, our deceitful modes of external and internal trade, our jealous competitions between different professions and callings, our aping of aristocratic distinctions, our licentiousness and sensuality, our profligate expenditures, public and private, have brought, and will continue to bring upon us.*

But Channing also wrote positively about how Americans should live to learn from — and overcome — these failures.

> *To live content with small means; to seek elegance rather than luxury, and refinement rather than fashion; to be worthy, not respectable, and wealthy, not rich; to listen to stars and birds, babes and sages, with open heart; to study hard; to think quietly, act frankly, talk gently, await occasions, hurry never; in a word, to let the spiritual, unbidden and unconscious, grow up through the common — this is my symphony.*

Channing's message lives on two centuries later, encouraging all of us in this present generation to draw lessons from our shortcomings in order to lead victorious lives. What follows are two points that should act as guideposts for you as you do your best to learn from failure.

LET IT NOT GO TO YOUR HEAD — Accept failure as a reality of life — yours, mine, everyone's. The only person who avoids failure is the one who never attempts anything. Such people are so full of doubt and fear that they spend their time and energy coming up with excuses: "I failed in the past . . . I can't take action now . . . the risks are too great . . ." Since failure is inevitable, your response to it is the key. Don't let it go to your head. Put it in perspective. Figure out what went wrong. If you dwell on the negative consequences of failure, you will be locked in your house of stagnation. But if you focus on failure as a learning experience, using it as a life lesson to build a better you, you will be looking at past mistakes and the concomitant confusion and depression in the rear view mirror. The words of George Washington are on point.

We ought not to look back unless it is to derive useful lessons from past errors, and for the purpose of profiting by dearly bought experience.

LET IT GO FROM YOUR HEART — If you really want to attain your goals, you have to go all in after them. As you go from your heart in pursuit of success, proceed with the understanding that failure is part of success. Go after your aspirations with confidence but also with the expectation that unanticipated obstacles will come to derail your plans — failure! Sometimes it's your fault, sometimes not; ultimately, it doesn't matter. What does matter is your learning from the failure so when you hit the road again, you're that much closer to success. It's okay to fail early, even to fail often, as long as you fail learning.

Turn Your Stumbling Blocks Into Stepping Stones   August 31st

Though we have had war, reconstruction and abolition as a nation, we still linger in the shadow and blight of an extinct institution. Though the colored man is no longer subject to be bought and sold, he is still surrounded by an adverted sentiment which fetters all his movements.
— Frederick Douglass

On September 24, 1883 Frederick Douglass delivered a speech about the ongoing challenges confronting African Americans. Douglass had helped lead the Abolitionist movement and had become the most influential black leader of post-Civil War America. In his remarks Douglass rejected the view that his political party — or any political party — could be the savior of his people.

If the Republican Party cannot stand a demand for justice and fair play, it ought to go down. We were men before that party was born, and our manhood is more sacred than any party can be. Parties were made for men, not men for parties.

He then made it clear that the only way towards progress for individual members of his race was self-reliance, not to look outside the group for help but to turn their own stumbling blocks into stepping stones.

If the 6 million colored people of this country, armed with the Constitution of the United States . . . have not sufficient spirit and wisdom to organize and combine to defend themselves from outrage, discrimination, and oppression, it will be idle for them to expect that . . . any other political party will organize and combine for them or care what becomes of them. Men may combine to prevent cruelty to animals, for they . . . cannot speak for themselves; but we are men and must speak for ourselves, or we shall not be spoken for at all.

Douglass' thoughts about individual progress for his race — which apply to any race —still ring true. The following strategies will help you turn your own stumbling blocks into stepping stones.

PROBLEMS — Start with examining yourself. Identify your problems and be committed to a daily plan of action to resolve them. Looking first to others to fix your issues will forever leave you in the same place, searching for answers.

POSSIBILITIES — Be forward-thinking. Don't be so focused on past problems that you miss opportunities that lie ahead. All things are possible for those who believe in the future and embrace hope for all of its possibilities.

PURPOSE — Be purpose-driven. Devise a specific strategy for overturning those stumbling blocks in your life. Your victory over them will rise from the strategy you apply to them. Change is the only constant in life so adapt your tactics to the shifting circumstances as you pursue your goals. If you have to break out in a new direction to get ahead, go for it! Meditate on this truth:

*If you always do what you have always done,
you will always get what you've always gotten.*

PERFECTION — Strive to become the best version of you. Though you'll never attain perfection, keep reaching for it anyway; make self-improvement a lifelong quest. Here's your question: what must I change about myself to get better today? Hold yourself accountable to this high standard, keep pushing yourself to step up to higher ground, and you'll find the motivation to achieve permanent progress. And keep Leo Tolstoy's point in mind.

Everyone thinks of changing the world but no one thinks of changing himself.

SEPTEMBER: OPTIMISM
DAILY SUCCESS PRINCIPLES

1. Keep Your Head To The Sky — Sally Ride — 1983
2. Use Your Prophetic Voice — Philip Freneau — 1783
3. Make It Through Your Valley — Langston Hughes — 1926
4. Be Motivated By Your Vision — Mary Antin — 1894
5. Embrace The Larger Perspective — James Weldon Johnson — 1928
6. Beware Your Dream Killers — Edward McCabe — 1890
7. Affirm Big Possibilities — Commission On Civil Disorders — 1968
8. Turn Your Dream Into Reality — Benjamin Franklin — 1790
9. Dream Your Impossible Dream — Martin Luther King, Jr. — 1963
10. Empower Your Dreams — Edward Everett — 1824
11. Make Your Dreams Comes Alive — Sinclair Lewis — 1930
12. Discern Your Gleams Of Light — Sarah Winnemucca — 1884
13. Be A Holistic Dreamer — George Santayana — 1920
14. Chart A New Course — Tench Coxe — 1787
15. Renew Your Vision — Joseph Holland — 1989
16. Realize Your Dreams — George Bancroft — 1830
17. Read The Trends And Act On Them — Massachusetts African Americans — 1777
18. Pursue Your Destiny — John O'Sullivan — 1845
19. Cast Vision For Others — Benjamin Rush — 1787
20. Illuminate Your Vision — Charles Beard — 1913
21. Reach For New Ideas — John Adams — 1776
22. Craft A Compelling Vision — George Henry Evans — 1846
23. Encourage Others To Dream — Joel Barlow — 1787
24. See Beyond Your Clouds — Hezekiah Niles — 1815
25. Push Your Boundaries — Continental Congress — 1780
26. Don't Turn Back The Clock — Earl Warren — 1954
27. Stick With Your Vision — George Washington — 1796
28. Fit Your Piece Into The Larger Puzzle — John Calhoun — 1820
29. Be A Visionary Warrior — Benjamin Franklin — 1754
30. Build With Your Vision — Samuel Davies — 1759

Keep Your Head To The Sky   **September 1st**

The stars don't look bigger, but they do look brighter.
Sally Ride

On June 18, 1983, Sally Ride launched with her crew on space shuttle Challenger STS-7, becoming the first American woman in space. One of Ride's responsibilities was to operate the robotics arm to deploy and retrieve the Shuttle Pallet Satellite, the first time that this communications satellite had been used on a space mission. Ride was only 32 years of age on the space shuttle — the youngest American to have traveled in space, then and now.

Ride succeeded not only because of her intelligence and hard work but because of her boundless optimism. Literally and figuratively, she kept her head to sky. Learn from her advice; practice what she preaches in the words that follow; they will help you keep your head to the sky.

HIGH-MINDED — *Three Secrets to Success: Be willing to learn new things. Be able to assimilate new information quickly. Be able to get along with and work with other people.*

Elevate your thinking by your openness to new information. Ride held her PhD in physics from Stanford, but to become an astronaut, she had to go back to school all over again. Each day presents a new opportunity to gain knowledge. Seize every moment to broaden your understanding. Like Ride, you could end up in higher places than you could have imagined.

HOW-TO — *. . . to making some mistake that could actually cost you and the crew either a mission or your lives. So there is a lot of pressure that's put on every astronaut to just make sure that he or she understands exactly what to do, exactly when to do it, and is trained and prepared to carry it out.*

Preparation is a key to success. Stay positive as you address the tasks at hand, so when you reach your launching pad, you'll be ready to soar.

HIKE — *The best advice I can give anybody is to try to understand who you are and what you want to do, and don't be afraid to go down that road and do whatever it takes and work as hard as you have to work to achieve that.*

Success is a journey: a marathon, not a sprint. Keep walking down the road of your destiny, no matter how endless it appears. Work hard; it will pave your way.

HUMOR — *I suggest taking the high road and have a little sense of humor and let things roll off your back. I think that's very important.*

Don't take yourself too seriously. Ride's "little sense of humor" helped maintain her far-reaching outlook. "Let things roll off your back"; laugh at them as they fall to the ground. This process will help you shake off burdens, lightening your mental load, making it easier to keep your head to the sky.

HIP — *We need to make science cool again.*

When you feel good about what you're doing, others will catch your positivity. Your optimism will be contagious.

HONOR — *It was a real honor for me to get to be the first woman astronaut. I think it's really important that young girls that are growing up today can see that women can be astronauts too.*

Attaining great goals will make you a role model. Live an inspired life. Others will follow suit.

HOPE — *You can't be what you can't see.*

Keep your head to the sky, so you can be what you can see.

Use Your Prophetic Voice   **September 2nd**

It is not easy to conceive what will be the greatness and importance of North America in a century or two to come if the present fabric of Nature is upheld, and the people retain those bold sentiments of freedom which actuate them at this day.
Philip Freneau

As a crew member on a privateer during the Revolutionary War, Philip Freneau was captured and held in captivity on a British ship for many weeks. Freneau had acquired a passion for writing as a student at Princeton in the 1760's, where he was close friends with James Madison. His time as a prisoner motivated his writing of patriotic poetry and prose throughout the war, for which he became known as "The Poet of the American Revolution".

Between 1781 and 1783 Freneau published the Philadelphia Freeman's Journal, through which he waged war with his pen with anti-

418

British writings. He published both negative and positive pieces. His publications lambasted the British military, but they also did inspirational battle by depicting the big picture of America's future, poetically rendering the nation's destiny.

> *Agriculture, the basis of a nation's greatness, will here, most probably, be advanced to its summit of perfection; and its attendant, commerce, will so agreeably and usefully employ mankind that wars will be forgotten; nations, by a free intercourse with this vast and fertile continent, and this continent with the whole world, will again become brothers after so many centuries of hatred and jealousy, and no longer treat each other as savages and monsters. The iron generation will verge to decay, and those days of felicity advance which have been so often wished for by all good men and which are so beautifully described by the prophetic sages of ancient times.*

Freneau used his pen to express his prophetic voice, depicting a promising future for America. It's also important for you to articulate your views of what lies ahead. To use your prophetic voice, be:

FEARLESS — Playing it safe means staying in the present. When you determine to look out over the unknown days of destiny, you dare to be a trailblazer — someone willing to go the road less traveled. You have to get the best possible roadmap for that uncertain journey. Refuse to be intimidated about setting your new course into uncharted territory. And fearlessly resist the doubters and naysayers. If your relative or teacher or boss or peer says you can't do it, prophesy your determination; defend your dream. Be tenacious. Life passes quickly; the moral battle for your dreams happens now, not yesterday, not tomorrow.

FERVENT — Freneau was passionate to write about America's future. Passion is so important because, without it, you can easily lose sight of the big picture for your life in the details of responsibility or drudgery of obligation. Avoid under-dreaming — having a negative or limited view of your future, or no glory plan at all. It's better to start with a wrong or fuzzy picture that can be adjusted and clarified than with a blank screen, which means you're without the fervor out of which true dreams arises. Err on the side of having too much vision rather than too little.

FOLLOWED — Be a leader in the struggle by crafting your goals and communicating them to others. Organize a group — at work, at school, in a club, through a community-based or faith-based entity; get people on board with your vision. The true test of your prophetic voice is whether people are willing to follow your lead.

FAITHFUL — Your prophetic voice will ring hollow without a firm faith in your dream. Believe in your divine destiny and your prophetic voice will rise. Hold on to these words from Eleanor Roosevelt to strengthen your faith.

The future belongs to those who believe in the beauty of their dreams.

Make It Through Your Valley   September 3rd

We hold these turns to be self-evident, that all men are created
equal, and they are endowed by their Creator with certain unalienable
Rights, that among these are Life, Liberty and the pursuit of Happiness.
America's Founding Fathers

On July 4, 1776, the signers of the Declaration of Independence cast a new vista for government and society, a visionary approach without precedent in the history of mankind. They possessed high ideals for this revolutionary social enterprise, which was, at its founding, much more dream than reality. The vision was to have the governmental powers rise from and be rooted in the will of the people.

That to secure these rights, Governments are instituted
among Men, deriving their just powers from the consent of the governed —
That when ever any Form of Government becomes destructive of these ends, it's
the Right of the People to alter or to abolish it, and to institute new
Government, laying it foundation of such principles and organizing its powers
in such form, as to them shall seem most likely to effect their Safety and
Happiness.

But realizing these founding ideals, so that every person could fulfill their God-given potential, regardless of the circumstances of birth, race or social position, has been an ongoing challenge throughout American history. Disappointments have often eclipsed attainments: incessant valleys have sought to vanquish the vision, but America is still making it through her valleys. To make it through your valleys, keep this 3-V principle in mind.

VISION — Don't let your vision be shaped or constrained by present circumstances. The Founders of 1776 didn't let the realities of their day limit their dreaming, so the American Dream was born. Let your American Dream soar, too.

VALLEY — A century and one-half after the Dream's declaration, Langston Hughes, the poet laureate of Harlem — in a poem entitled Harlem — mused:

> *What happens to a dream deferred?*
> *Does it dry up like a raisin in the sun?*
> *Or fester like a sore and then run?*
> *Does it stink like rotten meat?*
> *Or crust and sugar over like syrupy sweet?*
> *Maybe it just sags like a heavy load?*
> *Or does it explode?*

Disappointment, even despair, can be discerned from Hughes' deferred dream. Now here you are, a century after his poetic pondering, perhaps in pursuit of your own American Dream but stuck in a valley. Your valleys signify those forces that represent the greatest threats to you fulfilling your goals — the rough road ahead: the disappointments and setbacks, the doubts and fears that stand between you and your dreams. Your valleys exist to test your vision, to see how real and strong it is. Expect the obstacles to come. Be prepared for the adversities of life so that they don't take you by surprise. Like Hughes, you may be facing a deferred dream that is dried up, festering, stinking, crusting, sagging or exploding. Don't succumb to depression or defeat. Make it through your valley by daily renewing your vision.

VICTORY — However deep your valley, you can climb out of it if you work at that rising-up strategy day after day. Be patient, keep working, keep dreaming. Hughes answered his own poetic questions by affirming the key tactic:

> *Hold fast to dreams*
> *For without them*
> *Life is a broken-winged bird*
> *That cannot fly*

Perhaps when you overcome your valleys and fulfill your own dream, you can help America finally fulfill her Dream of Life, Liberty and the Pursuit of Happiness for all of her children!

Be Motivated By Your Vision   **September 4th**

No application made, no questions asked, no examinations, rulings,
exclusions; no machinations, no fees. The doors stood open for every one of us.
Mary Antin

In 1894 Mary Antin, a 13-year-old Russian immigrant, came to
Boston with her family. Almost twenty years later Antin's book "The
Promised Land" was published, in which she described her very first day in
America.

> *In our flat we did not think of such a thing as storing the coal in the*
> *bathtub. There was no bathtub. So in the evening of the first day my father*
> *conducted us to the public baths. As we moved along in a little procession, I*
> *was delighted with the illumination of the streets. So many lamps, and they*
> *burned until morning, my father said, and so people did not need to carry*
> *lanterns. In America, then, everything was free, as we had heard in Russia.*
> *Light was free; the streets were as bright as a synagogue on a holy day. Music*
> *was free; we had been serenaded, to our gaping delight, by a brass band of*
> *many pieces, soon after our installation on Union Place.*

Antin also wrote about her great vision for her American journey.

> *Education was free. That subject my father had written about*
> *repeatedly, as comprising his chief hope for us children, the essence of*
> *American opportunity, the treasure that no thief could touch, not even*
> *misfortune or poverty. It was the one thing that he was able to promise us when*
> *he sent for us; surer, safer than bread or shelter.*

Her dream of an American education was consummated a few
months later on her first day of school; consequently, her soul was full of
passion to excel in the classroom and beyond.

> *The apex of my civic pride and personal contentment was reached on*
> *the bright September morning when I entered the public school. That day I*
> *must always remember, even if I live to be so old that I cannot tell my name.*
> *To most people their first day at school is a memorable occasion. In*
> *my case the importance of the day was a hundred times magnified, on account*
> *of the years I had waited, the road I had come, and the conscious ambitions I*
> *entertained.*

Antin went on to attend Teachers College of Columbia
University and Barnard College and became a popular author and lecturer
to audiences across America. Like her, you should let your vision motivate

you, paving the way to educational and career success. Asking yourself these four questions will help.

WHAT MOTIVATES YOU? — Seek to understand what really drives you, the thing you care most about. For Anitin, it was education. She's a good role model. Whatever it is for you, spend as much time and energy on it as you can. Watch it take off and soar.

WHERE IS YOUR MOUNTAIN? — Get in touch with your obstacles, those forces — both internal and external — that can hold you back. Sometimes it's best not to try to climb over your mountain. Maneuver around it. Or go another way.

WHO IS YOUR MENTOR? — You will likely not make it alone. Mary Antin had her father. If you're not fortunate enough to have an engaged, supportive parent, reach outside of your family for help. Who is the one you can count on to pull you through?

WHEN IS YOUR MOMENT? — Antin's moment was her first day in an American school. What is your transformative moment, your turning point? If you've already had it, cherish it. If not, keep striving for it, make it happen; as Henry David Thoreau advises, your success will come.

Go confidently in the direction of your dreams, live the life you have imagined and you'll meet with success unexpected in common hours.

Embrace The Larger Perspective   **September 5th**

The question repeated generation after generation has been: what shall we do with the Negro? — ignoring completely the power of the Negro to do something for himself, and even something to America.
James Weldon Johnson

Dutch colonizers settled Harlem in the mid-seventeenth century under the leadership of Peter Stuyvesant, displacing the remaining members of the Weckquaesgeek, part of the Iroquois Nation, the first inhabitants of Manhattan Island. Slaves from the Dutch West India Company turned the Native American trail running through the lush bottomland meadows into the first road to Nieuw Haarlem. It is poetic justice that Africans first paved the way to the place that would eventually become the epicenter of African American culture. The village was anglicized to Harlem when the British captured the New Netherlands colony in 1674.

Over two hundred years later, at the turn of the twentieth century, Harlem possessed only a smattering of African Americans, who were confined to "Negro tenements". But the Harlem Renaissance, the greatest racial demographic transition in American history, was impending. The number of blacks grew from 10 percent of Harlem's population in 1910 to 70 percent in 1930 . . . home to countless writers, musicians, singers, dancers, painters and other creative artists . . . becoming the cultural Mecca of Black America.

Professor, author and songwriter James Weldon Johnson assessed Harlem's transformation in a 1928 article. Johnson's insight was that he brought a larger perspective to the problem of American race relations. Embracing a larger perspective as you tackle your own problems is crucial. Consider Johnson's words and the principles they represent as you develop the habit of seeing the picture for your life.

NEBULOUS PROBLEM — *The question of the races — white and black — has occupied much of America's time and thought. Many methods for a solution of the problem have been tried —most of them tried on the Negro, for one of the mistakes commonly made in dealing with this matter has been the failure of white America to take into account the Negro himself and the forces he was generating and sending out.*

Define your problem. Don't allow someone else to tell you what's going on with you. No matter how troubled your issues might be, face them head on. Dig deep to understand your crisis. That's the first step to overcoming it.

NEW THINKING — *It is a new thought that the Negro has helped to shape and mold and make America. . . . Today a newer approach is being tried . . . the art approach to the Negro problem. . . A generation ago the Negro was receiving lots of publicity, but nearly all of it was bad. There were front page stories with such headings as "Negro Criminal," "Negro Brute." Today, one may see undesirable stories, but one may also read stories about Negro singers, Negro actors, Negro poets. The connotations of the very word "Negro" have been changed. A generation ago many Negroes were half or wholly ashamed of the term. Today, they have every reason to be proud of it.*

Be creative in your problem-solving. Expand your thinking. Don't simply consider how your circumstances affect you personally. Like Johnson, embrace the larger perspective. View yourself within the broader cultural context to bring new meaning to your efforts. Whatever you're facing, see it as just one piece of the bigger puzzle. Your new perspective just might spark a renaissance for yourself and your community.

NOVEL INITIATIVE — *For many years and by many methods the Negro has been overcoming the coarser prejudices against him; and when we consider how many of the subtler prejudices have c r u m b l e d , a n d crumbled rapidly under the process of art creation by the Negro, we are justified in taking a hopeful outlook toward the effect that the increase of recognized individual artists fivefold, tenfold, twentyfold, will have on the most perplexing and vital question before the American people.*

Stay hopeful throughout your days of adversity. Resolve to do something positive every day to solve your problem. Strive to connect the dots of your individual experience to relevant collective initiatives. In the words of John Foster Dulles, success means putting your challenges in the rear-view mirror.

The measure of success is not whether you have a tough problem to deal with, but whether it is the same problem you had last year.

Beware Your Dream Killers   September 6th

Here the Negro can rest from mob law, here he can be secure from every ill of the southern policies.
Edward P. McCabe

In 1890, at the age of 40, African American attorney Edward P. McCabe moved to the Oklahoma Territory in pursuit of his dream. McCabe started his career on Wall Street but found himself stuck in clerk and porter jobs. Similar employment dead-ends plagued him after he relocated to Chicago so he moved further west. Working as a land agent in Kansas, he was appointed then elected Graham County clerk, which led to his election in 1882 as Kansas State Auditor, making him the the highest ranking African American elected official outside of the Reconstruction South.

With Oklahoma Territory opening to non-Native American settlement in 1889, McCabe moved to Washington, D.C. and lobbied President Benjamin Harrison to be appointed governor of the new territory, to no avail. He nevertheless moved to Oklahoma with the vision of an all-black state, creating a safe haven for African Americans seeking to gain better economic opportunities and to escape the racist realities pervading the late 19th century American South.

McCabe's first step was gaining the appointment as the first

Treasurer of Logan County, Oklahoma. He then purchased 320 acres to found the city of Langston, named after an African American Congressman committed to support a black college there. The Colored Agricultural and Normal School — later called Langston University — was established in 1897.

Within a year of Langston City's founding in 1890, in large part due to the land agents that McCabe sent out to recruit settlers, the town had over 200 black residents. Widespread African American settlement in the Oklahoma territory resulted from McCabe's effort. Between the city's founding and when statehood was granted in 1907, Oklahoma's black population doubled and during the same timeframe, approximately 30 new all-black towns were established. Different from the circumstances that prevailed in the South, Black Oklahomans owned the farms on which they worked. There was also greater mobility, as some moved from agricultural regions and coal mines to other locations within the state and found service jobs in urban areas.

Though his political aspirations to become governor of Oklahoma were left unfulfilled, McCabe succeeded in fostering better living conditions and greater economic opportunities for his fellow black Americans. He achieved this success because he was wary of factors that could have doused his dreams. You, too, should beware your dream killers by paying attention to:

DAMS — Early in his career institutional barriers blocked McCabe, but he didn't let them kill his dreams. Hewlett Packard engineer Steve Wozniak practiced this principle with great success. In 1975 Wozniak shared with his good friend Steve Jobs his dream of creating an easy-to-use personal computer for the mass market. They built and offered it to Hewlett Packard, who turned it down. So they founded Apple and turned the computer industry upside down. Whatever dams confront you, don't let them kill your dreams.

DISTANCE — Your dreams may seem so far away that you feel there's no hope to ever reach them. McCabe had to move from New York to Chicago to Kansas to Oklahoma in pursuit of his dream. Keep traveling — geographically and emotionally — until you close the gap between vision and reality.

DOUBTERS — People in your life can be dream killers, potentially the biggest ones. Avoid anyone who cast doubts on your dreams. Don't argue with them. Don't try to convince them of the beauty of your vision. Move forward towards fulfillment. Let your glorious outcomes prove them wrong.

DISAPPOINTMENTS — Things will happen that will disappoint you. McCabe went to Washington, D.C., to lobby the U.S. President for an appointment that would have been the biggest step towards his dream. It didn't happen; McCabe pursued his vision anyway. When disappointments come, follow the Apostle Paul's advice; get through it by taking a divine perspective.

And we know that all things work together for good to those who love God, to those who are the called according to His purpose.
— Romans 8:28

DIEHARD — The best way to deal with the above dream killers — or any forces that might derail your dreams — is to keep saying to them whenever they show up: GET OUT OF MY WAY! I WILL NEVER GIVE UP! I WILL KEEP HOPE ALIVE!!

Affirm Big Possibilities   September 7th

Just as Lincoln, a century ago, put preservation of the Union above all else, so should we put creation of a true union — a single society and a single American identity — as our major goal.
Kerner Commission Report

During the evening of July 12, 1967, the rioting in Newark erupted. The violence, looting and property destruction raged over the next four days, leaving in its wake hundreds injured and 26 dead. Though it was not the worst of the 159 urban riots in the long, hot summer of 1967 — surpassed by the calamities in Detroit — Newark symbolized the national crisis that resulted in the establishment of the National Advisory Commission on Civil Disorders. Known as the Kerner Commission, its mission was to investigate the causes of the widespread disturbances and recommend approaches to address them. The Commission's report, issued on March 1, 1968, projected the overarching values that informed its approach.

There are those who oppose these aims as "rewarding the rioters." They are wrong. A great nation is not so easily intimidated. We propose these aims to fulfill our pledge of equality and to meet the fundamental needs of a democratic and civilized society — domestic peace, social justice, and u r b a n centers that are citadels of the human spirit. . . .

427

The final words of the report affirmed the big possibilities of a visionary strategy for all sectors of society.

Our strategy is neither blind repression nor capitulation to lawlessness. Rather it is the affirmation of common possibilities, for all, within a single society.

In the throes of societal crisis, the Kerner Commission affirmed big possibilities for the nation. Whatever challenge you're presently facing, affirm big possibilities for your life through these success principles.

INITIATING CLEAR STRATEGIES — Your vision is your compass, keeping you on the pathway to success. Let your strategies flow from your goals. The Kerner Commission's objectives of "domestic peace, social justice, and urban centers that are citadels of the human spirit" informed its plans for moving the nation beyond its riot-torn realities. You have countless choices to make every day to forge your progress. Use the big picture for your life as a daily control tool, as a check to align your strategies with your goals.

INTENTIONAL ABOUT PURPOSE — At the 1968 Olympic Games in Mexico City, Tanzania's John Stephen Akhwari fell and injured himself during the marathon. Well over an hour after Ethiopia's Mamo Wolde had won the race, with only a fraction of the spectators remaining, Akhwari, the last runner, hobbled into the stadium. The small crowd cheered with a standing ovation as he — his leg bandaged and bleeding — crossed the finish line. When asked how he made it all the way, Akhwari responded, "My country did not send me to Mexico City to start the race. They sent me to finish the race." Stay focused on your finish line. Strong intention will propel you through the pain of the process to the glory of attainment.

IMAGINING NEW VICTORIES — Don't let your outlook be dictated by your surroundings. Even when you're confronted by a rising crisis, encircling gloom or even an unexpected injury, keep your focus on your mission. If your adversities intensify, make sure to increase your concentration on your goals commensurate with the difficulty of your challenges. Defeat disappointment and despair by envisaging new victories for your life, and committing yourself to attain them. Heed Helen Keller's words.

No pessimist ever discovered the secrets of the stars, or sailed to an unchartered land, or opened a new heaven to the human spirit.

Turn Your Dream Into Reality   September 8th

Slavery is such an atrocious debasement of human nature, that its very extirpation, if not performed with solicitous care, may sometimes open a source of serious evils.
Benjamin Franklin

On February 12, 1790, the Pennsylvania Abolition Society delivered a petition to the newly formed U.S. House of Representatives, imploring Congress to . . .

> *. . . take such measures in their wisdom, as the powers with which they are invested will authorize, for promoting the abolition of slavery, and discouraging every species of traffic in slaves.*

The document was signed by the aging, ailing Founding Father Benjamin Franklin. The antislavery cause was not new to Franklin. Decades earlier as a young Philadelphia printer he published tracts by Quaker abolitionists and, in the twilight of his illustrative career had moved the fight against slavery front and center. Franklin asserted the visionary approach, articulating the incongruity between the institution of slavery and the principles of the American Revolution, insisting on Congress to "devise means for removing this inconsistency from the Character of the American people." Franklin had further asserted:

> *I have conceived a higher opinion of the natural capacities of the black race than I had ever before entertained. Their apprehension seems as quick, their memory as strong, and their docility in every respect equal to that of white children.*

The salient responses to the Abolition Society petition came from two Deep South representatives, James Jackson of Georgia and William Loughton Smith of South Carolina. They not only threatened secession and emphasized that the recently ratified U.S. Constitution prohibiting Congress from legislating against the slave trade until 1808 but made a demographic point - where would the freed slaves go? Ninety percent of the total black population resided south of the Potomac River and since the first biracial society anywhere in the world had not been contemplated, relocation would transport the bulk of the freed slaves to an American colony in Africa or in the Caribbean; or to a homelands solution in the American West.

Franklin died two months later and the hope of immediately abolishing slavery died with him. Pragmatism ruled over perspective — to preserve the fragile, fractious republic, the key leaders went mostly silent on the issue, as the House issued a report moving emancipation off the federal agenda. This lack of vision yielded no decisive action against slavery during the period of America's Founding, which resulted in slavery becoming the defining problem over the next seventy years of American history, with 600,000 Americans eventually losing their lives as the crisis escalated into the Civil War.

The Founding Fathers failed to turn their egalitarian dream of 1776 into reality, with dire consequences. Don't make their mistake. Turn your dream into reality as you:

SHARE IT — Everyone has a dream. Too many keep it to themselves. Find a trusted family member or friend and describe your dream. Don't hold back. Give all the glorious detail. Talking about it will bring you in deeper touch with it, and will motivate you to make it real.

SIGN IT — Write your dream down. Keep journaling it to see how it changes over time. Inspirations can be elusive so when they come to mind, capture them: take good notes in the moment. Recording your dreams will help to give them reality.

SERVE WITH IT — No one fulfills a dream alone. Look to help others as you pursue it. You'll discover how real your dream becomes as you work together with others to attain it. And you may even find ways to help finish the American Experiment that the Founding Fathers launched centuries ago.

SOAR WITH IT — You must face challenges and overcome them to reach your dream. Be clear on what kinds of hurdles you're up against. Figure out how to rise above them. Follow Mark Twain's advice:

Twenty years from now you will be more disappointed by the things you didn't do than by the ones you did do. So throw off the bowlines. Sail away from he safe harbor. Catch the trade winds in your sails. Explore. Dream.

Dream Your Impossible Dream   September 9th

I have a dream that one day this nation will rise up and live out the true meaning of its creed: "We hold these truths to be self-evident, that all men are created equal."
Martin Luther King, Jr.

In 1931 Pulitzer Prize-winning historian James Truslow Adams coined the term American Dream. In his book "The Epic of America" he defined it in these words.

. . . that dream of a land in which life should be better and richer and fuller for everyone, with opportunity for each according to ability or achievement. It is a difficult dream for the European upper classes to interpret adequately, and too many of us ourselves have grown weary and mistrustful of it. It is not a dream of motor cars and high wages merely, but a dream of social order in which each man and each woman shall be able to attain to the fullest stature of which they are innately capable, and be recognized by others for what they are, regardless of the fortuitous circumstances of birth or position. . . . a genuine individual search and striving for the abiding values of life . . . common man to rise to full stature.

Just over thirty years later, in his March on Washington speech, Martin Luther King Jr. proclaimed this American Dream anew, taking Adams' version of the vision to a fuller expression. The social harmony of which King dreamed seemed impossible at that time; he dreamed it anyway. Heeds his words and follow his example; dream your impossible dream as you:

DREAM FOR YOUR DESTINY — *Let us not wallow in the valley of despair. I say to you today my friends — so even though we face the difficulties of today and tomorrow, I still have a dream. It is a dream deeply rooted in the American dream.*

Defy expectations and dream big. George Bernard Shaw said it best:

You see things and say, Why? But I dream things that never were and say, Why not?

DREAM FOR YOUR FAMILY — *I have a dream that my four little children will one day live in a nation where they will not be judged by the color of their skin but by the content of their character.*

DREAM FOR JUSTICE — *I have a dream that one day even the state of Mississippi, a state sweltering with the heat of injustice, sweltering with the heat of oppression, will be transformed into an oasis of freedom and justice.*

DREAM FOR UNITY — *I have a dream that one day down in Alabama, with its vicious racists, with its governor having his lips dripping with the words of interposition and nullification — one day right   there in Alabama little black boys and black girls will be able to join hands with little white boys and white girls as sisters and brothers.*

DREAM FOR NOW — *I have a dream today.*

What is your American Dream? If it seems like an impossible dream, too far away from your present circumstances to ever achieve, you're on the right track. Just keep dreaming it. Possess it. Embrace it. Let it reside deep inside of you, rooted in your heart and soul. This dream should not be your dream vacation, aspirational romance, or desire to win the lottery. Your true dream is so much more than that — the thing you were born to do. It's that big picture for your life that speaks to your highest ideals, fuels your virtuous lifestyle, adds value to what you do everyday, leads to great success and connects you to the larger purpose of uplifting others. Keep saying these words: I have a dream today!

Empower Your Dreams   September 10th

The vision is too magnificent to be fully borne . . .
— Edward Everett

Before his political rise as a U.S. Congressman, Massachusetts governor, U.S. Senator and Secretary of State, Edward Everett was a Harvard professor and accomplished orator. On August 26, 1824, Everett spoke before the Harvard chapter of Phi Beta Kappa; his remarks were so well received that they helped to build momentum for his election to Congress a few months later. He addressed the crowd on the uniqueness of America's social and political character and its positive influence on the development of a national literature. At one point in the speech Everett depicted the American Experiment as a trailblazer in the history of the governments of the world.

Hitherto, in the main, the world has seen but two forms of political government — free governments in small states, and arbitrary governments in large ones. Though various shades of both   have appeared at different times in the world, yet, on the whole, the political ingenuity of man has never before devised the method of extending purely popular institutions beyond small districts, or of governing large states by any other means than military power. . . . Such is the state of things existing in this country, and for the first time in the world, and for which we are indebted to the peculiar nature of our government as a union of confederated republics.

Later in his remarks, Everett articulated the rising destiny that he envisaged for America.

Should our happy Union continue, this great continent, in no remote futurity, will be filled up   with the mightiest kindred people known in history; our language will acquire an extension which no other ever possessed; and the empire of the mind, with nothing to resist its sway, will attain an expansion of which, as yet, we can but partly conceive. . . . bringing to bear on every point the   concentrated energy of such a host; calling into competition so many minds; uniting into one great national feeling the hearts of so many freemen, all to be guided, moved, and swayed by the master spirits of the time!

The thunderous applause that Everett received testified to the great extent to which he had moved the audience with his visionary speech. This same dynamic should be at work in your visions: they should motivate you and others. For your vision to be motivational, it has to be powerful. To empower your dreams, they have to be:

PERSONAL — There needs to be a custom fit. If you're trying on someone else's dream for size, you're wasting time. Your vision has to be so much who you are that it's second nature. You dream as you breathe.

PICTURESQUE — It's a pretty picture in your mind that becomes more beautiful as you share it with others. Like Everett, use eloquent words to depict your dreams; in this way it will generate the power of motivation, not only for your own life but as an inspiration for others. As William A. Ward stated, your imagination is key, so use it!

If you can imagine it, you can achieve it. If you can dream it, you can become it.

PENETRATING — Your dreams live in your heart and soul. You should feel them deep within. If you're not feeling the inner strength of it, you need to spend more time meditating on your vision, getting to know it better. No matter what changes on the outside, your deep-rooted dream remains unquenchable, possessing an inner truth that cannot be denied.

PROVIDENTIAL — Your dream is bigger than what you can make happen today or tomorrow. So keep believing it no matter what happens today or tomorrow. Embrace it as your divine destiny. Let the handiwork of God lead you — and inspire you — as you fulfill your vision. As you invite Providence into your dreams, you will discover new power.

Make Your Dreams Come Alive   September 11th

Life is hard and astonishingly complicated . . . No one great reform will make it easy. Most of us who work — or want to work — will always have trouble or discontent. So we must learn to be calm, train all our faculties, and make others happy.
Sinclair Lewis

On December 12, 1930, in Stockholm, Sweden, Sinclair Lewis was honored with the Nobel Price for Literature — the first American to receive that distinction. Not everyone was pleased. Some in the American intelligentsia criticized the Nobel Committee for selecting Lewis, who was known for his satirical depictions of American life in his novels "Babbit," "Main Street" and "Elmer Gantry". Lewis used much of his acceptance to combat his critics. But, at the end, he dispatched negativity and affirmed his dream for America's literary future.

I have, for the future of American literature, every hope and every eager belief. We are coming out, I believe, of the stuffiness of safe, sane, and incredibly dull provincialism. There are young Americans today who are doing such passionate and authentic work that it makes me sick to see that I am a little too old to be one of them.

Criticism can vanquish a vision, darken your view of the future. Lewis didn't let his critics dash his dreams, and you shouldn't let negative voices or adverse circumstances snuff out yours. To keep your dream alive, keep these points in mind.

DOWNCAST — It's easy to feel downcast when your expectations are defeated by your realities. Don't let disappointment dampen your emotional confidence. Heed Mark Twain's advice to gain a victorious perspective.

We should be careful to get out of an experience only the wisdom that's in it — and stop there; lest we be like the cat that sits down on a hot stove-lid. She'll never sit down on another hot   stove-lid again — and that is well; but also she'll never sit down on a cold one anymore.

DETERMINATION — Has anyone ever tried to pour water on your dream? You're not alone. Old Testament leader Joseph had a dream of future greatness when he was just a teenager. His brothers resented his grand envisioning so much that they conspired against him.

> *Here comes that dreamer. . . . let's kill him.*
> — Genesis 37:19-20

They eventually sold him into slavery. Joseph didn't let these family schemes discourage him; he rose to leadership in fulfillment of his dreams. Author Kenneth Hildebrand captures the determination underlying Joseph's dream — and that of all true dreamers.

> *The poorest of all men isn't the one without a penny to his name. He's the fellow without a dream. . . . He is like a great ship made for the mighty ocean but trying to navigate in a millpond. He   has no far port to reach, no lifting horizon, no precious cargo to carry. His hours are absorbed in routine and petty tyrannies. Small wonder he gets dissatisfied, quarrelsome and fed up. One of life's greatest tragedies is a person with a ten-by-twelve capacity and a two-by-four soul.*

DISCOVERY — Use your imagination to dream big, discovering new things about your future. See your Promised Land up ahead, keep focused on it, and let the brightness of that dream shed light on your pathway as you journey there. Robert Orben described the following dichotomy to underscore the importance of imagining the direction you see your life taking in the future.

> *Always remember that there are only two kinds of people in this world — the realists and the dreamers. The realists know where they're going. They dreamers have already been there.*

Your imagination is a gift, a resource; make the most of it to discover your dreams and make them come alive.

Discern Your Gleams Of Light   September 12th

The saddest day has gleams of light, the darkest wave hath bright foam beneath it. There twinkles o'er the cloudiest night, some solitary star to cheer it.
Sarah Winnemucca

In May 1860 the Pyramid Lake War erupted in the Utah Territory (presently northwest Nevada.) The Northern Paiutes — allied with the Shoshone and the Bannock — defended their lands against armed settlers fortified by U.S. military forces. To escape the fighting, Paiute teenage Sarah Winnemucca fled to California. While living in San Francisco, Winnemucca and other family members performed "A Paiute Royal Family", a stage play that helped them make ends meet.

In 1865 Winnemucca's mother was a casualty of the incessant violence against the Paiute tribe. Working through the gloom of lost loved ones, Winnemucca maintained her positive view of the future, teaching imprisoned Native Americans, starting a school for Native American children, advocating for the rights of her people, and writing books. In 1884 her memoir, "Life Among the Paiutes: Their Wrongs and Claims", was published. The first autobiography written by a Native American woman, the book chronicled her experience of relations between Nativer and European Americans. Her literary work prospered, which led to a speaking tour; she traveled east to give lectures in Pennsylvania, New England, and Washington, D.C. Winnemucca succeeded because she maintained her optimism through all of her challenges, as she explained:

When I think of my past life, and the bitter trials I have endured, I can scarcely believe I live, and yet I do; and, with the help of Him who notes the sparrow's fall, I mean to fight for my down-trodden race while life lasts. . . . I have not contended for Democrat, Republican, Protestant or Baptist for an agent. I have worked for freedom, I have laboured to give my race a voice in the affairs of the nation.

Winnemucca discerned gleams of light during the most difficult times of her life, and her search led to the pathways to get her through tough times. Discerning for your own gleams of light means you:

CAST ASIDE PROBLEMS — Don't bury your head under the weight of your problems. Put them aside. Winnemucca could have been overwhelmed in sorrow and hatred as a result of the tragedies and injustices that plagued her and her community. Instead she intentionally put her past problems in the rear view mirror and looked for the light. Helen Keller also found her gleams of light:

Optimism is the faith that leads to achievement.
Nothing can be done without hope or confidence.

CREATE POSSIBILITIES — Beware of being overly concerned about rules and regulations. You can get lost in the weeds of fine print, footnotes and red tape. Bring greater understanding to your vision by keeping your focus on the big picture for your life and the goals that support it. Creating possibilities for your future will help you find the gleaming light.

COORDINATE PARTNERS — It's easy to get disappointed, distracted or depressed when you're pursuing your vision on your own. Like Winnemucca who joined her family in a stage play, bring together a cohort and have all articulate the shared vision in their own words. Getting everyone on the same page is the first step to gaining the support you need to build individual positivity and collective momentum.

CULTIVATE POTENTIAL — Growing to your potential happens when you see success not as a single destination but as an ongoing journey. Your daily victories — no matter how apparently small — make you a success right now. Celebrate today's triumph. You are cultivating tomorrow's conquest.

Be A Holistic Dreamer   **September 13th**

Those who cannot remember the past are condemned to repeat it.
George Santayana

The Roaring Twenties refers to the 1920s, the epoch of expanding economic prosperity in America marked by the widespread use of automobiles, aviation, telephones, radio, motion pictures, and electrical appliances. Culture exalted celebrities like movies stars and sports heroes, flocking for the first time to fill stadiums and cinemas.

At the beginning of this period, renowned scholar and philosopher George Santayana published his observations about America in "Materialism and Idealism in American Life". In one passage Santayana established a historical context for the uniqueness of the American character.

The discovery of the New World exercised a sort of selection among the inhabitants of Europe. All the colonists, except the Negroes, were voluntary exiles. The fortunate, the deeply rooted, and the lazy remained at home; the wilder instincts or dissatisfaction of others tempted them beyond the horizon. The American is accordingly the most adventurous, or the descendant of the most adventurous, of Europeans. It is in his blood to be socially a radical . . .

Santayana wrote about optimism as a core American value, with imagination at its root.

What has existed in the past, especially in the remote past, seems to him not only not authoritative but irrelevant, inferior, and outworn. He finds it rather a sorry waste of time to think about the past at all. . . . his enthusiasm for the future is profound; he can conceive of no more decisive way of recommending an opinion or a practice than to say that it is what everybody is coming to adopt. This expectation of what he approves, or approval of what he expects, makes up his optimism. . . . the American is imaginative; for where life is intense, imagination is intense also. Were he not imaginative he would not live so much in the future.

As Santayana explained, having a vision for your life dynamically connects you to your future; but to get there, your dream must be holistic, connected to the other aspects of who you are. You must dream, think and do. Live your dreams holistically by becoming a:

DREAMER — Santayana emphasized imagination, rightly so; it is one of the greatest human attributes. Use it to shape your vision. Imagine the greatest things possible for your life and don't let your dreams be limited by what you perceive as your obstacles and weaknesses. Look inside yourself and arouse your natural gifts to awaken the Dreamer within. Albert Einstein affirmed this truth:

Imagination is more important than knowledge.

THINKER — It's not enough just to dream, to imagine the brightness of your future. You must think through your issues and options, clarifying your possibilities and perspectives. Your choices are the key; you have so many to make each and every day. Be a strategic thinker: align your choices with your values. Don't get stuck in the past but reflect on your experiences deeply enough to draw lessons from them. This approach will prepare you to make good decisions. Your victory lies in your strategy, so be wise. Reason through your deliberations and get sound advice, then you will develop the acumen to move forward in the fulfillment of your dreams.

DOER — Always be ready to cast new vision, but also be ready to put in the work to make it come true. Taking it easy has never been part of the formula of excellence. Work as hard as you think; think as hard as you work. And remember the Biblical mandate.

Faith without works is dead.
— James 2:20

Chart A New Course   September 14th

Machines ingeniously constructed will give us immense assistance . . . combinations of machines with fire and water have already accomplished much more than was formerly expected from them by the most visionary enthusiast on the subject . . .
Tench Coxe

When America attained its independence in the eighteenth century, its economy was primarily based on agriculture. Few anticipated the rise of American manufacturing, which would expand in the nineteenth century and become economically dominant in the twentieth.

One of the visionaries was Philadelphia merchant Tench Coxe. Coxe had served as one of the Pennsylvania delegates to the 1788 Continental Congress and the following year he was appointed Assistant Secretary to the first Secretary of the Treasury Alexander Hamilton. Coxe established his reputation as a leading proponent of industrialization in a speech at the first meeting of the Pennsylvania Society for the Encouragement of Manufactures and Useful Arts on August 9, 1787. He discussed the significance of the new machine technology and its value to American manufacturers. Coxe charted a new course for America, steering the ship of commerce in a direction that would eventually make the United States the greatest economy the world has ever known.

What about you? Where are you on the road map of success? Are you making daily progress towards your desired destinations? Or do you need to chart new course, make a bold move, reach for a higher destiny? Heed Coxe's words; they represent principles that will help you as you move forward to attain your dreams. Chart a new course of success for your own life by:

WATER — *Factories which can be carried on by watermills . . . supply the force of hands to a great extent without taking our people from agriculture.*

Realize you're already on the journey of your life, each day moving along in some direction, either towards or away from your goals. Don't allow yourself to be swept along by the rising tides of adverse circumstances or negative relationships. Determine to find and flow in streams that carry you forward. And don't be afraid of the deep waters. A big catch awaits.

FIRE — *By fire we conduct our breweries, distilleries, salt and potash works, sugar houses, potteries, casting and steel furnaces, works for animal and vegetable oils and refining drugs.*

Discover that thing you're most passionate about. Study it, live with it, let it burn within you, driving you to attain success. If you do what you love to do, you will be motivated to overcome whatever lies between you and your goals. You will not succumb to the whims of fortune. You will not let others dictate where you'll end up. You will determine your own direction. When you feel the fire of your commitment, make sure to keep it burning.

WIND — *By wind . . . machines we can make pig and bar iron, nail rods, tire, sheet-iron, gunpowder, printing and hanging paper; and they assist us in finishing scythes, sickles, and woolen cloths . . . How numerous and important then do the benefits appear which may be expected from this salutary design! . . . it will lead us once more into the paths of public virtue by restoring frugality and industry, those potent antidotes to the vices of mankind . . .*

Jesus said:

The wind blows where it wishes, and you hear the sound of it, but you cannot tell where it comes from and where it goes. So is everyone who is born of the Spirit
John 3:8

Spiritual guidance is key in charting a new course. Seek God. Incline your ear heavenward. If you take your spirituality seriously, you will cultivate your relationship with the Creator and be able to discern that Supernatural hand, intervening in your circumstances, pointing the way to your divinely charted course.

Renew Your Vision   **September 15th**

Your Vision Affirmation — I will see the big picture for my life, as glorious as the sky on a cloudless day, taking up a positive view of my future—motivated to overcome every obstacle in my way and soar beyond the storms on the wings of my dreams.
Joseph Holland

A downward path after getting seriously injured in an accident at his job site landed Arthur at Harkhomes. His despondency and frustration from his protracted recovery led to heavy drinking, which unsettled his wife; she moved out with their two children. Arthur ended up depressed, stopped working altogether, started drinking all day long, and got evicted from his apartment for not paying rent.

Listless and sullen, Arthur would be late for meals at Harkhomes, and sometimes he didn't eat at all. He would agree to see the physical therapist, then miss his appointment. He would be on his way to an A.A. meeting but would then sit outside the session instead of participating.

I kept asking him, "What is the big vision for your life?"

It took him months to answer the question, but he finally confessed: "I want my family back together in our own home."

Since Arthur had not seen his wife and two daughters since the breakup of the marriage,

I contacted his wife, and she gladly came with the girls. Arthur was totally surprised. At first he was embarrassed and angry that his family saw him in his current plight. But these negative feelings quickly passed, and the joy of being with his family again altered his mood. He smiled and joked and laughed for the first time since coming to Harkhomes.

Reconnecting him with his family renewed Arthur's vision. A recent photo of his wife and kids — a gift during their visit — rekindled his motivation; he taped to the wall by his cot as an ever-present reminder. Arthur's worked first on getting sober, then his job search resulted in an opportunity as a security guard, at which he prospered. When his company won a big new contract, he became a supervisor and, working as much overtime as possible, he ended up making nearly as much money as he had on the construction job. Arthur moved out of Harkhomes into his own room. He visited his family on his days off, provided support for his children, saved as much as possible, until he bought the home that reunited the family.

Arthur renewed his vision; and you can renew your vision if you:

REVIEW IT — Break down your big vision into the smaller pieces of that dream. Arthur first got sober, then a job, an apartment, a house. Your little wins will lead to your great victories.. Just get started; once you launch, you will be like a train with the momentum carrying towards your goal. The prophetic words of the Old Testament leader Zechariah are on point:

Do not despise these small beginnings . . .
Zechariah 4:10

REKINDLE IT — Light the fire of motivation under your life through the kindle of your dreams. Keep the flames ever burning by thing about your vision every day. Use your spiritual eyes — the faith in your heart to keep your head lifted up beyond the vicissitudes that will surely come.

REITERATE IT — Memorize your vision and keep saying to yourself and others. Old Testament leader Joseph practiced this success principle; his dream became deep-rooted within him.

Then he (Joseph) had another dream, and he told it to his brothers. "Listen," he said, "I had another dream, and this time the sun and moon and eleven stars were bowing down to me."
Genesis 37:9

RELAUNCH IT — Think about your legacy. Live today with tomorrow in mind. Arthur found motivation to put his life together back together when his plans looked to his children instead of just himself. Reflect on those things that you want to last beyond your lifetime. Keep launching your dream by passing it on to others.

Realize Your Dreams   September 16th

There is nothing which can better deserve your patronage, than the promotion of science and literature. Knowledge is in every country the surest basis of public happiness.
George Washington

On July 9, 1799, George Washington signed his last will and testament. In it he directed that funds be used for the fulfillment of one of his dreams for America — the establishment of a national university.

Just over thirty years later, in October 1830, several political and civic leaders, including former Treasury Secretary Albert Gallatin and educators George Ticknor, Joseph Cogswell and George Bancroft, met in New York City to discuss whether a new and improved university was needed to address problems in American higher education. Rising from their deliberations was New York University, which was founded the following year. Though not the national university that Washington envisaged, NYU was born to fulfill a vision for a better university, one with a higher quality library, broader curriculum and greater freedom of research.

Historian and diplomat George Bancroft issued a statement about the October 1830 meeting, outlining the reasons why America needed an urban academic community:

> *Finally, the question recurs whether the country in its present condition demands a university . . . the answer must be found in the numbers of our people, already surpassing that of any Protestant kingdom or state in the world, excepting England; in the character of our government, which can never interfere with the free inquiry and the pursuit of truth; in the relative age of our population, which in its rapid increase furnishes a larger proportion of persons to be educated than is found in older countries; in the basis of our social system, which regards intelligence as a conservative not less than as a productive principle in the body politic; in the forming character of all our institutions, which are as yet hardly fixed, but remain yet to receive the impress which they are to bear forever; in the period of our history, when the old states are in truth rapidly becoming the mothers of new ones; in the condition of our strength, since the weakness of today becomes tomorrow the confidence and admiration of the world; and, lastly, in the character of our population, proverbially ambitious and inquisitive, where elementary education is already universally diffused, and where, under the auspices of our political equality, the public walks of honor and emulation are crowded with throngs from every class of society.*

It's great to dream, but — like Bancroft and his colleagues — you have to bring your dreams out of your soul and into the real world. Realize your own dreams by:

COLLECTING THE DATA — The NYU Founders did their research across a range of issues to steep their dream in reality, so they knew what to do. Do your homework to move forward realistically. Spend more time studying and less time on social media. Gain knowledge and success will follow.

CRAFTING THE RATIONALE — Bancroft's statement clarifies advantages and objectives. You need to be clear on your purposes, so you can take your dream out of the sky and put it on the road. Write down your vision to give it emphasis, as the Old Testament prophet Habakkuk proclaimed:

Write down the revelation and make it plain
on tablets so that a herald may run with it.
Habukkuk 2:2

CULTIVATING OTHER DREAMS — The NYU
visionaries brought together a strong cohort, which led to their
success. Getting others on board with you, believing as you do and
sharing your commitment, will make your dream real. A team will
also be helpful in executing the agenda.

COMING TO A DECISION — You may not have
everything in place, but if you truly believe in your dream, move
forward with it anyway. As you begin to take concrete steps, it will
become more real — or not. At the very least you'll know whether
to pour yourself fully into your dream and to put it back on the
shelf for a future time. The most important thing is for you to
accept this truth: every day is a divine gift for you to take a step
forward towards your dreams. Keep in mind Abraham Lincoln's
precept.

The best thing about the future is that it comes only one day at a time.

Read The Trends <u>And</u> Act OnThem!   **September 17th**

The petition of a great number of blacks detained in a state of slavery in
the bowels of a free, Christian country shows that your petitioners apprehend
that they have in common with all other men a natural and unalienable right to that
freedom which the Great Parent of the universe has bestowed equally on all mankind.
African Americans of Massachusetts

At the time of the Declaration of Independence in 1776, there
were 700,000 Africans slaves in the Thirteen Colonies. But these slaves
perceived in the profound truth of the patriot's proclamation — We hold
these truths to be self-evident, that all men are created equal — that times
were changing. Some of them in the Massachusetts colony read this trend
and acted on it. They presented a petition to the Massachusetts House of
Representatives on January 13, 1777, calling for the abolition of slavery.

The petition elaborated the contradiction of the colonists waging a
war under the banner of equality and liberty while holding people in
bondage; it commenced with a summary of the slaves' deplorable
plight. . . .

444

But they were unjustly dragged by the hand of cruel power from their dearest friends and some of them even torn from the embraces of their tender parents, from a populous, pleasant and plentiful country . . . brought here either to be sold like beasts of burden and, like them, condemned to slavery for life.

. . . and concluded by appealing to the recently declared high ideals of the new nation.

They therefore humbly beseech Your Honors to . . . cause an act of legislation to be passed whereby they may be restored to the enjoyments of that which is the natural   right of all men, and the their children, who were born in this land of liberty, may not be held as slaves after they arrive at the age of twenty-one years. So may the inhabitants of this state, no longer chargeable with the inconsistency of acting themselves the part which they condemn and oppose in others, be prospered in their present glorious struggle for liberty and have those blessings for themselves.

Due in no small part to this petition and related initiatives, the cultural and political momentum in Massachusetts rose against the institution of slavery. Though its first constitution in 1780 kept slavery legal in the Commonwealth, court cases over the next several years ruled slavery unconstitutional, making Massachusetts the first state to effectively abolish slavery.

As the slaves did almost 250 years ago, you should read the trends of today and act on them. To do so, you need to tune in to your:

TROUBLES — Every era has its own peculiar set of problems. For example, though slavery is long gone, its legacies persist, among other social ills of these times. Pay attention to the news but also gather your info on the ground to get the best read on things. Take notes!

TREASURES — Resources to resolve problems aren't usually easy to find, so you have to be discerning to find solutions. Keep your eyes open for human as well as financial capital. Seize every opportunity to enhance your wealth. And when you get it, plan to pass it, as the Old Testament advises:

A good man leaves an inheritance to his children's children.
Proverbs 13:22

TEMPERAMENT — Don't let a negative mindset blind you to possibilities for progress. Make sure you're seeing the jar

half full so you can discover the breakthroughs. This juxtaposition
from Winston Churchill brings clarity to this principle.

A pessimist sees the difficulty in every opportunity;
An optimist sees the opportunity in every difficulty.

TACTICS — Be an activist, whether in the conference
room, legislative corridor, or street corner. It's not enough to know
something is wrong. Come up with a strategic plan and take action
to right that wrong!

Pursue Your Destiny   **September 18th**

And that claim is by the right of our manifest destiny to overspread and to possess
the whole of the continent which Providence has given us for the development of
the great experiment of liberty and federated self-government entrusted to us.
John O'Sullivan

In July 1845 "United States Magazine" editor John O'Sullivan
coined the term "manifest destiny" in an editorial about the annexation of
Texas. O'Sullivan's "manifest destiny" was his belief that God had blessed
America with a great mission to spread "the great experiment of liberty"
throughout North America and beyond. Though the idea behind his catch
phrase was not new — the Founders had referred to special calling of the
American Experiment — his wording caught on and endured, defining the
spirit of continental expansionism and global influence.

Just as O'Sullivan encouraged Americans to pursue their special
destiny, it's important for you to pursue your own special destiny; you can
do so by asking yourself some questions:

WHAT ARE MY DREAMS FOR MYSELF?

In a speech sixty-five years later, Theodore Roosevelt affirmed the
theme of destiny, declaring . . .

. . . *the history of America is now the central feature of the history*
of the world; for the world   has set its face hopefully toward our
democracy . . . each one of you carries on your shoulders not only the burden
of doing well for the sake of your own country, but the burden of doing well
and seeing that the nation does well for the sake of mankind.

Your destiny rises from your dreams. If you've lost hope for the future because of the casualties you've suffered, retreat: find a way to take a break from the battlefields of your life. Go to a place of solitude and spend some time alone with the big picture for your life. Dream in ways that inspire you to confront your daily challenges and work through them. Multi-task: dream as hard as you work and work as hard as you dream.

WHAT ARE MY DREAMS FOR MY COUNTRY?

On January 20, 1961, in his Inaugural Address, President John F. Kennedy expressed manifest destiny in this way:

> *Let every nation know that we shall pay any price, bear any burden, meet any hardship . . . to assure the survival and the success of liberty . . . And so, my fellow Americans — ask not what your country can do for you — ask what you can do for your country. . . . My fellow citizens of the world — ask not what America will do for you but what together we can do for the freedom of man. . . . With a good conscience our only sure reward, with history the final judge of our deeds, let us go forth to lead the land we love, asking His blessing and His help, but knowing that here on earth God's   w o r k must truly be our own.*

Focusing on your own dreams is necessary but not sufficient. Are you dreaming big enough? What do you need to imagine about your future to bring destiny to your dreams? Asking what you can do for your country is a great way to take your vision to the next level by connecting it to larger purposes. You don't have to run for President to make a difference. Just be willing to run up the mountainside of community service.

WHAT ARE MY DREAMS FOR THE WORLD?

Jesus said:

> *You are the light of the world. A city that is set on a hill cannot be hidden.*
> Matthew 5:14

Just like Jesus' dreams, yours can go global, too and really make a difference. Start small for today. Think huge for tomorrow.

Cast Vision For Others   September 19th

The state of property in America renders it necessary for our citizens to employ themselves in different occupations for the advancement of their fortunes. This cannot be done without the assistance of the female members of the community . . .
Benjamin Rush

    Women in colonial America possessed unequal social status and negligible political voice, with such notable exceptions as Abigail Adams and Mercy Otis Warren, the Anglo-American wives of prominent patriotic statesmen. Since the American Revolution had been waged based on egalitarian principles, these ideals sowed the seeds of women's rights after the war as the new nation emerged. Though the push for such rights didn't blossom until the suffrage movement of antebellum America, a handful of Revolutionary era male and female leaders called for change, starting with improvements to female education.

    Physician, teacher and statesman Benjamin Rush cast a new vision for female education, proposing a new model of instruction for elite women. He also helped to start the Young Ladies' Academy of Philadelphia, the first chartered women's institution of higher education in Philadelphia. In a speech there on July 28, 1787, which was later published as "Thoughts upon Female Education", Rush laid out his paradigm for educating young women. He began with a contextual remark, distinguishing his approach from the British experience.

    . . . the education of your ladies in this country should be conducted upon principles very different from what it is in Great Britain, and in some respects different from what it was when we were a part of a monarchical empire.

    Towards the conclusion of his address, he highlighted the moral benefit of his educational program for women.

    A philosopher once said, "let me make all the ballads of a country and I care not who makes its laws." He might with more propriety have said, let the ladies of a country be educated properly, and they will not only make and administer its laws, but form its manners and character. It would require a lively imagination to describe, or even to comprehend, the happiness of a country where knowledge and virtue were generally diffused among the female sex.

    Rush was one of the early voices on this significant issue, casting a new vision of women's role in American society, helping to seed a movement that would begin to flourish in the next century. You should also cast vision for others, especially for those individuals without a big dream for their own lives. To do so, embrace these principles.

CHARACTER — To cast vision for others, you have to be a visionary yourself. Check the character of your own dream before you start encouraging other dreamers. If your vision is bright, it will shed light for others. Carl Sandburg was right; it's the starting point.

Nothing happens unless first a dream.

COMMUNION — When you cast a big dream for others, you're communing with them through encouragement, speaking to their potential, raising a higher standard, giving them something good to go after. So help them to stretch for their dream. They will be affirmed and reach higher when someone whom they respect tells them to go for it.

COMMUNITY — Vision-casting for someone you know is a good thing. Also consider casting vision for community — for those you don't know, especially those who don't have the social status or political access to make things happen for themselves. Rush broke with the tradition of his times to raise his voice for women's rights. What group of people suffering under disadvantage or injustice can you speak for? Your advocacy could open doors of opportunity for them . . . or change the course of history.

Illuminate Your Vision   **September 20th**

I am convinced that the world is not a mere bog in which men and women trample themselves and die. Something magnificent is taking place here amidst the cruelties and tragedies, and the supreme challenge to intelligence is that of making the noblest and best in our curious heritage prevail.
Charles Beard

In 1913 Columbia University professor Charles Beard published the controversial historiography "Economic Interpretation of the Constitution". In the book Beard presented a novel perspective on America's founding, arguing that the Founding Fathers were motivated more by economic interests than philosophical views. The work's countless detractors notwithstanding, it gave Beard a national reputation; he used the notoriety and influence to propel his career as an independent scholar in history as well as in political science, which included becoming one of the founders of the New School for Social Research and serving as its first director.

Beard was once asked if he could summarize the lessons of history in a short book. He responded that he could achieve the task even more succinctly — in four sentences:

1. Whom the gods would destroy, they first make mad with power.

2. The mills of God grind slowly, but they grind exceeding small.

3. The bee fertilizes the flower it robs.

4. When it is dark enough, you can see the stars.

Beard's fourth lesson from history holds the most meaning for the individual life: it points to the power of your vision. No matter how gloomy your circumstances, you can still see through those clouds to your brighter days. In fact, the darker it gets, the stronger your inner light needs to shine. The following four lessons will help you illuminate your vision, making it the lighthouse for your present and the lodestar for your future.

CHANGE PRESUPPOSITIONS — Your first lesson: let go of the assumptions from your past that linger to burden your present and block your future. If all you've been exposed to is gloom and doom, you'll be inclined to think the worst will keep happening. Work on changing your way of thinking. Just because it's been that way in your past doesn't mean it has to stay that way in your future. Renewing your thinking will help illuminate your vision.

CHANGE POSITION — Your second lesson: get up and out! Let's be clear: changing your geography will not necessarily change your situation. But sometimes it does help to make a physical move. Getting out of your spatial rut may start shifting things around in your soul enough to begin to lift you out of your emotional rut. If you're feeling stuck, make a move. Something as simple as getting out of your house and going on a walk could bring you the fresh air of momentum to change your mood and propel you towards your breakthrough.

CUSHION PERILS — Your third lesson: declare your dreams. Adversities are not a maybe; they are a definite. The key is how you'll respond to them. The danger is that you'll let the trials of life trip you up and keep you down. Recite your vision to yourself. Share it with others. Describing in words — on paper and in speech — what you see for yourself in the future will not only make the big picture clearer; it will also help you battle and defeat inner doubts and active naysayers.

CATCH POWER — Your fourth lesson: vision fuels motivation. The more you think of the big picture for your future, the more potential energy you will generate for today's agenda. The words of Howard Thurman are relevant here.

> *Don't ask yourself what the world needs;*
> *ask yourself what makes you come alive.*
> *And then go and do that. Because what*
> *the world needs is people who have come alive.*

Reach For New Ideas   September 21st

> *Always stand on principle even if you stand alone.*
> John Adams

As a rising advocate for the patriot cause, John Adams was selected as a Massachusetts delegate to the First Continental Congress, which met in Philadelphia in September 1774. By the time of the Second Continental Congress in May 1775, Adams had lost all his loyalist leanings and was the leader of the New England contingent, stating, ". . . Powder and Artillery are the most efficacious, sure, and infallibly conciliatory measures we can adopt." To promote colonial unity, he nominated George Washington of Virginia as commander-in-chief of the army, even though the troops were assembled around Boston in the spring of 1775.

As the conflict with Britain intensified, Adams understood that a military conflict for independence entailed the formation of a new government. When prominent scholar and fellow Continental Congress delegate George Wythe requested Adams thoughts on the transition of the colonies to self-government, Adams responded with a letter in January 1776, sharing his vision for the new America. He reasoned that the government should be structured on the foundation of virtue.

> *All sober inquirers after truth, ancient and modern, pagan and Christian, have declared that the happiness of man, as well as his dignity, consists in virtue. . . . If there is a form of government, then, whose principle and foundation is virtue, will not every sober man acknowledge it better calculated to promote the general happiness than any other form?*

Throughout the letter to Wythe, Adam reached for the new idea of American government. As you review his points — articulated in his own words — consider the principles they project; use them as a ladder to reach for your own new ideas.

EXPLORE NEW TERRITORY — *The foundation of every government is some principle or passion in the minds of the people. The noblest principles and most generous affections in our nature, then, have the fairest chance to support the noblest and most generous models of government.*

Adams explored new territory, digging into the correlation between individual values and sound government. Think about old things in new ways. Challenge your mind to assess issues that it hasn't considered before. Good ideas don't just show up on your doorstep. You have to go out and find them. Your search starts in your soul. Dig deep! As Oliver Wendell Holmes asserted, you will never be quite the same.

Man's mind, once stretched by a new idea, never regains its original dimensions.

EXERCISE YOUR STRENGTH — *These colonies under such forms of government, and in such a union, would be unconquerable by all the monarchies of Europe.*

Adams' search for the new American idea proved to be a mighty initiative, bearing great fruit: the Declaration of Independence; the United States Constitution; the Revolutionary War victory; the establishment of the American Experiment, an innovative form of government that has stood the test of time. Reaching for new ideas worked wonders for Adams and the nation he helped to start. It can work wonders for you, too.

EXALT YOUR HOPE — *How few of the human race have ever enjoyed an opportunity of making an election of government . . . for themselves or their children! . . . I hope you will avail yourself and your country of that extensive learning and indefatigable industry which you possess to assist her in the formation of the happiest governments and the best character of a great people.*

Centuries later, another American political leader, New York governor and presidential candidate Alfred E. Smith, captured Adams' theme:

The American people never carry an umbrella.
They prepare to walk in eternal sunshine.

Let the hope of your dawning success eternally rise.

Craft a Compelling Vision   **September 22nd**

Vote yourself a farm!
— George Henry Evans

In the presidential campaign of 1860, one of the key planks of Abraham Lincoln's policy platform was homesteading. A homestead comprised an area of public land, approximately 160 acres, in the western United States, conditionally granted to a citizen committed to settle and farm the land. The slogan projecting this position — *VOTE YOURSELF A FARM!* — and the support it garnered proved to be a significant factor in Lincoln winning the White House.

Lincoln didn't come up with the pitch. To gain support for homesteading, editor and social reformer George Henry Evans coined the phrase in a 1846 newspaper article, in which he asserted:

> *Remember Poor Richard's saying: "Now I have a sheep and a cow, everyone bids me 'a good morrow.'" If a man have a house and a home of his own, though it be a thousand miles off, he is   well received in other people's houses; while the homeless wretch is turned away. The bare right to a farm, though you should never go near it, would save you from many an insult.*

As Evans and others published editorials and circulated handbills throughout the antebellum period, the compelling vision captured by — "Vote Yourself A Farm" — turned into a political movement. From 1844 to 1862, 55,000 Americans signed petitions that were sent to Congress, which called for free public lands for homesteaders. Influential figures like Horace Greeley and organizations like the Free Soil Party joined Evans in pushing for passage of homestead legislation. With the secession of the Southern states in 1861 — steadfast opponents of homesteading — the last major political obstacle dissipated.

On May 20, 1862, President Abraham Lincoln signed the Homesteading Act into law, which led to more than 270 million acres of public land — almost 10% of the total area of the United States — being granted free to 1.6 million homesteaders after five years of residence and improvements to the land. Women were eligible as were African Americans with the passage of a subsequent legislation in 1866 that explicitly included black Americans, resulting in one fourth of all Southern black farmers owning their farms by 1900.

The compelling vision crafted by George Henry Evans — even though he'd died before its fulfillment in the Homestead Act — fostered significant social change. This phenomenon relates to you on a personal level. Craft a compelling vision for your own life by incorporating:

CLARITY OF VISION — No message could be clearer than "Vote Yourself A Farm". Describe your vision, succinctly and powerfully, in language that you can embrace and communicate. Come up with your own winning slogan. Memorize it, recite it, proclaim it. Let it represent your new course, as Oliver Wendell Holmes declared:

The great thing in this world is not so much where we are but in what direction we are moving.

CHARACTER OF VISION — Homesteaders had deep roots, running back over a half-century to the agrarian dreams of the Jeffersonian Democrats. Connect the dots of dream to events of the past, activities of the present and prospects for the future. Place your vision into a context that will render it strong, that will resonate it far and wide.

CRUSADE OF VISION — Make your vision compelling enough to get others involved and excited. Visions become movements when leaders gain followers. Let the momentum of your dream rise like a wave, taking you and others to places where you can make a difference. Move it forward for personal as well as community impact.

COMMITMENT TO VISION — Unfortunately, George Henry Evans never witnessed the realization of his vision, yet his legacy rose through it, with some heralding him the "Father of the Homestead Act". Stay committed to your vision. Don't give up on it through the disappointments and setbacks. Your resolve will benefit you and could benefit countless generations.

Encourage Others To Dream   September 23rd

In the United States of America, the science of liberty is universally understood, felt and practiced as much by the simple as the wise, the weak as the strong. Their deep-rooted and inveterate habit of thinking is that all mean are equal in their rights . . .
                                   Joel Barlow

A few weeks after the 1787 Constitutional Convention opened in Philadelphia, lawyer and poet Joel Barlow delivered the Fourth of July address at the Society of Cincinnati in Hartford, Connecticut. In his speech Barlow expressed his belief that the American Revolution had established a model civilization that would be a light of humanity to the world. Barlow also encouraged his fellow citizens to dream of constituting an effective government that would be the pathway of nations.

> *The first great object is to convince the people of the importance of their present situation; for the majority of a great people, on a subject which they understand, will never act wrong. If ever there was a time in any age or nation when the fate of millions depended on the voice of one, it is the present period in these states. Every free citizen of the American empire ought now to consider himself as the legislator of half mankind.*

He told the audience to keep dreaming to touch others.

> *When he views the amazing extent of territory, settled and to be settled under the operation of his laws; when, like a wise politician, he contemplates the population of future ages, the changes to be wrought by the possible progress of arts in agriculture, commerce, and manufactures, the increasing connection and intercourse of nations, and the effect of one rational political system upon the general happiness of mankind — his mind, dilated with the great idea, will realize a liberality of feeling which leads to a rectitude of conduct. He will see that the system to be established by his suffrage is calculated for the great benevolent purposes of extending peace, happiness and progressive improvement to a large proportion of his fellow creatures.*

Barlow used his Independence Day address to share his dream of American greatness, seeking to motivate his fellow Americans to build on the achievement of the American Revolution to form a strong government. Follow his example. Encourage others to dream as you:

RE-IMAGINE — Barlow used specific imagery — "amazing extent of territory . . . general happiness of mankind . . . great benevolent purposes of extending peace" — to inspire his audience. Choose your words wisely: you can extinguish a person's dream with the wrong words; you can ignite it with the right ones. Use your imaginative powers to transform the old approach and raise a new vista. Such re-imagining will help people who are having trouble getting a hold of their future purpose; they will be motivated to wipe off their inner magnifying glass and delve for their divine destiny. The insight of Peter Drucker is germane to this point.

The best way to predict the future is to create it.

RE-ALIGN — Help people connect the dots between their virtues and their vision. Gain their trust so they will share their dream with you. Then help guide their thinking to enhance what they're doing today with what they're dreaming for tomorrow. Such realignment will encourage them to live out their dreams day by day.

RESTORE — There will always be faced with critics and cynics casting doubt on your dreams. In Barlow's day there were those who opposed his optimism, insisting that the American Experiment would soon fizzle out. No one knows what the future holds, so extend the benefit of the doubt. Let your fellow-visionaries know that their dreams are half-full glasses. Help them to restore the brightness of their dreams by chasing the clouds of doubts and fears away. Bring a sunny outlook to overshadow the pervasiveness of pessimism.

See Beyond Your Clouds   September 24th

The existing state of things, as well as the "prospect before us," is most happy for the American people.
Hezekiah Niles

In 1815 the United States faced many challenges: rebuilding after the recently ended war with Great Britain; effectively addressing the intractable crisis of slavery; handling rising national debt and other finances in the aftermath of the failure to renew Bank of the U.S.; managing the rush of settlers to the frontier and their widespread conflicts with Native Americans.

In the midst of such vexing problems, there were some who proclaimed this post-War of 1812/pre-Panic of 1819 period as the "era of good feeling". The leading spokesman of such rosy American views was Hezekiah Niles, the publisher of the Baltimore-based the Weekly Register, a national news magazine that was one of the most widely circulated magazines in the United States of that epoch. "The Prospect Before Us"— his editorial of September 2, 1815 — exemplified Niles' dramatic dreaming for America.

The republic, reposing on the laurels of a glorious war, gathers the rich harvest of an honorable peace. Everywhere the sound of the axe is heard, opening the forest to the sun . . . Our cities grow and towns rise up as by magic; commerce expands her proud sails in safety, and the striped bunting floats with majesty over every sea. The busy hum of 10,000 wheels fills our seaports . . . A high and honorable feeling generally prevails, and the people begin to assume, more and more, a national character; and to look at home for the only means, under divine goodness, of preserving their religion and liberty, with all the blessings that flow from their unrestricted enjoyment. The bulwark of these is in the sanctity of their principles, and the virtue and valor of these who profess to love them, and need no guarantee from the bloodstained and profligate princes and powers of Europe. Morality and good order ever prevail . . . for the Great Architect of the universe is worshiped on the altar of men's hearts, in the way that each believes most acceptable to Him . . .

Niles didn't get bogged down in the details. He poetically projected a big picture for his readers to embrace; it was a portrait of a nation on the road to high destiny. Accusations of hyperbole and myopia were beside the point. It was Niles' mission to reach beyond the nitty gritty and embrace a glorious perspective. If you're at a point in your life where the clouds of your challenges are blocking out the sunshine of your dreams, take Niles' approach. See beyond your clouds as you:

PREEN YOUR DREAMS — Follow Niles' example here. Use dramatic words to paint a pretty picture of your dreams. Write a poem about them . . . or draw prophetic art . . . sing a song about your vision; make them sound beautiful and memorable. Do your best to make your big dream come to life in some way. It's like creating the sun to break through your cloudy days. See yourself as part of the "some of us" in this quote from Oscar Wilde.

We are all in the gutter but some of us are looking at the stars.

PUT FUEL IN YOUR TANK — Spend as much time as possible doing things and going places that support your dreams. Create a reinforcing routine; visit as much as you can, even if it's just someplace known only to you and God. You will find inspiration there, and it will keep your vision active and alive.

PULL AWAY FROM DOUBTERS — Avoid those who would cast doubt on your dreams. When you're ready, confront them with confidence. Until then, don't let anyone rain on your parade. Replace the negative voices in your life with positive ones.

PULL TOGETHER YOUR DREAM TEAM — Find some folks who believe and dream as you do and hang out. Build around you a team of dreamers, especially those who are dreaming bigger than you. Lean on them for strength. You'll never be able to hold on to your dream if you're holding on alone.

Push Your Boundaries   September 25th

. . . the harder the conflict, the greater the triumph . . .
George Washington

1780 had been a challenging year for the colonial war effort against the British. As the war in the north trudged on inconclusively, the Continental Army suffered its worst defeat of the war at Charleston, South Carolina. After a 45 day siege at the hands of Cornwallis'14,000 British troops, the colonial forces surrendered on May 12th, resulting in the capture of four American ships and 5,400 patriot soldiers.

Despite these devastating losses the Continental Congress didn't lose sight of the big picture for the new nation, setting new boundaries for America. On October 10, 1780, the patriot leaders passed a landmark resolution that sought to clarify the western borders to their territories. In the midst of adversity they were optimistic enough to push their boundaries. Push your own boundaries by paying attention to their words and the principles they represent.

FORMULATION — *Resolved, that the unappropriated lands that may be ceded or relinquished to the United States by any particular states, pursuant to the recommendation of Congress on the 6th day of September last, shall be disposed of for the common benefit of the United States and be settled and formed into distinct republican states which shall become members of the federal Union, and shall have the same rights of sovereignty, freedom, and independence as the other states.*

It is important in life to respect tradition, follow rules, and set boundaries. Without these practices we would end up living in chaos. This truth holds for parents raising children in an orderly home as well as for the effective operation of larger organizations. But there comes a time to push those boundaries. The Founding Fathers established new policies for the westward expansion, so the nation could grow in orderly ways. Though far from perfect, this visionary approach paved the way for the fifty states of a relatively peaceful and prosperous nation centuries later. This principle is true for you. There comes a time to push your boundaries, setting new goals and bigger expectations for your life. Know your timing. When it's right, formulate a plan to move forward towards your new frontiers.

FASTIDIOUSNESS — *That each state which shall be so formed shall contain a suitable extent of territory, not less than 100 nor more than 150 miles square, or as near thereto as circumstances will admit.*

Pay close attention to details. Rules and traditions are good and necessary. Don't be reckless and throw out the baby with the bathwater. As you push forward, avoid trespassing into areas that belong to others. You will have less hassle and gain more ground if you stay in your lane.

FIGHT — *That the necessary and reasonable expenses which any particular state shall have incurred since the commencement of the present war, in subduing any of the British posts or in maintaining forts or garrisons within and for the defense, or in acquiring any part of the territory that my be ceded or relinquished to the United States, shall be reimbursed.*

Life is a fight for territory. Your progress may sometimes mean changing the rules, resisting the establishment and breaking with tradition. Taking the road less traveled will require you to see differently, looking to a horizon that your imagination hasn't previously touched. Turn on that light! No matter how strong the adversary appears, keep battling your way up . . . over . . . across . . . forward.

FUTURE — *That the said lands shall be granted and settled at such times and under such regulations as shall hereafter be agreed on by the United States in Congress assembled, or any nine or more of them.*

Unlike America — who is still working on her unfinished business — you don't have centuries to meet your goals and fulfill your destiny so start pushing your boundaries today. In the process, you may help America set important new boundaries and meet long-standing goals. The words of Ralph Waldo Emerson impart advice about how you should push your future boundaries.

Do not follow where the path may lead.
Go instead where is no path and leave a trail.

Don't Turn Back The Clock   September 26th

> *. . . separate educational facilities are inherently unequal.*
> Earl Warren

On May 17, 1954, the United States Supreme Court handed down its landmark decision in "Brown v. Board of Education", in which it overturned Plessy v. Ferguson's "separate but equal" precedent. The Court unanimously ruled that laws establishing racial segregation in public schools were unconstitutional. In his opinion Chief Justice Earl Warren asserted that it was more important to base the court's rationale on present circumstances than to look back to the nineteenth century context of the Fourteenth Amendment's application to public education.

In approaching this problem, we cannot turn the clock back to 1868 when the amendment was adopted, or even to 1896 when "Plessy v. Ferguson" was written. We must consider public education in the light of its full development and its present place in American life throughout the nation. Only in this way can it be determined if segregation in public schools deprives these plaintiffs of the equal protection of the laws.

Instead of arguing solely from precedent, Warren asseverated contemporary factors, elaborating the importance of equal educational opportunity.

Today, education is perhaps the most important function of state and local governments. Compulsory school-attendance laws and the great expenditures for education both demonstrate our recognition of the importance of education to our democratic society. . . . It is the very foundation of good citizenship. Today it is a principle instrument in awakening the child to cultural values, in preparing him for later professional training, and in helping him to adjust normally to his environment. In these days, it is doubtful that any child may reasonably be expected to succeed in life if he is denied the opportunity of an education. Such an opportunity, where the state has undertaken to provide it, is a right which must be made available to all on equal terms.

In its decision against turning back the clock, the Court looked to the present and future, sowing momentum for the Civil Rights Movement and paving the way for racial progress. You should use this legal ruling as a personal standard: avoid turning back the clock in your own life. To do so, make sure to:

REFLECT ON THE PAST — Understand the past but don't get stuck there. Think through the former things to draw lessons from them. Don't look at what you've lost; look at what you've learned. As soon as you've gathered those gems of wisdom, let go of the problems of yesteryear.

REPAIR THE PAST — If you've made past mistakes that have caused pain to others, do your best to repair the damage now, to make things right. Whatever happens, do no further harm. Remember Martin Luther King Jr.'s words.

Segregation is on its deathbed — the question now is, how costly will the segregationists make the funereal.

REFOCUS IN THE PRESENT — If you focus on your mission in life, you will bring motivation to your daily agenda. If you have a habit you've been wanting to break and you're frustrated with the failure to do so, concentrate even more on your goals and the motivation will rise to break that habit. Seize today, and all of its promise. Success will rise.

RENEW THE FUTURE — Possessing dynamic dreams for your future is not only an important factor in achieving personal success, it's also a key to community betterment. Move your consciousness beyond your own mission and aim to impact the collective good. Like the U.S. Supreme Court of 1954, you just might make a landmark decision that will make a difference for generations to come.

Stick With Your Vision   **September 27th**

. . . there is no truth more thoroughly established than that there exists in the economy and course of nature an indissoluble union between virtue and happiness.
George Washington

George Washington was the consummate visionary. A classic illustration arose from the climactic Revolutionary War battle in Yorktown in 1781. General Washington insisted on standing on top of a parapet to survey the field of action amidst an artillery attack with bullets flying all about him. In the last of his annual letters to the state governments as chief military commander, submitted in 1783, Washington made clear his vision for America:

The Citizens of America, placed in the most enviable condition. . . are now . . . acknowledged to be possessed of absolute freedom and Independency; They are, from this period, to be considered as Actors on a most conspicuous Theatre, which seems to be peculiarly designated by Providence for the display of human greatness and felicity.

Washington ascended from leading the Continental Army through eight hard years of battle to becoming the presiding officer at the Constitutional Convention in 1787 to serving as the first chief executive of the new federal government from 1789 - 1796. Notwithstanding the overblown accusations throughout his presidential tenure that he had become a quasi king as well as other unjustified charges, Washington did not become cynical, bitter or hostile but maintained his great vision for America, which he published on September 19, 1796, in his Farewell Address.

The name of American, which belongs to you in your national capacity, must always exalt the just pride of patriotism more than any appellation derived from local discriminations. With slight shades of difference, you have the same religion, manners, habits, and political principles. You have in a common cause fought and triumphed together; the independence and liberty you possess are the work of joint counsels, and joint efforts of common dangers, sufferings, and successes.

Washington stuck with his great vision for the United States throughout the eventful journey of his military and political career. Follow his example. You can stick with your vision as you possess:

FOCUS — Meditate on your vision, keep the future picture for your life ever bright and before you. The word picture can be used as both a noun and a verb — it's both something you have, and something you do. Possess your big dream in your soul, live it out day by day; you fail to do so at your peril, as this Biblical precept asserts.

Where there is no vision, the people perish.
Proverbs 29:18

FELLOWSHIP — Make sure to share your vision to others. Washington continuously communicated his vision for the people to see themselves as a collective unit with a common destiny as Americans above their identities as members of a state, city, or region; or of racial, ethnic, or gender-based constituencies. Cast a large vision to bring people together.

FOLLOW-THROUGH — Washington stuck with his vision, from his beginnings on the battlefield to his farewell from the White House. Hold onto your vision, no matter what confronts you, and you will find the strength to get through it.

FAITH — Washington believed that the American Experiment had been "peculiarly designated by Providence." Like him, possess faith in your own high calling. Your faith fuels your vision, so safeguard your life's mission against inner doubts and fears. There are times when the only time you can see your vision is by first believing it.

Fit Your Piece Into The Larger Puzzle   September 28th

Let it not be said that internal improvements may be wholly left to the enterprise of the states and of individuals. . . . in a country so new and so extensive as ours, there is required the resources and superintendence of this government to effect and complete.
John Calhoun

Early in his political career, South Carolina Congressman John Calhoun was devoted to nationalist visions, possessing a frontier passion for internal improvements, building out the nation's roads and waterways. To further this goal, Calhoun presented legislation before the U.S. House of Representatives on February 4, 1817; it was called the Bonus Bill because it offered bonuses from a new National Bank to finance such improvements. He advocated for all levels of governments — municipal, state and federal — working together to build a national transportation system. In his speech supporting the Bonus Bill, Calhoun laid out the big vision for his legislative initiative; near the closing of his remarks, he detailed his priorities.

The first great object was to perfect the communication from Maine to Louisiana. This might be fairly considered as the principal artery of the whole system. The next was the connection of the Lakes with the Hudson River. In a political, commercial and military point of view, few objects could be more important. The next object of chief importance was to connect at the great commercial points on the Atlantic — Philadelphia, Baltimore, Washington, Richmond, Charleston and Savannah — with the Western states; and finally, to perfect the intercourse between the West and New Orleans.

Though the Bonus Bill passed both the House and Senate, President Madison vetoed the bill on his last day in office. Its defeat notwithstanding, this legislation prefigured the nationwide transportation system that manifested over the next 150 years.

Just as Calhoun fit the pieces of the individual states into the large puzzle of the nation's roads and waterways, you must endeavor to see your life as part of the larger context. Answering these questions will help you connect the dots.

FAMILY — How can a be a better resource in support of my family?

FRIEND GROUP — What more can I do to serve those about whom I care the most?

FELLOWSHIP — Are there additional roles I can play to make my house of worship a more loving community?

FIELD OF ENDEAVOR (studies, job) — How do I fit into my department at school or work and how does that department relate to broader issues of the intellectual and/or commercial marketplace?

FAR REACHES (community, nation, world) — In this interconnected world, how can I take the positive things I'm doing as an individual to more people, extending my reach community-wide, nationwide, global?

FUTURE — Meditate upon these words from George Bernard Shaw.

Life is no brief candle to me. It is a sort of splendid torch which I have got hold of for the moment, and I want to make it burn as brightly as possible before handing it on to future generations.

How can I make the candle of my life keep burning for my legacy, to be a splendid torch for future generations?

Be A Visionary Warrior   September 29th

Do not anticipate trouble, or worry about what may never happen. Keep in the sunlight.
Benjamin Franklin

With the French and Indian War looming, the English Board of Trade summoned the Thirteen Colonies to consider joint defense measures. In June 1754 seven of the colonies — Connecticut, Maryland, Massachusetts, New Hampshire, New York, Pennsylvania, and Rhode Island — sent delegates to Albany to explore common interests. Benjamin

Franklin, one of the Pennsylvania representatives, devised a plan to unite the colonies under the auspices of the British Parliament. He wrote in a letter of December 1754 about the merits of the proposed union.

I should hope, too, that by such a union the people of Great Britain and the people of the colonies would learn to consider themselves as not belonging to a different community with different interests but to one community with one interest, which, I imagine, would contribute to strengthen the whole and greatly lessen the danger of future separations.

Franklin fought hard for his Albany Plan of Union, but it was rejected by Parliament, which was unwilling to yield any of its authority; and by the colonial assemblies, which were resistant to sacrificing any of their sovereignty. Facing opposition from both sides of the Atlantic, Franklin resolved to be visionary warrior. Despite the repudiation of his Albany Plan, his unifying approach seeded the American Revolution that first blossomed with the Declaration of Independence a dozen years later. You should be also be a visionary warrior. To fight for your vision, stock your arsenal with these success principles.

CONVICTIONS SEEDED — What you see for the future is determined by what you believe in the present. Don't let your current circumstances cloud your vision. Envisage from your heart. The deeper your faith, the brighter your vision. A person of vision and a person of faith go hand in hand, as the Apostle Paul articulated:

For our light and momentary troubles are achieving for us an eternal glory that far outweighs them all. So we fix our eyes not on what is seen, but on what is unseen, since what is seen is temporary, but what is unseen is eternal.
2 Corinthians 4:17-18

CONVERSATIONS SHORT — A visionary warrior lives out the maxim: actions speak louder than words. Though it's important to be able to articulate your vision, it's imperative to activate your vision. As Franklin did, develop a plan, write it down, share it with others. Then make sure you're taking concrete steps to realize it rather than just talking about it.

CONSCIOUSNESS SOARING — Great visions begin in your inner life. Dreams of social consequences first rise from individual consciousness. Find some quiet time to meditate on your vision. Let your imagination soar, lifting it to new heights. Reach for the stars; you may land on the moon; you're still far above the clouds. Louisa May Alcott highlighted this truth.

Far away in the sunshine are my highest aspirations. I may not reach them but I can look up and see their beauty, and try to follow where they lead.

CHARACTER STRONG — Franklin could have been intimidated by the recalcitrant Crown and the reluctant settlers, but he fought on and his visionary strategy eventually resulted in colonial collaboration and the birth of a new nation. Be aggressive with your vision. Make sure you keep fighting for it. Don't let it get blown away in the storms of opposition and adversity. Your inner strength will lead to daily victories.

Build With Your Vision   **September 30th**

Nothing has a more direct tendency to advance the happiness and glory of a community than the founding of public school and seminaries of learning for the education of youth, and adorning their minds with useful knowledge and virtue.
Samuel Davies

In 1759 the Reverend Samuel Davies was appointed the fourth president of the College of New Jersey (now Princeton University). The first of several colonial colleges rising from the First Great Awakening, it began in 1746 to educate "those of every religious denomination." In 1753 Davies had ventured with fellow Presbyterian minister and college trustee Gilbert Tennent to Great Britain to solicit funds for the fledgling school. During their eleven-month visit Davies preached sixty times, raising 4,000 pounds (over $230,000 in 21st century dollars), primarily through church collections. His efforts yielded sufficient funds to build Nassau Hall, the first permanent building as the college transitioned from its first location in Elizabeth to its new campus in Princeton.

Davies cast his vision with vigor, using it as a tool to build a great educational institution. Some of what he learned is stated below. Study his words and the principles they denote as you learn to build with your vision. Let it be your tool to:

BUILD CHARACTER — *The utmost care is taken to discountenance vice and to encourage the practice of virtue and a manly, rational, and Christian behavior in the students. Enthusiasm, on the one hand, and profaneness, on the other, are equally guarded against and met with the severest checks. . . .*

See yourself becoming a better person than you are today. Believe it; the vision will follow.

BUILD COMMUNITY — *Daily observation evinces that in proportion as learning makes its progress in a country, it softens the natural roughness, eradicates the prejudices, and transforms the genius and disposition of its inhabitants. New Jersey and the adjacent provinces already feel the happy effects of this useful institution.*

Aim not simply to improve yourself but to transform society.

BUILD KNOWLEDGE — *A general desire of knowledge seems to be spreading among the people.*

When you want to start something — a school project, a business venture, a college, a nation — first do the research. Study to know what you're doing; success will follow.

BUILD FAMILY — *Parents are inspired with an emulation of cultivating the minds of their offspring.*

If you want your life's work to endure to benefit future generations, build strong legacy; impart visionary qualities to members of your family.

BUILD CAREER — *Public stations are honorably filled by gentlemen who have received their education here.*

Pursing your vision will lead you up the economic ladder of achievement.

BUILD LEADERSHIP — *Many Christian assemblies are furnished with men of distinguished talents for the discharge of the pastoral office . . .*

Some will follow you — and invest in you — because they grasp your vision.

BUILD THE FUTURE — *Upon the success of which the happiness of multitudes in sundry colonies, and their numerous posterity, in the present and future ages far distant, in a great measure depends.*

No matter how old or young you are, building with your vision will brighten your future.

OCTOBER: PURPOSEFULNESS
DAILY SUCCESS PRINCIPLES

1. Sow Seeds Of Virtue — Peter Cooper — 1859
2. Plan To Influence Many — Patsy Mink — 1947
3. Be Bold With Your Plans — Noah Webster — 1789
4. Plan To Intervene Early — Benjamin Lindsey — 1909
5. Make Your Moment A Movement — Susan LaFlesche — 1865
6. Prepare For The Long Journey — Charles Lindbergh — 1927
7. Plan Outside The Box — Alexander Hamilton — 1779
8. Work Your Plan B — Dalip Singh Saund — 1946
9. Get Beyond Your Comfort Zone — Gustaf Unonius — 1841
10. Plan To Enlighten — Toni Morrison — 1987
11. Become A Lifelong Learner — Benjamin Rush — 1786
12. Plan To Make A Difference — Luis Munoz-Marin — 1949
13. Nip Your Problems In The Bud — John Quincy Adams — 1820
14. Plan To Build Heritage — Arturo Schomburg — 1911
15. Reckon With Your Ghosts — Joseph Holland — 1988
16. Plan To Break Barriers — James McCune Smith — 1853
17. Be Proactive — Samuel Sewall — 1700
18. Make The Most Of Your Potential — Horace Mann — 1848
19. Live Out Your Virtues Everyday — Benjamin Franklin — 1732
20. Develop Your Game Plan — John Tunis — 1928
21. Plan To Motivate — Thomas Paine — 1776
22. Plan To Revitalize Hope — John Collier — 1933
23. Cultivate Your Plan — Elias Pym Fordham — 1818
24. Plan To Be Self-Sufficient — James Madison — 1787
25. Get Things Right The First Time — Sargent Shriver — 1961
26. Be Pioneering — Christopher Andrews — 1854
27. Formulate Your Master Plan — Albert Einstein — 1939
28. Be Passionate In Your Purpose — William Lloyd Garrison — 1831
29. Plan To Expose Injustice — Jacob Riis — 1890
30. Stay Focused On Your Goals — Thomas Jefferson — 1787
31. Seize The Day! — Thaddeus Stevens — 1835

Sow Seeds of Virtue   October 1st

Feeling this great responsibility, I desire, by all that I can say and
by all that I can do, to awaken in the minds of the rising generation
a undying thirst for knowledge and virtue, in order that they may be
able, by wise and honorable measures, to preserve the liberties we enjoy.
                          Peter Cooper

In 1859 inventor, industrialist and philanthropist Peter Cooper
established in New York City Cooper Union for the Advancement of
Science and Art, an institution of higher education recognized throughout
its history as a leader in the fields of architecture, engineering, and art.
Cooper's founding vision was not only to prepare young men and women
of the working classes with free practical education for success in business;
he also intended to inculcate in Cooper Union students the virtues
necessary for success in life.

In a letter accompanying the Cooper Union Deed of Trust, Cooper
set forth the mission of the school in a national context.

Under a deep sense of the responsibility that rests on us, as a people, entrusted
as we are with greatest blessings that ever fell to the lot of man — the glorious yet fearful
power of framing and carrying on the government of our choice — it becomes us to
remember that this government will be good or evil in proportion as the people of our
country become virtuous or vicious.

To foster virtue among the student body, Cooper set forth his
intention that everyone attending the school participate in cultivating a
virtuous environment.

Desiring, as I do, that the students of this institution may become preeminent
examples in the practice of all the virtues, I have determined to give them an opportunity
to distinguish themselves for their good judgment by annually recommending to the trustees
for adoption such rules and regulations as they, on mature reflection, shall believe to be
necessary and proper to preserve good morals and good order throughout their connection
with this institution.

Just as Cooper sowed seeds of virtue for the students of the school
he founded, you should strive to sow seeds of virtue in your own life, which
means working purposefully to bring the vigorous virtues discussed in this
book to influence everything you say or do. To be intentional about
conducting a virtuous lifestyle, you have to be:

WILLING — Being virtuous is not about talent, skill,
ability or calling. It's a matter of your will. If you want to do the

right thing badly enough, you will do it. If you resolve in your heart to embrace virtue, you will conquer unrighteousness and evil. Jesus captured this truth in His Sermon on the Mount:

Blessed are the pure in heart, for they shall see God.
Matthew 5:8

WATCHFUL — Pay close attention to where you hang out and with whom you're associating. Watch the people, places and things of your life: they are the forces that can either make or break your virtue. If you sincerely want more virtue in your life, try hanging out in those places where virtuous people hang out.

WISE — As you go through your day, check to make sure you are living with a virtuous purpose. If you're just drifting along the rivers of life without the rudder of virtue, the capsizing of your destiny is inevitable. Being intentional about virtue is the wise approach; it's the moral compass that will steer you clear of trouble.

WINNING — Whatever your goals, doing the right thing as you pursue them is like a flashlight, guiding you through the gloom of disappointment and detractors along the pathway of daily victory. David Brinkley highlighted the triumphant mindset.

A successful man is one who can lay a firm foundation with the bricks others have thrown at him.

Plan To Influence Many   October 2nd

I always felt that we were serving a dual role in Congress, representing our own districts and, at the same time, having to voice the concerns of the total population of women in the country.
Patsy Mink

In 1947 Asian American and Hawaii native Patsy Takemoto Mink was a student at the University Nebraska, whose housing policy required students of color to live in different dormitories from white students. To protest this long-standing segregation, Mink organized the Unaffiliated Students of the University of Nebraska, a coalition of students, parents, employees, alumni, administrators, and sponsoring businesses. Her leadership helped to overturn the university's policies that had prevented non-white students from residing in regular dormitories and joining sororities and fraternities.

After graduating from the University of Chicago Law School, Mink returned to Hawaii, but her race and gender proved to be insurmountable obstacles in landing a law firm job. So she started a solo practice, becoming the first woman of Japanese heritage (Her grandparents had emigrated from Japan to the Territory of Hawaii.) to practice law in the Hawaiian territory.

As the debate over Hawaii's statehood proceeded in 1956, Mink was elected to the Hawaii Territorial Legislature, followed by her election to the Territorial Senate in 1958, and, after Hawaii became the 50th state in 1959, she was elected to the United States House of Representatives in 1964, becoming the first Asian American woman — and first woman of color — elected to Congress. Mink described her special mission in Washington, D.C.

. . . because there were only eight women at the time who were Members of Congress, I had   a special burden to bear to speak for all women, because they didn't have people who could express their concerns for them adequately.

Mink took the coalition-building skills that she'd learned early in life with her to Congress. As principal sponsor of the Title IX Amendment of the Higher Education Act, she brought the support together to pass this landmark legislation that prohibited gender discrimination by federally funded institutions. Mink also authored the Early Childhood Education Act and the Women's Educational Equity Act, laws through which she furthered her mission to bring equal rights not just to ethnic minorities but to all Americans.

Mink's plan to influence many started in college but was fulfilled throughout her trailblazing political career. Your own plan to influence many can happen through your:

EDUCATION — How much you know will influence others. Make sure to get as much formal education as you can; but when that's finished, don't stop there. Commit yourself to learn something new everyday. After Mink finished law school, she got a job as a legislative attorney so she could learn the inner workings of the political process.The more knowledge you add to your life, the more influential you'll be in making positive changes.

ENTHUSIASM — The way you feel will influence others. Expressing negative emotion will turn people off, driving them away. Expressing positive emotion will turn people on, bringing them into your coalition. Your success at a task, especially if your goal is to build a winning team, is directly related to the amount of enthusiasm you have for it.

ELEVATION — How you live your life will influence others. Mink excelled, and she elevated herself and countless others. People will be drawn to you if you are truly excellent at what you do. Don't settle for anything less than performing at your highest level. You'll feel better about yourself, you'll inspire some, and you'll make the world a better place. Vince Lombardi scored big with this point.

The quality of a person's life is in direct proportion to his commitment to excellence, regardless of their chosen field of endeavor.

Be Bold with Your Plans   October 3rd

If religious books are not widely circulated among the masses in this country, I do not know what is going to become of us as a nation. If truth be not diffused, then error will be.
Noah Webster

Referred to by some as the the "Father of American Scholarship and Education", Noah Webster was committed to laying the intellectual foundation and shaping a distinctive culture for the new American nation. Webster pioneered textbooks that taught generations of American children how to spell and read. In 1828 he published "An American Dictionary of the English Language," which evolved into the modern Merriam-Webster Dictionary. The dictionary furthered his purpose of Americanizing spellings and standardizing new words that were distinct to the American experience. In 1789 Webster published an essay in which he wrote about his big goals.

NOW is the time, and this the country, in which we may expect success in attempting changes favorable to language, science and government. Delay in the plan here proposed may be fatal; under a tranquil general government the minds of men may again sink into indolence; a national acquiescence in error will follow; and posterity be doomed to struggle with difficulties, which time and accident will perpetually multiply.

He stated the larger purpose in emphatic terms.

Let us then seize the present moment and establish a national language, as well as a national government. Let us remember that there is a certain respect due to the opinions of other nations. As an independent people, our reputation abroad demands that in all things we should be federal, be national; for if we do not respect ourselves, we may be assured that other nations will not respect us. In short, let it be impressed upon the mind of every American that to neglect the means of commanding respect abroad is treason against the character and dignity of a brave, independent people.

Though his work was much criticized during the early days of the United States — too radical by Hamilton and the Federalists and out of touch by Jefferson and the Republicans — Webster's plans were seminal and bold, helping to define Americanism through intellectual innovation. Follow his example. Be bold with your own plans as you:

DISRUPT THE STATUS QUO — Don't be content with things as they are. Don't hesitate to make waves, not for the sake of shaking things up but for the purpose of making things better. Webster shook things up and America got smarter. Those who are comfortable with or benefit from the status quo will dislike your disrupting it. Don't let that stop you from improving it.

DON'T DUCK THE RISKS — Planning to change things means taking on risks: the bigger the changes, the bigger the risks. You may not be able to avoid them, but you can prepare for them. Plan in advance for the risks. If you're doing something worthwhile, expect opposition. If you're living on the edge, don't be surprised by the loose rocks; carry a strong rope. Prepare mentally for the adversities; you will be better able to handle them.

DISPLAY DERRING-DO — This is your time to be heroic. It may be a once-in-a-lifetime moment. Find the inner strength to do what no one else is willing to do. Take note of Winston Churchill's counsel.

It's not enough to have lived. We should be determined to live for something.

DARE TO BE CREATIVE — A new national language seemed like madness to some. Webster dared to be creative and developed the educational tools to accomplish his goals. Like him, let your creative juices flow. If it hasn't been done before, dare to initiate — you be the first to do it!

Plan to Intervene Early   October 4th

> *... our court work for the children was going on very happily. It was a*
> *recreation for us all, and it kept me full of hope — for it was successful.*
> Benjamin Lindsey

In 1901 jurist Benjamin Lindsey, known as the "Kid's Judge", was appointed to the Juvenile Court of Denver, which had been established as a consequence of his advocacy for youth. Lindsey's pioneering work in criminal justice emphasized intervening early in the lives of challenged young people. His success proved paradigmatic: future juvenile courts across America replicated his practices. He described some of his lessons in a 1909 magazine article:

> *We were getting the most unexpected results. We were learning something new*
> *every day. We were deducing, from what we learned, theories to be tested in daily practice,*
> *and then devising court methods by which to apply the theories that proved correct. It had*
> *all the fascination of scientific research, of practical invention, and a work of charity*
> *combined. It was a succession of surprises and a continual joy.*

Lindsey assessed the problem and offered a solution.

> *The mistake of the criminal law had been to punish these little savages as if*
> *they had been civilized, and by so doing, in nine cases out of ten, make them criminal*
> *savages. Our work, we found, was to aid the civilizing forces — the home, the school,*
> *and the church — and to protect society by making the children good members of society*
> *instead of punishing them for being irresponsible ones. If we failed, and the child proved*
> *incorrigible, the criminal law could then be invoked. But the infrequency with which we*
> *failed was one of the surprises of the work.*

The effective methods that Lindsey used to deal with young people apply generally to how best to handle problem people and to youth in particular. The key to his success was to intervene as soon as possible. You should plan to intervene early not only with your own issues but especially with the problems of others. To intervene early, be sure to:

DISCERN DEEPLY — Read between the lines, see beyond the superficialities to the intangibles where the real problems lie. Focus on attitudes, hopes, emotions, dreams, motivation, atmosphere and faith. Yes, it's important to deal with the material things like lack of food, clothing or shelter but those deficiencies can be symptoms of deeper problems. Keep digging until you get to the root cause — in yourself as well as in others.

DEAL PRESENTLY — Once you get to the bottom line, act now. The longer you wait to deal with a problem, the harder it gets to deal with. If, like Lindsey, you're dealing with so-called bad apples, come at the person with three things: set high but clear expectations; extend   opportunities to make change; offer strong accountability. The earlier you do these things after discovering the problem, the better chance of success. Reflect on this truth:

The best time to plant a tree is twenty-five years ago . . .
. . . The second best time is today.

DECOUPLE STRATEGICALLY — Environment is key. If you or the person you're trying to help is in a counter-productive place, take steps to separate from it. Lindsey identified "home, school and church" as "civilizing forces". Figure out how you can move into positive and out of negative environments.

DETERMINE STRONGLY — Making a plan to intervene early will likely be the easier part of the process. Following through will be your challenge. If you're helping someone overcome, especially a young person, it could be a long haul. Take heart. Be determined to be there all the way to the destination. Someone's bright future is at stake.

Make Your Moment A Movement   October 5th

It was only an Indian and it did not matter. The doctor preferred
hunting for prairie chickens rather than visiting poor, suffering humanity.
Susan La Flesche

In June 1865 Susan La Flesche was born to biracial parents on the Omaha Reservation in eastern Nebraska. Her father, Iron Eye (also known as Joseph LaFlesche because he was of French Canadian as well as Ponca ancestry) was the leader of the Omaha tribe. Her mother's roots were also mixed: the offspring of a white Army surgeon and a woman of Omaha-Oto-Iowa heritage. When Susan was a child, she witnessed a sick Native American woman die because a white doctor refused to treat her.

This early experience turned out to be a defining moment for her. La Flesche made it her mission to become a doctor to bring quality health care to her people. She knew that gaining an education would fuel the pursuit of her dream. She journeyed to Virginia to attend Hampton Institute, a historically black college with the goal of also educating Native

American students. After graduating class salutatorian, La Flesche gained acceptance to Woman's Medical College of Pennsylvania, one of the handful of schools in the United States at that time providing medical education for women. La Flesche appealed to an auxiliary of the Women's National Indian Association to secure the funding for her medical education.

Finishing the demanding three years of study as valedictorian, La Flesche became the first Native American to earn a medical degree. Returning to the Omaha reservation as the physician of the government-run boarding school, La Flesche saw her work as more than providing health care.

From the outset the work of an Indian girl is plain before her . . . We who are educated have to be pioneers of Indian civilization. We have to prepare our people to live in the white man's way, to use the white man's books, and to use his laws if you will only give them to us . . . the shores of success can only be reached by crossing the bridge of faith.

La Flesche worked twenty hour days out of an schoolyard office, addressing the immediate health concerns of 1,200 residents as well as temperance, preventative medicine and public health issues.

I'm not accomplishing miracles, but I'm beginning to see some of the results of better hygiene and health habits. And we're losing fewer babies and fewer cases to infection.

La Flesche made a moment in her life into her mission, which in turn became a movement. You can do the same as you work to improve your:

MOMENT — In the midst of significant happenings, take a breath . . . slow down . . . grasp their full meaning. Life-changing moments can pass you by if you're moving too fast to embrace them.

MINDSET— Don't be easily distracted by non-priorities. Set your mind on what needs to be done today. La Flesche made it to the top wherever she went because she made every day count. Let this be your new mantra: attitude determines approach; approach determines success or failure. Abraham Lincoln nailed this principle:

Always bear in mind that your resolution to succeed is more important than any other thing.

MOMENTUM — Once you succeed at one thing, don't stop there. Draw lessons from each experience to plan the new move. Use the positive energy to attain the next goal, to conquer bigger territory. Commit yourself to learning then implementing best practices. Take them to people and places that need them the most. As you build momentum through your missionary devotion, your work will take on a life of its own.

La Flesche's mission became a . . .

MOVEMENT — She advanced food sanitation, school hygiene, and efforts to combat the spread of tuberculosis; chaired a Nebraska state health committee; and built the first privately funded hospital on a reservation, which became a national model. Follow her example!

Prepare For The Long Journey   October 6th

I didn't bring any extra clothes with me. I am wearing a borrowed suit now. It was a case of clothes or gasoline, and I took the gasoline.
Charles Lindbergh

On May 20, 1927, Charles Lindbergh took off from Long Island in the "Spirit of St. Louis", his single-engine, purpose-built Ryan monoplane. Thirty-three-and-one-half hours and 3,600 miles later, the twenty-five-year-old Lindbergh landed in Paris, completing the first solo, non-stop flight between North America and the European mainland — the most famous feat in the history of aviation.

After he arrived in Paris to the awaiting, adoring masses, Lindbergh gave a newspaper interview in which he dismissed the nickname "Lucky Lindy".

There's one thing I wish to get straight about this flight. They call me "Lucky," but luck isn't enough. As a matter of fact, I had what I regarded and still regard as the best existing plane to make the flight from New York to Paris. I had what I regard as the best engine, and I was equipped with what were in the circumstances the best possible instruments for making such efforts. . . .

Life is a marathon, not a sprint. Lindbergh's heroics hold lessons for all about the significance of preparing for the long journey of life. Heed the following precepts to enhance your preparation.

EXPERIENCE — Prepare for life's challenges by drawing lessons from your own past experiences. The key is to get in touch with your mistakes. Take some time to reflect on what went wrong on a previous project or initiative. Your preparation will be primed by your determination to apply what you've learned so you can handle similar situations in different ways. Timing is important, as John Wooden makes plain:

When opportunity comes, it's too late to prepare.

ENERGY — Focus on your energy level. Are you a high-energy or low-energy person? Either way, it's easy to get drained when you're multi-tasking with lots on your plate. Figure out the big priority for today and every day. Manage your food and rest to make sure your tank is full for it. You want to be able to handle it with excellence. Like Lindbergh flying across the Atlantic, you'll need your energy flowing positively and powerfully to be at your very best.

EXACTING — Success is not about guesswork. Pay attention to the details. Lindbergh flew without the typical navigation instruments and utilized with precision the earth inductor compass to plot his course. You can create your own system to chart your course and track your progress; just be sure to follow its directions without deviation. Lindbergh rejected the nickname "Lucky Lindy"; his action evokes a saying from Thomas Jefferson.

I'm a great believer in luck, and I find the harder I work the more I have of it.

EXTRA — Pack your extra! Lindbergh didn't pack a change of clothes so he would have room for extra gasoline. What is your extra — the vital thing that you'll need to be prepared for the length and vicissitudes of your quest? Jesus' parable of the ten virgins is relevant here: the five virgins with the extra oil made it; the five without the extra did not. Jesus concluded the parable with the admonition, which still rings true:

Therefore keep watch, because you do not know the day or the hour . . .
Matthew 25:13

Make sure you have extra oil handy to make it to the final destination of your long journey.

EXHALE — Don't wait to exhale. Be intentional and disciplined about making rest stops along the way. Create moments of separation and solitude in the hustle and bustle of your everyday. Find moments of peace to reflect and recenter. Be intentional and strategic about planning times of retreat and refreshment. The longer you journey, the greater the need to take a break along the way.

Plan Outside The Box   **October 7th**

I have not the least doubt that Negroes will make very excellent soldiers . . .
Alexander Hamilton

On December 29, 1778, local Patriot militia and Continental Army units resisted the Redcoats in the First Battle of Savannah, but the Americans lost the city. The British Invasion was just the first strike of its new campaign to take control of the Southern colonies. Consequently, during the first few months of 1779, the British made significant advances into Georgia and South Carolina, threatening to cut off the Southern colonies from the Northern ones.

In light of this dire turn of circumstances and with the understanding that the Continental Army could redeploy few troops to the southern theater of war, Colonel Alexander Hamilton — a chief assistant to General George Washington — devised a new plan. In a March 14, 1779 letter to John Jay, President of the Second Continental Congress at that time, Hamilton proposed arming and then freeing Negro slaves.

This is to raise two, three, or four battalions of Negroes, with the assistance of the government of that state, by contributions from the owners in proportion to the number they possess. . . . It appears to me that an expedient of this kind, in the present state of Southern affairs, is the most rational that can be adopted, and promises very important advantages. . . .

With this strategy, Hamilton planned outside of the box, offering the kind of proposal that no one else was putting forth at that time. You should try to emulate his thinking. Study his words and the principles rising from them.

PLAN FROM THE FACTS — *I foresee that this project will have to combat much opposition from prejudice and self-interest. The contempt we have been taught to entertain for the blacks makes us fancy many things that are founded neither in reason nor experience; and an unwillingness to part with property of so valuable a kind will furnish a thousand arguments to show the impracticability or pernicious tendency of a scheme which requires such a sacrifice. . . .*

Hamilton knew his proposal was a long shot facing high hurdles: "a thousand arguments to show the impracticability". The expected "much opposition from prejudice and self-interest" notwithstanding, Hamilton put forth a plan that represented outside of the box thinking, running the risk that it would fail, which it did. The important point is that he was aware of the facts and the risks they presented, but he didn't let the possibility of failure keep him back from an innovative approach towards a workable solution. Sometimes you will have to lose first before you win, especially if you're blazing new trails. Plan outside of the box anyway.

PLAN FROM YOUR HEAD — *An essential part of the plan is to give them their freedom with their   muskets. This will secure their fidelity, animate their courage, and I believe will have a good influence upon those who remain, by opening a door to their emancipation.*

Your imaginative powers are a divine gift, so use them as you innovate. Be creative and strategic as you revise and amend your plans. You'll get closer to producing the optimal one each time around.

PLAN FROM YOUR HEART — *This circumstance, I confess, has no small weight in inducing me to wish the success of the project; for the dictates of humanity and true policy equally interest me in favor of this unfortunate class of men.*

Be prepared for disappointments, mistakes and defeats. Accept that fact that success is a continual process of trial and error. Your failures are but milestones on the journey to attain your goals. You have to keep telling yourself: "I believe in this project. I'll work through these challenges." You will then be ready for the new opportunity, primed to make moves to fulfill the plan.

Work Your Plan B   **October 8th**

I knew if these bars of citizenship were lifted I would see wider gates of opportunity open to me, opportunity as existed for everybody else in the United States of America.
Dalip Singh Saund

In August 1920, 20-year-old Dalip Singh Saund left his his home state of Punjab, India, and journeyed to America. Saund arrived with other immigrants to Ellis Island, then headed westward to the University of California, Berkeley where he obtained his master's degree and PhD in mathematics.

Saund's desire for an academic career was confronted by the discrimination that prevailed against Asian people during this time. This unfair reality was difficult for him to accept, but he realized that an alternative direction was agricultural. Saund moved to Imperial Valley, the Southern California community where many other Indians were already established, to make his living as a farmer.

Indians could not own property in 1925 when Saund made this move; and they were not allowed to become U.S. citizens. So he set up his business under his wife's name, leasing land to grow alfalfa and other produce, which proved successful.

Saund was not content with such arrangements, so he took action. He organized meetings with other non-citizens, which led to the formation of the India Association of America, headquartered in Los Angeles; Saund was elected its first president. In part due to Saund's organizational initiatives, on July 3, 1946, a new law was signed by President Harry Truman allowing Indians to become American citizens.

On the heels of this success Saund was encouraged to engage politically. During his first campaign for judge in the town of Westmorland, a local resident fired a question at him: "Doc, tell us, if you're elected, will you furnish the turbans or will we have to buy them ourselves in order to come into your court?"

Saund responded:

> *My friend, you know me for a tolerant man. I don't care what a man has on top of his head. All I'm interested in is what he's got inside of it.*

Saund won that race, and a few years later gained a more important elective office, becoming the first native of Asia elected to the United States Congress.

Saund experienced great success because he didn't give up because his initial plan failed. He worked his Plan B. You should follow his example, and can do so as you:

DISCARD DISAPPOINTMENT— Life is full of disappointments. Be prepared for them. Manage your emotions when your things don't work out as initially planned. If you let frustration get the best of you, you'll never get out of the starting blocks.

DEVELOP OPTIONS — Be strategic and exhaustive in your planning. Don't get stuck on the one thing, that perfect scenario. Let your thinking be: If this doesn't work, then I'll try that. If that doesn't work, I'll attempt the other thing. If the other thing doesn't work, then . . .

DIRECT PURPOSE — Saund didn't get upset with the prejudice blocking his plans. As he worked his Plan B, he discovered a higher purpose for his life. As you work your Plan B, the same will happen for you. But as you work it, you have to know where you're headed, especially when you come to forks in the road of your life. Don't be like Alice, as she appears in the passage from Lewis Carroll's "Alice in Wonderland".

Alice came to a fork in the road. "Which road do I take?" She asked. "Where do you want to go?" responded the Cheshire cat. "I don't know," Alice answered. "Then," said the cat, "it doesn't matter."

DELIVER EXCELLENCE — Saund wanted to be a scholar; instead he became a successful farmer and a trailblazing politician. In everything he did his commitment to excellence was the key to his success. Let it also be the key to yours!

Get Beyond Your Comfort Zone   **October 9th**

I love the democratic social order where the majesty of the people really is a majesty before which a man can stand with the same veneration, yes, with even more, than before a royal throne; and I believe that the American people, left to themselves, will one day reveal that majesty to the world.
Gustaf Unonius

In 1841 Swedish pastor and pioneer Gustaf Unonius emigrated to the United States, establishing the first nineteenth-century Swedish colony in America. Leading a group of his fellow countrymen, Unonius settled on a lake now called Pine Lake in the village of Chenequa, Wisconsin. Unonius wrote letters back home about his experience, which were published in Swedish, Finnish and Danish newspapers, catalyzing Scandinavian immigration to the Midwest.

Unonius' letters evolved into his memoirs about life on the American frontier. In the following excerpt, he described the process of deciding on their lakefront settlement.

Without long deliberation, we decided . . . to settle on the shore of the little lake, where both the natural beauty and the good soil promised us a pleasant home, and where, among oak, beech, and hickory trees, the evergreen pines, untouched by the axe, would always stand as a pleasant reminder of the pine forest of our old homeland. We needed to take no steps to insure our claim except to inform our neighbors that we were planning to make our home here, and as a sign of our intention, start some improvement to indicate that this part of the section had been occupied. . . .

Because Unonius moved beyond his comfort zone onto the American frontier, he discovered not only the ideal location for his settlement but also blazed trails to the American frontier for countless others. You can follow his lead to move beyond your comfort zone as you:

FLY BEYOND YOUR EXPECTATIONS — Whatever your status quo is, don't be satisfied with it. Set your expectations high, and meet them. Endeavor to exceed them. Dream about trying new things and going new places Venture beyond the boundaries of your imagination. Like Unonius, you might just attain some ideal experiences.

FIX ON YOUR PRIORITIES — It's good to have choices and options. But don't let them keep you from concentrating on the most important thing on your agenda. Focusing on your priorities can be challenging because it means letting other things go. Your true priority is the key to the door of progress. The first thing you should do today is figure it out, focus on it and follow through. This approach is like planting a seed of progress, as Robert Louis Stevenson mused.

Don't judge each day by the harvest you reap but by the seeds you plant.

FORCE YOUR DOOR OPEN — Be aggressive in your approach, so you can get a seat at the front of the room, or you can be the one at the head of the line. You may feel uncomfortable being the first one to volunteer, but force yourself to shoot your hand up high! Asserting yourself at the right time could force the door of your big opportunity wide open.

FIND YOUR PURPOSE — You may not find the true purpose in life looking in the same old places. Break out of your routine. Seek a new and different environment. You may have to go on a hard mission to discover your highest mission.

Plan To Enlighten   October 10th

There is no time for despair, no place for self-pity, no need for silence, no room for fear. We speak, we write, we do language. That is how civilizations heal.
Toni Morrison

In 1987 professor and writer Toni Morrison published "Beloved", her most celebrated novel, for which she was awarded both the Pulitzer Prize and the American Book Award the following year. Inspired by a true story, the book tells the story of Sethe, who escaped from slavery with her two-year-old daughter. Morrison described her first few weeks of freedom.

Sethe had twenty-eight days — the travel of one whole moon — of unslaved life. From the pure clear stream of spit that the little girl dribbled into her face to her oily blood was twenty-eight days. Days of healing, ease and real-talk. Days of company: knowing the names of forty, fifty other Negroes, their views, habits; where they had been and what done; of feeling their fun and sorrow along with her own, which made it better. One taught her the alphabet; another a stitch. All taught her how it felt to wake up at dawn and decide what to do with the day.

But the slave hunters tracked Sethe down. About to be apprehended, she cut her daughter's throat but was captured before she could cut her own. The novel imagines the dead child returning years later as a ghost to haunt Sethe and her family.

"Beloved" exemplifies Morrison's literary plan to shed light on the gloomy history of American race relations. Her plan to use fiction to bring enlightenment to dire problems was fulfilled throughout her illustrious career. Her advice — in her own words — and the principles they represent are moral guideposts along your pathway of destiny. Seek to live them out as part of your own plan to enlighten.

GAIN WISDOM —*I know the world is bruised and bleeding, and though it is important not to ignore its pain, it is also critical to refuse to succumb to its malevolence. Like failure, chaos contains information that can lead to knowledge - even wisdom. Like art.*

GNARLY — *If you take racism away from certain people - I mean, vitriolic racism as well as the sort of social racist - if you take that away, they may have to face something really terrible, misery, self-misery, and deep pain about who they are.*

GET KNOWLEDGE — *It's important, therefore, to know who the real enemy is, and to know the function, the very serious function of racism, which is distraction. It keeps you from doing your work.   I t k e e p s y o u explaining over and over again, your reason for being. Somebody says you have no language and so you spend 20 years proving that you do. Somebody says your head isn't shaped properly so you have scientists working on the fact that it is. Someone says you have no art so you dredge that up. Somebody says you have no kingdoms and so you dredge that up. None of that is necessary. There will always be one more thing.*

GRAB-BAG — *I tell my students, 'When you get these jobs that you have been so brilliantly trained for, just remember that your real job is that if you are free, you need to free somebody else. If you have some power, your job is to empower somebody else. This is not just a grab-bag candy game.'*

GOAL — *Please don't settle for happiness. It's not good enough. Of course you deserve it, but if that's all you have in mind - happiness - I want to suggest to you that personal success devoid of meaningfulness, free of a steady commitment to social justice - that's more than a barren life. It's a trivial one.*

GREATNESS — *From my point of view, which is that of a storyteller, I see your life as something artful, waiting, just waiting and ready for you to make it art.*

GO FOR IT — *I want to discourage you from choosing anything or making any decision simply because it is safe. Things of value seldom are.*

GRACE — *Your life is already a miracle of chance waiting for you to shape its destiny.*

Become A Lifelong Learner   October 11th

> *This plan of general education alone will render*
> *the American Revolution a blessing to mankind.*
> Benjamin Rush

Benjamin Rush was by profession a physician but he had many involvements in late eighteenth century America. His support for education at all levels — with the goal of producing well-informed, fruitful citizens — was exemplary. Rush envisaged a comprehensive system of education that emphasized a balance of academic and utilitarian subjects, training in science as well as in the trades. Its overarching goal was to help complete the work of the American Revolution. On May 25, 1786, he wrote Richard Price, a British moral philosopher, explaining his approach.

> *Most of the distresses of our country and of the mistakes which Europeans have formed of us, have arisen from a belief that the American Revolution is over. This is so far from being the case that we have only finished the first act of the great drama. We have changed our forms of government, but it remains yet to effect a revolution in our principles, opinions, and manners so as to accommodate them to the forms of government we have adopted. This is the most difficult part of the business of the patriots and legislators of our country. It requires more wisdom and fortitude than to expel or to reduce armies into captivity.*

Rush intended his educational plan to be a new mission for America.

> *Call upon the rulers of our country to lay the foundations of their empire in knowledge as well as virtue. Let our common people be compelled by law to give their children (what is commonly called) a good English education. Let us have colleges in each of the states, . . . Let the law of nature and nations, the common law of our country, the different systems of government, history, and everything else connected with the advancement of republican knowledge and principles, be taught by able professors . . .*

Rush believed that an individual's commitment to education should be paramount. Take on this commitment by becoming a lifelong learner. These three precepts will help guide your journey.

DEDICATION — Commit to self-improvement. Check your work ethic: can you work harder than you're presently doing? . . . can you achieve more that your current goals? Think about what you can do today to get better at something you're involved with. It may seem just a little thing, like being on time for school, work or a meeting instead of late. Small improvements become big breakthroughs when they happen every day over time. Dedicate to self-improve with new habits. St. Francis of Assisi highlighted this principle when he wrote:

Start doing what is necessary; then do what is possible; and suddenly you are doing the impossible.

DISTANCE — Solitude is essential to learning. Distance yourself from the noise, whether it's a crowd of people or the distraction of your smartphone. Find your quiet space to study . . . and to contemplate. Library works, so does a room at home, without the TV on. To become a lifelong learner, be disciplined about spending time in those quiet places where your knowledge has room to breathe . . . and expand.

DESTINY — Like Rush, see your quest for new knowledge as a mission. It's about more than just you; it's about preparing yourself to be a better person, sharing your new knowledge with others, being a light in gloomy places, making a difference through your example, leaving a legacy of educational excellence for the generations that follow. Get in the habit of asking yourself the question:

What have I learned today that makes me a better person and makes the world around me a better place?

Plan To Make A Difference   **October 12th**

The Puerto Rican people, in fact, are more than just a politically mature people. I sincerely and proudly believe that in their hinterland of the world they constitute the best rural school of democracy in America today . . .
Luis Munoz-Marin

In 1898, as a consequence of America's victory in the Spanish-American War, Puerto Rico was ceded by Spain to the United States. Nineteen years later the Jones Act made the people of Puerto Rico U.S. citizens. During the 1930's, when significant numbers of Puerto Ricans migrated to New York and other large U.S. cities, journalist Luis Munoz-Marin returned from America back to his native Puerto Rico. Munoz-Marin discovered that countless Puerto Ricans were unemployed, victims of hurricane-ravaged sugar crops. He committed himself to make a difference, advocating for democratic practices, economic recovery and agricultural reform, which paved the way for the industrialization of the island's economy. Recognized for his exemplary community service, Munoz-Marin was elected to the Puerto Rican Senate and became Senate President in 1940. In May 1945, he made a speech that was broadcast over the CBS network, in which he emphasized that Puerto Rico's right to self-determination be recognized.

It is these people, so politically sound and so economically harassed, that are now contributing to the peace effort, as they are contributing to the war effort. They are now proposing to the Congress and the government of the United States a plan for self-determination. This plan may well serve as a basis for dealing with the colonial problem in many other parts of the world as well as in Puerto Rico. It should also help the United States in clarifying, maintaining, strengthening, and developing that leadership of hard-pressed mankind everywhere which is of such decisive importance to world justice and world peace.

On January 2, 1949, Munoz-Marin became the first elected governor of Puerto Rico, eventually earning the title of the "Father of Modern Puerto Rico". His rise to political prominence resulted from his plan to make a difference. Follow his example. Plan to make a difference by practicing these principles in your life.

CLEAR PURPOSE — Possessing a clear purpose for your life is one of the most important factors in keeping you on track in the midst of life's storms. Munoz-Marin purposefully returned to his homeland where he made a big difference. Make it your goal to shift your purpose beyond self-centeredness to include making a difference for others. Mother Teresa articulated the great impact that your purposefulness can have.

I alone cannot change the world, but I can cast
a stone across the waters to create many ripples.

CONCERN FOR OTHERS — Check your attitude: selfless is better than selfish. If you truly want to make a difference, you must develop the habit of putting the interests of others ahead of your own. Start this new habit by doing something today that prioritizes your selflessness over selfishness.

COMPELLING PRIORITIES — Align everything you do with your overall purpose. Munoz-Marin succeeded because he stayed focused on the priority of improving the lives of his fellow Puerto Ricans. Get in the habit of thinking ahead to what's most important; let nothing get in the way of getting that done.

CAPABLE HANDS/COMMITTED HEARTS — Don't face life alone. Plan to make a difference by working with others, those who have capable hands and committed hearts. Prepare for a life of service through the wisdom of   counsel. Before taking initiative, talk things over with someone you trust. You'll attain greater success if you can plan ahead by getting advice through a purposeful teammate, mentor, or friend. You have a better chance of really making a difference if you join forces with someone with a proven track record of doing so.

Nip Your Problems In The Bud   **October 13th**

*Take it for granted that the present is a mere
preamble — a title page to a great, tragic volume.*
John Quincy Adams

The Missouri Compromise of 1820 was controversial legislation that admitted Maine without slavery and Missouri with slavery, thus fulfilling the political strategy of   maintaining the balance of power between free and slave states. Future president John Quincy Adams, U.S. Secretary of State at the time, made an entry in his diary on March 3, 1820, reflecting on the complexities and challenges of that moment in American history.

It is among the evils of slavery that it taints the very sources of moral principle. It establishes the false estimate of virtue and vice; for what can be more false and heartless than this doctrine which makes the first and holiest rights of humanity to depend upon the color of the skin? It perverts human reason and reduces man endowed with logical powers to maintain that slavery is sanctioned by the Christian religion, that slaves are happy and contented in their condition, that between master and slave there are ties of mutual attachment and affection, that the virtues of the master are refined and exalted by the degradation of the slave . . .

Adams also recorded his second thoughts concerning his support of the Missouri Compromise and his reflections on its ominous consequences.

I have favored this Missouri Compromise, believing it to be all that could be effected under the present Constitution, and from extreme unwillingness to put the Union at hazard. But perhaps it would have been a wiser as well as a bolder course to have persisted in the restriction upon Missouri, till it should have terminated in a convention of the states to revise and amend the Constitution. This would have produced a new Union of thirteen or fourteen States unpolluted with slavery . . . rallying to their standard the other states by the universal emancipation of their slaves. If the Union must be dissolved, slavery is precisely the question upon which it ought to break. For the present, however, this contest is laid asleep.

In agreeing to the Missouri Compromise, Adams and other American leaders failed to nip the problem of slavery in the bud, so it got worse. Because it wasn't dealt with in 1820, the problem became a crisis, resulting in Civil War in 1860. Don't follow their bad example. Nip your problems in bud before they become the kind of issues that bring conflict and chaos into your life; do your best to:

PREFIGURE THE FUTURE CRISIS — Be visionary about the consequences if the problem isn't addressed. If the situation calls for a prophetic voice to declare what no one else dares to say, be like the Old Testament prophet Jeremiah: speak the truth no matter how bad it feels. Struggle to do the right thing, as he did:

> *But if I say, "I will not mention his word or speak anymore in his name," his word is in my heart like a fire, a fire shut up in my bones. I am weary of holding it in; indeed, I cannot.*
> — Jeremiah 20:9

PROCRASTINATE NOT! — "Contest is laid asleep", Adams wrote, putting off to the future what needed to be done in the present. Don't procrastinate. Seize the solution to your problem. Get it done now. Avoid regrets later on.

PROPOSE A STRATEGY — Adams had an alternative strategy to the Missouri Compromise — "a bolder course" — which he and others failed to propose and press forward. Make a plan to resolve the problem and follow through on it.

PUT FIRST THINGS FIRST — What's most important? For Adams, was it preserving the Union or fulfilling founding promises? He struggled with the decision but opted for the former; history proved it to be the wrong priority. Make sure you get your priorities right — and move forward accordingly.

Plan To Build Heritage   October 14th

We need the historian and philosopher to give us with trenchant pen, the story
of our forefathers, and let our soul and body brighten the chasm that separates us.
Arturo Alfonso Schomburg

In 1874 Arturo Alfonso Schomburg was born in Santurce, Puerto Rico to a German merchant living in Puerto Rico and a black midwife from St. Croix. While in grade school, Schomburg heard a teacher make the claim that blacks were without accomplishments or history. Several years later he immigrated to New York City and settled in Harlem, committed to prove his teacher wrong.

While holding various jobs to support his family, Schomburg began writing about African and Caribbean American history. An early and active participant in the Harlem Renaissance, Schomburg co-founded in 1911 the Negro Society for Historical Research, which for the first time created a coalition of West Indian, African and African American scholars to refute racist scholarship. Schomburg also served as president of the American Negro Academy, another umbrella organization of editors, activists and scholars to support black intellectual endeavors. Schomburg described his mission.

The American Negro must rebuild his past in order to make his future.
Though it is orthodox to think of America as the one country where it is unnecessary to
have a past, what is a luxury for the nation as a whole becomes a prime social necessity
for the Negro. For him, a group tradition must supply compensation for persecution, and
pride of race the antidote for prejudice. History must restore what slavery took away, for
it is the social damage of slavery that the present generation must repair and offset.

Impassioned to rebuild the past, Schomburg collected slave narratives, historical manuscripts and artwork as well as other African American artifacts. By 1926 he had amassed such a collection that the New York Public Library purchased it for $10,000 to include in its new Division of Negro History at its 135th Street Branch in Harlem. Schomburg curated the collection, and the Harlem branch was eventually named in his honor: the Schomburg Center for Research in Black Culture.

From an early age Schomburg had a plan to build heritage for people of African descent, and he executed on that over the course of his life with splendid outcomes. His example is worthy of your emulation. Your heritage is something special that you possess. Like Schomburg, it can be cultural; it can be family; or a creation of your hands that you want to preserve. Whatever your heritage, plan to build it using these principles.

FERVOR — Like Schomburg, be clear about your passion. He was devoted to renewing the black past, but fervent about working on it in the present. If you're constantly thinking about yesterday or tomorrow, you'll never get anything done today. Apply your passion to the hard work of heritage-building and it will become a labor of love waiting for you everyday.

FOUNDATION — Schomburg's fellow Harlem Renaissance leader Marcus Garvey once wrote:

A people without the knowledge of their past history,
origin and culture is like a tree without roots.

Knowledge is power. Knowing your heritage is a source of strength, a solid foundation for confidence and identity. Research your cultural roots. Understanding your family tree is not an idle exercise. Getting in touch with your personal and family history — whether positive or negative — will take you on an important inner journey where you will learn context for your life. Studying cultural history is just as important. Connecting to the great people of your cultural past is the best way to build heritage.

FRUITION — Schomburg's plan to build heritage was so fruitful that the Harlem building that bears his name has become "one of the world's leading cultural institutions devoted to the research, preservation, and exhibition of materials focused on African American, African Diaspora, and African experiences." Start working on your plan to build heritage. You, too, might create legacies that make a difference for future generations.

Reckon With Your Ghosts   October 15th

You can't ignore or outrun the ghosts of the past. They will always catch up with you.
Joseph Holland

Arriving straight from a park bench, Chip excelled at Harkhomes through his strong work ethic. He started working part-time at a construction site; he then took on remedial courses at a community college. Chip had also enrolled in membership classes at a local church and had even been appointed an assistant supervisor at Harkhomes. He did so well that when a local newspaper featured the work of the program, his story was the lead and his picture appeared along with the article.

I had asked Chip during intake — the same question I'd ask all new residents: "What are those things in your past you need to clean up so that they don't come back to haunt you?"

Chip shrugged, said nothing.

His silence led to his downfall. What Chip failed to tell me that day — or at any subsequent time — was that he was in violation of parole. In his drive to get ahead, he neglected it. It turned out to be the wrong detail to miss.

Not all publicity is good publicity. When Chip's parole officer saw his picture in the newspaper, he sent police officers to pick him up. If he had disclosed his parole situation with us beforehand, I would have been able to intervene with the authorities on his behalf and have him assigned to my supervision, as I had done for other residents with the same problem. Instead, my entreaties to the judge notwithstanding, Chip ended up in jail for six months; the hiatus derailed his progress. He never fully recovered his pre-incarceration rhythm of progress.

Chip failed to reckon with his ghosts. To make sure you reckon with yours, you have to:

LEAVE NO STONE UNTURNED — Plan with the past in mind. Pay attention to the consequences—financial, legal, relational, emotional—of your past. Address the breakdowns that happened yesterday, last week, last month, last year, in your youth, whenever. Think exhaustively about it. The cleanup plan involves completely straightening out the mess that the troubles of life have caused, whatever they might be; the bigger the prior breakdowns, the greater the need to reckon with your ghosts. It might feel a lot easier to leave your mess buried in the past than to resurrect the unpleasant stuff and figure out how to straighten it out. Don't risk it. You ignore the old things at your peril. Chip's myopia foredoomed his rise. He thought he could move on without addressing the problems of his past. His approach turned out to be disaster. His unfortunate outcome confronts you with a couple of fateful questions. What's your cleanup plan? Are you working on it?

LET THERE BE BALANCE — The course of life is sinuous, your journey typically not a straight line but a winding road, an obstacle course. Circumstances tend to come in completely unexpected ways replete with adversity. The bumps that knock you off course are inevitable, resulting in setbacks. Don't get stuck in the outstanding issues to be addressed, fallout to be rectified, damage to be cleaned up. Work on your cleanup plan, but don't be preoccupied with it. Strive to strike a balance in your agenda between yesterday's problem and today's priorities. Let the past go enough so that you have the time and energy to embrace your present agenda and future goals. Your strategy here is twofold: be purposeful about unpacking old baggage, be proactive about addressing new priorities, which will preclude the breakdowns of the past from becoming present or future obstacles. As you implement this approach, you will find that you'll need less time for the past and you'll possess more time and energy for the present and future.

Plan To Break Barriers   **October 16th**

With regard to ourselves, a consideration of our position in this country
teaches us that our inheritance is one that can only be ameliorated
by the combination of practical art with literary preparation.
James McCune Smith

The census of 1850 established the U.S. population at approximately 23 million, of which 15% or about 3.5 million were African Americans. The vast majority of blacks — 3.2 million — were chattel slaves in the American South. While Abolitionists fought to free these slaves, the 300,000 free blacks of the North were waging their own battles against pervasive racial inequities.

One such warrior was James McCune Smith, who graduated at the head of his class at Scotland's University of Glasgow and went on to become the first African American to hold a medical degree. Smith broke another barrier, becoming the first African American to run a pharmacy in the United States.

Working with Frederick Douglass, Smith helped to start the National Council of Colored People, the first permanent national organization for blacks, which held its inaugural convention July 6 - 8, 1953 in Rochester, New York. The convention's report emphasized a holistic approach — academic learning as well as practical training — to prepare blacks to elevate in American society.

We know that we cannot form an equally useful part of any people without the ability to contribute our full share to the wealth, activity, social comforts, and progress of such people. If, then, the necessary education to fit us to share in the responsibilities cannot be generally had, by the reason of the prejudices of the country, where best they can be taught, namely in the workshops and countinghouses, and the other varied establishments of the land that have to do with the machinery of activities carried on around us.

The report concluded by emphasizing the balanced educational initiative.

As a consequence, we have grown up to too large an extent — mere scholars on one side and muscular giants on the other. We should equalize those discrepancies. . . . Let us educate our youth in suchwise as shall give them means of success adapted to their struggling condition . . . we may hope to see them filling everywhere positions of responsibility and trust, and, gliding off the triple tide of wealth, intelligence and virtue, reach eventually to a sure resting place of distinction and happiness.

Following Smith's example, the convention offered a plan to help blacks break barriers. Prepare yourself to break through the barriers in your life as you:

FREE YOURSELF FROM STEREOTYPES — When I was in high school a guidance counselor advised me that I couldn't be a good student and good athlete. I went on to become an Academic All-American football player. Reject the negative assessments. Defy the prejudicial type-casting. Prove the naysayers wrong. No matter what others say to and about you, believe that you can do. Your success starts with breaking free from mental/emotional bondage.

FIND YOUR NICHE — If you've found your niche, keep growing within it. If you haven't discovered it yet, do self-research. Be honest about your strengths and weaknesses, then be active in managing your weaknesses and be proactive in cultivating your strengths.

FOCUS YOUR OBSTACLES — What's in your way? Smith was clear about the racist hurdles of his day, but he didn't let them stop his success journey. Know the giants in your path. Stare them down. Spend some time working on a plan to defeat them. Be intentional about overcoming your obstacles. Intentionality means being focused, not scattered; consistent, not haphazard.

FUEL YOUR AGENDA — Breaking through the barriers in your life is challenging. Some people never get through because they don't want it badly enough. Get in touch with your motivation. Search your heart. How much do you really want to succeed?

Be Proactive   **October 17th**

And it will be a vain attempt for us to offer Heaven to them if they take up prejudices against us, as if we did grudge them a living upon their own earth.
Samuel Sewall

When the first colonists arrived in New England during the 17th century, the Native American presence along the coasts where the newcomers established settlements was limited. As the settlers made their way into the interior, clearing land for farming and trapping and trading on Native American hunting grounds, the tensions sometimes escalated into armed conflict. King Philip's War (sometimes called the First Indian War) raged from 1675 to 1678 between Native Americans of the New England and colonists of the region.

Samuel Sewall, Puritan leader and prominent jurist, forged his most enduring legacy through his writings: his diary chronicling his own life in and around Boston as well as events and the lives of others; and The Selling of Joseph, a tract protesting slavery in the Massachusetts province. Sewall also wrote a letter of May 3, 1700 to Sir William Ashurst, an English banker and Member of Parliament, articulating his concerns about ongoing hostilities with Native Americans and proposing a new approach to establishing fair boundaries for their lands.

One thing more I would create leave to suggest. We have had a very long and grievous war with the Eastern Indians, and it is of great concernment to His Majesty's interests here that a peace be concluded with them upon firm and sure foundations; which in my poor opinion cannot well be while our articles of accord with them remain so very general as they do. I should think it requisite that convenient tracts of land should be set out to them; and that by plain and natural boundaries, as much as may be — as lakes, rivers, mountains, rocks — upon which for any Englishman to encroach   should be accounted a crime. Except this be done, I fear their own jealousies, and the French friars, will persuade them that the English, as they increase and think they want more room, will never leave till they have crowded them quite out of all their lands.

Sewall's plan was not approved by Ashurst and other British officials; the failure to do so prefigured the continual conflict between natives and settlers that ensued the succeeding centuries. Sewell made a proactive attempt to address an intractable problem. He exemplified proactivity, and it remains a viable strategy for you to implement as you plan to handle the challenges of your life. Be proactive about them as you:

LOOK BACK — Before making a move towards resolution, make sure to reflect on past experiences, drawing lessons from them to inform your present action. Sewall understood the recent history of relations between the two warring groups, which dictated his novel approach. Contextualize your plans before proceeding with them.

LOOK AROUND — Gather facts to inform your decision-making. Collect and examine enough relevant information to put you ahead of game. Knowing more than others positions you to be proactive. Pay attention to hard factors such as demographic and financial data as wells soft factors such as personality and timing.

LOOK AHEAD — Take a dual perspective as you survey the landscape that lies before. Be clear on the positive consequences that will benefit you by moving forward as well as on the negative ones that will persist and worsen if you don't make your move. Seek to nip problems in the bud by discerning them before they happen. By taking action now, you will avoiding greater challenges in the future.

LOOK INSIDE — Are you committed to this? Sewall was committed to his plan but not enough of his contemporaries were. Examine your mind and heart. Determine both your seriousness and sincerity about the plan. Be sure you're ready to do what it takes to make it a success, even if it means going up against opposing forces, even persuading uninformed and unintelligent leadership.

Make The Most Of Your Potential   **October 18th**

Individuals who, without the aid of knowledge, would have been condemned to perpetual inferiority of condition and subjected to all the evils of want and poverty, rise to competence and independence by the uplifting power of education.
Horace Mann

From 1837 to 1848 Horace Mann served as Secretary of the Massachusetts Board of Education, the position from which he implemented an extensive program of educational reform. During his tenure, Mann started three normal schools (the first in America) and fifty new common schools as well as increasing the length of the academic year. Mann's plan became a model for many other states, earning him the title — the "Father of the Common School Movement".

As Education Secretary each year Mann issued a report to the

Massachusetts legislature. His Fifth Report articulated one of his core messages: education as the great equalizer, helping the social disadvantaged make the most of their potential.

> *In great establishments, and among large bodies of laboring men . . . there it is found as an almost invariable fact, other things being equal, that those who have been blessed with a good common-school education rise to a higher and a higher point in the kinds of labor performed and also in the rate of wages paid, while the ignorant sink like dregs and are always found at the bottom. . . .*

He also explained the pecuniary value of education: it was the best way for an individual to gain property and generate revenue in American society.

> *Education is not only a moral renovator . . . it is also the most prolific parent of material riches. It has a right, therefore, not only to be included in the grand inventory of a nation's resources but to be placed at the very head of that inventory. It is not only the most honest and honorable but the surest means of amassing property. . . . It has more than the quality of an ordinary mercantile commodity, from which the possessor realizes but a single profit as it passes through his hands; it rather resembles fixed capital, yielding constant and high revenues.*

Mann's point went beyond education in school to an individuals' plan to make the most of their potential. To make the most of your potential, you need to:

TRUST IT — Always keep this point in mind: your potential is God's gift to you; what you do with it is your gift to Him. Be a good steward of your natural endowments. Your duty is to trust your special talents and do your best to develop them. Every day ask yourself this question: How can I get better at what I love to do?

TRAIN IT — Your potential will not grow without your resolve to train it. Mann's message was to "rise to a higher and a higher point" by working hard at education. Be committed to keep developing yourself — in and out of school — whatever your stage of life. Your potential will rise.

TREASURE IT — Consider Mann's point about your economic potential: gaining knowledge is the best way to prosper, "yielding constant and high revenues." Creating wealth begins with your intention to use every day as an opportunity to grow your potential so you can strategically gain financial profit from it.

TAP IT — Your potential is a limitless resource. Make it a daily discipline, not only to develop it but to draw motivation from it. Heed the wisdom of Olympic track legend Wilma Rudolph, apply it to your life.

Never underestimate the power of dreams and the influence of the human spirit. We are all the same in this notion: The potential for greatness lives within each of us.

Plan To Live Out Your Virtues Everyday   October 19th

I hope that some of my descendants may follow the example and reap the benefit.
Benjamin Franklin

More than any other Founding Father, Benjamin Franklin possessed a commitment to virtuous living, sown in his Puritan upbringing, which emphasized "inculcating virtue and character in themselves and their communities." Franklin came to believe that the American Experiment would only succeed if its citizens were virtuous. He regularly wrote about his passion for virtue, exploring the connection between individual and civic virtue in Poor Richard's Almanack, which he continually published from 1732 to 1758; several aphorisms follow:

He that hath a trade, hath an estate; and he that hath a calling, hath an office of profit and honor . . . diligence is the mother of good luck, and God gives all things to industry. Then plow deep, while sluggards sleep, and you shall have corn to sell and to keep. . . . Constant dripping wears away stones; and by diligence and patience the mouse ate in two the cable; and little strokes fell great oaks.

Through publishing Poor Richard and other writings, Franklin sought to embed virtue into the culture of the new American republic. It was his intention through these communications to help shape the character of colonial America.

Franklin was also intentional about role-modeling virtue. In 1726, when he was twenty, he established a daily plan of virtuous action, living out thirteen virtues, focused on putting into practice a different one every week. He continued to work on his inner life by practicing these principles for the rest of his life.

1) **Temperance** — *Eat not to dullness; drink not to elevation.*

2) **Silence** — *Speak not but what may benefit others or yourself; avoid trifling conversation.*

3) **Order** — *Let all your things have their places; let each part of your business have its time.*

4) **Resolution** — *Resolve to perform what you ought; perform without fail what you resolve.*

5) **Frugality** — *Make no expense but to do good to others or yourself; i.e., waste nothing.*

6) **Industry** — *Lose no time; be always employ'd in something useful; cut off all unnecessary actions.*

7) **Sincerity** — *Use no hurtful deceit; think innocently and justly, and, if you speak, speak accordingly.*

8) **Justice** — *Wrong none by doing injuries, or omitting the benefits that are your duty.*

9) **Moderation** — *Avoid extremes; forbear resenting injuries so much as you think they deserve.*

10) **Cleanliness** — *Tolerate no uncleanliness in body, clothes, or habitation.*

11) **Tranquility** — *Be not disturbed at trifles, or at accidents common or unavoidable.*

12) **Chastity** — *Rarely use venery but for health or offspring, never to dullness, weakness, or the injury of your own or another's peace or reputation.*

13) **Humility** — *Imitate Jesus and Socrates.*

Though the Vigorous Virtues of this book are twelve in number — one less than Franklin's Virtues — they share many similarities, the most important of which is an intentional and strategic plan of daily devotion. Like Franklin, plan to live out your virtues every day. Follow his selective approach. Practice all of the virtues all the time but really focus on incorporating one of the virtues into your lifestyle in new and creative ways every week: Integrity one week . . . Courage, then next . . . then try Teamwork . . . the following week, Compassion . . . You may not be able to keep the high virtuous standard 100% of the time, but if you strive for 50% at first, that's a lot more virtue flowing through your life than before. And simply by being purposeful about weekly virtuous living, you have begun to build a better you, and by extension, a better world.

Develop Your Game Plan   October 20th

For a series of five or six successive Saturdays in October and November each year, football proves its right to be called the King of American Sports.
John Tunis

On November 6, 1869, the first-ever college football game was played between Rutgers University and Princeton University (then known as the College of New Jersey). During the early 1900's the game was modernized through improvements introduced by such notable coaches as Amos Alonzo Stagg, Pop Warner and Knute Rockne and popularized by such star players as Jim Thorpe, Red Grange, Bronco Nagurski, the Four Horsemen and the Seven Blocks of Granite.

In November 1928 writer and broadcaster John Tunis published an article in Harper's Monthly about the rising spectacle of college football.

A baseball World's Series crowd of 80,000 is mentioned in the newspaper headlines; on the other hand, a football crowd of 80,000 is commonplace. At the approximate moment when the Yale Bowl is filled with a gathering of this size, larger numbers are watching Michigan play Illinois at Urbana, Pennsylvania take Chicago at Franklin Field, and California play Stanford at Berkeley.

Tunis also described the economic benefits of the game's popularity.

. . . the merchants of a college town and the Chamber of Commerce subscribed money to the Athletic Association, realizing that 100,000 persons in twenty-four hours can leave a good deal of surplus cash about . . . football is the godfather of games within and without the walls of the university, that with its gate receipts are built swimming pools and squash courts, that from its profits spring crews fully armed and golf and tennis teams fully clothed. A new baseball cage was built out of football earnings. The lacrosse team made a southern trip upon them. They helped finance the rifle and chess teams, the polo and the debating teams. They maintained and paid for all intramural sports . . . the intramural sports idea, "athletics for all," is hammered home for all it is worth to show how beneficial modern football really is. . . .

The success of college football has endured for a century, with countless favorable ramifications, for athletic programs at the college level and beyond. The planning that led to it holds some lessons for your life; the following points will help you develop your own game plan.

DISCOVER — Don't wing it. You will discover your best plans by thinking things through well in advance of taking action. Be visionary as well as practical. Create the time and space in your life — even if it means stepping back from the usual and familiar — for careful consideration. Crafting successful strategies don't happen by chance but through intention: align your capabilities and circumstances with your opportunities and resources.

DEPLOY — Take a concrete step to fulfill your most important goal today — every day. Your good intentions are not enough. Put your plan into action. Decide on your priority and move forward. Set a deadline and meet it. The key is to get started. Even if things don't go well at first and you have to begin again, use the lessons from your initial deployment as the foundation for the future. This is hard part, as Johann Wolfgang von Goethe explained:

Thinking is easy, acting is difficult and to put one's thoughts into action is the most difficult thing in the world.

DEVELOP — An effective game plan is the difference between a winning football team and a losing one. The success of college football transformed American sports into big business that yielded resources for other athletic programs. Research relevant models to improve your plans. Develop your plan by making a list of tasks you can take to make it better, and hold yourself accountable to timely completing it. Your enhanced plan will spell success for you and others.

Plan To Motivate   **October 21st**

Without the pen of the author of Common Sense,
the sword of Washington would have been raised in vain.
John Adams

In January 1776 Thomas Paine's Common Sense — a persuasive pamphlet advocating colonial independence — was published. It was an immediate bestseller: 100,000 copies sold in three months and 500,000 copies over the course of the American Revolution, making it proportionally the largest sale of any book in American history.

The pamphlet's appeal was making an impassioned case for independence in plain but poetic language. It was so influential that it was often read aloud in taverns, building momentum for separation from England, even fueling recruitment for the Continental Army. The following passage exemplifies its pointed, lively, rhetorical style.

Ye that tell us of harmony and reconciliation, can ye restore to us the time that is past? Can ye give to prostitution its former innocence? Neither can ye reconcile Britain and America. The last cord now is broken; the people of England are presenting addresses against us. There are injuries which nature cannot forgive; she would cease to be nature if she did. As well can the lover forgive the ravisher of his mistress as the continent forgive the murders of Britain. The Almighty has implanted in us these inextinguishable feelings, for good and wise purposes. They are the guardians of His image in our hearts, and distinguish us from the herd of common animals. The social compact would dissolve and justice be extirpated from the earth, or have only a casual existence, were we callous to the touches of affection. The robber and the murderer would often escape unpunished did not the injuries which our tempers sustain provoke us into justice.

The flourish of its concluding paragraph climaxed the clarion call to arms.

O! Ye that love mankind! Ye that dare oppose, not only the tyranny but the tyrant, stand forth! Every spot of the Old World is overrun with oppression. Freedom has been haunted round the globe. Asia and Africa have long expelled her. Europe regards her like a stranger, and England has given her warning to depart. O! Receive the fugitive, and prepare in time an asylum for mankind.

Paine's plan to motivate colonial America towards independence and liberty succeeded beyond measure. You, too, should plan to motivate others towards their goals. It will happen as you speak and write:

POETICALLY — Be intentional and strategic about the language you use. Choose words that paint a vivid picture. There was no way to miss or dismiss the power of Paine's analogy, comparing England to "the robber and the murderer . . ." The poetry of your advocacy will lighten the pathway of the followers you need to create a movement. Take time to craft an inspirational narrative.

PURPOSEFULLY — The reality is that you are both influencing someone and being influenced by someone all the time. In other words, you are both a leader and a follower; it varies, depending on the degree of influence you're exerting in the situations of your life. Just know that in some areas of your life you are leading; in other areas you are being led. You're usually able to choose whether it's your influence that prevails. Don't be obnoxious but seize the moment when the time is right. In short, be like Tom Paine. Be purposeful about proclaiming your goals. You can do it with your pen, your voice, your actions, or your example. And you will experience more success and fulfillment — and have more fun — as you use your influence to inspire others.

PROPELLINGLY — The influence of Common Sense not only reached far and wide but moved key people. After reading it, George Washington wrote:

A few more of such flaming arguments, as were exhibited at Falmouth and Norfolk, added to the sound doctrine and unanswerable reasoning contained in the pamphlet Commonn Sense, will not leave numbers at a loss to decide upon the propriety of a separation.

Make it a goal to motivate others. Like Paine, you just might inspire a liberating leader — and seed a history-making movement.

Plan to Revitalize Hope   October 22nd

Our task is to help Indians meet the myriad of complex, interrelated, mutually dependent situations which develop among them according to the very best light we can get on those happenings — much as we deal with our own perplexities and opportunities.
John Collier

In 1933 President Franklin Roosevelt appointed John Collier Commissioner of Indian Affairs. The next year Collier was instrumental in the passage of the Wheeler-Howard Indian Reorganization Act, which radically changed federal policy towards Native Americans. In a 1938 report Collier described this new direction. He began with the historical context.

For nearly 300 years white Americans, in our zeal to carve out a nation made to order, have dealt with the Indians on the erroneous, yet tragic, assumption that the Indians were a dying race — to be liquidated. We took away their best lands; broke treaties, promises; tossed them the most nearly worthless scraps of a continent that had once been wholly theirs. But we did not liquidate their spirit. The vital spark which kept them alive was hardy. . . .

Collier also delineated the specific goals of this unprecedented approach.

We, therefore, define our Indian policy somewhat as follows: So productively to use the moneys appropriated by the Congress for Indians as to enable them, on good, adequate lands of their own, to earn decent livelihoods and lead self-respecting, organized lives in harmony with their own aims and ideals, as an integral part of American life. Under such a policy, the ideal end result will be the ultimate disappearance of any need for government aid or supervision. This will not happen tomorrow; perhaps not in our lifetime; but with the revitalization of Indian hope . . . that aim is a probability, and a real one. . . .

Whatever plans you make for the future, make sure hope is at the center of them. If you've lost hope along life's journey, you must make plans to revitalize it. The following steps will do just that.

ACKNOWLEDGE PAST PROBLEMS — Damage done to you in the past, whether from abuse, disadvantage, or neglect, will take time to heal. The healing starts with you acknowledging the problem and really taking steps to understand it. And if you're having trouble unpacking the baggage, you don't have to go at it alone. Seek help, especially from those who are in some way responsible for creating your problems. Let them know that you're moving forward and you want their support. And remember — the best cure for past pain is present desire, which makes all the difference, as Abraham Lincoln expressed:

In the end, it's not the years of your life that count; it's the life in your years.

ACCEPT PRESENT RESPONSIBILITY — Collier represented a fresh approach to the Native American problem — the U.S. government taking ownership of it. Take ownership of your problems instead of pointing the finger of blame at others. Such responsibility will create the hope of moving beyond issues that have been holding you back.

AIM FOR FUTURE HEIGHTS — Expect the best for your life and you will make plans that aspire towards that high standard. If you instead expect the worst, your plans will likely be uninspired or nonexistent. Collier expected the best for his new federal strategy and his plans transformed historically poor policies towards Native Americans into better ones. Your attitude is key: expect bad things, they often happen to you; expect good things, you are more likely to make them happen, and you will find your hope revitalized and your actions energized. And your life just might surprise you with favorable outcomes once you resolve to expect the best from it. Why not start aiming for the best today?!

Cultivate Your Plan   October 23rd

. . . if he has no money, if he knows no mechanical trade, and he cannot work, he had better stay in a countinghouse in England.
Elias Pym Fordham

With the end of the War of 1812 — its second conflict with Great Britain during its Founding phase — America experienced the dawn of a new era. This historical epoch was marked by two phenomena: increasing westward expansion and surging European immigration. These mutually reinforcing forces were captured in correspondence by English immigrant Elias Pym Fordham, who had settled in Illinois. In a letter dated February 18, 1818, he offered advice to a friend.

I have consciously avoided giving to my young friends in England colored descriptions of this country; but I must beg leave to assure you that you cannot do a greater favor to any young man, who possesses from 800 to 5,000 pounds, with a proper degree of spirit, than by sending him out here.

In a subsequent letter he gave more elaborate counsel, offering the sound plan that he had cultivated for them to follow.

I will loosely classify English emigrants, and point out the sections of country in which each will find the greatest number of advantages. The English country gentleman may settle in Virginia, District of Columbia, Maryland, New Jersey, and the lower part of Pennsylvania; the genteel farmer in Kentucky; the rich yeoman in Kentucky, Missouri, Tennessee . . . the poor farmer, with a capital of 300 pounds and upwards in Illinois and Indiana; ditto, if unmarried, in Missouri, the lower parts of Kentucky . . .because in these countries he can have servants; mechanics, if masters of the most useful trade, and capitalists, always in the most settled parts of the western country, and generally in the slave states; ditto, inferior workmen or men without money, in the new towns on the frontiers; engineers, smiths, founders, millwrights, and turners may find employment in the larger towns on the Ohio; shopkeepers and makers and dealers of articles of luxury should never cross the mountains.

Fordham cultivated a plan for his countrymen coming to America. He charted the course for them before they arrived, giving them the best chance of success. You should follow this sound approach. Cultivate your own plan as you:

RISE UP — Plan early! I once heard a preacher say, "Never start your day until you have finished it." His point was have your plan of action in place before the dawn of a new day. Plan ahead — when you first wake up, maybe even the night before — think through your agenda and set your schedule. Maximize your time and energy by making a daily plan of action and executing it.

RECORD — Don't trust your memory. Have a notebook handy for those unanticipated moments in those unexpected places. Keep a written record of important thoughts, a folder for upcoming events. Refer to it as much as you need to, delete less important happenings, and plug in new priorities. One of the worst feelings is to forget a revelation that would have propelled you and others. Be diligent about writing stuff down.

REDUCE — Get to the bottom line. It's good to do research, talk things through, set decision-making protocols. You can acknowledge the value of all that, but also know when it's time to reduce the matter to its essence, align things with your core values and move forward. To execute your game plan, be a RIGHT NOW person.

REASSESS — Your game plan isn't sacred. Be flexible with it, so you can make changes, adjust priorities, revise strategies in accordance with the realities as they emerge. Know the difference between second-guessing and reassessing. Once you make a decision, don't doubt it; do your best to execute it. Once you complete your task, reflect on it, to see how you can improve your plan for the next game day.

Plan To Be Self-Sufficient   October 24th

Enlightened statesmen will not always be at the helm.
James Madison

With the United States as a new and growing nation in 1787, leaders from each state met in Philadelphia for a Federal Convention to create a governing instrument for the American Experiment. Though the putative purpose of the Convention was to revise the Articles of

Confederation of 1783, some of the delegates, in particular James Madison of Virginia and Alexander Hamilton of New York, had a different plan — create a new constitutional government rather than fix the existing one.

This strategic approach was challenging. The delegates held widely divergent views stemming from their clashing political ideas, sectional loyalties and personal agendas. While waiting for a Convention quorum to assemble, Madison drafted the Virginia Plan — a proposal featuring a bicameral legislative branch — and organized a coalition of delegates to support it. Madison also acted as Convention secretary and kept notes, which turned out to be the most complete record of the private proceeding.

The premise of the Virginia Plan was a constrained government and a strong citizenry. For almost four months Madison and his cohorts worked their plan, in group debates, committee drafts and one-on-one meetings. The end result was the Constitution of the United States, which — more than any other historical document — defined the legal structure and political character of America, which emphasized that individuals should be self-sufficient, independent of government. For your success, you need to take the same approach: plan to be independent of government, of family, of everyone and everything. To practice self-sufficiency, keep Madison's words and the principles they represent in mind.

CONTEXT — *The advancement and diffusion of knowledge is the only guardian of true liberty.*

Know your rights, safeguard them, act on them. Doing so will pave the way to your self-sufficiency.

CAPACITY — *We have staked the whole future our new nation, not upon the power of government; far from it. We have staked the future of all our political constitutions upon the capacity of each of ourselves to govern ourselves according to the moral principles of the Ten Commandments.*

Be a principled person; it's a cornerstone of your success.

COST — *It was incumbent on us then to try this remedy . . . to frame a republican system on such a scale and in such form as will control all the evils which have been experienced.*

Count the cost upfront to assess the factors for success. Madison came to Philadelphia early, writing and organizing before the Convention even began, then was there for four months. Be aware of the sacrifices that you must make to make to attain self-sufficiency, and be willing to endure them.

CONSCIENCE — *Knowledge will forever govern ignorance; and a people who mean to be their own governors must arm themselves with the power which knowledge gives.*

The key to attaining and maintaining success is your work ethic. Plan accordingly!

CHIMERICAL — *To suppose that any form of government will secure liberty or happiness without any virtue in the people, is a chimerical idea.*

Living out the vigorous virtues of this book will bolster you, giving you the strength to overcome any adversity of circumstance, insufficiency of resources or inadequacy of planning. The virtue of purposefulness is your antidote for chimera.

CREATOR — *The future and success of America is not in this Constitution, but in the laws of God upon which this Constitution is founded.*

Get in touch with the source of your greatness and you will readily draw on its power.

Get Things Right The First Time   October 25th

. . . we knew the Peace Corps would have only one chance to work. As with the parachute jumper, the chute had to open the first time.
Sargent Shriver

In March 1961 the Peace Corps was established by executive order of President John F. Kennedy; its purpose was to "make available to interested countries and areas men and women of the United States qualified for service abroad and willing to serve . . . to help the peoples of such countries . . ." Sargent Shriver, the founding director of the Peace Corps, reflected on its early days in a 1963 "Foreign Affairs" article.

An organization, we know, gains life through hard decisions so we hammered out basic policies in long, detailed discussions in which we sought to face up to the practical problems and reach specific solutions before we actually started operations. We knew that a few wrong judgments in the early hours of a new organization's life, especially a controversial government agency, can completely thwart its purposes — even as a margin of error of a thousandth of an inch in the launching of a rocket can send it thousands of miles off course.

Towards the end of the essay, Shriver reflected on the Peace Corps' mission in the light of the founding vision of America.

The Revolution placed on our citizens the responsibility for rendering their own social structure. It was a triumph over the idea that man is incompetent or incapable of shaping his destiny. It was our declaration of the irresistible strength of an universal idea connected with human dignity, hope, compassion, and freedom. . . . We still have our vision, but our society has been drifting away from the world's majority: the young and raw, the colored, the hungry, and the oppressed. The Peace Corps is helping to put us again where we belong. It is our newest hope for rejoining the majority of the world without at the same time betraying our cultural, historic, political, and spiritual ancestors and allies.

The founding work of Shriver endured and prospered. Since its inception, the Peace Corps has orchestrated almost a quarter million Americans serving in 141 countries. Shriver understood the importance of laying a strong organizational foundation by getting things right the first time around. This principle is timeless. For you to get things right the first time around, bring the following factors into your planning.

MANUFACTURE — Shriver explained: " . . . we hammered out basic policies in long, detailed discussions . . . before we actually started operations." Making effective plans is like making a new product. Successful outcomes are derived from rigorous processes. Be sure to hammer out your own plans before launching them.

MAINTENANCE — Whether its plans for your own life or for the organization that you lead, a daily plan of action is key. You can use a daily planning book, a whiteboard on your office wall or a sheet of scratch paper — whatever it is, get the agenda down at the beginning of each day. You will maintain your vision as you hold yourself accountable — every day — to your action plan.

MAGNITUDE — Like Shriver, be idealistic and reach for the big dreams that bring about social betterment. What matters just as much — sometimes more — than your natural talent and ability is your vision for the future and the motivation and commitment that rises from it. Heed Alvin Toffler's counsel to start getting things right the first time around:

You've got to think about big things while you're doing small things, so that all the small things go in the right direction.

MISSION — The words of Mahatma Gandhi summarize the mission-minded focus you should possess from the very beginning of your enterprise.

Be the change you want to see in the world.

Be Pioneering   October 26th

*. . .to compensate for these things he can feel that the labor of
the pioneer, aside from its pecuniary advantage to himself, is
of service to the state and a helpmate to succeeding generations. . . .*
Christopher Andrews

In 1837 the territory of Minnesota was officially opened when the U.S. government acquired it, along with neighboring lands, from the Chippewa and Sioux Native Americans. Settlers followed the forays of lumbermen and trappers into the area, heading north to the wilderness of Missouri and Iowa. The trickle of pioneers became a flood. Just over two decades later, when Minnesota entered the Union as the thirty-second state, its population was nearly 170,000.

Two years earlier in the fall of 1856, forester and future Civil War General Christopher Andrews traveled to the Minnesota and Dakota Territory by rail as far as Chicago, continuing by steamship to St. Paul, finally by stagecoach to St. Cloud, where he eventually settled. Andrews wrote twenty-six letters during his trip, recording his observations of the Territory's institutional development as well as its opportunities for pioneers. In the following excerpt he described the purposefulness of the pioneer.

The true pioneer is a model farmer. He lays out his work two weeks in advance. Every evening finds him further ahead. If there is a rainy day, he knows what to set himself about. He lays his plans in a systematic manner and carries them into execution with energy. He is a true pioneer, and therefore he is not an idle man, nor a loafer, nor a weak, addle-headed tippler. Go into his house, and though you do not see elegance, you can yet behold intelligence and neatness, and sweet domestic bliss.

Andrews also explained how the pioneers' efforts entailed personal sacrifice to attain larger purposes.

. . . he has left his dearest friends far away in his native village, where his

affections still linger. He has to endure painful separations and to forgo those many comforts which spring from frequent meetings under the parental roof and frequent converse with the most attractive scenes of youth.

The pioneers that Andrews depicted are paragons of planning. They succeeded in settling a new area of America because they laid out a plan for every day and stuck to it. To be pioneering in this sense is to be exemplary in your planning, striving to stay ahead of your challenges by preparing for them in advance. Use these tools to be pioneering and conquer new territory for your life.

MARTINET — Success doesn't just happen. You have to make it happen through commitment. Sometimes you have to be hard on yourself. Like the pioneering farmer who planned his work "two weeks in advance", be diligent and disciplined about making your plans. It might be really challenging at first but through developing a rigorous regimen of planning you will reap a reward.

MANAGEMENT — You can't manage anything without a plan, so if you want to better manage your life, bring the pioneering spirit to every day. Before the sun rises, know what new territory you want to conquer then go after it. And if the sun doesn't come out, have a plan for the rainy day.

MEASUREMENT — You have limitless potential, but you can't do everything at once. Set a goal — no matter how small or seemingly insignificant — measure your success with it. Hold yourself accountable. Don't move on until you have achieved it or you fully understand why you didn't.

MAHATMA — The words of Mahatma Gandhi best captures the character of the pioneering lifestyle. Embrace this truth, and live it out!

Live as if you were to die tomorrow. Learn as if you were to live forever.

Formulate Your Master Plan   October 27th

A single bomb of this type, carried by boat and exploded in a port, might very well destroy the whole port together with some of the surrounding territory.
Albert Einstein

On August 2 1939, physicist Albert Einstein sent a letter to U.S. President Franklin Roosevelt, advising him that scientific advances had raised the probability of the development of nuclear weapons. Einstein articulated his point in compelling terms.

In the course of the last four months it has been made probable . . . to set up a nuclear chain reaction in a large mass of uranium, by which vast amounts of power and large quantities of new radium-like elements would be generated. . . . The new phenomenon would also lead to the construction of bombs, and it is conceivable . . . that extremely powerful bombs of a new type may thus be constructed.

Given the fact that Nazi Germany had organized its nuclear physicists to develop atomic bombs, Einstein encouraged Roosevelt to support a similar American initiative. Einstein's master plan for Roosevelt posited two key recommendations:

a) approach government departments, keep them informed of the further development, and put forward recommendations for government action;

b) to speed up the experimental work . . . by providing funds . . . and perhaps also by obtaining the cooperation of industrial laboratories which have the necessary equipment.

Within a couple months Roosevelt responded by setting up the Advisory Committee on Uranium, which eventually led to the Manhattan Project, the secret research endeavor that took place at several sites across the U.S.; the first atomic tests were executed at the headquarters laboratory near Los Alamos, New Mexico. Einstein's master plan had far-reaching effects: American won the nuclear arms race with Germany and other nations. You can also formulate a winning master plan if you make it:

CONFIDENTIAL — Einstein shared his master plan with Roosevelt and a chosen few others. Your master plan is not for everyone; it is only for the trusted handful. First share your thinking with those who share your vision and mission and can add value to their development. Expand your support once your plan is solid, but your master plan should not go social-media or public until you're ready for full-blown execution.

CONSTRUCTIVE — Your master plan is also the strategy for fulfilling the dream for your life, so think big. Start by building the plan on the foundation of your own knowledge and experience. Think about your past failures and mistakes — study them: draw lessons that will help you formulate a plan that anticipates the obstacles that could derail your progress. Start with what you know. Build it out as you go forward.

COMPREHENSIVE — It was widely acknowledged that Einstein was a genius but you don't have to be the smartest person in the room to conceive a winning master plan. The key is to be comprehensive in your formulation, assiduous about covering every aspect of the idea. Leave no stone unturned. Be both detailed-oriented and future-oriented. Create a checklist of all the steps that you and others need to follow for a successful process in the present. Also, think ahead so that your plan encompasses both short-term and long-term agendas.

CONDITIONAL — Einstein reached out with his master plan to the President of the United States for support. You may not have to reach that high, but your master plan is so purposeful and far-reaching that it will need assistance for others to proceed. Without external support, you will not succeed. Plan for two kinds of resources: human — the people you'll need to bring on board; and financial — the money you'll need to raise to move things forward. Take the time to devise and draft your optimal plan — a compelling plan! — and the support that you need will find you.

Be Passionate In Your Purpose							**October 28th**

I desire to thank God that He enables me to disregard "the fear of man which bringeth a snare," and to speak His truth in its simplicity and power.
William Lloyd Garrison

The most influential media of the movement to abolish slavery was the Boston weekly newspaper the Liberator; its first edition was January 1831 and its last — December 1865, when the Thirteenth Amendment outlawing slavery was ratified. Its editor was William Lloyd Garrison, the champion abolitionist, who eschewed his gradualist thinking and with the launch of the Liberator demanded immediate emancipation. Garrison's editorial in the first issue established the historical context for his position.

> *Assenting to the "self-evident truth" maintained in the American Declaration of Independence, "that all men are created equal and endowed by their Creator with certain inalienable rights, among which are life, liberty, and the pursuit of happiness," I shall   strenuously contend for the immediate enfranchisement of our slave population.*

He followed with the key point, metaphorically — and passionately — articulating his position.

> *I am aware that many object to the severity of my language; but is there not cause for severity? I will be as harsh as truth and as uncompromising as justice. On this subject I do not wish to think or speak, or write with moderation. No! No! Tell a man whose house is on fire to give a moderate alarm; tell him to moderately rescue his wife from the hands of the ravisher; tell the mother to gradually extricate her babe from the fire into which it has fallen — but urge me not to use moderation in a cause like the present. I am in earnest; I will not equivocate; I will not excuse; I will not retreat a single inch — AND I WILL BE HEARD. The apathy of the people is enough to make every statue leap from its pedestal and to hasten the resurrection of the dead.*

Garrison's passion was no doubt part and parcel of his success in leading the movement to topple slavery. Let his example of great enthusiasm inspire your purposefulness. To be passionate in your purpose, practice these principles.

ALIGNMENT — If your values don't align with your initiative, you will never be passionate about it. Don't get involved in something you don't believe in. The sideline is better than the snare; and the heat of your passion better than the skepticism of the armchair. Like Garrison, once you believe in the cause, let your voice be dramatically heard.

ALACRITY — Be ready. When the calling of your life comes, answer it, and be forthright about it. There's a time to deliberate and a time to initiate. Know the difference. You'll find the answer as you delve more deeply on your inner trek of purpose. The words of Ralph Waldo Emerson remind us about the true source of greatness.

> *Nothing great was ever achieved without enthusiasm.*

APOTHEOSIS — Let your passion exalt you. Keep reaching for the stars, keep going for the higher ground. When you're passionate in your purpose, you will soar above the clouds of disappointment, and you won't get slowed down by the storms of adversity. Your passion will drive you to new heights.

ACTION — Garrison didn't wait for circumstances to turn in his favor before pressing his case against slavery. He went for it, and it was the power of his advocacy — and that of others like Frederick Douglass — that turned the tide towards justice. You will find the best course — and light the passion of your purpose — once you take action. The Chinese proverb rings ever true:

A journey of a thousand miles begins with a single step.

Your passion is the fuel to sustain you over the long and windy road of your purposeful journey.

Plan To Expose Injustice   **October 29th**

White people will not live in the same house with colored tenants, or even in a house recently occupied by Negroes, and that consequently its selling value is injured. The prejudice is not lessened by house agents, who have the maxim "once a colored house, always a colored house."
Jacob Riis

In 1890 journalist Jacob Riis published "How the Other Half Lives", which described the wretched housing conditions among the poor of New York City. The demand caused by the influx of immigrants and factory workers to the city positioned landlords to easily rent up their decrepit tenement buildings. In his writings Riis exposed the awful living conditions of the disadvantaged with the purpose of rectifying this injustice.

What made Riis' mission of improving slum life even more challenging was the racial dimension of the crisis. In his book Riis described the racism at work in the city's housing in no uncertain terms.

The color line must be drawn through the tenements to give the picture its proper shading. The landlord does the drawing, does it with an absence of pretense, a frankness of despotism, that is nothing if not brutal. The czar of all the Russians is not more absolute upon his own soil than the New York landlord in his dealings with colored tenants. Where he permits them to live, they go; where he shuts the door, stay out.

Riis made it clear that racial forces were not limited to housing but also effected employment opportunities.

How many colored carpenters or masons has anyone seen at work in New York? In the South there are enough of them, and, if the testimony of the most intelligent of their people is worth anything, plenty of them have come here. As a matter of fact, the colored man takes in New York, without a struggle, the lower level of menial service . . .

Riis' plan to expose these unjust conditions through his writing and photojournalism resulted in improvements to New York City's housing and water supply as well as the creation of new public parks. Riis was even successful in gaining Theodore Roosevelt's support for his cause.

You should heed Riis' example. Plan to expose injustice as it confronts you in your circumstances. Be strategic about this quest as you:

EXTRACT — Riis spent years visiting the slums of New York City, doing hands-on research, ascertaining the facts. Just because you experience or observe an injustice and feel it's wrong, that doesn't mean it's the cause for you. Do your research. Determine the fit between your values and the full range of issues before you take it on.

EXACT — Getting the timing right isn't easy, but it's crucial. As you make decisions about your initiative, understand that when to do it can be just as important as the what, the how and the where. Pay special attention to timing, to make sure all the factors indicate that this is a favorable moment for you to move forward to . . .

. . . EXPOSE — Be creative in bringing attention to your cause. Riis was a pioneer in photojournalism, which dramatically projected his issues and efficaciously fulfilled the maxim — a picture is worth a thousand words. Paint a vivid picture — literally and figuratively — to highlight injustice.

EXTEND — You need support for your cause. Riis gained then NYC Police Commissioner and future New York State Governor and U.S. President Theodore Roosevelt as an ally. Reach out to the influencers with the clout to overturn iniquity. In fact, Roosevelt's advise is apropos.

Do what you can, with what you have, where you are!

Stay Focused On Your Goals   **October 30th**

*Let me add that a bill of rights is what the people are entitled
to against every government of earth, general or particular;
and what no just government should refuse or rest on inference.*
Thomas Jefferson, in a letter to James Madison

On July 26, 1788 the New York Ratifying Convention approved the United States Constitution; only North Carolina and Rhode Island had not come on board. One of the key sticking points from holdouts was the omission of the provisions safeguarding individual liberties — the Bill of Rights. Some of the states who had voted in favor of the Constitution were now expecting the Bill of Rights to be incorporated into the Constitution as amendments.

As Minister to France, Thomas Jefferson was in Paris while the various proceedings transpired back home over what kind of government America should have. Jefferson set his own goals, advocating from afar, writing incessantly to his allies in the states to further his objectives.

On December 20, 1787, Jefferson wrote fellow Virginian James Madison, who wasn't interested in so soon amending the Constitution that he had just spent so much time and energy creating. Jefferson focused on his goal of the Bill of Rights as a constitutional amendment.

I will now tell you what I do not like. First, the omission of a bill of rights, providing clearly and without the aid of sophism for freedom of religion, freedom of the press . . .

Jefferson's purposeful correspondence persisted, writing again to Madison on July 31, 1788.

I sincerely rejoice at the acceptance our new Constitution by nine states. (It is a good canvas on which some strokes only want retouching.) What these are, I think are sufficiently manifested by the general voice from North to South which calls for a Bill of Rights. . . .

Madison responded to Jefferson in October 17, 1788 letter, expressing for the first time support for an individual liberties amendment, indicating that he now shared Jefferson's goal of advocating for the Bill of Rights.

What use then . . . can a Bill of Rights serve in popular government? I answer: . . . The political truths declared in that solemn manner acquire by degrees the character of fundamental maxims of free government, and, as they become incorporated with the national sentiment, counteract the impulses of interest and passion.

Just over three years later, the Bill of Rights was ratified as the first ten amendments to the Constitution, resulting in significant part from Madison and Jefferson staying focused on their goal. Like them, to achieve great things in life, stay focused on your goals; to do so, you must:

SEE IT — On your road to success, the first step — getting a clear picture of where you're headed — is the most important.

SHAPE IT — Break down the larger goal into smaller objectives. Jefferson had to write letters from afar. Figure out the little things you have to do to make progress and follow through on the agenda every day.

What good shall I do today?
— Ben Franklin asked himself every morning

What good have I done today?
— Ben Franklin asked himself every evening

SECURE IT — Don't pursue it alone. Jefferson and Madison worked together. Identify the right team members to work with you to help you stay focused and to make your goal happen.

SIMMER IT — Possess a big vision; it will keep the fire of activity burning under your goal over the time it takes to achieve it.

Seize The Day!   **October 31st**

Build not your monuments of brass or marble, but make them of everliving mind!
Thaddeus Stevens

On April 11, 1835, political leader Thaddeus Stevens rose to speak in the Pennsylvania House of Representatives in defense of a recently enacted education law threatened by repeal. Stevens was advocating for a statewide system of public education, which, during America's first half-century, was a hotly debated topic. The wealthy educated their children in private schools; the religious, in church schools; and those on the frontier, in home schools, believing in the innate wisdom of the common man over book learning. Stevens argued for public schools for all elementary school students, asserting a historical context to support his position.

> *. . . the ancient republics, who were most renowned for their wisdom and success, considered every child born subject to their control, as the property of the state, so far as its education was concerned: and during the proper period of instruction they were withdrawn from the control of their parents and placed under the guardianship of the commonwealth. There, all were instructed at the same school; all were placed on perfect equality, the rich and the poor man's sons; for all were deemed children of the same common parent of the commonwealth. . . .*

At a key point in his speech, Stevens reasoned that the American Experiment would fail without a plan to move forward towards education for every child.

> *If an elective republic is to endure for any great length of time, every elector must have sufficient information, not only to accumulate wealth and take care of his pecuniary concerns but to direct wisely the legislature, the ambassadors, and the executive of the nation — for some part of all these things, some agency in approving or disproving of them, falls to every freeman. If, then, the permanency of our government depends upon such knowledge, it is the duty of government to see that the means of information be diffused to every citizen.*

Stevens' plan prevailed as the repeal bill failed to pass, and from these early endeavors education for every American child evolved into the law of the land. But the availability of public education is only part of this success equation. The other part — the bigger part — is on the private side: your personal commitment to seize every day as an opportunity to learn, to advance your agenda, to become a better person. Begin to seize your days by practicing these three principles.

TERRITORY — Think about your life as a daily battle for territory, with knowledge as the most important daily expanse to conquer. Did I learn something new today? If you can't answer "Yes", then you didn't take any new knowledge territory, which means you're likely spending too much time watching TV shows and working social media than studying historical texts and reading inspirational books. Change your learning plan. Seize some new knowledge every day!

TIARA — Pursuit of destiny begins — and ends — with you. See each moment as a crown that you can adorn with a new jewels of wisdom as you move through the day. You can be in the best school, but without your own plan to seize the learning opportunities you can forfeit your educational advantage. You can be in the worst school, but if you possess a clear plan to embrace every chance to self-improve, you can overcome the institutional disadvantage. Develop a plan — and be committed to it — to add gems to knowledge crown every day. Let your practice be — Education Before Entertainment. And let your rule be — my bright and gleaming future starts with me.

TUTELARY — Stevens argued for "guardianship" to protect the educational opportunity of every child. You need to safeguard the opportunities that are before you today. Tomorrow is not promised. Circumstances outside of your control could show up tomorrow to derail your progress. Be vigilant about making the most of your immediate agenda, of not letting the precious hour of diligence slip away. Remember — what you possess on the inside determines what you produce on the outside. So . . .

. . . Above all else, guard your heart, for everything you do flows from it.
Proverbs 4:23

NOVEMBER: CIVILITY
DAILY SUCCESS PRINCIPLES

1. Leave Your Bows And Arrows Behind — William Bradford/ Samoset — 1620
2. Connect Beyond Your Cultural Identity — Crispus Attucks — 1770
3. Be Gracious To Your Adversaries — Ulysses Grant/Robert Lee — 1865
4. Work Towards Reconciliation — Mary Musgrove — 1732
5. Move Beyond Your Prejudices — Blanche K. Bruce — 1876
6. Bring Opposing Sides Together — Thomas Jefferson — 1790
7. Appreciate <u>And</u> Celebrate Diversity — Francis Pastorius — 1683
8. Use Soul Force — Martin Luther King, Jr. — 1963
9. Build Cultural Bridges — Joseph Heco — 1851
10. Agree to Disagree — Respectfully — Richard Henry Lee — 1787
11. Tell It Like It Is — Mark Twain — 1883
12. Learn Not To Hate — Andre Maurois — 1939
13. Speak Out Against Evil — Benjamin Franklin — 1764
14. Declare Common Interests — Red Cloud — 1870
15. Be An Effective Communicator — Cotton Mather — 1710
16. Make Peace With Yourself And Others — Joseph Holland — 1987
17. Extend Your Hand Of Forgiveness — Alexander Hamilton — 1784
18. Affirm Shared Values — Charles Ingersol — 1810
19. Reach Out To The Other Side — James Madison — 1789
20. Treat People As Individuals — Franz Boas — 1921
21. Look Out For The Interests Of Others — John Dickinson — 1768
22. Protest With Perspective — Niagara Movement Founders — 1905
23. Protest With Composure — California African American — 1855
24. Confront With Care — George Washington — 1783
25. Confront With Conviction — George Washington — 1783
26. Sow Your Ideas As Seeds — Richard Halverson — 1981
27. Share Your Stories With One Another — Hans Barlien — 1839
28. Learn To Work Together — Thomas Jefferson — 1776
29. Resist Cultural Divisiveness — Mississippi Black Codes — 1865
30. Be A Peacemaker — John Adams — 1797

Leave Your Bows And Arrows Behind   November 1st

. . . a while after he came again, and five more with him, and they brought again all the tools that were stolen away before, and made way for the coming of their great sachem, called Massasoit, who, about four or five days after, came with the chief of his friends and other attendants . . . after friendly entertainment and some gifts given him, they made a peace with him (which has now continued the twenty-four years) . . .
William Bradford

In 1620 the Pilgrims aboard the Mayflower left Plymouth, England, heading to Virginia but instead landed in Cape Cod. Their challenges — severe weather, scurvy infections, death from starvation, to name a few — abounded. Initial relations with Native Americans were also problematic; even some of the settlers' tools were stolen. Then an unexpected encounter with Samoset, a Native American who spoke a little English, paved the way for more interaction and new understanding between the groups. William Bradford, one of the early Pilgrim governors, wrote a history of the small New England colony that included the following account of the evolving peace, which stated these terms:

1. *That neither he nor any of his should injure or do hurt to any of their people.*
2. *That if any of his did hurt to any of theirs, he should send the offender that thy might punish him.*
3. *That if anything were taken away from any of theirs, he should cause it to be restored; and they should do the like to his.*
4. *If any did unjustly war against him, they would aid them; if any did war against them, he should aid them.*
5. *He should send to his neighbors confederates to certify them of this that they might not wrong them, but be likewise composed in the conditions of peace.*
6. *That when their men came to them, they should leave their bows and arrows behind them.*

The colonists' relations with the Native Americans improved when they became intentional about moving beyond the natural conflicts that inhere among different cultural groups. Their historic relationship is a model for contemporary interactions. Four lessons stand out, which you can live out as you:

LOOK DEEPLY — Look deep inside of your soul to talk about more than just the weather, your favorite TV show, or yesterday's headline. Be probing, even transparent so you can bring some personal insights to the table. If you stay on the surface, you'll miss diving to those inner places where wisdom and inspiration dwell.

LET GO — If you're holding any potentially antagonistic baggage, let it go! Work hard to release any prejudice or parochialism that could create relational waves. To be a source of civility instead of conflict, refuse to weaponize the interaction. Ask yourself the question: What do I have to   do to leave my emotional bows and cultural arrows behind?

LIVE BOLDLY — The rapprochement between the Native Americans and white settlers would've never happened but for the bold initiative of Samoset, whose intervention brought the warring parties together. Follow his example. You may have to run some risks to be an unifier. Manage the risks and move forward. Make some peace.

LEAN IN — Ask yourself another question: Where do I have to go to create some common ground on which I can walk together with others? . . . Across the tracks? . . . Across the street? . . . Across the hall? . . . Wherever you have to go, be intentional about leaning in to forgiveness. Fixing broken relationships or cultivating new ones won't just happen. You have to make reconciliation happen. Parker Palmer said it best:

> *The civility we need will not come from watching our tongues. It will come from valuing our differences. . . .*

. . . and sharing them constructively with others.

Connect Beyond Your Cultural Identity   November 2nd

First man to die for the flag we now hold high was a black man.
Stevie Wonder

In 1765 Great Britain imposed the Stamp Act — named for the stamp required to be attached to the items which it taxed — on its American colonies. Issued to raise public revenues for Britain's enormous war debt, the Act regulated newspapers, almanacs, pamphlets, legal documents, business papers, and even recreational items like playing cards and dice.

The colonial outcry over the Stamp Act and similar measures spawned protest groups like the Sons of Liberty; greater violence and vandalism resulted. Before this time detachments of British troops had marched inland to frontier forts, but in the fall of 1768, British soldiers landed and remained Boston for the purpose of controlling the growing colonial unrest.

But instead of mitigating tensions, the presence of troops exacerbated them. In the early evening of March 5, 1770, a crowd of Bostonians confronted a British sentry. In the chaos of flying snowballs and taunts, some of the soldiers opened fire, killing five colonists and wounding six others.

The first man to die in this incident known as the Boston Massacre was Crispus Attucks, an American stevedore of African and Native American descent. Born a slave in Framingham, Massachusetts in 1723, Attucks escaped slavery as a boy and became a waterfront laborer loading and unloading ships along the Atlantic seaboard. Not long before he was killed he had arrived in Boston from a trip to the Bahamas and was scheduled to soon depart on a ship for North Carolina.

The Boston Massacre came to symbolize the colonial struggle against British oppression — a rallying cry for freedom — leading inexorably to the formal declarations of freedom and war a half dozen years later.

Attucks connected with others beyond his cultural identity, sacrificing dearly for a common cause. His is a worthy example. You likely won't have to give up your life as you unite with others. Whatever challenge comes, do your best to connect beyond your cultural identity; to do so:

LOOK BACK — The fact that the first person killed in the Boston massacre and thus the first American killed in the American Revolution was a person of color speaks volume about the colorblindness at the heart of the American character. If people of different races died together at the very beginning to establish the American Experiment, it is certainly reasonable and imperative that people of different races get along with one another and work together to finish the Experiment. When was the last time you connected in a meaningful way with someone of a different race or background?

LEARN WELL — Studying about cultures different from your own will prepare you to connect with them. Commit to become culturally literate. Know enough to be able to communicate intelligently about your won culture while seeking to better understand the culture of others.

LET GO — Attucks let go of his identity as a former slave and connected with others who didn't look like him — all dedicated to a greater cause. Attucks' example signifies your duty, whatever your color or background, to transcend it to connect with others to build meaningful relationships with them. It is through cooperative effort that you can achieve great things, so you have to make yourself approachable to people who are different from you. What are you doing or saying — spoken or unspoken — to bring down barriers instead of heightening them?

LEGACY — The fact that Attucks was the first person killed in the Boston massacre made him a heroic figure of historic significance much to celebrated — the words on his Boston Commons monument . . .

And to honor Crispus Attucks who was the leader and voice that day:
The first to defy, and the first to die, with Maverick, Carr, and Gray.
Call it riot or revolution, or mob or crowd as you may, such deaths have been
seeds of nations, such lives shall be honored for aye...

Attucks — an African American/Native American man — died with white men, to set America on a road to freedom. With whom can you connect to take America further down that road towards that long-sought destination?

Be Gracious to Your Adversaries   November 3rd

The contrast between the two commanders was striking . . . General Grant,
then nearly forty three years of age. His hair and full beard were a nutbrown, with
a trace of gray in them. . . . Lee was fully six feet in height was Grant's senior by
sixteen years. His hair and full beard were a silver-gray, and quite thick . . .
Horace Porter

On April 9, 1865, at the Appomattox Court House in Virginia, Confederate General Robert E. Lee surrendered his Army of Northern Virginia to Union General Ulysses S. Grant. Their meeting, which effactually ended four years of bitter Civil War with over 600,000 casualties, was witnessed by Grant's aide-de-camp, Brigadier General Horace Porter. Porter's written account of this historic session evokes important principles about being gracious to your adversaries; seek to incorporate these points — captured in Porter's words — to bring win-win-win scenarios into your own life.

WIN THE WAR — . . . *Grant looked toward Lee, and his eyes seemed to be resting on the handsome sword that hung at that officer's side. He said afterward that this set him to thinking that it would be an unnecessary humiliation to require the officers to surrender their swords, and a great hardship to deprive them of their personal baggage and horses . . .*

Porter noted an important moment as Grant wrote out the terms of surrender. Grant's Union army had won the war, which put him in the position to dictate the peace. Fight hard to win your wars, but after your triumphs, maintain your humility, so you can, as Grant did, pay attention to the condition of the defeated. Instead of rubbing it in, look for way to lift your defeated foes up.

WIN THE PEACE — *When Lee came to the sentence about the officers' side arms, private house, and baggage, he showed for the first time during the reading of the letter a slight change of countenance and was evidently touched by this act of generosity. It was doubtless the condition mentioned to which he particularly alluded when he looked toward General Grant as he finished reading and said with some degree of warmth in his manner: "This will have a very happy effect upon my army."*

Without solicitation, Grant added conciliatory points to his written terms before handing the document to Lee for review. Take the initiative to be gracious to your adversary in some meaningful way. Grant's gesture established a tone of civility, making it easier for erstwhile enemies to become future friends. Find ways to extend courtesies and offer support even when you don't have to.

WIN THE FUTURE — *I will instruct the officers I shall appoint to receive the paroles to let all the men who claim to own a horse or mule take the animal home . . . Lee now looked greatly relieved, and though anything but a demonstrative man, he gave every evidence of his appreciation of his concession, and said, "This will have the best possible effect upon the men. It will be very gratifying and will do much toward conciliating our people."*

Grant had responded positively to Lee's request that all his soldiers — not just the officers — be permitted to keep their horses. Grant's magnanimity towards Lee demonstrates the importance of being gracious to your enemies, as it set a positive tone not only for that historic meeting but for future North-South relations. Heed Grant's example. Avoid taking a hard line, even if you're justified in doing so. Look for ways to accommodate your foes, not only by granting their requests but also initiating concessions. Let go of past hostilities and embrace future possibilities. Your cordial gesture will speak volumes about your character: humble enough to prioritize reconciliation and civility over looking good and being right. If you go out of your way to show graciousness to your opponents, particularly to those whom you've defeated in some way, you are sowing seeds of peace that will pave the way for social harmony.

Work Towards Reconciliation   **November 4th**

Tomochichi's interpreter was one Mrs. Musgrove. She understands both languages, being educated amongst the English. She can read and write, and is a well-civilized woman. She is likewise to teach us the Indian tongue.
John Wesley

In January 1733, having been granted a Royal charter by King George II to establish a colony in Georgia, James Oglethorpe arrived in America with more than one hundred settlers. Oglethorpe soon met with Tomochichi, chief of the Yamacraws, to negotiate settlement rights for land south of the Savannah River. The parties needed an interpreter and chose Mary Musgrove, who had been born Coosaponakeesa among the Creek Indians of that region to a Yamacraw Native American mother and an English–trader father. Musgrove eventually became an adviser and mediator to Oglethorpe, traveling with him as a liaison to various Native American leaders.

For her work Musgrove had been promised compensation by the English colonists; she sent a petition to London requesting it. Lieutenant Colonel Alexander Heron, one of her Majesty's leaders in the Georgia colony, endorsed Musgrove's request.

I have personal knowledge of her merit since my first arrival in this country, and I am highly sensible of the singular service she has done the country — a great part of the expense of her own private fortune — in continuing the Creek Indians in friendship and alliance with the English.

Musgrove received 2100 pounds as well as the title to St. Catherines Island for her labors, which fostered reconciliation in pre-Revolutionary America. Her example is noteworthy. You, too, should work towards reconciliation as you:

CONNECT TO OTHERS STRATEGICALLY — Do research in advance to learn the objectives of each group so that you can emphasize common interests. Think about ways to overcome the natural barriers that exists between different people and highlight them. John F. Kennedy enriches our understanding of this principle:

So let us begin anew — remembering on both sides that civility is not a sign of weakness, and sincerity is always subject to proof. Let us never negotiate out of fear, but let us never fear to negotiate. Let both sides explore what problems unite us instead of belaboring those problems which divide us.

COMMUNICATE WITH OTHERS EFFECTIVELY — Musgrove served as an interpreter so she had to listen intently to make the communication between the parties effective. How are your listening skills? Do you talk more than you listen? Do you state what you've heard before commenting on it? If you're a good listener, you know what questions to ask to deepen the understanding between different groups. Seek to unearth the gems of similarity that are typically buried under traditions of difference; introduce them to the conversation — that's what brings people together.

COME TO OTHERS CREDIBLY — If you practice what you preach, your credibility will precede you, making you the bridge over the troubled waters of opposing sides. Gaining the trust of people who don't trust each other can only happen if you're trustworthy. Protect your reputation. Safeguard your character. Be the person whose righteousness is the light that draws individuals out of the darkness of conflict.

CAST VISION FOR OTHERS PROPHETICALLY — When divergent backgrounds clash, cast a vision of the future. Let your mediation reach for perspectives that help others see beyond the narrow boundaries of their self-interest. Shift self-centered agendas from the center of attention; instead put the focus on how the different pathways connect and move forward together.

Move Beyond Your Prejudices   November 5th

We simply demand the practical recognition of the rights given us in the Constitution and laws, and ask from our white fellow citizens only the consideration and fairness that we so willingly extend to them. Let them generally realize and concede that citizenship imports to us what it does to them, no more and no less . . .
Blance K. Bruce

On March 4, 1875, Blanche K. Bruce began his term in the U. S. Senate, one of fourteen African Americans elected to Congress from 1869 to 1877 and the first to serve a full term in the Senate. Born into slavery in

Virginia — the offspring of his enslaved mother and her white master — Bruce attended Oberlin College before his careers as a successful Mississippi planter and political officeholder at local and federal levels.

On March 31, 1876, Bruce delivered a speech to the Senate in which he affirmed the equal footing that black and white citizens share on their American journey, describing the members of his race as . . .

. . . free from prejudices and have no uncharitable suspicions against their white fellow citizens, whether native-born or settlers from the Northern states. They not only recognize the equality of citizenship and the right of every man to hold, without proscription, any position of honor and trust to which the confidence of the people may elevate him; but, owing nothing to race, birth, or surroundings, they, above all other classes in the community, are interested to see prejudices drop out of both politics and the business of the country, and success in life proceed only upon the integrity and merit of the man who seeks it. . . .

Bruce posited a high standard: whatever prejudices you possess, strive to move beyond them. You and I need to heed his approach; to address discord in the community at its root, it begins with you and me. We all have prejudices of some kind. You prejudge me based on race. I prejudge you based on class. He prejudges her based on gender. She prejudges him based on religion or ethnicity or association or nationality or . . . To move beyond your prejudices, you have to:

ACKNOWLEDGE the fact that your prejudices are real. As long as you bury your head in the sand about your personal biases and pretend they don't exist ("Who? . . . Me?") those biases will be a source of tension and conflict in your dealings with others different from you. Keep it real!

ASSESS the reasons for your prejudices. Dig into your upbringing, schooling, your various cultural exposures or lack thereof. Be honest with yourself. Get in touch with the gulf, so you can demolish the inner barriers that exist in your heart and soul and start building bridges to others.

ACCEPT your differences from others. It's okay. In the real world, diversity is the norm, not the exception. If that's not your world and you're stuck within a narrow circle of people just like you, it's time to get out of your comfort zone, which introduces the last and most important point.

ASCEND beyond your prejudices. Be intentional about moving beyond your biases, broadening your cultural horizons. Plan some new experiences that foster broader and deeper understanding of our diverse world and people who are different than you. Take an initiative in a new direction. For example, break your routine one Sunday: if you're white, go to a black church; if you're black, go to a white church. You won't move beyond the old thing if you keep doing the same thing. To move beyond your prejudices, you have to be creative and connect with others in personally trailblazing ways. Try speaking to someone you've never spoken to before, in the spirit of which Mother Teresa spoke.

Kind words can be short and easy to speak, but their echoes are truly endless.

Bring Opposing Sides Together   November 6th

*On considering the situation of things, I thought the first
step towards some conciliation of views would be to bring Mr.
Madison and Colo. Hamilton to a friendly discussion of the subject.*
Thomas Jefferson

On June 20, 1790, Secretary of State Thomas Jefferson, recently returned from a five-year tour of duty as Minister to France, hosted a dinner at his new residence at 57 Maiden Lane in New York City. Jefferson's guest for the private dinner meeting were political adversaries James Madison and Alexander Hamilton, who had differing points of view on an important policy issue.

The first Secretary of the Treasury, Hamilton proposed a financial plan, one of the main tenets of which was the assumption of state debts by the federal government. He believed the nascent U.S. economy was so deeply troubled by foreign and domestic debt that a centralized solution by the new federal government — based on his recently published Report on the Public Credit — was the only way forward.

A former collaborator on The Federalist Papers, Congressman Madison had become critical of Hamilton over his scheme for funding the domestic debt, decrying it in the House as a repudiation of the American Revolution. His fellow Virginians such as Henry Lee were so virulently opposed to the Hamiltonian approach that they battled it with the same fervor as the earlier fight against the English Parliament's right to tax the colonies. At one point Lee queried Madison:

Is your love for the constitution so ardent that it should produce ruin to your native country (i.e., Virginia)?

At dinner Jefferson floated a compromise: Madison use his Congressional influence to pass Hamilton's fiscal program; in return Hamilton gather support for Madison's long-held objective — locating the permanent residence of the national capital on the Potomac River. This give-and-take eventually became political reality, with momentum generated by gentlemanly conversation.

Jefferson bringing Madison and Hamilton together moved them beyond conflict to conciliation. You can succeed with the same strategy as you:

DINE — Create a comfortable environment where adversaries can feel less defensive and let their guards down. A public setting like a popular restaurant or busy park won't work. Set up a meeting in a private space removed from the hustle/bustle of a Grand Central Station. Serving a meal helps mellow the mood. Bring people to a place that is quiet enough so that they can discern the voice of conciliation when it speaks, even if it whispers.

DISCUSS — Hurling heckles, insults and threats versus sharing stories, insights and jokes — the former things happen when people are at a distance; the latter when they are close enough to exchange views without shouting across the aisle. Tell adversaries that they're welcome to the table to talk. Help facilitate discussion with an ice-breaker or a couple of intentionally targeted questions. Once the rhythm of dialogue starts to flow, stay out of its way. The momentum of positive exchange is your best friend.

DEAL — Be a dealmaker. Practice the art of compromise to bring factions to consensus. With an assist from Jefferson, Hamilton and Madison found the will and the way to overcome profound differences for the sake of the common good. Since this Founding period, E pluribus unum ("Out of many, one) has been the motto of the United States, found on its Great Seal of the United States and on its currency. But the intensity of partisanship, public discourse and cultural wars challenges the social reality of this national theme. The question of how Americans live together with our deepest differences — cultural, racial, ethnic — is not new, but it cannot and will not happen unless we are intentional about doing it. You can move the culture towards a spirit of unity by treating people — no matter how different they may be in race, ethnicity, religion, gender, region or political views — with dignity, courtesy and respect. Heed Theodore Roosevelt's words.

The most important single ingredient in the formula of success is knowing how to get along with people. Without it, most achievements are not possible, and even what we do achieve can feel hollow.

Appreciate And Celebrate Diversity   November 7th

William Penn is one of the sect of Friends, or Quakers, still he will compel no man to belong to his particular society; but he has granted to everyone free and untrammeled exercise of their opinions and the largest and most complete liberty of conscience. . . .
Francis Pastorius

In 1683 Francis Pastorius founded Germantown, Pennsylvania, the first permanent   German American settlement in colonial America. The settlement was such a success that it attracted countless other Germans coming to the colonies. Pastorius was the agent of the Frankfort Land Company, which sponsored German Mennonite settlements in the New World. He wrote a report to the company in 1700; he highlighted the religious pluralism that was characteristic of the Pennsylvania colony, which set the precedent for the free exercise of religion that was constitutionalized in the United States of America later in the century. Pastorious attributed the advancements of the colony to the leadership of its governor, William Penn.

This wise and truly pious ruler and governor did not, however, take possession of the province thus granted without having first conciliated, and at various councils and treaties duly purchased from, the natives of this country the various regions of Pennsylvania. He, having by these means obtained good titles, I have purchased from him some 30,000 acres for my German colony.

He also wrote about the various groups, including his own Mennonites, peacefully co-existing there.

The native Indians have no written religious belief or creed . . . The English and the Dutch adhere to the Calvinistic persuasion. The colonists of William Penn are nearly all Quakers. The Swedes and Germans are Evangelical Lutherans . . . We at Germantown built a little chapel for ourselves in 1686, but did not so much care for a splendid stone edifice as for having a humble but true temple devoted to the living God . . .

The Pennsylvania settlers accepted the fact that there were many differences among them and learned to appreciate their respective distinctiveness, which created the stability and viability for their diverse community as well as lifting a beacon for the advent of the United States. Theirs is a timeless and direly needed example that you can follow as you:

CLARIFY DIFFERENCES — God created you one of a kind, with a unique set of features, thoughts, feelings, and habits. Others were created just like you — distinct in their own way. Whatever your own opinions of people, the natural difference of human creation is the reality. Instead of complaining about what you don't understand about your neighbors, seek to clarify those inherent differences, which can more easily happen as you . . .

CULTIVATE DIALOGUE — When was the last time you meaningfully interacted with someone of a different race, ethnicity, religion, or class background? . . . Cultivate social harmony by communicating across cultural barriers.

COOPERATE DAILY — Resolve to take the first step — today! — into a cultural arena different from yours where you can be a social sponge, soaking in new knowledge from those of divergent persuasions. You will create comity instead of conflict, togetherness instead of tension, and you will spread joy wherever you go, in the words of Gregory Berns.

The small, brave act of cooperating with another person, of choosing trust over cynicism, generosity over selfishness, makes brain cells light up with quiet joy.

CELEBRATE DIVERSITY — You have the natural tendency — we all do — to value, perhaps even to trumpet, the identity of those who are like you. Jettison the perspective that everyone should be more like you. Don't be part of the growing problem of cultural strife. Be part of the solution of overcoming divisiveness. Learn to understand and appreciate others, especially those of a different background, race, gender, religion or culture from you. Appreciate the wonderful diversity of your fellow human beings. Celebrate that diversity!

Use Soul Force   **November 8th**

Being to advise or reprehend anyone, consider whether it ought to be in public or in private, presently or at some other time, also in what terms to do it; and in reproving show no signs of choler, but do it with sweetness and mildness.
From George Washington's 1745 Notebook

Historical research indicates that, when he was fourteen years old attending school in Fredericksburg, Virginia, George Washington wrote some 110 principles into a notebook as his very own code of personal conduct. The fact that these precepts became the moral compass guiding his private and public conduct attributed in no small part to his history-making leadership.

Such rules of civility are neither old-fashioned or outdated; they are timeless. Over two hundred years later another great American leader declared similar themes of comity and graciousness. In his 1963 March on Washington speech Martin Luther King, Jr. proclaimed:

Let us not seek to satisfy our thirst for freedom by drinking from the cup of bitterness and hatred. We must forever conduct our struggle on the high plane of dignity and discipline. We must not allow our creative protest to degenerate into physical violence. Again and again we must rise to the majestic heights of meeting physical force with soul force. The marvelous new militancy which has engulfed the Negro community must not lead us to a distrust of all white people, for many of our white brothers, as evidenced by their presence here today, have come to realize that their destiny is tied up with our destiny. And they have come to realize that their freedom is inextricably bound to our freedom. We cannot walk alone.

Civility is the constant from 18th century to 20th century America — from Washington's no signs of choler to King's soul force. Civility doesn't mean you must change your message or your views, but you may have to adjust your approach. Use "soul force"; do so by using a:

SERENE MOOD — If you're upset with someone, with until your temper settles down before making your approach. A salty attitude blocks soul force, fomenting misunderstanding and even arguments, leading away from civility.

SWEET VOICE — George Washington learned at a young age to "do it with sweetness and mildness". Pay attention to the tone of your words. Strive for meaningful dialogue instead of menacing soundbites; a face-to-fact chat instead of a Facebook charade. Bring your uniqueness to the conversation but bring it with your understanding up and your barriers down. If you find yourself in the midst of conflict, seek the common ground and endeavor to get others to step on it. But it's important that you take the first step so that others can follow your lead.

SAFE SPACE — You create a safe space by filling it with forgiveness. To release soul force, forgive someone. Create an environment of congeniality, sensitivity and love, and people will begin to connect to you and each other, refusing to walk alone. Seek to make these other words from King words come to life:

Forgiveness is not an occasional act; it is a permanent attitude.

STRONG HAND — Learning to speak and interact with people who think and act differently from you is a daily challenge. But through the centuries, great leaders like Washington and King used soul force: they resisted a hostile and violent approach; instead they treated others — no matter how different they were — with dignity, affirmation and respect. Think of America society not so much as a melting pot but a tossed salad; not so much as a homogenized blend simmering in a pot but as ingredients mixed in a bowl, each retaining its own special flavor as part of an inspired unity. So even in the face of hostility, use soul force. You will be more successful in both your independent and collective work; and you just might help to heal 21st century America.

Build Cultural Bridges   November 9th

Yokohama, Nagasaki, and the China ports all sent their quota of bearded foreigners on the hunt for the Almighty Dollar.
Joseph Heco

In 1851 the American freighter Auckland rescued out of the Pacific seventeen survivors from a Japanese sightseeing ship wrecked by a severe storm. Among the survivors who were brought to San Francisco was 13-year-old Joseph Heco (born Hikozō Hamada). A year later Heco was in the group that journeyed back across the Pacific with Commodore Matthew Perry endeavoring to open up diplomatic relations with Japan. Heco was soon back in San Francisco training to be an interpreter. His language skills opened the door to influential politicians in California and Washington, D.C., eventually leading to introductions to Presidents Pierce and Buchanan. In March 1862, he met President Abraham Lincoln, the first person of Asian descent to have done so. And Heco became the first naturalized Japanese American citizen in United States history.

Heco returned many times to his homeland, working as an interpreter for the United States Consuls at Kanagawa, Nagasaki and Yokohama. He left diplomacy for a business career, working with American trading firms opening up commercial relations with the Japanese. Heco also became a journalist, writing "Record of a Castaway", an account of his experiences in America as well as helping to publish in 1864 the first Japanese language newspaper, the Kaigai Shinbun, earning him the reputation as the father of Japanese journalism.

Throughout his multi-faceted career, Heco built cultural bridges, creating new channels of understanding where there had been only waters of separation. His life exemplifies principles of civility and connectivity that you should incorporate into your own. Do your best to build cultural bridges by practicing these principles.

CONFIDENCE IN YOURSELF — You can't build a bridge if you don't believe you have the skills to build it. Heco returned to Japan as a diplomat, journalist and a businessman; in each role he possessed the self-confidence to be the linchpin bringing people of different cultures together. See yourself as the key to the door of intercultural understanding and unlock that door!

COMMUNICATE VALUE — Let others know that you value them, especially if they're from the other side of the cultural tracks. Learn something important to share about their background. Pass on a compliment about their world. The foundation of the bridge that you're building is sincere messaging: I appreciate who you are and want to get to know you better.

CENTER OF ATTENTION — Take the spotlight off of you. Make them the focus. Listen more than talk. Ask questions more than sharing stories. It's important to let them know about you, but find out about them first.

CREDIBILITY EXTENDED — Practice what you preach. As an American citizen, Heco went back to his homeland and shared some of what he'd learned, helping to start the first newspaper there. In serving them in this way, he added value to their work. Credibility is important when establishing new relationships. Do something to earn it.

CAST HOPE — Don't build a bridge to nowhere. Talk about where the fellowship is going, the purpose of coming together. If you can create mutual excitement about common goals, it's lot easier to get everyone moving in the same direction.

Agree to Disagree — Respectfully   November 10th

My opinion in this case is only the opinion of an individual,
and so far only as it corresponds with the opinions of the honest
and substantial part of the community is it entitled to consideration.
Richard Henry Lee

A signatory to the Declaration of Independence, Richard Henry Lee had already gained renown for his 1775 motion in the Second Continental Congress calling for the colonies' independence from Great Britain. Lee is also remembered for his strong opposition to the United States Constitution. Lee made his anti-Federalist arguments in Letters from the Federal Farmer to the Republican, a series of essays that he published as the debate raged over the enactment and ratification of the Constitution in 1787. In a letter of October 12th of that year, he stated his opposition in no uncertain terms.

There appears to me to be out only a premature deposit of some important powers in the general government, but many of those deposited there are undefined and may be used to good or bad purposes as honest or designing men shall prevail.

But in correspondence three days later he summarized his position with a sincere statement of his conciliatory disposition.

I have in the course of these letters, observed that there are many good things in the proposed Constitution, and I have endeavored to point out many important defects in it. I have admitted that we want a federal system — that we have a system presented, which, with several alterations, may be a tolerable good one . . . To say that these conventions ought not to attempt, coolly and deliberately, the revision of the system, or that they cannot amend it, is very foolish or very assuming. If these conventions, after examining the system, adopt it, I shall be perfectly satisfied, and wish to see men make the administration of the government an equal blessing to all orders of men.

Although his anti-constitutional position did not prevail, Lee won nevertheless. Because he had agreed to disagree — and he did with respect — he rose in leadership, serving as one of the first United States senators from Virginia from 1789 to 1792. During part of that time he was elevated as the second President pro tempore of the upper house putting him a great position to proclaim his views inside the new government, shaping federal policies for years to come.

Lee's example is a good one for you to follow. You can agree to disagree by keeping these points in mind:

CRATERS — If you throw bombs with your words and actions, you will leaves craters of division in their wake. If you create a big enough hole, the relationship breakdown could reach the point of return. Avoid throwing the bomb: state your disagreement but do it with respect. Mark Twain's quip is relevant here.

It were not best that we should all think alike;
it is difference of opinion that makes horse races.

COMPLIMENTS — In expressing his disagreement, Lee made sure to acknowledge the merits of the contrary point of view as well as affirming the larger purposes. Compliment your opposition. Depersonalize the debate. Make it about logic and not about personality.

CAMRADERIE — This is a moral point. What's the right thing to do? For you to be right or for you to connect with others? To prove your point or to avoid greater tension? To hold to your opinion or build harmony in the community? To ego trip or make peace? This can be hard thing to do because it may mean holding your tongue even if you're right. Asses your position. If you're asserting tangential points rather fundamental issues, be willing to agree to disagreer. You viewpoint should be inflexible only when your core values are at stake.

Tell It Like It Is   **November 11th**

Kindness is the language that the deaf can hear and the blind can see.
Mark Twain

In 1883 writer and entrepreneur Mark Twain (His real name was Samuel L. Clemens.) published "Life on the Mississippi", which drew on his experiences as a Southern riverboat pilot. Twain's eclectic background — Midwestern roots; cross-country traveler; journeyman printer; frontier miner; and wandering journalist — brought wit and satire to his writings. "Life on the Mississippi" differed from his best-known works — "The Adventures of Tom Sawyer" (1876) and its sequel, "The Adventures of Huckleberry Finn" (referred to by some as the first great American novel, 1885) — in its cultural insightfulness. The selections below are from Chapter 48, "Political Liberty in the South", which came to be known as "the suppressed chapter", because Twain's publishers canceled the section in proofs because they considered some of the material offensive to Southerners.

In the following passage Twain contrasted Southern and Northern temperaments.

There is a superstition, current everywhere, that the Southern temper is peculiarly hot; whereas, in truth, the temper of the average Southerner is not hotter than that of the average Northerner. The temper of the Northerner, through training, hereditary, and fear of the law, is kept under the better command, that is all. In a wild country where born instincts may venture to the surface, this fact shows up. In California, Nevada, and Montana, the most of the desperadoes, and the deadliest of them, were not from the South but from the North.

Twain elaborated the cultural differences that he'd observed among Americans during his journeying, but he emphasized — in spite of these differences — that people respected one another and found ways to work together.

What a lovely thing it is to see all these variegated nationalities exhibiting miracles which makes all other miracles cheap in comparison — that is, voting and feeling all one way, in spite of an eternal law of nature which pronounces such a thing impossible. And how pretty it is to see all these Germans and Frenchmen, who bitterly differ in all things else, meet sweetly together on the platform of a single party in the free and unembarrassed political atmosphere of New Orleans. How odd it is to see the mixed nationalities of New York voting all sorts of tickets, and the very same mixed nationalities of New Orleans voting all one way — and letting on that that is just the thing they wish to do, and are entirely unhampered in the matter, and wouldn't vote otherwise, oh, not for anything.

In his own signature style, Twain was committed to tell it like it is. It's not an easy thing to do because it means you're devoted to tell the truth as you see it, no matter how unpleasant it might be. It's a good idea for you to, as much as possible, to tell it like it is. These three principles will guide you on that mission.

WORDS — In every situation, in every relationship, it's your choice: you can tell it like it is — or not. Use your words to reveal things that help people understand one another, that encourage them to be kind to one another. Commit yourself to use your voice for healing instead of hurting, for hope instead of hard knocks. Be clear on the power your words possess, as the Old Testament makes clear.

The tongue has the power of life and death . . .
Proverbs 18:21

WAYS — Embrace the facts. Be intentional about living your life in ways that affirm reality, that respect things as they truly are. People are drawn to the truth. If you center your life there, you will be like the magnet bringing folks together.

WISE — A wise person looks for ways to empathize, uplift and honor others, especially those who are different from you. Like Twain, use your truth-telling as a bridge where people can find a crossing-over towards civility. Be intentional and strategic about telling it like it is. You will help peace triumph over discord, creating a better world.

Learn Not To Hate   November 12th

Most of the citizens of the United States are united by a common faith; they believe in their institutions and in the virtues of liberty. They believe in the possibility of a better future for a free people.
Andre Maurois

During the 1930s French novelist Andre Maurois was a frequent visitor to America, traveling extensively about the country. In 1939 Maurois published a book about his experiences through the states, which contained the following selection about the diversity of the nation.

This is an immense country made up of overpopulated islands sprinkled among the prairies, the forests, and the deserts. Among these islets of skyscrapers there is hardly any common life. The newspapers of Minneapolis are not read in Cincinnati. The great man of Tulsa is unknown in Dallas. The Negro of Georgia, the Swede of Minnesota, the Mexican of San Antonio, and the German of Chicago, Marquand's patricians, and Steinbeck's tramps are all citizens of the United States, but there is slight resemblance among them. . . .

Maurois went on to state his concern about divisive factors and articulated his ideas about how best to address them.

. . . It seems to me that the weakest point in the recent American experiences was that they were almost all directed against someone. One class was ranged against another. No government can thus construct an enduring system. A government has the right to be firm; it has the right to be severe and to demand a respect for the laws; but it

has not the right to hate. We will not emerge from our present difficulties by class war, but by love and a mutual effort of intelligence and understanding.

As Maurois affirmed, no one — not even the government — has the right to hate. You should make it our business not to hate, which is easier said than done because of our natural biases. You can learn not to hate; to do so, you must:

BREAK DOWN PREJUDICES — We all have prejudices of one kind or another. It's your responsibility to understand them and to own them — "Yes, I really did say that"; then to transform them — "No, I won't say that anymore." The key is to go on an inner journey of honesty and discover what your prejudices are. Acknowledge them by writing them down; where they come from; how long you've had them. You can't get rid of them until you've come to terms with them.

BIND UP NEGATIVITY — Meditate on these truths from Nelson Mandela:

No one is born hating another because of the color of his skin, or his background, or his religion. People must learn to hate, and if they can learn to hate, they can be taught to love, for love comes more naturally to the human heart than the opposite.

BUILD OUT BRIDGES — Once you've determined your prejudices, you overcome in two ways: increase both outgoing and incoming relational traffic. The former happens when you intentionally put yourself in a position — go to a neighborhood you haven't been to before — to interact people different from you. The latter is about your approachability. If you turn people off by your attitude, language or demeanor, change your ways. Being approachable means shaping your personality as an open window with a fresh breeze blowing through. Because of your gentle, understanding and affirming responses, people feel comfortable in coming to you with whatever's on their mind. If you're a welcomer, you won't be a hater.

BRING THE LOVE — The best way to overcome hate is with love. If you've had a negative attitude towards someone in the past, resolve to flip the script in the future. Changing to a positive attitude can be as simple as transforming your scowl into a smile. Do an act of kindness — bring a homebound relative or friend something to eat — to manifest your new loving approach.

Speak Out Against Evil   November 13th

*Let us rouse ourselves, for shame, and redeem the honor of our province
from the contempt of its neighbors; let all good men join heartily that justice
may be done . . . otherwise we can, as a people, expect no blessing from Heaven.*
Benjamin Franklin

During the years after the French and Indian War and the run-up
to the Revolutionary War, the unsettled frontier of Pennsylvania witnessed
hostilities between Native Americans and a new wave of Scots-Irish
immigrants encroaching on their land in violation of previously signed
treaties. One of the leaders of the settlers in this region was the Reverend
John Elder — the "Fighting Parson" — who delivered sermons from the
pulpit with his rifle in his hand!

Elder organized the settlers at Paxtang into a mounted militia
known as Paxton Boys, who suspected that the Conestoga Indians — long
regarded as friendly to the settlers — were secretly providing aid and
intelligence to other tribes who were scalping and pillaging. On December
14, 1763, the Paxton Boys attacked the Conestoga village and murdered the
entire tribe — men, women and children.

Most colonists were rightly outraged by the Conestoga Massacre.
Benjamin Franklin's voice of indignation was especially strong. He spoke
out against this evil in an 1764 article; throughout the narrative he
addressed the Paxton Boys directly in no uncertain terms.

*O, ye unhappy perpetrators of this horrid wickedness! Reflect a moment on the
mischief ye have done, the disgrace ye have brought on your country, on your religion, and
your Bible, on your families and children! Think on the destruction of your captivated
country folks which probably may follow in resentment of your barbarity! Think on the
wrath of the united Five Nations, hitherto our friends, but now provoked by your
murdering one of their tribes, in danger of becoming our bitter enemies. Think of the
mild and good government you have so audaciously insulted; the laws of your King, your
country, and your God, that you have broken; the infamous death that hangs over your
heads; for justice, though slow, will come at last. All good people everywhere detest your
actions. You have imbrued your hands in innocent blood; how will you make them clean?
The dying shrieks and groans of the murdered will often sound in your ears. Their
specters will sometimes attend you, and affright even your innocent children! Fly where you
will, your consciences will go with you. Talking in your sleep shall betray you, in the
delirium of a fever you yourselves shall make your own wickedness known.*

Like Franklin, when the evil is clearly before you, speak out against
it. To make your voice effectively heard, speak in ways that are:

STRAIGHT ON — Direct your words at the culprits. Call them out by name. Evil warrants a head-on assault. As Franklin did, go for the jugular.

SINGLE-MINDED — Don't come with a laundry list. Speak to the main issue and leave other matters for another day's battle.

SEARING — Don't mince words. Don't apologize. Strike at the heart of the matter with language that helps people see the wrong committed and that also inspires them to take strong and certain action against it. Let your address burn through to the heart of the matter. Note the strength of Jesus' language against the evildoers of his day. Follow suit.

Woe to you, . . . hypocrites! For you are like whitewashed tombs which indeed appear beautiful outwardly, but inside are full of dead men's bones and all uncleanness.
— Matthew 23:27

SOON — Proclaim your indictment against the evildoers right away. You will come across as more natural and connected if you address the offensive incident as soon as possible after it occurs. Let the perpetrators know that judgment day is fast approaching.

Declare Common Interests   November 14th

You ask anybody who has gone through our country to California; ask those who have settled there, you will find we have treated always them well. You have children; we have children. You want to raise your children and make them happy and prosperous; we want to raise ours and make them happy and prosperous.
Red Cloud

On July 16, 1870, Chief Red Cloud, head of the largest tribe of the Teton Sioux Nation, spoke at a reception in his honor at Cooper Union in New York City. Several years earlier, Red Cloud gained a reputation as a Native American war leader for fiercely defending the land of his people in Montana and Wyoming in what became known as Red Clouds War. Because of his successful attacks, Red Cloud signed the Treaty of Fort Laramie (also called the Sioux Treaty of 1868) ending that military conflict. Though he continued his criticism of the policies of the U.S. government and its Native American agents, Red Cloud's Cooper Union speech reached beyond the past and present antagonisms. Red Cloud began the speech with some points of unity.

My Brethren and my friends who are here before me this day, God Almighty has made us all, and He is here to bless what I have to say to you today. The Good Spirit made us both. He gave you lands and He gave us lands; He gave us these lands; you came in here, and we respected you as brothers. God Almighty made you but made you all white and clothed you; When He made us He made us with red skins and poor; now you have come.

As Red Cloud concluded, he made his remarks personal, reiterating the family values and reaching for common ground.

Look at me. I am poor and naked, but I am the Chief of the Nation. We do not want riches, we do not ask for riches, but we want our children property trained and brought up. . . . Our riches will . . . do us no good; we cannot take away into the other world anything we have — we want to have love and peace. . . .

Given the injustices that he and his people had suffered — and would continue to endure — Red Cloud would have been justified in articulating a critical, even condemnatory position towards his white audience. Instead he projected civility over confrontation by declaring common interests. You should do the same. As you declare common interests, strive to:

TREAT OTHERS WITH RESPECT — Endeavor to extend sincere words of affirmation to others whenever you can. Though it's good to be respectful one-on-one, it's better to make the praise public, increasing its value by bringing private commentary into collective awareness. Like Red Cloud, choose your words carefully; make sure they embrace life-affirming, unifying themes.

TAME YOUR TRADITIONS — By all means hold onto to your traditions, asserting their importance, just don't be so excessive about your embrace that you become myopic about the values and mores that others hold dear. Maintain a balanced perspective between what you and what others hold dear.

TAKE THE BLAME — When things don't go well, you can either spread the blame around to others or share in it yourself. Be humble enough to take more than your fair share of the blame in order to help others feel better about their role and any contributions that they might have made.

TREAD FORWARD TOGETHER — Find the common ground and tread on it. Red Cloud did it — "You have children; we have children". Declare what you possess in common with others and find ways to move towards it together.

Be An Effective Communicator   **November 15th**

It is very certain that the devotions and conferences carried on in such
a society will not only have a wonderful tendency to produce the "comfort
of love" in the hearts of good men toward one another but that their
ability to serve many valuable interests will also thereby be much increased . . .
Reverend Cotton Mather

The American Revolution was sparked by various Boston events — the Tea Party, the Massacre, Revere's Ride, among others — around 1770. A half-century earlier in Boston, a neighborhood-based initiative spearheaded by Reverend Cotton Mather, a religious and civic leader in colonial New England, sowed the seed for unified community activism that eventually made Boston the hotbed of independence fervor. Mather affirmed the value of communication in public discussion. He advocated bringing people together into small societies for constructive interaction and mutual support; in a phrase — "talking things out" — which became a tradition in New England and beyond. Mather outlined his plan for discussion groups in Essays To Do Good, published in 1710.

The members of such a society should consider themselves as bound up in one
"bundle of love," and count themselves obliged, by very close and strong bonds, to be
serviceable to one another. If anyone in the society should fall into affliction, all the rest
should presently study to   relieve and support the afflicted person in every possible
way. If anyone should fall into temptation, the rest should watch over him, and with
the "spirit of meekness," with "meekness of wisdom," endeavor to recover him. . . . It is
not easy to calculate the good offices which such a society may do to many other persons,
besides its own members. The prayers of such well-disposed societies may fetch down
marvelous favors from Heaven on their pastors; their lives may be prolonged, their gifts
augmented, their graces brightened, and their labors prospered, in answer to the
supplications of such associated families. . . . yea, the country at large may be the better
for them. . . .

Mather's paradigm influenced activities in other colonies, in particular Philadelphia, where Benjamin Franklin implemented Mather's plan in the Junto, his adult discussion groups. It was all about effective communication for history-makers like Mather and Franklin; this should be your priority as well. You will be an effective communicator as you:

LISTEN BEFORE SPEAKING — This principle is not only about courtesy and respect, two virtues you should always exhibit. Promoting understanding starts with hearing correctly, then you respond accordingly. Sometimes it's wise to repeat what you've heard before responding, to make sure you've got it right. And sometimes the best answer is no answer at all.

LIGHT UP THE CONVERSATION WITH CLARITY — Be deliberate; collect your thoughts before sharing them. Be simple and straightforward in the language you use. Impressing people with your intelligence can lead them into the darkness of confusion. You can't resolve things and move forward together if people don't know what you're saying.

LOVE THE TRUTH — It has been said that a single lie can negate a hundred truths. Don't sacrifice your credibility on the altar of expediency. You jeopardize communication by uttering falsehood. When you speak the truth, you sow authenticity and bring sunshine into the relationship.

LESSEN CONFLICT WITH QUESTIONS — Work through the conflict by asking the right questions of the offended person, for example: "What really happened here?" . . . "Why do you feel the way you do?" . . . "Is there something I can do to help resolve things?" . . . "Is there something that could have been done differently?" Don't query for query's sake. Be strategically inquisitive. Use the answers to the questions to talk things out and build better relations.

Make Peace With Yourself And Others   November 16th

Being at peace with yourself makes it easier to be at peace with the world.
Joseph Holland

Recently divorced, Lincoln had left South Carolina to escape the heartache of a bitter breakup. He arrived in New York City in search of a better life but found just the opposite: work hard to find; hanging with the wrong crowd; relapsed into drinking and womanizing; incarcerated for fighting; kicked out by fair-weather relatives. Homeless, he found his way to

Harkhomes.

After less than a month at Harkhomes, Lincoln reported that he'd grown tired of New York City and was returning home.

"How are you going to avoid the problems of the past?" I asked, urging him not to go.

Refusing to listen, Lincoln borrowed enough money for a bus ticket and headed back south.

Soon after his return, he ran into his ex-wife and her brother. An altercation ensued, tempers flared, punches were exchanged, and Lincoln ended up in jail for violating his order of protection. The indignity of a couple days behind bars was too much for Lincoln, so once again northward he came, less than two weeks after his departure.

This time around, a humbled Lincoln heard and heeded my counsel: "You're too full of regret. You've got to forgive yourself, and you've got to make peace with yourself."

Lincoln started praying every day for emotional healing and scheduled counseling sessions for anger management. As his emotional fog lifted, Lincoln realized: "I'm all alone up here." Lincoln concluded that his support networks back home — his family, friends, school cronies, coworkers, and church members — provided the best foundation for his new life. He reached out to them, apologizing for being out of touch, with the intentions of cultivating a broader base of support that would cushion him against the circumstances from which he had twice taken flight. Within three months, with some money in his pocket, less petulant and more determined, he was back on a bus to South Carolina, this time for good.

Lincoln's newfound peace with himself and others paved his pathway of permanent progress. Heeding his example, you can experience similar successes if you:

LOOK IN — Having twice taken flight, Lincoln had every reason to stay away from home. But he realized the problem wasn't home; the problem was him. Once he got clear and got control, the terrain was no longer treacherous. Look inside to transform yourself; your past mine fields will turn into future gold mines.

LOOK OUT — Your answer lies within and without. Look at old things in novel ways and obstacles will turn into opportunities. The resources you need to move towards your goals are out there. To find them, you may have to open some new doors, reconnect with your support network, even meet some new people. Go for it! Heed Golda Meir's admonition.

You cannot shake hands with a clenched fist.

LOOK AROUND — Lincoln's turning point was a revelation that pointed to relationships already in his network. The opened eyes of a new perspective highlighted human resources that became Lincoln's bridge over troubled waters. He first made peace with himself then was able to make peace with others. What resources do you have in your social universe that you only need a fresh, peaceful outlook to behold?

LOOK UP — Lincoln found the extra strength he needed through prayer. Looking up for help is always a good idea. Do all that you can but realize that there are times when divine intervention will be the key to your breakthrough.

Extend Your Hand Of Forgiveness   November 17th

To say that, by espousing the cause of Great Britain, they became aliens ... is to admit that subjects may at pleasure, renounce their allegiance to the state of which they are members and devote themselves to a foreign jurisdiction; a principle contrary to law and subversive of government.
Alexander Hamilton

On January 14, 1784, the Treaty of Paris was ratified by the American Congress, formally ending the Revolutionary War. The United States was free from foreign rule, but it had to create a government from scratch. One of the most urgent issues was the treatment of Loyalists — Americans who had supported the British Redcoats during the Revolution. In November 1783 the last enemy troops evacuated their New York City headquarters. 7,000 Loyalists fled the city to England, Canada and elsewhere, fearing American vengeance.

This flight took place despite the treaty stipulations that no revenge be taken against those colonists who sided with the Tories during the war. The military conflict transformed into a war of words in the press. Concerned about these Americans losing voting and property rights, Alexander Hamilton defended their fair treatment in newspaper articles throughout 1784, advocating that the treaty be enforced, arguing for principles of toleration and forgiveness.

How does it appear that the persons who are thus to be stripped of t h e i r citizenship have been guilty of such an adherence to the enemy, as, in legal contemplation, amounts to a crime? Their merely remaining in their possessions, under the power of the conqueror, does not imply this, but is executed by the laws and customs of all civilized nations. To adjudge them culpable, they must be first tried and convicted;

and this the Treaty forbids. These are the difficulties involved by recurring to subtle and evasive, instead of simple and candid, construction, which will teach us that the stipulations in the Treaty amount to an amnesty and acts of oblivion.

Hamilton's insistence that the new Americans extend fair and just treatment to all of their fellow citizens, even those with contrary past affiliations, underscored a fundamental virtue — to act with forgiveness, even towards your former enemies. Living out this vigorous virtue is a difficult thing to do. These principles will help; do your best to:

REFLECT — Take deep breath and think about your own shortcomings. Reflect on all of your bad days, the mistakes you made that aroused anger, the moments when you offended, insulted, or betrayed someone. Focus on your own need for forgiveness. Such an inner journey will prepare you to:

RELEASE — The old saying is trite but true: confession is good for the soul. It's good because it allows you to release burdens that may be blocking you from extending your hand of forgiveness. If you don't have a trusted friend or cleric to whom you can confess, pray to God on your own. This scriptural promise from the Apostle John is as good as gold.

If we confess our sins, He is faithful and just to forgive us our sins and to cleanse us from all unrighteousness.
1 John 1:9

RECONCILE — Yes, take the spiritual approach to this relational challenge. The words of the Alexander Pope speak volumes here . . .

To err is human, to forgive, divine.

. . . as do those of Jesus:

Love your enemies. Bless them who curse you. Do good to those who hate you. Pray for those who despitefully use you and persecute you.
Matthew 5:44

Humbling yourself to "pray for those who despitefully use you" will empower you to extend a hand of forgiveness.

Affirm Shared Values   November 18th

Were it not for the slaves of the South, there would be but one rank. By the facility of subsistence and high price of labor, by the universal education and universal suffrage, almost every man is a citizen, sensible of his individual importance.
Charles Ingersoll

In the first years of the nineteenth century, the political divisiveness that had begun a decade earlier continued to escalate. Though Philadelphia lawyer and Congressman Charles Ingersoll had been raised in the tradition of George Washington and Alexander Hamilton as a Federalist, he sided with Thomas Jefferson and James Madison in their Democratic-Republican party. Nevertheless he disliked the growing partisanship and anonymously wrote a series of letters in 1810 about the national character that all Americans shared, affirming common values.

Natural equality perhaps does not exist. Birth, affluence, and talents create distinctions, notwithstanding political regulations to the contrary. The pride of family, the vanity of wealth, and other adventitious advantages are not without their sensation in society, even in this young republic. But patrician and plebeian orders are unknown . . . Luxury has not yet corrupted the rich, nor is there any of that want which classifies the poor. There is no populace. All are people. What in other countries is called the populace, a compost heap,   whence germinate mobs, beggars, and tyrants, is not to be found in the towns; and there is no peasantry in the country.

Ingersoll's view of the American way of life might have been regarded as utopian even in the nation's early years; but he emphasized civility — the factors that united people rather than the forces that separated them. Though much has changed in the two centuries since his writing, his approach remains important. Seek to affirm the values you share with others as you:

ACCEPT PEOPLE'S DIFFERENCES — There's no way to get around individual uniqueness — that's the way God made us. Don't insist that others become more like you, conforming to your way of doing things. Affirm who they are, and who you are. As you accept the distinctiveness inherent in human relationships, you will find easier to interact with others.

APPRECIATE PEOPLE'S ATTRIBUTES — Understanding people, especially those who are culturally different from you, is a challenge. Take time to do it, and focus on their attributes instead of deficiencies. Look for the good. It may require some study, not only into the particular person's personality and background but also into the history of the relevant ethnic group or religious persuasion. Invest time and energy in perceiving the beautiful aspects that everyone possesses. It will yield social dividends of understanding and connectivity.

ALERT CONFLICTUAL ISSUES — You will not agree with everyone on everything. Since some kind of conflict is inevitable, stay alert for issues that conflict with your core values. Know the difference between a semantical divergence and a fundamental clash. Stand up for your most deeply held convictions. If someone disagrees with you concerning them and conflict results, you just have to deal with it. . . . it is what it is . . . The best way to deal with it is to acknowledge it, then to search together for the common ground.

AFFIRM SHARED VALUES — Even as you recognize your differences with others, you should also emphasize the things you have in common with them. In fact, focus on the latter more than the former. If you look for it, you will find you have just as much as — if not more — of what brings you together with people than what separates you from them. So dig beneath the superficialities and stereotypes to discover the solid rock of shared values — you will uncover gems of social harmony and inner peace — the precious things of life that money can't buy.

Reach Out To The Other Side   November 19th

It cannot be a secret to the gentlemen in this House that, notwithstanding the ratification of this system of government by eleven of the thirteen United States, in some cases unanimously, in others by large majorities; yet still there is a great number of our constituents who are dissatisfied with it.
James Madison

The Bill of Rights refers to the first ten amendments to the U.S. Constitution, which were proposed after the constitution's ratification in 1789. On June 8th of that year, James Madison — the erstwhile opponent of the Bill of Rights who had decided to become its sponsor — was the representative who introduced the amendments to the House of Representatives. In anticipation of the spirited debate and intense negotiations that ensued over the summer, Madison underscored the importance of Bill of Rights as part of a strategy to reach out to the two states which hadn't yet ratified the constitution.

. . . . We ought not to disregard their inclination, but, on principles of amity and moderation, conform to their wishes and expressly declare the great rights of mankind secured under this Constitution. . . . But perhaps there is a stronger motive than this for our going into a consideration of the subject. It is to provide those securities for liberty which are required by a part of the community. I allude in a particular manner to those two states that have not thought fit to throw themselves into the bosom of the Confederacy. . . . I have no doubt, if we proceed to take those steps which would be prudent and requisite at this juncture, that in a short time we should see that disposition prevailing in those states which have not come in, that we have seen prevailing in those states which have embraced the Constitution.

Madison's outreach was vindicated. After the Bill of Rights was passed by Congress and presented to the states for approval, the two outliers — North Carolina, then Rhode Island —   voted to ratify the Constitution and formally join the Union.

Is there someone on the other side of the political or cultural fence and reconciliation with this person would be a good thing? Is there someone else you know and it would be good for that person to join your cause or for you to join theirs? Or perhaps an outlier who needs to be brought in from the cold? Reach out to that person using these four principles.

TEMERITY — Be bold. Do what others dare not. Try to connect with someone who's considered too difficult or just out of touch. To build an important bridge, you may have to navigate into waters regarded as off limits by everyone else.

TONE — How you say it can be just as pivotal as what you say. Be deliberate. Choose the right words. Check your body language. Pay attention to your mood. They can make all the difference. And make sure you leave unsaid the wrong thing. You never want to add fuel to the fire.

TACTICS— Your victory is in the strategy. Have something of value to put on the table. Madison understood that the two holdout states wanted to see the Bill of Rights passed. What carrot can you use to facilitate reconciliation?

TIMING — Though temerity, tone and tactics are important, timing is crucial. If the relational storms are blowing, wait for the calm breeze. Read the signs of times and discern the social dynamics. Seize the opportune moment.

Treat People As Individuals   November 20th

We may, perhaps, expect an increasing number of strong minds will
free themselves from race prejudice and see in every person a man entitled
to be judged on his merits. The weak-minded will not follow their example.
Franz Boas

In 1915, after many decades of inactivity, the Ku Klux Klan reorganized but made little progress until the "Red Scare" of 1920 sparked the group. By 1924 the Klan expanded into several states and its membership reached four million.

Opposition to the Klan took many forms. Columbia University anthropology professor Franz Boas raised an intellectual voice, disputing the Klan-promoted superiority of his own Caucasian race. In his 1921 article Boas asserted that the best way to move beyond racial prejudice was to treat people as individuals:

It is easier to point out the causes of conflict between whites and Negroes than to formulate a   remedy. . . . it is clear that the only fundamental remedy for the situation is the recognition that the Negroes have the right to be treated as individuals, not as members of a class. But how can this be brought about in a population that is so deeply saturated with class-consciousness as our own? Even if, in the education of the young, the importance of individual differences were emphasized so that an intelligent understanding could be attained of the irrationality of the assumption that all Negroes are inferior, we should not effectively overcome the general human tendency of forming groups that in the mind of the outsider are held together by his emotional attitude toward them. . . .

The truth is that we all have biases of some kind, prejudging others based on race, gender, nationality, ethnicity, religion, occupation . . . the list goes on. We must acknowledge that prejudice of any sort is wrong. It limits us and hurts others. Put bias to the side. Begin to treat others as individuals. These principles will help as you:

LET GO — Be honest with yourself about your prejudices and let them go. Keep it simple. Make up your mind to be a person of civility and treat people as the unique and special individuals they are. Start by   examining where your biases come from: family, neighborhood, clubs, friend groups, house of worship

...? You can't put prejudice in the trash if you don't realize you've been carrying it in your pocket; get hold of it and toss it in the garbage.

LEAN — Don't be weak-minded. Make the decision to rid yourself of prejudice, then lean into it. Go outside your comfort zone to interact with members of groups different from your own. If you don't stretch, you won't grow. Lean into colorblindness: choose to put aside the lens of race to see others for who they truly are.

LISTEN — To get to know someone who's different from you it's best to listen more than talk. You will not only learn some new things but — just as importantly — you will show respect, which will affirm and strengthen the relationship.

LIKE — Start by giving other people the benefit of the doubt. Let them prove themselves unworthy of your positivity. If it's someone not to be liked, reach that conclusion after experiencing the person, not because of emotional baggage you're bringing to the interaction. Instead of looking for the dirt — things that support your prejudicial thinking — look for the gems — those not-so-obvious qualities that distinguish the person, establishing the individuality that you can affirm. Start there, you may end up liking the individual, the differences notwithstanding. Consider Mark Twain's pondering about what really matters.

I'm quite sure that . . . I have no race prejudices, and I think I have no color prejudices. Indeed, I know it. I can stand any society. All I care to know is that a man is a human being — that is enough for me; he can't be any worse.
Mark Twain

Look Out For The Interests Of Other   November 21st

My Dear Countrymen, I am a farmer, settled near the banks of the River Delaware in the province of Pennsylvania . . . My farm is small; my servants are few and good; I have a little money at interest; I wish for no more . . . I am completing the number of days allotted to me by divine goodness.
John Dickinson

In 1765 the British Parliament passed the Quartering Act, which required colonial legislatures to provide lodging, food and supplies for the

British troops stationed there. Refusal by several colonies to support the act increased tensions, especially in New York, headquarters of the British Army. On July 2, 1767, Parliament suspended the New York Assembly for non-compliance, making it an example.

Founding Father John Dickinson became known as Penman of the Revolution; he published in 1767 and 1768 a dozen Letters from a Farmer in Pennsylvania. Not from New York, Dickinson addressed Parliament's suspension of colonial legislature there in one of his letters, in which he emphasized virtues, which premised his political thinking.

From infancy I was taught to love humanity and liberty. Inquiry and experience have since confirmed my reverence for the lessons then given me by convincing me more fully of their truth and excellence. Benevolence toward mankind excites wishes of their welfare, and such wishes endear the means of fulfilling them. These can be found in liberty only . . . her sacred cause ought to be espoused by every man, on every occasion, to the utmost of his power. . . .

As a Pennsylvanian, he could have easily left New York's issues off his agenda. But his letter climaxed with a call for unity, rising from a core value to look out for the interests of others.

But whoever seriously considers the matter must perceive that a dreadful stroke is aimed at the liberty of these colonies. I say of these colonies; for the cause of one is the cause of all. If the Parliament may lawfully deprive New York of any of her rights, it may deprive any or all the other colonies of their rights: and nothing can possibly so much encourage such attempts as a mutual inattention to the interest of each other. To divide and thus to destroy is the first political maxim in attacking those who are powerful by their union. He certainly is not a wise man who folds his arms and reposes himself at home, seeing with unconcern the flames that have invaded his neighbor's house without using any endeavors to extinguish them.

Dickinson was looking out for the interests of others. You should do the same by keeping these precepts in mind:

PANOPTIC — Train your perspective to see the whole community, not just your individual domain. Put others first in your thinking by paying attention to what's important to family members, neighbors, schoolmates, coworkers, etc. When you look out for the interests of others — even before your own — you are sacrificing in ways that will yield long-term benefits.

PERIPATETIC — Take the road less traveled; being in their environment will help you pay attention to the interests of others. For those closet to you, sometimes just being a sounding board is enough. For those out in the community, crossing the neighborhood tracks or the political aisles just might blaze some new trails of unity.

PONDER — Consider how you can best serve others. If you're not sure what their best interests are, ask them. Pay attention to what they're saying — and what they're not saying. Just as important — observe them: figure out where they spend their time, how they spend their money, what they're journaling about; it will tell you what matters to them the most, what their highest aspirations are. Reach out with relevance.

PRODUCE — Don't just look out for others; live out in ways that will positively impact them. You can't produce neighborliness when you're forever alone at home, on the couch watching TV. Get out of the house and and do things that close the gap between you and your neighbors. Greater civility will rise from your concrete steps towards interaction with others.

Protest With Perspective   November 22nd

We note with alarm the evident retrogression in this land on the subject of manhood rights and human brotherhood; we pray God this nation will not degenerate into a mob of boasters and oppressors, but will return to the faith of the fathers, that all men were created free and equal, with certain unalienable rights.
Niagara Movement Founders

In July 1905 a group of twenty-nine African American ministers, teachers, journalists, businessmen and lawyers founded the Niagara Movement to advocate better education, greater political access, and expanded economic opportunities for African Americans. These founders sought a black civil rights agenda less accommodating than the policies of the Booker T. Washington-controlled National Afro-American Council. Led by W.E.B. DuBois and William Monroe Trotter, the Movement was the forerunner of the National Association for the Advancement of Colored People, into which it merged several years later.

The Niagara Movement founders took a hard line against racial injustice, outlining the ways that blacks were worthy of fairer treatment.

We repudiate the monstrous doctrine that the oppressor should be the sole authority as to the rights of the oppressed. The Negro race in America, stolen, ravished, and degraded, struggling up through difficulties and oppression, needs sympathy and receives criticism; needs help and is given hindrance; needs protection and is given mob violence; needs justice and is given charity; needs leadership and is given cowardice and apology; needs bread and is given a stone. This nation will never stand justified before God until these things are changed.

One of their final points offered gratitude to supporters for the difference they had made.

At the same time we want to acknowledge with deep thankfulness the help of our fellowmen from the Abolitionist down to those who today still stand for equal opportunity and who have given and still give of their wealth and of their poverty for our advancement.

The Niagara Movement's founding statement registered a powerful protest against racism in America, but it did so with perspective, shifting its points of view to incorporate distinct yet significant positions. You can bring perspective to whatever you're protesting against as you:

REACH BACK — The Niagara Movement's founders encouraged America to reach back and connect to its founding principles to support their case. Make sure you ground your point of view in relevant history. Use past accounts and examples to resonate your voice of protest in historical truth. First reach back, then:

RIDE FORWARD — Don't ignore or dismiss the facts on the ground but be clear on the goals of your cause. Protesting for the sake of protesting is the noise of anarchy. Be more concerned with vision-casting than vile-complaining. Protesting with perspective means you come prepared with a plan of action to address the problem and move your agenda forward. You should be ready to make yourself heard but you should also be ready to be taken seriously because of the power of the plan you're proposing.

ROUND UP OTHERS— Cultivate supporters by showing them gratitude. The Niagara Movement founders followed words like "monstrous doctrine" with "deep thankfulness". Don't get so caught up in an angry crusade that you forget to express the softer sentiments.

REFLECT WITHIN — An old saying carries an important truth: people won't go along with you unless they can get along with you. You may be an expert on some things, but certainly not on everything. So don't act like the smartest person in the room. Be approachable, teachable, willing to learn from others. Raise your voice in protest only after listening to other voices in peace. Abide in these words from T.D. Jakes.

It is important that we rebuild an atmosphere of
forgiveness and civility in every aspect of our lives.

Protest With Composure   November 23rd

The colored citizens of this commonwealth would respectfully represent
before you their state and condition: and they respectfully ask a candid
and careful investigation of facts in relation to their true character.
California Blacks of 1855

The discovery of gold in California in January 1848 transformed the trickle of westward emigrants into a deluge. The resulting Gold Rush brought 80,000 miners to the area by the end of 1849 — approximately one-quarter of them were from outside the United States — to make their fortunes. As the hub for the gold seekers from all over the world, San Francisco burgeoned from a village into a city of 20,000 inhabitants within several years.

In 1850 California entered the Union as a free state, but, as in other places African Americans were not free. Blacks suffered such economic, social and legal constraints that they organized a state convention to address their grievances. On November 22, 1855, they gathered at the Colored Methodist Church in Sacramento to begin three days of deliberations. The delegates issued several resolutions as well as a general statement published for the people of California; they made their protest with composure; heed their words and their example as you:

PREFACE YOUR ISSUE — *Our population numbers about 6,000 persons, who own capital to the amount of near $3 million. This has been accumulated by our own industry since we migrated to the shores of the Pacific.*

The African Americans made it clear from the outset that they were a significant minority group with some financial clout due to their industriousness. From the outset create a positive context for the advocacy of your issues.

POSITION YOUR ARGUMENT — *Most of us were born upon your soil; reared up under the influence of your institutions; become familiar with your manners and customs; acquired most of your habits; and adopted your policies. We yield allegiance to no other country save this. With all her faults we love her still.*

The California blacks went on to affirm the common ground that they shared with the people of California as well as their love for America, the disadvantages of racism notwithstanding. Strike a conciliatory posture, before shifting to a more confrontational tone.

PRESS YOUR POINT — *People of California! We entreat you to repeal that unjust law. We ask it in the name of humanity, in the enlightened age in which we live, because of the odium it reflects upon you as a free and powerful people; we ask you to remove it from your civil code; we ask it that our homes and firesides may be protected; we ask it that our just earning as laborers may be secured to us, and none offered impunity in withholding from us our just hire; that justice may be meted out to all without respect to complexion; the guilty punished; the innocent protected; the shield of wise and wholesome and equal laws extended over all in your great state . . .*

They climaxed their appeal for fairness and equality by focusing on the chief offense: a recently passed law that excluded their courtroom testimony in cases in which whites were involved. When confronted with unfairness and injustice, it's imperative to voice your protest. How you express your protest is likely to be as important as the substance of your protest. The 19th century blacks of California got it right, so heed their example. Avoid voicing your protest full of anger, finger-pointing and violence. Make your case compelling and do it with composure. Begin by emphasizing the common ground — search hard for it — with the offending party, then the ask: press your point! Your audience will likely be listening.

Confront With Care   **November 24th**

Let your heart feel for the afflictions and distress of everyone . . .
George Washington

After the Revolutionary War had ended, many new challenges confronted America. One of the greatest was the unpaid military. Without the financial resources to compensate them, the incipient government had to send the soldiers who had fought for independence home without pay. Disgruntlement among the troops was widespread, which crystallized in what became known as the Newburgh Address. One of the officers, Major

John Armstrong, called for a meeting during which he planned to propose that the military supplant the civilian authority that had so miserably failed to fulfill its obligations.

On March 15, 1783, General George Washington preempted Armstrong's planned meeting with his own gathering. He addressed the army officers, taking issue with any notion that military forces take over the civilian establishment, promising that Congress would do the Army justice. He confronted Armstrong's initiative by first reminding the men of his own character and devotion.

This much, gentlemen, I have thought it incumbent on me to observe to you, to show upon what principles I opposed the irregular and hasty meeting which was proposed to have been held on Tuesday last, and not because I wanted a disposition to give you every opportunity consistent with your own honor and the dignity of the Army to make known your grievances. If my conduct heretofore has not evinced to you that I have been a faithful friend to the Army, my declaration of it at this time would be equally unavailing and improper. But as I was among the first who embarked in the course of our common country; as I have never left your side one moment but when called from you on public duty; as I have been the constant companion and witness of your distresses and not among the last to feel and acknowledge your merits; as I have ever considered my own military reputation as inseparably connected with that of the Army; as my heart has ever expanded with joy when I have heard its praises, and my indignation has raised when the mouth of detraction has been opened against it, it can scarcely be supposed at this late stage of the war, that I am indifferent of its interests.

Washington started by confronting his men with care. His is a timeless example. Follow it as you:

EXALT BONDS — It takes wisdom to effectively confront wrongful action. To avert a coup attempt, Washington had to nip feelings of insurrection in the bud. He did this by affirming his special relationship to the soldiers, the sacrifices he had made on their behalf, the loyalty he had demonstrated over time, exalting the love that their shared service of country represented. Sharing about their extraordinary bond softened the blow of confronting them about a difficult matter. Whatever you have in common with the person you plan to confront, start there to create a comfort level for what is to come.

EXPRESS UNDERSTANDING — For most people, confrontations are not easy. If you're one of those who shies away from confronting wrongdoing, you're in the majority. There may be someone in your life right now that you need to confront about something that's not quite right. Don't avoid it, and don't come across as unloving. Be wise. Express your understanding of the difficult situation. Show them sensitivity by listening as much as talking. If they feel like you understand them, they are more emotionally disposed to accept what you have to say.

EXTEND LOVE — The truth may hurt, but it will hurt less when it's cushioned: it's coming from someone who cares. His supportive track record was one of Washington's chief points to his soldiers. Be sure to remind the person you're confronting of the good you've done for them in the past, that you have a demonstrated history of keeping their best interests in mind. Your message should be said as well as felt: "I'm not here to criticize but I'm coming in love."

Confront With Conviction   November 25th

. . . let me entreat you, gentlemen, on your part, not to take any measures which, viewed in the calm light of reason, will lessen the dignity and sully the glory you have hitherto maintained.
George Washington

During his March 15, 1783 meeting with army officers about their uncompensated status, General George Washington moved in his comments from soft to hard. This transition in tone from tender to tough was necessary. It was not enough for his men to know that he respected and appreciated them — a sentiment that he had communicated at the outset of his talk. He was their leader. It was his job to hold them accountable to the highest standard of conduct. Washington confronted those officers who were contemplating the coup, showing that he knew when and how to take off the gloves.

And let me conjure you, in the name of your common country, as you value your own sacred honor, as you respect the rights of humanity, and as you regard the military and national character of America, to express your utmost sorrow and detestation of the man who wishes, under any specious pretenses, to overturn the liberties of our country, and who wickedly attempts to open the floodgates of civil discord and deluge our rising empire in blood.

He concluded his remarks that day by confronting them with the challenging truth that their individual reputation, the standing of the military and the destiny of the nation were all at stake.

By thus determining, and thus acting, you will pursue the plain and direct road to the attainment of your wishes. You will defeat the insidious design of your enemies, who are compelled to resort from open force to secret artifice. You will give one more distinguished proof of unexampled patriotism and patient virtue . . . and you will, by the dignity of your conduct, afford occasion for posterity to say, when speaking of the glorious example you have exhibited to mankind, had this day been wanting, the world had never seen the last stage of perfection to which human nature is capable of attaining.

Whomever in your life you need to confront, embrace Washington's approach: yes, do it with care; but also, when necessary, do it with conviction by following these steps:

STAND — Washington took a stand. Right or wrong conduct is not subject to negotiation or compromise. Wrongdoing comes in countless shapes and sizes. When you see it, don't back away from it. Take a stand! Your firm positioning will move both the individual and the circumstance towards righteousness.

SERIOUSNESS — Washington was dead serious. Be clear on the gravity of your situation. Check your mood. This is no time for jokes. Let the seriousness of your tone be proportionate to the direness of the challenge you're facing. If the pounding of your fist or a scowl on your face is in order, act accordingly. When it's time to be tough, take off the gloves.

STANDARDS — Washington held to high standards. In times of crisis, don't moderate your approach because you're concerned about hurting someone's feelings. You may need to confront someone who tells too many dirty jokes (one may be too many); or who drinks or does drugs so much that they're late for school or work or delinquent on responsibilities; or who curses all the time and uses other inappropriate language; or who looks lustfully at others and shows them disrespect in other ways; or who comes to the house of worship but cheats and lies incessantly when they're not there. Elevate your standards and hold others accountable to them.

SACRED — Like Washington, summon your troops to the higher ground of righteous conduct. Always doing the right thing is a sacred calling. The best way to confront others is to lead them by your exalted example. They will be better people, and the world a better place!

Sow Your Ideas As Seeds   November 26th

> *You can offer your ideas to people as bullets*
> *or as seeds. You can shoot them or sow them.*
> Richard Halverson

In 1812, former President John Adams had been out of office for eleven years, but he continued to be actively engaged from the sidelines, never lost for words about politics. In November of that year Adams wrote a letter on the origins and character of American political parties, describing American politics as constantly — even inherently divisive.

> *You say "Our divisions began with Federalist and anti-Federalism." Alas! They began with human nature; they have existed in America from its first plantation. In every colony, divisions always prevailed. In New York, Pennsylvania, Virginia, Massachusetts, and all the rest, a court and country party have always contended. Whig and Tory disputed very sharply before the Revolution, and in every step during the Revolution. Every measure of Congress, from 1774 to 1787, exclusively, was disputed with acrimony, and decided by as small majorities as any question is decided in these days . . . Every Federalist in the nation will vote for the former, and every Republican for the latter. The light troops on both sides will skirmish; the same Northern and Southern distinctions will still prevail; the same ruling and riding; the same railing and reviling; the same lying and libeling, cursing and swearing will still continue. The same caucusing, assembling, and conventioning.*

Adams painted a cynically bleak picture of political divisiveness; such partisanship has persisted throughout American history, even to this day. Though poor communication is a culprit, it doesn't have to be that way in political or personal interaction. Richard Halverson, U.S. Senate Chaplain during the 1980's observed party divisions firsthand. He shared some insights describing a better way.

> *Ideas used as bullets kill inspiration and motivation. Ideas used as seeds take root, grow and bear fruit in the life in which they are planted. But there's a risk: Once it becomes part of those in whom it's planted, you'll probably get no credit for originating the idea. But if you willing to do without the credit . . . you'll reap a rich harvest.*

Halverson offered excellent advice: you should strive to sow your ideas as seeds instead of shooting them as bullets. When the divisiveness is longstanding, chronic or even intractable, reasonable interaction can be challenging. To improve your communication with others, especially with those who may already have a disagreement with you, heed Halverson's counsel to sow your ideas as seeds to grow civility; do you best to be:

SINCERE — Building trust is crucial, so lose the hidden agendas. Openness — even transparency — is the best policy, but until a comfort level for honest communication is reached, avoid sending loaded messages through third parties and surreptitious social media posts. Mahatma Gandhi compellingly articulated this principle.

A "No" uttered from the deepest conviction is better and greater than a "Yes" merely uttered to please, or what is worse, to avoid trouble.

SUITABLY TIMED — Don't sit on things you need to say. The quicker you can communicate towards reconciliation, the better.

SELF-CONTROLLED — Anger is your worst enemy. If you're upset about what was said about you, wait until you simmer down. Never say anything that takes the communication from the frying pan into the fire.

SENSITIVE — Listen . . . And as you listen . . . Be discerning . . . Be positive . . . Be humble . . . Be affirming . . . Be supportive . . . Be inspiring . . . Keep listening . . .

Share Your Stories With One Another   **November 27th**

Give my greetings to all those who are eager for information and tell them that I am as happy here as any person can be, and that those who want to come here may, with a little effort, live just as happily.
Hans Barlien

In the 1830's the first big waves of Irish and German immigration hit America, which provoked opposition among those who already had roots in the young nation. The nativist movement claimed to defend "Americanism" against the "un-American" ways of the newcomers. Yet the surge of immigrants was unabated, especially to the frontier.

One such group was from Norway, ahead of the influx to America from other Scandinavian countries, which happened after the Civil War. Norwegian farmer Hans Barlien traveled to the United States in 1837, arriving in Missouri in September. Barlien is recognized for establishing the first Norwegian immigrant settlement in the state of Iowa; he did so by sharing his story with the folks back home. His letter to Reverend Jens Rynning, dated April 23, 1839, was likely circulated hand to hand when it was received in Christiania, Norway; it was published in the newspaper Morgenbladet as well.

. . . I have also found land in abundance that is fertile, healthful, and profitable in every respect. . . . You can claim the necessary land without buying it; and when in ten, twenty, or thirty years it comes up for sale, you can keep what you have claimed at $1.25 an acre, which will be very easy to do then even though you have to to start out with nothing.

His main point stressed the diversity and safety of the New World.

All kinds of people from all nations of the world live together here like brothers and sisters; and in spite of the fact that there are no garrisons of soldiers, police and the like, you never hear anything about theft, begging, or any noticeable ill will between neighbors. To me everybody is good, kind, and accommodating. Nobody here can take anything away from you by force; but he can do this by cunning, power of money, and forestallment. This I hope to prevent on our claims by the help of Congress and so, in time, to succeed in uniting the Norwegians who are still here.

Just a Barlien shared his story, you should share yours; you will do it in a special way as you:

TELL A TALE — Everyone has a story to tell — but not everyone will share it. Be the exemplary story teller. Break the ice. Share it with others in ways that motivate them to tell their own stories. After you tell yours, you may have to simply ask them — "What's your story?" or "Where are you from?" or "What are you up to these days?" Share your story as the key to help others open the door to their own.

TRANSFORM A LIFE — Like Barlien, telling your story could initiate communication to help people not only tell their own stories but to make decisions to better their lives. Sharing stories with one another will allow you to connect in a meaningful way, at a deeper level, even to discover common ground. Such a process will reveal you two possess more of what brings you together than what drives you apart. Transformation happens when people come together in new ways.

TRANSPORT A PEOPLE — Barlien shared his, and he did it in such an inspirational way that many not only shared their stories but their own lives, sparking an intercontinental movement that culminated with his founding an American settlement. Meditate on the words of J.K. Rowling.

There's always room for a story that can transport people to another place.

TURN ON HOPE — Start sharing your success story — how you overcame obstacles on your victorious journey — far and wide. Tell it to impart hope to those who need to see beyond their gloomy moments to brighter days ahead. Who knows what kind of movement you might spark?

Learn To Work Together   November 28th

In matters of style, swim with the current;
in matters of principle, stand like a rock.
Thomas Jefferson

On June 7, 1776, Richard Henry Lee of Virginia submitted resolutions to the Continental Congress calling for the independence of the Thirteen Colonies from Britain. Two days of debate among the delegates ensued, but opponents of independence delayed any voting on the resolution for three weeks. The notes of Thomas Jefferson revealed what happened next.

On Monday, the 1st of July, the House resolved itself into a committee of the whole and resumed the consideration of the original motion made by the delegates of Virginia, which, being again debated through the day, was carried in the affirmative by the votes of New Hampshire, Connecticut, Massachusetts, Rhode Island, New Jersey, Maryland, Virginia, North Carolina, and Georgia. South Carolina and Pennsylvania voted against it. Delaware had but two members present, and they were divided. The delegates from New York . . . thought themselves not justifiable in voting on either side and asked leave to withdraw from the question. . . .

Jefferson then recorded a movement of delegates at the Congress that represented the will to work together.

Mr. Edward Rutledge of South Carolina then requested the determination might be put off to the next day, as he believed his colleagues, though they disapproved of the resolution, would then join in it for the sake of unanimity. . . accordingly postponed to the next day, when it was again moved and South Carolina concurred in voting for it. . . . a third member had come post from the Delaware counties and turned the vote of that colony in favor of the resolution. . . . Pennsylvania also, her vote was changed . . . and within a few days the convention of New York approved of it . . .

Two days later on July 4th, the delegates unanimously declared independence by making public a document that Jefferson had also drafted. It took some time and effort, but the Founding Fathers learned to work together. You can, too, as you:

LIFT OFF — The process towards an unanimous Declaration of Independence evokes the legend of the quails in the forest. They were tracked down by a crafty hunter. His plan was simple: imitate their call, cast a net over them, and cart them off to market. After losing many of his fellow quail to the hunter, one of them came up with a plan: "When the hunter tosses the net over us, don't scatter but unite. Let's come together in one section of the net and start flapping our wings. We'll have strength to lift the net and fly off." After the birds achieved their successful escape, the quail catcher's wife queried, "Why are you home empty-handed?" He responded, "When they all got together there was no stopping them!" Like these exemplary birds, the colonial delegates learned to work together and with the strength of their unity, there was no stopping their independence movement, yielding countless beneficiaries over the centuries since. Learn to work together with others, and there will be no stopping you.

LEAN IN — Break your usual routine, go someplace to pick up some new knowledge about others. Lean into someone's space to let them know that you care, that it's unity you seek, as the Apostle Paul encouraged:

Be of one mind, united in thought and purpose.
1 Corinthians 1:10

LEVER UNITY —When you learn to work together, you will raise the bar of excellence.With your strength of unity, achieving great things, the sky's the limit, so why not raise the make some history while you're at it?

Resist Cultural Divisiveness   November 29th

*That it shall not be lawful for any freedman, free Negro, or mulatto to
intermarry with any white person; nor for any white person to intermarry with
any freedman, free Negro, or mulatto; and any person who shall so intermarry shall
be deemed guilty of felony and shall be confined in the state penitentiary for life . . .*
Mississippi Black Codes

The 13th Amendment abolished slavery, but its social reality persisted through the Black Codes — the legal strategy perpetrated by southern whites to oppress blacks socially, politically and economically. These statutes were passed by the white-dominated legislatures of the south; they were slavery thinly disguised, intended to nullify the outcomes of the Civil War. Yet instead of attempting to resist or counter these initiatives, the administration of President Andrew Johnson took a passive approach towards Reconstruction, which emboldened southern political leaders to enact unjust measures to keep the Negro in his place.

In November 1865, Mississippi became the first state to legislate Black Codes, with a wide range of harsh provisions. There was a life sentence for intermarriage, practically ensuring the social separation of the races. Another one punished vagrants, very broadly defined:

. . . that all freedman, free Negroes, and mulattoes in this state over the age of eighteen years found on the second Monday in January 1866, or thereafter, with no lawful employment or business, or found unlawfully assembling themselves together either in the day-or night time . . . shall be fined . . . and imprisoned at the discretion of the court.

All the southern states followed Mississippi's example and passed some form of Black Codes, which in part precipitated Congress to enacts laws placing the South under military rule. The Compromise of 1877 ended the federal military intervention, with southern states persisting with various forms of discrimination, thus beginning the Jim Crow "separate but equal" era, which lasted until the Civil Rights Movement of the mid-20th century.

The failure of post-Civil War leaders — South and North — to resist laws and mores of cultural divisiveness led to the perpetuation of racial incivility and injustice through the 20th century and into the 21st, legacies of which persist to this very day. Don't make the same mistake. Resist cultural divisiveness by NOT doing certain things.

DON'T BE:

ANTIQUARIAN — Let go of past: old ways of thinking that no longer fit with present realities. If you attempt — like southern leaders with the Black Codes —   to force outmoded practices on new circumstances, bad things happen. Trust God's words — "Behold, I do a new thing" (Isaiah 60:1), and act accordingly.

AGORAPHOBIC — Lose your fear of situations that bring you in contact with people who are different from you. Look for opportunities to cross cultural boundaries as a way to expand your personal horizons.

ASININE — It is not smart to come up with rationales to mistreat or disadvantage others. It is wisdom to think of ways to uplift rather than oppress them. Use your intelligence to devise innovations that further justice and freedom.

ACIDULOUS — Watch your tone when interacting with others, especially when you're reaching across the cultural divide. It's not only what you say or do, but how you speak and act, that will determine whether you bring people together or drive them apart. Resolve to be a source of reconciliation and peace in all your interactions. And, beyond your own initiatives, be ready to resist the culturally divisive conduct of others and foster peace instead; blessings will follow.

Blessed are the peacemakers, for they will be called children of God.
Jesus (Matthew 5:9)

Be A Peacemaker   **November 30th**

Every problem is an opportunity in disguise.
— John Adams

In 1797 the United States and France were on the verge of war. John Adams, who had succeeded George Washington as President the year before, dispatched John Marshall and Elbridge Gerry to join C.C. Pinckney in Paris to negotiate a commercial agreement to protect U.S. shipping. But the French foreign minister Charles Maurice de Talleyrand kept the American diplomats waiting for weeks, then deployed three of his operatives (designated X, Y and Z by the Americans) to demand a bribe of fifty thousand pounds sterling for the negotiations to continue. The talks broke down and undeclared naval war broke out, with incidents at sea, primarily in the Caribbean.

This diplomatic incident, which became known as the XYZ Affair, stoked the pressure for Adams to declare war on France. Ideologically, Adams was committed to his predecessor's Proclamation of Neutrality, which established that the United States was neutral in the conflict between France and Great Britain. Practically, this task of maintaining the peace was so huge and complex, even overwhelming and intimidating, but Adams became a historic peacemaker by practicing three principles:

MANAGE THE PROCESS — When Adams received word of Tallyrand's ultimatum, he decided not to make the outrageous dispatches immediately public. He knew the popular reaction would be extremely patriotic and bellicose — an outcry for total war against France — so he bought time for peace, as his contemporary Ben Franklin advised in a 1783 letter to Josiah Quincy.

May we never see another war! For in my
opinion there never was a good war or a bad peace.

MANEUVER THE TEAM — Adam had included in his peace delegation Eldridge Gerry — known as a maverick — who opted to remain in Paris to carry on unofficial discussions with French diplomats to nip the looming war in the bud. And he had appointed his son, John Quincy, as minister to Prussia, who was now in position to favorably work the diplomatic backchannels of Europe.

MOVE DESPITE OPPOSITION — In February 1797 Adams sent another peace delegation to Paris — an unilateral move that was widely and roundly opposed. Adams' Secretary of State Thomas Pickering was "thunderstruck", stating "it was done without any consultation with any member of the government and for a reason truly remarkable — because he knew we should all be opposed to the measure." Such resistance notwithstanding, Adams' initiative restored the peace, settled by the Convention of 1800 — the Treaty of Morfontaine — which solidified the precedent of U.S. isolation from European wars, which defined American foreign policy for the next century.

When your crisis looms, you can follow Adams' principles and be a peacemaker in your own life as you:

MANAGE YOUR PROCESS - Don't be governed by urgency. When the crisis drives you, you will lose opportunities to make good decisions. Buy time: it's better to wait for the storm to pass. Let the conflict settle down, then intervene.

MANEUVER YOUR TEAM - Share the task with influential people, who can help you be the glue to bring it all together. The most important step is to determine who will be on your peace delegation. Pick even-tempered, circumspect team members with a commitment to practice civility.

MOVE DESPITE YOUR OPPOSITION - It is better to be principled than popular. The thought of people lining up against you may be intimidating, even overwhelming — don't think about! You may at first have to sacrifice a little acclaim for the greater peace.

Whether you realize it or not, you have a part to play in the peacefulness of your "country", whether at home, school, work, wherever. So manage, maneuver and move in ways that make peace. You will be happier, so will those around you.

DECEMBER: FAITH
DAILY SUCCESS PRINCIPLES

1. Exercise Great Faith — Harriet Tubman — 1850
2. Discover The Divine — Benjamin Franklin — 1787
3. Remember: You Are Not Alone — Pearl S. Buck — 1927
4. Possess Strong Faith — Abraham Lincoln — 1865
5. Be A Faithful Voice — Phillis Wheatley — 1773
6. Be True To Your Faith — John F. Kennedy — 1960
7. Make Sure To Acknowledge God — George Washington — 1789
8. Let Your Faith Ignite A Movement — Lucy Farrow — 1906
9. Affirm The Faith Of Others — Henry Brackenridge — 1819
10. Leave A Legacy Of Faith — Mary McLeod Bethune — 1904
11. Embrace Your Calling — Patrick Henry — 1775
12. See The World In A New Light — Frederick Douglass — 1838
13. Foster Freedom Through Faith — John Witherspoon — 1777
14. Write Down Your Revelations — Julia Ward Howe — 1861
15. Discern Your Blessing In Disguise — Joseph Holland — 1982
16. Practice What You Preach — Benjamin Rush — 1766
17. Fight Faithfully For Fairness — Richard Allen — 1816
18. Heed The Voice Of God — Jarena Lee — 1783
19. Examine Your Faith — Thomas Jefferson — 1787
20. See The Hand Of God — John Sweet Rock — 1862
21. Strengthen Faith Through Unity — Harold Ockenga — 1942
22. Put Your Faith To The Test — Simon Greenleaf — 1846
23. Take A Holistic Approach To Your Faith — Billy Graham — 1957
24. Rise Up In Faith — Jonathan Edwards — 1741
25. Sing Songs of Faith — Carols/War Songs/Spirituals — 1791
26. Cry Out To God For Help — John Jay/George Washington — 1786
27. Let Your Faith Fuel Your Conduct — James Bryce — 1888
28. Let Repentance Lead To Reform — Federal Council Of Churches — 1908
29. Be Faithful In Fellowship — Theodore Roosevelt — 1917
30. Take The Road Less Traveled — Francis Asbury/Henry Hosier — 1780
31. Don't Lose Sight Of Your Faith — John Spalding — 1877

Exercise Great Faith   **December 1st**

*'Twant me, 'twas the Lord. I alway told hem, 'I trust to you. I don't know
where to go or what to do, but I expect you to lead me,' and he always did.*
Harriet Tubman

Like most slaves, Harriet Tubman couldn't read or write, so her
mother told her Bible stories, which helped her develop a passionate faith in
God. Whipped and beaten by her masters as a child, Tubman rejected New
Testament scriptures instructing slaves to be obedient; she instead
embraced Old Testament accounts of deliverance. Tubman grew into a
devout Christian; she interpreted her dreams and visions as revelations from
God.

Her spiritual perspective was the key to her amazing work leading
slaves to freedom. On the Underground Railroad throughout the 1850's,
Tubman traveled by night, looking to the North Star for divine guidance,
praying every step of her journeying. During her first foray — her own
escape from slavery — she recalled the heavenly experience of crossing
over into Pennsylvania.

*When I found I had crossed that line, I looked at my hands to see if I was the
same person. There was such a glory over everything; the sun came like gold through the
trees, and over the fields, and I felt like I was in Heaven.*

Her faith in God led to supernatural outcomes, without which she
and her freedom-seeking passengers would not have survived. During one
journey, the safe house that she was counting on to harbor her escaping
slaves had been discovered and shuttered. Her only option was to rush the
terrified group to a nearby swamp. A biographer's account follows.

*She ordered them to lie down in the tall, wet grass, and here she prayed again,
and waited for deliverance . . . It was after dusk when a man came slowly walking along
the solid pathway on the edge of the swamp. He was clad in the garb of a Quaker. He
seemed to be talking to himself, but ears quickened by sharp practice caught the words he
was saying: My wagon stands in the barnyard of the next farm across the way. The horse
is in the stable; the harness hangs on a nail. And the man was gone. Night fell, and
Harriet stole forth to the place designated. Not only a wagon, but a wagon well
provisioned stood in the yard; and before many minutes the party were rescued . . . on
their way rejoicing to the next town. . . . How the good man who thus came to their rescue
had received any intimation of their being in the neighborhood Harriet never knew. But
these sudden deliverances never seemed to strike her as at all strange or mysterious; her
prayer was the prayer of faith, and she expected an answer.*

MOMENT — Tubman declared the prayer of faith and things happened in her favor. Faith happens in a moment in time. The Bible lets us know that though faith is immaterial, it is nevertheless real.

Now faith is the substance of things hoped for, the evidence of things not seen.
Hebrews 11:1

Faith is the key to your relationship with God. When you exercise faith, you open the door to supernatural grace entering into your life. Your faith releases the miraculous into your life.

MONUMENTAL — Great faith happens through divine experiences over time. You build up your faith through walking daily with God. When the Red Sea parted for Moses, it wasn't his first day on the job leading the Israelites. The more godly time you put it, the greater your supernatural outcomes will be.

MIRACLE — Tubman experienced miraculous outcomes because she exercised great faith. She was called Black Moses because, like her Biblical namesake, she possessed a special connection to God and a singular calling to lead her people. Tubman had no formal education, leadership background, or social standing. But she had a spiritual relationship and divine anointing, which was the key to her amazing success as the conductor of the Underground Railroad. Harriet Tubman's life of faith exemplifies the simple yet profound truth: when you have nothing left but God, you discover God is enough. If you exercise great faith, you will experience supernatural outcomes that will foster freedom for yourself and others. Are you ready for your miracle? Start believing God for great things!

Discover The Divine   **December 2nd**

And have we now forgotten that powerful friend? Or do we imagine that we no longer need His assistance? . . . the longer I live, the more convincing proofs I see of this truth — that God governs in the affairs of men. If a sparrow cannot fall to the ground without his notice, is it probable that an empire can rise without his aid?
Benjamin Franklin

At the the Constitutional Convention in June 1787, Benjamin Franklin endeavored to break an impasse by introducing the practice of daily common prayer. He started his argument with a reflection.

> *In the beginning of the contest with G. Britain, when we were sensible of danger we had daily prayer in this room for the Divine Protection. Our prayers, Sir, were heard, and they were graciously answered. All of us who were engaged in the struggle must have observed frequent instances of a Superintending providence in our favor. . . .*

He concluded with a specific proposal.

> *I therefore beg leave to move that henceforth prayers imploring the assistance of Heaven, and its blessings on our deliberations, be held in this Assembly every morning before we proceed to business, and that one or more of the Clergy of this City be requested to officiate.*

Though Franklin's motion failed on that day, he and James Madison succeeded in reaffirming the Christian precept that we all are created equal in God's eyes when they defeated the initiative by proslavery delegates to incorporate slavery into the Constitution as a federally sanctioned institution. Franklin challenged his fellow delegates to delve into the dynamic between their destiny and the divine. It's good thing for you to do, too. You can begin to discover the divine for yourself as you:

SEARCH INSIDE — Though Franklin was raised by pious Puritans and regularly attended the Old South Church in Boston growing up, he moved away from church-going and traditional religious practices and views as an adult. He nevertheless supported First Great Awakening leader George Whitefield, publishing all of his sermons and journals in his Gazette, devoting 45 issues to his activities, with many of the preacher's words gracing the front page. Franklin maintained a firm belief in God.

> *I never doubted, for instance, the existence of the Deity; that He made the world, and governed it by His providence; that the most acceptable service of God was the doing good to man; that our souls are immortal . . . and virtue rewarded, either here or hereafter.*

Like Franklin, you may have had a religious upbringing and you're now trying to figure it out on your own. Launch your inner journey to faith today. The more seriously you take this journey, the greater the possibility you will delve deeply enough inside to discover the divine. You may find God in the sanctity of a house of worship or in the solitude of your bedroom. Keep digging. Try praying. Ask God to reveal Himself to you. The Lord will likely show up in unexpected ways!

SURVEY OUTSIDE — Ask friends and family members of faith what they believe. Be open to supernatural ideas. Go to a house of worship; do more listening than talking but ask questions about subjects you don't understand. Remember — God was there for America's Founders. God will be there for you. Don't settle for what you've been told or taught. Endeavor to accept that some mysteries of faith, like the divinity and humanity of Christ, are beyond perfect understanding. You will unearth God as you dig into your most deeply held values that shape your view of the world.

SANCTIFY AROUND — Stop doing ungodly things. If you've been lying, cheating, envying, womanizing, stealing, self-aggrandizing, etc. — take a break. Step back from your worldly routine and go on a spiritual vacation. Turn off the TV, put down your smartphone, leave social media alone . . . if only for a little while . . . but long enough to get quiet, reflect on things you haven't thought about for a while. All the noise in your head and in your circumstances can make it more difficult for you to discover the divine. Put this scriptural directive into practice.

Be still and know that I am God.
Psalm 46:10

Remember: You Are Not Alone   December 3rd

Inside myself is a place where I live all alone and
that is where I renew my springs that never dry up.
Pearl S. Buck

In the 1930's the literary career of Pearl S. Buck soared with success. "The Good Earth" — Buck's novel that dramatized family life in a Chinese village in the early 20th century — was the best-selling work of fiction in the U.S. during 1931 and 1932; the book won the Pulitzer Prize in 1932. She published more great literature and in 1938, she became the first American woman to win the Nobel Prize for Literature.

The previous decade was more challenging for Buck. The daughter of missionaries raised in China, she returned there after college, serving as a Presbyterian missionary for 18 years. Life-threatening crisis surrounded her family during the Nanking Incident of 1927, when several Westerners were murdered in the midst of the violent conflict between various warlords, Communist forces and Chiang Kai-shek's Nationalist troops. As the battle intensified and approached the city of Nanjing where Buck resided with her husband and two daughters, the family prayerfully took refuge in the hut of a poor Chinese family. Terrified, they spent an entire day in hiding as the military conflict raged around them. Their hideout proved effective, the battle moved on, and the Bucks were rescued by American gunboats, fleeing to Shanghai then sailing to Japan.

During their peril, the Bucks called out in faith and made it to safety. Their experience evokes James T. Fields' "The Captain's Daughter" and the faithful principles that the poem projects.

CIRCUMSTANCE FOR FAITH:

We were crowded in the cabin,
Not a soul would dare to sleep —
It was midnight on the waters,
And a storm was on the deep.

'Tis a fearful thing in winter
To be shattered by the blast,
And to hear the rattling trumpet
Thunder, "Cut away the mast!"

CRISIS OF FAITH:
So we shuddered there in silence—
For the stoutest held his breath,
While the hungry sea was roaring
And the breakers talked with Death.

As thus we sat in darkness,
Each one busy with his prayers,
"We are lost!" the captain shouted
As he staggered down the stairs.

CALL OUT IN FAITH:
But his little daughter whispered,
As she took his icy hand,
"Isn't God upon the ocean,
Just the same as on the land?"

CONTENTMENT OF FAITH:
Then we kissed the little maiden,
And we spoke in better cheer,
And we anchored safe in harbor
When the morn was shining clear.

The Bucks remembered that they weren't alone. The Captain's Daughter did likewise. Their historic and poetic prayers were answered in amazing ways. When was the last time you renewed the divine presence within?

Possess Strong Faith   **December 4th**

If God now wills the removal of a great wrong, and wills also that we of the North as well as you of the South, shall pay fairly for our complicity in that wrong, impartial history will find therein new cause to attest and revere the justice and goodness of God.
Abraham Lincoln

In March 1865, as President Abraham Lincoln prepared to give his second inaugural address, the Civil War that had withered the nation was indicating signs of the Confederacy's collapse: the siege of Lee's army at Petersburg; the devastation of South Carolina and Georgia by Sherman's southern campaign; and the advance of Union troops across Virginia. Lincoln sensed Providence at work amidst the crisis as he looked beyond military triumph and political unity to the moral reconstruction of America. He believe that his cause would succeed, trusting in the Biblical promise. His March 4th speech was filled with divine perspective, as he summoned his fellow Americans to possess strong faith. His words evoked three important tenets of faith.

PURPOSE — *Each looked for an easier triumph, and a result less fundamental and astounding. Both read the same Bible, and pray to the same God, and each invokes His aid against the other. It may seem strange that any men should dare to ask a just God's assistance in wringing their bread from the sweat of other men's faces, but let us judge not that we be not judged. . . . The Almighty has his own purpose.*

Lincoln acknowledged his limited understanding yet still affirmed his belief in the sovereignty of divine purpose.

PRAYER — *Fondly do we hope, fervently do we pray, that this mighty scourge of war may speedily pass away. Yet, if God wills that it continue until all the wealth piled by the bondman's two hundred and fifty years of unrequited toil shall be sunk, and until every drop of blood drawn with the lash, shall be paid by another drawn with the sword, as was said three thousand years ago, so still it must be said "the judgements of the Lord, are true and righteous altogether.*

Lincoln's faith was so strong that it sustained his hope and fueled his prayers that — even through the pervasive calamity — divine justice would prevail.

> PEACE — *With malice toward none, with charity for all, with firmness in the right as God gives us to see the right, let us strive on to finish the work we are in, to bind up the nation's wounds, to care for him who shall have borne the battle and for his widow and his orphan, to do all which may achieve and cherish a just and lasting peace among ourselves and with all nations.*

Lincoln concluded his remarks on the high ground of contrition, compassion and confidence, affirming his faith that America would heal her wounds, unite in peace and rise towards the fulfillment of her divine destiny. His belief that his cause would succeed vindicated the Biblical promise.

> *And without faith it is impossible to please God, because anyone who comes to him must believe that he exists and that he rewards those who earnestly seek him.*
> Hebrews 11:6

The power of Lincoln's message still resonates in our times. Your future success will rise from your present belief. Progress doesn't start with your activities. It begins with your faith. If you believe positively about your situation (spirit as renewed faith), you will think positively about it (soul as renewed attitude), then you will act positively — and victoriously (body as renewed lifestyle). In a phrase: believe to succeed. This holistic strategy worked for Lincoln in the nineteenth century to bring America through her greatest challenge. If you just believe, it will work for you now. Your success tomorrow depends on the strong faith you possess today.

Be A Faithful Voice   December 5th

> *The world is a severe schoolmaster, for its frowns are less dangerous than its smiles and flatteries, and it is a difficult task to keep in the path of wisdom.*
> Phillis Wheatley

In 1761 Phillis Wheatley was brought from West Africa to Boston when she was seven years old and sold into slavery. Her owners taught her to read the Bible and Wheatley grew in her Christian faith. When not busy with her domestic duties, she became a voracious reader of history, geography, British literature, even the Greek and Latin classics of Virgil, Ovid, Terence, and Homer.

Inspired to write, Wheatley had created a collection of 28 poems by the time she was eighteen. But her efforts for a colonial publisher — apparently unwilling to support literature from a slave — were in vain. Wheatley travelled to England where her initiatives bore fruit. In 1773 her *Poems on Various Subjects, Religious and Moral* was published in London, making her the first published African American poet in modern times.

Wheatley combined her literary passion with her religious faith and social values. In *On Being Brought from Africa to America*, her best-known poem, she reminded the Great Awakening movement of her era that black people were as good an audience for the gospel as anyone else.

> *'Twas mercy brought me from my Pagan land,*
> *Taught my benighted soul to understand*
> *That there's a God, that there's a Saviour too:*
> *Once I redemption neither sought nor knew.*
> *Some view our sable race with scornful eye,*
> *"Their colour is a diabolic die."*
> *Remember, Christians, Negros, black as Cain,*
> *May be refin'd, and join th' angelic train.*

Though she lived a short life (She died at thirty-one.) with many hardships, Wheatley kept writing through it all, faithful to her artistic calling, ever a creative voice. She was part of the eighteenth century abolitionist movement, using her gifts and influence to keep the flame of justice burning. Wheatley proved to be a faithful voice to her generation, and you should be one to yours. To do so, you have to practice:

DEVOTION — No one of her day expected Wheatley, a little African slave girl, to rise up as a faithful voice creating poetry that shed hope for her people and for the young nation. But she was devoted to her faith, which released amazing outcomes through her life, fulfilling this scriptural promise.

> *Now to him who is able to do immeasurably more than all we ask*
> *or imagine, according to his power that is at work within us . . .*
> Ephesians 3:20

No one may expect for you to be a faithful voice, bringing creative truth to your daily circumstances. Don't listen to what popular opinion has to say about your calling. If Phillis Wheatley had listened to it, her poetry would have never been published. Be ready to reject negative advice and listen for that still, small voice from within, which will inspire you to inspire others in unexpected and uplifting ways.

DECLARATION — Phillis never stopped writing; she was both prolific and profound, as the following verse from her demonstrates.

Proceed, great chief, with virtue on thy side,
Thy every action let the goddess guide.

Let the expressions of your voice be heard in manifold ways — writing, speaking, video, social media — and let your voice resound with your faith-inspired purpose.

DYNAMICS — Make your declarations dynamic, stimulating transformative development among your listeners. Let them be compelled by your voice, and transformed in the process. And let your success be measured by the number of lives you uplift.

Be True to Your Faith   **December 6th**

I do not intend to apologize for these views to my critics
of either Catholic or Protestant faith, nor do I intend to
disavow either my views or my church in order to win this election.
John F. Kennedy

On September 12, 1960, John F. Kennedy, as the Democratic Presidential nominee, addressed the Greater Houston Ministerial Association. Kennedy was responding to a statement issued five days earlier by a group of 150 Protestant ministers and laypeople asserting that Kennedy as President would be unduly influenced by the Catholic Church. In his speech answering this charge, Kennedy cast a vision for American of religious equality and harmony.

I believe in an America where religious intolerance will someday end; where all men and all churches are treated as equal; where every man has the same right to attend or not attend the church of his choice; where there is no Catholic vote, no anti-Catholic vote, no bloc voting of any kind; and where Catholics, Protestants and Jews . . . will refrain from those attitudes of disdain and division which have so often marred their works in the past, and promote instead the American ideal of brotherhood.

Kennedy emphasized his theme of religious transcendence by

expounding a historical context.

> . . . *this is the kind of America for which our forefathers died when they fled here to escape religious test oaths that ended office to members of less favored churches; when they fought for the Constitution, the Bill of Rights . . . when they fought at the shrine I visited today, the Alamo. For side by side with Bowie and Crockett died Fuetes and McCafferty and Bailey and Bedilio and Carey — but no one knows whether they were Catholics or not.*

The frankness in which Kennedy dealt with his faith on the campaign trail turned the issue in his favor, which was not an insignificant factor in his electoral success in November 1960. Kennedy was true to his faith, and you should be true to yours. To do so, commit to:

PLOW INTO WHAT YOU BELIEVE — Dig beneath the surface of Sunday school lessons and worship services. Know what you believe and why you believe it. It's not good enough to show up weekly in your house of worship or recite the Lord's prayer. Do research into your religious world view. Become a lifelong learner of your faith so that your understanding will grow and your wisdom will flourish. These words from Anatole France will encourage you in your faithful mission.

> *To accomplish great things, we must not only act,*
> *but also dream; not only plan but also believe.*

PROFESS WHAT YOU BELIEVE — If you've been in the closet with your faith, that's the wrong place to be. Jesus emphasized the importance of professing your faith.

> *Whoever acknowledges me before others, I will*
> *also acknowledge before my Father in heaven.*
> Matthew 10:32

Kennedy's profession of his faith proved to be a key factor in his winning the Presidency. Don't let timidity put a lid on your destiny.

PRACTICE WHAT YOU BELIEVE — Be consistent, aligning what you say with what you do. Jesus' advice is also crucial here.

*Therefore everyone who hears these words of mine and puts them
into practice is like a wise man who built his house on the rock. The
rain came down, the streams rose, and the winds blew and beat against
that house; yet it did not fall, because it had its foundation on the rock.*
Matthew 7:24-25

Practicing your faith will not only bring you spiritual credibility; it will
also help you make it through the storms of life.

Make Sure To Acknowledge God   December 7th

*No people can be bound to acknowledge and adore the Invisible Hand
which conducts the affairs of men more than those of the United States.
Every step by which they have advanced to the character of an independent
nation seems to have been distinguished by some token of providential agency . . .*
George Washington

On April 30, 1789, George Washington gave the First Inaugural
Address at Federal Hall in New York City, marking the commencement of
the United States Presidency. After being formally introduced to the House
of Representatives and the Senate, Washington moved to the second floor
balcony to deliver his remarks. Throughout the speech, Washington
affirmed the divine handiwork at the founding of the nation. As you review
his historic words and the principles that they highlight, remember that
Washington made sure to acknowledge God throughout America's
founding. As you reflect on his words and the precepts they highlight,
consider the foundational principle of acknowledging the handiwork of
God in your own life.

DIVINE SUPPLY — *. . . it would be peculiarly improper to omit in
this first official act my fervent supplications to that Almighty Being who rules
over the universe, who presides in the councils of nations, and whose
providential aids can supply every human defect, that His benediction may
consecrate to the liberties and happiness of the people of the United States a
government instituted by themselves for these essential purposes . . . In tendering
this homage to the Great Author of every public and private good, I assure
myself that it expresses your sentiments not less than my own, nor those of my
fellow citizens at large less than either.*

Your own efforts are always necessary but sometimes not sufficient
to attain your biggest dreams. Washington recognized the importance of
divine supply — supernatural resources beyond his own human limitations

to achieve epochal goals. When you come to the end of your abilities and options, remember the words of the Apostle Paul.

And my God shall supply all your need
according to His riches in glory by Christ Jesus.
Philippians 4:19

DIVINE SYNERGY — . . . *there is no truth more thoroughly established than that there exists in the economy and course of nature an indissoluble union between virtue and happiness; between duty and advantage; between the genuine maxims of an honest and magnanimous policy and the solid reward of pubic prosperity and felicity; since we ought to be no less persuaded that the propitious smiles of Heaven can never be expected on a nation that disregards the eternal rules of order and right which Heaven itself has ordained; and since the preservation of the sacred fire of liberty and the destiny of the republican model of government are justly considered, perhaps, as deeply, as finally, staked on the experiment entrusted to the hands of the American people.*

Washington correlated the future success of the American Experiment to the ongoing favor of God, blessings released by the virtuous conduct of the people. Do your best to live virtuously, perhaps even to live out the vigorous virtues of this book; it will bring divine favor into your life — and into the life of the nation.

DIVINE SUPPLICATION — . . . *I shall take my present leave; but not without resorting once more to the benign Parent of the human race in humble supplication that, since He has been pleased to favor the American people with opportunities for deliberating in perfect tranquility . . .*

Washington could not conclude his Inaugural Address without — once again — affirming the primacy of Providence in the promise of America. You may not understand what's going on in your life right now. There was much that was unclear to Washington as he led the country through the American Revolution, but he acknowledged that God was intimately aware of every detail of the struggle. You may be in the throes of a situation where it makes no sense what's happening to you. Despite all the challenges, acknowledge God, reach out with your supplications, and Providence will provide the blessings to get you through it with victorious, historic outcomes. That was Washington's testimony. Why not make it your own?

Let Your Faith Ignite A Movement   December 8th

She came with love and power, holding up
the blood of Jesus Christ in all His fullness.
— Azusa Street Church Bulletin about Lucy Farrow

In 1851 Lucy Farrow, the niece of prominent abolitionist Frederick Douglass, was born into slavery in Norfolk, Virginia. After emancipation, Farrow moved to Mississippi, then to Houston, where, as a woman of strong faith, she pastored a small church while working other jobs to support her family.

Farrow worked as a cook during Charles Parham's 1905 Houston crusade. Parham was so impressed with Farrow that he invited her back to Kansas as a governess for his children and to mentor her in ministry. Through Parham's teachings, Farrow experienced glossolalia: speaking in tongues as the sign of receiving the baptism in the Holy Spirit.

While she was in Kansas, Farrow brought in young minister William Seymour to help run her church. In February 1906 Seymour moved to Los Angeles to start his own holiness church, holding Bible studies and prayer services in friends' homes. He soon sent for Farrow to assist him. Arriving in early April, she was called the "Anointed Handmaiden" because her praying through the laying on of hands resulted in physical healing miracles, which played a significant role in the revival that resulted. The church bulletin reported the divine dynamics.

There was a great deal of opposition, but they continued to fast and pray for the baptism with the Holy Spirit, till on April 9th the fire of God fell in a cottage on Bonnie Brae. Pentecost was poured out upon workers and saints. Three days after that, Bro. Seymour received his Pentecost. Two who had been working with him in Houston came to Los Angeles just before Pentecost fell. They came filled with the Holy Ghost and power. One of them had received her personal Pentecost, Sister Lucy Farrow, and said the Lord had sent her to join us in holding up this precious truth.

The crowds at the house grew so large that Seymour and Farrow moved the meetings to a former church building on Azusa Street. The "Azusa Street Revival" attracted not only throngs of worshippers — up to 1,500 daily — but also denominational and racial diversity. Within two years Azusa had spawned countless missionaries throughout America and fifty nations. From this humble birthplace to a century later, the modern-day Pentecostal Movement has become the fastest-growing form of Christianity with 500 million charismatic believers across the globe.

Lucy Farrow let her faith ignite a movement; you can, too, by committing yourself to:

DIVINE PRESENCE — You enter into God's presence by gathering with other believers. You create a more intense spiritual environment by unifying, so come together. Jesus explained:

For where two or three gather in my name, there am I with them.
Matthew 18:20

DAILY PRAYER — For great things to happen, praying weekly in your house of worship is necessary but not sufficient. Farrow and Seymour sparked a movement at Azusa Street because they prayed daily in the spirit of Paul's counsel.

Pray without ceasing.
1 Thessalonians 5:17

DIRECTED PASSION — People from different regions, classes, denominations, and races flocked to Azusa Street because they got excited about what was going on there. Passion rising from good work is contagious, especially when miracles like feelings from sickness, injury and disease are taking place. Do your best to serve in ways that meet important practical and spiritual needs; people will be blessed; their excitement will draw others.

DOUGHTY PROCLAMATION — Facing opposition and hardship, Farrow kept going, proclaiming what she believed. A former slave in the era of Jim Crow, a woman before the 19th Amendment, she rose up in faith to overcome greater obstacles than are before you today. Let her example encourage you to keep striking your match of faith. Your flame will glow; it could ignite your own movement.

Affirm The Faith Of Others   December 9th

Supported by the spirit of the law and the strong argument of inconvenience,
I would contend in behalf of the citizen, that in requiring him to subscribe to a
religious test, for any purpose, his just, constitutional rights are infringed and violated.
Henry Brackenridge

In 1819 judge and writer Henry Brackenridge spoke out against a Maryland law that limited the civil rights of Jews, restricting them from practicing law or holding elective office in the state. In a speech in January of that year, Brackenridge argued that Jews had a right to be placed on the same legal footing as other citizens. He began his remarks with a theological point.

If, as members of society, we have duties whose performance the temporal power may justly enforce, we have, as rational beings, other duties of a much higher nature to our Creator, of which He is the judge, and to whom, alone, should be referred the punishment or reward of their fulfillment or neglect. Religion, therefore, merely as such, is a matter entirely between man and his God.

From this spiritual premise, Brackenridge asserted that each person should be free to exercise their own faith; society should get out the way of the individual's religious freedom.

If my position, then, be correct, it will follow that it must be left to every citizen, as he is to stand or fall by his own merits or demerits, to entertain that belief or offer that worship which in his conscience he thinks most acceptable; and should any of his fellow citizens desire to release him from what he conceives to be the bondage of error, let it be an appeal to the reason, and not by a resort to coercion — a coercion which can only affect outward actions, and serve to exhibit power on the one side and feebleness on the other . . . The human frame may be bound in chains; it may be imprisoned and enslaved; it may yield to the dagger of the assassin or the murderer's bowl; but the immortal mind soars beyond the reach of earthly violence.

Brackenridge joined Maryland state legislator Thomas Kennedy and others in a thirty-year fight for legislation vindicating civil rights for Jews. The "Jew Bill" was finally passed by the Maryland House of Delegates in 1825.

Like Brackenridge, you should have an inclusive view of religion, embracing your own beliefs while affirming the faith of others. As you encourage their beliefs, seek to:

KNOW YOUR FAITH — Be articulate about your religious views. You should be able to share them with others and defend them from attack. Affirming your own faith opens the door to conversations in which you can affirm others' faith. The Apostle Paul made this relevant point.

Let your conversation be always full of grace, seasoned
with salt, so that you may know how to answer everyone.
Colossians 4:6

KICK YOUR BIASES TO THE CURVE — We all have our biases, including you and me. Religious ones can be particularly toxic, which the long history of violent sectarian conflicts demonstrates. Be tough on your biases. If you have one, don't lollygag. Kick it to the curve, and keep moving.

KNOCK OUT PREJUDICE — When you see prejudice in individuals or society, speak out against it. Like Brackenridge, throw a knockout punch; bring a lawsuit; lobby for new legislation; pummel discrimination of every institutional sort to its knees. When you're dealing with a prejudiced person, take a gentler approach: first listen, then confront in ways that seeks to value the individual's faith while correcting the prejudicial thinking.

KINDLE UNDERSTANDING — Strike the delicate balance: don't shy away from talking about your faith but share it in an inoffensive way that encourages meaningful dialogue, promotes understanding and fosters peace.

Leave A Legacy Of Faith   **December 10th**

Believe in yourself, learn, and never stop wanting to build a better world.
Mary McLeod Bethune

Born in 1875 on a small South Carolina rice and cotton farm, Mary McLeod Bethune started working the fields with her sixteen siblings at age five. Determined to learn, McLeod Bethune was the only family member to walk five miles to the one-room black schoolhouse. Her commitment to educating herself evolved into a calling to educating others, especially young black women. In October 1904 she rented a small house in Daytona, Florida and launched the Educational and Industrial Training School for Negro Girls. Her students rose at 5:30 a.m. for Bible study and labored at class work through the day, finishing at 9 p.m. In addition to traditional academic regimen of english, math and science, the curriculum emphasized employable skills and self-sufficiency such as millinery, dressmaking and cooking. In 1931 she merged her school with an all-boys school to form Bethune-Cookman College, and within ten years this coeducational junior college attained full college status with a four-year curriculum. By this time McLeod Bethune was working with President Franklin Roosevelt as a member of his "Black Cabinet", helping him shape public policy concerning black people. Bethune-Cookman University operates to this day as a private, co-ed, historically black university located in Daytona Beach, Florida; its 2018 enrollment was well over 4,000 students.

Part of McLeod Bethune's rich legacy are success principles that she lived and taught. Take special note of the following precepts, stated in her own words; seek to live them out.

LEAN INTO YOUR FAITH — *Faith is the first factor in a life devoted to service. Without it, nothing is possible. With it, nothing is impossible.*

LIFT YOURSELF UP — *I plunged into the job of creating something from nothing . . . Though I hadn't a penny left, I considered cash money as the smallest part of my resources. I had faith in a living God, faith in myself, and a desire to serve.*

LEARN TO BELIEVE IN OTHERS — *World peace and brotherhood are based on a common understanding of the contributions and cultures of all races and creeds.*

LEVEL PLAYING FIELD — *What does the Negro want? His answer is very simple. He wants only what all other Americans want. He wants opportunity to make real what the Declaration of Independence and the Constitution and the Bill of Rights say . . . While he knows these ideals are open to no man completely, he wants only his equal chance to obtain them.*

LET YOUR TRADITIONS ENLIGHTEN — *If we have the courage and tenacity of our forebears, who stood firmly like a rock against the lash of slavery, we shall find a way to do for our day what they did for theirs.*

LINGER NOT IN THE LIGHT — *In each experience of my life, I have had to step out of one little space of the known light, into a large area of darkness. I had to stand awhile in the darkness, and then gradually God has given me light. But not to linger in. For as soon as that light has felt familiar, then the call has always come to step out ahead again into new darkness.*

LIFELONG QUEST — *The drums of Africa still beat in my heart. They will not let me rest while there is a single Negro boy or girl without a chance to prove his worth.*

LOOK IN FOR TREASURE — *Invest in the human soul. Who knows, it might be a diamond in the rough.*

LOOK OUT FOR HOPE — *There is a place in God's sun for the youth "farthest down" who has the vision, the determination, and the courage to reach it.*

LOVE TO SERVE — *The progress of the world will call for the best that all of us have to give.*

LEAVE A LEGACY OF FAITH — *I leave you love. I leave you hope. I leave you the challenge of developing confidence in one another. I leave you respect for the use of power. I leave you faith. . . .*

Embrace Your Calling   December 11th

. . . we shall not fight our battles alone. There is a just God who presides over the destinies of nations; and who will raise up friends to fight our battles for us. The battle, sir, is not to the strong alone; it is to the vigilant, the active, the brave.
Patrick Henry

On March 23, 1775, the Second Virginia Convention met at St. John's Church in Richmond to consider whether to arm the Virginia militia to fight the British. Six months earlier fifty-six delegates from twelve colonies — Georgia did not participate — attended the First Continental Congress in Philadelphia. Patrick Henry, member of the Virginia House of Burgesses, attended both of these gatherings.

At the Philadelphia meeting, concerned about a series of British actions, including the blockade of Boston, the quartering of British troops, and new taxes, Henry spoke out in favor of colonial unity.

Let the freeman be represented by numbers alone. The distinctions between Virginians, Pennsylvanians, New Yorkers, New Englanders are no more. I am not a Virginian, but an American!

During the Richmond convention, in light of the buildup of British forces in New England, Henry had much more to say, courageously proclaiming a call to arms.

Mr. President, it is natural to man to indulge in the illusions of hope. . . . There is no longer any room for hope. If we wish to be free — if we mean to preserve inviolate those inestimable privileges for which we have been so long contending . . . we must fight! . . . An appeal to arms, and to the God of Hosts, is all that is left us! . . . Gentlemen may cry, peace, peace — but there is no peace. The war is actually begun! The next gale that sweeps from the north will bring to our ears the clash of resounding arms! Our brethren are already in the field! . . . Is life so dear, or peace so sweet,   as to be purchased at the price of chains and slavery? Forbid it, Almighty God! I know not what course others may take; but as for me, give me liberty, or give me death!

Henry's famous plea was rooted in his sense of divine calling. He embraced this calling and spoke out about it, encouraging others to join him on what appeared to be an impossible mission. His example still speaks volumes centuries later. Embrace your own calling. To do so, you must first:

PERCEIVE IT — Henry's vision of liberty for America was so clear and strong that it had conquered all his doubts and filled him with a spirit of sacrifice: the willingness to give his all for his cause, even his own life. His commitment was consistent with one of Jesus' greatest teachings.

Greater love has no one than this: to lay down one's life for one's friends.
John 15:13

Get in touch with your commitments, the things beyond yourself that you treasure the most. Your calling will rise from your deeply held values.

PRACTICE IT — Much credit is given to Henry for his fiery speech — a major factor in convincing convention delegates, including future U.S. Presidents George Washington and Thomas Jefferson, to pass a resolution authorizing Virginian troops for the Revolutionary War. It was indeed a turning point. Without the support of the most populous, wealthy and influential colony the fight for independence would have been foredoomed. Henry had credibility with his fellow delegates because he'd been practicing what he preached. Be sure to live out your calling in practical ways. If you truly believe it, you will do things in support of it. Your credibility will rise from concrete activities.

PROCLAIM IT — Henry proclaimed his calling, inspiring others to embrace it, leading to the most successful social revolution and political innovation in the history of humankind. Have you embraced your calling deeply enough to proclaim it? Are you ready to inspire others towards history-making endeavors?

See The World In A New Light   December 12th

> *My point here is, first, the Constitution is, according to its reading, an anti-slavery document; and, secondly, to dissolve the Union, as a means to abolish slavery, is about as wise as it would be to burn up this city, in order to get the thieves out of it . . . I would unite with anybody to do right; and with nobody to do wrong.*
> Frederick Douglass

Before he escaped from slavery in 1838, Frederick Douglass had heard his slave master's wife reading the Bible, and he began reading and copying bible verses and listening to sermons. While still a slave, Douglass had converted to Christianity, an experience he described in his autobiography, "Life and Times of Frederick Douglass":

I was not more than thirteen years old, when in my loneliness and destitution the preaching of a white Methodist minister was the means of causing me to feel that in God I had such a friend. I consulted a good old colored man who told me to pray, and to "cast all my care upon God." Though for weeks I was a poor, broken-hearted mourner, traveling through doubts and fears, I finally found my burden lightened, and my heart relieved. I saw the world in a new light.

Douglass later joined the AME Zion church and became a licensed preacher, holding various positions including steward, Sunday School superintendent, and sexton. His religious convictions premised his political views, making him a firm believer in the equality of all peoples as well as a strong adherent to the egalitarian values of the American Experiment. He believed that his individual spiritual experience was inextricably linked to social reform, exhorting . . .

. . . let the religious press, the pulpit, the Sunday school, the missionary associations of the land array their immense powers against slavery and slave-holding; and the whole system of crime and blood would be scattered to the winds.

Douglass saw the world in the a new light, and with such vision he was able to make a difference for others. He went through a faithful process to be transformed. You can also see the world in a new light and make a difference by following these steps in your faithful process.

BROKEN-HEARTED — Douglass described himself as "a poor, broken-hearted mourner, traveling through doubts and fears." To get to the light, you may have to travel through the darkness. Like Douglass, there might be some emotional baggage for you to release; or counterproductive relationships to leave behind. Whatever is causing your heart to break, you'll have to faithfully move beyond it.

BURDEN LIGHTENED — Douglass then reported: "I finally found my burden lightened." This is your spiritual breakthrough, when putting your life in God's hands lightens your load. God's Spirit upon your life gives you the wisdom and strength to overcome past problems. Declare this scriptural promise over your life.

For my yoke is easy and my burden is light.
Matthew 11:30

BELIEF STRENGTHENED — When Douglass' vision was renewed, his faith was strengthened. Like him, you'll likely have to work to get to the point of renewal. The rigor is worth the reward. Your greater faithfulness equips you to move forward on your success journey.

BLESSING OTHERS — Your faith in God can be the decisive factor in whether you rise above your circumstances and fulfill your divine destiny — or not. Frederick Douglass is just one of countless testimonies whose faith enlightened and empowered them to uplift the community on their way to historic achievements. Take your faith seriously, see the world in a new light, and you will find bright pathways of success and service.

Foster Freedom Through Faith   **December 13th**

The people in general ought to have regard to the moral character of those whom they invest with authority either in the legislative, executive, or judicial branches.
John Witherspoon

In 1768 prominent Presbyterian minister John Witherspoon emigrated from Scotland to the American colonies, becoming the sixth president of the College of New Jersey, later known as Princeton University. In addition to fundraising to expand the library collection and purchase scientific equipment, Witherspoon taught courses in history, divinity, eloquence and moral philosophy. His diligence transformed the college from a training ground for the ministry into an institution of higher education to prepare leaders of the new nation. His visionary work so distinguished him that he was the only clergyman to sign the Declaration of Independence in 1776.

In November 1777 as Revolutionary War forces approached Princeton, Witherspoon evacuated the College of New Jersey to protect students and faculty. The school suffered extensive property damage and Witherspoon lost personal papers and books. He led the postwar rebuilding effort at the college while serving in the Continental Congress throughout the founding period, serving on countless committees, helping to organize the executive departments and draft the Articles of Confederation; he also argued in favor of the U.S. Constitution's adoption during the New Jersey ratification debates. Most notably, Witherspoon advocated faith as the foundation of freedom, asserting that public morality and sound government derived from the virtue of the citizenry as individuals lived out their faith.

Study the following statements fromWitherspoon and the principles they impart; they will help you foster freedom through your faith.

BEYOND FOUR WALLS — John Witherspoon is known for many things—a thorn in the side of the Moderate Party in the Scottish Kirk, a successful president at Princeton, an influential moral philosopher, and, most famously, the only clergyman to sign the Declaration of Independence. What the Presbyterian pastor is not known for is being a particularly insightful, significant, or even consistent Reformed preacher and thinker.

Scholar Kevin DeYoung described Witherspoon's legacy, which featured work outside the four walls of the church. Though spending time at your house of worship is important, you should also prioritize exercising your faith in other ways than worship. Reaching those outside of your faith extends divine influence.

BREAK YOUR SILENCE — You are all my witnesses, that this is the first time of my introducing any political subject into the pulpit. At this season, however, it is not only lawful but necessary, and I willingly embrace the opportunity of declaring my opinion without any hesitation, that the cause in which America is now in arms, is the cause of justice, of liberty, and of human nature.

Witherspoon recounted the moment when he spoke out for the first time for political freedom. Be bold. Use whatever platform you've develop to declare greater rights for others.

BOLSTER YOUR VALUES — There is not a single instance in history, in which civil liberty was lost, and religious liberty preserved entire. If therefore we yield up our temporal property, we at the same time deliver the conscience into bondage.

Witherspoon emphasized the dynamic between civil rights and religious freedom. One doesn't exist without the other. Work to preserve both.

BUILD UP LEADERS — Those who wish well to the State ought to choose to places of trust men of inward principle, justified by exemplary conversation.

Witherspoon was committed to train virtuous leaders. His students played many different roles in the young nation: 12 Continental Congress members, 49 U.S. congressmen, 28 U.S. senators and 37 judges, 3 of whom became U.S. Supreme Court justices. Also among his students were prominent founders James Madison, Philip Freneau, William Bradford, and Hugh Henry Brackenridge.   Help others lead lives of faith and virtue. It is one of the best ways to foster freedom.

Write Down Your Revelations   **December 14th**

. . . the long lines of the desired poem began to twine themselves in my mind . . .
— Julia Ward Howe

In November 1861, when visiting a Union army camp near Washington, D.C. with her husband and her minister, poet Julia Ward Howe joined the troops in singing some songs. One of them was the marching song "John Brown's Body". Her minister queried, "Mrs. Howe, why do you not write some good words for that stirring tune?"

That night, laying in bed, unable to sleep, a revelation of a song came to Howe. She took a few minutes in silence to meditate on the inspiration then arose to write down the words. What she experienced that night evolved into "The Battle Hymn of the Republic", which became the most famous song of the Union, with the soldiers as well as the general public. Its lyrics follow.

Mine eyes have seen the glory of the coming of the Lord;
He is trampling out the vintage where the grapes of wrath are stored;
He hath loosed the fateful lightning of His terrible swift sword;
His truth is marching on.

I have seen Him in the watch-fires of a hundred circling camps;
They have builded Him an altar in the evening dews and damps;

I can read His righteous sentence by the dim and flaring lamps;
His day is marching on.

He has sounded forth the trumpet that shall never call retreat;
He is sifting out the hearts of men before His judgment seat:
Oh! be swift, my soul, to answer Him! be jubilant, my feet!
Our God is marching on.

In the beauty of the lilies Christ was born across the sea,
With a glory in His bosom that transfigures you and me:
As He died to make men holy, let us die to make men free,
While God is marching on.

When the words of this song were revealed to Howe, she didn't recite them to her husband, deliberate over their meaning or wait until morning to act; she immediately wrote them down. When your revelation comes, take these steps to walk into the fullness of it.

CLOSET — Find a quiet place to meditate. Like Howe, it may be your bed; or it could be your prayer pillow at your home altar, or perhaps a secluded spot in your favorite park. Solitude is the key to the door of the divine moment. You may not hear God's voice if you insist on staying in the middle of a Grand Central Station.

CLARITY — Take your time as you grasp the full meaning of the revelatory moment. Don't rush through this divine process. Be patient as the vision unfolds. Abide in the moment, for as long as it takes to get the compete picture.

CREATE — What God is showing you is likely not just for you. Be deliberate about putting it into a form for others to partake. Let your creative juices infuse the revelation, imparting triumphant truth to the world. Like Howe, you may produce something to inspire a nation.

CELEBRATE — Divine revelation is a special victory, so celebrate it. Sing your song, recite your poem, publish your writing, so that others may experience your excitement. Take note of the instruction that the Prophet Habakkuk received from the Lord, indicating the positive response generated by the documentation of the prophetic voice.

Write down the revelation and make it plain
on tablets so that a herald my run with it.
Habakkuk 2:2

Discern Your Blessing In Disguise   December 15th

Faith is the force that produces the miraculous in our lives.
Joseph Holland

During the summer of 1981, after my second year at Harvard Law School, I worked at a Washington, D.C., law firm while renting from a close family friend whom I knew as absentminded Aunt Marie. I'd been saving money for a top-of-the-line stereo system, so one Friday after work, I withdrew the twelve hundred dollars, only to find out at the store that my model was out of stock. Since the bank had closed, I hid the money in my room at Aunt Marie's house, intending to buy the stereo on Monday.

What I didn't know — because she forgot to tell me — was that Aunt Marie was having some rooms painted the next day. When I returned home Saturday evening, I'd found the furniture rearranged and covered, my room painted, and the painters come and gone. My money was missing! "I can't believe this is happening to me!" — I felt like an idiot, leaving so much cash unsecured?! I told Aunt Marie, who summarily dismissed my concerns. I searched again, never found the money, and chalked it up as a very tough life lesson.

Eighteen months later, after I'd graduated law school and moved to Harlem — broke, behind on rent, with no job in sight — Aunt Marie called: "I found your money." I was speechless. Aunt Marie explained how she'd discovered the twelve hundred dollars in an envelope tucked inside a favorite blouse she'd removed and put to the side before the painters started. She'd been reorganizing her wardrobe, seen the misplaced blouse, picked it up, and my cash had fallen out. She promised to send me a check by overnight mail.

I discerned my blessing in disguise! Absentminded Aunt Marie became to me like one of Elijah's ravens. What had seemed like bad luck at the time had actually been God's handiwork. Providence had prevented me from spending the money on a stereo I really didn't need to preserve it for a more important future purpose that I didn't know I had — manna from heaven to survive during my first year out of school in Harlem. Four months rent that I didn't have — that I direly needed in that moment — was now on the way.

To discern your blessing in disguise, you first have to mountain-moving faith. Mark Jesus' words.

Have faith in God. Truly I tell you, if anyone says to this mountain,
'Go, throw yourself into the sea,' and does not double in their heart
but believes that what they say will happen, it will be done for them.
Mark 11:22-23

Possessing this caliber of faith, you then must:

ACCEPT PREDICAMENT — Life has a way of resisting your control, of defying predictability, of introducing predicaments, of upsetting your best-laid plans. Accept the fact that the constants of life are uncertainty, challenge and change, which will help you to:

AVOID PARALYSIS — Keep in mind that too much analysis leads to paralysis. Don't think yourself into a box. Do your best to resolve the challenges of life without divine intervention. But when you've exhausted every possible strategy to fix the situation, and nothing has worked, then it's time to:

ADOPT PRAYER — Prayer is vital because there are some things that you'll understand in God's presence that you won't understand any other way. If you don't pray, you run the risk of missing or dismissing the divine interventions that could pop up along the pathways of your life. But if do pray, you increase your chances of seeing a silver lining in the clouds, and when your miracle manifests, be ready to:

ACCLAIM PROVIDENCE — Your faithfulness will bring the revelation that things are darkest before the dawn. It will be in those extreme moments — when all hope seems lost — that you will discern Providential handiwork transforming the adversities of your life into blessings in disguise. And when God shows up to save your day, answering your prayers through supernatural intervention, give the Lord the praise that's due.

Practice What You Preach   **December 16th**

*I am as perfectly satisfied that the Union of the United States in its
form and adoption is as much the work of a Divine Providence as
any of the miracles recorded in the Old and New Testament.*
Benjamin Rush

The Philadelphia physician and Declaration of Independence
signatory Benjamin Rush was also a man of God. Rush believed that the
American Experiment was the work of God. He connected the dots
between personal faith, virtuous living and American liberty in the
following statement.

*The only foundation for a useful education in a republic is to be laid in
Religion. Without this there can be no virtue, and without virtue there can be no liberty,
and liberty is the object and life of all republican governments.*

Nowhere was his wholistic commitment more evident than in his
opposition to slavery. During his medical studies at the University of
Edinburgh in Scotland in 1766, Rush was outraged when he observed one
hundred slave ships in the Liverpool harbor. The experience made an
indelible impression. In 1773, while practicing medicine and teaching
college chemistry, he wrote an anti-slavery pamphlet, An Address to the
Inhabitants of the British Settlements in America, upon Slave-Keeping. In it
he attacked slavery using the scientific argument that Africans were not by
nature intellectually or morally inferior to Europeans.

Perhaps Rush's most significant anti-slavery activity was his support
of Richard Allen, who founded in 1794 the African Methodist Episcopal
Church, the first independent black denomination in the United States.
Allen's goal was to create for free blacks a religious environment without
racial prejudice, so that blacks, whether slave or free, could worship
together in dignity. He also established Sabbath schools in his churches to
teach literacy. In his autobiography, Allen wrote about Rush.

*By this time we had waited on Dr. Rush and Mr. Robert Ralston, and told
them of our distressing situation. They pitied our situation, and subscribed largely
towards the church, and were very friendly towards us and advised us how to go on. . . .
Dr. Rush did much for us in public by his influence. I hope the name of Dr. Benjamin
Rush and Mr. Robert Ralston will never be forgotten among us. They were the two first
gentlemen who espoused the cause of the oppressed and aided us in building the house of
the Lord for the poor Africans to worship in. Here was the beginning and rise of the
first African church in America.*

Benjamin Rush practiced what he preached. You should do the

same; it will happen when you:

MATCH YOUR CONDUCT AND WORDS —
Hyprocrisy means saying one thing and doing another thing that
conflicts with your statement. Slow down. Assess your actions to
make sure that there's alignment with your words, especially with
your declarations of faith. It's crucial that you live your life
consistent with your beliefs and values. Your failure to do so could
cause you and others to stumble. Dallas Willard made this telling
point.

*You can live opposite of what you profess, but you can't live opposite of
what you believe. Invariably what you believe is revealed by what you do.*

MASTER YOUR PROCESS — The journey of your life
involves countless difficulties, trials and unknowns. Being
consistent in what you say and what you do will help generate the
staying power to get you to where you want to go in life. The
struggle you're going through may be uncomfortable, even
agonizing, but it is essential part of the process of success. What
you're becoming on the inside is being shaped by what you're
experiencing on the outside. Be strong in faith; you're being
prepared to fulfill your divine destiny.

MELIORATE YOUR COMMUNITY — An important
institution to build the African American faith community took
shape because of Rush's faithful contributions. Like Rush, you can
bring this vigorous virtue to life by demonstrating your faith in
others. It was especially significant that Rush — a Founding Father
— invested in a project lead by Allen — a former slave. Follow his
example. Let your faith inspire you to reach out in unprecedented
ways. As you practice what you preach, you might just bring
inspiration through your example to those still stumbling towards
their American dreams.

Fight Faithfully For Fairness   December 17th

The Lord was pleased to strengthen us, and remove all fear
from us, and disposed our hearts to be as useful as possible.
— Richard Allen

In 1760 Richard Allen was born into slavery in Delaware; when he was still a boy, his mother and two of his five siblings were sold to another plantation owner. Allen attended meetings of the local Methodist Society. Encouraged by the fellowship, he taught himself to read and write. After the Revolutionary War Allen's owner was touched by the message of Methodist ministers that slavery was sinful. Allen was able to buy his freedom in 1780 and changed his name from "Negro Richard" to "Richard Allen."

While working several jobs to make ends meet, Allen spent all his free time involved in church activities, and in 1784 was qualified to preach in Baltimore at the Christmas Conference, the founding of the Methodist Church in North America. Allen moved to Philadelphia and began ministering at St. George's Methodist Episcopal Church but was directed to preach only at early-morning, separate services for black parishioners. Consequently, he lead an exodus of African American worshippers away from St. George's in 1787 because of its segregated congregations.

Allen and his wife Sara operated a station on the Underground Railroad and participated in the formation of the Free African Society, a non-denominational mutual aid society that assisted fugitive slaves and new migrants to Philadelphia. Determined to have the members of his race treated fairly in holy spaces, Allen organized a group of blacks to purchase a lot in the city on which they constructed Mother Bethel African Methodist Episcopal Church; the church has been in operations on that site since its founding, the oldest real estate holding in America continuously owned by African Americans.

Out of this fight for fairness grew the African Methodist Episcopal Church (A.M.E.), the first independent black denomination in the United States. Allen formed the A.M.E. in 1816 by uniting five African-American Methodist congregations from Pennsylvania, New Jersey, Delaware and Maryland; he was elected the first bishop. Now the oldest such institution in black America, the A.M.E. is composed of 7,000 congregations throughout the United States and around the world.

Like Allen, commit yourself to faithfully fight for fairness by living out these principles.

FOREFRONT — Your attitude is key, so let a positive, constructive, cheerful mindset be at the forefront of your daily perspective and conduct. Strive to have a godly outlook, remembering the words of the Apostle Paul.

. . . have the same mindset as Christ Jesus . . .
Philippians 2:5

FELLOWSHIP — You will not succeed in your fight for fairness if you do it alone. Like Allen spend time building a righteous army before taking the battlefield. You will lay a foundation for lasting spiritual and social progress through the strength of your fellowship.

FAVOR — Your faithful endeavors will release divine favor into your circumstances. Your detractors and enemies will be miraculously transformed into your supporters and friends. That was Allen's testimony, as he explained.

Many of the white people who have been instruments in the hands
of God for our good, even such as have held us in captivity,
are now pleading our cause with earnestness and zeal.

FAITH — Leave room for God to move on your behalf. Faith means avoiding the tendency to over-plan your agenda and all the stress that comes along with that approach. The biggest factor in your successful fight for fairness will be divine influence, which won't happen unless you . . .

. . . live by faith, not by sight.
2 Corinthians 5:7

Heed The Voice Of God   December 18th

If the man may preach, because the Savior died for him, why not the woman,
seeing he died for her also? Is he not a whole Savior, instead of half of one?
Jarena Lee

Though she was born free in 1783 in Cape May, New Jersey, Jarena Lee experienced the trauma of being raised as an African American girl in a society where the discriminatory culture of slavery was pervasive. Lee was so distressed as a seven-year-old live-in maid in a white household that she contemplated suicide on several occasions.

The transformative moment came one Sunday after Lee had

moved to Philadelphia as a teenager, still working as a domestic servant for white families. She attended Bethel Church and heard a sermon by Richard Allen, the founder of the African Methodist Episcopal (A.M.E.) Church. Inspired by the powerful message, Lee made a decision that day to convert to Christianity.

Through her devoted prayer life, Lee began to sense God commissioning her to preach the Gospel. She resisted this divine call, knowing the challenge of pursuing ministry in a male-dominated church, especially in light of the ban against female ministers in the A.M.E. church. But then she heard the voice of God.

Between four and five years after my sanctification, on a certain time, an impressive silence fell upon me, and I stood as if someone was about to speak to me, yet I had no such thought in my heart. But to my utter surprise, there seemed to sound a voice which I thought I distinctly heard, and most certainly understood, which said to me, "Go preach the Gospel!" I immediately replied aloud, "No one will believe me." Again I listened, and again the same voice seemed to say—"Preach the Gospel; I will put words in your mouth, and will turn your enemies to become your friends."

Emboldened by the revelatory moment, Lee approached Richard Allen, requesting the opportunity to preach. Allen denied her request, but in 1819 during a morning worship service at Bethel Church in Philadelphia, her oratorical opportunity arrived. When a guest preacher stumbled in his message, at a loss for words, Lee intervened, coming to her feet, preaching the sermon instead. Allen was so impressed with Lee's ministry that he commissioned her to preach.

Lee heeded the voice of God, which led to itinerant ministry, traveling extensively to preach in churches throughout the Midwest. Follow her example. Heed the voice of God in your life by practicing these principles.

SILENCE — Let an "impressive silence" fall upon you. Turn off the TV. Shut down your smart phone. Skip the social event. Go to a place of solitude. Have you ever been alone with God, intentionally setting yourself apart for divine interaction? That's where you'll discern His voice.

SOTTO VOCE — The Lord spoke to Elijah in a "still, small voice" (1 Kings 19:12). If you're always using your words in prayer, not taking time to listen, you'll likely miss the divine whisper. Spend some time during the day in a prayerful state of mind, even meditating on God's Word. That's the best way to incline your ear heavenwards . . . to abide in an awareness of divine presence.

SURRENDER — Humility is the key to discernment. Give up the idea that you know what's best for you. Jesus told his Heavenly Father in the Garden of Gethsemane:

. . . not as I will, but as You will.
Matthew 26:39

Whenever you sense divine prompting, surrender. The wisest thing to do is to submit to God's sovereignty.

SERVICE — It's not enough to simply discern the divine voice. Like Lee, act on what you hear. She exemplifies the ideal approach, consistent with the Prophet Isaiah's testimony.

Then I heard the voice of the Lord saying, "Whom shall I send?
And who will go for us?" And I said, "Here am I. Send me!"
Isaiah 6:8

Examine Your Faith   December 19th

The moral sense, or conscience, is as much a part of man as his leg
or arm. It is given to all human beings in a stronger or weaker
degree, as force of members is given them in a greater or less degree.
Thomas Jefferson

In 1787 Thomas Jefferson lived in Paris and was traveling Europe, busy in his duties as United States Minister to France, having succeeded Benjamin Franklin in that role. But he took time to write a letter to his nephew Peter Carr — whose parents had died — encouraging the young man to examine his faith. After instructing his youthful relative to read books, including the Bible, Jefferson focused on his main point.

Religion. Your reason is now mature enough to examine this object. In the first place, divest yourself of all bias in favor of novelty and singularity of opinion. . . . Fix reason firmly in her seat, and call to her tribunal every fact, every opinion. Question with boldness even the existence of a God; because, If there be one, he must more approve of the homage of reason, than that of blindfolded fear.

Jefferson concluded the letter by directing Carr to take an open, introspective, and fearless approach in scrutinizing the options of faith.

Do not be frightened from this inquiry by any fear of its consequences. If it ends in a belief that there is no God, you will find incitements to virtue in the comfort and pleasantness you feel in its exercise . . . If you find reason to believe there is a God, a consciousness that you are acting under his eye, and he approves you, will be a vast additional incitement; . . . if that Jesus was also a God, you will be comforted by a belief of his aid and love.

Jefferson challenged his nephew Carr to examine his faith. Examining your faith to determine your beliefs is a critical step to success and fulfillment in life. To scrutinize your faith and get more closely in touch with what you truly believe, honestly answer these questions.

WHAT — What is your worldview or belief system? What are you deepest convictions and most strongly held views?

WHICH — Which type of person are you most like: the devout, the fatalist, the astrologist, the egoist, the atheist, or the pragmatist?

WHERE — Where does your belief system come from? From your family? Your school? Your friend group? Your mentor?

WHY — Why do you believe? Are you rock solid in what you believe or do you have questions and doubts?

HOW — How is your worldview influencing your lifestyle? Do you believe in miracles? Have you ever experienced a miracle or known someone who has?

As you meditate on these questions and sincerely answer them, you will delve more deeply into what faith means to you; and you will make new discoveries about the supernatural, the natural and yourself. And as you examine your faith, reflect on this Old Testament prayer; consider praying it yourself.

Search me, O God, and know my heart;
Try me, and know my anxieties;
And see if there is any wicked way in me,
And lead me in the way everlasting.
Psalm 139:23-24

See The Hand Of God   December 20th

The Abolitionists saw this day of tribulation and reign of terror
long ago, and warned you of it; but you would not hear! You now say
that it is their agitation which has brought about this terrible civil war!
John Swett Rock

Boston physician and lawyer John Swett Rock was one of the first African Americans to earn a medical degree as well as the first black person to be admitted to the bar of the United States Supreme Court. Rock was also an ardent abolitionist. On January 23, 1862, as the Civil War raged, Rock addressed the Massachusetts Anti-Slavery Society. Though he discussed the nation's dire circumstances throughout the speech, Rock concluded on a faithful note.

I do not regard this trying hour as a dark one. The war that has been waged on us for more than two centuries has opened our eyes and caused us to form alliances, so that instead of acting on the defensive, we are now prepared to attack the enemy. This is simply a change of tactics. I think I see the finger of God in all this. . . . Yes, there is the handwriting on the wall: "I come not to bring peace, but the sword. Break every yoke, and let the oppressed go free. I have heard the groans of my people and am come down to deliver them! . . ."

Rock saw the hand of God in the occurrences and outcomes of the Civil War. Spiritual handiwork abounds; you just have to keep your eyes open for it. Cecil Frances Alexander's poem "All Things Beautiful" points to some divine signs.

SUNSHINE:
All things bright and beautiful,
All creatures great and small,
All things wise and wonderful,
The Lord God made them all.

SPARROW:
Each little flower that opens,
Each little bird that sings,
He made their glowing colors,
He made their tiny wings.

STREAMS:
The purple-headed mountain,
The river running by,
The sunset, and the morning,

That brighten up the sky;

SEASONS*:*
The cold wind in the winter,
The pleasant summer sun,
The ripe fruits in the garden,
He made them every one.

SIGHT*:*
He gave us eyes to see them,
And lips that we might tell
How great is God Almighty,
Who has made all things well.

Have you seen the hand of God at work in your circumstances? Have you been looking for it? If not, endeavor to discern the divine signs highlighted in Alexander's poem. Have you ever sought to perceive God in the dawn of a new day? Or in the miracle you needed to make it through?

Strengthen Faith Through Unity   **December 21st**

Have we put aside our prejudices, our differences, our controversies, even, if I may say it, our hates, that we may be of one mind?
Harold Ockenga

On April 7, 1942, Congregational minister Harold Ockenga gave the keynote address at the National Conference for United Action Among Evangelicals in St. Louis. Men and women of faith had come from across America to resolve a vexing problem. Though they shared common beliefs, their churches manifested excessive individualism, resisted organizational hierarchies and lacked concerted action. Ockenga spoke to this concern as the paramount issue.

I believe we must first of all seek unity. This means that this millstone of rugged independence which has held back innumerable movements before, in which individual leaders must be the whole hog or none, must be utterly repudiated by everyone one of us.

Ockenga drummed this theme throughout his remarks, challenging the integrity of the attendees and the churches they represented to leave their cultural and theological baggage behind for the sake of unity.

I summon you to unity. If the prayer of Jesus on Solomon's porch, that they may be one, was actually answered at Pentecost, then let us demonstrate our unity instead of our division. It is folly to speak of the union of the true Church and then declare that those who profess to believe in the doctrines of the true Church can never work in unity.

Those in attendance heeded Ockenga's message, for out of the convention arose a new association, the National Association of Evangelicals, which eventually grew into a nationwide organization representing millions of believers in 45,000 local churches from dozens of different denominations. Ockenga strengthened his own faith and the strength of others by bringing people together. You can also strengthen faith through unity by practicing these principles.

CONVICTION — Believe the truth of divine creation that makes us all one in the eyes of God.

So God created mankind in his own image, in the image of
God he created them; male and female he created them.
Genesis 1:27

Like Ockenga, speak passionately from your heart. Proclaim your beliefs as a clarion call for unity.

CONNECTION — For people of faith the common ground would be easier to find, but cultural barriers can block religious comity. Take time to get to know someone of a different faith, to find some intersections that allow you to connect with them in meaningful ways. If you perceive an opportunity to bond with someone, seize it. And take the advice of the Apostle Paul.

Make every effort to keep the unity of the Spirit through the bond of peace.
Ephesians 4:3

CORRECTION — Ockenga asked the question — "Have we put aside . . . our hates?" This is the question you must ask yourself — have you put aside your prejudices, your differences, your controversies, even your hates? Don't blame others for dissension and disunity. Be intentional about addressing your own issues, those inner roadblocks that cause others to steer clear of your negativity and faithlessness. Let unity start with your determination to correct your attitude, so you can build bridges of ecumenism.

COMMUNITY — Strength rises from community. You are stronger working together with others than making an attempt on your own. Make your strategy two-fold: have faith in yourself, and have faith in others. When you encounter people plagued with self-doubt, take time to express your faith in who they are and their potential for greatness. The best way to build a community of faith is to sow seeds of faith into an individual's life. Great oaks grow from little acorns.

Put Your Faith To The Test   **December 22nd**

A person who rejects Christ may choose to say that I do not accept it, he may not choose to say there is not enough evidence.
Simon Greenleaf

In 1846 Simon Greenleaf was named Dane Professor of Law at Harvard University, the summit of his long and prodigious career as a lawyer and jurist. Greenleaf was instrumental in the expansion of the Harvard Law Library and published "Treatise on the Law of Evidence", a classic of American jurisprudence. Considered one of the greatest authorities on legal evidence of his era, Greenleaf also put his faith to the test, examining his beliefs in light of the laws of evidence. You can also put your faith to the test by studying the principles from Greenleaf's experience — imparted in his own words — and applying them to your life.

PREJUDICE — *In examining the evidence of the Christian religion, it is essential to the discovery of truth that we bring to the investigation a mind freed, as far as possible, from existing prejudice, and open to conviction.*

Don't prejudge things. Enter the spiritual universe with an open mind; leave any intellectual or emotional baggage at the door.

PIERCING — *If a close examination of the evidences of Christianity may be expected of one class of men more than another, it would seem incumbent upon lawyers who make the law of evidence one of our peculiar studies. Our profession leads us to explore the mazes of falsehood, to detect its artifices, to pierce its thickest veils, to follow and expose its sophistries, to compare the statements of different witnesses with severity, to discover truth and separate it from error.*

Be lawyerly: prove your case by digging deeply into its facts. Study all the evidence; determine whether it supports the stated conclusions.

PROOF — *In the ordinary affairs of life we do not require nor expect demonstrative evidence, because it is inconsistent with the nature of matters of fact, and to insist on its production would be unreasonable and absurd.*

If you go overboard in your search for truth, you'll drown in oceans of information. Set reasonable expectations. No one can know everything — not even you.

PROBITY — *Either the men of Galilee were men of superlative wisdom, and extensive knowledge and experience, and of deeper skill in the arts of deception than any and all others, before them or after them, or they have truly stated astonishing things which they saw and heard.*

Check your motives. Examine your faith to meet your goals, not to cater to the needs and demands of others.

PREPARATION — *There should be a readiness, on our part, to investigate with candor to follow the truth wherever it may lead us, and to submit, without reserve or objection, to all the teachings of this religion, if it be found to be of divine origin.*

Resist the urge to search for the sake of searching; you could stay in the hunt forever. Be ready to embrace the truth once you discover it.

PERFECTION — *The object of man's worship, whatever it be, will naturally be his standard of perfection. He clothes it with every attribute, belonging, in his view, to a perfect character; and this character he himself endeavors to attain.*

Set your standards high in all that you do. Be the best you can be. Strive for perfection, as Jesus directed.

Be perfect, therefore, as your heavenly Father is perfect.
Matthew 5:48

Take A Holistic Approach To Your Faith   December 23rd

It is the Holy Spirit's job to convict, God's job to judge and my job to love.
Billy Graham

In the summer of 1957, evangelist Billy Graham brought revival to New York City, perhaps attaining the summit of his world-renowned ministry: 16 weeks at Madison Square Garden with a standing-room-only crowd of 20,000 every night; 3,000 ushers; 4,000-member choir; thousands to counsel those who answered Graham's call for conversion; hour-long TV broadcasts; even the New York Times printed the texts of his sermons; 100,000 people at Yankee Stadium for a midsummer service, breaking the record set by the Joe Louis–Max Baer fight; and another 100,000 for the Labor Day weekend finale in Times Square.

The success of his crusades notwithstanding, Graham faced criticism for what some considered to be his overly aggressive approach to religion. These critics claimed that people responded to Graham under the influence of heightened emotion, later to regret their decisions. Graham's answer to this charge was published in "Look" magazine. He explained that, though emotion was central to an individual's Christian faith, it had to be balanced with one's intellectual and spiritual dimensions.

Ministers and newspaper people have remarked time after time about the quietness, dignity, and absence of hysteria in our meetings. We never have any shouting or outbursts of any kind. However, there is emotion involved in everything people do. Love and hate are elements of emotion. We are trying to get men to love Christ and to hate their sins. To that extent, there is emotion involved, though we do not find in our meetings that it results in any demonstrative outbursts. I find it   hard to think, however, that the preaching of John the Baptist, Christ and the Apostles set no emotion aflame . . . He may give intellectual assent to the claims of Christ and may have had emotional religious experiences; however, he is not truly converted until he has surrendered his will to Christ as Lord, Savior, and Master.

Graham's comments point to the importance of taking a holistic approach to what you believe: balancing the emotional, mental and spiritual dimensions of your faith. To take a holistic approach to your faith, you should:

EXERCISE YOUR INTELLECT — You don't have to be a theologian to know what you believe. Whatever your doctrine, study it, with the commitment that the Apostle Paul encouraged his mentee Timothy to take.

Study to show yourself approved unto God, a workman that
needs not to be ashamed, rightly dividing the word of truth.
2 Timothy 2:15

Deepen your understanding of the tenets of your faith, so that you can articulate and live it, fully and consistently.

EMBRACE YOUR WILL — There are times when all you can do is simply believe. It is a matter of your will. It may be time of tragedy, a moment of extremity, a season of life when you don't see any way you can make it. Take that inner journey deep inside your spirit, embrace your will to believe, and let your faith rise from the recesses of your soul.

EMOTE YOUR SPIRIT — This is not about running around your place of worship. Speak words of testimony about your spiritual experience even when you don't feel like it. Recall the great things that God has done for you and sing songs of praise to acknowledge them. Rejoice over your divinely ordained victories. Your challenges may not change right away, but your mood will.

EXPRESS YOUR FAITH — If you truly believe something, you will sincerely live it out. Hypocrites say one thing but do another. Let the consistency between your lifestyle and spirituality speak volumes to others, making your faith come alive. Always keep in mind:

As the body without the spirit is dead, so faith without works is dead.
James 2:26

Rise Up In Faith   December 24th

Many are daily coming from the east, west, north and south; many
that were very lately in the same miserable condition that you are in,
are now in a happy state . . . rejoicing in hope of the glory of God.
— Jonathan Edwards

The First Great Awakening, the 18th century religious revival beginning in the 1730's and permeating the Thirteen Colonies for decades thereafter, had a profound impact on the culture and politics of the Colonial America. The ecclesiastical environment of this era helped to create the ideological milieu that led to America's Founding. Gaining freedom from personal sin, which was the thrust of this religious awakening, was easily translated by American revolutionaries of this period into a political awakening – gaining freedom from political sins like taxation without representation. The core value of spiritual freedom spawned constitutional principles: freedom of speech, of the press, of religion, the inalienable rights of life and liberty.

Two clergymen, one American, Jonathan Edwards, and one Anglican, George Whitefield, sparked the spiritual awakening. Whitefield did a revivalist tour throughout the colonies in 1739-40, attracting large crowds and gaining countless conversions. His favorite place to preach was Philadelphia. Benjamin Franklin and other prominent colonists heard him and were so impressed they had a chapel specially built for him in the city, a building that eventually became the first home of the University of Pennsylvania.

On July 8, 1741, Edwards delivered at Enfield, Connecticut, his most famous sermon, Sinner in the Hands of an Angry God. Edwards' preaching that day is often cited as the "fire and brimstone" style characteristic of colonial revivals. The truth is his terrifying eloquence had a tempered purpose — to bring his audience to the compelling conclusion: they were without hope without the grace of God. A highlight of the sermon appears below.

And now you have an extraordinary opportunity, a day wherein Christ has thrown the door of mercy wide open, and stands in the door calling and crying with a loud voice to poor sinners; a day wherein many are flocking to Him, and pressing into the kingdom of God. . . . How awful is it to be left behind at such a day! To see so many others feasting, while you are pining and perishing! To see so many rejoicing and singing for joy of heart, while you have cause to mourn for sorrow of heart, and howl for vexation of spirit! How can you rest one moment in such a condition?

Edwards challenged his listeners to rise up in faith through a relationship with God. To rise up in your faith, strive to be:

HUMBLE BEFORE GOD — Humility is the antidote for pride, the elemental sin that's the self-centered root of a host of problems. Don't seek to exalt yourself; let God exalt you in His own time and way, as the Apostle Peter counseled:

Humble yourselves, therefore, under God's mighty hand, that he may lift you up in due time.
1 Peter 5:6

HONEST WITH GOD — The things that you conceal from others, don't even think about hiding them from God. Use your prayer time to put everything on the spiritual table: the good, the bad, the ugly. Tell it all to God. You will receive wisdom on the changes you need to make and the best ways to make them.

HUNGRY FOR GOD — Check your spiritual appetite. Survey the time you spend each week doing worldly versus godly things. Assess the priorities of your life. If you want better outcomes, shift your energies to righteous activities. You will reap what you sow.

HOPEFUL IN GOD — Hope is your most important resource, the inner light to keep you going through the darkest of times. You should think about it in this way: you can live forty days without food; four days without water; four minutes without air; but only four seconds without hope. No matter what you're going through, look to God to hold on to your hope. You will gain the spiritual strength to weather the storm.

Sing Songs Of Faith   **December 25th**

O come all ye faithful, joyful and triumphant . . .
— Christmas Carol

On December 15, 1791, the Bill of Rights was ratified by the necessary number of states; the ten amendments become part of the United States Constitution, making it the first nation in the Western world to make an effective separation between church and state. The First Amendment states:

Congress shall make no law respecting an establishment of religion, or prohibiting the free exercise thereof.

This and other governmental actions regarding religion sprang from the spiritual culture of America, beginning with the countless settlers of faith who migrated to escape religious persecution in their home countries. With the First Great Awakening expanding and deepening the religious climate, hymns and other religious songs became a common practice in America. Such songs fostered individual and collective strength. As you sing your own songs of faith, you will bolster yourself and others. Take note of the following songs and the success principles that they resound.

VALOR — One of the favorite Revolutionary War songs, which the soldiers sang in camp and played by the fife and drum corp, was William Billings' Let Tyrants Shake.

> *Let tyrants shake their iron rod,*
> *And slavery clank her galling chains,*
> *We fear them not, we trust in God,*
> *New England's God forever reigns.*
>
> *When God inspired us for the fight,*
> *Their ranks were broke, their lines were forced,*
> *Their ships were shattered in our sight,*
> *Or swiftly driven from our coast.*
>
> *What grateful offering shall we bring,*
> *What shall we render to the Lord?*
> *Loud Hallelujahs let us sing,*
> *And praise His name on every chord.*

VIGOR — Songs of faith took on a different cultural form as Negro spirituals — songs created by African Americans that imparted Christian values and voiced the hardships of slavery. A spiritual of enduring meaning follows.

> *I don't feel no ways tired*
> *Come too far from where I started from*
> *Nobody told me that the road would be easy*
> *I don't believe He's brought me this far to leave me.*

VICTORY — This song of faith promises triumph to those who don't give up.

> *We've come this far by faith*
> *Leaning on the Lord*
> *Trusting in His Holy Word*
> *He's never failed us yet . . .*

Sing your own song of faith. You can sing with others in a house of worship; to encourage yourself during a disappointing time; to reinvigorate while you're in the shower; meditatively in solitude of your quiet time; or victoriously after a moment of achievement. Don't just sing songs of faith during the Christmas season. Commit yourself to songs of faith everyday and your life will be uplifted. And don't worry if you're out of tune. Your spiritual audience cares less about the quality of the melody than the sincerity of your heart.

Cry Out To God For Help   December 26th

Your sentiments, that our affairs are drawing rapidly to a crisis, accord with my own.
George Washington, in a letter to John Jay

1786 was a troubled time in the newly independent America. Great Britain refused to evacuate its Great Lakes posts, as promised in the 1783 Treaty of Paris, until the U.S. government paid its debts to Britain. Falling farm wages, decreasing imports and exports, money shortages and high taxes all manifested the increasing economic malaise. In Shay's Rebellion, debt-ridden farmers in Western Massachusetts took up arms against governmental authorities to protest economic injustice. In an attempt to rectify the dysfunctional federal government, a special convention was called for September in Annapolis but only delegates from five states were present; the others showed up late or not all.

Correspondence between two eminent leaders of the War of Independence — John Jay and George Washington — revealed the extreme distress. In a letter dated June 27, 1786, Jay wrote to Washington:

What I most fear is that the better kind of people, by which I mean the people who are orderly and industrious, who are content with their situations and not uneasy in their circumstances, will be led by the insecurity of property, the loss of confidence in their rulers, and the want of pubic faith and rectitude to consider the charms of liberty as imaginary and delusive.

On August 1st Washington responded:

What a triumph for our enemies to verify their predictions! What a triumph for the advocates of despotism to find that we are incapable of governing ourselves and that systems founded on the basis of equal liberty are merely ideal and fallacious!

Showing deep consternation, Washington concluded his letter by crying out to God for help.

Would to God that wise measures may be taken in time to avert the consequences we have but too much reason to apprehend.

Like these legendary leaders, when you're having a bad day or a bad week — even a bad year — don't forget to cry out to God for help. When you're in deep distress and could use divine assistance, be sure to:

EXTEND TO OTHERS — Don't try to figure everything out on your own. Jay and Washington were trusted friends who had weathered storms together. When you're in a crisis, don't treat it like a walk in the park or a casual social media post. Find someone close and trusted to share with one-on-one.

EXHUME YOUR FEARS — Don't talk about the weather or small talk about who won the game last night. Get to the point. Bring what's bothering you the most to the surface. Jay wrote to Washington: What I most fear . . . Make sure you're articulating your fears during your heartfelt conversation. Holding back will only increase your stress.

EXERCISE YOUR FAITH — Thinking through solutions is a good practice, but, like Washington and Jay, you could very well come to the end of your rationales. When that happens, don't give up. Where logic ends, let your faith begin. Resolve to believe that a brighter day is coming.

EXALT YOUR PETITIONS — Go forth on two tracks: horizontal (talking with friends); and vertical (crying out to God!) Your friend may not understand you or give you an appropriate response. Not so with God, who can handle your frustrations, your questions, your fears, even your anger and depression. Whatever your emotional baggage, leave it on the spiritual table. It's better to step into the ring and wrestle with God, crying out for help, than to spectate from your seat wondering what to do with your mess. Heed this scriptural advice.

Get up, cry out in the night, even as the night begins.
Pour out your heart like water in prayer to the Lord.
Lamentations 2:19

Let Your Faith Fuel Your Conduct   December 27th

No one can help admiring the depth of your insight into our
peculiar conditions, and the absolute fairness of your criticisms.
— Theodore Roosevelt in a letter to James Bryce

In 1888 British academic and diplomat James Bryce published

"The American Commonwealth", in which he analyzed culture and politics in 19th century America. Bryce later served as British ambassador to the United States from 1907 to 1913. Many acclaimed the scholarship and insightfulness of his writings. In one selection concerning faith, Bryce described the dynamic between the religious views held by Americans and their practice stemming therefrom.

They are also a religious people. It is not merely that they respect religion and its ministers, for that one might say of Russians or Sicilians, not merely that they are assiduous churchgoers and Sunday school teachers, but that they have an intelligent interest in the form of faith they profess, are pious without superstition and zealous without bigotry. The importance which they still . . . attach to dogmatic propositions does not prevent them from feeling the moral side of their theology. Christianity influences conduct, not indeed half as much as in theory it ought, but probably more than it does in any other modern country, and far more than it did in the so-called ages of faith.

Bryce elaborated the point by highlighting the social impact of individual faith.

Nor do their moral and religious impulses remain in the soft haze of self-complacent sentiment. The desire to expunge or cure the visible evils of the world is strong. Nowhere are so many philanthropic and reformatory agencies at work.

Bryce's observations about religious life in late 19th century America may be out of sync with contemporary ecclesiastical realities, but the principles to which he points about personal faith precipitating positive social impact hold true. As you live out the following precepts, you will find your faith fueling your conduct.

PERSPECTIVE — Let your faith shape your perspective, adding sunshine to your outlook, no matter how gloomy things appear. The Apostle Paul shares this life lesson:

I've learned to be content in whatever situation I'm in.
Philippians 4:11

His faith allowed him to maintain a positive outlook in the midst of hardship and crisis. Strive to look at things through the lens of your faith. You will begin to experience hope instead of despair, not only for your life; you'll possess such abundant aspiration that it will overflow into the lives of others.

POWER — If you want more power for your life to achieve your dreams, begin with what you believe. You generate willpower by believing you can do it. When you resolve to possess such faith, you've not only taken a big mental stride towards accomplishing the thing; you're also well on your way to gaining the wisdom to figure out how to do it. And exercising faith releases spiritual power in support of your goals. The Apostle Paul is on point here as well.

> *Now to Him who is able to do immeasurably more than all we*
> *ask or imagine, according to his power that is at work within us.*
> Ephesians 3:20

PRACTICE — The practical outcomes of faith are as important as its religious doctrines and spiritual resources. Words and thoughts alone, theory and theology without more, fall short of the faithful standard of uplifting lives. Faith is a vigorous virtue, but only if you act on it. Practicing your faith energizes your life, blesses others and leads to amazing outcomes.

Let Repentance Lead to Reform   **December 28th**

> *In the mighty task of putting conscience and justice*
> *and love into a "Christian" civilization, the church,*
> *with all its splendid achievements, has sometimes faltered.*
> The Federal Council of Churches, First Convention Report

In December 1908 the Federal Council of Churches held its first convention. The delegates met in Philadelphia and issued "The Church and Modern Industry", which acknowledged that Protestant churches in America had largely missed the opportunity to be at the vanguard of social change sweeping across the country. This paper was consistent with the new Social Gospel movement: a handful of clergymen — Josiah Strong, Walter Rauschenbusch, Richard T. Ely and Washington Gladden — challenged their fellow preachers to address social problems such as poverty, alcoholism, crime, racial tensions, slums, and labor unrest.

In its "Modern Industry" policy statement, the convention delegates first acknowledged the need for repentance from past shortcomings.

> *Christian practice has not always harmonized with Christian principle. But by*
> *the force of economic law and of social custom individual life has been, at times, swerved*
> *from the straight course, and the organized church has not always spoken when it should*
> *have borne witness, and its plea for righteousness has not always been uttered with*

boldness. . . .

This new clerical sense of social responsibility called for reforms.

We note as omens of industrial peace and goodwill the growth of a spirit of conciliation, and of the practice of conference and arbitration in settling trade disputes. We trust profoundly that these methods may supplant those of the strike and the lockout, the boycott, and the blacklist. . . . We believe no better opportunity could be afforded to Christian men, employers and wage earners alike, to rebuke the superciliousness of power and the obstinacy of opinion than by asserting and illustrating before their fellows in labor contests the Gospel which deals with men as men and has for its basis of fraternity the Golden Rule.

The Convention delegates advocated for social change but first affirmed their need to change their individual ways. You should also let your repentance lead to reform as you:

ACKNOWLEDGE YOUR SHORTCOMINGS — Repentance is the first and hardest step. If you're unwilling to confront where you fell short, you'll stay stuck in the rut of complacency and denial. Honesty with yourself leads to helping others. Turning away from sin will lead to opportunities to serve others, as Jesus declared:

Therefore produce fruit consistent with repentance.
Luke 3:8

ALERT YOUR CONSCIENCE — Make your changes permanent by turning habits into lifestyle. Turning away from negative behavior one week is frustrating if you turn right back to it the next week. Set up conscience alerts: mental yellow-flashing lights that warn you that the danger of reversion is approaching. That's when you activate your spirit. Pray for wisdom and strength to heed every moral signal as you stay on the high road without detours or U-turns.

ACCEPT YOUR RESPONSIBILITY — Let go of the misconception that helping someone else will somehow hurt your opportunities for success. Take responsibility through your initiative: step outside of your comfort zone and create an environment for personal growth and social change. They should go hand in hand.

ASSERT YOUR REFORMS — The Social Gospel principles of Federal Council of Churches first convention endured, finding expression in the Civil Rights Movement of the 1960s as well as influencing more modern movements like Christians Against Poverty in the United Kingdom and the Christian Community Development Association in the United States. This legacy indicates that progress follows repentance. Your personal progress will rise from your resolve to learn from past mistakes and go in a new directions. Become a living example of the personal reforms you proclaim. More people will pay attention to what you're saying if you're already living it; they will be encouraged to make changes in their own lives.

Be Faithful In Fellowship   **December 29th**

The man who does not in some way . . . connect himself
with some active, working church misses many opportunities for
helping his neighbors, and therefore, incidentally, for helping himself.
Theodore Roosevelt

In 1917 former President Theodore Roosevelt published an article in "Ladies Home Journal" entitled "Shall We Do Away with the Church?". In the piece he responded to the rhetorical question by emphasizing the importance of attending church, elaborating ten reasons. Roosevelt makes a strong case for you — for all of us — to engage in spiritual fellowship. It's a Biblical case:

And let us consider how we may spur one another on
toward love and good deeds, not giving up meeting together,
as some are in the habit of doing, but encouraging one another . . .
Hebrews 10:24-25

Of his ten points of encouragement to be faithful in fellowship, five follow, emphasizing aspects of fellowship as success principles — articulated in his own words — for you to apply in your life.

CULTIVATION — *Church work and church attendance mean the cultivation of the habit of feeling some responsibility for others and the sense of braced moral strength, which prevents a relaxation of one's own moral fiber.*

COMMITMENT — *Yes, I know all the excuses. I know that one can worship the Creator and dedicate oneself to good living in a grove of trees, or by a running brook, or in one's own house, just as well as in church. But I also know as a matter of cold fact the average man does not thus worship or thus dedicate himself. If he stays away from church he does not spend his time in good works or in lofty meditation. He looks over the colored supplement of the newspaper. . . .*

COUNSEL — *He may not hear a good sermon at church. But unless he is very unfortunate, he will hear a sermon by a good man who, with his good wife, is engaged all the week long in a series of wearying, humdrum and important tasks for making hard lives a little easier.*

CHARITY — *He will meet and nod to, or speak to, good, quiet neighbors. . . . He will come away feeling a little more charitable toward all the world, even toward those excessively foolish young men who regard church-going as rather a soft performance.*

COMMUNITY — *In this actual world a churchless community, a community where men have abandoned and scoffed at or ignored their religious needs, is a community on the rapid downgrade.*

Wherever your religious faith brings you together with others — storefront or cathedral, temple or schoolroom, synagogue or mosque, sanctuary or catering hall — it's important to come together in spirit. No one can gain true success without trusted teammates. If you share a spiritual bond with someone — you listen, sing, study, pray and experience God together — your relationship deepens. You become like family. You will be able to really rely on that person. Don't continue on the journey of life without fellow travelers of faith. When you come to those roadblocks and detours, your spiritual brothers and sisters will always be there for you to strengthen your faith, providing the bedrock of fellowship to bolster you through.

Take The Road Less Traveled   December 30th

Whither am I going? To the New World. What to do?
To gain honor? No, if I know my own heart. To get money?
No: I am going to live to God, and to bring others so to do.
Francis Asbury

In October 1771 young clergyman Francis Asbury left England for America and eventually became one of the first two bishops of the Methodist Episcopal Church in the United States. During his first year in the colonies Asbury preached in twenty-five different settlements, primarily on the eastern shore between the Delaware River and the Chesapeake Bay, the focus of his ministry during its early years. Asbury could have continued to minister on the Eastern seaboard but he took roads less traveled, carrying the evangelical message by horse-drawn carriage westward to those hearty souls pioneering on the American frontier. He preached as well as conducted meetings and conferences, in myriad places — from private gardens to public squares — averaging 6,000 miles of travel each year.

In 1780 Asbury met the freedman Henry "Black Harry" Hosier, who became Asbury's driver. Though illiterate, Hosier memorized Bible passages as Asbury read them aloud during their travels. Hosier learned so well along the way that he became a preacher in his own right, even a cross-over success, as popular among white audiences as his own race, delivering the first sermon in American history by a black directly to a white congregation. Hosier's trailblazing laid the foundation for African American Methodism, of which Sojourner Truth, Harriet Tubman and Frederick Douglass all became members.

Asbury's life and work evoke Robert Frost's The Road Not Taken. The poem not only connects thematically to Asbury's life but also suggests principles for you to ponder as you consider taking the road less traveled in your life.

EXPLORE:
Two roads diverged in a yellow wood,
And sorry I could not travel both
And be one traveler, long I stood
And looked down one as far as I could
To where it bent in the undergrowth;

Life presents choices, some really difficult ones like which path is best to take. Consider all options but resist following the crowd; instead go the way of faith, which will lead you in mysterious ways to marvelous outcomes.

EXTEND:
Then took the other, as just as fair,
And having perhaps the better claim,
Because it was grassy and wanted wear;
Though as for that the passing there
Had worn them really about the same,

If Asbury had traveled the usual route he wouldn't have mentored Henry Hosier and sown revival in new directions. As you take the less traveled course look for ways to extend your kindness and influence.

EXCEL:
I shall be telling this with a sigh
Somewhere ages and ages hence:
Two roads diverged in a wood, and I —
I took the one less traveled by,
And that has made all the difference.

When you come to the fork in your life's road today — or in the future — make the intrepid decision to take the road less traveled. It will make all the difference for you, and could even make a historic difference for others as well.

Don't Lose Sight Of Your Faith   December 31st

Man is born to act, and thought is valuable mainly as a guide to action. Now, the chief inspiration to action, and above all to right action, is found in faith, hope, and love.
John Spalding

In May 1877 John Spalding was appointed the first bishop of the Roman Catholic Diocese of Peoria, Illinois. In the thirty-one years Spalding served in the position, he became an advocate for education, starting several Catholic schools in Peoria as well as co-founding the Catholic University of America in Washington, D.C. In his 1895 book "Means and Ends of Education", he argued that faith and morality should play a central role in education. Spalding highlighted the importance of faith and character in education by pointing to the founder of his faith as the paradigm of virtue.

If the thinkers, from Plato and Aristotle to Kant and Pestalozzi, who have dealt with the problems of education, have held that virtue is its chief aim and end, shall we thrust from the school the one ideal character who, for nearly 1,900 years, has been the chief inspiration to righteousness and heroism; to whose words patriots and reformers have appealed in their struggles for liberty and right; to whose example philanthropists have looked in their labors to alleviate suffering; . . .by whose courage and sympathy the world has been made conscious that the distinction between man and woman is meant for the propagation of the race, but as individuals they have equal rights and should have equal opportunities?

Spalding's point about not losing sight of faith in education also applies in a personal context. It's important that you don't lose sight of your faith. Focusing on these points will help you keep your faith in plain view.

SECURITY — Faith is the most important implement in your personal toolbox to hammer away your fears. Think about it this way:

Fear knocked on the door. Faith answered. No one was there.

SURE ENOUGH— The Sure Enough Syndrome states: if you expect to fail, sure enough, you will. If you expect to succeed, sure enough, you will. What you believe determines what you think determines what you do. Spalding stressed faith as the source of virtuous conduct. If you want to act differently, start by believing differently.

STRENGTH — Life has a way of resisting your control, of defying predictability, of introducing unfavorable circumstances, of upsetting your best-laid plans. This doesn't mean you should live with a sense of frustration and futility but with the awareness that the constants in life are challenge and change. If you don't believe so, you run the risk of missing or dismissing the providential interventions that could pop up along the pathways of your life. Be a person of faith—then you will find a purpose in opposition, a silver lining in the clouds, calm in uncertainty, and an opportunity for serendipity in the midst of life's storms. Your faithfulness produces the strength to believe that when things are darkest in your life, the dawn of breakthrough approaches.

SALVATION —The ultimate purpose of your faith is bring you into a personal relationship with God through Jesus Christ. Your true spiritual journey begins in that moment of confession of faith. This New verse explains the basis of salvation by faith.

For God so loved the world that he gave his one and only Son,
that whoever believes in him shall not perish but have eternal life.
John 3:16

Not losing sight of your faith in this way will cultivate for your life present-day abundance and everlasting blessings.

ABOUT THE AUTHOR

Joseph Holland (josephholland.com) is an author, attorney, speaker entrepreneur, and ordained minister with outreach ministries to the homeless and other needy people.

Mr. Holland has been a Harlem-based lawyer and small business owner as well as having served as a government official in legislative and executive capacities, as vice-president of the Harlem Business Alliance (hbany.org), and as a co-founder of the Beth Hark Christian Counseling Center (bethhark.org). He presently ministers as an elder at Bethel Gospel Assembly in Harlem.

Holland's writings include an inspirational self-help book "The Touchstone Tools: Building Your Way To An Inspired Life" (touchtonetools.com); his spiritual memoir - "From Harlem With Love: An Ivy Leaguer's Inner-City Odyssey"; his first stage play - "Cast Me Down", which enjoyed a Off-Broadway run; and his second stage play, "Homegrown," which experienced two extended runs at Harlem's landmark - The National Black Theatre. He has also created a motivational video series, "Holistic Hardware: Tools That Build Lives".

Holland is a graduate of Cornell University, where he earned a B.A. and M.A. and was an All-American football player. Holland has served as a member of the University's Board of Trustees since 1988. He holds his J.D. degree from Harvard Law School.

Made in USA - North Chelmsford, MA
1028697_9781705354285
12.02.2019 1653